P9-CBY-670

Ideas and Movements
That Shaped America

Ideas and Movements
That Shaped America

FROM THE BILL OF RIGHTS
TO "OCCUPY WALL STREET"

VOLUME 2: F-O

Michael S. Green and Scott L. Stabler, Editors

ABC-CLIO™

An Imprint of ABC-CLIO, LLC
Santa Barbara, California • Denver, Colorado

SWOSU-Sayre / McMahan Library

Copyright © 2015 by ABC-CLIO, LLC

All rights reserved. No part of this publication may be reproduced, stored in a retrieval system, or transmitted, in any form or by any means, electronic, mechanical, photocopying, recording, or otherwise, except for the inclusion of brief quotations in a review, without prior permission in writing from the publisher.

Library of Congress Cataloging-in-Publication Data
Ideas and movements that shaped America : from the Bill of Rights to "Occupy Wall Street" / Michael S. Green and Scott L. Stabler, editors.
    3 v. ; cm
  Includes bibliographical references and index.
  Contents: v. 1. A-E — v. 2. F-O — v. 3. P-Z.
  ISBN 978-1-61069-251-9 (alk. paper) — ISBN 978-1-61069-252-6 (ebook)
 1. Social movements—United States—History—Encyclopedias. 2. Social movements—United States—History—Sources. 3. Ideology—United States—History—Encyclopedias. 4. Ideology—United States—History—Sources.
5. United States—History—Philosophy—Encyclopedias. 6. United States—History—Philosophy—Sources. 7. United States—Politics and government—Philosophy—Encyclopedias. 8. United States—Politics and government—Philosophy—Sources.
  I. Green, Michael S., editor.   II. Stabler, Scott L., editor.
  HM881.I43   2015
  303.48'40973—dc23   2014041512

ISBN: 978-1-61069-251-9
EISBN: 978-1-61069-252-6

19 18 17 16 15   1 2 3 4 5

This book is also available on the World Wide Web as an eBook.
Visit www.abc-clio.com for details.

ABC-CLIO, LLC
130 Cremona Drive, P.O. Box 1911
Santa Barbara, California 93116-1911

This book is printed on acid-free paper ∞
Manufactured in the United States of America

Contents

Volume 2: F–O

Volume 3: P-Z

F

FASCISM

Although *fascist* became an indiscriminate term of opprobrium suggesting repression and brutality, fascism, properly defined, is a distinct ideology and political style that surfaced in Italy after World War I under Benito Mussolini and spread across Europe, the Americas, and the developing world. Fascism sought to create new models for the state based on national community and the principal of charismatic leadership, called for an end to class divisions, and drew from an aesthetic of symbols, mass meetings, military, and the mass media. Fascism was antiliberal, anticommunist, and anticonservative, albeit willing to join conservatives in alliances of convenience.

Most American groups deemed "fascist" by their opponents fell short of fascism. The Ku Klux Klan and the Black Legion were reactionary conservatives, Huey Long was a Populist demagogue, and Gerald L. K. Smith was an anti-Semitic Protestant Fundamentalist.

Father Charles E. Coughlin, however, closely adhered to the model of Roman Catholic fascism prevalent in Spain, Portugal, and pre-Nazi Austria. Through his fiery radio broadcasts, Coughlin drew a large following of tens of millions during the Great Depression, and organized Christian Front paramilitary groups and the Union Party, which ran William Lemke for president in the 1936 election. Coughlin was America's loudest apologist for some of Mussolini's and Adolf Hitler's policies, and called for a program of work and income guarantees, the nationalization of some industries and wealth redistribution through taxation. Although he originally supported the New Deal, by 1934 Coughlin attacked Roosevelt and Jewish financial interests while keeping overtly Nazi groups at arm's length. The controversy he generated eventually caused many radio stations to cancel his program. In 1942, he was silenced by the Catholic hierarchy and disappeared from public view.

Significant among the welter of groups emulating aspects of fascism in the 1930s were the gray-uniformed Silver Shirts. Led by William Dudley Pelley, they numbered 15,000 at their peak in 1934. Pelley advocated a "Great Corporation of the United States" with all citizens as shareholders, but with citizenship restricted to people of Northern European descent. Pelley preached hatred against blacks and Jews, and inspired a pair of popular novels warning of the danger of American fascism, Nathaniel West's *A Cool Million* and Sinclair Lewis's *It Can't Happen Here*.

After the San Diego Silver Shirts sought the aid of U.S. Marine Corps drill instructors in a 1934 plot to assassinate public officials and stage an armed march on their city, the U.S. House of Representatives established the predecessor of the un-American Activities Committee that probed communism in the late 1940s to investigate extremist groups. The "Brown Scare" fueled by Pelley's notoriety and rising public

Father Coughlin was a radio priest during the Great Depression era. Coughlin began promoting hatred of such targets as the New Deal, Jews, union labor, and communism. He was eventually silenced by the Roman Catholic Church. (Library of Congress)

anxiety over the rise of Hitler led to government surveillance and antifascist demonstrations by moderate, liberal, and leftist groups.

Pelley was convicted of sedition in 1942 and indicted with other far Right leaders for "conspiring to impair the morale and the loyalty of the armed forces." The United States failed to prove its assertion that Pelley and two dozen other defendants were Nazi agents plotting to establish a puppet regime after a German victory. The trial brought together a loose association of rightist agitators, including Elizabeth Dilling, an anti-Semitic, anticommunist, pro-German leader of the "Mothers' Movement" for American neutrality in World War II. Dilling's book-length index of alleged Communists, *The Red Network* (1941), foreshadowed the

blacklists of the McCarthy era. Among others indicted for conspiracy were Gerhard Wilhelm Kunze, August Klaprott, Herman Max Schwinn, and Hans Diebel, leaders of the largest avowedly Nazi group to emerge in the United States, the German-American Bund.

The Bund may have numbered as many as 20,000 members, largely German Americans. With their brown shirts, Hitler salutes, and swastika emblems, the Bund styled itself after the German Nazis but added a few American touches, including an invocation of George Washington as the "First Fascist." The Bund maintained training camps in New York, New Jersey, Pennsylvania, and Wisconsin; their rallies in public auditoriums often led to clashes with communist protestors. Although the Bund disbanded after the United States declared war on Germany in 1941, many of its leaders were prosecuted or forced to relocate away from coastlines under military regulations.

Despite America's victory over Nazi Germany, the swastika would never disappear entirely. The American Nazi Party, founded in 1959 by George Lincoln Rockwell, a U.S. Navy veteran, eagerly embraced Nazi uniforms and iconography. The neo-Nazis drew their strength largely for its "White Power" message in opposition to the civil rights movement, and engaged in noisy protests against the desegregation of public schools. In 1967, the party, which numbered around 500, was renamed the National Socialist White Peoples Party. In that same year, the leader of a schismatic Nazi group assassinated Rockwell. The line between American Nazis, the Ku Klux Klan, and other white supremacists has always been blurry. David Duke was a Nazi before becoming the "modernizing" leader of a Klan group.

Rockwell's brown-uniformed successors continue to surface, but elements of Nazi ideology and symbolism live on most virulently among younger generations of neo-Nazi skinheads, whose markers include hair buzzed to the scalp and Doc Marten boots. America's skinhead subculture and its international affiliates support a network of racist rock bands, white power rock festivals, websites, and publications; skinheads have engaged in violence against minority groups, notably the 2012 massacre at Milwaukee's Sikh Temple that left six parishioners dead.

The Silver Shirts also played a role in the evolution of the American Right. After World War II, former members became active in the John Birch Society and the Christian Anti-Communist Crusade; in 1968, Silver Shirt veteran

Henry L. Bean founded the Posse Comitatus, the model for a number of extremist groups in its refusal to pay taxes or acknowledge any authority above the county level and its survivalist ethos. Posse members have engaged in shoot-outs with police and its members are linked to the anti-Semitic Christian Identity movement. Mussolini would have difficulty recognizing the descendants of American fascism as his heirs. Their ideology is closer to militant libertarianism than classic fascism.

See also

Anticommunism; Capitalism; Commercialization; Communism

GLEN JEANSONNE AND DAVID LUHRSSEN

Further Reading

Beekman, Scott. 2005. *William Dudley Pelley: A Life in Right-Wing Extremism and the Occult.* Syracuse, NY: Syracuse University Press.

Brinkley, Alan. 1982. *Voices of Protest: Huey Long, Father Coughlin, and the Great Depression.* New York: Knopf.

Goodrick-Clarke, Nicholas. 2002. *Black Sun: Aryan Cults, Esoteric Nazism and the Politics of Identity.* New York: New York University Press.

Jeansonne, Glen. 1996. *Women of the Far Right: The Mothers' Movement and World War II.* Chicago: University of Chicago Press.

Payne, Stanley G. 1995. *A History of Fascism 1914–1945.* Madison, WI: University of Wisconsin Press.

Fascism—Primary Document

Introduction

In the 1930s, the rise of Benito Mussolini and Generalissimo Francisco Franco's takeover in Spain made Americans more aware of the term fascism. *Some Americans saw signs of it developing in their country. Major General Smedley Butler testified before a congressional investigating committee that a group of businessmen had plotted to create a fascist regime in the United States and overthrow President Franklin Roosevelt.*

Document: Testimony of General Smedley Butler Before the McCormack-Dickstein Committee (1934)

(The witness was duly sworn by the chairman.)

The Chairman: General, you are a retired Commandant of the Marine Corps?

General Butler: No, I was never Commandant.

The Chairman: You were in the Army how long? **The Chairman:** As I remember, you are a Congressional Medal of Honor man; received the Congressional Medal of Honor on two occasions?

General BUTLER: Yes.

The CHAIRMAN: General, you know what the purpose of your visit here is today?

General BUTLER: Yes.

The CHAIRMAN: Without my asking you any further questions, will you just go ahead and tell in your own way all that you know about an attempted Fascist movement in this country?

General BUTLER: May I preface my remarks by saying, sir, that I have one interest in all of this, and that is to try to do my best to see that a democracy is maintained in this country.

The CHAIRMAN: Nobody who has either read about or known about General Butler would have anything but that understanding.

General BUTLER: It is nice of you to say that, sir.

But that is my only interest.

I think I had probably better go back and give you the background. This has been going on for a year and a half. Along—I think it must have been about the 1st of July 1933, two men came to see me. First there was a telephone message from Washington, from a man who I did not know well. His first name was Jack. He was an American Legionnaire, but I cannot remember his last name—cannot recall it now accurately. Anyhow, he asked me if I would receive 2 soldiers—2 veterans—if they called on me that afternoon. I said I would.

About 5 hours later a Packard limousine came up into my yard and 2 men got out. This limousine was driven by a chauffeur. They came into the house and introduced themselves. One said his name was Bill Doyle, who was then the department commander of the Legion in Massachusetts. The other said his name was Jerry MacGuire.

The CHAIRMAN: Where did MacGuire come from?

General BUTLER: MacGuire said he had been State commander the year before of the department of Connecticut and was then living in Connecticut. Doyle was living in Massachusetts.

The CHAIRMAN: Had you met either of these men before?

General BUTLER: Never had seen them before, as I recollect. I might have done so; but as far as my impression then was, they were absolute strangers. The substance of the conversation, which lasted about 2 hours, was this: That they were very desirous of unseating the royal family in control of the American Legion, at the convention to be held in Chicago, and very anxious to have me take part in it. They said that they were not in sympathy with the then administration—that is, the present administration's treatment of the soldiers.

They presented to me rather a confused picture, and I could not make up my mind exactly what they wanted me to do or what their objective was, but it had something to do with weakening the influence of the administration with the soldiers.

They asked me to go to the convention, and I said I did not want to go—that I had not been invited and did not care anything about going.

Then MacGuire said that he was the chairman of the distinguished-guest committee of the American Legion, on Louis Johnson's staff; that Louis Johnson had, at MacGuire's suggestion, put my name down to be invited as a distinguished guest of the Chicago convention. . . . I thought I smelled a rat, right away—that they were trying to get me mad—to get my goat. I said nothing.

They said, "We represent the plain soldiers, and we want you to come to this convention." They said, "We want you to come there and stampede the convention in a speech and help us in our fight to dislodge the royal family."

The CHAIRMAN: When you say you smelled a rat, you mean you had an idea that they were not telling the truth?

General BUTLER: I could not reconcile and from the very beginning I was never able to reconcile their desire to serve the ordinary man in the ranks, with their other aims. They did not seem to be the same. It looked to me us if they were trying to embarrass the administration in some way. They had not gone far enough yet but I could not reconcile the two objectives; they seemed to be diametrically opposed. One was to embarrass the administration of the American Legion, when I did not want to go anyhow, and the other object will appear here in a little while. I do not know that at that moment I had formed any particular opinion. I was just fishing to see what they had in mind. So many queer people come to my house all the time and I like to feel them all out.

Finally they said, "Now, we have arranged a way for you to come to this convention."

I said, "How is that, without being invited?"

They said, "Well, you are to come as a delegate from Hawaii."

I said. "I do not live in Hawaii."

"Well, it does not make any difference. There is to be no delegate from one of the American Legion posts there in Honolulu, and we have arranged to have you appointed by cable, by radio, to represent them at the convention. You will be a delegate."

I said, "Yes; but I will not go in the back door."

They said, "That will not be the back door. You must come."

I said "No; I will not do this."

"Well," they said, "are you in sympathy with unhorsing the royal family?"

I said. "Yes; because they have been selling out the common soldier in this Legion for years. These fellows have been getting political plums and jobs and cheating the enlisted man in the Army, and I am for putting them out. But I cannot do it by going in through the back door."

"Well," they said, "we are going to get them out. We will arrange this."

Doyle and MacGuire's Second Visit

That was all that happened the first day, as I recollect it. There were several days of it, and I will tell you everything that happened, but I cannot check it with the specific days. So they went away. Two or three days later they came back in the same car, both together, the second time. Doyle dropped out of the picture, he appeared only twice.

The Chairman. What was the second talk?

General BUTLER: The substance of the second talk was this, that they had given up this delegate idea, and I was to get two or three hundred legionnaires from around that part of the country and bring them on a special train to Chicago with me; that they would sit around in the audience, be planted here and there, and I was to be nothing but an ordinary legionnaire, going to my own convention as an onlooker; not as a participant at all. I was to appear in

the gallery. These planted fellows were to begin to cheer and start a stampede and yell for a speech. Then I was to go to the platform and make a speech. I said, "Make a speech about what?"

"Oh," they said, "we have one here."

This conversation lasted a couple of hours, but this is the substance of it. They pulled out this speech. They said, "We will leave it here with you to read over, and you see if you can get these follows to come."

I said, "Listen. These friends of mine that I know around here, even if they wanted to go, could not afford to go. It would cost them a hundred to a hundred and fifty dollars to go out there and stay for 5 days and come back."

They said, "Well, we will pay that."

I said," How can you pay it? You are disabled soldiers. How do you get the money to do that?"

"Oh, we have friends. We will get the money."

Then I began to smell a rat for fair. I said, "I do not believe you have got this money."

It was either then or the next time, or one of the times, they hauled out a bank-deposit book and showed me, I think it was $42,000 in deposits on that occasion, and on another occasion it was $64,000.

The Chairman: They took out a bank book and showed you what?

General Butler: They took out a bank book and showed me deposits of $42,000 on one occasion and $64,000 on another.

The Chairman: Do you know on what bank that was?

General Butler, I do not. They just flipped the pages over. Now, I have had some experience as a policeman in Philadelphia. I wanted to get to the bottom of this thing and not scare them off, because I felt then that they had something real. They had so much money and a limousine. Wounded soldiers do not have limousines or that kind of money. They said, "We will pay the bill. Look around and see if you cannot get two or three hundred men and we we'll bring them out there and we will have accommodations for them."

Third Visit with MacGuire

This was getting along about the first of August, I should say. Well, I did not do anything about it. MacGuire made one other trip to see me, this time by himself, to see how things were getting along, I said that I had been busy and had not had time to get the Soldiers together. Then on this occasion I asked him where he got this money. He was by himself when I asked him that. Doyle was not around.

"Where did you get all this money? It cannot be yours."

He said that it was given to him by nine men, that the biggest contributor had given $9,000 and that the donations ran all the way from $2,500 to $9,000.

I said, "What is the object?"

He said the object was to take care of the rank and file of the soldiers, to get them their bonus and get them properly cared for.

Well, I knew that people who had $9,000 to give away were not in favor of the bonus. That looked fishy right away.

He gave me the names of two men; Colonel Murphy, Grayson M.-P. Murphy, for whom he worked, was one. He said, "I work for him. I am in his office."

I said to him, "How did you happen to be associated with that kind of people if you are for the ordinary soldier and his bonus and his proper care? You know damn well that these bankers are not going to swallow that. There is something in this, Jerry MacGuire, besides what you have told me. I can see that."

He said, "Well, I am a business man. I have got a wife and family to keep, and they took good care of them, and if you would take my advice, you would be a business man, too." I said, "What has Murphy got to do with this?

"Well," he said, "don't you know who he is?"

I said, "Just indirectly. He is a broker in New York. But I do not know any of his connections."

"Well," he said "he is the man who underwrote the formation of the American Legion for $125,000. He underwrote it, paid for the field work of organizing it, and had not gotten all of it back yet."

"That is the reason he makes the kings, is it? He has still got a club over their heads."

"He is on our side, though. He wants to see the soldiers cared for."

"Is he responsible, too, for making the Legion a strike breaking outfit?"

"No, no. He does not control anything in the Legion now."

I said: "You know very well that it is nothing but a strike breaking outfit used by capital for that purpose and that is, the reason they have all those big club-houses and that is the reasons I pulled out from it. They have been using these dumb soldiers—to break strikes."

He said: "Murphy hasn't anything to do with that. He is a 'very fine fellow."

I said, "I do not doubt that, but there is some reason for him putting $125,000 into this."

Well, that was the end of that conversation. I think it was then that he showed me the deposit of $64,000.

The CHAIRMAN: MacGuire had the money?

General BUTLER: MacGuire had the bank book. He did not have any money yet. No money had appeared yet. There was nothing but a bank book showing deposits. It was in his name.

The CHAIRMAN: In his name?

General BUTLER: Yes.

The CHAIRMAN: Not in Doyle's name?

General BUTLER: No. Doyle had faded out of the picture and his name was never mentioned again and has never been mentioned since I do not know but what Doyle just rode along with him.

Source: U.S. House of Representatives, Special Committee on Un-American Activities, Public Statement, 73rd Congress, 2nd session. Washington, DC: Government Printing Office, 1934, pp. 1–12.

FEDERAL RESERVE SYSTEM

See NATIONAL BANK/FEDERAL RESERVE SYSTEM

FEDERALISM

Governments are organized and classified in many different ways. One such classification scheme is based on the relation between the central government and various subgovernments, or what are in America called states. Using this scheme, political scientists have identified three forms of government—unitary, confederal, and federal.

The governments of England and France are examples of unitary governments. Unitary governments have no permanent subgovernments with powers comparable to those of the individual states in America. The central government exercises direct control over the subgovernments, which are designed for administrative convenience.

By contrast, in a confederal government, power is divided between a national government and various subunits. On many matters such subunits are considered to be sovereign, or supreme. There have been two confederal governments in American history. One was based on the Articles of Confederation, which existed between 1781 and 1789 and preceded the adoption of the U.S. Constitution. The other was the Confederate States of America, in which eleven Southern states joined during the Civil War.

Under a confederal government, primary power is concentrated in the states, each of which has its own constitution. If the national government wants to do something, it acts through the states rather than directly upon individuals. Thus, under the Articles of Confederation, the national government requested that the states supply revenues and soldiers rather than directly asking the people for them. The men who authored the U.S. Constitution were convinced that the central government under the Articles of Confederation failed to meet the country's needs. Likewise, some scholars believe that the relative weakness of the central government under the Confederacy was one of the factors that led to its eventual defeat in the Civil War.

A federal government, like that in the United States, falls somewhere between the unitary and confederal models. Like a confederal government, a federal government divides power between a central authority and various subgovernments. States are considered sovereign to the extent that they have fixed boundaries and their own constitutions. The U.S. Constitution further guarantees that American states cannot be deprived of their equal representation in the U.S. Senate (where each has two senators) without the states' consent. In a federal government, both the central and state governments have power—as in taxation—to act directly on the people. Contemporary nations with federal governments other than the United States include Mexico, Canada, and Switzerland.

The framers of the U.S. Constitution wanted a national government that was stronger than the one they had observed under the Articles of Confederation, but many were highly devoted to their own states and wary of establishing a form of government similar to that which they had rebelled against in Great Britain. A federal system emerged as an alternative that might work in a nation spread over a large land area where a blend of uniformity and diversity was desired. The theory of balancing state and national

Governor George Wallace (left, in doorway) confronts U.S. deputy attorney general Nicholas Katzenbach (right) on the steps of the University of Alabama in an attempt to block integration on June 11, 1963. (Library of Congress)

power also appealed to the framers, who thought such a division of power might prove an additional safeguard for liberty.

The framers attempted to delineate national and state powers in the U.S. Constitution, primarily in Article IV of the Constitution. Article IV states that the national government has an obligation to guarantee states a republican, or representative, form of government and must come to the aid of states that face the threat of invasion or domestic upheaval. Article IV also maintains that states have obligations to one another—as in returning criminals who have fled (a process known as extradition), in respecting the rights—or privileges and immunities—of citizens from other states, and in recognizing the legal judgments of such states (what the Constitution refers to as full faith and credit).

In a federal government, some powers are exercised exclusively by the national government. Under the U.S.

Constitution, only the national government can wage war, enter into treaties, coin money, and naturalize citizens. Article I, Section 10 specifically prohibits states from exercising some of these powers. Moreover, Article VI of the Constitution asserts that the national Constitution and the laws and treaties made under its authority are the supreme law of the land and cannot be overridden by individual states.

However, there are areas in which states hold not exclusive, but primary, power. The Tenth Amendment to the U.S. Constitution refers to powers reserved to the states, which political scientists traditionally have referred to as state police powers. Thus, when it comes to criminal laws, laws regulating public morals, education, control of private property, administration of welfare systems, and the like, states are expected to take the lead.

As the economy has become more complex and states have become more interrelated, it has been more difficult to identify areas in which the nation or the states exercise exclusive powers. Instead, states often exercise power jointly, or concurrently, with the national government. Such combinations allow the federal government to gain leverage over the states by placing conditions on the money it distributes to the states through various grant programs. Political scientists have described the U.S. government as a three-layer cake, with the national, state, and local authorities all exercising separate and discrete functions. However, political scientist Morton Grodzins suggested that the more apt analogy might be that of a marble cake. To cite but a single example, locally elected school boards might supervise local schools that are largely financed by city or county taxes. States might provide additional funding or regulation of the schools. The national government might provide funds for school lunches, remedial education, or the like. While local, state, and national powers all have some influence on the system, none has exclusive control.

Relationships among governments in a federal system can become quite complicated, and they have provided frequent controversy over the course of American history. Almost as soon as the U.S. Constitution was proposed, anti-Federalist opponents of the document began their critique. One of their key arguments, borrowed in part from the French philosopher Baron de Montesquieu, was that it would be impossible to have a democratic government over a land area as large as that envisioned for the new republic. To counter such a statement, one of James Madison's most decisive arguments on behalf of the new government was his *Federalist No. 10* in which he argued that a government that expanded over a larger geographical area would in fact be more conducive to freedom because a government could not possibly suppress liberty on such a wide scale. One of the results of the anti-Federalists' criticisms of the Constitution was the adoption of the Bill of Rights, which limited the power of the new national authority. Eventually, the guarantees to safeguard liberty in the Bill of Rights would also be applied to the states.

Advocates of states' rights and nationalism often clashed in the early American republic. The first two political parties—the Federalist Party led by Alexander Hamilton on one side, and the Democratic-Republican Party led by Thomas Jefferson and Madison on the other—were formed largely over the question of the constitutionality of a national bank. Although the U.S. Constitution did not specifically grant such a power to Congress, Hamilton persuaded President George Washington that the power to establish a national bank could be derived as an implied power from such other granted rights as the power to raise taxes and spend money. By contrast, Jefferson and Madison feared that broad interpretations of congressional powers might eventually erode state authority. Although the national bank became a reality, such concerns over its powers remained a controversial issue until it was finally dismantled in the 1830s amid much political acrimony.

In 1798, the Federalist Party adopted the Alien and Sedition Acts, another controversial maneuver to establish national control at the expense of individual states. The latter law significantly restricted freedom of speech, which the First Amendment had sought to guarantee. Madison and Jefferson subsequently authored the Virginia and Kentucky Resolutions in which they urged states to interpose themselves against enforcement of this law, or essentially to override the national authority. During the 1807 embargo imposed by Jefferson's administration and the subsequent War of 1812, the shoe was on the other foot. This time, Northern Federalist states complained that the embargo was an excessive use of federal powers. Their opposition crystallized in a series of resolutions for greater state control adopted by the Hartford Convention (December 1814 to January 1815), although the ending of the war at almost the exact same time made the resolutions moot and left the issue of federal-state relations unresolved.

The issue of slavery ultimately brought issues of state and national power to the forefront. Building in part on the doctrine asserted in the Virginia and Kentucky Resolutions, Southern proponents of slavery, fearing national intervention on the subject, began to develop doctrines by which they could resist such power. During a dispute over higher tariffs that developed during the late 1820s, South Carolinian John C. Calhoun developed the doctrine of nullification, whereby states could attempt to nullify, or void, federal laws with which they disagreed. Taken to its most extreme conclusion, this theory led to the doctrine of secession, whereby states asserted their power to leave the Union altogether.

Although he opposed the spread of slavery, President Abraham Lincoln cited the preservation of the Union as his chief reason for pursuing the resulting Civil War. Ultimately, the North prevailed, and the doctrines of nullification and secession suffered a defeat with the Confederacy's loss in 1865, although the attitudes behind them have not gone completely away. At the war's end, three amendments were adopted that affirmed national powers, without however, bringing an end to the federal system. The Thirteenth and Fifteenth Amendments, respectively, abolished slavery and prohibited the use of race as an obstacle to voting, thus overriding individual state governments on these issues.

The Fourteenth Amendment, however, ultimately had the greatest impact on federalism. This amendment guaranteed that all persons born or naturalized in the United States were U.S. citizens, thus overturning *Dred Scott v. Sandford* (1857), in which Chief Justice Roger B. Taney had argued that African Americans were not, and could not become, U.S. citizens. This amendment also limited the powers of the states by preventing them from denying such rights as due process and equal protection of the laws to their citizens.

Over time, the due process clause became the vehicle by which the U.S. Supreme Court declared that, like the national government, the states would be bound by the provisions for liberty found in the Bill of Rights. After the Civil War, the Supreme Court declared in *Texas v. White* (1869) that the nation "looks to an indestructible Union, composed of indestructible states." The Civil War, however, did not bring questions regarding the limits of national and state powers to an end.

Although state and national powers have waxed and waned since the end of the Civil War, the general direction has been in favor of expanded national authority. As the economy has become more interdependent, opportunities for national exercises of power under congressional control over interstate and foreign commerce have expanded. Similarly, two world wars and the Cold War led to increased national expenditures and greater national control over the economy, all of which led to expanded powers for the national government.

At no time have states appeared more inadequate than when confronting the Great Depression. President Franklin D. Roosevelt subsequently pushed for a variety of new national programs under the rubric of the New Deal to revitalize the economy and contain the despair that was sweeping the nation. Initially, the U.S. Supreme Court resisted many of these programs, arguing that New Deal legislation exceeded federal authority, thus undermining the rights

reserved to the states under the Tenth Amendment. After being reelected in 1936 by a popular landslide, however, Roosevelt proposed a plan to pack the Supreme Court with new justices, who would ostensibly concur in the New Deal effort. Although Congress did not approve of the plan, the Court backed down rather than face a showdown with Roosevelt and subsequently began accepting the constitutionality of his New Deal programs, especially as the older justices retired or died and Roosevelt was able to appoint their successors. Once again, the states lost power to the growing federal government.

National powers were also expanded when the U.S. Supreme Court decided in *Brown v. Board of Education* (1954) and subsequent cases to declare the system of racial segregation unconstitutional. Such Southern governors as Orval Faubus of Arkansas, George Wallace of Alabama, and Lester Maddox of Georgia sought to resist these Supreme Court judgments with all the trappings of state power at their commands. In some cases, presidents met such defiance by calling in federal troops, as President Dwight D. Eisenhower did in Little Rock, Arkansas, in 1957 and as President John F. Kennedy did in Birmingham, Alabama, in 1963. In both instances, federal troops forced state schools to integrate in the face of state resistance. Over time, federal court decisions prevailed, in large part because of a developing consensus that they represented sound morality and good policy.

At about the same time, the U.S. Supreme Court began to incorporate an increasing number of provisions of the Bill of Rights into the due process clause of the Fourteenth Amendment and apply them to the states. Again, some states saw such restrictions as improper impositions on their rights, but over time, most came to recognize that the result was greater freedom for all. During this period, the U.S. Supreme Court was extremely generous in interpreting the powers of the national government. For example, the Court upheld the Civil Rights Act (1964)—a law prohibiting racial discrimination in places of public accommodation—and numerous other laws on the basis of congressional authority to control interstate commerce. It looked as though there might be little, if anything, that Congress could not regulate.

In recent years, however, the Supreme Court has begun again to examine the extent to which national laws can usurp state prerogatives. A number of cases have relied on the Eleventh Amendment to limit lawsuits that can be brought against the states without their consent. The Supreme Court eventually reversed a decision holding that a federal minimum wage law could not apply to state employees, but in a number of subsequent decisions, the Court paid renewed attention to the preservation of states' rights. Thus, in *New York v. United States* (1992), the Supreme Court overruled a national environmental law that appeared to commandeer states to be part of a regulatory system that they opposed.

In *United States v. Lopez* (1995), the Court subsequently overturned a congressional law that restricted the possession of guns near schools. The Court saw little connection between this law and the control of interstate commerce and saw the law as an improper attempt by Congress to interfere with matters of criminal law and education, areas that were traditionally left to the states. Similarly, in a 5–4 decision in *United States v. Morrison* (2000) the Supreme Court struck down a provision of the Violence Against Women Act that enabled women to sue their alleged attackers in federal court. Even though Congress had attempted to quantify the effects of domestic violence on commerce, the Court majority ruled that such effects were too indirect to warrant national control. By contrast, the dissenters argued that the Court did not need to protect the rights of the states against congressional encroachment. In the dissenters' judgment, state interests were already adequately protected by the structure of the federal government, and especially by state representation in Congress.

These recent decisions indicate that the debate over the proper relation between the national government and the states, as well as the courts' role in adjudicating this debate, is unlikely ever to be conclusively resolved. This relationship will often vary from one issue to another. Both governments must operate with sensitivity to the rights of the other. Although the Constitution has established broad guidelines, the people's representatives must decide on a day-to-day basis exactly what powers each government should exercise.

See also

African American Civil Rights Movement; Anti-Federalism; Conservativism; Judicial Activism; Judicial Review; Separation of Powers; States' Rights (Antebellum, Memory, Contemporary); Welfare State

JOHN R. VILE

Further Reading

Dye, Thomas R. 1990. *American Federalism: Competition Among Governments*. New York: Lexington Books.

Farber, Daniel. A. 2007. *Retained by the People: The "Silent" Ninth Amendment and the Constitutional Rights Americans Don't Know They Have*. New York: Basic Books.

Gerston, Larry L. 2007. *American Federalism: A Concise Introduction*. Armonk, NY: M.E. Sharpe.

LaCroix, Alison L. 2011. *The Ideological Origins of American Federalism*. Cambridge, MA: Harvard University Press.

Massey, Calvin R. 1995. *Silent Rights: The Ninth Amendment and the Constitution's Unremunerated Rights*. Philadelphia, PA: Temple University Press.

Federalism—Primary Document

Introduction

Clinton v. City of New York *addressed the issue of the presidential line-item veto. Although many states provide for an item veto by which their governors may annul individual items in appropriations bills, at the national level, the United States makes no specific provision for such a mechanism. After continuing concern over the budget deficits that have plagued the nation in recent years, Congress adopted the Line-Item Veto Act in April 1996, giving the president power to exercise such authority. In 1998 in* Clinton v. City of New York, *the U.S. Supreme Court ruled that the Line-Item Veto Act was unconstitutional because it inappropriately gave the president the power to repeal or amend statutes enacted by the Congress.*

Document: *Clinton v. City of New York* (June 25, 1998)

JUSTICE STEVENS delivered the opinion of the Court.

The Line Item Veto Act (Act) was enacted in April 1996 and became effective on January 1, 1997. The following day, six Members of Congress who had voted against the Act brought suit in the District Court for the District of Columbia challenging its constitutionality. On April 10, 1997, the District Court entered an order holding that the Act is unconstitutional. In obedience to the statutory direction to allow a direct, expedited appeal to this Court, see §§692(b)-(c), we promptly noted probable jurisdiction and expedited review. We determined, however, that the Members of Congress did not have standing to sue because they had not "alleged a sufficiently concrete injury to have established Article III standing," *Raines v. Byrd* (1997); thus, "in . . . light of [the] overriding and time-honored concern about keeping the Judiciary's power within its proper constitutional sphere," we remanded the case to the District Court with instructions to dismiss the complaint for lack of jurisdiction.

Less than two months after our decision in that case, the President exercised his authority to cancel one provision in the Balanced Budget Act of 1997, and two provisions in the Taxpayer Relief Act of 1997. Appellees, claiming that they had been injured by two of those cancellations, filed these cases in the District Court. That Court again held the statute invalid, and we again expedited our review. We now hold that these appellees have standing to challenge the constitutionality of the Act and, reaching the merits, we agree that the cancellation procedures set forth in the Act violate the Presentment Clause, Art. I, §7, cl. 2, of the Constitution. . . .

The Line Item Veto Act authorizes the President himself to effect the repeal of laws, for his own policy reasons, without observing the procedures set out in Article I, §7. The fact that Congress intended such a result is of no moment. Although Congress presumably anticipated that the President might cancel some of the items in the Balanced Budget Act and in the Taxpayer Relief Act, Congress cannot alter the procedures set out in Article I, §7, without amending the Constitution.

Neither are we persuaded by the Government's contention that the President's authority to cancel new direct spending and tax benefit items is no greater than his traditional authority to decline to spend appropriated funds. The Government has reviewed in some detail the series of statutes in which Congress has given the Executive broad discretion over the expenditure of appropriated funds. For example, the First Congress appropriated "sum[s] not exceeding" specified amounts to be spent on various Government operations. In those statutes, as in later years, the President was given wide discretion with respect to both the amounts to be spent and how the money would be allocated among different functions. It is argued that the Line Item Veto Act merely confers comparable discretionary authority over the expenditure of appropriated funds. The critical difference between this statute and all of its predecessors, however, is that unlike any

of them, this Act gives the President the unilateral power to change the text of duly enacted statutes. None of the Act's predecessors could even arguably have been construed to authorize such a change.

Although they are implicit in what we have already written, the profound importance of these cases makes it appropriate to emphasize three points.

First, we express no opinion about the wisdom of the procedures authorized by the Line Item Veto Act. Many members of both major political parties who have served in the Legislative and the Executive Branches have long advocated the enactment of such procedures for the purpose of "ensur[ing] greater fiscal accountability in Washington."

The text of the Act was itself the product of much debate and deliberation in both Houses of Congress and that precise text was signed into law by the President. We do not lightly conclude that their action was unauthorized by the Constitution.

We have, however, twice had full argument and briefing on the question and have concluded that our duty is clear.

Second, although appellees challenge the validity of the Act on alternative grounds, the only issue we address concerns the "finely wrought" procedure commanded by the Constitution. We have been favored with extensive debate about the scope of Congress' power to delegate law-making authority, or its functional equivalent, to the President. The excellent briefs filed by the parties and their amici curiae have provided us with valuable historical information that illuminates the delegation issue but does not really bear on the narrow issue that is dispositive of these cases. Thus, because we conclude that the Act's cancellation provisions violate Article I, §7, of the Constitution, we find it unnecessary to consider the District Court's alternative holding that the Act "impermissibly disrupts the balance of powers among the three branches of government."

Third, our decision rests on the narrow ground that the procedures authorized by the Line Item Veto Act are not authorized by the Constitution. The Balanced Budget Act of 1997 is a 500-page document that became "Public Law 105–33" after three procedural steps were taken: (1) a bill containing its exact text was approved by a majority of the Members of the House of Representatives; (2) the Senate approved precisely the same text; and (3) that text was signed into law by the President. The Constitution explicitly requires that each of those three steps be taken before a bill may "become a law." If one paragraph of that text had been omitted at any one of those three stages, Public Law 105–33 would not have been validly enacted. If the Line Item Veto Act were valid, it would authorize the President to create a different law, one whose text was not voted on by either House of Congress or presented to the President for signature. Something that might be known as "Public Law 105–33 as modified by the President" may or may not be desirable, but it is surely not a document that may "become a law" pursuant to the procedures designed by the Framers of Article I, §7, of the Constitution.

If there is to be a new procedure in which the President will play a different role in determining the final text of what may "become a law," such change must come not by legislation but through the amendment procedures set forth in Article V of the Constitution.

The judgment of the District Court is affirmed.

It is so ordered.

Source: *Clinton v. City of New York*, 524 U.S. 417 (1998); Justia. com. http://supreme.justia.com/cases/federal/us/524/417/.

FEMINIST MOVEMENT

The feminist movement has been a major force in shaping American society and culture, but it has done so in a variety of ways, depending on the rights at issue, the era in which the movement was at work, and the people leading the fight at the time. Scholars of feminism and some of the participants in the movement divide it into three "waves," all committed to promoting women's rights, but involving different groups seeking different forms of advancement. The successes and failures of feminism have been tied to political and socioeconomic forces both outside and inside the movement.

The first wave of feminism lasted for more than seventy years and concentrated on suffrage—for the most part. While feminists and students of their actions point to the Seneca Falls Convention of July 19 and 20, 1848, as a beginning point, the goals expressed by those present had been percolating for some time. That year was literally a revolutionary one throughout the world, with uprisings across Europe. The United States proved less revolutionary but certainly reform-minded: opponents of the expansion of slavery broke with the Democratic and Whig parties to join longtime antislavery men in forming the Free-Soil Party. The abolitionist movement had been one of the reforms in which women had been involved, along with a variety of others growing out of the Second Great Awakening and responses to changes caused by expansion and industrialization that affected women employed outside the home and working in the domestic sphere. Their role in improving the lives of others helped inspire women to be more aware of the possibilities of reform for themselves.

Leading the approximately 100 women's rights advocates who gathered at Seneca Falls, New York, were Elizabeth Cady Stanton, a mother of four from upstate, and Lucretia Mott, a Quaker active in the abolitionist movement. Stanton devised the "Declaration of Sentiments, Grievances, and Resolutions," which reworked Thomas Jefferson's words in the Declaration of Independence to proclaim: "We hold these truths to be self-evident: that all men and women are created equal." The Seneca Falls Declaration included thirteen proposals for women's rights. The key one for Stanton in particular was the "sacred right of franchise," which would prove to be the major goal of the first wave of feminism—and the source of considerable division and dispute.

In 1850, Stanton met Susan B. Anthony, and the two of them became the leading advocates of the right to vote. Success eluded them in their lifetimes. They argued in favor of including women in the Fourteenth and Fifteenth Amendments, but the latter focused on "race," with Radical Republicans and other advocates of black civil rights calling it "the negro's hour." Some feminists objected that they were white and better educated, but to no avail, and cost themselves some backing among civil rights supporters in the process.

The introduction and passage of the Fifteenth Amendment also fostered divisions among the first wave of feminists. In 1869, with Congress approving that measure, Stanton and Anthony formed the National Woman Suffrage

Rosalynn Carter and Betty Ford, center, at the National Women's Conference in Houston on November 19, 1977. The event is considered by many historians to be a milestone in the feminist movement. The bipartisan attendance at the conference, and the presence of women like Carter and Ford, lent credibility to the movement. With such mainstream support, it became less of a stigma to be considered a feminist. (Bettmann/Corbis)

Association, which sought to alter federal laws and opposed the amendment's passage on the grounds that its framers failed to include women. Abolitionist and longtime women's rights supporter Lucy Stone countered with the American Woman Suffrage Association, which preferred to leave the Fifteenth Amendment alone and targeted the states.

Eventually, in 1890, the two groups merged, becoming the National American Woman Suffrage Association, and adopted the tactic of concentrating on action at the state level. With an increase in voluntarism among women in the late 19th and early 20th centuries, and the accompanying rise of the Progressive movement and its focus on expanding democracy through political reforms, the women's suffrage movement won more support in territories and states. Influenced by a more vocal women's suffrage movement in England, Alice Paul formed the Congressional Union, later

known as the National Woman Party, in 1913, and engaged in rallies and picketing to push harder for the vote. Two years later, Carrie Chapman Catt assumed leadership of NAWSA and expanded its efforts in the states. Adding to their pressure, President Woodrow Wilson, who had opposed suffrage, finally supported American entrance into World War I in 1917 "to make the world safe for democracy"—which women at home lacked, especially at a time when their participation in the war effort was needed. This combination of factors prompted Congress to pass the constitutional amendment that women's rights advocates had been seeking for so long. The Nineteenth Amendment took effect on August 26, 1920, in time for women to vote in the presidential election that November.

While suffrage was its overarching goal, the first wave of feminism focused on other issues of importance to women.

In its earlier years, the movement also concentrated on changing laws governing marriage, divorce, child custody, and property ownership, all of which baldly discriminated against women, and achieved some success. By the late 19th and early 20th centuries, as more women worked outside the home, wages and working conditions received increased attention. Ironically, some divisions existed at the time, and more have developed since, over whether women required any different kind of treatment. In 1908, attorney and future Supreme Court Justice Louis Brandeis, whose wife and her sister were active in reform movements, successfully argued before the high court in favor of shorter working hours for women in *Muller v. Oregon*. Many feminists opposed the decision because it endorsed discrimination on the basis of gender, even though some well-meaning reformers intended it to protect women. Indeed, success bred its share of problems: the passage of the women's suffrage amendment also eliminated one of the forces unifying a diverse group of people behind a rights movement whose members differed on some of its ultimate goals, and suffrage did not automatically or easily translate into political offices or political power.

While the quest for women's civil rights and those supporting it did not go away, the feminist movement was less united and active from the achievement of suffrage until the rights revolution of the 1960s. Backers of women's rights could count some victories: more women in prominent governmental roles during the New Deal, including Eleanor Roosevelt's advocacy as First Lady and the appointment of Secretary of Labor Frances Perkins; the contributions that women made in the military and on the home front during World War II; and more women winning elective office in the 1950s. But advancement proved limited until the modern black civil rights movement of the 1950s and the student movement of the early 1960s, much like the reform movements a century before, helped bring social issues back to the forefront.

Some of the second wave goals mirrored those of the first wave, but with some modern twists. Feminists sought to ease and eliminate gender discrimination in the workplace, to achieve equal pay for equal work, and to obtain opportunities for promotions and more executive positions. This obviously had been a problem during the first wave, but, by the 1960s, matters had grown worse as more women had been able to obtain jobs outside traditional women's spheres like nursing and teaching, but found few avenues to advancement. For example, more women became reporters for newspapers and television, but often had to cover "women's subjects" like fashion and food, and had little success in moving into major print editing or broadcast anchoring positions. Thus, the postwar economic boom, which rejuvenated the American economy but also inspired critiques of what economist John Kenneth Galbraith called "the affluent society," prompted a critique from women's perspective, too.

Anger or unhappiness over these issues helped empower feminists to act in the 1960s, but so did other factors. One was the publication of a book, Betty Friedan's *The Feminine Mystique* (1963), which described "the problem that has no name"—the feelings among housewives of ennui, or boredom, or lack of appreciation or challenges beyond the household. Another was that women became involved in other movements, most notably for black civil rights and student rights, and resented it when the leaders, who were almost exclusively male, ignored or minimized their issues. At the same time, the leadership roles that women did assume—from attorney Constance Baker Motley with the NAACP's legal fight against segregation to Rosa Parks in the Montgomery Bus Boycott to Diane Nash in the student civil rights movement—made clear that women could and would assert themselves. Technological improvements also aided the rise of the second wave: products for the home meant that women who had to tend to the home might have more time on their hands, and mass communication tools made it easier to organize and win attention for the rights and needs of women.

Women's efforts combined with sympathetic men in the reform climate of the 1960s to move the federal government to act. Upon taking office in 1961, President John F. Kennedy named longtime activist Esther Peterson to run the federal Women's Bureau, and her efforts led to the appointment of a Presidential Commission on the Status of Women, chaired by Eleanor Roosevelt. The commission proposed a raft of recommendations, although they did not extend to a constitutional amendment guaranteeing equal rights for women. But Congress passed and Kennedy signed the Equal Pay Act of 1963, a step on the long and often tortuous road to paying women what men earned for the same job. The next year, the combination of rights movements led to passage of Title VII of the Civil Rights Act of 1964, which barred discrimination on grounds of "sex," and led to the creation of the

Equal Employment Opportunity Commission, which heard a variety of complaints from women. Title VII and whether it would have teeth also inspired a major step forward in the feminist movement: the formation of a new advocacy group, the National Organization for Women (NOW), which concentrated first on lobbying and grew into its name as a truly national organization. Other Great Society programs advanced by President Lyndon Johnson and a sympathetic Congress helped women, directly and indirectly—for example, job training in inner cities and assistance with childcare—while the rise of affirmative action also aided women's quest for equal treatment.

The rights revolution within the Supreme Court, led by Chief Justice Earl Warren (1953–69), also boosted second wave feminism. In 1965, *Griswold v. Connecticut* became the first of several decisions promoting access to contraception and family planning. In 1973, the Court ruled in *Roe v. Wade* that the due process clause of the Fourteenth Amendment and the implicit right to privacy protected a woman's right to an abortion, at least for part of her pregnancy.

These measures combined to promote not just feminism, but women's liberation, referring to a more radical form of feminism that encouraged the idea of female autonomy. In 1970, NOW called for a national strike for equality. In the wake of the Stonewall Riot and the rise of the gay rights movement, lesbians became more vocal in seeking equality and, indeed, acceptance. The "battle of the sexes," including the tennis match in which Billie Jean King defeated Bobby Riggs (1973), brought attention to women's advances in sports, among other areas. Women became more active and successful in politics, including a fight for the passage of the Equal Rights Amendment (ERA) to the U.S. Constitution. That effort failed as only thirty-five of the required thirty-eight (three-fourths of the states) approved the amendment.

These developments also produced a reaction from conservatives, including women opposed to second wave feminism. Phyllis Schlafly formed Stop ERA and the Eagle Forum, and supported conservative Republicans, most notably Ronald Reagan, in warning that feminism and the ERA endangered the traditional family and would have ill effects by promoting women's presence in the military and promoting equality in education through Title IX programs. They predicted that the ERA would lead to higher divorce rates—which did, in fact,

go up, although the ERA's failure to pass clearly had nothing to do with it; rather, changes in the law that made it easier for women to exit unhappy marriages and to earn enough to support themselves had a bigger impact. The movement against the right to an abortion, including such groups as the Moral Majority, often worked in concert or merged with groups opposed to second wave feminism, and had the effect of supporting conservative politicians.

The third wave of feminism has unfolded in the last decade of the 20th century and the beginning of the 21st century. Its advocates have felt that one of the major problems with the second wave (and the same could be said of the first wave) is that it emphasized the issues facing middle-class and especially upper-middle-class women without enough attention to poorer women and to the image of women, and that the second wave failed to respond properly to the antifeminist reaction on the political right. Thus, third wave feminists have paid far more attention to the problems of minority women and to the objectification of women in general, and some of them have argued that, indeed, the word *feminism* is a misnomer because it promotes the idea that gender and its concepts are unchanging. The third wave has focused more intently on combating violence against women and such workplace issues as sexual discrimination and harassment.

Accompanying the third wave has been an increased political presence—still less than feminists would prefer, but with hopeful signs. Since 1997, three women have served four years each as secretary of state: Madeline Albright for President Bill Clinton, Condoleeza Rice for President George W. Bush, and Hillary Rodham Clinton for President Barack Obama. Yet Hillary Rodham Clinton's life and career have reflected and affected the problems of women in politics: her husband's candidacy in 1992 brought attention to her status as both a prominent attorney and a wife and mother, with political attacks against her for supposedly not emphasizing the latter; her election as a U.S. senator from New York in 2000 followed her husband's impeachment and revelations about his sex life; her candidacy for president in 2008 led to attacks against her that included traditional political in-fighting but also obvious gender bias.

Important legislation passed in the late 20th and early 21st centuries has reflected all three waves of feminism. In

1993, the Family and Medical Leave Act required employers to protect jobs and provide unpaid leave for, among other reasons, pregnancy and childcare. The next year, the Violence Against Women Act funded more extensive investigations of crimes against women and an office in the U.S. Justice Department to concentrate on the issue. In 2009, the Lilly Ledbetter Fair Pay Act amended the Civil Rights Act of 1964 to help women file lawsuits against employers who deny them equal pay—and followed a Supreme Court decision against Ledbetter's lawsuit against her employer. Dissenting from the Court's majority, Justice Ruth Bader Ginsburg, perhaps the leading architect of women's rights cases during the second wave, took the unusual step of reading her dissent from the bench and urging Congress to act—and it did.

That the bill was politically controversial, that it was even required, and that Ginsburg took that unusual step suggest that feminism remains controversial and the divisions that have existed and continue to exist within the movement. Politicians and the public—not just men—remain divided over the rights that women seek and the effect those rights will have. Within the feminist movements, women and their supporters often have divided over tactics and strategies. In the process, though, feminism has led to legal action, to advancements at home and at work, and to changes in people's hearts and minds.

See also

Abolition; Affirmative Action; African American Civil Rights Movement; Birth Control Movement; Divorce; Gay Rights; Judicial Activism; Moral Majority; Privacy; Pro-Choice Movement; Second Great Awakening; Sex in American Society; Student Rights Movement; Women's Rights Movement (19th Century); Women's Suffrage

RAVINDRA PRATAP SINGH

Further Reading

DuBois, Ellen Carol. 1978. *Feminism and Suffrage: The Emergence of an Independent Women's Movement in the U.S., 1848–1869.* Ithaca, NY: Cornell University Press.

Evans, Sara M. 1997. *Born for Liberty: A History of Women in America.* 2nd ed. New York: The Free Press.

Kessler-Harris, Alice. 2001. *In Pursuit of Equity: Women, Men, and the Quest for Economic Citizenship in 20th Century America.* New York: Oxford University Press.

Matthews, Glenna. 1992. *The Rise of Public Woman: Woman's Power and Woman's Place in the United States, 1630–1970.* New York: Oxford University Press.

Feminist Movement—Primary Document

Introduction

More than any other document to come out of the radical feminist era, The SCUM Manifesto by Valerie Solanas (1936–1988) reflected the rage of many radical feminists. From her self-publication of the radical SCUM Manifesto in 1967 to her attempted assassination of artist Andy Warhol in 1968, Solanas, who served three years in prison for the latter, became a fringe outlaw of the feminist movement.

Document: *The SCUM Manifesto (Society for Cutting Up Men)* by Valerie Solanas (1967)

Life in this society being, at best, an utter bore and no aspect of society being at all relevant to women, there remains to civic-minded, responsible females only to overthrow the government, eliminate the money system, institute complete automation and destroy the male sex.

It is now technically feasible to reproduce without the aid of males (or, for that matter, females) and to produce only females. We must begin immediately to do so. Retaining the male has not even the dubious purpose of reproduction. The male is a biological accident: the Y (male) gene is an incomplete X (female) gene, that is, it has an incomplete set of chromosomes. In other words, the male is an incomplete female, a walking abortion, aborted at the gene stage, To be male is to be deficient, emotionally limited; maleness is a deficiency disease and males are emotional cripples.

The male is completely egocentric, trapped inside himself, incapable of empathizing or identifying with others, or love, friendship, affection of tenderness. He is a completely isolated unit, incapable of rapport with anyone. His responses are entirely visceral, not cerebral; his intelligence is a mere tool in the services of his drives and needs; he is incapable of mental passion, mental interaction; he can't relate to anything other than his own physical sensations. He is a half-dead, unresponsive lump, incapable of giving or receiving pleasure or happiness;

consequently, he is at best an utter bore, and inoffensive blob, since only those capable of absorption in others can be charming. He is trapped in a twilight zone halfway between humans and apes, and is far worse off than the apes because, unlike the apes, he is capable of a large array of negative feelings—hate, jealousy, contempt, disgust, guilt, shame, doubt—and moreover, he is *aware* of what he is and what he isn't.

Although completely physical, the male is unfit even for stud service. Even assuming mechanical proficiency, which few men have, he is, first of all, incapable of zestfully, lustfully, tearing off a piece, but instead is eaten up with guilt, shame, fear, and insecurity, feeling rooted in male nature, which the most enlightened training can only minimize; second, the physical feeling he attains is next to nothing; and third, he is not empathizing with his partner, but he is obsessed with how he's doing, turning in an A performance, doing a good plumbing job. To call a man an animal is to flatter him; he's a machine, a walking dildo. It's often said that men use women. Use them for what? Surely not pleasure.

Eaten up with guilt, shame, fears and insecurities and obtaining, if he's lucky, a barely perceptible physical feeling, the male is, nonetheless, obsessed with screwing. . . . He'll screw a woman he despises, any snaggle-toothed hag, and furthermore, pay for the opportunity. Why? . . .

Completely egocentric, unable to relate, empathize or identify, and filled with vast, pervasive, diffuse sexuality, the male is psychically passive. He hates his passivity, so he projects it onto women, defines the make as active, then sets out to prove that he is (prove that he is a Man') His main means of attempting to prove it is screwing. . . . Since he's attempting to prove an error, he must 'prove' it again and again. Screwing, then, is a desperate compulsive, attempt to prove he's not passive, not a woman; but he *is* passive and *does* want to be a woman.

Being an incomplete female, the male spends his life attempting to complete himself, to become female. He attempts to do this by constantly seeking out, fraternizing with and trying to live through a fuse with the female, and by claiming as his own all female characteristics—emotional strength and independence, forcefulness, dynamism, decisiveness, coolness, objectivity, assertiveness, courage, integrity, vitality, intensity, depth of character, grooviness, etc.—and

projecting onto women all male traits—vanity, frivolity, triviality, weakness, etc. It should be said, though, that the male has one glaring area of superiority over the female—public relations. (He has done a brilliant job of convincing millions of women that men and women and women are men). The male claim that females find fulfillment through motherhood and sexuality reflects what males think they'd find fulfilling if they were female. . . .

Source: Solanas, Valerie, *S.C.U.M (Society for Cutting Up Men) Manifesto*. New York, 1967. Womynkind.org. http://www.womynkind.org/scum/htm.

FITNESS MOVEMENT
Origins and Development

Originating in Britain in the first half of the 19th century, the fitness movement blossomed in the United States in the second half of the century. The movement was particularly noticeable during and after the Civil War, when Americans turned to fitness by participating in gymnastics, calisthenics, physical education, and sports. The movement was particularly vigorous in the Northeast among the middle and upper classes. The move to the cities led many to jettison strenuous activity. Too many Americans became sedentary. They turned to exercise and athletics to combat the lack of activity and saw physical activity as a cure-all.

Religious sentiments supported the fitness movement. The body was more than a container for the soul. Exercise and diet could improve and even perfect the body so that it would be more pleasing to God. Some enthusiasts went so far as to say that a fit body would make the afterlife more pleasurable. By being fit, one increased one's chances of entering heaven.

In the 19th century, Americans were still far from the notion that a fit body was sexually attractive, a notion that seems ubiquitous today. Local governments responded to the fitness movement by building gymnasiums to entice the public to exercise. The construction of these buildings intensified after 1860. In 1861, for example, Poughkeepsie, New York, built its first gym. These gyms appealed to Americans

Female students exercising with dumbbells at Western High School in Washington, D.C., ca. 1899. Men and women alike were caught up in a movement to get into better shape. (Library of Congress)

not merely as venues for the attainment of fitness but also as social centers where people exchanged greetings, met new people, and forged new friendships. As rural Americans moved to the cities they sought gathering places. Churches remained important, and gyms provided new avenues to build social ties. The gym's boosters promoted it and fitness as ways to combat the poor health and moral conditions of the city.

By the late 19th century, ministers reinforced the importance of fitness by promoting "Muscular Christianity," a movement that linked physical fitness with moral fitness (Green, 182). These ministers assumed that the best Christians were fit. Fitness, seen in this context, was not an end in itself. It provided religious benefits and sharpened the mind. With a sound body and mind one was prepared to enter the fray that was American capitalism. Like the trappings of industry, the body was a machine made more efficient by the pursuit of fitness. Jobs that made demands on the intellect must be balanced by exercise that placed strenuous demands on the body.

The extension of the fitness movement to women was controversial. Some advocates thought that the delicate constitution of women could not bear the stresses of exercise. Others, convinced that women had a fragile nervous system, advocated exercise as the instrument of a calm disposition. Still others thought that women must be fit to bear and raise children. Fitness was therefore a precondition to procreation. Some authorities insisted that women exercise without the intrusion of men for fear of sexually stimulating them. Others favored coeducational exercise. One proponent of the women's fitness movement counseled women to listen to music during exercise to pass the time pleasantly.

The use of dumbbells as an early form of weight training gained adherents among men and women. One authority preferred the use of light dumbbells to promote flexibility. Rather than iron, these dumbbells were wooden. Those in pursuit of fitness ran laps inside a gym, tossed four pound beanbags, performed calisthenics, and did both isotonic and isometric exercises. The 19th century also saw the introduction of a warm-up as a preparation for a workout. Using the analogy of a machine, experts warned that one would not turn a machine from off to maximum output in a matter of seconds. In the same way, the body must not jump into the full vigor of a workout without the preparation of a warm up for fear of injury. As a rule, 19th-century Americans did not have an aversion to sweat or body odor. These traits would develop in the 20th century.

Many Americans pursued fitness to build stamina rather than brute strength. The man who lifted heavy weights, it was thought, risked disfiguring his body. With origins in the 19th century, American bodybuilders (one might consider bodybuilding a type of fitness activity) disregarded this caveat and lifted maximum loads. Bodybuilding was perhaps an unusual type of fitness activity. Its participants did not seek to increase the number of jumping jacks one could do or lengthen the distance they could cover by bicycle. They sought the perfect physique. Whether they became better athletes in the process was beside the point. The gym of the late 19th century had to have a well-equipped weight room. Strongman Eugene Sandow emerged as an advocate of bodybuilding and, among bodybuilders, remains an inspiration today.

At the turn of the 20th century, Theodore Roosevelt became known as an advocate of the strenuous life. A boxer, wrestler, tennis player, and all round athlete, the president was the epitome of fitness and a glaring contrast to William McKinley and William Howard Taft, his predecessor and successor, respectively.

About this time, if not a little earlier, the bicycle craze swept the United States and became part of the fitness movement. Americans took to the bicycle as they would later to the Model T. The bicycle was an appropriate activity for men and women, many thought. Young couples bicycled to the park and away from the watchful eye of parents to share intimate moments. For prudes, however, a woman straddling a bicycle adopted too provocative a pose. The cost of a bicycle priced it out of the reach of the working class but it nevertheless seems to have mesmerized Americans of all walks of life. Because one rode in the open air and to scenic locales whenever possible, bicycling seemed a wholesome way to pursue fitness. Men seeking to display their fitness pedaled a Century (a ride of 100 miles) in a single day.

The Fitness Movement in the 20th and 21st Centuries

In the 20th century and into the 21st century bodybuilding attracted many adherents. It was more than a method of becoming fit. It made its practitioners large, well-muscled men, exactly what advertisers wanted. It also, its advocates maintained, made a man more attractive to a woman. It acquired a tincture of sexuality that no other fitness activity could match. In the 1970s, Austrian-born bodybuilder Arnold Schwarzenegger won several Mr. Olympia crowns. He used bodybuilding to launch a career as an actor and politician, ultimately serving as governor of California. Since then, bodybuilding has become an obsession to some Americans, who micromanage their diets, acquire a dark tan, and become so ubiquitous as to earn the moniker "gym rat." The bodybuilder's reliance on anabolic steroids has infected sports even beyond bodybuilding. New York Yankee Alex Rodriguez is the latest to face the accusation of taking illegal performance-enhancing drugs.

After World War II, Americans engaged in a recrudescence of the fitness movement that had galvanized the 19th century. Physicians applauded Americans who exercised and reduced their intake of fat and other calories. The fit American could expect a low incidence of heart disease and cancer. Educated, middle-class Americans embraced this movement though the poor grew more sedentary and fatter. By the 1980s, the most heartless critics blamed the poor for their lack of fitness. Their deleterious genes caused them to be inactive and unhealthy.

The new fitness movement, much like the old, was critical of tobacco and alcohol. In the 1950s, President Dwight D. Eisenhower took a practical approach to fitness. Having been a collegiate football player and army general, Eisenhower grew concerned that too many Americans were not fit enough for military service. To countermand this trend, the president in 1955 created the Presidential Council on Physical Fitness. Eisenhower's concern was to build fitness among youth, though in the 1970s President Jimmy Carter focused his efforts on promoting adult fitness. During the Eisenhower administration, both Jack LaLanne's television shows and Vic Tanny's health clubs promoted working out.

In the 1970s, Canadian American physician Kenneth Cooper and jogger James Fixx emerged as the spokespersons for the fitness movement. Both men were able writers and used this skill to emphasize the importance of aerobic exercises. Fixx in particular was unimpressed by bodybuilding.

Today, the fitness movement appears to have merged with a body sculpting movement. As the baby boomers have aged, they have had trouble maintaining their youthful figures. Doubts about sexual attractiveness and performance have led them to pursue fitness as a means of losing fat, building muscle, and recapturing their sexual allure. Bikini clad women often grace the cover of today's fitness magazines, strengthening the link between fitness and sexuality. Unquestionably, the fitness movement has remained an important part of American culture and economics as it has spread in numerous directions.

See also

Feminist Movement; Suburbanization; Urbanization

CHRISTOPHER CUMO

Further Reading

Engs, Ruth Clifford. 2001. *Clean Living Movements: American Cycles of Health Reform*. Westport, CT: Praeger.

Green, Harvey. 1986. *Fit for America: Health, Fitness, Sport and American Society*. Baltimore, MD: The Johns Hopkins University Press.

Fitness Movement—Primary Document

Introduction

The Body Builder, *by Robert J. Roberts, was published in 1916. Reproduced next is the introduction to the book written by Luther H. Gulick. Roberts dedicated the book to "my fellow physical directors in the Young Men's Christian Associations," and his ideas about fitness, body building, and gymnastics were heavily influenced by the ideals of "Muscular Christianity," which linked physical fitness with moral fitness. The introduction summarizes the main points of the book, explaining Roberts's early emphasis on the importance of physical activity, and why he believed that exercises should be "safe, short, easy, beneficial, and pleasing."*

Document: Luther H. Gulick's Introduction to *The Body Builder* by Robert J. Roberts (1916)

The best thing ever said about exercise was said by Robert J. Roberts: "All exercises must be safe, short, easy, beneficial, and pleasing."

I am happy to write this introduction, for in so doing I can pay my proper tribute to him and at the same time can extend his idea.

Roberts' platform—just ten words—"all exercises must be safe, short, easy, beneficial, and pleasing," grew out of his long teaching and great common sense in observation of men and the effects of different exercises upon them. He had taught so-called fancy gymnastics; he was thoroughly familiar with the heavy work of the weight lifters; he took into account not only the immediate effect of exercises, but, by means of watching men for a series of years, he formed important conclusions with reference to the ultimate effects of exercises. Let us examine his platform.

All exercises must be safe. Approximately one man out of ten is qualified by nature to take up the more difficult forms of gymnastics—those forms which by common repute are not safe. Roberts maintains that his work is for the masses; that he is not endeavoring to build up a system for the favored few—he wants everybody. He wants to be able to handle people in large numbers and quickly. This can be done only where the exercises are safe.

All exercises must be short. When Roberts first formulated this, there had been little or no work done upon blood pressure. The effect upon the heart and arteries of prolonged muscular activity was then unknown scientifically. We knew but little as to the way in which the muscle is nourished—the way it gets rid of its waste. He observed as an important fact that a large number of short exercises—other things being equal—did more good than a short number of long exercises. Science has since demonstrated the correctness of his observations.

All exercises must be easy. Big muscles are built up by doing work that is hard. Those men who build up the biggest muscular system are those who handle heavy weights. The muscles become harder. Fatty tissues tend to disappear. We believe that the size of the muscular fiber itself increases. It is a general fact that the heavier the work that a muscle has to do, the coarser are its fibers. Health of body and of muscles is not related to the hardness of the muscles or the size of the fibers. A large number of easy exercises are productive of more good than are hard exercises. Blood pressure is not raised by the easy exercises as it is by the hard exercises. Overwork is less probable.

Taking again the standard of exercises for the average man, it is clear that to handle large masses with benefit and safety, the individual exercises given to them should be easy.

All exercises must be beneficial. This now seems a truism to those of us who have grown up since the teachings of Roberts have been embodied in the very tissues of physical education in America, but as I look back at my own early experience in the gymnasium and realize that a large part of the work which I did was difficult but not beneficial, I realize what an enormous change has taken place. I remember the great struggles with which I mastered certain purely technical muscular stunts which could have no possible benefit. I mastered them because they were difficult and not because they were useful. I think that most of the muscular stunts that I mastered were positively harmful, but neither I nor my teachers thought about these things. Exercises for the great mass of people for the purpose of wholesome living should be beneficial.

Lastly: All exercises should be pleasing. Roberts did not make the mistake, which was so common among the early teachers of gymnastics, of thinking that the body was something by itself, separated from the mind. He recognized that exercise had a better effect on happy than on unhappy men; that laughter aided digestion as well as circulation. The men who have frequented his classes now for a generation have been happy in their work. It was not merely that the results were secured through regularity in attendance, brought about by the enjoyment men had in it, but the fact that the work was pleasing added to its effectiveness and aided in mental recuperation.

There is not a point to be disputed in this platform of Roberts when one understands that it applies to everyday gymnastics, for everyday conditions, for everyday people. But few men have ever crowded the experience of a lifetime so adequately into a sentence: All exercises should be safe, short, easy, beneficial, and pleasing.

Luther H. Gulick.

Source: Roberts, Robert J. *The Body Builder*. New York: Association Press, 1916, pp. vii–x.

FORDISM

The term "Fordism" was coined by Marxist political theorist and sociologist Antonio Gramsci in 1934 to refer to an economic system epitomized by the American industrialist and innovator, Henry Ford. Henry Ford's meteoric rise from tinkerer to industrial powerhouse in the early 20th century centered on a production and business plan that focused on set tenets, namely, the standardization of nearly every part that went into production, the creation of repetitive work tasks that low-skilled employees were easily trained to do, specialized tools to aid the moveable assembly line, and the development of an American standard of living for average factory workers so that workers could afford to purchase the products made in the factories. Ford's production and economic plans also affected the social lives of Americans as companies mimicking Ford's plans for success demanded increasingly faster rates of production, intruded into the personal lives of workers, created a vast consumer culture, and shaped political developments and foreign relations in the 20th century. The tenets of Fordism demanded high efficiency in production output and high wages paid to workers in

This Ford assembly line produced a large number of Model Ts in 1913—indeed, one every three minutes. The idea came from William C. Klann, who visited a Chicago slaughterhouse and saw a "disassembly line." (National Archives)

efforts to promote a self-sustaining consumerist culture that would continue to drive production demands. Ford's phenomenal success as an automobile manufacturer inspired many industrialists and politicians and became a dominant business model for American companies from the 1920s to the early 1970s.

In the autumn of 1908, Henry Ford released the first run of Model T automobiles from his small Piquette Plant manufacturing facility in Detroit, Michigan. Within less than two years from the first run of what many Americans nicknamed the "Flivver" or "Tin Lizzie," Ford moved his productions to a newly built and specially designed manufacturing complex just outside of Detroit's city limits in the small community of Highland Park. The Highland Park Ford Plant was his first attempt at developing a factory around the production of a moveable assembly line. Ford hired industrial architect Albert Kahn to design the plant and facilities, including offices and a foundry. Kahn's brilliant design for the Highland Park Plant reduced the amount of time to assemble a Model T from about twelve hours and fifteen minutes at Piquette to an hour and a half at Highland Park. The time savings reduced the manufacturing costs and Ford priced and marketed the Model T to reflect these industrial improvements. By seven years after the Model T's introduction into the daily lives of numbers of Americans, Ford's insistence on industrial efficiency and the standardization of parts and labor procedures allowed the Ford Motor Company to cut the cost of the Model T to $350, about half its introductory price of $700. By 1917, Americans could buy a new Model T for $350 but could not request any special options, as Ford's insistence on standardization did not allow for any personal differences, including exterior paint color. The massive price reduction, however, allowed more Americans the ability to own an automobile, which a few decades before only the most wealthy could buy.

The Highland Park Plant's production levels justified Ford's insistence on building manufacturing complexes that increased productivity and integrated the production materials used in the final assemblies through a process called vertical integration. Popularized by other industrialists such as Andrew Carnegie, vertical integration allowed the Ford Motor Company increased controls over the raw materials and supplies that went into an assembled Model T. Vertical integration allowed companies and industrialists to control supply chains through the strategic planning, purchasing, and production of materials used in a final product. Ford's Model T required several different assembled and finished products, including rubber tires, molded wood trims, formed steel frames, car body panels, and carefully worked glass for instrument panels and windshields. Vertical integration planning permitted the Ford Motor Company to control nearly every aspect of the parts and products going into the final assembly of the automobiles and thereby help to lower the manufacturing costs for Ford, which enabled the company to lower the price point on his Model T.

Ford's plans for market dominance and his devotion to controlling nearly every aspect of the manufacturing processes for the Model T through strategic planning and vertical integration were showcased in his mega-manufacturing

complex, the River Rouge Plant. The River Rouge Complex opened in 1928. Ford and Kahn partnered again in the design of the massive factories located near the Rouge River in Dearborn, Michigan. The Rouge, as many employees and local area residents came to call the sprawling complex, combined Ford's and Kahn's best plans for vertical integration and assembly and included ninety-three buildings and almost 16 million square feet of manufacturing floor space. The Rouge Complex's construction also included over one hundred miles of railroad track to move equipment, materials, and supplies as well as an iron-ore plant to process the steel required in manufacturing the body and frame of the automobile, an electric plant to provide the energy needed for production, and its own shipping and receiving docks on the Rouge River. Even though the final assembly of the Model T still occurred at the Highland Park Plant, the Rouge Complex allowed Ford to vertically integrate his business and by the 1930s, the Rouge Complex converted raw materials into the standardized parts that made up the Model T. The River Rouge Complex epitomized the best practices of Fordism and vertical integration during the early 20th century.

Ford not only wanted to price and market the automobile to the masses through designing and implementing factories and production practices intended to cut costs and increase output, but he also desired a workforce that could be easily replaced. One of the tenets of Fordism included detailed implementation of a step-by-step manufacturing process broken down into basic, repetitive, and easily trainable tasks. The Ford Motor Company, like many larger companies during the early 20th century, experienced high rates of worker turnover, resulting in a vast amount of new workers with few skills who needed training. Rather than spend the time and energy training new workers just to have them take those skills elsewhere, Ford's standardization of parts allowed the production and assembly processes to be broken down in easily learned repetitive jobs. Since the assembly line moved on a regulated basis, employees hustled to complete rudimentary tasks such as tightening the nuts on the back tire of a Model T, screwing a seat into place, or attaching the steering wheel. For the employees, this system meant eight to ten hours a day, five to six days a week, of completing the same task over and over again until their employment ended. This system of easily trainable tasks for production combined with the automated assembly line meant that workers never learned the entire processes involved in building the parts and assembling the automobile but improved upon their abilities to do simplified tasks quickly and accurately. Ford's industrial engineers studied workers on the assembly lines at factories such as the River Rouge Complex and the Highland Park Plant and determined that speeding up the assembly lines' pace increased production. Workers were required to maintain the speeds of the lines and when workers could not keep up with the steadily increasing pace of the line, new workers replaced them. Eventually, the increasing speed-up of the assembly lines and other abuses by the Ford Motor Company toward employees in the factories led to the rise of one of America's most powerful 20th century unions, the United Auto Workers.

A key tenet of Fordism is the payment of high wages to factory employees so that those workers could afford to purchase the products they made in factories such as the River Rouge Complex. During the 1930s, when hundreds of smaller automobile manufacturers went bankrupt and laid-off thousands of employees, Ford's River Rouge Complex alone employed over 100,000 workers in low-skilled tasks. Those Ford Motor Company workers, however, often labored in difficult and sometimes dangerous jobs and faced layoffs that could last up to several months during car model transitions when the factories would have to change out equipment. Since few federal or state-level regulations existed for issues such as workplace safety or employee compensation for layoffs and injuries, many Ford workers suffered during difficult economic times. Ford, however, preferred to pay the majority of workers good wages for their work and in 1914 offered the unheard of sum of $5 per eight-hour day for factory workers (the modern equivalent is almost $120). Ford's $5 Day helped promote a massive population increase in the greater metropolitan area of Detroit and was a significant contributing factor in pulling poor Southerners, especially African Americans, north for jobs and opportunities unavailable in the South. Detroit's African American population grew by over 400 percent in the years 1910 to 1920, and many of the city's new residents looked to jobs at Ford Motor Company or one of its competitors as an opportunity for social and economic advantages. News of Ford's $5 Day reached thousands of the working poor in Europe as well

and provided significant reasons to immigrate to the United States during World War I.

Ford's $5 Day, however, was available only to selected factory workers. In order to determine who qualified for Ford's $5 Day, the company hired professionally trained sociologists to staff the Ford Sociological Department and to interview factory workers and assess their worthiness for the $5 Day. Workers, according to Ford's Sociological Department's guidelines for qualifying for the $5 Day, had to be male and responsible for either a family of their own or elderly parents, had to maintain a savings account in a bank, either owned or desired to own homes, and pledged to abstain from alcohol and other activities that distracted from issues related to work and family. If factory workers qualified, the sociologists visited their homes unannounced to speak with wives, friends, and neighbors about the workers' habits and temperaments. Ford's Sociological Department became an intrusive and sometimes obstructive force in the lives of many factory workers but also helped establish an American standard of living for the average Ford factory worker.

The establishment of a standard of living for American workers meant that the Ford Motor Company could set wages for the average factory worker so that he or she could afford to purchase the automobiles made at River Rouge and Highland Park. Ford's Sociological Department not only studied how workers worked and what paces to set the assembly lines, but also investigated wages and benefits to maximize employees' abilities to become consumers. A central tenet of Fordism is the payment of high wages to average workers to promote consumerism and within a few years following the introduction of the $5 Day, Ford Motor Company controlled about 60 percent of American automobile sales and had created a reliable, although low-skilled, workforce.

Ford found success through ideas of mass production of a reliable product at a fair price for the average working-class American and following World War I, Ford expanded operations into Europe with similar goals in mind. Ford believed not only that expanding automobile factories in Europe could bring significant profits to his company, but also that he could help modernize countries such as the Soviet Union through the business tenets of Fordism. Since Fordism included promoting mass consumerism, high wages to workers, and standardization in industry, communist leaders adopted these tenets in the Soviet Union to formulate plans for modernization and industrialism.

By the 1930s, Ford's business plan of standardizing parts and work procedures, designing factories for optimal production efficiency, paying high wages to workers to sustain a consumerist economy, and keeping costs low to maintain product price points within the reach of average workers led to phenomenal success for Ford Motor Company. In 1934, Italian political theorist and sociologist Antonio Gramsci, then jailed for his objections to Mussolini's Italian fascist regime, coined the term "Fordism." Gramsci, a Marxist intellectual, believed that Fordism could not be achieved in the fascist state because it undermined class systems; therefore, Gramsci believed that Fordism ultimately organized a planned economic state that eliminated many socioeconomic class divisions. Fordism in the United States did not eliminate socioeconomic class divisions among citizens, but Fordism did help develop a vibrant middle class that consumed increasing amounts of mass-produced goods.

The tenets of Fordism began to collapse in the 1970s. Facing the oil embargo with the Middle East oil producing countries, increased technologies that required trained workers with specialized skills, and the rise of service-industry jobs marked the end of Fordism. By the end of the 1970s, the tenets of Fordism no longer applied to the changing working world.

See also

Capitalism; Communism; Labor Movement; Unionization

ANITA ANTHONY-VANORSDAL

Further Reading

Biggs, Lindy. 1996. *The Rational Factory: Architecture, Technology, and Work in America's Age of Mass Production*. Baltimore, MD: Johns Hopkins University Press.

De Grazia, Victoria. 2005. *Irresistible Empire: America's Advance Through Twentieth-Century Europe*. Cambridge, MA: Belknap Press of Harvard University.

May, George. 1975. *A Most Unique Machine: The Michigan Origins of the American Automobile Industry*. Grand Rapids, MI: Eerdmans.

Meyer, Stephen. 1981. *The Five Dollar Day: Labor Management and Social Control in the Ford Motor Company, 1908–1921*. Albany, NY: State University of New York Press.

Fordism—Primary Document

Introduction

In 1922, American automobile manufacturer and leading industrialist Henry Ford penned My Life and Work. *The following excerpt from Chapter V, "Getting Into Production," details the importance involved in vertical integration, standardization of parts and manufacturing processes, and the benefits to industrial planning for both employees and the Ford Motor Company. While Ford admits that the processes involved in the success of his company developed over time, his concentration on the development of better, more efficient methods for industrial manufacturing raised wages for factory employees, reduced costs and potential accidents, and eliminated much of the time spent in useless activities.*

Document: *My Life and Work* by Henry Ford with Samuel Crowther (1922)

Chapter V: "Getting Into Production"

The more economical methods of production did not begin all at once. They began gradually—just as we began gradually to make our own parts. "Model T" was the first motor that we made ourselves. The great economies began in assembling and then extended to other sections so that, while to-day we have skilled mechanics in plenty, they do not produce automobiles—they make it easy for others to produce them. Our skilled men are the tool makers, the experimental workmen, the machinists, and the pattern makers. They are as good as any men in the world—so good, indeed, that they should not be wasted in doing that which the machines they contrive can do better. The rank and file of men come to us unskilled; they learn their jobs within a few hours or a few days. If they do not learn within that time they will never be of any use to us. These men are, many of them, foreigners, and all that is required before they are taken on is that they should be potentially able to do enough work to pay the overhead charges on the floor space they occupy. They do not have to be able-bodied men. We have jobs that require great physical strength—although they are rapidly lessening; we have other jobs that require no strength whatsoever—jobs which, as far as strength is concerned, might be attended to by a child of three.

It is not possible, without going deeply into technical processes, to present the whole development of manufacturing, step by step, in the order in which each thing came about. I do not know that this could be done, because something has been happening nearly every day and nobody can keep track. Take at random a number of the changes. From them it is possible not only to gain some idea of what will happen when this world is put on a production basis, but also to see how much more we pay for things than we ought to, and how much lower wages are than they ought to be, and what a vast field remains to be explored. The Ford Company is only a little way along on the journey.

A Ford car contains about five thousand parts—that is counting screws, nuts, and all. Some of the parts are fairly bulky and others are almost the size of watch parts. In our first assembling we simply started to put a car together at a spot on the floor and workmen brought to it the parts as they were needed in exactly the same way that one builds a house. When we started to make parts it was natural to create a single department of the factory to make that part, but usually one workman performed all of the operations necessary on a small part. The rapid press of production made it necessary to devise plans of production that would avoid having the workers falling over one another. The undirected worker spends more of his time walking about for materials and tools than he does in working; he gets small pay because pedestrianism is not a highly paid line.

The first step forward in assembly came when we began taking the work to the men instead of the men to the work. We now have two general principles in all operations—that a man shall never have to take more than one step, if possibly it can be avoided, and that no man need ever stoop over.

The principles of assembly are these:

(1) Place the tools and the men in the sequence of the operation so that each component part shall travel the least possible distance while in the process of finishing.

(2) Use work slides or some other form of carrier so that when a workman completes his operation, he drops the part always in the same place—which place must always be the most convenient place to his hand—and if possible have gravity carry the part to the next workman for his operation.

(3) Use sliding assembling lines by which the parts to be assembled are delivered at convenient distances.

The net result of the application of these principles is the reduction of the necessity for thought on the part of the worker and the reduction of his movements to a minimum. He does as nearly as possible only one thing with only one movement. The assembling of the chassis is, from the point of view of the non-mechanical mind, our most interesting and perhaps best known operation, and at one time it was an exceedingly important operation. We now ship out the parts for assembly at the point of distribution.

> **Source:** Ford, Henry, in collaboration with Samuel Crowther. *My Life and Work*. Garden City, NY: Doubleday, Page and Company, 1922. Available online at Project Gutenberg. http://www.gutenberg.org/cache/epub/7213/pg7213.html.

FOREIGN ALLIANCES

The influence of founding father George Washington's Farewell Address (1796), which advised Americans against forming permanent alliances, was far reaching. In fact, American history was characterized by a reluctance to form alliances and a penchant for isolationism. Turning over a new leaf out of necessity, Americans became more open to alliances after the outbreak of World War II and the Cold War era. However, Americans never completely abandoned their distrust of alliances, which they still regarded as temporary arrangements.

During the American Revolutionary era, Thomas Paine wrote a widely popular pamphlet entitled *Common Sense* (1776). Among several arguments for independence, Paine stated that the connection between the American colonies and Great Britain was allowing the mother country to pull the colonies into European wars. He encouraged the colonists to break the existing connection and advised them to refrain from making any new exclusive connections with any other European nation. During the war of independence, American leaders realized that they needed help against Britain, which was the most powerful country in the world. Consequently,

This cartoon, showing Uncle Sam protecting Latin Americans, has a small caption at the bottom: "Keep off! The Monroe doctrine MUST be respected." (Library of Congress)

they reluctantly negotiated an alliance with France. Before the alliance, General Washington regretted the fact that many of the colonial volunteers were ill-equipped. However, after the alliance was negotiated, France formally declared war against Britain and began fortifying the American effort. Within months, France sent troops, a fleet of ships, money, weapons, and much-needed gunpowder.

France maintained that the Franco-American alliance was permanent, but after American independence had been achieved, the Americans began the process of weaning themselves away from French-related responsibilities. Aware that the French were going behind their backs in dealing with the English, American diplomats negotiated a peace treaty with Britain without consulting the French. The action was a direct violation of the French alliance. In the years following the American Revolution, France became engaged in a revolution and a series of wars and asked the United States for help. Washington refused to comply, and instead issued

a Proclamation of Neutrality (1793). Washington and other American leaders refused to honor an alliance that would pull them into a foreign war. Furthermore, as part of his farewell address, President Washington defended his decision for neutrality and warned the young republic against entering into permanent alliances with foreign powers. The parting advice from the greatly admired American icon was very influential. President John Adams followed his predecessor's advice by avoiding wars and alliances, even at great personal political detriment.

In 1801, during his first inaugural address, Thomas Jefferson announced that he would seek "entangling alliances with none." After Napoleon Bonaparte wrestled the Louisiana Territory from Spain, Jefferson became uneasy about having a strong French presence as a neighbor. Under the circumstances, Jefferson grudgingly considered making an alliance with Britain for protection against the land-grabbing Napoleon, but, ultimately, the Louisiana Purchase (1803) rendered an alliance unnecessary. Jefferson did not want the United States to expand as it did with the new territory, because he feared that democracy would become more difficult with the nation's geographical growth. However, he considered alliances and Napoleon's empire-building activities bigger threats to the safety of the nation. During the War of 1812, which came about because the British refused to respect American neutrality rights among other issues, President James Madison ran the war against Britain without entering into any alliances. In the end, the nation was able to stand on its own, and although the issues that brought about the war remained unresolved after the war, Americans gained a patriotic zeal and a greater conviction against alliances. With the Treaty of Ghent (1814), the war was officially declared over and a new era of a tenuous and unofficial American-British alliance began.

The natural boundary provided by the Atlantic Ocean fostered a continued aloofness to alliances with European nations and a quest for isolation. In 1823, the Monroe Doctrine declared the American continent and the Western Hemisphere closed to further European colonization, because the political systems of European powers were too different to those of the United States, which were, therefore, "dangerous" to the American political system. Basically, the doctrine's net effect was to further isolate the United States from Europe. During the American Civil War (1861–1865), the Confederate States of America unsuccessfully attempted to negotiate an alliance with Britain. As it turned out, the British needed the North's wheat more than the South's cotton. European nations, as they had done for centuries, remained actively involved in alliance politics, because they saw it as the best way to achieve a balance of power. However, both the inconclusive Crimean War (1853–1856) and the French withdrawal from Mexico in 1867 convinced many American political leaders that alliance diplomacy caused more problems than it solved. In fact, by the end of the 19th century, many Americans believed that alliances caused wars instead of helping to avoid them.

During the early 20th century, imperial-minded leaders like President Theodore Roosevelt (1901–1909) and Senator Henry Cabot Lodge of Massachusetts sought to expand America's reach in the world by acquiring territory overseas and entering into alliances. However, the American people resisted and held fast to anti-alliance sentiments. In fact, many Americans believed that the alliance system that existed in Europe had been a major cause of World War I (1914–1918). The United States resisted formally entering the Great War. When President Woodrow Wilson finally did send the American Expeditionary Force in 1917, it remained exclusively under the command of U.S. officers. The United States refused to join the alliance between the British, French, and Russians. Instead, the U.S. participation in the war was conducted as a coalition force (a temporary force with the primary mission of providing military assistance against a common enemy). Even before the war's end, Wilson devised a plan for peace. In spite of Wilson's efforts, the U.S. Senate rejected the Treaty of Versailles, which blocked U.S. membership in the League of Nations. Wishing to avoid future entanglements with European nations, Congress declared the end of the war with an independent resolution of Congress.

In the 1930s, the Great Depression intensified American isolationist tendencies. In the meantime, aggression was sweeping across Europe. Adolf Hitler (Germany) and Benito Mussolini (Italy) were actively engaged in territorial conquests. In 1939, Germany's invasion of Poland drew a declaration of war from Britain and France. The United States remained officially neutral until 1941 when both President Franklin D. Roosevelt and Congress began openly supplying weapons to the allies. American sentiment against sending troops to Europe remained strong until late in 1941 when the Japanese bombed Pearl Harbor, Hawaii. Throughout the war, Roosevelt worked very closely with Winston Churchill (Britain) and to a lesser extent with Joseph Stalin (Russia). The Grand Alliance (as it came to be called) between Roosevelt and Churchill was very often a one-sided affair with Roosevelt dictating strategy. Furthermore, Roosevelt never abandoned the idea that the wartime alliance with these nations was merely a temporary necessity in a time of crisis. In truth, Roosevelt had no way of knowing that postwar developments would thrust the world into a conflict between communist and noncommunist nations, which would make alliances more necessary than ever before.

Indeed, the Cold War (a deterioration of U.S.-Soviet relations after World War II) led to the creation of the Eastern bloc (the Warsaw Pact led by the Soviet Union) and the Western bloc (the North Atlantic Treaty Organization [NATO] supported by the United States). The United States devised the Truman Doctrine and Marshall Plan to rebuild Western Europe with the aim of helping these countries fend off communist influence. From 1945 to 1989, the Soviets and the

Americans engaged in an arms race that eventually evolved into a space race. While the Soviet allies sought to expand communism, American allies attempted to contain its spread all over the world. The end of the Cold War did not signal an end to America's involvement with alliances. By the late 1900s and early 2000s, the United States employed alliances to continue to spread its influence in a world enveloped in globalism (an interconnected world). For example, the terrorist attacks in 2001 made it painfully clear or clearer to Americans that isolationism had become impractical. On the surface, the U.S. participation in alliances after World War II might have seemed to be a radical change of course. However, in truth, it was not. As a world power, the United States remained in control of the alliances it entered and served its purposes. Basically, none of the postwar alliances really entangled the United States in any way. Instead, U.S. involvement in alliances remained as it had been since Washington's time—only when necessary and always temporary.

See also

Anticommunism; Containment; Diplomacy; Foreign Interventionism; Free Trade; Imperialism; Isolationism; Monroe Doctrine

ROLANDO AVILA

Further Reading

Bailey, Thomas Andrew. 1980. *A Diplomatic History of the American People.* Englewood Cliffs, NJ: Prentice-Hall.

Gilbert, Felix. 1961. *To the Farewell Address: Ideas of Early American Foreign Policy.* Princeton, NJ: Princeton University Press.

Hastedt, Glenn P. 2004. *Encyclopedia of American Foreign Policy.* New York: Facts on File.

Neustadt, Richard E. 1970. *Alliance Politics.* New York: Columbia University Press.

Sabrosky, Alan Ned, ed. 1988. *Alliances in U.S. Foreign Policy: Issues in the Quest for Collective Defense.* Boulder, CO: Westview Press.

Foreign Alliances—Primary Document

Introduction

Before leaving office after a second term, President George Washington issued an open letter with parting advice to the American people. The letter came to be known as Washington's Farewell Address. Among other things, Washington cautioned Americans against forming permanent alliances with other nations because he felt that the best course of action for the recently created and militarily weak nation was to avoid being pulled into wars in which the United States had little to gain but much to lose. In fact, during the French Revolutionary Wars (1792–1802), France, counting on the Treaty of Alliance of 1778 that allied France and the United States during the American Revolution (1775–1783), asked Americans for help. Washington declined to aid France militarily by arguing that the Treaty of Alliance had been a temporary agreement. As an official statement for his stand, Washington declared a Proclamation of Neutrality in 1793. The following year, Congress supported Washington's decision with the passage of the Neutrality Act of 1794. Washington's attitudes toward alliances lined up with American foreign policy for many years, but especially during the early years of the republic and the years between the two world wars in the 20th century.

Document: President George Washington's Farewell Address (September 17, 1796)

Friends and Fellow-Citizens:

Observe good faith and justice towards all nations; cultivate peace and harmony with all. Religion and morality enjoin this conduct; and can it be, that good policy does not equally enjoin it—It will be worthy of a free, enlightened, and at no distant period, a great nation, to give to mankind the magnanimous and too novel example of a people always guided by an exalted justice and benevolence. Who can doubt that, in the course of time and things, the fruits of such a plan would richly repay any temporary advantages which might be lost by a steady adherence to it? Can it be that Providence has not connected the permanent felicity of a nation with its virtue? The experiment, at least, is recommended by every sentiment which ennobles human nature. Alas! is it rendered impossible by its vices?

In the execution of such a plan, nothing is more essential than that permanent, inveterate antipathies against particular nations, and passionate attachments for others, should be excluded; and that, in place of them, just and amicable feelings towards all should be cultivated. The nation which indulges towards another a habitual hatred or a habitual fondness is in some degree a slave. It is a slave to its animosity or to its affection, either of which is sufficient to lead it astray from its duty and its interest. Antipathy in one nation against another disposes each more readily to offer insult and injury, to lay hold of slight causes of umbrage, and to be haughty and intractable, when accidental or trifling occasions of dispute occur. Hence, frequent collisions, obstinate, envenomed, and bloody contests. The nation, prompted by ill-will and resentment, sometimes impels to war the government, contrary to the best calculations of policy. The government sometimes participates in the national propensity, and adopts through passion what reason would reject; at other times it makes the animosity of the nation subservient to projects of hostility instigated by pride, ambition, and other sinister and pernicious motives. The peace often, sometimes perhaps the liberty, of nations, has been the victim.

So likewise, a passionate attachment of one nation for another produces a variety of evils. Sympathy for the favorite nation, facilitating the illusion of an imaginary common interest in cases where no real common interest exists, and infusing into one the enmities of the other, betrays the former into a participation in the quarrels and wars of the latter without adequate inducement or justification. It leads also to concessions to the favorite nation of privileges denied to others which is apt doubly to injure the nation making the concessions; by unnecessarily parting with what ought to have been retained, and by exciting jealousy, ill-will, and a disposition to retaliate, in the parties from whom equal privileges are withheld. And it gives to ambitious, corrupted, or deluded citizens (who devote themselves to the favorite nation), facility to betray or sacrifice the interests of their own country, without odium, sometimes even with popularity; gilding, with the appearances of a virtuous sense of obligation, a commendable deference for public opinion, or a laudable zeal for public good, the base or foolish compliances of ambition, corruption, or infatuation.

As avenues to foreign influence in innumerable ways, such attachments are particularly alarming to the truly enlightened and independent patriot. How many opportunities do they afford to tamper with domestic factions, to practice the arts of seduction, to mislead public opinion, to influence or awe the public councils. Such an attachment of a small or

weak towards a great and powerful nation dooms the former to be the satellite of the latter.

Against the insidious wiles of foreign influence (I conjure you to believe me, fellow-citizens) the jealousy of a free people ought to be constantly awake, since history and experience prove that foreign influence is one of the most baneful foes of republican government. But that jealousy to be useful must be impartial; else it becomes the instrument of the very influence to be avoided, instead of a defense against it. Excessive partiality for one foreign nation and excessive dislike of another cause those whom they actuate to see danger only on one side, and serve to veil and even second the arts of influence on the other. Real patriots who may resist the intrigues of the favorite are liable to become suspected and odious, while its tools and dupes usurp the applause and confidence of the people, to surrender their interests.

The great rule of conduct for us in regard to foreign nations is in extending our commercial relations, to have with them as little political connection as possible. So far as we have already formed engagements, let them be fulfilled with perfect good faith. Here let us stop. Europe has a set of primary interests which to us have none; or a very remote relation. Hence she must be engaged in frequent controversies, the causes of which are essentially foreign to our concerns. Hence, therefore, it must be unwise in us to implicate ourselves by artificial ties in the ordinary vicissitudes of her politics, or the ordinary combinations and collisions of her friendships or enmities.

Our detached and distant situation invites and enables us to pursue a different course. If we remain one people under an efficient government. the period is not far off when we may defy material injury from external annoyance; when we may take such an attitude as will cause the neutrality we may at any time resolve upon to be scrupulously respected; when belligerent nations, under the impossibility of making acquisitions upon us, will not lightly hazard the giving us provocation; when we may choose peace or war, as our interest, guided by justice, shall counsel.

Why forego the advantages of so peculiar a situation? Why quit our own to stand upon foreign ground? Why, by interweaving our destiny with that of any part of Europe, entangle our peace and prosperity in the toils of European ambition, rivalship, interest, humor or caprice?

It is our true policy to steer clear of permanent alliances with any portion of the foreign world; so far, I mean, as we are now at liberty to do it; for let me not be understood as capable of patronizing infidelity to existing engagements. I hold the maxim no less applicable to public than to private affairs, that honesty is always the best policy. I repeat it, therefore, let those engagements be observed in their genuine sense. But, in my opinion, it is unnecessary and would be unwise to extend them.

Taking care always to keep ourselves by suitable establishments on a respectable defensive posture, we may safely trust to temporary alliances for extraordinary emergencies.

Harmony, liberal intercourse with all nations, are recommended by policy, humanity, and interest. But even our commercial policy should hold an equal and impartial hand; neither seeking nor granting exclusive favors or preferences; consulting the natural course of things; diffusing and diversifying by gentle means the streams of commerce, but forcing nothing; establishing (with powers so disposed, in order to give trade a stable course, to define the rights of our merchants, and to enable the government to support them) conventional rules of intercourse, the best that present circumstances and mutual opinion will permit, but temporary, and liable to be from time to time abandoned or varied, as experience and circumstances shall dictate; constantly keeping in view that it is folly in one nation to look for disinterested favors from another; that it must pay with a portion of its independence for whatever it may accept under that character; that, by such acceptance, it may place itself in the condition of having given equivalents for nominal favors, and yet of being reproached with ingratitude for not giving more. There can be no greater error than to expect or calculate upon real favors from nation to nation. It is an illusion, which experience must cure, which a just pride ought to discard.

In offering to you, my countrymen, these counsels of an old and affectionate friend, I dare not hope they will make the strong and lasting impression I could wish; that they will

control the usual current of the passions, or prevent our nation from running the course which has hitherto marked the destiny of nations. But, if I may even flatter myself that they may be productive of some partial benefit, some occasional good; that they may now and then recur to moderate the fury of party spirit, to warn against the mischiefs of foreign intrigue, to guard against the impostures of pretended patriotism; this hope will be a full recompense for the solicitude for your welfare, by which they have been dictated.

George Washington

United States—September 17, 1796

Source: United State Government Printing Office Homepage. http://www.gpo.gov/fdsys/pkg/GPO-CDOC-106sdoc21/pdf/GPO-CDOC-106sdoc21.pdf.

FOREIGN INTERVENTIONISM

Foreign interventionism is a subject of continuing debate in the field of foreign policy that also has domestic and political implications and effects. It is a term for a strategy of proactive activity undertaken by a nation or state, to help or manipulate the economy, politics, social, and cultural activities of another country, usually lesser than the intervening country. The United States has grown out of its policy, pursued through its first century-plus, of non-interventionism, or isolationism, the direct opposite of interventionism, to occupy super power status. As such, it often has arrogated for itself the duty of being caretaker of the world. The United States has therefore intervened in the affairs of other countries since the end of the 19th century. The intervention had been in two forms: aggressive and non-aggressive. In the aggressive way, military forces of the United States are normally applied to force nations to acquiesce to the whims of the United States, while other means such as aid, diplomacy, talks, and sanctions have been the non-aggressive means of achieving policy ends.

President James Monroe promoted isolationism in response to the circumstances of his time. The Monroe Doctrine was a policy of the United States introduced on December 2, 1823. It stated that further efforts by European nations to colonize land or interfere with states in North or South

America would be viewed as acts of aggression, requiring U.S. intervention. At the same time, with interventionism came isolationism: the doctrine noted that the United States would neither interfere with existing European colonies nor meddle in the internal concerns of European countries. The Monroe idea became known as the Monroe Doctrine and was invoked by other American presidents including Theodore Roosevelt, Woodrow Wilson, John F. Kennedy, Lyndon B. Johnson, Ronald Reagan, and many others who followed Monroe. Yet it would be William McKinley who would lead the United States—or be led, according to his critics—into foreign intervention in Cuba in 1898. The Spanish-American War

Workers clean and landscape underneath a sign showing U.S. president Barack Obama, top right, and Ghana president John Atta Mills, top left, along a road where Obama passed during his visit, in Accra, Ghana, on July 10, 2009. Obama arrived for his first visit to sub-Saharan Africa since taking office. (AP Photo/Rebecca Blackwell)

led to the United States acquiring Guam and the Philippines, where it faced an insurgent rebellion from 1899 to 1902.

After World War I, public opinion in favor of U.S. isolationism was still so high that even though the necessary points and structures needed for the enactment of the League of Nations were more American than European, the United States was not a member of the League of Nations. Little did Americans realize that isolationism does not hold, in itself, the shield of defense and in their state of neutrality, they could not avoid World War II and the threats and attacks of the Axis powers, Germany, Italy, and Japan.

Opposed to isolationism and recalling the failures surrounding the League of Nations, President Franklin D. Roosevelt initiated talks on a successor agency to the League of Nations during World War II. The United Nations (UN) Charter was drafted at a conference in April–June 1945; this charter took effect on October 24, 1945, and the United Nations began its operations. The UN was essentially a restatement and reworking of the ideas behind the League of Nations but with an enforcement mechanism.

From the hot war of World War II, the United States found itself in the Cold War with the Union of Soviet Socialist Republics (USSR). The nation's next round of interventionism came to the fore in the Marshall Plan and the pursuit of the policy of Containment. The Marshall Plan (officially the European Recovery Program or ERP) was the American initiative to aid Europe, in which the United States gave economic support to help rebuild European economies after the end of World War II. The plan was in operation for four years beginning in April 1948. The goals of the United States were to rebuild war-devastated regions, remove trade barriers, modernize industry, and make Europe prosperous again while limiting the spread of Soviet-style communism and expanding American markets. The initiative was named after Secretary of State George Marshall. The plan had bipartisan support in Washington, where the Republicans controlled Congress and the Democrats controlled the White House. The plan was largely the creation of State Department officials, especially William L. Clayton and George F. Kennan, with help from the Brookings Institution, as requested by Senator Arthur H. Vandenberg, chairman of the Senate Foreign Relations Committee, who had evolved from an isolationist to a believer in internationalism and, when necessary, interventionism. Marshall spoke of an urgent need to help the European recovery in his address at Harvard University in June 1947.

Containment was a U.S. policy to prevent the spread of communism abroad, a component of the Cold War. This policy was a response to a series of moves by the Soviet Union to enlarge communist influence in Eastern Europe, China, Korea, Africa, and Vietnam. The basis of the doctrine was articulated in a 1946 cable by Kennan, then a U.S. diplomat in the Soviet Union. The word *containment* is associated most strongly with the policies of President Harry Truman (1945–1953), including the establishment of the North Atlantic Treaty Organization (NATO), a mutual defense pact. Although President Dwight Eisenhower (1953–1961) toyed with the rival doctrine of *rollback*, he refused to intervene in the Hungarian uprising of 1956. President Lyndon Johnson (1963–1969) cited containment as a justification for his policies in Vietnam.

The policy continued in the late 20th century. President Richard Nixon (1969–1974), working with advisor Henry Kissinger, followed a policy called détente, or relaxation of tensions. This involved expanded trade and cultural contacts, as well as the Strategic Arms Limitation Talks. President Jimmy Carter (1977–1981) at first emphasized human rights rather than anticommunism. He dropped this stance and returned to containment when the Soviets invaded Afghanistan in 1979.

After settling Europe, poverty and instability in most parts of Middle East, Asia, and Africa became the next line of problems the West and the United States attempted to solve. In 1970, the world's richest countries agreed to give 0.7 percent of their GNI (gross national income) as official international development aid, annually. Since that time, despite billions given each year, rich nations have rarely met their actual promised targets. For example, the United States is often the largest donor in dollar terms, but ranks among the lowest in terms of meeting the stated 0.7 percent of its GNI target.

The U.S. Congress passed the Foreign Assistance Act on September 4, 1961, reorganizing U.S. foreign assistance programs and separating military and nonmilitary aid. The act mandated the creation of an agency to administer economic assistance programs, the U.S. Agency for International Development (USAID), which was established by President Kennedy two months later. USAID became the first U.S. foreign assistance organization whose primary focus was long-term economic and social development.

Of this foreign support, in 2011, for instance, $17.8 billion was spent on defense, $31.7 billion on economic activities, and $14.1 billion on aid. Most Americans are of the opinion that U.S. aid to poor countries is grossly misplaced since a chunk of it goes to support terrorist and Islamic nations. Tall on the list of countries the United States supports is Afghanistan, followed by Israel, then Iraq, Pakistan, Egypt, Haiti, and Kenya—and, obviously, the United States has been involved militarily in Iraq and Afghanistan in particular.

Nevertheless, no matter how horrific or troubling this aid seems, America always has something to gain from it. Its prestige as a world economic and political leader, the creation of markets, extraction and mining corporations around the world, with majority of these found in developing countries, and the re-instatement of democratic institutions are just some of the benefits to America and the developed nations.

Some foreign intervention methods are physically passive and non-aggressive: economic sanctions, embargo, boycott, trade sanctions, political sanctions, and international sanctions. Ideologies for supporting or opposing varying degrees of foreign intervention in international relations can have philosophical, religious, or scientific origins. Within political philosophy there are variations giving ideological foundation and reasoning to different degrees of foreign interventionism. The non-aggression principle holds that aggression is inherently illegitimate, but does not preclude defense against aggression.

Efforts in foreign intervention may include diplomacy to dispute resolution. Aid normally functions as bait in these interventionist schools of thought. Aid in some instances has acted as a kind of bulwark against terrorism and countries that receive the aid are told in overt and covert terms to respect the terms and conditions that go with it, of which the most important is the upholding of American principles and democracy. Those nations are supposed to allow America a free hand in many important internal political affairs which external powers are constitutionally banned from contributing.

Nevertheless, the spate of poverty and squalor in Africa put governments in a very ambivalent position. Africa receives a greater share, at 36 percent, of total global aid than any other part of the world. Over the past four decades, aid to Africa has quadrupled from around $11 billion to $44 billion, with a net increase of almost $10 billion during the period 2005–2008 alone. This is supposed to reduce poverty, the rate of spread of deadly diseases such as AIDS and malaria, and improve agriculture, health, education, and the general living conditions of the people. Although a chunk of this aid finds its way into the pockets of corrupt and greedy politicians, the role the little aid plays in the general lives of many Africans is immense.

Using Ghana as a case study, even though the country is touted as one of the fastest-growing economies in the world, the gross domestic product (GDP) in Ghana was worth just $40.71 billion in 2012. The GDP value of Ghana represents 0.07 percent of the world economy. From 1960 until 2012, Ghana GDP averaged $7.8 billion reaching an all-time high of $40.7 billion in December 2012 and a record low of $1.2 billion in December 1960. The GDP measures the national income and output for a given country's economy. This tiny GDP of Ghana puts the nation at ninth position in Africa and second to Nigeria in West Africa. This is the worth of a nation with about 25.37 million people.

Relations between the United States and Ghana started with U.S. recognition of Ghana as a sovereign state in 1957, when the latter gained its independence from Great Britain. A promising sociopolitical relationship begun, Ghana received aid from the United States in diverse forms. This relationship was marred by the alignment of the first president of Ghana, Dr. Kwame Nkrumah, to the communist countries: Russia, Bolivia, Cuba, and Venezuela. Most Ghanaians are of the belief that the Central Intelligence Agency (CIA) masterminded the overthrow of Nkrumah. After 1966, the relationship became better, but became again particularly unsteady in the early 1980s, apparently because of Ghana's relations with Libya. Libya came to the aid of Ghana soon afterward by providing much-needed economic assistance. Libya also has extensive financial holdings in Ghana. In July 1985, a distant relative of Rawlings, Michael Soussoudis, was arrested in the United States and charged with espionage. Despite Soussoudis's conviction, he was exchanged the following December for several known U.S. CIA agents in Accra, but not before diplomats had been expelled in both Accra and Washington. In spite of these incidents, relations between the United States and Ghana had improved markedly by the late 1980s. Former U.S. president Jimmy Carter visited Ghana in 1986 and again in 1988 and was warmly received by Ghana's government. Presidents Bush, Clinton, and Obama have all visited Ghana in their tenures in office to deepen these fruitful diplomatic relations. Carter's Global 2000 agricultural program is quite popular with Ghanaian farmers and helps promote good relations with the United States. In 1989, the United States forgave $114 million of Ghana's foreign debt, part of a larger debt relief effort by Western nations.

The United States has strongly favored Ghana's economic and political reform policies and, since the birth of the Fourth Republic and Ghana's return to constitutional rule, has offered assistance to help Ghana institutionalize and consolidate its steps toward democratic governance. By 1994, U.S. development aid totaled about $38 million; in addition, the United States supplied more than $16 million in food aid. Thousands of Ghanaians have been educated in the United States. Close relations are maintained between educational and scientific institutions, and cultural links, particularly between Ghanaians and African Americans, are strong.

U.S. development assistance to Ghana in fiscal year 2007 totaled more than $55.1 million, with programs in small farmer competitiveness and health, including HIV/AIDS and maternal child health, education, and governance. Ghana was the first country in the world to accept Peace Corps volunteers, and the program remains one of the largest. Currently, there are more than 150 volunteers in Ghana. Almost half of Peace Corps volunteers work in education, and the others in agro-forestry, small business development, health education, water sanitation, and youth development. Ghana's $547 million compact with the Millennium Challenge Corporation is the most recent achievement in the U.S.-Ghanaian development partnership.

Today, the United States has 294 embassies across the world and many of these are in places most Americans think are high-risk areas such as North Africa and the Middle East. The entire world seems to enjoy the benevolence of the United States, a nation that could boast of a quarter of the whole world's wealth and spends not less than $700 billion on its military and security annually. But this benevolence has not gone unchallenged at home or abroad.

The rationale behind U.S. foreign interventionism from time immemorial had attracted unending debates that never seem to ever have a convergent end, yet this albatross, as critics often perceive it as being, needs to be viewed always from the points of view of the recipients and the donors.

See also

JOSEPH OSEI

Further Reading

Adler, Selig. 1957. *The Isolationist Impulse: Its Twentieth Century Reaction.* New York: The Free Press.

Agorsah, E. Kofi, and Childs, G. Tucker. 2005. *Africa and the African Diaspora: Cultural Adaptation and Resistance.* Portland, OR: Author House.

Bailey, Thomas. 1980. *A Diplomatic History of the American People.* 10th ed. Englewood Cliffs, NJ: Prentice Hall.

Cohen, Warren I. 1995. *The Cambridge History of American Foreign Relations: Volume 4, America in the Age of Soviet Power, 1945–1991.* Cambridge, UK: Cambridge University Press.

Fawcett, Louise, ed. 2013. *International Relations of the Middle East.* 3rd ed. New York: Oxford University Press.

Herring, George C. 2008. *From Colony to Superpower: U.S. Foreign Relations Since 1776.* New York: Oxford University Press.

Iriye, Akira. 1995. *The Cambridge History of American Foreign Relations: Volume 3, The Globalizing of America, 1913–1945.* Cambridge, UK: Cambridge University Press.

Maurer, Noel. 2013. *The Empire Trap: The Rise and Fall of U.S. Intervention to Protect American Property Overseas, 1893–2013.* Princeton, NJ: Princeton University Press.

Owusu, Maxwell. 1994. "Guiding Principles and Objectives." In La Verle Berry, ed. *A Country Study: Ghana.* Washington, DC: Library of Congress.

Robinson, William I. 1996. *Polyarchy: Globalization, US Intervention, and Hegemony*, PA. Pittsburgh: Syndicate Press of University of Cambridge.

Foreign Interventionism—Primary Document

Introduction

In 1917, President Woodrow Wilson asked Congress to declare war on Germany and thus bring the United States into World War I. Wilson hoped that by entering the war the United States could help "make the world safe for democracy." But Wilson, like other presidents before him, had tried to export American ideals beyond the nation's borders. An incident in 1914, during the Mexican Revolution, which had begun in 1910, led Wilson to ask Congress for authority to send the U.S. Navy to Mexico. In the following speech, Wilson explained to Congress his views, and what he saw as the importance of American intervention in foreign affairs that affected the United States.

Document: President Woodrow Wilson's Address to Congress on the Mexican Crisis (April 20, 1914)

Gentleman of the Congress: It is my duty to call your attention to a situation which has arisen in our dealings with General Victoriano Huerta at Mexico City which calls for action, and to ask your advice and cooperation in acting upon it. On the ninth of April a paymaster of the U.S.S. *Dolphin* landed at the Iturbide Bridge landing at Tampico with a whaleboat and boat's crew to take off certain supplies needed by his ship, and while engaged in loading the boat was arrested by an officer and squad of men of the army of General Huerta. Neither the paymaster nor anyone of the boat's crew was armed. Two of the men were in the boat when the arrest took place and were obliged to leave it and submit to be taken into custody, notwithstanding the fact that the boat carried, both at her bow and at her stern, the flag of the United States. The officer who made the arrest was proceeding up one of the streets of the town with his prisoners when met by an officer of higher authority, who ordered him to return to the landing and await orders; and within an hour and a half from the time of the arrest orders were received from the commander of the Huertista forces at Tampico for the release of the paymaster and his men. The release was followed by apologies from the commander and later by an expression of regret by General Huerta himself. General Huerta urged that martial law obtained at the time at Tampico; that orders had been issued that no one should be allowed to land at the Iturbide Bridge; and that our sailors had no right to land there. Our naval commanders at the port had not been notified of any such prohibition; and. even if they had been, the only justifiable course open to the local authorities would have been to request the paymaster and his crew to withdraw and to lodge a protest with the commanding officer of the fleet, Admiral Mayo regarded the arrest as so serious an affront that he was not satisfied with the apologies offered but demanded that the flag of the United States be saluted with special ceremony by the military commander of the port.

The incident cannot be regarded as a trivial one, especially as two of the men arrested were taken from the boat itself, that is to say, from the territory of the United States; but had it stood by itself it might have been attributed to the ignorance or arrogance of a single officer. Unfortunately, it was not an isolated case. A series of incidents have recently occurred which cannot but create the impression that the representatives of General Huerta were willing to go out of their way to show disregard for the dignity and rights of this government and felt perfectly safe in doing what they pleased, making free to show in many ways their irritation and contempt. A few days after the incident at Tampico an orderly from the U.S.S. *Minnesota* was arrested at Vera Cruz while ashore in uniform to obtain the ship's mail and was for a time thrown into jail. An official dispatch from this government to its embassy at Mexico City was withheld by the authorities of the telegraphic service until peremptorily demanded by our Chargé d'Affaires in person. So far as I can learn, such wrongs and annoyances have been suffered to occur only against representatives of the United States. I have heard of no complaints from other governments of similar treatment. Subsequent explanations and formal apologies did not and could not alter the popular impression, which it is possible it had been the object of the Huertista authorities to create, that the Government of the United States was being singled out, and might be singled out with impunity, for slights and affronts in retaliation for its refusal to recognize the pretensions of General Huerta to be regarded as the constitutional provisional President of the Republic of Mexico.

The manifest danger of such a situation was that such offenses might grow from bad to worse until something happened of so gross and intolerable a sort as to lead directly and inevitably to armed conflict. It was necessary that the apologies of General Huerta and his representatives should go much further, that they should be such as to attract the attention of the whole population to their significance, and such as to impress upon General Huerta himself the necessity of seeing to it that no further occasion for explanations and professed regrets should arise. I, therefore, felt it my duty to sustain Admiral Mayo in the whole of his demand and to insist that the flag of the United States should be saluted in such a way as to indicate a new spirit and attitude on the part of the Huertistas.

Such a salute General Huerta has refused, and I have come to ask your approval and support in the course I now purpose to pursue.

This Government can, I earnestly hope, in no circumstances be forced into war with the people of Mexico. Mexico is torn by civil strife. If we are to accept the tests of its own constitution, it has no government. General Huerta has set his power up in the City of Mexico, such as it is, without right and by methods for which there can be no justification. Only part of the country is under his control. If armed conflict should unhappily come as a result of his attitude of personal resentment toward this government, we should be fighting only General Huerta and those who adhere to him and give him their support, and our object would be only to restore to the people of the distracted republic the opportunity to set up again their own laws and their own government.

But I earnestly hope that war is not now in question. I believe that I speak for the American people when I say that we do not desire to control in any degree the affairs of our sister republic. Our feeling for the people of Mexico is one of deep and genuine friendship, and everything that we have so far done or refrained from doing has proceeded from our desire to help them, not to hinder or embarrass them. We would not wish even to exercise the good offices of friendship without their welcome and consent. The people of Mexico are entitled to settle their own domestic affairs in their own way, and we sincerely desire to respect their right. The present situation need have none of the grave implications of interference if we deal with it promptly, firmly, and wisely.

No doubt I could do what is necessary in the circumstances to enforce respect for our government without recourse to the Congress, and yet not exceed my constitutional powers as President; but I do not wish to act in a matter possibly of so grave consequence except in close conference and cooperation with both the Senate and House. I, therefore, come to ask your approval that I should use the armed forces of the United States in such ways and to such an extent as may be necessary to obtain from General Huerta and his adherents the fullest recognition of the rights and dignity of the United States, even amidst the distressing conditions now unhappily obtaining in Mexico.

There can in what we do be no thought of aggression or of selfish aggrandizement. We seek to maintain the dignity and authority of the United States only because we wish always to keep our great influence unimpaired for the uses of liberty, both in the United States and wherever else it may be employed for the benefit of mankind.

Source: Woodrow Wilson: "Address to a Joint Session of Congress on the Tampico Incident," April 20, 1914. Online by Gerhard Peters and John T. Woolley, *The American Presidency Project.* http://www.presidency.ucsb.edu/ws/?pid=65376.

FREE LOVE MOVEMENT

The 19th-century free love movement sought to separate state governance from such sexual matters as marriage, birth control, and adultery. It insisted that such matters were properly the concern of the individuals involved and no one else. The movement grew out of feelings of discontent with fundamental issues of personal freedom, the government, and the status quo.

Except for the issue of slavery, nothing in 19th-century life attracted as much reform energy as the issues of sex, marriage, and the family. During the period beginning around 1780 through the 19th century, gender roles and behavior often changed rapidly and significantly. New ideas of romantic love in marriage and more premarital sexual activity (indicated by a rise in premarital pregnancy) signaled the early start to the free love movement. Discontent for gender roles found expression in and out of the home through organized feminism, free love, birth control, and sexuality.

The combination of the two ideas of freedom and love was first used by Oneida Community writers in about 1849, and it probably originated with them. The Oneida Community—which referred to its spiritual practice as Bible communism—lasted from 1848 until 1880. The free love movement also appealed to the mission and practitioners of spiritualism, another religious organization. According to C. M. Overton, editor of *The Social Revolutionist,* a free love journal, spiritualism incorporated free love as one of its doctrines. Free love spiritualists believed that people control their own love relations by the laws of attraction, affinity, or free love and not by outside laws and rigid social norms. Free love spiritualists also believed that they should not sacrifice their individual happiness for the good of the community.

The free love movement of the 1870s was an outgrowth of deep changes throughout many layers of society, including moral codes, male-female roles, definitions of self and selfishness, and marriage and civilization. Women's rights were a central concern to the free love movement since most sexual laws, including marriage laws and anti-birth control measures, discriminated against women. The movement used the strategies of civil disobedience and education to galvanize attention and gain support. In addition, it inspired women to begin to speak outside of the home in favor of the movement and its ideas. Victoria Woodhull was an early champion of the free love movement of the 1870s. In the style of social

This Thomas Nast engraving, captioned "Get Thee Behind Me, (Mrs.) Satan!" appeared in *Harper's Weekly* in 1872. The cartoon satirized the free love platform of Victoria Woodhull, the presidential candidate of the Equal Rights Party. (Library of Congress)

reformers at that time, she and her sister, Tennessee Celeste Claflin, along with reformer Stephen Andrews, started a newspaper called *Woodhull and Claflin's Weekly*. The paper advocated free love, equal rights for women, and a variety of other causes.

Although Woodhull is most noted as the vanguard of the free love movement, others argue that the most important American free love journal was *Lucifer the Light Bearer* (1883–1907), edited by Moses Harman. Harman's *Lucifer* pursued a consistent long-term policy of baiting the law, particularly the postal obscenity laws put in place by Anthony Comstock. Harman established an "open word" rule for *Lucifer*, whereby no contributions would be edited because of explicit language; however, this policy led to his own imprisonment.

After the Civil War, abolitionist Ezra Heywood turned his attention toward the labor movement and eventually toward free love. Like Harman's *Lucifer*, Heywood's *The Word*—subtitled "A Monthly Journal of Reform"—was connected to radical individualism both by editors and by contributors, including Josiah Warren, Benjamin Tucker, and J.K. Ingalls. Initially, *The Word* presented free love as a minor theme expressed within its calls for labor reform, but the publication later evolved into an explicitly free love periodical. Moreover, it antagonized lawmakers by printing birth control material and openly discussing sexual matters. As a result, Heywood was imprisoned under the Comstock laws for his pro-birth control stand from August to December 1878.

Nichols' Monthly, edited by Stephen Pearl Andrews and Dr. and Mrs. Thomas L. Nichols, became the organ of fierce spiritualistic free lovers eager for advance on a large scale. They held a free love convention at Berlin Heights in the fall of 1856 and another in the fall of 1857. The following year, thirty participants pledged themselves to dispose of their property and move to Berlin Heights as soon as possible. However, the public had cried its disapproval, and by January 1858, there was a decline in membership. After this, though many spiritualistic free lovers continued to live at Berlin Heights, the free love movement centered there fell into complete disorganization.

Although the free love movement had all but disappeared by the turn of the 20th century, its challenges to 19th-century social norms had a lasting effect and in many ways opened the door for 20th-century challenges. With each subsequent decade, growing urbanization, increases in technology, the introduction of jazz and rock and roll as accepted musical styles, and greater mobility led to different, and often less stringent, societal norms. By the 1960s, these changes had resulted in another free love movement, this one touted by the counterculture as a way to rebel against the Vietnam War.

See also

Birth Control Movement; Counterculture; Feminist Movement; Marriage; Pro-Choice Movement; Right to Life; Utopian Movements; Women's Rights (19th Century)

Danielle Greene

Further Reading

Baugess, James S., and Abbe A. Debolt, eds. 2011. *Encyclopedia of the Sixties: A Decade of Culture and Counterculture*. Santa Barbara, CA: Greenwood Press.

Foster, Lawrence. 1984. *Religion and Sexuality: The Shakers, the Mormons, and the Oneida Community*. Champaign, IL: University of Illinois Press.

Kern, Louis J. 1981. *An Ordered Love: Sex Roles and Sexuality in Victorian Utopias—the Shakers, the Mormons, and the Oneida Community*. Chapel Hill, NC: University of North Carolina Press.

Klaw, Spencer. 1994. *Without Sin: The Life and Death of the Oneida Community*. Reprint ed. New York: Penguin Books.

Noyes, George Wallingford, ed. 1931. *John Humphrey Noyes: The Putney Community*. No publisher.

Olson, James S., ed. 1999. *Historical Dictionary of the 1960s*. Westport, CT: Greenwood Press.

Wolf, Leonard, ed. 1968. *Voices from the Love Generation*. Boston: Little, Brown.

Free Love Movement—Primary Document

Introduction

Victoria Woodhull (1838–1927) was an early leader of the free love movement in the 1870s. Woodhull and her sister, Tennessee Celeste Claflin (1844–1923), along with reformer Stephen Andrews (1812–1886), started a newspaper called Woodhull and Claflin's Weekly. *This paper advocated free love, equal rights for women, and other social causes. These excerpts from the newspaper demonstrate the variety of articles printed, including letters to the editors, jokes arguing for women's rights, editorials, defenses of free love, and arguments for why girls should be taught the same as boys were in public schools.*

This paper was very popular within the free love movement and exemplifies some of the prominent ideas behind the movement. Finally, Victoria Woodhull was also a suffragist and the first woman to run for president of the United States for the new Equal Rights Party in 1872.

Document: *Woodhull and Claflin's Weekly* (August–October 1871)

Aug. 5, 1871

A Letter to Victoria Woodhull.
Dear Victoria:

Passing an evening lately with my friend and fellow reformer, Mrs. Loomis, she proposed, after an appetizing conversation on progressive subjects, that we should adjourn to a neighboring restaurant, our mental banquet promoting the desire for the more material pabulum.

But in these days of male domination, women are not allowed to sup at a public eating-house after a certain hour (nine o'clock) unless under the aegis of male attire; and any belated female, tired and hungry, and with no means of satisfying her wants at home, can find no welcome in any of our first-class, pretentious restaurants unless accompanied by a voucher of the male sex. The waiters informed us that we—two women without male accompaniment—could have nothing; and no insistency of ours availed against the iron despotism of this masculine institution. I have been an *habitue* of this restaurant for several years; but an appeal to the head clerk was met by the response that such was the rule, and his duty was solely to enforce it. The waiters grinned and leered as if in enjoyment of our discomfiture. My friend, Mrs. Loomis, discoursed eloquently at the counter on the equal rights of women and men; but she might as well have preached charity to churchmen, or the golden rule to the Board of Brokers....

I sought to appeal to a higher tribunal, and called for the proprietor with whom I am acquainted, but he was absent. Finding that there was no possibility of satisfying our demand, without the appendage of a puppet in pants, we concluded that only the expedient of calling upon the first mannikin [*sic*] we should meet, to serve as a male

duenna, would answer our purpose, since it seemed that a little man flesh by the side of a woman invested her with respectability which fitted her to pay her way in an eating saloon. We had already observed near us, as we awaited our expulsion from the premises, a lady of no uncertain notoriety in a profession more sinned against than sinning, who flaunted proudly her gorgeous array, under the redeeming protection of that uniform of virtue, male attire.

Quitting the saloon in disgust, in crossing the street, the Providence that presides over the destinies of woman's rights brought us in contact with the landlord, who, at my request, gallantly offered us his guarantee, and we returned triumphantly, one on each side of the proprietor to the dismay of the waiters, and the surprise of the rest of the immaculate assemblage. Thus, at the very nick of time came to us the best male friend we could have desired, sent doubtless by our guardian spirits, to relieve us from the pain of going supperless, and solving the annoyance to which we had been subjected as champions of the rights of women, adding also to his opportune intervention by defraying the expense of our refreshment, and then accompanying us to the door of my friend's residence, where I remained until the small hours of the night in philosophical disquisition on our evening's adventure, interesting, as it did to us, the diabolical injustice and cruel inhumanity of man to woman....

Why should it be presumed that when women are accompanied by men they are reputable, and when alone otherwise? What a comment upon the utter falsity of the social conditions under which we live!...

It is said that women of the class against whom these regulations are directed might become riotous if admitted at a late hour of night into a public restaurant. That these women have become masculinized, as it were, and have lost much of their femininity by their contact with men, is too true. But are they any more likely to breed disturbance than men themselves? When well treated, they are uniformly well behaved, and many have an exceeding beauty and grace of manner—and, indeed, a largeness of soul—rarely to be met with among their prudish sisters....

Yours for freedom,

Frances Rose McKinley

Aug. 12, 1871

Free Love.
To the Editor of the N.Y. Tribune:

SIR: During some five or six years past, and especially of late, the Newspaper Press has made free use of my name in connection with what it denominates the Doctrine of Free Love. Every variety of interpretation has been put upon my opinions, usually the least favorable which the imagination of the writer could devise, with a view, apparently, of cultivating still further the natural prejudice existing in the public mind against any one bold enough to agitate the delicate and difficult question of the true relations of the sexes, and the legitimate *role* which the Passions were intended to play in the economy of the Universe. During the same period, I have allowed the Press to make what havoc it pleased of my reputation, uttering no word of explanation or reply, for the reason that neither Press nor People were, as I believe, prepared to do justice in the premises, and I preferred to "bide my time," rather than seek or accept the stinted half justice which I might, perhaps, have supplicated and obtained. Most or all of my *co-doctrinaires* have pursued the same course. Two results have followed. First, in the absence of any readiness on the part of the public to know the truth on the subject, false, extravagant and ridiculous notions have flooded the country in its stead; secondly, in the absence of any opportunity for a judicious popular advocacy of Social Freedom, and despite abuse, the doctrine itself has made unprecedented progress, until at this day its advocates are numbered by thousands, while there are included among them an unusual proportion of the wealthy, intelligent and refined. . . .

America, and through it, the world, have been recently startled, shocked and horrified even, by the announcement of a new freedom, the Freedom of Love. It may be well to reflect that every new idea, fraught with any genuine greatness or value, has, in other times, startled, shocked and horrified the public in whose ears it was first uttered, and to inquire whether we, in one day, may not be, perchance, repeating the same ridiculous farce, the nightmare of the world's infancy, the panic of ignorance and "verdancy," with which the race

has always hitherto accorded a reception to every new dispensation of truth.

Is there anything to terrify the imagination in the idea of Freedom? Is not freedom already recognized and worshipped as a goddess, and her image stamped upon the coin of the realm? Is it Love that is viewed as a monster, whose very name paralyzes with fear? There are ancient writings, not a little revered among us, which declare that "Love is the fulfilling of the law," and again, that "God is Love." How, then, does it happen that Free Love, of the Freedom of Loving Hearts, should be a word of terror to mankind, so that the world forgets her propriety, and is made to misbehave herself, with unseemly alarm, at the mere mention of an entymological combination the elements of which, uttered separately, fall with the soothing cadence of a lullaby upon the same excitable nerves.

Free Love is simply the antithesis of enslaved Love. This is equally true in all the senses of which the word is susceptible, whether confined to the amative and sentimental relation of the sexes, or enlarged to signify the whole affectional nature of man.

In beginning an agitation for the emancipation of the human race from the tyranny which prescribes what it is lawful for them to fell, the writer of this intended the freedom of the whole range of the affections, and adopted, as the technicality to express that idea, the term "Freedom of the Affections." . . .

Without restraining the meaning of the word to the relations of the sexes, it is admitted that those relations are included and mainly intended by it, and that the freedom proposed contemplates the entire abolition of the institution of Marriage *as a legal tie to be maintained and perpetuated by force.*

The first popular objection to Free Love, to be anticipated as existing in the public mind, is the prevalent belief that the Bible has prescribed an indissoluble monogamy, or the life-marriage of one man and one woman, as the only form of the union of the sexes which God approves. This belief results from the interpretation which some of the words of Christ in relation to marriage have almost uniformly received. . . . The Scriptures have been held, at various periods with equal unanimity, to teach that the sun revolves around the earth; that kings reign of divine right, and must not, for any cause, be resisted; and that the world was created in six literal days. With the progress of astronomy, politics and geology, each of these convictions has given way before the scientific discovery of adverse facts and principles....

In this country; and in this age, we have, in one sphere of social affairs, a successful and triumphant practical illustration of the theory that the recognition of the rights of the individual is the talisman of order and harmony in society....Not only is he permitted "to worship God according to the dictates of his own conscience," but, equally, to neglect or refuse to worship Him altogether; and the result is peace and fraternity; in the place of the inquisition, the burning fagot and war.

For one, *I reject and repudiate the interference of the State in my morals*, precisely as I do the interference of the church to prescribe my religious deportment or believe. The outrage on human rights is in my view no less in kind to assume to determine whom men and women may love, and what manifestation they may make of that sentiment, than it is to burn them at Geneva or Smithfield for heretical practice or faith.

Such, then, is Free Love—neither more nor less. It is simply a branch or single application of the larger doctrine of the Sovereignty of the Individual. It decides absolutely *nothing* with regard to the form or continuity of the love relation. Whosoever believes that the parties immediately concerned are the proper parties to determine the form and duration of that relation; whosoever wishes to discard legislative enactments, and adopt a "higher law" as the appropriate regulator of affairs of the heart, is, a Free Lovite, *no matter what he expects will be the result* as the operation of that law.

The attempt to degrade Free Love into the partisanship of an unbridled licentiousness is partly the result of an honest confusion of ideas, and partly the effect of natures conscious as yet of no greater elevation of sentiment in themselves than the promptings of unregulated desire. This fog will rapidly disappear ...

[T]he second grand objection to freedom in this application, an objection also founded upon a popular religious dogma—namely, the belief that man is, in himself, radically bad. Under this belief the passions, especially, are abused as

infernal and diabolical. No belief ever held by mankind is so essentially anti-progressives as this....

The third and last grand objection to Amorous Liberty relates to the maintenance and culture of Children. This objection assumes that the isolated family offers the only mode of properly caring for offspring. The family, as now constituted, is, in fact, a very hot-bed of selfishness, which, while it provides for one's own children badly enough, permits the children of others, equally good, to starve at one's door, with the comfortable assurance that the responsibility belongs with someone else. A grand social revolutions is soon to occur. In this generation THE PEOPLE *float* in palaces upon their rivers and bays; in the next they will *live* in palaces upon land. Then the nursery will be a Unitary Institution, scientifically organized and adapted to the new social state. Let the reader refer, upon this subject, to a tract called "The Baby World."

Finally, the words Free and Freedom are everywhere honored, except in the connections "Free Niggers," "Free Women," "Free Thinking" and "Free Love." They are scoffed at in those relations because they stand opposed to Tyrannies that are still respectable—Slavery, Marriage and the Authority of the Church. When Tyranny of all kinds shall have disappeared, Freedom of all kinds will be revered, and none will be ashamed to confess that they believe in the Freedom of Love.

STEPHEN PEARL ANDREWS

Oct. 28, 1871

The Boston Exclusives Again.

People who do not stand upon principles and guide all their actions by them are always found contradicting and stultifying themselves. People who tell lies must resort to habitual lying in order to be consistent and not expose themselves; but such persons are, sooner or later, certain to be detected, since it is natural for people to speak the truth rather than to lie; and sometimes they will forget themselves and act in accordance with their natural inclination.

We are forcibly reminded of this general rule of life from comparing the present attitude of some of the "Boston Exclusives" with that assumed by them in past time. Last week was presented the protest against marriage laws made by Lucy Stone, who is most vehement against us for now advocating their amendment; This week we contrast the position of the editor-in-chief of the organ of the Exclusives with that she occupied in 1869.

On the 15th of July, at a Woman Suffrage Convention at Plano, Ill., Mrs. Livermore, then a resident of Chicago, made the following speech upon the proposition that "the men and women most forward in this movement are of immoral character," are such as we do not most desire to pin our teeth to: "Mrs. Livermore," says the Aurora *Herald*, "denied the above *in toto*. She was herself President of the Woman Suffrage Association in the west, and Mrs. Jane Willing, of Rockford, was the Secretary. The well-known advocates of the cause were of the purest morality. No purer girl lives than Anna Dickinson? No more tender mother than Mrs. Cady Stanton; no truer woman Susan B. Anthony; and hosts of the great and good men throughout the land."

"But what difference does it make to the hungry man whether his food comes to him on a dish of gold or silver, or of wood? In either case it satisfies hunger as well. What difference does it make who buys it? And so with the truth—whether presented by an angel or a devil, the truth is all the same; *and blind is the man who cannot see that*. Is Woman Suffrage right? That is the question. What matters it who advocates it, whether Free Lovers, Spiritualists, or the Methodists, orthodox or heterodox? It makes no difference. 'Truth is truth wherever we find it.'" The *Herald* afterward says: "To Mrs. Livermore was tendered the thanks of the Convention for her instructive speeches, accompanied by a roll of greenbacks."

Mrs. Livermore at that time belonged to the class who were the objects of abuse, who were called all sorts of bad names by the then "respectables." But a change has come over the spirit of her life. She has contracted the disease of respectability and can abuse as vilely as the most pious of former times. Then Mrs. Stanton and Miss Anthony were good women and true. Now they are not fit for the prae [*sic*] excellent Bostonians to mingle with at all; indeed, they will have nothing to do with anything that either these ladies associate with. They are even doing the cause "great injury," according to the paper Mrs. Livermore edits, because they hold more advanced social ideas than are considered admissible by the clique of which she is chief. But Mrs. Livermore considered the truth of suffrage to be acceptable even from Free Lovers and Spiritualists then, while now they are not even to be permitted to so much as approach the platform upon which "the immaculates" stand. They are even so discourteous as to tell them in a call for a convention that they are not wanted. We presume Mrs. Livermore and the rest of her set are not as hungry for suffrage now as she was then, since they will not accept it through anything that has a taint of Wood about it. Suffrage must be tendered to them on golden plates; and be most graciously offered by satin-clothed servants; their tastes have so improved upon what they were that anything short of this will not agree with their present delicate sensibilities....

For our part we should be very glad to have the movement for suffrage receive the support of all persons who are honest advocates of it; but we maintain now, as Mrs. Livermore did in 1869, that whoever rejects aid, let it come from whatever source it may, is not for suffrage but against it; and Mrs. Livermore and all the rest of that clique know it is so. And when they say that the 150,000 readers of a paper which advocates suffrage earnestly and persistently, are not representatives of the movement, and, in fact do not belong to it at all, simply because they patronize that paper which advocates Lucy Stone's former marriage theory in preference to the *Journal*, they know they speak a lie of which they are liable to convict themselves, whenever the spirit of truth predominates over their assumed policy of falsehood.

Source: Woodhull and Claflin's Weekly. http://victoria-woodhull.com/wcwarchive.htm.

FREE SILVER
See BIMETALLISM

FREE SPEECH MOVEMENT
In 1964, the free speech movement (FSM) erupted at the University of California, Berkeley—the first massive countercultural protest by college students. Few expected it, and even

fewer realized that it would ignite similar protests on other campuses.

Students at Berkeley had for some time felt constrained by university regulations that restricted political expression. They had only one place outside the classroom where they could present their ideas: a small piece of land, called a free speech area, at the entrance to the college on Bancroft Strip. There, they made speeches and distributed pamphlets. On September 14, 1964, however, the university announced that it would end the free speech zone. The decision came after several students picketed the nearby *Oakland Tribune* for having engaged in racial discrimination. The newspaper's owner complained about students inciting radicalism, and so the administration decided to crack down.

On campus, discontent grew as angry students claimed that the episode proved that the university, and American society as a whole, wanted to crush dissent. On October 1, the tense situation boiled over when university police arrested a student, Jack Weinberg, for violating the restrictions on political speech. Dozens of students immediately gathered in front of Sproul Hall, the main administration building, where they surrounded the police car holding Weinberg.

Mario Savio, a philosophy student, addressed the crowd and won recognition as the leader of the protest. About 200 students soon occupied Sproul Hall, began a sit-in, and did not disperse until the administration promised to establish a committee, which would include faculty and students, to study college rules. The protest became known as the FSM

A leader of the Free Speech Movement, Mario Savio, rallies a crowd at the University of California, Berkeley, on December 4, 1964. Savio and 800 others had been arrested only days before for similar demonstrations. (Corbis)

later that week, after representatives from several student clubs met and established a formal organization.

On November 20, the University of California Board of Regents eased the speech restrictions, and the crisis appeared to be over. Several days later, however, the administration announced that it would prosecute the protest leaders. In response, on December 2, new sit-ins occurred at Sproul Hall, with 400 students occupying the building until riot police dragged them out. At the same time, graduate teaching assistants went on strike, and in the turmoil, the college canceled many classes. Finally, on December 8, the faculty generally agreed with the students' demands, and the regents decided to further extend the right of free speech.

In all, the students sought freedom of political expression and some educational reforms, and for the most part, they were neither ideologues nor under the control of outside agitators. They presented, one analyst observed, "a clear-eyed and courageous response to concrete, felt injustices." Perhaps most important, in the increasingly technological society of the United States, they wanted to feel human. About Clark Kerr, the university chancellor, the students insisted, "By our action we have proved [him] wrong in his claim that human beings can be handled like raw material without provoking revolt. We have smashed to bits his pretty little doll house. The next task will be to build in its stead a real house for real people."

On campuses across the nation, students held Berkeley-style protests in reaction to oppressive conditions. Most universities reformed, but often minimally. Meanwhile, the FSM splintered, with some members stressing the speech issue and others launching a broad attack on what they viewed as a sterile and oppressive society. Within a short time, the Vietnam War emerged as the overriding concern. By 1966, the FSM disbanded and was replaced by radicalized movements disgusted with liberal moderation and by a Hippie culture that rejected political action as futile.

See also

Antiwar Movement (Vietnam Era); Counterculture; Hippies

NEIL HAMILTON

Further Reading

Cohen, Robert, and Reginald E. Zelnik, eds. 2002. *The Free Speech Movement: Reflections on Berkeley in the 1960s.* Berkeley, CA: University of California Press.

Goines, David Lance. 1993. *The Free Speech Movement: Coming of Age in the 1960s.* Berkeley, CA: Ten Speed Press.

Free Speech Movement—Primary Document

Introduction

Reproduced here is a statement issued in October 1964 by various student organizations protesting the university administration's closure of the "free speech zone" at the corner of Bancroft and Telegraph near the University of California, Berkeley campus. From this beginning sprang the free speech movement on the Berkeley campus.

Document: Statement Issued by University of California at Berkeley, Student Organizations (October 2, 1964)

We are students—American students—who believe in the right and duty to hold, relate, and advocate positions and actions that reflect our desire to promote a continually improving world. The University especially is under a moral obligation to ensure that full discussion of the important ideas and issues affecting our society and world continue.

But to discuss is not enough. The democratic process is one of carrying into action the ideas and issues freely aired in free discussion. Free speech means not only freedom to discuss issues in abstract intellectual terms, but means freedom to advocate actions based on such discussions.

The intersection at Bancroft and Telegraph represents the most frequently travelled area near the campus. And because each of us takes seriously this obligation to be informed participants in our society—and not armchair intellectuals—we feel that this location alone guarantees not only our right to speak, but to be heard! It is a valueless right to have free speech if our corresponding rights to reach people with our ideas and to advocate action on them are not protected.

All of us subscribe to Chancellor Strong's statement that "The University is no ivory tower shut away from the world, and from the needs and problems of society". To eliminate the use of Bancroft and Telegraph is to shut this University up in an ivory tower. It is to limit the freedom of ideas which is necessary to produce truly educated citizens of a democratic society.

We believe that the continued use of the Bancroft and Telegraph privileges will cause Chancellor Strong's goals of "exposure to critical questions and search for knowledge" to be furthered.

And therefore, we respectfully submit for consideration as policy the following:

1. Tables for the student organizations at Bancroft and Telegraph will be manned at all times.

2. The organizations shall provide their own tables and chairs; no University property shall be borrowed.

3. There shall be no more than one table in front of each pillar and one at each side of the entrance way. No tables shall be placed in front of the entrance posts.

4. No posters shall be attached to posts or pillars. Posters shall be attached to tables only.

5. We shall make every effort to see that provisions 1–4 are carried out and shall publish such rules and distribute them to the various student organizations.

6. The tables at Bancroft and Telegraph may be used to distribute literature advocating action on current issues with the understanding that the student organizations do not represent the University of California—thus these organizations will not use the name of the University and will disassociate themselves from the University as an institution.

7. Donations may be accepted at the tables.

> **Source:** Online Archive of California. http://www.oac.cdlib.org/view?docId=kt7z09n93b&brand=oac4&doc.view=entire_text.

FREE TRADE
Definitions

Free trade and protectionism are two sides of the same coin. Free trade seeks the reduction and ultimate elimination of tariffs between two trading partners. At its grandest, free trade seeks the elimination of tariffs worldwide. *Protectionism*, as the term suggests, seeks to protect domestic industries by creating a tariff to raise the cost of imports. With imports at a high price, domestic businesses can increase the cost of their products. For much of American history businessmen promoted a high tariff but the situation on the farm was much different. Farmers had to pay high prices for manufactured goods, but because they sold their crops on a competitive world market, they often had to settle for low prices. Accordingly American farmers have tended to promote free trade.

The Conflict Between Free Trade and Protectionism

Free trade was not an idea new to the United States. In 1776 English economist Adam Smith advocated free trade in his classic book, *The Wealth of Nations*. Scottish economist David Ricardo was likewise a promoter of free trade, though he was aware that it, conspiring with other factors, would reduce wages.

The United States was not an immediate convert. Between the Civil War and 1877, the United States pursued protectionism to protect its nascent industries. The new Republican Party quickly became the party of business (President Calvin Coolidge would say that the business of America was business) and the party of a high tariff. In the late 19th century the United States experimented with free trade, crafting agreements with the nations of Latin America. Between 1897 and 1912, however, the United States reverted to protectionism, though in several instances it negotiated free trade with nations that reciprocated this policy. In 1909 for example, the Payne-Aldrich Act invited other nations to forge free trade agreements with the United States. A proponent of free trade, President Woodrow Wilson badgered Congress to reduce the tariff as much as possible. The recession that followed World War I, particularly severe to American farmers, caused the United States to flirt briefly with the idea of raising the tariff again. During the

Since the end of World War II the United States has consistently promoted free trade. Protectionism is an anachronism.

The North American Free Trade Agreement (NAFTA)

A free trader, President Bill Clinton signed NAFTA in 1993, and it took effect on January 1, 1994. The idea of a free trade zone among the United States, Canada, and Mexico was not original to Clinton. In the 1980s, President Ronald Reagan promoted similar ideas, and in 1989 the United States and Canada agreed to reduce and ultimately eliminate tariffs between the two. Since enactment of NAFTA, trade among the United States, Canada, and Mexico has tripled. Between 1994, the year NAFTA took effect, and 2006 alone, trade among the United States, Canada, and Mexico leapt from $7.3 billion to $20.1 billion. Today, one-third of U.S. trade is with Canada and Mexico. In Canada and Mexico the figure approaches 80 percent.

U.S. billionaire Ross Perot warned that NAFTA would cost the United States jobs. He predicted that the United States would lose 5 million jobs. Although Perot expected U.S. jobs to go to Mexico, in the context of free trade these jobs have gone to China. Factory workers in the Rust Belt have long blamed NAFTA for their woes. In the 2008 presidential campaign, Senator Barack Obama blamed NAFTA for the erosion of high-paying blue-collar jobs in the United States. He believes that NAFTA helps businesses rather than workers. Yet as president, Obama sought neither to modify nor to jettison NAFTA.

The General Agreement on Tariffs and Trade (GATT)

In 1994, at the behest of the new World Trade Organization (WTO), a number of nations gathered in Morocco to finalize what would become GATT. The director general of the meeting, Peter Sutherland, hailed GATT as "the greatest trade agreement in history" (Dunkley, 3). Although it had taken seven years to forge, GATT had the support of the United States and many other countries. GATT aims to promote free trade by reducing and ultimately eliminating tariffs throughout the world, making the planet the largest free trade zone in history. Partisans have predicted the dawn of a global age and the stimulus of the world's economy. Others

President Bill Clinton gestures while addressing the U.S. Chamber of Commerce in Washington, November 1, 1993. The president prodded corporate America to do more to build congressional support for the North America Free Trade Agreement, saying Europe and Japan would be the big winners if the pact failed. It passed. (AP Photo/Doug Mills)

Great Depression the United States and many other nations retreated to protectionism in hopes of staving off bankruptcy for their businesses. One scholar has asserted that the retreat of free trade during the Great Depression made it longer and more severe and retarded U.S. economic growth. He has noted that periods of protectionism coincide with stagnation whereas free trade has galvanized economic growth. Those who learned these lessons would become the advocates for the North American Free Trade Agreement (NAFTA) and the General Agreement on Tariffs and Trade (GATT).

In 1930, the United States enacted the Smoot-Hawley tariff, a misguided measure that putatively sought to protect farmers, an action that prompted other nations to raise their tariffs, worsening the Great Depression. Consequently the United States may deserve blame for exacerbating the crisis.

fear economic, social, and environmental ruin as multinational corporations supersede governments and heed only the profit motive. The harm that Big Oil has done to the planet is clear. Among American journalists the reaction to the implementation of GATT has been generally positive. U.S. corporations have also praised GATT, which doubtless makes easier the transition from high-cost U.S. labor to low-cost Third World labor. From an objective viewpoint, it should not matter whether agribusiness and chemical giant Monsanto makes its agro chemicals in the United States or India because it will be able to export these chemicals back into the United States, where agribusiness will consume them in large quantities. Even the critics of free trade on a global scale admit that this movement is inevitable. The historical and economic momentum has pushed the world toward globalism, with the United States being the principal enabler.

At least one U.S. economist has warned that the cost of transitioning to free trade over the long term will surpass the benefits of this shift. Yet no one can doubt that GATT came to fruition at an auspicious moment. Enacted the same year as NAFTA, GATT witnessed the crumbling of the Soviet Union, which opened Eastern Europe and Central Asia to the possibility of free trade. The United States had entered a decade of economic growth and was bullish about the future of free trade. Capitalism, and with it the corollary of free trade, had triumphed over communism.

Once a cornerstone of economic policy, the tariff has become a stumbling block to economic progress in the United States since the end of World War II. By the 21st century the United States had emerged as the leading exponent of free trade. Several nations, however, perceive U.S. policy as an attempt to force free trade on the rest of the world and so resent the United States. The United States promotes free trade as the logical extension of worldwide economic policies. Partisans declare that free trade makes easier investment in foreign companies and especially in multinational corporations. In the United States the manufacture of computers and software, agribusiness and the retail market (e.g., McDonald's) it has spawned, and Big Oil have all benefited from free trade. There is less agreement about the American automobile industry. Doubtless competition from Toyota, Honda, and other imports has hurt U.S. auto sales, but it also follows that, operating in the bubble of free trade, Ford can easily make cars and trucks in Mexico rather than in Michigan, saving labor costs. In this context, free trade has hurt the U.S. labor movement. Non-union Walmart and similar large operations have thrived in an environment of free trade. Multinational corporations have profited from free trade, but workers have lost ground.

Alternatives to Free Trade

These drawbacks have led one American economist to propose three alternatives to it. First, managed trade promotes a modest tariff for nations that cannot yet compete in a global economy. As these nations raise their gross domestic product (GDP), they can move cautiously toward free trade. Managed trade assumes a minimum level of government intervention in the economy, for example, to retrain workers so they can adapt to an environment of free trade. Second, fair trade, which has adherents in the United States and which appears to overlap with managed trade, recognizes that other nations may intervene in the domestic economy to protect it from global competition. The supporters of this model acknowledge that the world's economies do not engage one another on a level-playing field. Because they do not think that the world will correspond to the same set of rules for everyone in the short term, proponents of fair trade are willing to tolerate government intervention until economic conditions approach the same standard of fairness. Fair traders worry that inequality leaves weak nations vulnerable to multinational corporations. In the absence of government intervention, fair traders fear that corporations will squeeze the maximum labor for the lowest cost from workers, be they in the United States or Indonesia. Third, self-reliant trade hopes to preserve the trading rights of the world's indigenous and often poor people. U.S. oil companies have heartlessly taken land from the indigenes of South America, much to the criticism of self-reliant traders. Self-reliant trade allows indigenes to preserve their lifeways.

The issue of free trade has remained controversial. Supporters believe it to be part of the increasingly globalized economy and beneficial to individual economies. Opponents charge that it not only is of no or little economic benefit, but also that it costs jobs because more cheaply made foreign products cut into the sales of what is domestically produced, and, even more, that companies within the United States can export jobs to countries where they can pay far lower wages.

Neither the controversy over the benefits and dangers of free trade nor the political impact of the discussion figured to end any time soon.

See also
Capitalism; Diplomacy; Taxation

CHRISTOPHER CUMO

Further Reading
Dunkley, Graham. 2000. *The Free Trade Adventure: The WTO, the Uruguay Round and Globalism—A Critique.* London: Zed Books.

Irwin, Douglas A. 2012. *Trade Policy Disaster: Lessons from the 1930s.* Cambridge, MA: MIT Press.

Lake, David A. 1988. *Power, Protection, and Free Trade: International Sources of U.S. Commercial Strategy, 1887–1939.* Ithaca, NY: Cornell University Press.

Free Trade—Primary Document

Introduction

The North American Free Trade Agreement (NAFTA) created a free trade zone among the United States, Canada, and Mexico, intended to eliminate limitations on trade and investment. President George H. W. Bush's administration began the negotiations, but he left office before they could be completed and his successor, Bill Clinton, signed the agreement. Both houses of Congress approved the bill, but only after much debate, and the voting did not break down in a partisan way: both parties divided over the issue. Clinton said, "NAFTA means jobs, American jobs, and good-paying American jobs. If I didn't believe that, I wouldn't support this agreement." But many on both sides of the aisle feared that it would fail to protect both American industry and American labor.

Document: North American Free Trade Agreement (NAFTA) (1994)

Article 102: Objectives

1. The objectives of this Agreement, as elaborated more specifically through its principles and rules, including national treatment, most-favored-nation treatment and transparency, are to:

a) eliminate barriers to trade in, and facilitate the cross-border movement of, goods and services between the territories of the Parties;

b) promote conditions of fair competition in the free trade area;

c) increase substantially investment opportunities in the territories of the Parties;

d) provide adequate and effective protection and enforcement of intellectual property rights in each Party's territory;

e) create effective procedures for the implementation and application of this Agreement, for its joint administration and for the resolution of disputes; and

f) establish a framework for further trilateral, regional and multilateral cooperation to expand and enhance the benefits of this Agreement.

2. The Parties shall interpret and apply the provisions of this Agreement in the light of its objectives set out in paragraph 1 and in accordance with applicable rules of international law.

Source: NAFTA Secretariat. www.nafta-sec-alena.org/en/view.aspx?x=343&mtpiID=122#102.

FREEDOM OF RELIGION

The freedom to worship or not to worship as one pleases is one of America's proudest traditions. The early Pilgrims and Puritans, who settled in New England, came to America in large part to secure their own religious liberties. Ironically, they were themselves often intolerant of rival religious sects. Indeed, some of these colonies initially required church membership as a condition for voting, and many of the early colonies established a state church, for the support of which mandatory tax monies were collected.

In the U.S. Constitution of 1787, the framers provided that no individual would have to take a religious oath as a condition to running for or holding public office. In deference to such religious groups as the Quakers—who had convictions against swearing oaths—the framers also permitted individuals who became president either to swear or affirm when they took their oaths of office. Excepting the provision that is sometimes appended to the document referring to "the year of our Lord," the Constitution does not directly mention God. By contrast, the Declaration of Independence refers on a number of occasions to God or a supreme being.

When the Constitution was being discussed, anti-Federalist opponents raised the possibility that the new central government might attempt to establish a national church (which would have conflicted with existing state establishments) or restrict religious freedoms. As a result, the Bill of Rights, which was adopted soon after the Constitution's ratification, contained two provisions relative to religion in the First Amendment. The first provision prohibits Congress from passing laws leading to "an establishment of religion." The second provision restrains Congress from "prohibiting the free exercise thereof." Thus, the national government could neither establish a state church nor restrain people from worshipping whatever religion they chose. Originally, these guarantees applied only to the national government. However, through a process known as incorporation, the U.S. Supreme Court subsequently employed the due process clause of the Fourteenth Amendment to apply these provisions to the states as well.

Although there is general agreement about the broad purposes of these amendments, there is controversy about the details and application to specific cases. Scholars also disagree about what should be done where there is apparent tension between the two clauses.

The establishment clause is clearly designed to prohibit the imposition of a national church (the last state establishments came to an end in the early 19th century). However, there is continuing dispute as to whether it was intended to abolish all aid programs that might aid religion in general (as opposed to a particular religion) or prefer religious over nonreligious groups. Drawing from an analogy that Thomas

First-graders share a moment of silent prayer at the start of their day in a South Carolina school on September 8, 1966. Though the Supreme Court had banned school prayer as unconstitutional four years before, many state legislatures supported the practice of providing a brief moment of silence during the school day that could be used for prayer. (UPI/Bettmann/Corbis)

Jefferson once made in which he referred to a "wall of separation of church and state," some interpreters of the establishment clause advocate strict separation of church and state. Others argue for "strict neutrality," and still others argue for accommodation between church and state, seeing nothing wrong with providing benefits that aid religion in general.

In dealing with cases under the establishment clause, the Supreme Court has formulated three standards, collectively known as the Lemon Test because they were first articulated in the case of *Lemon v. Kurtzman* (1971), in which the Court overturned provisions of state aid programs designed to fund parochial school teachers. The components of this three-pronged test require that: a law must "have a secular [nonreligious] legislative purpose"; its primary, or main, effect "must be one that neither advances nor inhibits religion"; and the law must not create "an excessive government entanglement with religion." However, in some cases, the Court has decided that historical practices or other considerations outweigh the application of these tests. Moreover, some justices prefer to use an "endorsement test" in which they uphold legislation relative to religion in cases where they think such legislation is not intended to endorse one religion over another or to make individuals feel like insiders or outsiders on the basis of their religious beliefs or lack of them.

In an early case in which the Court applied the establishment clause to the states, it decided in *Everson v. Board of Education* (1947) that a New Jersey plan for subsidizing transportation to parochial schools did not violate the establishment clause. Although referring to the need for separation of church and state and denying that state tax monies should go to religious institutions, the Court majority said that general aid for bus transportation, which went to parents rather than schools, was little different from the state's provision of fire or police protection to churches. The Court has subsequently permitted states to provide secular textbooks to parochial schools and some remedial education services. As in the *Lemon* case, however, the Court has generally overturned more direct legislative attempts to supplement the salaries of parochial school teachers or finance building projects at such institutions, where funding might appear to be a form of state sponsorship or approval.

The Court has closely monitored religious exercises in public school settings. In *Engel v. Vitale* (1962), it struck down a prayer composed for public school students by the New York State Board of Regents. The Court concluded that

it was not the government's business to participate in public religious activities. The Court came to a similar conclusion in *Abington v. Schempp* (1963), this time striking down a school rule providing for daily readings from the Bible and recitations of the Lord's Prayer. In *Lee v. Weisman* (1992), the Court applied this same rule to prayers at high school graduation ceremonies led by local clergymen. Many scholars believe it is permissible for schools to have a minute of silence in which prayers might be offered, but the Court struck down a moment of silence law in *Wallace v. Jaffree* (1985) where it appeared that the state of Alabama was trying to prefer such religious exercises to other activities. The Court also decided in *Santa Fe Independent School District v. Doe* (2000) that students could not lead or initiate public prayers at high school football games because that would violate the Establishment Clause.

The Supreme Court has struck down a number of other provisions as unduly leading to an establishment of religion. In *Edwards v. Aguillard* (1987), for example, the Court struck down a Louisiana law that appeared to favor the teaching of creation over the doctrine of evolution. Similarly, in *Board of Education v. Grumet* (1994), the Court voided the creation of a special public school district designed to meet the needs of handicapped students who were members of an ultra-orthodox Jewish sect.

There are occasions, however, where the Court has waived strict application of the Lemon Test. In *Marsh v. Chambers* (1983), for example, the Court ruled that the state of Nebraska could continue hiring a chaplain to lead the state legislature in prayer—a practice that the justices traced all the way back to the first Congress. Similarly, the Court sometimes permits the inclusion of religious figures in seasonal displays. In *Lynch v. Donnelly* (1984), it permitted the inclusion of a manger scene in a Christmas display that included numerous secular figures as well. By contrast, in *Allegheny County v. Greater Pittsburgh ACLU* (1989), the Court ruled that such a display standing alone in a courthouse did constitute an improper symbolic endorsement of religion.

There are similar anomalies in judicial interpretations of the free exercise clause. In *West Virginia Board of Education v. Barnette* (1943), for example, the Court overturned a 1940 precedent and concluded that the First Amendment protected Jehovah's Witness children from having to salute the American flag in public school classrooms. Similarly, in *Sherbert v. Verner* (1963), the Court ruled that it was unfair for a state to deny unemployment benefits to a member of the Seventh-Day Adventist Church who lost her job because she refused to work on Saturday, which she considered the Sabbath. The Court ruled that the state failed to show a compelling state interest that would justify denying such benefits in her case. Similarly, in *Wisconsin v. Yoder* (1972), the Court ruled that a state could not force Amish children to attend school beyond the eighth grade. The Amish thought such education was detrimental to their own beliefs and the way of life they attempted to follow. The Court may have considered the fact that, although formal educations came to an end, Amish children continued in apprenticeships after this time.

In recent years, there has been renewed controversy over the meaning of the free exercise clause, particularly as the Religious Right has gained supporters and momentum for a reintroduction of Christianity into many aspects of society. In the 19th century, the Court ruled that religious belief was not sufficient justification for violating state laws against polygamy. Just as clearly, the free exercise clause would not allow individuals to practice child-sacrifice. But what exactly are the limits of practices dictated by religious beliefs? The Court faced such an issue in the case of *Department of Human Services of Oregon v. Smith* (1990). Two Native Americans were fired from their jobs as drug counselors because they continued to ingest small amounts of peyote, a mildly hallucinogenic drug, as part of their Navaho religious ritual. When the state subsequently denied them unemployment compensation, they appealed to the U.S. Supreme Court but lost their case. The five to four majority argued that the law against the use of illegal drugs was not directly aimed at a religion (in which case it might have been illegal discrimination against such a group) but was an incidental byproduct of a generally applicable law that did not interfere with any other rights. In such cases, the Court majority did not think that the legislature had to make special exceptions for religious believers. Some of the justices who concurred in the opinion argued that this law was valid only because the state established a compelling interest in regulating illegal drugs. Dissenters argued that even this interest was not enough to overbalance the free exercise rights of Native Americans.

Congress subsequently adopted the Religious Freedom Restoration Act in 1993 under which it attempted to require that the courts defer to religious liberties except in cases where it could show a compelling state interest to do otherwise. The U.S. Supreme Court struck this law down in *Boerne v. Flores* (1997), however, when it decided that churches were equally subject—like secular institutions—to general zoning laws. Still, the Court has been wary of laws that specifically single out religious groups for discriminatory treatment. In *Church of the Lukumi Babalu Aye, Inc. v. Hialeah* (1993), the Court voided an ordinance passed in Hialeah, Florida, that specifically discriminated against churches—in this case of the Santeria religion—that practiced animal sacrifices.

On a number of occasions, the Court appears to have weighed free exercise rights more heavily than establishment clause fears. In *Board of Education v. Mergens* (1990), the Supreme Court upheld an equal access law in which Congress had guaranteed the same rights to extracurricular religious clubs to meet in public schools as it gave to nonreligious clubs. Similarly, in *Lamb's Chapel v. Center Moriches Union Free School District* (1993), the Court ruled that a school could not prohibit religious groups from the same opportunity to use school property after hours that it extended to nonreligious groups. In *Zobrest v. Catalina Foothills School District* (1993), the Court allowed a state to fund a sign language interpreter for a student attending a parochial high school. In *Rosenberger v. University of Virginia* (1995), the Court allowed religious organizations on campus to have the same access to student activity fee monies as nonreligious groups.

Early in the 21st century, other cases and questions arose in connection with religious freedom. The passage of the Affordable Care Act, usually called Obamacare, in 2010 prompted religious institutions and organizations to object to some of its provisions, including whether to provide birth control coverage. After the U.S. Supreme Court upheld the constitutionality of the legislation, lawsuits raised questions about those individual requirements, with the Court ruling in *Burwell v. Hobby Lobby Stores, Inc.* (2014) that a closely held corporation's owners could be exempt from a law to which they objected on religious grounds. Some religious groups also objected to the spread of same-sex marriage, starting with the Massachusetts Supreme Court upholding it in 2004, as a limitation on their freedoms.

Many observers think religions actually flourish in circumstances, like those in America, where churches depend on private, as opposed to state, support. When compared to citizens in many Western democracies, Americans are unusually religious. They will continue to argue about which kinds of general programs are constitutional and which are not, but it seems clear that Americans will continue to value a system in which individuals are free to worship and in which they—rather than the state or national governments—choose which, if any, places of worship they will support.

See also

Children's Rights; Conservatism; Freedom of Speech; Great Awakening; Health Care Reform; Islamic Fundamentalism; Judicial Activism; Moral Majority; Peace Movement (Late 19th Century); Prohibition; Reproductive Rights; Right to Die; Right to Life; Temperance Movement; Zionism

JOHN R. VILE

Further Reading

Abraham, Henry J., and Barbara A. Perry. 2003. *Freedom and the Court: Civil Rights and Liberties in the United States*. 8th ed. Lawrence, KS: University Press of Kansas.

Guliuzza, Frank, III. 2000. *Over the Wall: Protecting Religious Expression in the Public Square*. Albany, NY: SUNY Press.

Hunter, James Davison, and Os Guiness, eds. 1990. *Articles of Faith, Articles of Peace: The Religious Liberty Clauses and the American Public Philosophy*. Washington, DC: Brookings Institution Press.

Swanson, Wayne R. 1992. *The Christ Child Goes to Court*. Philadelphia, PA: Temple University Press.

Freedom of Religion—Primary Document

Introduction

The Virginia Statute for Religious Freedom was among the three achievements for which Thomas Jefferson asked to be remembered on his tombstone at Monticello, Virginia—the others were writing the Declaration of Independence and founding the University of Virginia. Drafted in 1777, but not adopted until January 16, 1786, the Statute for Religious Freedom served as a precursor to the establishment and the free exercise clauses of the First Amendment of the U.S. Constitution, and contributed to how they have been interpreted.

Document: Virginia Statute for Religious Freedom (January 16, 1786)

I. WHEREAS Almighty God hath created the mind free; that all attempts to influence it by temporal punishments or burthens, or by civil incapacitations, tend only to beget habits of hypocrisy and meanness, and are a departure from the plan of the Holy author of our religion, who being Lord both of body and mind, yet chose not to propagate it by coercions on either, as was in his Almighty power to do; that the impious presumption of legislators and rulers, civil as well as ecclesiastical, who being themselves but fallible and uninspired men, have assumed dominion over the faith of others, setting up their own opinions and modes of thinking as the only true and infallible, and as such endeavouring to impose them on others, hath established and maintained false religions over the greatest part of the world, and through all time; that to compel a man to furnish contributions of money for the propagation of opinions which he disbelieves, is sinful and tyrannical; that even the forcing him to support this or that teacher of his own religious persuasion, is depriving him of the comfortable liberty of giving his contributions to the particular pastor whose morals he would make his pattern, and whose powers he feels most persuasive to righteousness, and is withdrawing from the ministry those temporary rewards, which proceeding from an approbation of their personal conduct, are an additional incitement to earnest and unremitting labours for the instruction of mankind; that our civil rights have no dependence on our religious opinions, any more than our opinions in physics or geometry; that therefore the proscribing any citizen as unworthy the public confidence by laying upon him an incapacity of being called to offices of trust and emolument, unless he profess or renounce this or that religious opinion, is depriving him injuriously of those privileges and advantages to which in common with his fellow-citizens he has a natural right, that it tends only to corrupt the principles of that religion it is meant to encourage, by bribing with a monopoly of worldly honours and emoluments, those who will externally profess and conform to it; that though indeed these are criminal who do not withstand such temptation, yet neither are those innocent who lay the bait in their way; that to suffer the civil magistrate to intrude his powers into the field of opinion, and to restrain the profession or propagation of principles on supposition of their ill tendency, is a dangerous fallacy, which at once destroys all religious liberty, because he being of course judge of that tendency will make his opinions the rule of judgment, and approve or condemn the sentiments of others only as they shall square with or differ from his own; that it is time enough for the rightful purposes of civil government, for its officers to interfere when principles break out into overt acts against peace and good order; and finally, that truth is great and will prevail if left to herself, that she is the proper and sufficient antagonist to error, and has nothing to fear from the conflict, unless by human interposition disarmed of her natural weapons, free argument and debate, errors ceasing to be dangerous when it is permitted freely to contradict them.

II. Be it enacted by the General Assembly, that no man shall be compelled to frequent or support any religious worship, place or ministry whatsoever, nor shall be enforced restrained, molested or burthened in his body or goods, nor shall otherwise suffer on account of his religious opinions or belief; but that all men shall be free to profess and by argument to maintain, their opinion in matters of religion, and that the same shall in no wise diminish, enlarge or affect their civil capacities.

III. And though we well know that this assembly, elected by the people for the ordinary purposes of legislation only, have no power to restrain the acts of succeeding assemblies, constituted with powers equal to our own, and that therefore to declare this act to be irrevocable would be of no effect in law; yet as we are free to declare, and do declare, that the rights hereby asserted are of the natural rights of mankind, and that if any act shall hereafter be passed to repeal the present, or to narrow its operation, such act will be an infringement of natural right.

Source: Hening, William Waller. *Statutes at Large.* Vol. XII. Richmond, VA: Pleasants, 1810–1823, pp. 84–86.

FREEDOM OF SPEECH

As a part of basic human rights, fundamental freedoms are the cornerstones of political and democratic rights in modern democratic republics. One of these freedoms, of speech, is the right to hold and express one's ideas and opinions among other persons by means of oral, written, signs, and gestures or audio-visual communication. While addressing military officers in 1783, George Washington said, "If freedom of speech is taken away then dumb and silent we may be led, like sheep to the slaughter." Freedom of speech is synonymous with freedom of expression, literally meaning that a person can freely speak and communicate views to a part of society or people at large. Yet this freedom is not absolute. Democracies impose reasonable restrictions on freedom of speech in the larger public interest so as to protect others' rights and to uphold societal standards of decency and morality. The English writer John Milton wrote, "Give me the liberty to know, to utter, and to argue freely according to conscience, above all liberties." The conscience here implies a self-imposed restriction on freedom of speech. Therefore, the right of freedom of speech cannot be said to be absolute.

History of Freedom of Speech in the United States

The United States was a pioneer country in ensuring and protecting freedom of speech for its citizens. What we refer to as freedom of speech is a specific statement in the First Amendment of the U.S. Constitution—"Congress shall make no law … abridging the freedom of speech"—but it also is part of a set of guarantees in the form of freedom of press and "the right of the people peaceably to assemble." In the original document, there was no provision for protecting freedom of speech, but, realizing the ever-increasing significance of the freedom of speech, and the desire of those voting on the Constitution's ratification for a Bill of Rights, the founding fathers paved the way for this protection to be explicit rather than implicit, and James Madison introduced the amendments at the first meeting of the new U.S. Congress. The ten amendments that comprise the Bill of Rights took effect in 1791. These amendments have been the subject of debate ever since, and the freedom of speech included in the First Amendment has been no exception. Congress has passed restrictive laws, and the Supreme Court has held on several occasions that reasonable restrictions could be imposed on freedom of speech, justifying these actions under the qualifying term *peaceably* in connection with assembly and for the common defense, among other reasons.

During the colonial period in America, there were controls on freedom of speech, especially any speech considered blasphemous. Massachusetts Bay, founded by the Puritans, was particularly stringent. After the adoption of the Constitution and the beginning of the new government, Americans debated just how far their freedoms extended in the light of European warfare and domestic discord that they saw as threatening the young republic. In 1798, Congress passed and President John Adams signed the Alien and Sedition Acts. The sedition law restricted the publication of "false, scandalous and malicious writings or writings against the Government of United States, or either houses of the congress of the United States, or the President of the United States, with intent to defame them or either of them into contempt or disrepute or to excite against them or either or any of them, the hatred of the good people of the United States, or to stir up sedition within the United States or to excite any unlawful combination therein for opposing or resisting any law of the United States or any act of the President of the United States." Thus, less than a decade after the Bill of Rights became part of the Constitution, Congress had chosen to abridge freedom of speech and other First Amendment guarantees. The Alien and Sedition Acts were a major issue in the presidential election of 1800 because of instances of Adams's Federalist Party using the anti-free speech law against political rivals who supported Thomas Jefferson's Republican Party. The act expired after Jefferson won the election and became president.

Freedom of speech would face other restrictions, demonstrating that while it remained an important American value, it also was a contested and hotly debated value. In 1836, the House of Representatives approved what was known as the "gag rule," and renewed it annually through 1844. It stopped abolitionists and their elected officials from presenting antislavery petitions by simply tabling any such materials. The Senate agreed not to pass such a rule, but instead to vote on whether it would consider even receiving a petition, effectually accomplishing the same goal. In the same period, the federal government barred antislavery literature from being mailed into the Southern slave states, and antislavery speakers faced violence from mobs, which also attacked presses and offices; in a famous (or infamous) act in 1837, a mob killed abolitionist editor Elijah P. Lovejoy outside St. Louis. In none of these cases did Congress pass a law specifically limiting free speech, but free speech suffered obvious restrictions.

Wars also proved dangerous to free speech. During the Civil War, President Abraham Lincoln suspended the writ of habeas corpus to permit the jailing of those he and his administration considered threats to their effort to preserve the Union, and an estimated 14,000 civilians went to prison, sometimes for taking action, in other cases because they spoke against the war. In May 1863, General Ambrose Burnside sent soldiers to arrest Democratic politician Clement Vallandigham, one of the so-called Copperheads who opposed the war, for sedition; Lincoln ordered him released into the Confederate lines. Labor and Socialist Party leader Eugene V. Debs went to prison for violating the Espionage Act of 1918 in speaking out against World War I: the law barred interfering with supporting enemies in wartime or interfering in military operations or recruitment. The U.S. Supreme Court upheld it in *Schenck v. U.S.* in 1919, with Justice Oliver Wendell Holmes Jr., declaring that the freedom of speech did not extend to "falsely shouting fire in a crowded theater"—a statement that came to be used as a benchmark for imposing restrictions on the freedom of speech. Perhaps for this reason, perhaps because of the unity fostered by the attack on Pearl Harbor, the United States endured fewer threats to and debate about free speech during World War II.

Other threats to free speech materialized during the Cold War between the United States and the communist Soviet Union and China. Congress passed, and then overrode President Harry Truman's veto of, the McCarran Internal Security Act of 1950, which required communist groups to register with the federal government, which then could investigate them for promoting a "totalitarian dictatorship." The short-lived popularity of Senator Joseph McCarthy, who claimed that communists had infiltrated the federal government, had what would be termed a "chilling effect" on freedom of speech.

Others contested this approach to free speech. The nonpartisan, nonprofit American Civil Liberties Union (ACLU), founded in 1920, had as its mission "to defend and preserve the individual rights and liberties guaranteed to every person in this country by the Constitution and laws of the United States," and filed numerous lawsuits in that connection. The U.S. Supreme Court did not consistently support freedom of speech, both upholding and overturning various legislative acts. The ACLU's first major case before the court, *Gitlow v. New York* (1925), led to the Court setting the standard that a federal or state government may punish or suppress speech that impinges on the national interest. A majority of the Court tended to stand by this precedent until the "rights revolution" that occurred during the chief justiceship of Earl Warren (1953–1969). With colleagues Hugo Black (1937–1971) and William O. Douglas (1939–1975), who dissented from many of the decisions upholding limitations on free speech in the 1940s and early 1950s, and newer colleagues, Warren expanded civil rights and liberties, according to some observers and critics—or, as his defenders would say, simply acknowledged the existing rights that previous figures had ignored or reduced. In the process, the Warren Court implicitly encouraged legal challenges to efforts to limit free speech, whether for stated concerns about national security or over standards of decency.

Changes in technology have led to other definitions and redefinitions of free speech. In a 9–0 decision, the U.S. Supreme Court extended full protection of the First Amendment to the Internet in *Reno vs. American Civil Liberties Union* (1997). It was a landmark decision since it struck down part of the Communications Decency Act of 1996. In *Ashcroft vs. American Civil Liberties Union* (2002), again the Supreme Court ruled that any limitation on the Internet was unconstitutional. In both cases, the Court consisted mainly of more conservative appointees than there were on the Court during the Warren period.

Exceptions to Freedom of Speech in the United States

Although the First Amendment guarantees free speech and expression, the Supreme Court has put limitations on this freedom in the form of exceptions created over time. The exceptions are based on certain types of speech and expression and their context, and thus that free speech is subject to reasonable limitation, much as Holmes argued in the *Schenck* case. The nature of speech and expression involving incitement, making false statements of fact, obscenity that corrupts public morals, offensive speech, threats, child pornography, and speech owned by others are examples of forms of speech that can be and often are exempted from protection of the First Amendment. Some restrictions are based on the special capacity of government as employer, educator, subsidizer or speaker, regulator of the bar, controller of the military and the airwaves, prison warden, and regulator of immigration. The government is not permitted to fire an employee based on the employee's speech if the speech is on a matter of public concern, the speech is not said as part of that employee's job duty (*Garcetti vs. Ceballos* 2006), or the damage caused by the speech is not outweighed by the speech's value to the employee and public (*Connick vs. Myers* 1983). Commercial speech by means of false or misleading advertising also is punishable, and Congress has limited the advertising of such products as tobacco. In *Tinker v. Des Moines Independent Community School District* (1969), the Supreme Court extended broad First Amendment protection to school speeches by children attending schools unless there is "substantial interference with school discipline or the right of others." But in *Morse v. Frederick* (2007), the Court held that school officials may limit student speech at a school function if they see it as promoting illegal drug use; during the 2002 Olympic torch relay, an Alaska student held up a sign saying "BONG HITS 4 JESUS," and the Court upheld his suspension for doing so.

National security is another area in which the government has sought to limit free speech and, again, the public often has supported these efforts, with notable and frequent exceptions. Publishing, gathering, or collecting national security information is not protected speech in the United States. Any unauthorized creation, publication, sale, or transfer of photographs or sketches of vital defense installations or equipment as designated by the president are prohibited. Such information is kept in the category of military secrets. The Invention Secrecy Act of 1951 prevents inventors from publishing or sharing vital information, and the Voluntary Tender Act of 1971 authorized the Commissioner of Patents to withhold certification from inventors that might harm the U.S. national security. The Atomic Energy Act of 1954 imposed restrictions for disseminating data or information concerning design, manufacture, or utilization of atomic weapons or production of nuclear material.

Censorship has been another contested issue. The Alien Registration Act of 1940, also known as the Smith Act, made provisions to punish anyone who "knowingly or willfully advocates, abets, advises, or teaches the duty, necessity, desirability or propriety of overthrowing the Government of the United States or of any State by force or violence, or for anyone to organize any association which teaches, advises, encourages such an overthrow, or for anyone to become a member of or to affiliate with any such association." As early as 1915, the Supreme Court decided in *Mutual*

Film Corporation vs. Industrial Commissioner of Ohio that motion pictures were purely commercial and not an art, and thus not covered by the First Amendment. During the Warren era, the Court began trying to define obscenity as being "utterly without redeeming social value," leading to a variety of cases in which the Court tried to determine reasonable standards and determine who can regulate them. Thus, it has become possible to find an assortment of pornography on the Internet, but the Federal Communications Commission has disciplined television networks for showing nudity or using language that regulators deemed unacceptable.

The First Amendment seems clear. As Justice Black once said, "I read 'no law . . . abridging' to mean no law abridging," stamping him as a seeming absolutist on free speech. But he objected to picketing as conduct rather than speech and therefore within the scope of regulation. Thus, the First Amendment and its guarantee of free speech remain, as they have from their 18th-century beginnings, subject to debate and threat.

See also

Bill of Rights; Constitutionalism; Freedom of the Press; Judicial Activism; Judicial Review; Sedition

D.N.N.S. Yadav

Further Reading

Ashcroft v. American Civil Liberties Union, 535 U.S. 564 (2002).

Cohen, Henry. 2009. *Freedom of Speech and Press: Exceptions to the First Amendment*. Washington, DC: Congressional Research Service.

Connick v. Myers, 461 U.S. 138 (1983).

Eldridge, Larry D. 1994. *A Distant Heritage: The Growth of Free Speech in Early America*. New York: New York University Press.

First Amendment Lawyer-Basic First Amendment and Censorship Information. www.firstamendment.com. Accessed April 21, 2014.

Garcetti v. Ceballos, 547 U.S. 410 (2006).

Gitlow v. New York, 268 U.S. 652 (1925).

Godwin, Mike. 1998. *Cyber Rights: Defending Free Speech in the Digital Age*. New York: Times Books.

Mutual Film Corporation v. Industrial Commissioner of Ohio, 236 U.S. 230 (1915).

Reno v. American Civil Liberties Union, 521 U.S. 844 (1997).

Tedford, Thomas L. 1985. *Freedom of Speech in the United States*. Carbondale, IL: Southern Illinois University Press.

Tinker v. Des Moines Independent Community School District, 393 U.S. 503 (1969).

Volokh, Eugene. 2008. *The First Amendment and Related Statutes: Problems, Cases and Policy Arguments*. New York: Foundation Press.

Freedom of Speech—Primary Documents

Document 1: Introduction

The First Amendment to U.S. Constitution was adopted on December, 15, 1791, as part of the Bills of Rights, which comprised the first ten amendments to the Constitution. The First Amendment codifies " freedom of speech" as a constitutional right. But the right to freedom of speech is not an absolute right. The Supreme Court of the United States has recognized several categories of speech that are excluded from this freedom. The Court has made clear that governments may enact statutory provisions relating to restrictions on such freedom of speech, including when it creates a danger that falls within the state's power to protect against, or when the people may indeed "peaceably assemble."

Document 1: First Amendment to the U.S. Constitution (December 15, 1791)

Congress shall make no law respecting an establishment of religion, or prohibiting the free exercise thereof; or abridging the freedom of speech, or of the press; or the right of the people peaceably to assemble, and to petition the Government for a redress of grievances.

Source: Available at http://billofrightsinstitute.org/founding-documents/bill-of-rights/

Document 2: Introduction

In 1798, in the midst of war tensions with France, the Federalists who controlled Congress passed four acts known as the Alien and Sedition Acts. These measures increased residency requirements for citizenship and restricted speech that was critical of the federal government. The acts were ostensibly intended to protect national security, but many historians see them as an attempt to limit support for the opposition Jeffersonian Republicans. The fourth act, entitled An Act for the Punishment of Certain Crimes Against the United States, punished with fines and imprisonment speech critical of the president, Congress, and government. The Sedition Acts were allowed to expire after the Jeffersonians had come to power.

Document 2: An Act for the Punishment of Certain Crimes Against the United States (July 14, 1798)

CHAP. LXXIV.—*An Act in addition to the act, entitled "An act for the punishment of certain crimes against the United States."*

SECTION 1. *Be it enacted by the Senate and House of Representatives of the United States of America, in Congress assembled,* Penalty on unlawful combinations to oppose the measures of government, &c.

That if any persons shall unlawfully combine or conspire together, with intent to oppose any measure or measures of the government of the United States, which are or shall be directed by proper authority, or to impede the operation of any law of the United States, or to intimidate or prevent any person holding a place or office in or under the government of the United States, from undertaking, performing or executing his trust or duty; And with such intent counselling &c. insurrections, riots, &c. and if any person or persons, with intent as aforesaid, shall counsel, advise or attempt to procure any insurrection, riot, unlawful assembly, or combination, whether such conspiracy, threatening, counsel, advice, or attempt shall have the proposed effect or not, he or they shall be deemed guilty of a high misdemeanor, and on conviction, before any court of the United States having jurisdiction thereof; shall be punished by a fine not exceeding five thousand dollars, and by imprisonment during a term not less than six months nor exceeding five years; and further, at the discretion of the court may be holden to find sureties for his good behaviour in such sum, and for such time, as the said court may direct.

SEC. 2. *And be it further enacted,* Penalty on libelling the government, That if any person shall write, print, utter or publish, or shall cause or procure to be written, printed, uttered or published, or shall knowingly and willingly assist or aid in writing, printing, uttering or publishing any false, scandalous and malicious writing or writings against the government

of the United States, or either house of the Congress of the United States, or the President of the United States, with intent to defame the said government, or either house of the said Congress, or the said President, or to bring them, or either of them, into contempt or disrepute; or to excite against them, or either or any of them, the hatred of the good people of the United States, or to stir up sedition within the United States, or to excite any unlawful combinations therein, for opposing or resisting any law of the United States, or any act of the President of the United States, done in pursuance of any such law, or of the powers in him vested by the constitution of the United States, or to resist, oppose, or defeat any such law or act, or to aid, encourage or abet any hostile designs of any foreign nation against the United States, their people or government, then such person, being thereof convicted before any court of the United States having jurisdiction thereof, shall be punished by a fine not exceeding two thousand dollars, and by imprisonment not exceeding two years.

SEC. 3. *And be it further enacted and declared,* Truth of the matter may be given in evidence. The jury shall determine the law and the fact, under the court's direction.

Limitation. That if any person shall be prosecuted under this act, for the writing or publishing any libel aforesaid, it shall be lawful for the defendant, upon the trial of the cause, to give in evidence in his defence, the truth of the matter contained in the publication charged as a libel. And the jury who shall try the cause, shall have a right to determine the law and the fact, under the direction of the court, as in other cases.

SEC. 4. *And be it further enacted,* That this act shall continue and be in force until the third day of March, one thousand eight hundred and one, and no longer: *Provided,* that the expiration of the act shall not prevent or defeat a prosecution and punishment of any offence against the law, during the time it shall be in force.

APPROVED, July 14, 1798.

Source: United States Statutes at Large, Volume 1. *United States Congress. Public Acts of the Fifth Congress,* Second Session, Chapter LXXIV.

FREEDOM OF THE PRESS

Freedom of the press is closely related to freedom of speech. Originally used in reference to printed media like books and newspapers, freedom of the press today is understood to embrace the electronic media as well. Americans have long valued the right to express their opinions. This right is useful as a way of helping individuals develop their talents and widen their knowledge and also as a mechanism for disseminating vital information about political candidates and the positions they take on matters of public policy.

Like freedom of speech, freedom of the press is guaranteed by the First Amendment to the U.S. Constitution, which prohibits Congress from making laws "abridging the freedom . . . of the press." As the reference to Congress indicates, this clause was originally adopted as a way of limiting the national government after anti-Federalist opponents of the Constitution expressed fears that Congress would attempt to suppress such liberties. With the adoption of the Fourteenth Amendment in 1868 (which prohibits states from denying individuals the due process of law), and the selective incorporation of the provisions of the Bill of Rights in ensuing cases, the U.S. Supreme Court extended the guarantees in the First Amendment to the states as well.

Even before the ratification of the First Amendment in 1791, Americans had established freedom of the press as an important right. In 1735, John Peter Zenger was exonerated in a famous case—usually designated simply as the *Zenger* case—that arose in the colony of New York. Zenger was prosecuted for seditious libel after he published articles critical of the colonial governor. In contrast to the law in England, the New York jury accepted the arguments of Zenger's attorney that individuals could defend themselves against libel charges by showing that the allegations were truthful.

In *Schenck v. United States* (1919), the U.S. Supreme Court upheld a conviction under the Espionage Act of 1917 against an individual who had mailed pamphlets to potential

The New York Times resumed publication of its series of articles based on the secret Pentagon papers in its July 1, 1971, edition, after it was given the green light by the U.S. Supreme Court. The Nixon administration had gone to Court to stop publication, claiming threats to national security. (AP Photo/Jim Wells)

draftees urging them to resist the military draft in the midst of World War I. Justice Oliver Wendell Holmes formulated the "clear and present danger" test to indicate that freedom of speech, like the corresponding freedom of the press, was not absolute. Although both freedoms are intended to have broad protection, both can be regulated when they endanger the rights of others. In subsequent cases, however, the Supreme Court indicated that it would rarely uphold laws restricting freedom of speech or freedom of the press unless such laws are designed to prevent the possibility of "imminent lawless action."

American courts have established a strong presumption against what is known as prior restraint of the press. Drawing from the English roots of this basic freedom, American courts have ruled that, historically, the primary meaning of freedom of speech is that a publication cannot be censored before being published. This doctrine was clearly established by the U.S. Supreme Court in the case of *Near v. Minnesota* (1931). In that case, Minnesota closed down a scandal-mongering newspaper known as *The Saturday Press*. Although the Court agreed that some of the allegations made in this newspaper might be considered libelous, it ruled that the proper solution was not a state decision to close the newspaper but the opportunity for individuals to vindicate themselves by bringing libel suits against the newspaper. The Court has followed this principle in most subsequent cases dealing with freedom of the press.

One of the most important such cases was *New York Times Co. v. United States* (1971). In this case, several prominent newspapers obtained copies of a top-secret report on American participation in the Vietnam War. These papers, which were highly critical of many aspects of American participation in the war, were illegally leaked to the press by one of the authors of the study, Daniel Ellsberg, who had since turned against the war. When the newspapers began to publish daily edited installments of these documents, known as the Pentagon Papers, the U.S. attorney general sought an injunction to restrict further publication. In a highly fractured opinion, a majority of the U.S. Supreme Court ruled that the injunction was unconstitutional. Although the government thought publication was detrimental to U.S. security interests, it did not offer proof of identifiable harm that would result from publication. By contrast, some justices indicated that it might be willing to enjoin publication of a newspaper that attempted to publish information about troop deployments,

which might be used by an enemy in time of war. Consistent with the presumption against such prior restraint, the Court's decision did not mean that the government could not subsequently prosecute Ellsberg for leaking top-secret documents. In this case, however, the government's prosecution was dropped when it was discovered that some of the agents working out of the White House had illegally searched the office of Ellsberg's psychiatrist.

The Supreme Court has ruled that neither freedom of speech nor press protects the publication of obscenity, but the Court has had difficulty defining pornography and has tried to draw standards that do not have a chilling effect on otherwise acceptable speech. The Court's primary standards for judging pornography were articulated in *Miller v. California* (1973). In that case, the Court directed juries to define obscenity by applying three standards: "(a) whether 'the average person, applying contemporary community standards' would find that the work, taken as a whole, appeals to the prurient [lustful] interest; (b) whether the work depicts or describes, in a patently offensive way, sexual conduct specifically defined by the applicable state law, and (c) whether the work, taken as a whole, lacks serious literary, artistic, political, or scientific value." Under this three-part test, obscenity standards can vary from one jurisdiction to another, leading some publishers to charge that they do not always have fair notice in advance of what will and will not be considered pornographic.

Just as freedom of speech does not give individuals the right to make verbal statements falsely accusing others of wrongs (known as slander), so too does freedom of the press fail to relieve publishers of the obligation of checking the accuracy of printed stories for similarly detrimental materials (known as libel). The Supreme Court reiterated this principle in the case of *New York Times Co. v. Sullivan* (1964) by deciding that publications need sufficient breathing room to comment on issues of public policy, making it especially difficult for public figures to collect libel awards. At issue in this case was an advertisement in *The New York Times* entitled "Heed Their Rising Voices," which accused Alabama officials of various violations of the rights of civil rights demonstrators. Although the Montgomery police commissioner had sued and won half a million dollars in state court after proving that the advertisement contained various factual inaccuracies, the U.S. Supreme Court overturned this judgment, declaring that it was especially important for the media not to censor criticisms of public officials. The Court thus established the very high standard of actual malice in such cases—that is, it ruled that public officials alleging libel must prove that the statements printed about them were published with knowledge that they were false or with reckless disregard of their truth or falsity. In *Masson v. New Yorker Magazine, Inc.* (1991), the Court subsequently allowed a prominent scholar to collect a libel judgment when the individual was able to show that the writer of a negative magazine article about him had attributed direct quotations to him that he did not make.

Just as the Court has stood against prior restraint, it has also struck down gag orders in which judges attempted to assure the fairness of trials by quelling stories about ongoing proceedings. In *Nebraska Press Association v. Stuart* (1976), the Court ruled that there were other means of protecting the fairness of criminal trials—including sequestering the jury, changing the trial venue, or conducting more vigorous examinations of potential jurors—than by such censorship. On a related issue, the Court decided in *Cox Broadcasting Corporation v. Cohn* (1975) that newspapers could not be punished for publishing information—in that case the name of a rape victim who had died—that was available in the public record.

Reporters sometimes rely on sources who do not want to be identified. Such individuals may refuse to provide information to reporters if they think they might be identified and (in the case of illegal activities) arrested. In *Branzburg v. Hayes* (1972), *In re Pappas* (1972), and *United States v. Caldwell* (1972), the Court ruled, however, that news reporters were subject, like all other citizens, to grand jury calls, and they had no constitutional right to withhold information about their sources. Many states have subsequently adopted so-called shield laws protecting reporters from having to testify in most cases. In the wake of another Court decision subjecting newsrooms to police searches and seizures, Congress adopted a law ensuring that such searches are not routinely used.

Since reporters serve in part as eyes and ears for the community, some journalists have argued that they are entitled to special access to facilities from which the general public is excluded. In *Houchins v. KQED, Inc.* (1978), the Supreme Court refused to recognize such a generalized right of access—in this case, to a prison—although the justices in the majority acknowledged that legislators could provide for such special access if they so chose.

Early in the 20th century, American courts treated commercial speech as a category that was entitled to less protection than other forms of press or speech, but, in recent years, courts have provided increasing protection for advertising. In *Bigelow v. Virginia* (1975), the Supreme Court voided a law that prohibited advertising about the availability of legalized abortions in other states at a time when the procedure was illegal in Virginia. In *Bates v. State Bar of Arizona* (1977), the Court struck down laws that once prohibited lawyers from advertising. Similarly in *44 Liquormart, Inc. v. Rhode Island* (1996), the Court voided a Rhode Island law that was designed to restrict advertisements for alcoholic beverages.

A freedom that was given wide protection in early America has thus been increasingly expanded over the course of the nation's history. Such freedom can arguably lead to abuses, but abuses are generally considered a small price to pay compared to the benefits this freedom brings.

See also

Freedom of Speech; Judicial Activism; Judicial Review; Sedition; Yellow Journalism

JOHN R. VILE

Further Reading

Epps, Garrett. 2008. *Freedom of the Press: The First Amendment: Its Constitutional History and the Contemporary Debate.* Amherst, NY: Prometheus Books.

Finkelman, Paul. 2010. A Brief Narrative of the Case and Tryal of John Peter Zenger: with Related Documents. New York: Bedford/St. Martin's.

Friendly, Fred W. 2003. *Minnesota Rag: The Dramatic Story of the Landmark Supreme Court Case That Gave New Meaning to Freedom of the Press.* Minneapolis, MN: University of Minnesota Press.

Lewis, Anthony. 1992. *Make No Law: The Sullivan Case and the First Amendment.* New York: Vintage.

O'Brien, David M. 2014. *Constitutional Law and Politics: Civil Rights and Civil Liberties.*, Vol. 2. 9th ed. New York: W. W. Norton and Company.

Powe, Lucas A., Jr. 1992. *The Fourth Estate and the Constitution: Freedom of the Press in America.* Berkeley, CA: University of California Press.

Freedom of the Press—Primary Document

Introduction

The brief per curiam (unsigned) opinion in New York Times Co. v. United States *is generally recognized as a milestone in*

defining freedom of the press. At issue was a classified study known as the Pentagon Papers, which had been leaked to the press by one of its authors, Daniel Ellsberg. The study showed that American policy makers had not always told the truth about the Vietnam War and included some confidential communications between the United States and other governments. President Richard Nixon and Attorney General John Mitchell feared that many of the facts published from the Pentagon Papers by The New York Times, the Washington Post, *and other newspapers threatened the national interest. They sought and obtained an injunction (or order) against further publication. In concurrence, Justice Hugo L. Black (1886–1971) issued a capstone to his thirty-four years of insisting on as absolute as possible an interpretation of the First Amendment's guarantees.*

Document: *The New York Times Co. v. United States* (June 30, 1971)

PER CURIAM.

We granted certiorari in these cases in which the United States seeks to enjoin *The New York Times* and the *Washington Post* from publishing the contents of a classified study entitled "History of U.S. Decision-Making Process on Viet Nam Policy."

"Any system of prior restraints of expression comes to this Court bearing a heavy presumption against its constitutional validity." *Bantam Books, Inc. v. Sullivan* (1963); see also *Near v. Minnesota* (1931). The Government "thus carries a heavy burden of showing justification for the imposition of such a restraint." *Organization for a Better Austin v. Keefe* (1971). The District Court for the Southern District of New York in *The New York Times* case and the District Court for the District of Columbia and the Court of Appeals for the District of Columbia Circuit in the *Washington Post* case held that the Government had not met that burden. We agree.

The judgment of the Court of Appeals for the District of Columbia Circuit is therefore affirmed. The order of the Court of Appeals for the Second Circuit is reversed and the case is remanded with directions to enter a judgment affirming the judgment of the District Court for the Southern District of New York. The stays entered June 25, 1971, by the Court are vacated. The judgments shall issue forthwith.

So ordered.

MR. JUSTICE BLACK, with whom MR. JUSTICE DOUGLAS joins, concurring.

I adhere to the view that the Government's case against the *Washington Post* should have been dismissed and that the injunction against *The New York Times* should have been vacated without oral argument when the cases were first presented to this Court. I believe that every moment's continuance of the injunctions against these newspapers amounts to a flagrant, indefensible, and continuing violation of the First Amendment. Furthermore, after oral argument, I agree completely that we must affirm the judgment of the Court of Appeals for the District of Columbia Circuit and reverse the judgment of the Court of Appeals for the Second Circuit for the reasons stated by my Brothers DOUGLAS and BRENNAN. In my view it is unfortunate that some of my Brethren are apparently willing to hold that the publication of news may sometimes be enjoined. Such a holding would make a shambles of the First Amendment.

Our Government was launched in 1789 with the adoption of the Constitution. The Bill of Rights, including the First Amendment, followed in 1791. Now, for the first time in the 182 years since the founding of the Republic, the federal courts are asked to hold that the First Amendment does not mean what it says, but rather means that the Government can halt the publication of current news of vital importance to the people of this country.

In seeking injunctions against these newspapers and in its presentation to the Court, the Executive Branch seems to have forgotten the essential purpose and history of the First Amendment. When the Constitution was adopted, many people strongly opposed it because the document contained no Bill of Rights to safeguard certain basic freedoms. They especially feared that the new powers granted to a central government might be interpreted to permit the government to curtail freedom of religion, press, assembly, and speech. In response to an overwhelming public clamor, James Madison offered a series of amendments to satisfy citizens that these great liberties would remain safe and beyond the power of government to abridge. Madison proposed what later became the First Amendment in three parts, two of which are set out below, and one of which proclaimed: "The people shall not be deprived or abridged of their right to speak, to write, or to publish their sentiments; and the freedom of the press, as one of the great bulwarks of liberty, shall be inviolable." The amendments were offered to curtail and restrict the general powers granted to the Executive, Legislative, and Judicial Branches two years before in the original Constitution. The Bill of Rights changed the original Constitution into a new charter under which no branch of government could abridge the people's freedoms of press, speech, religion, and assembly. Yet the Solicitor General argues and some members of the Court appear to agree that the general powers of the Government adopted in the original Constitution should be interpreted to limit and restrict the specific and emphatic guarantees of the Bill of Rights adopted later. I can imagine no greater perversion of history. Madison and the other Framers of the First Amendment, able men that they were, wrote in language they earnestly believed could never be misunderstood: "Congress shall make no law . . . abridging the freedom . . . of the press. . . ." Both the history and language of the First Amendment support the view that the press must be left free to publish news, whatever the source, without censorship, injunctions, or prior restraints.

In the First Amendment the Founding Fathers gave the free press the protection it must have to fulfill its essential role in our democracy. The press was to serve the governed, not the governors. The Government's power to censor the press was abolished so that the press would remain forever free to censure the Government. The press was protected so that it could bare the secrets of government and inform the people. Only a free and unrestrained press can effectively expose deception in government. And paramount among the responsibilities of a free press is the duty to prevent any part of the government from deceiving the people and sending them off to distant lands to die of foreign fevers and foreign shot and shell. In my view, far from deserving condemnation for their courageous reporting, *The New York Times*, the *Washington Post*, and other newspapers should be commended for serving the purpose that the Founding Fathers saw so clearly. In revealing the workings of government that led to the Vietnam war, the newspapers nobly did precisely that which the Founders hoped and trusted they would do.

The Government's case here is based on premises entirely different from those that guided the Framers of the First Amendment. The Solicitor General has carefully and emphatically stated:

Now, Mr. Justice [BLACK], your construction of . . . [the First Amendment] is well known, and I certainly respect it. You say that no law means no law, and that should be obvious. I can only say, Mr. Justice, that to me it is equally obvious that 'no law' does not mean 'no law', and I would seek to persuade the Court that is true. . . . [T]here are other parts of the Constitution that grant powers and responsibilities to the Executive, and . . . the First Amendment was not intended to make it impossible for the Executive to function or to protect the security of the United States.

And the Government argues in its brief that in spite of the First Amendment, "[t]he authority of the Executive Department to protect the nation against publication of information whose disclosure would endanger the national security stems from two interrelated sources: the constitutional power of the President over the conduct of foreign affairs and his authority as Commander-in-Chief."

In other words, we are asked to hold that despite the First Amendment's emphatic command, the Executive Branch, the Congress, and the Judiciary can make laws enjoining publication of current news and abridging freedom of the press in the name of "national security." The Government does not even attempt to rely on any act of Congress. Instead it makes the bold and dangerously far-reaching contention that the courts should take it upon themselves to "make" a law abridging freedom of the press in the name of equity, presidential power and national security, even when the representatives of the people in Congress have adhered to the command of the First Amendment and refused to make such a law. See concurring opinion of MR. JUSTICE DOUGLAS. To find that the President has "inherent power" to halt the publication of news by resort to the courts would wipe out the First Amendment and destroy the fundamental liberty and security of the very people the Government hopes to make "secure." No one can read the history of the adoption of the First Amendment without being convinced beyond any doubt that it was injunctions like those sought here that Madison and his collaborators intended to outlaw in this Nation for all time.

The word "security" is a broad, vague generality whose contours should not be invoked to abrogate the fundamental law embodied in the First Amendment. The guarding of military and diplomatic secrets at the expense of informed representative government provides no real security for our Republic. The Framers of the First Amendment, fully aware of both the need to defend a new nation and the abuses of the English and Colonial governments, sought to give this new society strength and security by providing that freedom of speech, press, religion, and assembly should not be abridged. This thought was eloquently expressed in 1937 by Mr. Chief Justice Hughes—great man and great Chief Justice that he was—when the Court held a man could not be punished for attending a meeting run by Communists.

The greater the importance of safeguarding the community from incitements to the overthrow of our institutions by force and violence, the more imperative is the need to preserve inviolate the constitutional rights of free speech, free press and free assembly in order to maintain the opportunity for free political discussion, to the end that government may be responsive to the will of the people and that changes, if desired, may be obtained by peaceful means. Therein lies the security of the Republic, the very foundation of constitutional government.

> **Source:** Justia.com. http://supreme.justia.com/cases/federal/us/403/713/case.html.

FRIEDMANISM
See MONETARY POLICY

THE FRONTIER

Perhaps no other spatial area of the United States has done more to shape the ways that Americans think about themselves and their past than the frontier. The frontier has affected Americans' thoughts about their geography, their culture, their politics, and their folklore. Although it cannot be defined as one place for all time, but rather a moving border between *civilization* and *wilderness*—although both of those terms are problematic—many Americans grew up with visions of the frontier in their imaginations. As the domain of the cowboys and Indians, the frontier was always populated—it included farmers, ranchers, shopkeepers, and all manner of artisans. The frontier was always rife with contradictions in both reality and imagination. It was the place where the ideal of American individualism found its fullest expression, yet a place where the vast majority of people could not have survived without community. It was the location of opportunity for anyone with the drive to make something of themselves, yet a place where many people went broke and had to return home penniless. But most of all, it was quintessentially American—where many argued that America differentiated itself from the ways of the "Old World."

People on the Frontier: Westward Movement and Manifest Destiny

The frontier began when the first Europeans set foot upon the North American continent and established separate settlements, distinct from the Native tribes that filled the land. For the English who would create the colonies from which the United States would be formed, the permanent frontier began with Jamestown in 1607. Expansion into the surrounding areas took the form of trading posts where local Indian peoples traded the furs desired by the Europeans for manufactured goods. Before long, however, the desire for land pushed the frontier further out from the initial settlements, pushing the Indian people out of their homelands. Seventeenth-century wars such as the Pequot War and King Philip's War always resulted in the loss of land by the Indians, a pattern that would be repeated for nearly 300 years. The frontier was never the movement of European Americans into a "virgin wilderness"; rather, it always involved the loss of land and sovereignty on the part of the Indian groups that already lived there.

By the time the United States declared independence in 1776, the frontier was the line along the Appalachian Mountains, and the nation gained its first frontier icon in the person of Daniel Boone, who pushed through the Cumberland Gap from Virginia into Kentucky, opening up an entirely new frontier region. With the Louisiana Purchase of 1803 roughly doubling the land base of the United States, the stage was set for a further expansion. With the completion of Lewis and Clark's voyage to the Pacific during 1804–1806, and the peace after the War of 1812, many began to feel that the United States had a special mission—a "manifest destiny"—to spread its enlightened institutions across the continent, and anything or anyone (especially Indian peoples) who got in the way were only impeding progress. Between the War of 1812 and the start of the Civil War in 1861, Indian tribes were relocated from the American South and from what was then called the Northwest (what we today would call the upper Midwest) to the area west of the Mississippi River, where they were told they would possess the land forever.

But forever ended all too quickly, as Americans quickly came across the Mississippi after the Civil War, looking to establish farms and ranches, and take advantage of the gold rushes that continually occurred as Americans moved further west. Farmers claimed homesteads, and the completion of the Transcontinental Railroad brought even more settlers. The amount of land the Indians held shrank as the federal government passed the General Allotment Act, which gave plots of land to individual Indians, forcing them to become farmers when many of them had no experience, no water, and not good enough land to make it work. The "surplus" land left over after allotment was then available to European Americans for settlement. Finally, in 1889, the "surplus" lands in what had been Indian Territory, now the state of Oklahoma, were opened up for non-Indian settlement. It is not without irony that the census the following year would be the one that declared that there was no more frontier—no more land that was unsettled. What would happen next would take the frontier from the American West into the American imagination.

Daniel Boone and his band of pioneers cross the Cumberland Gap in 1769. In that year, Boone had explored Kentucky as part of hunting expeditions. This is another classic frontier painting by George Caleb Bingham (1852). (Bettmann/Corbis)

Thought on the Frontier: Frederick Jackson Turner and His Legacy

When Frederick Jackson Turner wrote *The Significance of the Frontier in American History* in 1893, he outlined the ways in which many historians would view the West for the next century. He argued that the presence of free land beyond the western edge of settlement, the actions of settlers in leaving Eastern cities and moving out to that frontier, and the accommodations that those settlers made once they arrived on that frontier were what made the history of the United States unique from Europe. They explained not only the American love of freedom, but also the freedom of American political, economic, and social structures. The Turner thesis gave the identification of America with the West a degree of intellectual legitimacy. There were, however, historians in Turner's day, such as Charles Beard, who disputed the fact that the frontier was the formative factor in the development of the American character and American democracy. However, even today popular histories still conflate the West with Turner's moving frontier where free land acts as the Americanizing force.

By the 1940s, most historians had rejected the Turner thesis as a basis for American history as a whole, but it lived on in Western history through the work of historians such as Ray Allen Billington and Martin Ridge. Billington argued that the frontier was an indispensable factor in explaining the shaping of the American character. Certainly, the mingling of races in the United States, the diversified economy, and the late but accelerated industrialization of the nation each contributed to the development of the American character, but the westward movement of the frontier was the most important factor. He argued that the social order of the Old West was different from that of New England, that as European cultures met the forest environment of the Old Northwest, they were fundamentally altered into something totally different.

Antagonism toward colonial authority became a characteristic of the early frontier. The typical frontiersman was French thinker Hector St. John de Crèvecoeur's "new man." He was materialistic, suspicious of intellectuals, and above all adaptable, optimistic, and individualistic. Much as Turner had described it, according to Billington, frontiering was a process through which the customs and institutions brought over from Europe were adapted to suit conditions in the America. As Americans went out onto the frontier, they tended to revert to the primitive. However, this process ended when settlement of the region began in earnest. But, however convincing their arguments may have been in explaining the character of the frontier regions, they held very little weight with the dominant parts of the profession, acting to relegate Western history to the backwater of the profession for many years.

Forgetting the "F-Word": The New Western Historians

During the 1980s, however, a "New Western History" developed, concentrating on aspects of America's Western past that Turner and Billington had never considered adequately in their work. Dominated by historians such as Patricia Nelson Limerick, Elliot West, William Robbins, Donald Worster, and Richard White, this school of historians has proven to be nearly as dominant within the historical profession as was Turner. However, neo-Turnerians such as William Cronon, John Mack Faragher, Walter Nugent, and David Weber reinterpreted Turner's thought for a new era, merging it with the emphases of the New Western History. The core controversy between the New Western and the neo-Turnerians has been over whether to view the frontier as a "place" or a "process." Neo-Turnerians have disregarded Turner's blindness to underrepresented groups, the importance of the economic factors, and the impact of the federal government, but they insist on the linkage between various frontiers and that the frontier experience was important in determining the later regional identities of these areas.

Both John Mack Faragher's *Sugar Creek* and William Cronon's *Nature's Metropolis* explore the connections between different regions that at one time were frontiers. Dean May's *Three Frontiers* investigates the consequences of the frontier process in the context of three different regions with diverse social and economic motivations. Although these groups have developed a mutual rapport and respect for each other's work, the controversy over the West as a place (New Western) versus the frontier as a process (Neo-Turnerians) has occupied numerous books and formed the basis for many scholarly conferences.

New Western historians assert that factors other than the process of the frontier make the history of the West distinctive. Patricia Nelson Limerick argues that it is the idea of conquest and persistence of the conquered. Even though the actions of white Westerners were innocent and justifiable in their own eyes, they did not intend to despoil Indian lands; their actions had the result of forcibly removing or surmounting the native peoples of the West. Further, that the history of the West is also the history of the conquest of women and minorities by white males. Rather than doing away with the ideas of Social Darwinism that were popularized among Eastern industrialists, Westerners seeking to conquer a new land proved through their actions that profit did rule the actions of men. In sum, Limerick argues that the idea of conquest has been present throughout American history and has followed whites out West, linking them inextricably to the Eastern institutions that they supposedly eschew.

Picking up from Wallace Stegner's study of John Wesley Powell, Donald Worster, in his *Rivers of Empire*, argues that aridity is the defining characteristic of the West. While acknowledging that the West is, in popular thinking, a land of untrammeled freedom, he portrays a West that, due to aridity and the need to control scarce water, is a land of authority and power relations. He describes the West as a modern hydraulic society, where the social order was based on the manipulation of water. Like Limerick, Worster asserts that the West has always been linked to the East. In order to conquer the large rivers of the region, Westerners needed capital from Eastern banks, European investors, and most prominently, the federal government. Through bureaucracies such as the Bureau of Reclamation and the Army Corps of Engineers as well as through federal legislation and court decisions, the federal government has been the dominant body in determining who gets what water for what purpose in the West. The connections between capitalist expansion and environmental change can be seen in Worster's work on agriculture and the consequences of capitalist exploitation during the Dust Bowl years on the Great Plains.

Richard White has provided the New Western History's overriding narrative of the region's history, *It's Your Misfortune and None of My Own*. White constantly keeps in the forefront the idea that the West had a series of shifting relationships with other regions. He has also emphasized mythology, class divisions, racial and ethnic differences, urbanization, industrialization, environmentalism, and many other factors affecting Western development while refusing to credit the westward-moving frontier with any modicum of influence. To the contrary, White credits the northward-moving Hispanic frontier with a much greater degree of influence over the shape of Southwestern culture.

Other historians have had made important contributions to the thought about the frontier in their emphases as well. William Robbins emphasizes the role of capitalism in Western development. William Deverell explored the economic, social, and political roles that the railroad played in the development of California politics. Richard Lowitt has emphasized that the West was the site of growing federal power during the 20th century because of its natural resources, its low population density, and the fact that many Western states had fairly weak state governments. Some of the largest federal bureaucracies have been exclusively Western, and the federal government during the depression years of the 1930s and the war years of the early 1940s was instrumental in forming the modern West. As a result of the New Deal's impact on the West, by the end of the 1930s, people in the West were ready to accept government as an agency for human welfare, and expect it to support their ventures. Gerald Nash has pointed to World War II as the critical moment where federal influence formed the basis for Western development. Because of the necessities of war, it created the industrial infrastructure of the region that resulted in a massive migration to the West both during and after the war.

New Western Historians have sought to illuminate the experiences of those not included in Turner's West. In his book *Walls and Mirrors*, David Gutiérrez has illustrated the long history of Spanish and Mexican settlers in the West. He points out the fact that relations between Mexican Americans and Mexican immigrants have been negotiated in the politics of ethnicity in the Southwest. Mexican American identity is a creation of the West, and it has been constantly changing throughout the 20th century, largely because of the continued presence of new immigrants into the region. Similarly, Ronald Takaki's *Strangers from a Different Shore* has brought to light the roles that Asian Americans played in the formative period of Western development during the 1860s through the 1890s, as well as their persistence in the 20th-century West. Quintard Taylor has shown that African Americans played a previously overlooked role in the development of the West in the years before the Great Migration in the early 20th century.

The Persistence of the Frontier in American Thought

Despite the proponents of the New Western History making the frontier a contested region, its popularity as a trope in American popular culture, as well as the popular cultures of many other peoples, has not waned. Depictions on television or film of the "wild west," the agricultural West, and the ranching West are still replete with stereotypes of individualism and the struggle of European Americans against a hostile environment, though the depictions in recent decades have become more nuanced, not shying away from including Native Americans, Mexican Americans, and African Americans—though one still seldom sees Mexican American or African American cowboys, though they constituted between 30 percent and 50 percent of the ranching workforce. American presidents, including Theodore Roosevelt, Lyndon Johnson, Ronald Reagan, and George W. Bush, have also used the trope of the frontier to show themselves as stereotypically American—rugged, self-reliant, and ready for anything.

See also

Manifest Destiny; Western Expansion/Exploration; Western Lore

STEVEN L. DANVER

Further Reading

Billington, Ray Allen. 1966. *America's Frontier Heritage.* New York: Holt Rinehart and Winston.

Billington, Ray Allen, and Martin Ridge. 2001. *Westward Expansion: A History of the American Frontier.* 6th ed. Albuquerque, NM: University of New Mexico Press.

Cronon, William, George Miles, and Jay Gitlin, eds. 1992. *Under an Open Sky: Rethinking America's Western Past.* New York: W. W. Norton.

Etulain, Richard W., ed. 2002. *Writing Western History: Essays on Major Western Historians.* Reno, NV: University of Nevada Press.

Hausladen, Gary J. 2006. *Western Places, American Myths: How We Think About the West.* Reno, NV: University of Nevada Press.

Hine, Robert V., and John Mack Faragher. 2000. *The American West: A New Interpretive History.* New Haven, CT: Yale University Press.

Limerick, Patricia Nelson. 1987. *The Legacy of Conquest: The Unbroken Past of the American West.* New York: W. W. Norton.

Limerick, Patricia Nelson, Clyde A. Milner, II, and Charles E. Rankin, eds. 1991. *Trails: Toward a New Western History.* Lawrence, KS: University Press of Kansas.

Slotkin, Richard. 1998. *The Fatal Environment: The Myth of the Frontier in the Age of Industrialization, 1800–1890.* Norman, OK: University of Oklahoma Press.

Smith, Henry Nash. 1950. *Virgin Land: The American West as Symbol and Myth.* Cambridge, MA: Harvard University Press.

Turner, Frederick Jackson. 1994. *The Frontier in American History.* Reprint ed. Tucson, AZ: University of Arizona Press.

Unruh, John David. 1993. *The Plains Across: The Overland Emigrants and the Trans-Mississippi West, 1840–1860.* Urbana, IL: University of Illinois Press.

White, Richard. 1991. *"It's Your Misfortune and None of My Own": A New History of the American West.* Norman: University of Oklahoma Press.

The Frontier—Primary Document

Introduction

Historian Frederick Jackson Turner likely did more than anyone to shape the perception of the frontier in both academic circles and the popular perception. In a paper presented to a meeting of the American Historical Association in Chicago in 1893, Turner explained his "frontier" thesis of American history. Turner's thesis, that the existence of the frontier between civilization and wilderness was the primary driving factor explaining the development of the exceptional identity and institutions of the United States, was seen as a motif around which American history as a whole could be based. Although later scholars have added many other formative factors to Turner's thesis, and disputed the argument behind it, it remains influential over 120 years after it was first argued.

Document: Frederick Jackson Turner's "The Significance of the Frontier in American History" (July 12, 1893)

. . . Having now roughly outlined the various kinds of frontiers and their modes of advance, chiefly from the point of view of the frontier itself, we may next inquire what were the influences on the East and on the Old World. A rapid enumeration of some of the more noteworthy effects is all that I have time for.

First, we note that the frontier promoted the formation of a composite nationality for the American people. The coast was preponderantly English, but the later tides of continental immigration flowed across to the free lands. This was the case from the early colonial days. The Scotch-Irish and the Palatine Germans, or "Pennsylvania Dutch," furnished the dominant element in the stock of the colonial frontier. With these peoples were also the freed indented servants, or redemptioners, who at the expiration of their time of service passed to the frontier. Governor Spotswood of Virginia writes in 1717, "The inhabitants of our frontiers are composed generally of such as have been transported hither as servants, and, being out of their time, settle themselves where land is to be taken up and that will produce the necessaries of life with little labor." Very generally these redemptioners were of non-English stock.

In the crucible of the frontier the immigrants were Americanized, liberated, and fused into a mixed race, English in neither nationality nor characteristics. The process has gone on from the early days to our own. Burke and other writers in the middle of the eighteenth century believed that Pennsylvania was "threatened with the danger of being wholly foreign in language, manners, and perhaps even inclinations." The German and Scotch-Irish elements in the frontier of the South were only less great. In the middle of the present century the German element in Wisconsin was already so considerable that leading publicists looked to the creation of a German state out of the commonwealth by concentrating their colonization. Such examples teach us to beware of misinterpreting the fact that there is a common English speech in America into a belief that the stock is also English.

In another way the advance of the frontier decreased our dependence on England. The coast, particularly of the South, lacked diversified industries, and was dependent on England for the bulk of its supplies. In the South there was even a dependence on the Northern colonies for articles of food. Governor Glenn of South Carolina writes in the middle of the eighteenth century:

> Our trade with New York and Philadelphia was of this sort, draining us of all the little money and bills we could gather from other places for their bread, flour, beer, hams, bacon, and other things of their produce; all which, except beer, our new townships begin to supply us with, which are settled with very industrious and thriving Germans. This no doubt diminishes the number of shipping and the appearance of our trade, but it is far from being a detriment to us.

Before long the frontier created a demand for merchants. As it retreated from the coast it became less and less possible for England to bring her supplies directly to the consumer's wharfs and carry away staple crops, and staple crops began to give way to diversified agriculture for a time. The effect of this phase of the frontier action upon the northern section is perceived when we realize how the advance of the frontier aroused seaboard cities like Boston, New York, and Baltimore, to engage in rivalry for what Washington called "the extensive and valuable trade of a rising empire."

The legislation which most developed the powers of the national government, and played the largest part in its activity, was conditioned on the frontier....

So long as free land exists, the opportunity for a competency exists, and economic power secures political power. But the democracy born of free land, strong in selfishness and individualism, intolerant of administrative experience and education, and pressing individual liberty beyond its proper bounds, has its dangers as well as its benefits. Individualism in America has allowed a laxity in regard to governmental affairs which has rendered possible the spoils system and all the manifest evils that follow from the lack of a highly developed civic spirit....

From the conditions of frontier life came intellectual traits of profound importance. The works of travelers along each frontier from colonial days onward describe certain common traits, and these traits have, while softening down, still persisted as survivals in the place of their origin, even when a higher social organization succeeded. The result is that, to the frontier, the American intellect owes its striking characteristics. That coarseness and strength combined with acuteness and inquisitiveness, that practical, inventive turn of mind, quick to find expedients, that masterful grasp of material things, lacking in the artistic but powerful to effect great ends, that restless, nervous energy, that dominant individualism, working for good and for evil, and withal that buoyancy and exuberance which comes with freedom—these are traits of the frontier, or traits called out elsewhere because of the existence of the frontier.

Since the days when the fleet of Columbus sailed into the waters of the New World, America has been another name for opportunity, and the people of the United States have taken their tone from the incessant expansion which has not only been open but has even been forced upon them. He would be a rash prophet who should assert that the expansive character of American life has now entirely ceased. Movement has been its dominant fact, and, unless this training has no effect upon a people, the American energy will continually demand a wider field for its exercise. But never again will such gifts of free land offer themselves.

For a moment, at the frontier, the bonds of custom are broken and unrestraint is triumphant. There is not *tabula rasa*. The stubborn American environment is there with its imperious summons to accept its conditions; the inherited ways of doing things are also there; and yet, in spite of environment, and in spite of custom, each frontier did indeed furnish a new field of opportunity, a gate of escape from the bondage of the past; and freshness, and confidence, and

scorn of older society, impatience of its restraints and its ideas, and indifference to its lessons, have accompanied the frontier.

What the Mediterranean Sea was to the Greeks, breaking the bond of custom, offering new experiences, calling out new institutions and activities, that, and more, the ever retreating frontier has been to the United States directly, and to the nations of Europe more remotely. And now, four centuries from the discovery of America, at the end of a hundred years of life under the Constitution, the frontier has gone, and with its going has closed the first period of American history.

Source: Turner, Frederick Jackson. "The Significance of the Frontier in American History." In *The Frontier in American History*. New York: Henry Holt and Company, 1920, pp. 1–38.

G

GAY RIGHTS

Denied the same constitutional rights as other Americans for nearly two centuries, gay men and lesbians after "coming out" in the 1970s have secured legal access to equal employment, partner benefits, and the right to engage in homosexual behavior in public and private. Despite recent gains, homosexuals continue to face severe repression, as witnessed in the 1998 murder of gay college student Matthew Shepard and the recent inclusion of sexual orientation in hate crime legislation.

Prior to the 1960s, the rights of homosexual men and women in America were not completely protected by the U.S. Constitution. The persecution of gays and lesbians in the United States traces back to laws criminalizing homosexual behavior in early modern England. In 1533, Parliament passed the Buggery Act, which made homosexual intercourse a capital offense punishable by hanging. Defined as the "carnal knowledge...by mankind with mankind, or with brute beast, or by womankind with brute beast," buggery became the basis for laws against homosexuality formed in colonial America. Interestingly, although male homosexual acts were a capital offense in the new colonies, lesbian sexual acts were not. Regardless, homosexuals of either gender rarely expressed their sexual preferences in public, and issues related to homosexuality remained out of the public eye. With few people admitting to being homosexuals, most states did not enforce the sodomy laws enshrined in their legal codes.

In the early 20th century, many homosexuals became more open about their sexuality as urbanization and migration brought thousands of single people from their rural homes to large urban centers like New York and Chicago. In response to a visible gay culture, government authorities moved to clamp down on homosexual behavior. For the first time in America, moral reform societies identified homosexuality as a specific social problem to eradicate. No longer just a moral transgression, homosexuality was now viewed as deviant behavior outside of the patriarchal social order and a threat to the stability of American culture. Accordingly, police began to arrest gay men on sodomy charges in Manhattan in large numbers beginning in 1918, when 238 men were jailed and fined. By 1920, more than 500 gay men were being arrested annually in New York City alone.

Though gay men were now open targets of law enforcement, it was not until the 1930s that concerted antigay campaigns began to flourish, most of which developed in reaction to the perceived lawlessness of the Prohibition era. Homosexuality became linked in the popular mind to a criminal underworld populated by prostitutes, child molesters, and murderers. The anticommunist purges of the U.S. Congress in the 1950s, led by Senator Joseph McCarthy, painted an even more threatening picture of the "homosexual menace"

Hillary, left, and Julie Goodridge, lead plaintiffs in the landmark Massachusetts gay marriage lawsuit, are pronounced "married" by Unitarian Rev. William Sinkford for their ceremony in Boston during the first day of state-sanctioned gay marriage in the United States, May 17, 2004. (AP Photo/Elise Amendola)

as actively spread by communists to recruit the innocent to a life of depravity. The use of illegal drugs like marijuana and heroin became synonymous with individuals engaged in homosexual behavior.

As a result of both a culture of conformity and widespread public views regarding the supposedly antisocial proclivities of homosexuals, numerous restrictions against gays and lesbians in public life began to appear in the 1950s. In addition to being subjected to sodomy laws, gay men and

lesbians were barred from federal, state, and local government employment, including the military, and from teaching positions in public schools. Denied custody and visitation rights of their children and the right to be in bars, homosexuals faced an increasingly restrictive social world in the immediate post–World War II era. For example, in 1950, the U.S. Senate appointed a committee to conduct an investigation into employment by the federal government of homosexuals and other "sex perverts." President Dwight D. Eisenhower issued an executive order for the dismissal of all government employees who were believed to be homosexuals.

By limiting the presence of gays and lesbians in the public sphere, state authorities sought to push homosexual behavior to the realm of invisibility. In the 1960s, several states passed regulations aimed at eliminating the representation of homosexuality in such live entertainment venues as cabarets, live-performance theaters, and the stage. Some states went so far as to prohibit males from performing female impersonations. Even Hollywood passed a code prohibiting reference to homosexuality in movies, despite the prevalence of homosexuals throughout the movie industry. The licensing of the sale of alcohol and the subsequent creation of police-like agencies to monitor the flow of liquor and "morality" represented the state's most powerful weapon in limiting the presence of openly gay men in public life. Indeed, the first gay rights legal case involved a bar owner in the 1960s who fought successfully against the state of California to reinstate his liquor license, which the state had taken away because the bar was charged with catering to homosexuals.

Although the success of gays and lesbians in securing civil rights has increased markedly since the 1970s after activists began to challenge federal and state laws, aspects of homosexual behavior remained criminalized in many parts of the United States until the landmark decision in *Lawrence v. Texas* (2003), which ruled antisodomy laws unconstitutional. Sodomy statutes were at the heart of state efforts to deny gays and lesbians protection of the First Amendment right to freedom of association. Laws against sodomy existed in all states before the 1960s, and they remained on the books in thirteen states at the time of the *Lawrence* decision, mostly in the South. Sodomy laws, though rarely enforced against consenting adults acting in private, were used to deny custody and visitation rights to lesbian and gay parents. Associating homosexuality with deviancy and citing sodomy laws as proof, employers and landlords argued that they should not be forced to hire or rent to criminals. In 1986, the U.S. Supreme Court, in a narrow 5–4 vote, upheld the constitutionality of sodomy laws in the case of *Bowers v. Hardwick* (1986) by arguing that the right to privacy did not extend to homosexual behavior. The Court reversed itself seventeen years later, however, when the *Lawrence* decision overturned *Bowers*.

In addition to sodomy laws, the primary method of regulating gay sexual activity has been laws against solicitation, loitering, lewd and lascivious behavior, and indecent exposure. Because gay men are stereotyped as oversexed and part of a predator class of people like pedophiles, they are particularly vulnerable to being charged with those crimes. Gay men are often arrested for engaging in sex acts in such public places as parked cars, parks, and restrooms, while heterosexual couples are told simply to go home or find a hotel when caught in the same predicament. Those statutes have been challenged but rarely overturned.

Nevertheless, throughout this period, the public's attitude toward homosexuality underwent a dramatic shift. While the majority of Americans no longer view homosexuals as criminals, homosexuality continues to make many people uncomfortable. Extremists on both sides of the homosexuality debate have often been vocal and confrontational, with those supporting homosexuality demanding that Americans not only accept it but condone it, and those opposed to homosexuality enacting outrageous displays of hatred and violence toward gays and lesbians.

Bias crimes—acts committed against individuals due to their race, gender, disability, or sexual orientation—became increasingly prevalent in American society during the late 20th century, fueled by widespread media coverage. In response, Congress passed the Hate Crimes Statistics Act in 1990 mandating that the U.S. Justice Department acquire data on crimes evidencing prejudice based on race, religion, sexual orientation, or ethnicity. The Criminal Justice Information Division of the Federal Bureau of Investigation collects the data and published a report in 1996 detailing more than 1,016 cases of sexual orientation bias-motivated crimes, representing almost 12 percent of all reported bias incidents. The murder of gay college student Matthew Shepard in Wyoming in 1998 prompted the Senate to pass new hate crime legislation in 2000 that included provisions against sexual orientation crimes.

Yet even those states that allow tougher sentences for crimes committed under a bias of sexual orientation often fail to make judges impose tough sentences on the perpetrators. Some judges have actually imposed lesser sentences for crimes committed against lesbians and gays. In 1988, a Texas judge sentenced the murderer of two gay men to thirty years in prison, effectively giving him parole in seven years. The judge later declared that he had given the murderer a lighter sentence because the victims were "queers" who would not have been killed if they were not out cruising the streets and trying to spread AIDS.

Following the 1969 Stonewall Riots in New York, during which gay men at a gay bar called the Stonewall Inn defended themselves against a police raid, gays and lesbians have become more willing to "come out" and let others know they are homosexuals. The election of openly gay men, like former San Francisco supervisor Harvey Milk in 1977 and longtime Democratic representative Barney Frank of Massachusetts, to positions of political power has catalyzed many gays and lesbians to fight for greater civil rights.

The election of President Bill Clinton in 1992 was a political watershed for gays and lesbians. Clinton actively courted gay and lesbian votes and initially supported a proposal to allow gays and lesbians to openly serve in the military. Yet Clinton backed down in the face of severe congressional and public criticism and supported instead a "don't ask, don't tell" policy that allowed gays and lesbians to serve in the military only if they remained closeted. From 1994, when the policy was instated, to 2000, the number of people discharged for homosexuality increased by 73 percent, and reports of harassment of homosexuals increased significantly. In one sensational case, the U.S. Navy received criticism for sending undercover agents posing as gay men into bars to search for illegal drug trafficking, with the result that more gay men were ousted from the navy. However, Clinton did support a 1995 act that reversed a long-standing Central Intelligence Agency policy of denying security clearances "solely on the basis of the sexual orientation of the employee."

The movement to get legal recognition of same-sex relationships and provide partner benefits for same-sex cohabiting couples had prompted heated controversy and achieved minimal gains by the late 1990s. In early 2000, the state of Vermont became the first to legalize same-sex civil unions. In June 2000, the nation's three largest car makers announced that they would extend full health benefits to the same-sex domestic partners of their nearly 500,000 American employees, a move that gay activists hope will convince other companies to follow suit.

The drive for recognition of gay unions made a significant leap in 2003, when the Supreme Court of Massachusetts found that the state's ban on gay marriages violated the state's constitution. Following the decision, thousands of same-sex couples were wed there. Another wave of gay marriages took place when San Francisco mayor Gavin Newsom began issuing marriage licenses to same-sex couples. While the U.S. Supreme Court refused to hear an appeal to the Massachusetts ruling, the Supreme Court of California put a stop to the marriages in San Francisco after just a month. The court later ruled that, because California law defined marriage as being between a man and a woman, Newsom had gone beyond his authority and the licenses he issued were illegal. Though the court nullified the marriages performed under Newsom, it did not rule on whether the state constitution left room for gay marriages.

If the election of 2004 was any indication, there was something of a backlash against gay marriage following its legalization in Massachusetts and the month-long boom in San Francisco, particularly among the so-called red states, which have populations that are generally more conservative than such states as Massachusetts and California. In the election, eleven states voted to amend their constitutions to ban gay marriage. These states joined six others that had previously done the same. In addition, amending the U.S. Constitution to ban gay marriage on a federal level became a hot topic in political debates.

Part of the difficulty that gays and lesbians have faced in securing the legalization of same-sex relationships stems from the rise of the Christian Right and misinformation generated during the early phase of the AIDS epidemic in the 1980s, when gay men were thought to be the only carriers of the disease. AIDS generated a backlash among conservative Americans, who used the disease as an excuse to justify violence against homosexuals and their exclusion from civil rights and hate crime legislation. Colorado's Amendment 2 (1992), which was later declared unconstitutional by the U.S. Supreme Court in *Romer v. Evans* (1996), sought to deny sexual orientation as a possible basis for discrimination and thus protection under Colorado law.

But in the early 2010s came rapid changes in the legality and perception of gay marriage. After President Barack Obama declared his support for gay marriage and several states passed laws approving it, the Supreme Court in 2013 held the Defense of Marriage Act of 1996 unconstitutional as a violation of the rights of gays and lesbians and for interfering in the rights of states. By the beginning of 2015, thirty-five states had recognized the right to same-sex marriage, by popular vote, legislative act, or a judicial decision.

The most difficult minority group to protect under existing laws, more than 30 million gays and lesbians in the United States are actively seeking legal recognition of social, economic, and political rights. The increased protection afforded by recent hate crime legislation is one step closer to the full acceptance of gays and lesbians as human beings in America. Yet the Supreme Court decision in *Boy Scouts of America v. Dale* (2000), upholding the right of the Boy Scouts to ban gays as scout leaders, means that other groups may now discriminate against gays and lesbians as well.

But popular culture increasingly promoted the acceptance of gay culture and the recognition of gay rights. In 2013, Jason Collins became the first active athlete in a major sport—professional basketball—to come out as gay; the next year, Michael Sam, a defensive star for the University of Missouri football team, made it public that he was gay, and was thus the first openly gay player to be drafted by a National Football League team, the St. Louis Rams. Late in 2014, Dale Scott, a veteran of nearly three decades as a major league umpire, came out as gay.

See also

Constitutionalism; HIV/AIDS Awareness; Judicial Activism; Marriage; Privacy; Prohibition; States' Rights (Antebellum, Memory, Contemporary)

JASON NEWMAN

Further Reading

D'Emilio, John. 1983. *Sexual Communities: The Making of a Homosexual Minority in the United States, 1940–1970.* Chicago: University of Chicago Press.
D'Emilio, John, and Estelle Freedman. 2012. *Intimate Matters: A History of Sexuality in America.* 3rd ed. Chicago: University of Chicago Press.
Faderman, Lillian. 1998. *Surpassing the Love of Men: Romantic Friendship and Love Between Women from the Renaissance to the Present.* New York: HarperCollins.

Gay Rights—Primary Document

Introduction

In December 1999, the Vermont Supreme Court ruled in Baker v. Vermont *that the state's marriage statutes were unconstitutional because they were denied to same-sex couples. After heated debate, the state legislature followed the court's lead and passed the Vermont Civil Unions Act, which Governor Howard Dean signed on April 26, 2000. Effective on July 1, 2000, the law created the legal status of "civil unions" for gay and lesbian couples under which they could obtain the same benefits, protections, and responsibilities as married couples in the state. Seven years after Vermont became the first state to grant civil unions to same-sex couples, eight states passed similar legislation that allowed civil unions or domestic partnerships. Because marriage laws vary according to states, civil unions may not be recognized in other states. The following is the full text of Vermont Civil Unions Act.*

Document: Vermont Civil Unions Act (2000)

It is hereby enacted by the General Assembly of the State of Vermont:

Sec. 1. Legislative Findings

The General Assembly finds that:

(1) Civil marriage under Vermont's marriage statutes consists of a union between a man and a woman. This interpretation of the state's marriage laws was upheld by the Supreme Court in Baker v. State.

(2) Vermont's history as an independent republic and as a state is one of equal treatment and respect for all Vermonters. This tradition is embodied in the Common Benefits Clause of the Vermont Constitution, Chapter I, Article 7th.

(3) The state's interest in civil marriage is to encourage close and caring families, and to protect all family members from the economic and social consequences of abandonment and divorce, focusing on those who have been especially at risk.

(4) Legal recognition of civil marriage by the state is the primary and, in a number of instances, the exclusive source of numerous benefits, responsibilities and protections under the laws of the state for married persons and their children.

(5) Based on the state's tradition of equality under the law and strong families, for at least 25 years, Vermont Probate Courts have qualified gay and lesbian individuals as adoptive parents.

(6) Vermont was one of the first states to adopt comprehensive legislation prohibiting discrimination on the basis of sexual orientation (Act No. 135 of 1992).

(7) The state has a strong interest in promoting stable and lasting families, including families based upon a same-sex couple.

(8) Without the legal protections, benefits and responsibilities associated with civil marriage, same-sex couples suffer numerous obstacles and hardships.

(9) Despite longstanding social and economic discrimination, many gay and lesbian Vermonters have formed lasting, committed, caring and faithful relationships with persons of their same sex. These couples live together, participate in their communities together, and some raise children and care for family members together, just as do couples who are married under Vermont law.

(10) While a system of civil unions does not bestow the status of civil marriage, it does satisfy the requirements of the Common Benefits Clause. Changes in the way significant legal relationships are established under the constitution should be approached carefully, combining respect for the community and cultural institutions most affected with a commitment to the constitutional rights involved. Granting benefits and protections to same-sex couples through a system of civil unions will provide due respect for tradition and long-standing social institutions, and will permit adjustment as unanticipated consequences or unmet needs arise.

(11) The constitutional principle of equality embodied in the Common Benefits Clause is compatible with the freedom of religious belief and worship guaranteed in Chapter I, Article 3rd of the state constitution. Extending the benefits and protections of marriage to same-sex couples through a system of civil unions preserves the fundamental constitutional right of each of the multitude of religious faiths in Vermont to choose freely and without state interference to whom to grant the religious status, sacrament or blessing of marriage under the rules, practices or traditions of such faith.

Sec. 2. Purpose

(a) The purpose of this act is to respond to the constitutional violation found by the Vermont Supreme Court in

Baker v. State, and to provide eligible same-sex couples the opportunity to "obtain the same benefits and protections afforded by Vermont law to married opposite-sex couples" as required by Chapter I, Article 7th of the Vermont Constitution.

(b) This act also provides eligible blood-relatives and relatives related by adoption the opportunity to establish a reciprocal beneficiaries relationship so they may receive certain benefits and protections and be subject to certain responsibilities that are granted to spouses.

Sec. 3. 15 V.S.A. Chapter 23 is Added to Read:

CHAPTER 23. CIVIL UNIONS

Sec. 1201. DEFINITIONS

As used in this chapter:

(1) "Certificate of civil union" means a document that certifies that the persons named on the certificate have established a civil union in this state in compliance with this chapter and 18 V.S.A. chapter 106.

(2) "Civil union" means that two eligible persons have established a relationship pursuant to this chapter, and may receive the benefits and protections and be subject to the responsibilities of spouses.

(3) "Commissioner" means the commissioner of health.

(4) "Marriage" means the legally recognized union of one man and one woman.

(5) "Party to a civil union" means a person who has established a civil union pursuant to this chapter and 18 V.S.A. chapter 106.

Sec. 1202. Requisites of a Valid Civil Union

For a civil union to be established in Vermont, it shall be necessary that the parties to a civil union satisfy all of the following criteria:

(1) Not be a party to another civil union or a marriage.

(2) Be of the same sex and therefore excluded from the marriage laws of this state.

(3) Meet the criteria and obligations set forth in 18 V.S.A. chapter 106.

Sec. 1203. Person Shall Not Enter a Civil Union with a Relative

(a) A woman shall not enter a civil union with her mother, grandmother, daughter, granddaughter, sister, brother's daughter, sister's daughter, father's sister or mother's sister.

(b) A man shall not enter a civil union with his father, grandfather, son, grandson, brother, brother's son, sister's son, father's brother or mother's brother.

(c) A civil union between persons prohibited from entering a civil union in subsection (a) or (b) of this section is void....

Source: Vermont State Legislature Web site. Available online at http://www.leg.state.vt.us/docs/2000/acts/act091.htm.

GREAT AWAKENING

By the close of 1735, a peculiar development had occurred in Northampton, Massachusetts, as approximately 300 followers of Congregationalist minister Jonathan Edwards began undergoing radical spiritual conversions. Some reported experiencing bouts of mysterious illnesses, leaving them full of despair and uncertainty, while others reported experiencing sensations that included moaning, wailing, and uncontrollable writhing, after which they all claimed to have gained a newfound spirituality. As Edwards soon realized, residents of other British colonies had also been experiencing similar behavior. Often termed the *Great Awakening* by contemporary historians of colonial American religion, evangelical Christian revivalism took hold throughout the British colonies from the late 1720s through the eve of the American Revolution.

Twentieth-century scholars of American religious history have grappled with the meaning of the Great Awakening in the sweep of American history. For several decades, the Great Awakening had been understood as a fairly united religious movement whose common denominator—Protestantism—was interpreted as the intellectual forerunner of American Revolutionary thought. More recently, however, historians have begun to question whether a "Great Awakening" actually occurred as well as the relationship between the Great Awakening and Revolutionary thought. For example, how could American thinkers steeped in reason and science, including Benjamin Franklin and Thomas Jefferson, claim intellectual lineage with Edwards, Presbyterian Gilbert Tennent, and Methodist revivalist George Whitefield? Looking beyond American intellectual history, the new social dynamics—or the methods and modes of 18th-century revivalism engineered by preachers and ministers—in many ways set the stage for the American Revolution. Innovations that included an individual focus on conversion, ministerial itinerancy, the transatlantic use of print promotion, and the rejection of rigid ecclesiastical hierarchies all influenced the ways in which the American Revolution would eventually be mapped out.

Although Edwards is frequently identified as the founder of the Great Awakening, inward spirituality and outward religiosity owe a debt to Dutch Reformed minister Theodorus Frelinghuysen. Knowing little about the Dutch colonies in America, Frelinghuysen agreed to serve as a Dutch Reformed minister, leaving Holland and arriving in Raritan Valley, New Jersey, in 1720. Thereafter, Frelinghuysen transformed the theological foundation of the Dutch Reformed Church. He introduced a new method of prayer that was derisively called the "howling prayer" because of all of the howling and wailing involved. Invoking the antinomian tradition of Anne Hutchinson a century earlier, Frelinghuysen believed firmly that prayer and spirituality resided in the heart. That focus on inward spirituality made church leadership obsolete, and as a result, the Dutch Reformed Church rejected Frelinghuysen's religious adaptations. Further north, at about the same time, Congregational minister Solomon Stoddard had enlisted the support of his grandson, Jonathan Edwards.

Both the influence of Stoddard and the philosophy of the Enlightenment had an enormous impact on Edwards's theological development. Something of a religious upstart himself, Stoddard rejected the Puritan belief in the "elect," or that conversion could only be legitimized by church leaders. Edwards's own theological training at Yale focused primarily on traditional Congregationalism; nevertheless, he also displayed keen interest in the philosophy of John Locke and the science of Isaac Newton. Those two philosophical currents intertwined in a new type of religious experience—sensationalism—the belief that conversion could only occur by melding psychology and religious belief, or faith.

Eventually, Edwards reasoned that Congregational preaching also needed invigorating. Passive listening would no longer sustain the interest of a congregation. As a result, Edwards developed a mode of preaching that incorporated visceral imagery to influence the consciousness of his congregation. In his 1741 sermon titled "Sinners in the Hands of an Angry God," Edwards used fiery imagery to illuminate the traditional Congregational belief in a wrathful God: "The God that holds you over the pit of hell, much as one holds a spider, or some loathsome insect over the fire, abhors you, and is dreadfully provoked: his wrath towards you burns like fire; he looks upon you as worthy of nothing else, but to be cast into the fire."

By stressing that conversion occurred through grace alone, much like Stoddard before him, Edwards rejected two of the pillars of Puritanism—the covenant of grace and the elect. In "Justification by Faith Alone" (1738), Edwards focused on a belief in faith and rejected the notion that human action, or "good works," influenced salvation. In addition, Edwards noted the widespread incidents of revivalism in his 1737 sermon, which was published in book form, titled *A Faithful Narrative of the Surprising Work of God:*

> As what other towns heard of and found in this, was a great means of awakening them; so our hearing of such a swift and extraordinary propagation, and extent of this work, did doubtless for a time serve to uphold the work amongst us.... But this shower of divine blessing has been yet more extensive: there was no small degree of it in some part of the Jerseys ...

By the mid-1730s, evangelicalism had begun to emerge in the middle colonies, especially in Pennsylvania and New Jersey. A religious congregation led by William Tennent and his sons, Gilbert and William, drew the consternation of traditional Presbyterians. Profoundly dismayed by the lack of formal seminary training available to Presbyterians, the elder Tennent established the "log college" system in Neshaminy,

Buck County (north of present-day Philadelphia), Pennsylvania. Originally a negative term, a *log college* referred to the type of homespun theological training that defied the elitism of such institutions as Yale University and Harvard University. In fact, institutions like the College of New Jersey, established in 1746 and later renamed Princeton University, owed its intellectual foundation to the log college. As the Presbyterian Church gained adherents, it eventually splintered into two factions—the Old Lights and the New Lights, the group that supported the fiery emotional practices of the Tennents. Scorn for evangelicalism seemed only to strengthen the resolve of the religious upstarts, however. Gilbert Tennent, for example, delivered one of his most celebrated sermons at that time entitled *The Danger of an Unconverted Ministry* (1740).

While some early ministers in the British colonies offered theological viewpoints clearly at odds with the established Church of England, other early missionaries simply sought reforms in order to better serve Anglicans in a new American context. Educated at Oxford University, Anglicans Charles and John Wesley were sent to evangelize in the newly formed Georgia colony as part of the Society of the Propagation of the Gospel (SPG). Neither brother had the intention of forming a new religion; they only sought to personalize their own religious tradition and make it less hierarchical. Though formally trained, John Wesley relied on lay people to serve as his preachers, and Charles sought to make religion more accessible through the use of hymns. Meetings organized by the Wesleys were meant to supplement the traditional Anglican Sunday service, but by the 1760s, a new form of Anglicanism, called Methodism because of its methodical nature, stretched into the middle colonies.

Adopting new modes of religious expression, including extemporaneous speaking, itinerancy, and the use of print to publicize events, Whitefield irrevocably transformed American religion. Educated at Oxford University, Whitefield interacted in the same religious circle as the Wesleys; however, Whitefield became utterly convinced that conversion was necessary to achieve salvation. Like the Wesleys, Whitefield received a commission from the SPG to minister in the Georgia colony, where he established an orphanage. Whitefield's success in the American colonies was unprecedented. American religious historian Frank Lambert suggests that part of Whitefield's success is owed to his own self-promotion. He used the colonial press to popularize his sermons and to advertise his arrival in America. Franklin's *Pennsylvania Gazette* was a huge promoter of Whitefield, although Franklin's interest in Whitefield was purely economic. In fact, Whitefield and Franklin, a deist, became unlikely allies when Franklin agreed to publish Whitefield's sermons in his many colonial newspapers.

The use of colonial print publishing further expanded the bounds of Whitefield's itinerancy. Whitefield's published sermons allowed for a broader base of followers. For example, evangelicalism spread into the Piedmont region of Virginia where one of Whitefield's promoters served as a lay preacher. Although the minister was scarcely trained in preaching, he found that reading Whitefield's printed sermons made for a captive audience. Whitefield's ministry expanded considerably once he established ties with local merchants. One Philadelphia merchant provided Whitefield with a sloop to travel the New England-Georgia circuit, and other merchants from both New England and Great Britain donated to his Savannah orphanage. Whitefield's success, in part, came from his ability to adapt to the changing market.

Evangelical religious experiences in America, although not entirely homegrown, reflected the vicissitudes occurring throughout the American colonies. The organizational modes of worship introduced by American Methodists, especially in such Anglican-dominated colonies as Virginia, appeared to have had some effect on the political culture of the region. By democratizing religious practices, Protestant ministers and preachers paved the way for the intellectuals of the coming American Revolution. Echoing the sentiments of Methodists and Presbyterians, Revolutionary thinkers would call into question the power wielded by the Church of England and by extension, King George III.

Indeed, some scholars have argued that it was evangelicals who first united religious freedom with political freedom. For example, Isaac Backus, a Baptist minister who openly supported the American Revolution, penned the treatise entitled *An Appeal to the Public for Religious Liberty* (1773), which merged Whig politics and evangelical religion. Other scholars more modestly suggest that, if anything, the impact of the Great Awakening helped bring freedom of religion to the consciousness of the framers of the U.S. Constitution. It was no mere coincidence that Jefferson drafted the Virginia Statute of Religious Freedom (1786) following the dissolution of Anglicanism in Virginia and as a precursor to the drafting of the Bill of Rights.

Recent scholarship on colonial evangelicalism challenges the understanding of the Great Awakening as a spontaneous religious experience. In fact, revivals were well advertised in the colonial press; planned events often received press attention across the Atlantic Ocean and throughout the emerging American colonies. Edwards initiated the idea of a "correspondence religious experience," where written words (published sermons) assumed the power of the spoken word. Revivalism offered up innovative models that would be replicated in the pages of *The Pennsylvania Gazette* and tracts by Thomas Paine, summoning American colonists to take up arms against the British Crown. Although intellectuals of the American Revolution took their cues from the ideas of Thomas Hobbes, Locke, and Jean-Jacques Rousseau, debts owed to the revivalists of the Great Awakening extend beyond belief—the new social dynamics engineered by colonial evangelicals gave these thinkers new modes and methods of political expression.

See also

Enlightenment; Second Great Awakening

ABC-CLIO

Further Reading

Butler, Jon. 1990. *Awash in a Sea of Faith: Christianizing the American People*. Cambridge, MA: Harvard University Press.

Heyrman, Christine L. 1997. *Southern Cross: The Beginnings of the Bible Belt*. Chapel Hill, NC: University of North Carolina Press.

Jonathan Edwards Center. http://edwards.yale.edu/ Accessed May 5, 2014.

Kidd, Thomas S. 2007. *The Great Awakening: A Brief History with Documents*. New York: Bedford/St. Martin's.

Kidd, Thomas S. 2009. *The Great Awakening: The Roots of Evangelical Christianity in Colonial America*. New Haven, CT: Yale University Press.

Lambert, Frank. 1990. "'Pedlar in Divinity': George Whitefield and the Great Awakening, 1737–1745." *Journal of American History*.

Noll, Mark A. 2002. *America's God: From Jonathan Edwards to Abraham Lincoln*. New York: Oxford University Press.

Great Awakening—Primary Document

Introduction

The Reverend Jonathan Edwards led the Great Awakening of the 1740s in America. A dynamic speaker and formidable theologian, Edwards fired the spirit of revivalism throughout western New England. His 1741 sermon, "Sinners in the Hands of an Angry God," became his most famous work and was widely republished throughout colonial North America.

Document: Jonathan Edwards's Sermon "Sinners in the Hands of an Angry God" (1741)

. . . The God that holds you over the pit of hell, much as one holds a spider, or some loathsome insect over the fire, abhors you, and is dreadfully provoked: his wrath towards you burns like fire; he looks upon you as worthy of nothing else, but to be cast into the fire; he is of purer eyes than to bear to have you in his sight; you are ten thousand times more abominable in his eyes, than the most hateful venomous serpent is in ours. You have offended him infinitely more than ever a stubborn rebel did his prince; and yet it is nothing but his hand that holds you from falling into the fire every moment. It is to be ascribed to nothing else, that you did not go to hell the last night; that you was suffered to awake again in this world, after you closed your eyes to sleep. And there is no other reason to be given, why you have not dropped into hell since you arose in the morning, but that God's hand has held you up. There is no other reason to be given why you have not gone to hell, since you have sat here in the house of God, provoking his pure eyes by your sinful wicked manner of attending his solemn worship. Yea, there is nothing else that is to be given as a reason why you do not this very moment drop down into hell.

O sinner! Consider the fearful danger you are in: it is a great furnace of wrath, a wide and bottomless pit, full of the fire of wrath, that you are held over in the hand of that God, whose wrath is provoked and incensed as much against you, as against many of the damned in hell. You hang by a slender thread, with the flames of divine wrath flashing about it, and ready every moment to singe it, and burn it asunder; and you have no interest in any Mediator, and nothing to lay hold of to save yourself, nothing to keep off the flames of wrath, nothing of your own, nothing that you ever have done, nothing that you can do, to induce God to spare you one moment.— And consider here more particularly,

1. Whose wrath it is: it is the wrath of the infinite God. If it were only the wrath of man, though it were of the most potent prince, it would be comparatively little to be regarded. The wrath of kings is very much dreaded, especially of absolute monarchs, who have the possessions and lives of their subjects wholly in their power, to be disposed of at their mere will. Prov. 20:2. "The fear of a king is as the roaring of a lion: Whoso provoketh him to anger, sinneth against his own soul." The subject that very much enrages an arbitrary prince, is liable to suffer the most extreme torments that human art can invent, or human power can inflict. But the greatest earthly potentates in their greatest majesty and strength, and when clothed in their greatest terrors, are but feeble, despicable worms of the dust, in comparison of the great and almighty Creator and King of heaven and earth. It is but little that they can do, when most enraged, and when they have exerted the utmost of their fury. All the kings of the earth, before God, are as grasshoppers; they are nothing, and less than nothing: both their love and their hatred is to be despised. The wrath of the great King of kings, is as much more terrible than theirs, as his majesty is greater. Luke 12:4,5. "And I say unto you, my friends, Be not afraid of them that kill the body, and after that, have no more that they can do. But I will forewarn you whom you shall fear: fear him, which after he hath killed, hath power to cast into hell: yea, I say unto you, Fear him."

2. It is the fierceness of his wrath that you are exposed to. We often read of the fury of God; as in Isa. 59:18. "According to their deeds, accordingly he will repay fury to his adversaries." So Isa. 66:15. "For behold, the Lord will come with fire, and with his chariots like a whirlwind, to render his anger with fury, and his rebuke with flames of fire." And in many other places. So, Rev. 19:15, we read of "the wine press of the fierceness and wrath of Almighty God." The words are exceeding terrible. If it had only been said, "the wrath of God," the words would have implied that which is infinitely dreadful: but it is "the fierceness and wrath of God." The fury of God! the fierceness of Jehovah! Oh, how dreadful that must be! Who can utter or conceive what such expressions carry in them! But it is also "the fierceness and wrath of almighty God." As though there would be a very great manifestation of his almighty power in what the fierceness of his wrath should inflict, as though omnipotence should be as it were enraged, and exerted, as men are wont to exert their strength in the fierceness

of their wrath. Oh! then, what will be the consequence! What will become of the poor worms that shall suffer it! Whose hands can be strong? And whose heart can endure? To what a dreadful, inexpressible, inconceivable depth of misery must the poor creature be sunk who shall be the subject of this!...

Source: Edwards, Jonathan. "Sinners in the Hands of and Angry God: A Sermon Preached at Enfield, July 8th 1741." Boston: Printed and Sold by S. Kneeland and T. Green, 1741.

GREAT SOCIETY

Vice President Lyndon B. Johnson (LBJ) assumed the presidency after the November 1963 assassination of President John F. Kennedy. Weeks later, on January 8, he set out in his State of the Union Message (1964) to define his own presidency. In his first address before Congress, President Johnson laid out his plans for an ambitious, multifaceted program of social and economic reforms designed to promote social equality and economic fairness for all Americans. Over the next four years, these programs, which came to be known as the Great Society, expanded the role of the federal government in the nation's domestic policies, transformed the relationship between citizen and government, and alleviated the suffering of millions of disadvantaged Americans.

Lyndon Johnson was raised in poverty in rural Texas in the early 20th century, and in later years he attributed his firm belief in social equality to his early experiences living among the rural white poor and teaching poverty-stricken Mexican American students when he was a young man. Elected to the House of Representatives in a special election in 1937, Johnson was an ardent supporter of Franklin Roosevelt's New Deal, after which he would model the Great Society nearly three decades later. Designed to alleviate the suffering of millions of Americans during the Great Depression of the 1930s, the New Deal fundamentally changed the traditional perception that the federal government should play little role in the everyday lives of Americans. A vast network of social programs including Social Security, and new federal legislation such as the Agricultural Adjustment Act (1938) and the creation of the Tennessee Valley Authority, expanded the reach of the government and greatly strengthened its economic

regulatory powers. As a member of Congress, LBJ embraced the activist approach of the New Deal, and when he became president he sought to expand its remaining programs by creating more federal agencies that would provide a safety net for the poor. The Great Society also aimed to improve education, protect the environment, and renew the nation's urban areas, which were mired in poverty, racism, and crime. Significantly, Johnson's plan also was designed to promote racial equality and civil rights, a goal that would prove to be highly controversial.

The plan that Johnson laid out in his 1964 State of the Union address was ambitious. Importantly, whereas the New Deal that inspired it took place as a response to the deepest economic crisis in U.S. history, President Johnson proposed his Great Society so that the unprecedented affluence that the country was enjoying in the 1960s might be extended to those citizens who traditionally had been left behind. His central goal was bold: he declared "unconditional war on poverty" and committed himself to eliminating poverty as it then existed. The president's antipoverty initiative was to be "cooperative," involving communities, local governments, and the courts. It took various forms; among its most significant and effective programs were Head Start, Medicare, Medicaid, and VISTA (Volunteers in Service to America). These programs reflected the range of problems that Johnson sought to address. Head Start established early childhood education programs in underprivileged communities; Medicare and Medicaid provided health insurance coverage for the previously uninsured; and VISTA, a domestic counterpart to the Peace Corps, was a service agency that created jobs and provided a number of programs including literacy and community health care initiatives.

Such Great Society initiatives targeted the economic status of the nation's poor, including whites and nonwhites. Another arm of the Great Society specifically focused on African Americans, whose long struggle for civil rights was at its peak in the mid-1960s. LBJ proposed sweeping legislation that would ensure the basic civil rights that had been denied to most black Americans since the end of the Civil War. The Civil Rights Act (1964), which had its roots in the Kennedy administration, outlawed segregation and discrimination against blacks and created an Equal Employment Opportunity Commission to ensure fairness in hiring practices. The Voting Rights Act (1965) rededicated the federal government

President Lyndon B. Johnson signs the Medicare program into law on July 30, 1965. On the right is former president Harry Truman, who became the first person to apply for the federal health care program and had been the first president to support a national health insurance program. (Lyndon B. Johnson Library)

to protecting the right to vote for blacks, who had been disenfranchised through a number of means, including literacy tests, in the century following the 1870 ratification of the Fifteenth Amendment to the Constitution.

The Johnson administration enlisted various agencies and institutions to make the Great Society a reality. John Gardner, who was appointed secretary of health, education, and welfare in 1965, was responsible for overseeing the implementation of many Great Society programs. He played a central role in ensuring the enforcement of civil rights protections and in creating and implementing Medicare and similar health programs. President Johnson envisioned that the Great Society would enlist not only leading figures such as Secretary Gardner, but also private citizens who would create and administer local and community projects and programs. This approach led to problems, as evidenced in the highly controversial Community Action Program

(CAP). One of the antipoverty measures of the Great Society, the goal of CAP was "maximum feasible participation" by community members in administering its programs. CAP fell under the direction of the Office of Economic Opportunity and it empowered local community leaders and soon became linked to civil rights goals. This angered local officials, including many of the country's mayors, and particularly Southern white politicians who saw CAP's empowerment of blacks as a direct threat to white social and political supremacy. The resulting backlash precipitated the end of the CAP and underscored the pervasive resistance of many whites to what was known at the time as the "uplift" of black Americans.

Despite such resistance, the 1964 national election had resulted in Johnson's overwhelming victory and a Democratic congressional landslide, which ensured that the president would enjoy strong support, and thus passage and funding, for most of his Great Society proposals. He also had the power of the Supreme Court behind him. Led by Chief Justice Earl Warren, the Court's liberal activism reflected the activism of the executive and legislative branches. The Warren Court upheld individual freedoms and civil liberties as promoted by the Johnson administration, most notably when it affirmed the constitutionality of the Civil Rights and Voting Rights Acts. In this way, the Supreme Court became something of an agent of the liberalism of the Great Society.

Liberal court activism and the Great Society generally antagonized conservative Republicans. They opposed the Great Society from its inception, contending that it unnecessarily expanded the size and power of the federal government and simply cost too much money. Despite this persistent opposition, it was not until the 1980s that significant efforts were made by President Ronald Reagan to roll back the programs of the Great Society (as well as those of the New Deal). Nevertheless, the institutional legacy of the Great Society persisted, and by the early 21st century, most of Lyndon Johnson's programs remained fixtures in the federal apparatus and in communities around the nation.

See also

African American Civil Rights Movement; Capitalism; Conservatism; Federalism

ABC-CLIO

Further Reading

Andrew, John A., III. 1999. *Lyndon Johnson and the Great Society*. Chicago: Ivan R. Dee.

Bornet, Vaughn D. 1984. *The Presidency of Lyndon B. Johnson*. Lawrence, KS: University Press of Kansas.

Dallek, Robert. 1998. *Flawed Giant: Lyndon Johnson and His Times, 1961–1973*. New York: Oxford University Press.

Goodwin, Doris Kearns. 1991. *Lyndon Johnson and the American Dream*. New York: St. Martin's Griffin.

Milkis, Sidney M., and Jerome M. Mileur, eds. 2005. *The Great Society and the High Tide of Liberalism*. Amherst, MA: University of Massachusetts Press.

Great Society—Primary Document

Introduction

On May 22, 1964, U.S. president Lyndon B. Johnson outlined his plan to create an American welfare state in this speech, which he delivered at the University of Michigan in Ann Arbor.

What he proposed would be largely enacted by a mostly Democratic Congress, with help from many Republicans, over the next four years.

Document: President Lyndon Johnson's "Great Society" Speech (May 22, 1964)

I have come today from the turmoil of your Capitol to the tranquility of your campus to speak about the future of our country. The purpose of protecting the life of our nation and preserving the liberty of our citizens is to pursue the happiness of our people. Our success in that pursuit is the test of our success as a nation. For a century we labored to settle and to subdue a continent. For half a century we called upon unbounded invention and untiring industry to create an order of plenty for all of our people. The challenge of the next half century is whether we have the wisdom to use that wealth to enrich and elevate our national life and to advance the quality of our American civilization.

Your imagination, your initiative, and your indignation will determine whether we build a society where progress is the servant of our needs or a society where old values and new visions are buried under unbridled growth. For, in your time, we have the opportunity to move not only toward the rich society and the powerful society but upward to the Great Society.

The Great Society rests on abundance and liberty for all. It demands an end to poverty and racial injustice, to which we are totally committed in our time. But that is just the beginning. The Great Society is a place where every child can find knowledge to enrich his mind and to enlarge his talents. It is a place where leisure is a welcome chance to build and reflect, not a feared cause of boredom and restlessness. It is a place where the city of man serves not only the needs of the body and the demands of commerce but the desire for beauty and the hunger for community.

It is a place where man can renew contact with nature. It is a place which honors creation for its own sake and for what it adds to the understanding of the race. It is a place where men are more concerned with the quality of their goals than the quantity of their goods. But, most of all, the Great Society is not a safe harbor, a resting place, a final objective, a finished work; it is a challenge constantly renewed, beckoning us toward a destiny where the meaning of our lives matches the marvelous products of our labor.

So I want to talk to you today about three places where we begin to build the Great Society—in our cities, in our countryside, and in our classrooms. Many of you will live to see the day, perhaps fifty years from now, when there will be 400 million Americans, four-fifths of them in urban areas. In the remainder of this century, urban population will double, city land will double, and we will have to build homes, highways, and facilities equal to all those built since this country was first settled. So, in the next forty years, we must rebuild the entire urban United States.

Aristotle said, "Men come together in cities in order to live, but they remain together in order to live the good life." It is harder and harder to live the good life in American cities today. The catalog of ills is long: there is the decay of the centers and the despoiling of the suburbs. There is not enough housing for our people or transportation for our traffic. Open land is vanishing and old landmarks are violated. Worst of all, expansion is eroding the precious and time-honored values of community with neighbors and communion with nature. The loss of these values breeds loneliness and boredom and indifference. Our society will never be great until our cities are great. Today the frontier of imagination and innovation is inside those cities, and not beyond their borders. New experiments are already going on. It will be the task of your generation to make the American city a place where future generations will come, not only to live but to live the good life.

I understand that if I stay here tonight I would see that Michigan students are really doing their best to live the good life. This is the place where the Peace Corps was started. It is inspiring to see how all of you, while you are in this country, are trying so hard to live at the level of the people.

A second place where we begin to build the Great Society is in our countryside. We have always prided ourselves on being not only America the strong and America the free but America the beautiful. Today that beauty is in danger. The water we drink, the food we eat, the very air that we breathe are threatened with pollution. Our parks are overcrowded. Our seashores overburdened. Green fields and dense forests are disappearing.

A few years ago we were greatly concerned about the Ugly American. Today we must act to prevent an Ugly America. For once the battle is lost, once our natural splendor is destroyed, it can never be recaptured. And once man can no longer walk with beauty or wonder at nature, his spirit will wither and his sustenance be wasted.

A third place to build the Great Society is in the classrooms of America. There your children's lives will be shaped. Our society will not be great until every young mind is set free to scan the farthest reaches of thought and imagination. We are still far from that goal. Today, 8 million adult Americans, more than the entire population of Michigan, have not finished five years of school. Nearly 20 million have not finished eight years of school. Nearly 54 million, more than one-quarter of all America, have not even finished high school.

Each year more than 100,000 high-school graduates, with proved ability, do not enter college because they cannot afford it. And if we cannot educate today's youth, what will we do in 1970 when elementary-school enrollment will be 5 million greater than 1960? And high-school enrollment will rise by 5 million? College enrollment will increase by more than 3 million? In many places, classrooms are overcrowded and curricula are outdated. Most of our qualified teachers are underpaid, and many of our paid teachers are unqualified. So we must give every child a place to sit and a teacher to learn from. Poverty must not be a bar to learning, and learning must offer an escape from poverty.

But more classrooms and more teachers are not enough. We must seek an educational system which grows in excellence as it grows in size. This means better training for our teachers. It means preparing youth to enjoy their hours of leisure as well as their hours of labor. It means exploring new techniques of teaching, to find new ways to stimulate the love of learning and the capacity for creation.

These are three of the central issues of the Great Society. While our government has many programs directed at those issues, I do not pretend that we have the full answer to those problems. But I do promise this: We are going to assemble the best thought and the broadest knowledge from all over the world to find those answers for America. I intend to establish working groups to prepare a series of White House conferences and meetings on the cities, on natural beauty, on the quality of education, and on other emerging challenges. And from these meetings and from this inspiration and from these studies we will begin to set our course toward the Great Society.

The solution to these problems does not rest on a massive program in Washington, nor can it rely solely on the strained resources of local authority. They require us to create new concepts of cooperation, a creative federalism, between the national Capitol and the leaders of local communities.

Woodrow Wilson once wrote: "Every man sent out from his university should be a man of his nation as well as a man of his time." Within your lifetime powerful forces, already loosed, will take us toward a way of life beyond the realm of our experience, almost beyond the bounds of our imagination. For better or for worse, your generation has been appointed by history to deal with those problems and to lead America toward a new age. You have the chance never before afforded to any people in any age. You can help build a society where the demands of morality and the needs of the spirit can be realized in the life of the nation.

So will you join the battle to give every citizen the full equality which God enjoins and the law requires, whatever his belief, or race, or the color of his skin? Will you join in the battle to give every citizen an escape from the crushing weight of poverty? Will you join in the battle to make it possible for all nations to live in enduring peace as neighbors and not as mortal enemies? Will you join in the battle to build the Great Society, to prove that our material progress is only the foundation on which we will build a richer life of mind and spirit?

There are those timid souls who say this battle cannot be won, that we are condemned to a soulless wealth. I do not agree. We have the power to shape the civilization that we want. But we need your will, your labor, your hearts if we are to build that kind of society.

Those who came to this land sought to build more than just a new country. They sought a free world. So I have come here today to your campus to say that you can make their vision our reality. Let us from this moment begin our work so that in the future men will look back and say: It was then, after a long and weary way, that man turned the exploits of his genius to the full enrichment of his life.

Source: Lyndon B. Johnson: "Remarks at the University of Michigan," May 22, 1964. Online by Gerhard Peters and John T. Woolley, *The American Presidency Project.* http://www.presidency.ucsb.edu/ws/?pid=26262.

GUN CONTROL MOVEMENT

Gun control (government policies that influence or determine the availability and use of firearms) has been a feature of American life since the formative years of the republic. From colonial times to the early 1900s, local and state laws, often supported by the U.S. Supreme Court, were the source of all gun control in the nation. However, beginning in 1934, the federal government took an active lead in gun control legislation. While high-profile gun-related violence cases and public outcry for stricter measures sometimes led to a national gun control movement, which spurred on new federal gun control laws, gun rights proponents like the National Rifle Association (NRA), who saw gun ownership as a basic American right, pushed against gun control measures. With few exceptions, since the introduction of federal gun control laws, Democratic administrations have tended to support and influence gun control measures while Republican administrations have opposed and blocked them.

During the 17th century, colonial governments required adult white male Protestant land-owning citizens to keep guns for the purpose of maintaining militias. In other words, early gun control measures included requiring certain citizens to own guns. On the other hand, the government banned slaves, indentured servants, and Roman Catholics from owning guns. Also, supplying firearms to Native Americans was strongly discouraged by stiff penalties, including death. Leading up to the American Revolution, many Americans sought to arm themselves against a British government that

The Mall in Washington, D.C., was filled with women—and some men—bearing their messages calling for gun controls at the Million Mom March on May 14, 2000. The next year, the organization that created the event merged with the Brady Campaign against gun violence. (Harry Hamburg/NY Daily News Archive via Getty Images)

they believed was trampling on their rights. During the early years of the American republic, Congress passed the Uniform Militia Act (1792) and the Calling Forth Act (1792), which established the federal government's power to marshal state militias in times of crisis. However, the poor performance of most militias during the War of 1812 convinced the American leadership that a well-trained professional army was needed. Consequently, government reliance on citizen militias waned after the War of 1812. Officially, the Militia Act (1903) replaced the citizen militia system with the National Guard.

Due in great part to industrialization, after the American Civil War (1861–1865), gun ownership dramatically increased across the nation. Gun violence, especially in Eastern cities, led to calls for gun control measures. Some towns and cities prohibited the carrying of any type of firearms. In some cases, visitors were required to check their weapons in at a designated location. Upon exiting the town or city, visitors would then claim their property with a ticket or token. Various types of local and state controls on firearms, such as a ban on carrying concealed weapons, continued throughout the 19th century. Although the federal government did not pass any laws pertaining to gun control during this time, the U.S. Supreme Court supported local and state controls. With *Miller v. Texas* (1894), the Court ruled that state laws prohibiting the carrying of weapons did not violate the Second Amendment. Also, three years later the Court ruled in *Robertson v. Baldwin* (1897) that laws barring concealed weapons did not violate the Second Amendment.

High-profile violence cases sometimes brought about new restrictions on gun ownership. For example, in 1911, the state of New York passed the Sullivan Dangerous Weapon

Law, which at the time was one of the strictest gun control measures in the nation. The new state law regulated the sale, ownership, and carrying of firearms. Under the law, a license was required in order to carry and conceal a weapon, and the penalty for lawbreakers was elevated to a felony. The Sullivan Law had been proposed due to the high rate of gun violence in the large city, and it gained great popular support after an assassination attempt in 1910 on New York City Mayor William J. Gaynor. Although the law gave police greater authority, it did not stop gun violence. In fact, the rise of organized crime after World War I (1914–1918) led to an increase in gun violence in many major cities across the country.

After World War I, war-type handheld machine guns, sawed-off shot guns, sawed-off rifles, and silencers became the weapons of choice by organized crime groups. During the 1920s and 1930s in cities like Chicago with a significant organized crime presence, shootouts between rival criminal groups and law enforcement officials were highly publicized. Following an assassination attempt on president-elect Franklin D. Roosevelt (Democrat) in 1933, with Roosevelt's support, Congress passed the first federal gun control law in American history. The shooter, an anarchist, missed Roosevelt, but he killed Chicago Mayor Anton Cermak, who was with Roosevelt at the time. In the wake of mob-style violence and Roosevelt's assassination attempt, the National Firearms Act (1934) targeted gun control measures for gangster-type weapons such as machine guns and sawed-off long guns. Under the law, prospective buyers were required to submit to a background check with the Federal Bureau of Investigation (FBI). Four years later, Congress sought to strengthen the 1934 federal gun control efforts with the Federal Firearms Act (1938), which required that all gun manufacturers, gun dealers, and gun importers be licensed by the government. The next federal gun control law did not appear until thirty years later.

The 1960s were a time of social unrest. Violent and nonviolent protests occurred all over the country as militant and peaceful groups sought social equality. Random gun violence occurred as well. In Texas in 1966, a lone gunman armed with several weapons fired from a University of Texas (Austin) tower, killing sixteen and wounding thirty-two. In the midst of the social pressures that the nation was experiencing, the assassinations of President John F. Kennedy (1963), Senator Robert Kennedy (1968), and civil rights leader Martin Luther King Jr. (1968) led Congress to pass the Gun Control Act (1968). The law, which was supported by President Lyndon B. Johnson (Democrat), brought about rigorous and numerous gun control measures, which included barring convicted felons, fugitives, drug addicts, minors, and mentally ill people from purchasing firearms, banning interstate and mail order sales of firearms and ammunition to private individuals, requiring serial numbers on all new firearms, requiring government oversight of stricter licensing and recordkeeping requirements for gun dealers, and increasing penalties for crimes committed using firearms. These and other gun control measures included in the Gun Control Act remained in force for approximately twenty years.

The NRA, the most powerful antigun control political force in the world, was formed in 1871 by Lieutenant Colonel William C. Church and Captain George W. Wingate to promote marksmanship. The organization's first significant spike in membership occurred after the Spanish American War (1898), due in large part to President Theodore Roosevelt's support, which facilitated the organization's attainment of land for target practice and army surplus rifles and ammunition. Not surprisingly, federal involvement in gun control increased the controversy surrounding the issue. In 1974, Nelson Shields organized the National Council to Control Handguns. Concerned by the new federal gun control measures introduced in the late 1960s and the creation of another pro-gun control group, in 1977, the NRA leadership expanded its agenda to include the defense of Second Amendment rights. Consequently, as gun control activists attempted to push for stronger gun control measures, the NRA continually pushed back, and in the 1980s the NRA exerted strong influence over political issues.

Surprisingly, in spite of being shot in an assassination attempt that almost cost him his life, Ronald Reagan (Republican) refused to support new gun control measures while he was president. In fact, it was not until he left office that he reversed his position on some gun control issues. In 1986, Congress passed the Firearms Owner's Protection Act, which overturned some of the provisions of the Gun Control Act (1968). Senator James A. McClure (Republican) and Representative Harold L. Volkmer (Democrat), the main sponsors of the bill, argued that the Gun Control Act restricted the gun-owning rights of law-abiding citizens while not doing enough to deter criminals from gun possession. Seen as benefits to law-abiding citizens, the new law erased the ban on mail order ammunition sales, it eased up recordkeeping requirements by dealers, and it prohibited the Bureau of Alcohol, Tobacco, and Firearms (ATF), the firearms enforcement branch of the federal government, from establishing a centralized database of guns and gun owners with the use of gun dealer records. In an attempt to curtail criminal gun violence, the law prohibited the manufacture and sale of machine guns to private citizens and it increased the penalties to gun-carrying drug traffickers.

During the attempt on Reagan's life, presidential press secretary James Brady was seriously wounded. Wishing to make America safer from gun violence, Brady and his wife Sarah sought new gun control measures, but they faced stiff opposition from the Reagan administration and the NRA. However, several high-profile acts of gun violence during the 1980s and 1990s served to turn the tide of public sentiment on the issue. In 1984, a gunman injured or killed forty-four people in a fast-food restaurant in San Ysidro, California. In 1991, in Killeen, Texas, a gunman killed twenty-two people and wounded twenty-three others at a cafeteria. At a U.S. Post Office in Oklahoma (1986) and at the Royal Oak Post Office in Michigan (1991) more than thirty people combined were wounded or killed. These and other cases of gun violence caused alarm, but none did so more acutely than the shootings at public schools. For example, in 1989, a gunman armed with an AK-47 killed five children and wounded twenty-nine others as they played in a schoolyard in Stockton, California.

President Bill Clinton (Democrat) supported new gun control measures, and in 1993 Congress passed the Brady Handgun Violence Prevention Act, which placed a five-day waiting period on all handgun purchases and required a background check of prospective purchasers by local law enforcement officers. In 1997, the Supreme Court ruled in *Printz v. United States* that local law enforcement officers were not required to run background checks. Also, in 1998, a computerized instant background check system eliminated the five-day waiting period. While the Brady Act targeted the control of handguns, the 1994 Violent Crime Control and Law Enforcement Act (VCCLEA) banned various kinds of assault-type weapons. The VCCLEA, which was put in

force for ten years, was passed shortly after the April 1993 fifty-one-day siege of a Branch Davidian compound in Waco, Texas, by ATF agents, which left seventy-four Davidians dead. The attack on the Davidians by government officials in Waco convinced some Americans that they needed to arm themselves against a government that had become overly powerful. The NRA, too, criticized the government's use of force in Waco, and sounded a call to arms. In 2004, Congress did not renew the VCCLEA, which erased the ban on assault weapons.

In 2000, the largest gun control demonstration in history occurred. The Million Mom March, which was held on Mother's Day at the capitol, was made up of more than 7 million people. In 2001, the National Council to Control Handguns, which had been pushing for gun control measures since 1974, changed its name to the Brady Coalition. On the opposing front, with Charlton Heston, a famous charismatic former actor, as the head of the NRA, their membership reached 4 million. In 2008, the NRA won a tremendous victory in its struggle against gun control activists. In legal terms, for many years the meaning of the Second Amendment had been a matter of contention between the two opposing sides of the gun control controversy. While gun control supporters claimed that the original intent of the Second Amendment was to protect gun ownership rights for militia use only, those who opposed gun control laws claimed that the Second Amendment protected the right of individuals to own guns for self-protection. In 2008, the U.S. Supreme Court dismissed the historical interpretation adopted by gun control activists and ruled in *District of Columbia v. Heller* (2008) that individual gun ownership was, in fact, the original intent of the amendment.

In the midst of the gun control controversy in the late 1990s and early 2000s, acts of gun violence continued unabated. Some of the most highly publicized shootings took place at Columbine High School (1999) in Littleton, Colorado, where two students shot and killed twelve students, one teacher, and themselves; at Virginia Tech (2007) where a student went on a rampage of the college campus and left thirty-three people dead and twenty-three wounded; at the military base at Fort Hood, Texas (2009), a Muslim army doctor went on a shooting spree leaving forty-three people dead or wounded; at a movie theater in Aurora, Colorado (2012), with seventy victims; and Sandy Hook Elementary (2012) in Sandy Hook, Connecticut, which left twenty-eight dead and two injured–mostly children. These shootings and several others brought attention to gun violence, and gun control activists sought to get stricter laws passed while public sentiment was in favor of change. For example, after the Sandy Hook shooting, President Barack Obama (Democrat) publicly vowed to enact new gun control measures. One unintended effect of his stated mission, however, was the increase of firearm and ammunition sales around the country as Americans braced for possible gun restrictions. The net effect was that there were more guns in America after his promise than before it.

In January 2013, Obama introduced a series of executive and congressional actions. The twenty-three executive actions included strengthening the background check system in various ways, such as requiring states to make previously protected confidential mental health information available for background checks so that dangerous people would not slip "through the cracks" undetected, directing the Centers for Disease Control and Prevention to conduct research on gun violence, and launching a campaign to better educate the populace on gun responsibilities and gun safety. In short, none of the twenty-three executive orders brought about any significant changes to limit the rights of Americans to own guns. Not surprisingly, Obama left the more constitutionally controversial changes for Congress to make. Among the congressional laws the president requested were a new ban on assault-type weapons, a ban on armor-piercing bullets, and limiting magazines to ten rounds each. To Obama's frustration, he encountered much more Republican congressional resistance (and from some Democrats) to his proposed gun control measures than he had expected and, as a consequence, none were approved.

See also
Bill of Rights; Conservatism

ROLANDO AVILA

Further Reading
Carter, Gregg Lee. 1997. *The Gun Control Movement*. New York: Twayne Publishers.

DeConde, Alexander. 2001. *Gun Violence in America: The Struggle for Control*. Boston: Northeastern University Press.

Goss, Kristin A. 2006. *Disarmed: The Missing Movement for Gun Control in America*. Princeton, NJ: Princeton University Press.

Spitzer, Robert J. 2002. *The Politics of Gun Control*. New York: Chatham House.

Utter, Glenn H. 2000. *Encyclopedia of Gun Control and Gun Rights*. Phoenix, AZ: Oryx Press.

Vizzard, William J. 2000. *Shots in the Dark: The Policy, Politics, and Symbolism of Gun Control*. Lanham, MD: Rowman & Littlefield.

Winkler, Adam. 2011. *Gunfight: The Battle over the Right to Bear Arms in America*. New York: W.W. Norton.

Gun Control Movement—Primary Document

Introduction

In 2008, the U.S. Supreme Court ruled in District of Columbia v. Heller *that the Second Amendment assured citizens of a right to bear arms. The ruling certainly did not end the controversy over the extent of Second Amendment rights. It represented a victory for gun rights advocates, but the majority opinion by Justice Antonin Scalia also made clear that those rights were and are not absolute. Scalia also devoted a significant part of the opinion to analyzing the amendment's language, which states, "A well regulated Militia, being necessary to the security of a free state, the right of the people to keep and bear Arms, shall not be infringed." Scalia devoted lengthy parts of his opinion to addressing dissents by Justices John Paul Stevens and Stephen Breyer.*

Document: *District of Columbia v. Heller* (2008)

From the opinion for the majority by Justice Scalia:

. . . . The debate with respect to the right to keep and bear arms, as with other guarantees in the Bill of Rights, was not over whether it was desirable (all agreed that it was) but over whether it needed to be codified in the Constitution. During the 1788 ratification debates, the fear that the federal government would disarm the people in order to impose rule through a standing army or select militia was pervasive in Antifederalist rhetoric. See, *e.g.*, Letters from The Federal Farmer III (Oct. 10, 1787), in 2 The Complete Anti-Federalist 234, 242 (H. Storing ed. 1981). John Smilie, for example, worried not only that Congress's "command of the militia" could be used to create a "select militia," or to have "no militia at all," but also, as a separate concern, that "[w]hen a select militia is formed; the people in general may be disarmed." 2 Documentary History of the Ratification of the Constitution 508–509 (M. Jensen ed. 1976) (hereinafter Documentary Hist.). Federalists responded that because Congress was given no power to abridge the ancient right of individuals to keep and bear arms, such a force could never oppress the people. See, *e.g.*, A Pennsylvanian III (Feb. 20, 1788), in The Origin of the Second Amendment 275, 276 (D. Young ed., 2d ed. 2001) (hereinafter Young); White, To the Citizens of Virginia, Feb. 22, 1788, in *id.*, at 280, 281; A Citizen of America, (Oct. 10, 1787) in *id.*, at 38, 40; Remarks on the Amendments to the federal Constitution, Nov. 7, 1788, in *id.*, at 556. It was understood across the political spectrum that the right helped to secure the ideal of a citizen militia, which might be necessary to oppose an oppressive military force if the constitutional order broke down.

It is therefore entirely sensible that the Second Amendment's prefatory clause announces the purpose for which the right was codified: to prevent elimination of the militia. The prefatory clause does not suggest that preserving the militia was the only reason Americans valued the ancient right; most undoubtedly thought it even more important for self-defense and hunting. But the threat that the new Federal Government would destroy the citizens' militia by taking away their arms was the reason that right—unlike some other English rights—was codified in a written Constitution. Justice Breyer's assertion that individual self-defense is merely a "subsidiary interest" of the right to keep and bear arms, see *post*, at 36, is profoundly mistaken. He bases that assertion solely upon the prologue—but that can only show that self-defense had little to do with the right's *codification;* it was the *central component* of the right itself.

Besides ignoring the historical reality that the Second Amendment was not intended to lay down a "novel principl[e]" but rather codified a right "inherited from our English ancestors," *Robertson* v. *Baldwin*, 165 U.S. 275, 281 (1897), petitioners' interpretation does not even achieve the narrower purpose that prompted codification of the right. If, as they believe, the Second Amendment right is no more than the right to keep and use weapons as a member of

an organized militia, see Brief for Petitioners 8—if, that is, the *organized* militia is the sole institutional beneficiary of the Second Amendment's guarantee—it does not assure the existence of a "citizens' militia" as a safeguard against tyranny. For Congress retains plenary authority to organize the militia, which must include the authority to say who will belong to the organized force. That is why the first Militia Act's requirement that only whites enroll caused States to amend their militia laws to exclude free blacks. See Siegel, The Federal Government's Power to Enact Color-Conscious Laws, 92 Nw. U.L. Rev. 477, 521–525 (1998). Thus, if petitioners are correct, the Second Amendment protects citizens' right to use a gun in an organization from which Congress has plenary authority to exclude them. It guarantees a select militia of the sort the Stuart kings found useful, but not the people's militia that was the concern of the founding generation....

Like most rights, the right secured by the Second Amendment is not unlimited. From Blackstone through the 19th-century cases, commentators and courts routinely explained that the right was not a right to keep and carry any weapon whatsoever in any manner whatsoever and for whatever purpose. See, *e.g.*, *Sheldon*, in 5 Blume 346; Rawle 123; Pomeroy 152–153; Abbott 333. For example, the majority of the 19th-century courts to consider the question held that prohibitions on carrying concealed weapons were lawful under the Second Amendment or state analogues. See, *e.g.*, *State* v. *Chandler*, 5 La. Ann., at 489–490; *Nunn* v. *State*, 1 Ga., at 251; see generally 2 Kent *340, n. 2; The American Students' Blackstone 84, n. 11 (G. Chase ed. 1884). Although we do not undertake an exhaustive historical analysis today of the full scope of the Second Amendment, nothing in our opinion should be taken to cast doubt on longstanding prohibitions on the possession of firearms by felons and the mentally ill, or laws forbidding the carrying of firearms in sensitive places such as schools and government buildings, or laws imposing conditions and qualifications on the commercial sale of arms.

We also recognize another important limitation on the right to keep and carry arms. *Miller* said, as we have explained, that the sorts of weapons protected were those "in common use at the time." 307 U.S., at 179. We think that limitation is fairly supported by the historical tradition of prohibiting the carrying of "dangerous and unusual weapons." See 4 Blackstone 148–149 (1769); 3 B. Wilson, Works of the Honourable James Wilson 79 (1804); J. Dunlap, The New-York Justice 8 (1815); C. Humphreys, A Compendium of the Common Law in Force in Kentucky 482 (1822); 1 W. Russell, A Treatise on Crimes and Indictable Misdemeanors 271–272 (1831); H. Stephen, Summary of the Criminal Law 48 (1840); E. Lewis, An Abridgment of the Criminal Law of the United States 64 (1847); F. Wharton, A Treatise on the Criminal Law of the United States 726 (1852). See also *State* v. *Langford*, 10 N.C. 381, 383–384 (1824); *O'Neill* v. *State*, 16 Ala. 65, 67 (1849); *English* v. *State*, 35 Tex. 473, 476 (1871); *State* v. *Lanier*, 71 N.C. 288, 289 (1874).

It may be objected that if weapons that are most useful in military service—M-16 rifles and the like—may be banned, then the Second Amendment right is completely detached from the prefatory clause. But as we have said, the conception of the militia at the time of the Second Amendment 's ratification was the body of all citizens capable of military service, who would bring the sorts of lawful weapons that they possessed at home to militia duty. It may well be true today that a militia, to be as effective as militias in the 18th century, would require sophisticated arms that are highly unusual in society at large. Indeed, it may be true that no amount of small arms could be useful against modern-day bombers and tanks. But the fact that modern developments have limited the degree of fit between the prefatory clause and the protected right cannot change our interpretation of the right.

We turn finally to the law at issue here. As we have said, the law totally bans handgun possession in the home. It also requires that any lawful firearm in the home be disassembled or bound by a trigger lock at all times, rendering it inoperable.

As the quotations earlier in this opinion demonstrate, the inherent right of self-defense has been central to the Second Amendment right. The handgun ban amounts to a prohibition of an entire class of "arms" that is overwhelmingly chosen by American society for that lawful purpose. The prohibition extends, moreover, to the home, where the need for defense of self, family, and property is most acute. Under any of the standards of scrutiny that we have applied to enumerated constitutional rights, http://www.law.cornell.edu/supct/html/07-290.ZO.html—27 banning from the home "the most preferred firearm in the nation to 'keep' and use for protection of one's home and family," 478 F.3d, at 400, would fail constitutional muster.

Few laws in the history of our Nation have come close to the severe restriction of the District's handgun ban. And some of those few have been struck down. In *Nunn* v. *State*, the Georgia Supreme Court struck down a prohibition on carrying pistols openly (even though it upheld a prohibition on carrying concealed weapons). See 1 Ga., at 251. In *Andrews* v. *State*, the Tennessee Supreme Court likewise held that a statute that forbade openly carrying a pistol "publicly or privately, without regard to time or place, or circumstances," 50 Tenn., at 187, violated the state constitutional provision (which the court equated with the Second Amendment). That was so even though the statute did not restrict the carrying of long guns. *Ibid.* See also *State* v. *Reid*, 1 Ala. 612, 616–617 (1840) ("A statute which, under the pretence of regulating, amounts to a destruction of the right, or which requires arms to be so borne as to render them wholly useless for the purpose of defence, would be clearly unconstitutional").

It is no answer to say, as petitioners do, that it is permissible to ban the possession of handguns so long as the possession of other firearms (*i.e.*, long guns) is allowed. It is enough to note, as we have observed, that the American people have considered the handgun to be the quintessential self-defense weapon. There are many reasons that a citizen may prefer a handgun for home defense: It is easier to store in a location that is readily accessible in an emergency; it cannot easily be redirected or wrestled away by an attacker; it is easier to use for those without the upper-body strength to lift and aim a long gun; it can be pointed at a burglar with one hand while the other hand dials the police. Whatever the reason, handguns are the most popular weapon chosen by Americans for self-defense in the home, and a complete prohibition of their use is invalid.

We must also address the District's requirement (as applied to respondent's handgun) that firearms in the home be rendered and kept inoperable at all times. This makes it impossible for citizens to use them for the core lawful purpose of self-defense and is hence unconstitutional. The District argues that we should interpret this element of the statute to contain an exception for self-defense. See Brief for Petitioners 56–57. But we think that is precluded by the unequivocal text, and by the presence of certain other enumerated exceptions: "Except for law enforcement personnel . . . , each registrant shall keep any firearm in his possession unloaded and disassembled or bound by a trigger lock or similar device unless such firearm is kept at his place of business, or while being used for lawful recreational purposes within the District of Columbia." D.C. Code §7–2507.02. The nonexistence of a self-defense exception is also suggested by the D.C. Court of Appeals' statement that the statute forbids residents to use firearms to stop intruders, see *McIntosh* v. *Washington*, 395 A. 2d 744, 755–756 (1978).

Apart from his challenge to the handgun ban and the trigger-lock requirement respondent asked the District Court to enjoin petitioners from enforcing the separate licensing requirement "in such a manner as to forbid the carrying of a firearm within one's home or possessed land without a license." App. 59a. The Court of Appeals did not invalidate the licensing requirement, but held only that the District "may not prevent [a handgun] from being moved throughout one's house." 478 F. 3d, at 400. It then ordered the District Court to enter summary judgment "consistent with [respondent's] prayer for relief." *Id.*, at 401. Before this Court petitioners have stated that "if the handgun ban is struck down and respondent registers a handgun, he could obtain a license, assuming he is not otherwise disqualified," by which they apparently mean if he is not a felon and is not insane. Brief for Petitioners 58. Respondent conceded at oral argument that he does not "have a problem with . . . licensing" and that the District's law is permissible so long as it is "not enforced in an arbitrary and capricious manner." Tr. of Oral Arg. 74–75. We therefore assume that petitioners' issuance of a license will satisfy respondent's prayer for relief and do not address the licensing requirement.

Justice Breyer has devoted most of his separate dissent to the handgun ban. He says that, even assuming the Second Amendment is a personal guarantee of the right to bear arms, the District's prohibition is valid. He first tries to establish this by founding-era historical precedent, pointing to various restrictive laws in the colonial period. These demonstrate, in his view, that the District's law "imposes a burden upon gun owners that seems proportionately no greater than restrictions in existence at the time the Second Amendment was adopted." *Post*, at 2. Of the laws he cites, only one offers even marginal support for his assertion. A 1783 Massachusetts law forbade the residents of Boston to "take into" or "receive into" "any Dwelling House, Stable, Barn, Out-house, Ware-house, Store, Shop or other Building" loaded firearms, and permitted the seizure of any loaded firearms that "shall be found" there. Act of Mar. 1, 1783, ch. 13, 1783 Mass. Acts p. 218. That statute's text and its prologue, which makes clear that the purpose of the prohibition was to eliminate the danger to firefighters posed by the "depositing of loaded Arms" in buildings, give reason to doubt that colonial Boston authorities would have enforced that general prohibition against someone who temporarily loaded a firearm to confront an intruder (despite the law's application in that case). In any case, we would not stake our interpretation of the Second Amendment upon a single law, in effect in a single city, that contradicts the overwhelming weight of other evidence regarding the right to keep and bear arms for defense of the home. The other laws Justice Breyer cites are gunpowder-storage laws that he concedes did not clearly prohibit loaded weapons, but required only that excess gunpowder be kept in a special container or on the top floor of the home. *Post*, at 6–7. Nothing about those fire-safety laws undermines our analysis; they do not remotely burden the right of self-defense as much as an absolute ban on handguns. Nor, correspondingly, does our analysis suggest the invalidity of laws regulating the storage of firearms to prevent accidents.

Justice Breyer points to other founding-era laws that he says "restricted the firing of guns within the city limits to at least some degree" in Boston, Philadelphia and New York. *Post*, at 4 (citing Churchill, Gun Regulation, the Police Power, and the Right to Keep Arms in Early America, 25 Law & Hist. Rev. 139, 162 (2007)). Those laws provide no support for the severe restriction in the present case. The New York law levied a fine of 20 shillings on anyone who fired a gun in certain places (including houses) on New Year's Eve and the first two days of January, and was aimed at preventing the "great Damages . . . frequently done on [those days] by persons going House to House, with Guns and other Firearms and being often intoxicated with Liquor." 5 Colonial Laws of New York

244–246 (1894). It is inconceivable that this law would have been enforced against a person exercising his right to self-defense on New Year's Day against such drunken hooligans. The Pennsylvania law to which Justice Breyer refers levied a fine of 5 shillings on one who fired a gun or set off fireworks in Philadelphia without first obtaining a license from the governor. See Act of Aug. 26, 1721, §4, in 3 Stat.at Large 253–254. Given Justice Wilson's explanation that the right to self-defense with arms was protected by the Pennsylvania Constitution, it is unlikely that this law (which in any event amounted to at most a licensing regime) would have been enforced against a person who used firearms for self-defense. Justice Breyer cites a Rhode Island law that simply levied a 5-shilling fine on those who fired guns in *streets* and *taverns*, a law obviously inapplicable to this case. See An Act for preventing Mischief being done in the town of Newport, or in any other town in this Government, 1731, Rhode Island Session Laws. Finally, Justice Breyer points to a Massachusetts law similar to the Pennsylvania law, prohibiting "discharg[ing] any Gun or Pistol charged with Shot or Ball in the Town of *Boston*." Act of May 28, 1746, ch. X, Acts and Laws of Mass. Bay 208. It is again implausible that this would have been enforced against a citizen acting in self-defense, particularly given its preambulatory reference to "the *indiscreet* firing of Guns." *Ibid.* (preamble) (emphasis added).

A broader point about the laws that Justice Breyer cites: All of them punished the discharge (or loading) of guns with a small fine and forfeiture of the weapon (or in a few cases a very brief stay in the local jail), not with significant criminal penalties. http://www.law.cornell.edu/supct/html/07-290.ZO.html—29 They are akin to modern penalties for minor public-safety infractions like speeding or jaywalking. And although such public-safety laws may not contain exceptions for self-defense, it is inconceivable that the threat of a jaywalking ticket would deter someone from disregarding a "Do Not Walk" sign... to flee an attacker, or that the Government would enforce those laws under such circumstances. Likewise, we do not think that a law imposing a 5-shilling fine and forfeiture of the gun would have prevented a person in the founding era from using a gun to protect himself or his family from violence, or that if he did so the law would be enforced against him. The District law, by contrast, far from imposing a minor fine, threatens citizens with a year in prison (five years for a second violation) for even obtaining a gun in the first place. See D.C. Code §7–2507.06.

Justice Breyer moves on to make a broad jurisprudential point: He criticizes us for declining to establish a level of scrutiny for evaluating Second Amendment restrictions. He proposes, explicitly at least, none of the traditionally expressed levels (strict scrutiny, intermediate scrutiny, rational basis), but rather a judge-empowering "interest-balancing inquiry" that "asks whether the statute burdens a protected interest in a way or to an extent that is out of proportion to the statute's salutary effects upon other important governmental interests." *Post*, at 10. After an exhaustive discussion of the arguments for and against gun control, Justice Breyer arrives at his interest-balanced answer: because handgun violence is a problem, because the law is limited to an urban area, and because there were somewhat similar restrictions in the founding period (a false proposition that we have already discussed), the interest-balancing inquiry results in the constitutionality of the handgun ban.

We know of no other enumerated constitutional right whose core protection has been subjected to a freestanding "interest-balancing" approach. The very enumeration of the right takes out of the hands of government—even the Third Branch of Government—the power to decide on a case-by-case basis whether the right is *really worth* insisting upon. A constitutional guarantee subject to future judges' assessments of its usefulness is no constitutional guarantee at all. Constitutional rights are enshrined with the scope they were understood to have when the people adopted them, whether or not future legislatures or (yes) even future judges think that scope too broad. We would not apply an "interest-balancing" approach to the prohibition of a peaceful neo-Nazi march through Skokie. See *National Socialist Party of America* v. *Skokie*, 432 U.S. 43 (1977) *(per curiam)*. The First Amendment contains the freedom-of-speech guarantee that the people ratified, which included exceptions for obscenity, libel, and disclosure of state secrets, but not for the expression of extremely unpopular and wrong-headed views. The Second Amendment is no different. Like the First, it is the very *product* of an interest-balancing by the people—which Justice Breyer would now conduct for them anew. And whatever else it leaves to future evaluation, it surely elevates above all other interests the right of law-abiding, responsible citizens to use arms in defense of hearth and home.

Justice Breyer chides us for leaving so many applications of the right to keep and bear arms in doubt, and for not providing extensive historical justification for those regulations of the right that we describe as permissible. See *post*, at 42–43. But since this case represents this Court's first in-depth examination of the Second Amendment, one should not expect it to clarify the entire field, any more than *Reynolds* v. *United States*, 98 U.S. 145 (1879), our first in-depth Free Exercise Clause case, left that area in a state of utter certainty. And there will be time enough to expound upon the historical justifications for the exceptions we have mentioned if and when those exceptions come before us.

In sum, we hold that the District's ban on handgun possession in the home violates the Second Amendment, as does its prohibition against rendering any lawful firearm in the home operable for the purpose of immediate self-defense. Assuming that Heller is not disqualified from the exercise of Second Amendment rights, the District must permit him to register his handgun and must issue him a license to carry it in the home.

We are aware of the problem of handgun violence in this country, and we take seriously the concerns raised by the many *amici* who believe that prohibition of handgun ownership is a solution. The Constitution leaves the District of Columbia a variety of tools for combating that problem, including some measures regulating handguns, see *supra*, at 54–55, and n. 26. But the enshrinement of constitutional rights necessarily takes certain policy choices off the table. These include the absolute prohibition of handguns held and used for self-defense in the home. Undoubtedly some think that the Second Amendment is outmoded in a society where our standing army is the pride of our Nation, where well-trained police forces provide personal security, and where gun violence is a serious problem. That is perhaps debatable, but what is not debatable is that it is not the role of this Court to pronounce the Second Amendment extinct.

Source: Justia.com. http://supreme.justia.com/cases/federal/us/554/07-290/.

H

HARLEM RENAISSANCE MOVEMENT

Overview

The Harlem Renaissance was a movement of African American self-assertion against white supremacy. When the movement was in its heyday, it was known as the Negro Renaissance. The phrase *Harlem Renaissance* was a creation of later scholars. In the 1920s and 1930s, the period of the Harlem Renaissance, the word *Negro* was a term of pride, though it has lost its luster with the current generation of African Americans.

One would be wrong to think of the Harlem Renaissance as a single movement. Rather it was a series of social, intellectual, artistic, literary, and musical movements that overlapped in time and theme. One sees pride in the Harlem Renaissance's creation of Negro History Week, which has blossomed into Black History Month. The movement, in an American context, valued democracy, not the kind that disenfranchised blacks and women, and African American culture.

Because of racism many African Americans of the Harlem Renaissance viewed the United States as a quasi-democracy. World War I gave the movement its impetus. Blacks who had fought for freedom in Europe returned to the United States determined to stamp out Jim Crow. The increase in the number of magazines and publishing houses after the war gave these New Negro writers an outlet for their work. Blues and Jazz became popular and emblematic of the Harlem Renaissance.

One scholar situates the origin of the Harlem Renaissance in 1924, the year in which black writer Charles S. Johnson hosted a party for blacks and whites to celebrate the publication of the novel *There Was Confusion* by African American female author Jessie Fausert. The party represented a moment for reflection on the cultural and artistic progress that African Americans were making. It seemed as though a new period of creativity had begun. An issue devoted to black culture in the journal *Survey Graphic* sold 42,000 copies in 1925, twice the sales of other issues. *The Crisis*, the magazine of the National Association for the Advancement of Colored People (NAACP), and other magazines like it, held literary competitions in hopes of stimulating black creativity. As early as 1920 W.E.B. DuBois, editor of *The Crisis*, foresaw the coming of the Harlem Renaissance. Otherwise one must concede that the Harlem Renaissance began in 1918, as the overview proposed. The only art and literature of any merit, DuBois believed, must uplift blacks.

Another authority marks the origin of the Harlem Renaissance in 1918, the end of World War I. The movement ended about 1937, toward the end of the New Deal. One myth holds that the Harlem Renaissance ended in 1929 or 1930 with the stock market crash and the onset of the Great Depression.

Poet, novelist, playwright, activist, Langston Hughes was all of these and one of the towering figures of the Harlem Renaissance. The great-grandson of white slave owners, he also wrote books for children. (Library of Congress)

Americans concentrated on economic matters rather than black literature and art. Yet this view is erroneous. The 1930s witnessed the publication of more black literature than during the 1920s despite the fact that the number of publications declined overall in the 1930s. African Americans won more Guggenheim Fellowships in the 1930s than in the 1920s. The Federal Writers Project, the Federal Theater Project, and the Federal Arts Project of the New Deal employed black authors, playwrights, and artists.

Some critics wondered whether the Harlem Renaissance matched the quality of white cultural contributions. Had black authors penned anything as great as *Moby Dick* or *The Sound and the Fury*? The Harlem Renaissance had

contributed little to mollify elitists. In the 1980s interpretations of the Harlem Renaissance began to soften. Black feminists called attention to the contributions of African American women to the Harlem Renaissance. No longer was it acceptable to dismiss black authors and artists as inferior to their white counterparts. The emphasis on globalism fostered interest in black literature that transcended geographical boundaries. Queer theorists took particular interest in the sexual themes in the Harlem Renaissance. Today, the Harlem Renaissance is a subject of intense interest.

The Harlem Renaissance was an attempt to give voice to all the African American experience. Even though its participants were black, they engaged white intellectuals and authors in a discussion of what it meant to be an American in the early 20th century. Although there has been a temptation to see black heterosexual men as leaders of the Harlem Renaissance, many of its creative voices were gay, lesbian, or bisexual. Central to the Harlem Renaissance were the interracial parties that brought blacks and whites together. Georgia Douglas Johnson, Gwendolyn Bennett, and Anne Spencer, writing poetry about love, intimacy, and motherhood, proved that black women occupied a distinguished place in the Harlem Renaissance. These poets and others dreamed of a new type of citizenship, one that granted the vote to all Americans and ended Jim Crow. Given that today black religious leaders are conspicuous in opposing gay and lesbian marriage, it may come as a surprise that the Harlem Renaissance was a pluralistic movement, once comfortable with gay and lesbian culture.

The Harlem Renaissance emerged at a pivotal movement. The 1920s witnessed the culmination of a trend decades old in which the United States became more urban and less rural and agricultural. It was this new urban America that black intellectuals, authors, and artists sought to transform. By the 1930s black intellectuals had become more hostile to the status quo and wondered whether the United States would ever be a land of opportunity for all Americans. The New Negro was now an activist for equality. He or she resented that the business elites were overwhelmingly white at a time when white automaker Henry Ford was among the richest men in the United States.

The connection between black and white high culture was evident in the fact that in the 1930s actor Paul Robeson starred in Eugene O'Neill's plays. Robeson also struck up friendships with some of Africa's leaders, revealing the Harlem Renaissance to be a transnational movement. Traveling to Europe, Robeson starred in William Shakespeare's *Othello*. Reading the literature of socialists, he became a critic of racism and fascism. Fascinated by indigenous cultures, Robeson was indignant that European colonialism suppressed the rights of indigenes.

The Vogue and the New Negro Movement

What is in vogue, however, is in fashion, and fashion is transient. A movement of contradictions, the Harlem Renaissance was a search for black identity and recognition of lost identity. Some historians are uncomfortable with the term *renaissance* because the Harlem Renaissance was not a rebirth but rather a stage of evolution of black consciousness. Poet, prose writer, and arguably the best-known member of the Harlem Renaissance, Langston Hughes noted that the Harlem Renaissance "was the period when the Negro was in vogue" (Hutchinson, 28). The Harlem Renaissance was the first significant literary and cultural movement in African American history.

The Harlem Renaissance, in some corners, was the New Negro movement, a movement that according to one scholar invented itself in the 1920s. The New Negro was a phrase to sum up the new black identity. The New Negro was a liberated black man or woman, one who had transcended the slave past. In this sense the New Negro movement was conscious of its historical roots. It was a movement for racial progress. With its arrival, African Americans wrote themselves into American history.

The Harlem Renaissance was a national and international movement. More than anywhere else, Langston Hughes longed to be in Harlem, originally a Dutch settlement, then German, Irish, Jewish, and finally black when whites fled this tiny part of Manhattan. If Harlem was the center of the movement, its intellectuals, artists, and writers hailed from Chicago, Detroit, Philadelphia, and Washington, D.C. The authors of the Harlem Renaissance sought connections to their counterparts in the Caribbean and Africa. In the 1920s Harlem was known as the Black Mecca. What attracted Hughes and others to Harlem, aside from its nightlife, was the fact that in the 20th century New York replaced Boston as a center of publishing.

Whites also visited Harlem for its nightlife. The nightclubs and cabarets that hosted whites were as segregated as the South. Blacks had to sit in separate sections and, because of this, resented the whites who came to Harlem.

By 1926 tensions had emerged in the Harlem Renaissance. Intellectuals like DuBois thought that art was legitimate only if it served as racial propaganda. On the other hand, writers Langston Hughes and Wallace Thurman thought that there should be no constraints on art and literature. They proposed to depict African Americans as they wished. Hughes's 1926 essay "The Negro Artist and the Racial Mountain" announced his commitment to artistic freedom. Writer George S. Schuyler wrote in 1926 that black art and literature did not really exist, a puzzling viewpoint given the prodigious activity of the Harlem Renaissance.

White author Carl Van Vechten dispelled the idea of segregation in arts and letters. He guided Hughes's first book of poetry, *The Weary Blues*, to publication and mentored Hughes the rest of his life. He mentored as well other luminaries of the Harlem Renaissance, including Nella Larsen, Zora Neale Hurston, and James Weldon Johnson. Charlotte Mason, another white author, praised the work of Hughes, Hurston, and philosopher Alain Locke. In 1926 Van Vechten published the novel *Nigger Heaven*, his only novel aimed at an African America audience. It described his vision of Harlem. Hughes hated the book, but he wrote favorable reviews of it despite his own sentiment. His review in *The Crisis*, however, made no secret of his disgust with the novel. Whatever Hughes's opinion, the novel went through nine printings in only four months, more than any Harlem Renaissance novel. *The New York Times* criticized *Nigger Heaven* for its use of the word *nigger*. DuBois disliked it for this reason. Van Vechten defended the novel as an attack on segregation and racism and had meant the reader to see the title as irony. The phrase *nigger heaven* was used freely in Harlem to refer to the balcony of theaters to which blacks were confined. Although he was white, Van Vechten thought his friendship with Hughes and others would insulate him from criticism. He thought that readers and critics would excuse his use of the term *nigger*, a word that blacks could use among themselves but a word that whites were forbidden to utter. Less controversial, Van Vechten believed that blacks should write about what interested them but always with an eye on the market if they wished to make a living.

Black Female Poets of the Harlem Renaissance

Female writers grappled with what it meant to be black and female. Marita Bonner's 1925 essay "On Being Young—A Woman—and Colored" described her struggle to define who she was. She chose Buddha, one of Asia's religious reformers in antiquity, as a symbol of the black female poet, prose writer, and artist. She appreciated that Buddha, like her, had dark skin. Women poets of the Harlem Renaissance struggled to define themselves in the context of gender, class, and race. Some compared themselves to educated white women. Others sought to differentiate themselves from white women. Female poets of the Harlem Renaissance fought to reclaim the femininity that racists tried to deny black women. Not all female poets struggled with issues of race, class, and gender. Some wrote about nature in the manner of Henry David Thoreau. On the other hand some nature poems confronted the issue of race, attempting to instill racial pride in the reader.

Some poems were pessimistic. In "Black Women" Georgia Douglas Johnson insisted that no black woman should give birth to a child in racist America. Some black female poets sought to address white women. In 1918, Mae V. Cowdery, in "A Brown Aesthete Speaks," took on the idea that many black women secretly aspired to be white. The black woman who aspired to education and high culture was not imitating uptight white women. The black woman who straightened her hair was experimenting with fashion. She was not trying to be white. Some black poets sought to promote solidarity with white women. Others signaled the chasm that separated black from white. Cowdery referred to her white readers as friends.

Black and white women experimented with style and fashion, complicating the division between black and white women. Cowdery noted that whereas some black women straightened their hair, other white women donned the tight curls of black women. In 1929 Alice Dunbar-Nelson's "The Proletarian Speaks" admitted candidly that both black and white women desire beauty. Even when poor, even when working class, women still want to be beautiful. Dunbar-Nelson was a bisexual who, while married to a succession of men, had affairs with women. Black female poets understood that many whites wished to strip away their femininity, as happened when both black men and women had to use the colored restroom. Poet Anne Spencer admitted that the unremitting toil of women's work often effaced their femininity. Poet Angelina Grimke's "The Black Finger" described the black woman, not the white woman, as the archetype of beauty.

Other poets tried to grapple with the white stereotype that black men and women were sexually hyperactive compared to the more restrained lives of whites. Others found delight in the white man's discovery that black women are beautiful and sexy. Yet others felt compelled to take on the stereotype that black women were promiscuous. Dunbar-Nelson decried "sewer literature" that aimed to portray a messy world as dignified (Hutchinson, 154). She favored honesty over elegance. Georgia Douglas Johnson protested against the attempts to apply white norms to black women. Cowdery and Helene Johnson wrote poetry that celebrated healthy, nonrepressed black women at the same time that they came to grips with the primitivist movement that sought to depict black women as obsessed with sex. Other black female poets indulged in primitivism, in their own sexuality. Still others wrote poetry that saw no contradiction in the notion that a black woman could be downtrodden but still beautiful. Oppression did not rob black women of their beauty. Others tried to address issues of sex, race, class, and gender by surveying nature. Tall trees became a phallic image, playing into the stereotype that black men were well endowed. Although often ignored, black women poets were a vital part of the Harlem Renaissance Movement.

See also

African American Civil Rights Movement; Back to Africa Movement; Feminist Movement; Jim Crow; Pan-Africanism

CHRISTOPHER CUMO

Further Reading

Hutchinson, George, ed. 2007. *The Cambridge Companion to the Harlem Renaissance*. Cambridge, UK: Cambridge University Press.

Wintz, Cary D. 1996. *Black Culture and the Harlem Renaissance*. College Station, TX: Texas A & M University Press.

Harlem Renaissance Movement—Primary Document

Introduction

In this excerpt from his first volume of autobiography, The Big Sea *(1940), Langston Hughes recalls the optimism and*

celebration of blacks during the Harlem Renaissance. The Big Sea covers the years from Hughes's birth in 1902 to the spring of 1931, including his experiences in Mexico, in Africa, and in Paris. It also describes in detail his discovery of Harlem and his varied experiences as a recognized leader of the Harlem Renaissance.

Document: *The Big Sea: An Autobiography* by Langston Hughes (1940)

The 1920s were the years of Manhattan's black Renaissance . . . . White people began to come to Harlem in droves. For several years they packed the expensive Cotton Club on Lenox Avenue. But I was never there, because the Cotton Club was a Jim Crow club for gangsters and monied whites. They were not cordial to Negro patronage, unless you were a celebrity like Bojangles. So Harlem Negroes did not like the Cotton Club and never appreciated its Jim Crow policy in the very heart of their dark community. Nor did ordinary Negroes like the growing influx of whites toward Harlem after sundown, flooding the little cabarets and bars where formerly only colored people laughed and sang, and where now the strangers were given the best ringside tables to sit and stare at the Negro customers—like amusing animals in a zoo.

The Negroes said: "We can't go downtown and sit and stare at you in your clubs. You won't even let us in your clubs." But they didn't say it out loud—for Negroes are practically never rude to white people. So thousands of whites came to Harlem night after night, thinking the Negroes loved to have them there, and firmly believing that all Harlemites left their houses at sundown to sing and dance in cabarets, because most of the whites saw nothing but the cabarets, not the houses . . . .

It was a period when, at almost every Harlem upper-crust dance or party, one would be introduced to various distinguished white celebrities there as guests. It was a period when almost any Harlem Negro of any social importance at all would be likely to say casually: "As I was remarking the other day to Heywood—," meaning Heywood Broun. Or: "As I said to George—," referring to George Gershwin. It was a period when local and visiting royalty were not at all uncommon in Harlem. And when the parties of A'Lelia Walker, the Negro

heiress, were filled with guests whose names would turn any Nordic social climber green with envy. It was a period when Harold Jackman, a handsome young Harlem schoolteacher of modest means, calmly announced one day that he was sailing for the Riviera for a fortnight, to attend Princess Murat's yachting party. It was a period when Charleston preachers opened up shouting churches as sideshows for white tourists. It was a period when at least one charming colored chorus girl, amber enough to pass for a Latin American, was living in a penthouse, with all her bills paid by a gentleman whose name was banker's magic on Wall Street. It was a period when every season there was at least one hit play on Broadway acted by a Negro cast. And when books by Negro authors were being published with much greater frequency and much more publicity than ever before or since in history. It was a period when white writers wrote about Negroes more successfully (commercially speaking) than Negroes did about themselves. It was the period (God help us!) when Ethel Barrymore appeared in blackface in *Scarlet Sister Mary!* It was the period when the Negro was in vogue.

Source: Hughes, Langston. *The Big Sea: An Autobiography.* New York: Hill & Wang, 1940. Available online at http://www.npenn. org/55777011985858/lib/55777011985858/ch%2013/sec%20 4%20PS%20Hughes.pdf.

HEALTH CARE REFORM

The U.S. health care system is an incredibly complex network of private and public institutions. It includes scores of state and federal government agencies, along with thousands of private and public hospitals and clinics, insurance companies, drug companies, and professional organizations, as well as countless thousands of individual doctors, nurses, technologists, and other health care providers. America's health care system is considered one of the best—and perhaps the single most technologically advanced—in the world. Yet, the United States has a lower life expectancy and a higher infant mortality rate than several other developed countries, and health care reform has been one of the most controversial political issues of the late 20th and early 21st centuries.

Most experts agree that the relatively poor showing of the United States in these respects is not due to the care provided by American medical practitioners, but rather the result of the way in which that care is distributed among the population. For those in a position to take full advantage of the U.S. health care system, it provides the most complete, up-to-date, and proficient care available anywhere in the world. Many Americans, however, are unable to take full advantage of these resources—a problem that became increasingly acute in the 1980s and came to a political head in the early 1990s.

By the early 1990s, there was a growing feeling among the American populace that the health care system was in crisis. That crisis was made up of a combination of factors, the most important being the alarming escalation of health care costs. The dramatic rise in these costs was driven partly by the soaring price of drugs and partly by the development and increased use of extremely expensive technological advances. Costs had become so high that, except for the very wealthy, most Americans could no longer afford to pay for an extended illness or emergency requiring high-tech care out

of their own pockets. Even routine medical and dental care was too expensive for millions of Americans to afford. Those who could afford to pay for an occasional visit to the doctor were often reluctant to do so, fearful of the unpredictable costs they might incur.

Most Americans were covered by some kind of medical insurance through their (or a family member's) employment, but rising health care costs, together with internal problems at some insurance companies, drove up private insurance premiums. At the same time, many businesses cut back on the types of medical services they would pay for or eliminated medical care as a benefit of employment altogether. In addition, more people were pressed to join health maintenance organizations (HMOs) and other forms of managed care, in which the patient's choices of medical care providers and courses of treatment were limited to those approved by the particular plan to which they belonged.

First Lady Hillary Rodham Clinton holds up a pamphlet entitled "Coronary Artery Bypass Graft Surgery" while testifying on Capitol Hill before the House Energy Committee, September 28, 1993. The committee was holding hearings on health care reform. (AP Photo)

Worse, many Americans were not insured at all. Estimates of those without health insurance at any given time ranged as high as 37 million people. Some—perhaps most—of the uninsured had access to medical treatment in an emergency, since most hospitals and many physicians will treat anyone in medical crisis, regardless of their ability to pay. However, they received no preventive care, resulting in minor problems that were more likely to develop into more serious and expensive conditions. When a medical crisis drove uninsured people to the emergency room, the high costs of emergency service had to be borne by the public through higher cost for paying patients to compensate for this pro bono treatment.

If acute medical problems were expensive to deal with, long-term care for the aged or the chronically ill was far too expensive for most people to afford. Such government programs as Medicare and Medicaid provided help to the elderly and the poor, but only after such patients had exhausted most or all of their own economic assets.

Two decades after a failed attempt to enact it during Richard Nixon's administration (1969–1974), health care reform emerged as a central issue in the 1992 presidential campaign. Democratic candidate Bill Clinton campaigned strongly on the need for reform, arguing that health care services needed to be made available to all Americans at the same time that costs had to be restrained. Once elected, Clinton put his wife, Hillary Rodham Clinton, at the head of a panel of hundreds of health care experts, politicians, and others charged with designing a major reform of the U.S. health care system. The health care panel was the subject of political controversy long before it announced its reform plan. In order to reduce the inevitable political pressures on the panel, the group met in private, and the names of the panel members were not released, measures that led to angry charges of closed-door government, as well as to suspicion about the panel's makeup and intentions among medical providers and others who were nervous about health care reform.

Hillary Clinton became the center of the political storm over the design of the health care reform bill. Many Americans objected to the president's selection of his wife to lead the health care reform effort. Although Bill Clinton had campaigned side by side with his wife and promised that she would be an important element of his administration, traditionalists objected to a first lady being given a formal position of substantial political power.

In addition, although most Americans—along with a majority of senators and representatives—agreed that change was needed, there was little agreement about what form the change should take. The key disputes had to do with the scope of proposed reforms and the method of paying for them. Some Democrats, including Bill and Hillary Clinton, insisted that health care should be universal. They favored a broad-ranging plan that would make available to everyone a more-or-less complete program of care. Most Republicans, along with many conservative Democrats, favored a more limited approach, with some wanting only catastrophic coverage and others supporting government help only for those who could not pay for their own insurance privately. The most liberal reformers called for a "single-payer" plan, similar to Canada's national health insurance system, under which the government provides comprehensive medical insurance for all citizens. Most others favored paying for the plan, however broad it turned out to be, with some combination of private and governmental insurance plans.

The ambitious plan that the health care reform panel crafted and Bill Clinton proposed to Congress in September 1993 would have covered all Americans under a vast managed care program of "health alliances." The plan was to be paid for largely by employers as a part of the benefits package offered to their employees. Small businesses and the self-employed would be subsidized for the expense, and the unemployed would be covered by insurance provided by the government. The costs of health care were to be held down by negotiations between the "alliances" (some of which would be established by the states and some by large employers), the insurance companies, and health care providers.

In an apparent attempt to satisfy all the conflicting points of view on health care reform, the Health Care Reform Bill became so complex that it took up 1,342 printed pages. Unfortunately for the plan's legislative future, most special interest groups quickly focused on those elements of the plan to which they objected, rather than those they liked. As a result, the plan was met with heavy criticism from almost every side and received very little political support.

Large employers were upset by a provision that required them to pay 80 percent of the health care insurance premiums of their employees. Doctors became alarmed by elements of the plan that they felt smacked of "socialized medicine." Insurance companies objected to further government intrusion in their industry. Roman Catholic authorities and others opposed to abortion furiously resisted the plan's provisions to cover abortions. Drug companies derided provisions to hold down the price of their products. These and other interest groups launched public attacks on the plan, while only the American Federation of Labor-Congress of Industrial Organizations launched a counterattack in its favor. Even those groups that hoped to see health care reform passed concentrated their efforts on changing elements of the plan to which they objected, rather than supporting the plan as a whole. As a result, the public and Congress heard a mounting crescendo of criticism, and the overall impression of the plan was negative.

The congressional debate over the Health Care Reform Bill ultimately involved eleven separate committees, as well as at least ninety-seven lobbying organizations—most of which worked to oppose the plan. With the issue in doubt in Congress, the health insurance industry launched a major public relations campaign to alarm voters about the plan. Network television viewers were bombarded with an effective series of television spots featuring actors playing an ordinary middle-aged, middle-class couple named Harry and Louise, who were pictured expressing serious concerns about what the bill would mean for ordinary Americans like themselves. Would they lose the right to choose their own doctor? Would they end up paying more for health insurance than they were already?

Realizing that the bill's chances of passage were small, House majority leader Richard Gephardt and Senate majority leader George Mitchell each introduced bills of their own, as did Senate minority leader Bob Dole. It soon became obvious, however, that none of these, nor any of the alternatives proposed by other members of Congress, were likely to pass. The final demise of health care reform was assured in political wrangling and compromise over the Omnibus Violent Crime Control and Prevention Act of 1994. In late September 1994, Mitchell announced that health care reform was dead.

Nearly two years later, in August 1996, Congress passed and Bill Clinton signed a pale shadow of health care reform entitled the Health Insurance Portability and Accountability Act, which allows insured workers who lose their jobs to continue their insurance coverage provided they can pay for it. This legislation resolved one of the significant side issues that

had been addressed by the health care reform effort of 1994 but left unsolved the main problems—the escalating costs and limited availability of medical care. Clinton also later worked to pass a patients' bill of rights, which would ensure a minimum standard of care for anyone seeking medical help. Efforts to legislate this bill of rights continued well into the George W. Bush administration, with several versions of the concept but were ultimately unsuccessful.

During the election of 2000, the debate over health care largely focused on such issues as how to make it—including increasingly expensive prescription drugs—affordable and available to seniors citizens. As president, Bush signed the Medicare Prescription Drug Improvement and Modernization Act (2003) in an effort to address these issues. In addition to restructuring parts of the Medicare system, the act first provided for drug discount cards, to be followed in 2006 by prescription drug coverage through private plans. Like most of the health care legislation presented in the preceding decade, however, not everyone was satisfied with the act, and even those who were realized that a great deal more had to be done to improve health care for seniors—and the rest of the population. In addition, while the problem of expensive prescription medication for seniors had ostensibly been addressed, it was still an issue for anyone else who needed such medication.

Various attempts have since been made to bring down the cost of prescriptions, but none was fully successful. One of the most promising avenues for lowering costs was drug reimportation. Typically, prescription drugs are notably less expensive in such countries as Canada, and many legislators proposed creating a program that would allow people to purchase drugs from these countries through their health insurance coverage. However, the concept met with a great deal of resistance from pharmaceutical companies and some health care providers. While several states began working on reimportation programs, no such program materialized at the federal level, despite becoming an important element of the debate over health care reform during the election of 2004; like many issues that year, the health care debate was largely overshadowed by foreign policy issues, particularly the Iraq War.

Legislators continued looking for ways to lower health costs without having to create such an ambitious and controversial plan as Clinton's Health Care Reform Bill. The cost of malpractice lawsuits—including premiums for malpractice insurance and the cost of trials and payouts—has increasingly been an issue for health care providers, forcing the cost of medical care to increase. Particularly high malpractice costs in certain states have even led some physicians to leave medicine or relocate. Thus, in addition to raising the cost of health care, the cost of malpractice lawsuits could theoretically lead to a shortage of health care providers in some states, lowering the quality of care there. Legislation to curb malpractice lawsuits—primarily by limiting the monetary damages that could be awarded—reached Congress in 2005 but stalled in the Senate. As in the case of reimporting prescription drugs, many states have moved to curb malpractice suits on their own.

When Barack Obama took office in 2009, he dealt with the effects of the Great Recession and the wars in Iraq and Afghanistan, but he also decided to pursue health care reform. The bill that ultimately went through Congress and became law on March 23, 2010, was based in part on a proposal by the conservative Heritage Foundation and health care reform enacted in Massachusetts in 2006 under Governor Mitt Romney, the Republican who was Obama's opponent for reelection in 2012. The extensive legislation required numerous compromises as Republicans were almost united in opposition to the measure. Indeed, a more conservative wing of the Republican party, known as the Tea Party, led the fight against the Patient Protection and Affordable Care Act, generally called "Obamacare," and successful Republican efforts to regain control of the House of Representatives in 2010. House Republicans repeatedly passed measures to repeal the health care bill, but to no avail. In 2012, in *National Federation of Independent Business v. Sebelius*, the U.S. Supreme Court ruled that the health care bill was constitutional under the taxing power but could not force states to participate in the expansion of Medicaid or face the loss of Medicaid funding.

"Obamacare" did encourage states to expand Medicaid. The provision that the Supreme Court upheld under the taxing power, the individual mandate, required everybody not already covered by health insurance (by an employer, or a federal or state program) to obtain coverage or pay a penalty. The Affordable Care Act barred insurers from denying coverage due to preexisting conditions, set minimum standards for health insurance policies, created insurance exchanges

to provide coverage, and subsidized those below the federal poverty level. Many of the provisions were taking effect in 2014, and surveys showed increasing numbers of Americans accepting the Affordable Care Act, and taking advantage of it. But it also continued to face challenges, especially provisions requiring coverage of contraception, to which religious groups objected. Whatever its successes and failures, support and opposition, Obamacare proved that Americans continued to debate how best to get their health care and health insurance.

See also

Great Society; States' Rights (Antebellum, Memory, Contemporary); Welfare State

ABC-CLIO

Further Reading

Arnould, Richard J., Robert F. Rich, and William D. White, eds. 1993. *Competitive Approaches to Health Care Reform.* Washington, DC: The Urban Institute.

Davidson, Stephen M. 2013. *A New Era in U.S. Health Care: Critical Next Steps Under the Affordable Care Act.* Stanford, CA: Stanford Briefs.

Helms, Robert B., ed. 1993 *American Health Policy: Critical Issues for Reform.* Washington, DC: American Enterprise Institute Press.

Holahan, John, et al. 1991. *Balancing Access, Costs, and Politics: The American Context for Health System Reform.* Washington, DC: The Urban Institute.

Kronenfeld, Jennie J. 1997. *The Changing Federal Role in U.S. Health Care Policy.* Westport, CT: Praeger.

Skocpol, Theda. 1996. *Boomerang: Clinton's Health Security Effort and the Turn Against Government in U.S. Politics.* New York: W.W. Norton.

Health Care Reform—Primary Document

Introduction

On September 9, 2009, President Barack Obama addressed a joint session of Congress and the nation on the topic of health care reform. The speech followed Congress's summer recess, during which debate over health care reform had grown increasingly contentious, with protesters disrupting town hall meetings held by Congress members to discuss the subject. Obama's address was interrupted by Representative Joe Wilson (R-South Carolina), who shouted, "You lie!" when the president said the health care plan he was proposing would not insure illegal immigrants; Wilson later apologized and was rebuked by the House. The following is the official White House transcript of Obama's speech.

Document: President Barack Obama's Speech on Health Care to Congress (September 9, 2009)

... What this plan will do is make the insurance you have work better for you. Under this plan, it will be against the law for insurance companies to deny you coverage because of a preexisting condition. (Applause.) As soon as I sign this bill, it will be against the law for insurance companies to drop your coverage when you get sick or water it down when you need it the most. (Applause.) They will no longer be able to place some arbitrary cap on the amount of coverage you can receive in a given year or in a lifetime. (Applause.) We will place a limit on how much you can be charged for out-of-pocket expenses, because in the United States of America, no one should go broke because they get sick. (Applause.) And insurance companies will be required to cover, with no extra charge, routine checkups and preventive care, like mammograms and colonoscopies—(applause)—because there's no reason we shouldn't be catching diseases like breast cancer and colon cancer before they get worse. That makes sense, it saves money, and it saves lives. (Applause.)

Now, that's what Americans who have health insurance can expect from this plan—more security and more stability.

Now, if you're one of the tens of millions of Americans who don't currently have health insurance, the second part of this plan will finally offer you quality, affordable choices. (Applause.) If you lose your job or you change your job, you'll be able to get coverage. If you strike out on your own and start a small business, you'll be able to get coverage. We'll do this by creating a new insurance exchange—a marketplace where individuals and small businesses will be able to shop for health insurance at competitive prices. Insurance companies will have an incentive to participate in this exchange because it lets them compete for millions of new customers. As one big group, these customers will have greater leverage to bargain with the insurance companies for better prices

and quality coverage. This is how large companies and government employees get affordable insurance. It's how everyone in this Congress gets affordable insurance. And it's time to give every American the same opportunity that we give ourselves. (Applause.)

Now, for those individuals and small businesses who still can't afford the lower-priced insurance available in the exchange, we'll provide tax credits, the size of which will be based on your need. And all insurance companies that want access to this new marketplace will have to abide by the consumer protections I already mentioned. This exchange will take effect in four years, which will give us time to do it right. In the meantime, for those Americans who can't get insurance today because they have preexisting medical conditions, we will immediately offer low-cost coverage that will protect you against financial ruin if you become seriously ill. (Applause.) This was a good idea when Senator John McCain proposed it in the campaign, it's a good idea now, and we should all embrace it. (Applause.)

Now, even if we provide these affordable options, there may be those—especially the young and the healthy—who still want to take the risk and go without coverage. There may still be companies that refuse to do right by their workers by giving them coverage. The problem is, such irresponsible behavior costs all the rest of us money. If there are affordable options and people still don't sign up for health insurance, it means we pay for these people's expensive emergency room visits. If some businesses don't provide workers health care, it forces the rest of us to pick up the tab when their workers get sick, and gives those businesses an unfair advantage over their competitors. And unless everybody does their part, many of the insurance reforms we seek—especially requiring insurance companies to cover preexisting conditions—just can't be achieved.

And that's why under my plan, individuals will be required to carry basic health insurance—just as most states require you to carry auto insurance. (Applause.) Likewise—likewise, businesses will be required to either offer their workers health care, or chip in to help cover the cost of their workers. There will be a hardship waiver for those individuals who still can't afford coverage, and 95 percent of all small businesses, because of their size and narrow profit margin, would be exempt from these requirements. (Applause.) But we can't have large businesses and individuals who can afford coverage game the system by avoiding responsibility to themselves or their employees. Improving our health care system only works if everybody does their part.

And while there remain some significant details to be ironed out, I believe—(laughter)—I believe a broad consensus exists for the aspects of the plan I just outlined: consumer protections for those with insurance, an exchange that allows individuals and small businesses to purchase affordable coverage, and a requirement that people who can afford insurance get insurance.

And I have no doubt that these reforms would greatly benefit Americans from all walks of life, as well as the economy as a whole. Still, given all the misinformation that's been spread over the past few months, I realize—(applause)—I realize that many Americans have grown nervous about reform. So tonight I want to address some of the key controversies that are still out there.

Some of people's concerns have grown out of bogus claims spread by those whose only agenda is to kill reform at any cost. The best example is the claim made not just by radio and cable talk show hosts, but by prominent politicians, that we plan to set up panels of bureaucrats with the power to kill off senior citizens. Now, such a charge would be laughable if it weren't so cynical and irresponsible. It is a lie, plain and simple. (Applause.)

There are also those who claim that our reform efforts would insure illegal immigrants. This, too, is false. The reforms—the reforms I'm proposing would not apply to those who are here illegally.

AUDIENCE MEMBER: You lie! (Boos.)

THE PRESIDENT: It's not true. And one more misunderstanding I want to clear up—under our plan, no federal dollars will be used to fund abortions, and federal conscience laws will remain in place. (Applause.)

Now, my health care proposal has also been attacked by some who oppose reform as a "government takeover" of the entire health care system. As proof, critics point to a provision in our plan that allows the uninsured and small businesses to choose a publicly sponsored insurance option, administered by the government just like Medicaid or Medicare. (Applause.)

So let me set the record straight here. My guiding principle is, and always has been, that consumers do better when there is choice and competition. That's how the market works. (Applause.) Unfortunately, in 34 states, 75 percent of the insurance market is controlled by five or fewer companies. In Alabama, almost 90 percent is controlled by just one company. And without competition, the price of insurance goes up and quality goes down. And it makes it easier for insurance companies to treat their customers badly—by cherry-picking the healthiest individuals and trying to drop the sickest, by overcharging small businesses who have no leverage, and by jacking up rates....

Source: Barack Obama: "Address Before a Joint Session of the Congress on Health Care Reform," September 9, 2009. Online by Gerhard Peters and John T. Woolley, *The American Presidency Project.* http://www.presidency.ucsb.edu/ws/?pid=86592.

HIGHER EDUCATION MOVEMENT
Origins

The higher education movement arose in ancient Greece. In the fourth century BCE, Greek philosopher Plato may have been the first to found an institution of higher learning, the Academy in Athens. When he was not promoted to director of the academy upon Plato's death, his pupil Aristotle founded the Lyceum. The curriculum anticipated the modern university in emphasizing not only logic and rhetoric, but also the sciences. The rise of Christianity did not mean the end of higher education. Although Emperor Justinian closed the academy on the charge of paganism, the Church would found the university in the Middle Ages. The emphasis on theology and ancient languages was not surprising, but some universities became renowned for their colleges of medicine or law.

Higher Education in Colonial America and the Early Republic

The first English inhabitants of what would become the United States created a higher education movement that sought to emulate the universities of their homeland. This movement gained momentum in the 1630s and 1640s with the publication of several pamphlets urging New Englanders to create their own colleges. In Massachusetts, colonists founded Harvard College in the late 1630s. Early on, Harvard emphasized theology, making certain that faculty and students read passages from the Bible twice daily. College authorities were strict, requiring that students receive permission before venturing beyond the town of Cambridge. Harvard's chief aim in its early years was to train clerics for service in towns throughout New England.

The colleges that followed Harvard in colonial America and the early republic adhered to instruction in theology. The College of New Jersey, later Princeton University, announced that in addition to theology, it would train students in several professions. Because of the importance of the classics, potential students had to be fluent in Greek and Latin before admission. During their first year, students, intent on reading the Bible in its original languages, studied Hebrew and Greek, and in addition logic and rhetoric, a curriculum that would not have been unfamiliar in the Middle Ages and Renaissance. Indeed, the Roman orator Cicero would have been comfortable with an emphasis on Greek, Latin, logic, and rhetoric. After the freshman year, students would read Aristotle, a cornerstone of the medieval university. In the late 18th century, students could study the sciences as a sideline, but the emphasis remained on the classics and theology. In the late 18th and early 19th centuries came a spike in the founding of new colleges and universities as states began to fund higher education. By the early 19th century, North Carolina, Tennessee, Vermont, and Georgia had a state college. Before the Civil War, Ohio alone had thirty-seven colleges and universities.

Growing Pains in the 19th-Century United States

Nineteenth-century U.S. colleges and universities might be accused of undervaluing the sciences. Institutions of higher education had few laboratories and little emphasis on experimental methods. Faculty were less well educated than they are today. The typical professor was a young man whose knowledge extended no farther than the textbook he used. One might argue that the use of textbooks rather than primary sources produced an inferior product. By contrast, the modern introduction to philosophy, for example, takes for granted that students will read some of Plato's dialogues, at least in translation, and perhaps selections from Thomas Aquinas, Immanuel Kant, John Locke, and maybe Bertrand Russell. Friedrich Nietzsche, Soren Kierkegaard, Martin Heidegger, and Jean Paul Sartre are usually consigned to a course on existentialism.

By the late 19th century the higher education movement had gained new momentum. Enrollment rose from 52,000 in 1870 to 137,000 in 1890 and to 600,000 in 1920. The number of U.S. colleges and universities and of faculty likewise rose. U.S. colleges and universities in the West and at Oberlin College in Ohio pioneered the admission of women. In the 19th century and into the 20th century, colleges and universities tended to point women in the direction of the humanities because some professors doubted that women could endure the rigors of the sciences and mathematics. When women entered the sciences, they were often steered to descriptive disciplines like botany. Indeed, Freda Detmers, one of Ohio State University's first female Ph.Ds, took her degree in botany. Even then the path upward was difficult for women. Detmers took a junior position at the Ohio Agricultural Experiment Station, which was then separate from Ohio State University. Her supervisor was a man with only a B.S. Detmers was never promoted and resigned after less than five years' service.

The rise of graduate education was perhaps the dominant movement after the Civil War. The Americans who entered German universities for their doctorates returned to the United States determined to instill in American higher education a focus on specialization, research, and publication. Harvard and Yale adopted the German model in the 1860s and early 1870s. Johns Hopkins University has attracted graduate students since 1876. The student was an apprentice to his or her advisor, a system that prevails today.

The Higher Education Movement Comes to the Farm

The emphasis on the classics irritated farmers who wished for a practical education for their sons and daughters. With soil exhaustion the bugaboo of farmers in the East and

South and competition intense against the inundation of food from foreign lands, farmers felt in crisis. One way they sought to combat this crisis was to demand that the states and even the federal government fund colleges and universities that emphasized the teaching of agriculture and other practical subjects. Southerners in Congress opposed this idea because they did not believe that federal patronage of higher education was constitutional. Their departure from Congress with the Civil War left the North free to exert its will. In 1862, Congress passed the Morrill Act, otherwise known as the Land Grant Act, which gave each state federal land to sell. The proceeds from this sale would endow an agricultural and mechanical, otherwise known as a land grant, college or university in every state, but tensions quickly flared. Farmers believed that the agricultural and mechanical colleges and universities emphasized agriculture less than they should, but sought to emulate the universities that taught the classics. Tensions peaked in Ohio, where in 1877 the Ohio A & M College became Ohio State University (OSU), causing an uproar among farm leaders who accused the new university of trying to become the Harvard of the West. They noted that students who attended Ohio State University did not come home to farm, but instead took a job in a town or city. Not only were the A & M colleges like OSU not teaching agriculture properly, they were conducting little research to benefit farmers. The farmers' movement, turning its attention to research, demanded that each A & M college establish a research unit that would devote itself exclusively to agricultural science. This unit became the Agricultural Experiment Station, though in Ohio, we have seen, farmers' distrust of OSU caused the state to establish an agricultural experiment station separate from the university. The two merged only in 1982.

The Higher Education Movement and African Americans

In the 1840s and 1850s a movement arose, chiefly in the North, to offer African Americans higher education. The movement primarily envisioned segregated higher education, though from its early days Oberlin College has admitted students without regard to race or gender. In 1842, Quakers founded the Institute for Colored Youth, possibly the earliest black college. Throughout the South, many whites resisted the call to offer higher education to blacks. The tiresome white logic asserted that blacks were inferior to whites and so could not take advantage of higher education. Colleges and universities would do a disservice to blacks by welcoming them.

Fortunately the farmers' movement coincided with the movement to offer blacks higher education. Farmers believed that the A & M colleges in the South should enroll black students. Florida A & M University (founded 1887) and its like-minded colleges and universities became renowned for their instruction of blacks. This movement drew strength from the conviction that what blacks needed most was practical knowledge. The A & M colleges and universities, having a practical curriculum, were therefore ideal for blacks, so said the logic of self-help.

The Higher Education Movement as a Business Model

Today's higher education movement has emulated the business model of cost containment. Colleges and universities have outsourced food services and maintenance. College and university faculty have come under attack as being too costly. The tenure system appears to be in the process of disintegration as tenure track appointments have given way to part-time positions that offer neither job security nor medical coverage nor a pension. The money saved on downsizing the faculty can be transferred to the erection of opulent buildings and dormitories to attract students.

See also
Agrarianism; Education

CHRISTOPHER CUMO

Further Reading

London, Herbert I. 2010. *Decline and Revival in Higher Education.* New Brunswick, NJ, and London: Transaction Publishers.
Lucas, Christopher J. 2006. *American Higher Education: A History.* London: Palgrave Macmillan.
Thelin, John R. 2004. *A History of American Higher Education.* Baltimore, MD and London: The Johns Hopkins University Press.

Higher Education Movement—Primary Document

Introduction

In 1862, Congress passed and President Abraham Lincoln signed the Morrill Land Grant College Act. Representative

Justin Morrill of Vermont had tried before to make it possible to help states create colleges that would promote education in agriculture and the mechanical arts. To aid the states, the federal government would give each of them 30,000 acres of public land for each of its representatives and senators. While some of the states wasted their bounty, others sold the land and used it to finance the creation of new colleges and universities, eventually including Cornell, Nebraska, Clemson, Washington State, and the University of Nevada, Reno.

Document: Morrill Land Grant College Act (1862)

Be it enacted by the Senate and House of Representatives of the United States of America in Congress assembled, That there be granted to the several States, for the purposes hereinafter mentioned, an amount of public land, to be apportioned to each State a quantity equal to thirty thousand acres for each senator and representative in Congress to which the States are respectively entitled by the apportionment under the census of eighteen hundred and sixty: *Provided,* That no mineral lands shall be selected or purchased under the provisions of this Act.

SEC. 2. *And be it further enacted,* That the land aforesaid, after being surveyed, shall be apportioned to the several States in sections or subdivisions of sections, not less than one quarter of a section; and whenever there are public lands in a State subject to sale at private entry at one dollar and twenty-five cents per acre, the quantity to which said State shall be entitled shall be selected from such lands within the limits of such State, and the Secretary of the Interior is hereby directed to issue to each of the States in which there is not the quantity of public lands subject to sale at private entry at one dollar and twenty-five cents per acre, to which said State may be entitled under the provisions of this act, land scrip to the amount in acres for the deficiency of its distributive share: said scrip to be sold by said States and the proceeds thereof applied to the uses and purposes prescribed in this act, and for no other use or purpose whatsoever: *Provided,* That in no case shall any State to which land scrip may thus be issued be allowed to locate the same within the limits of any other State, or of any Territory of the United States, but their assignees may thus locate said land scrip upon any of the unappropriated lands of the United States subject to sale

at private entry at one dollar and twenty-five cents, or less, per acre: *And provided, further,* That not more than one million acres shall be located by such assignees in any one of the States: *And provided, further,* That no such location shall be made before one year from the passage of this Act.

SEC. 3. *And be it further enacted,* That all the expenses of management, superintendence, and taxes from date of selection of said lands, previous to their sales, and all expenses incurred in the management and disbursement of the moneys which may be received therefrom, shall be paid by the States to which they may belong, out of the Treasury of said States, so that the entire proceeds of the sale of said lands shall be applied without any diminution whatever to the purposes hereinafter mentioned.

SEC. 4. And be it further enacted, That all moneys derived from the sale of the lands aforesaid by the States to which the lands are apportioned, and from the sales of land scrip hereinbefore provided for, shall be invested in stocks of the United States, or of the States, or some other safe stocks, yielding not less than five per centum upon the par value of said stocks; and that the moneys so invested shall constitute a perpetual fund, the capital of which shall remain forever undiminished, (except so far as may be provided in section fifth of this act,) and the interest of which shall be inviolably appropriated, by each State which may take and claim the benefit of this act, to the endowment, support, and maintenance of at least one college where the leading object shall be, without excluding other scientific and classical studies, and including military tactics, to teach such branches of learning as are related to agriculture and the mechanic arts, in such manner as the legislatures of the States may respectively prescribe, in order to promote the liberal and practical education of the industrial classes in the several pursuits and professions in life.

SEC. 5. *And be it further enacted,* That the grant of land and land scrip hereby authorized shall be made on the following conditions, to which, as well as to the provisions hereinbefore contained, the previous assent of the several States shall be signified by legislative acts:

First. If any portion of the fund invested, as provided by the foregoing section, or any portion of the interest thereon, shall, by any action or contingency, be diminished or lost, it shall be replaced by the State to which it belongs, so that the capital of the fund shall remain forever undiminished; and the annual interest shall be regularly applied without diminution to the purposes mentioned in the fourth section of this act, except that a sum, not exceeding ten per centum upon the amount received by any State under the provisions of this act may be expended for the purchase of lands for sites or experimental farms, whenever authorized by the respective legislatures of said States.

Second. No portion of said fund, nor the interest thereon, shall be applied, directly or indirectly, under any pretence whatever, to the purchase, erection, preservation, or repair of any building or buildings.

Third. Any State which may take and claim the benefit of the provisions of this act shall provide, within five years from the time of its acceptance as provided in subdivision seven of this section, at least not less than one college, as described in the fourth section of this act, or the grant to such State shall cease; and said State shall be bound to pay the United States the amount received of any lands previously sold; and that the title to purchasers under the State shall be valid.

Fourth. An annual report shall be made regarding the progress of each college, recording any improvements and experiments made, with their cost and results, and such other matters, including State industrial and economical statistics, as may be supposed useful; one copy of which shall be transmitted by mail [free] by each, to all the other colleges which may be endowed under the provisions of this act, and also one copy to the Secretary of the Interior.

Fifth. When lands shall be selected from those which have been raised to double the minimum price, in consequence of railroad grants, they shall be computed to the States at the maximum price, and the number of acres proportionally diminished.

Sixth. No State while in a condition of rebellion or insurrection against the government of the United States shall be entitled to the benefit of this act.

Seventh. No State shall be entitled to the benefits of this act unless it shall express its acceptance thereof by its legislature within three years from July 23, 1866:

Provided, That when any Territory shall become a State and be admitted into the Union, such new State shall be entitled to the benefits of the said act of July two, eighteen hundred and sixty-two, by expressing the acceptance therein required within three years from the date of its admission into the Union, and providing the college or colleges within five years after such acceptance, as prescribed in this act.

SEC. 6. And be it further enacted, That land scrip issued under the provisions of this act shall not be subject to location until after the first day of January, one thousand eight hundred and sixty-three.

SEC. 7. *And be it further enacted*, That the land officers shall receive the same fees for locating land scrip issued under the provisions of this act as is now allowed for the location of military bounty land warrants under existing laws: *Provided*, their maximum compensation shall not be thereby increased.

SEC. 8. *And be it further enacted*, That the Governors of the several States to which scrip shall be issued under this act shall be required to report annually to Congress all sales made of such scrip until the whole shall be disposed of, the amount received for the same, and what appropriation has been made of the proceeds.

Source: Morrill Act. Available at http://www.ourdocuments.gov/doc.php?flash=true&doc=33.

HIPPIES

The Hippie movement took shape in the mid-1960s and had intricate ties to the Beat Generation of the 1950s. The Beats existed as a counterculture that sought to challenge the prevailing norms of American society and the Hippies followed this ideology. The Hippies rose to prominence in San Francisco and their ethos spread not only through the country but also throughout the world. In their book *It's Happening* (1966), J. L. Simmons and Barry Winograd saw the emerging youth movement as one that was built on the attitudes of irreverence, experience, and tolerance. Much like the Beats, the Hippies never established a singular message from their movement, though they pushed for allowing everyone to, in essence, do his or her own thing.

The term *Hippie* is derived from the words *hip* and *hep*, both part of the jazz slang of the 1940s. From there those who were involved with the movement, commonly fifteen to twenty-five years of age, embraced a mind-set that focused on a number of views and ethics—and some that were in contradiction with themselves. With that acknowledgment, part of the hope of the Hippies was to embrace everything.

Welcoming so many ideas brought a number of different facets to the movement. Hippies encouraged drug use, freedom in sexuality, broader musical tastes, a combination of Eastern and Western religious thought, spirituality, and new fashions, among other things. The Hippie movement both espoused a counterculture mind-set and established the norm of "cool" in culture generally. Although the Hippies, overall, tended to be white, middle-class males, their openness toward and inclusion of other groups was one of its promising facets.

Writer Ken Kesey was one of the early prominent figures in the Hippie movement. Graduating from the University of Oregon in 1957 with a degree in speech and communication, he moved on to the creative writing program at Stanford University. There he began working on *One Flew Over the Cuckoo's Nest*, a novel that would give him national attention and financial security.

In 1964, Kesey and group of like-minded individuals, called the Merry Pranksters, who were living a communal lifestyle in California, took a bus trip to the World's Fair in New York City. Though part of the reason for doing so was to celebrate Kesey's latest publication, *Sometimes a Great Notion*, the trip itself became integral to the developing Hippie culture. Kesey and the Pranksters tried to play against the strait-laced culture they faced as they traversed the country.

Hippies sing and dance at a "love-in" near Los Angeles, California, in March 1967. (Bettmann/Corbis)

One interesting aspect of the trip is that Neal Cassady, the driver of their day-glo painted bus named Furthur, was also Jack Kerouac's driving partner for his excursions that became *On the Road*.

Once in New York, Kesey and the Merry Pranksters sought out Timothy Leary, the Harvard psychologist who promoted the use of psychedelic drugs like lysergic acid diethylamide, or LSD, also known as acid. While the meeting between Kesey, the Pranksters, and Leary never materialized, the LSD culture became the inherent characteristics of the Hippie movement. Kesey and the Merry Pranksters epitomized the use of acid and marijuana, and a free-wheeling attitude. Tom Wolfe chronicled the bus trip across the country and back in *The Electric Kool-Aid Acid Test*, published in 1968, a work that has been widely regarded as the onset of new journalism. Though the book arrived late in the Hippie movement, it was still able to provide a glimpse into the attitudes of its incipience.

Upon their return to San Francisco, the Merry Pranksters began holding what they called Acid Tests—large parties open to almost anyone where the use of acid and other drugs was encouraged. These parties occurred between 1965 and 1966 and featured musicians who would become intrinsic elements of the Hippie scene. Bands like the Grateful Dead, Jefferson Airplane, and Big Brother and the Holding Company all emerged from these "tests." In addition, a number of bands throughout the country found a home in the style of music that went against the regular radio-play songs of the day. The Beatles, Bob Dylan, the Allman Brothers Band, and Buffalo Springfield all found homes in the Hippie movement.

In late 1966, California pushed against the Hippie movement by declaring LSD a controlled substance, an obvious attempt to corral the wayward youngsters. The response by the Hippies was to start hosting Be-Ins, which was a different way of calling something a concert and a party. The name also implied that that to be at a Be-In was to be hip, or with the in crowd. This concept existed in a bi-coastal manner, as both California and New York held Be-In events in 1967.

The Monterey Pop Festival, which took place in mid-June 1967, in California, took the idea of the Be-Ins and turned them into a large-scale production. This festival was a triggering event for what became known as the Summer of Love. It was here that Jimi Hendrix, The Who, Big Brother, and the Holding Company (featuring Janis Joplin), the Mamas and the Papas, and Otis Redding first played to large crowds. The three-day event brought in 60,000–90,000 people and allowed the nascent Hippie culture to spread.

This summer constituted a number of aspects that would both heighten and start the downfall of the Hippie movement. The variance of music and its impact was welcomed, as the Beatles' *Sergeant Pepper's Lonely Hearts Club Band* became one of the featured works, while others like the Velvet Underground and a number of other bands and artists were able to attract attention during this era. Unfortunately, the "free-love" attitude was also marked by an increasing sense of commercialism toward those involved.

As articles in notable publications like *Time* magazine focused on the Hippie movement, it brought increased attention and people to the scene in San Francisco, many with no place to live or any ties to the area. The movement there became unduly inflated and frustrated the original ideals that had perpetuated the movement.

These negative effects did not derail the Hippie movement at its core. Many still embraced and furthered its hopeful messages. The artwork of the time shows a significant stylistic trend in its use of colors and patterns. Much of the art, like the music, would later be called psychedelic in nature. The art used free-form design and welcomed the use of neon and day-glo colors. The music ostensibly paralleled these paradigms, taking standard forms and combining them with the be-bop jazz ideals of free expression, bringing jam sessions and a flowing style to many artists' work. Bands like the Doors, Jimi Hendrix, and Cream all evoked this sense of style to great success.

In the following two years—after the 1967 Summer of Love—the Hippie movement grew in stature, in part because businesses saw a chance to capitalize on the youth market. Movies like *Easy Rider* and *Alice's Restaurant* both used Hippies as their focus in confronting the straight, conservative culture. However, for every positive exploration of the culture, there were also strange attempts to use it as a marketing tool, as a band like the Monkees highlighted. Assembled from auditions, and built for a television show, the Monkees were able to become a household name and a commercial success, as the band was the best-selling American artist in 1967.

One of the grand spectacles of the movement was the Woodstock Music and Art Fair, which was held in Bethel, New York, from August 15 to 17, 1969. The festival drew nearly 500,000 people to the farmland, and featured the following bands: Canned Heat, Richie Havens, Joan Baez, Janis Joplin, the Grateful Dead, Creedence Clearwater Revival, Crosby, Stills, Nash & Young, Carlos Santana, the Who, Jefferson Airplane, and Jimi Hendrix. Though marred by rain, the event was considered a success, as it continued the mantra of peace, love, and understanding.

The close of the year would also signify the beginning of the end of the Hippie movement. On December 6, 1969, the Altamont Speedway Free Festival took place in California. Much like Woodstock, it drew a large crowd, roughly 300,000 people, but rather than being marred by rain, it became the site of a murder, two accidental deaths, a number of violent attacks, and a large amount of property damage. Headlined by the Rolling Stones, the event featured security by the Hell's Angels biker gang. The nonviolent, live and let live ideals that had shaped the Hippie movement had given way to a sense of lawlessness and violence.

Though elements of the Hippie movement persisted, it became a more problematic group, and many of those involved became tied to different social and politic causes, namely the civil rights movement and the Vietnam War. The protests surrounding these issues took on more violent components and much of what had been positive "vibes" in the youth movement became darker.

The Hippie era also suffered from the loss of notable figures like Jimi Hendrix, Jim Morrison of the Doors, Janis Joplin, Mama Cass, Otis Redding and, later, Duane Allman. In addition, violence seemed to occupy more of the headlines in late 1969 and 1970, with the murders by the Charles Manson "family" and the killing of students at Kent State University by the Ohio National Guard. Combined with other conflicts on college campuses, and race riots throughout the country, and the continuing Vietnam War, the Hippie era could no longer sustain its drive and optimism.

Author Hunter S. Thompson may have best summarized the Hippie movement with what is referred to as the Wave Speech from *Fear and Loathing in Las Vegas*. In those words he recognizes that there was hopefulness in the movement and a belief that those involved were doing something special. He ends by recognizing that it had been a wave that soon receded and the culture of the country had changed. Ultimately, the Hippies have had a lasting impact in music, art, fashion, and some of the sensibilities that exist in America, and in some parts the communal nature is still alive and well.

See also

Beat Movement; Counterculture; Enlightenment; Free Love Movement; Internet Nation; Transcendentalism; Youth Movement

P. HUSTON LADNER

Further Reading

Grunenberg, Christoph, and Jonathan Harris. 2005. *Summer of Love: Psychedelic Art, Social Crisis and Counterculture in the 1960s*. Liverpool, UK: Liverpool University Press.

Heath, Joseph, and Andrew Potter. 2004. *Nation of Rebels: Why Counterculture Became Consumer Culture*. New York: Collins.

Miller, Timothy S. 2011. *The Hippies and American Values*. Knoxville, TN: University of Tennessee Press.

Wolfe, Tom. 2008. *The Electric Kool-Aid Acid Test*. New York: Picador.

Hippies—Primary Document

Introduction

Haight-Asbury in San Francisco, California, was the epicenter of the Hippie movement. Besides Woodstock, it is the place that most denotes the 1960s counterculture. The following article looks to mock those who fear the hippies' long hair and unconventional clothing.

Document: "Notes to Tourists: Roll Down Your Windows" (1967)

Many tourists upon seeing the unshaven, unconventionally clothed Love Generation roll up their car windows and lock the doors. This is not necessary and can be mightily inconvenient. Some of the hippies do bite, but all of them have taken their rabies shots so their bite is not too bad. Honestly though, you must consider that the unconventional attire would make it easy to describe your assailant to the police. By the way, if it appears to you that there are no police in the area, have no fears—probably one out of every twenty males that you see between the ages of 25 and 35 is an officer of some kind or the other.

Source: "Notes to Tourists: Roll Down Your Windows. *Haight-Ashbury Maverick.*" newspaper article, 1967. Available online at http://caho-test.cc.columbia.edu/ps/102015.html.

HIV/AIDS AWARENESS

Early mass media campaigns to promote HIV/AIDS awareness required sensitivity to legal and ethical treatment of human subjects. AIDS entered the headline news in 1981 when the first cases of a strange illness among gay men were reported. Some quickly dubbed the mystery ailment "gay cancer" or "gay pneumonia." Public health officials tried to respond to this specific community misunderstood and marginalized by the vast majority of the public with mixed results. Because HIV-positive status was so stigmatized for its prevalence in high-risk communities, it initiated a movement within gay rights activism to garner protected status for AIDS patients. By 1984, scientists recognized AIDS as a new viral disease that destroys the immune system and the etiological agent human immunodeficiency virus (HIV) as its cause.

AIDS made national headlines in the United States when a teenager named Ryan White (1971–1990) in the Midwest was diagnosed with HIV in 1984 after receiving infected blood through transfusion. White's crusade ignited the fears within the heterosexual majority and created a public health debate on the vulnerability of nation's blood supply. A hemophiliac attending public school in Kakoma, Indiana, White fought to remain in school despite widespread opposition and became an early "poster boy" for the epidemic. A foundation was established in his name to create awareness of the disease that is now part of AIDS United (http://www.aidsunited.org/about/).

The San Francisco AIDS Foundation (http://www.sfaf.org/), established in 1982 in the city's Castro District, developed ad campaigns to educate the community on AIDS prevention and the importance of HIV testing among individuals in high-risk groups. Internationally, governments began to develop mass media campaigns to address the growing threat the epidemic posed for high-risk groups of intravenous drug use and prostitutes. The Foundation compiled, synthesized, and disseminated information to local HIV-positive gay men. The Foundation produced some of the most provocative and effective HIV prevention and education campaigns in the world.

Local television news teams covered grassroots political activism–related gay civil rights in San Francisco. The *AIDS Lifeline* was a mass media campaign initiated by Group W executives Tom Goodgame and Nance Guilmartin. KPIX (CBS 5, San Francisco) partnered with the San Francisco AIDS Foundation to produce early "activist television." With the resulting corporate/nonprofit collaboration, production of the *AIDS Lifeline* commenced in 1983. The station supported the campaign by programming AIDS information into news, entertainment, talk shows, documentaries, and call-in programs. The San Francisco AIDS Foundation and KPIX copublished flyers and booklets containing practical information on AIDS-related agencies. This material was mailed in response to more than a half-million requests and was translated into several languages.

The *AIDS Lifeline* (http://www.landispr.com/clients/casehistories/aids_lifeline.htm) also spawned a series of seventy-six public service announcements (PSAs) featuring celebrity speakers reading scripts by Holly Smith, from the San Francisco AIDS Foundation, and poet Rod McKuen, a popular culture icon from the 1960s. The concept behind these spots was to present comforting messages designed to shape the public perception of AIDS to reduce fear.

After preliminary issues of public health were addressed, the need to educate public policy makers of the critical need for AIDS support was desperate. Local activists responded first to the needs of a newly emerging HIV/AIDS community. On October 27, 1985, protesters chained themselves to the old Federal Building in San Francisco, to protest government inaction and to make "Four Moral Appeals." These demands were funding AIDS research, federal recognition of AIDS-related complex (ARC) as a critical issue of the AIDS crisis, timely U.S. Food and Drug Administration (FDA) approval of AIDS and ARC treatments already available in other countries, and condemnation of perceived AIDS discrimination from President Ronald Reagan and all federal officials. Conversely, the British government played an important function in determining support for HIV/AIDS awareness in the United Kingdom that included mass media campaigns, setting up AIDS hotlines, support groups, and creating dialogs in communities about AIDS. Prime Minister Margaret Thatcher and Health Secretary Norman Fowler developed policies that directed mass media campaign and Diana, princess of Wales, served as a role model for compassion in relating to HIV-positive patients.

Local ordinances passed in 1985 banning AIDS discrimination allowed HIV/AIDS patients to participate in shaping perceptions of AIDS. Following the announcement that Rock Hudson had AIDS in 1985, Los Angeles became the first

A contingent of AIDS victims carry a banner and ride in a motorized cable car up Market St. in San Francisco, June 26, 1986, as they lead an estimated 300,000 participants in the Thirteenth Annual Gay Freedom Day Parade. The colorful, festive event was dedicated to the victims of the deadly AIDS disease. (AP Photo/Eric Risberg)

major city in the United States to pass an ordinance banning AIDS discrimination. San Francisco's ordinance changed the environment for lobbying for funding by opening the door to media coverage and creating a more realistic community face for fighting AIDS.

The intangible truth was that the AIDS community was fragile and rapidly dying. The most meaningful rituals adopted by the San Francisco AIDS community became their marches and vigils. These events were visually dramatic so that they would get picked up in the broadcast media. In June 1987, Cleve Jones started piecing a quilt in a San Francisco storefront, launching the Names Project AIDS Memorial Quilt (http://www.aidsquilt.org/). The AIDS Memorial Quilt remains significant for its commemoration of the lives of the earliest HIV/AIDS victims. After the protests and vigils ceased, drugs were developed to turn AIDS into

a "manageable" chronic disease, and once HIV/AIDS care became institutionalized, the most enduring monument of the epidemic was the Names Project due to its sheer size and scope. The quilt grew to weigh fifty-five tons by 1990; it could not be ignored nor forgotten, for stories of too many lives had been stitched into its cloth.

KPIX's pioneering coverage of the AIDS epidemic spawned a cooperative network of over 100 media outlets (in over 50 percent of the markets in the United States), which shared local stories that could be used as news segments. Thus, an important transition took place where local media outlets reporting on a local theme moved into national and international reporting. *The New York Times* featured a story, "In San Francisco, TV Battles on the Front Lines Against AIDS," that described the collaborative efforts of KPIX staff to create "frank, instructive programming."

Small grassroots consumer groups, such as the Healing Alternatives Buyers Club established in 1987, screened products and provided information for HIV-positive clients. They networked with specialists to share information about treatments when patients had already explored every treatment alternative and were weakened by overmedication. Some large pharmaceutical companies exploited the epidemic to increase profits by quoting higher expenses for research and development of potential HIV/AIDS treatments than what was actually used, and some East Coast pharmaceutical distributors "jacked up" prices for therapies for West Coast markets.

HIV/AIDS activists lobbied the medical community for faster access to experimental therapies in legitimate clinics. "Guerilla clinics," which emerged after FDA crackdowns on unapproved therapies, were provided free of charge when doctors would not provide treatment for fear of losing their licenses. Underground networks provided individuals with AIDS with information and referrals to clinics, arguing that there should be a government-supported clearinghouse for AIDS research. To many it was inconceivable that underground clinics were necessary in the United States, but they asserted that radical actions were compelled by unethical regulations. In Orange County, grassroots efforts to disseminate information on the epidemic resulted in the formation of the AIDS Global Education Information System (AEGIS [http://www.aegis.com/en/aegis]).

By the early-1990s, stressed caregivers working with HIV/AIDS patients indicated that troubles in recruiting volunteers had eclipsed the ongoing fight over federal funding for AIDS services. Volunteers were economically indispensable in the absence of government funding since they subsidized efforts to provide assistance to AIDS patients. The 1991 announcement that basketball superstar Earvin "Magic" Johnson was HIV-positive also brought increased attention to AIDS, and that he survived and thrived spoke to the medical advances made against HIV/AIDS. The legacy of the early HIV-AIDS awareness activism is that today different at-risk communities are initiating preventative programs within their own communities. Multicultural campaigns and college awareness days are among a few examples where AIDS prevention and HIV testing is available. Until a viable cure is found, HIV prevention must be continually reinforced with each generation.

See also
Disability Rights Movement; Gay Rights

MEREDITH ELIASSEN

Further Reading

Ball, Steven, ed. 1998. *The HIV-Negative Gay Man: Developing Strategies for Survival and Emotional Well-Being*. New York: Harrington Park Press.

Gillett, James B. 2011. *A Grassroots History of the HIV/AIDS Epidemic in North America*. Spokane, WA: Marquette Books.

Green, Edward C. 2011. *AIDS, Behavior, and Culture: Understanding Evidence-Based Prevention*. Walnut Creek, CA: Left Coast Press.

Hogan, Mary Ann. 1988. "In San Francisco, TV Battles on the Front Lines Against AIDS." *The New York Times*, February 21, pp. 31, 37.

Kolata, Gina. 1991. "Patients Going Underground to Buy Experimental Drugs." *The New York Times*, November 4. http://www.nytimes.com/1991/11/04/us/patients-going-underground-to-buy-experimental-drugs.html?pagewanted=all&src=pm. Accessed June 16, 2014.

Pheland, John M. 2005. "Activist Television: Sociological and Public Policy Implications of Public Service Campaigns." March 21. http://www.religion-online.org/showarticle.asp?title=158. Accessed June 16, 2014.

Schulman, David I. 1988. "AIDS Discrimination: Its Nature, Meaning and Function." *Nova Law Review* (Spring): 1113. http://www.aegis.com/law/journals/1988/ALAW0003.html. Accessed June 16, 2014.

Smith, Reginald. 1985. "S.F. Board Votes to Ban Bias Against AIDS Patients." *San Francisco Chronicle*, November 6, p. 1.

United States. General Accounting Office. 2000. *HIV/AIDS: Use of Ryan White CARE Act and Other Assistance Grant Funds: Report to Congressional Requestors*. Washington, DC: General Accounting Office.

White House Office of National AIDS Policy. 2010. *National AIDS Strategy for the United States*. Washington, DC: White House Office of National AIDS Policy.

HIV/AIDS Awareness—Primary Document

Introduction

Preserving the anonymity of HIV-positive informants, cameramen often used "cutaway" shots and silhouettes to conceal the identities of AIDS patients prior to the existence of AIDS discrimination legislation. Patterned after similar laws in Los Angeles and West Hollywood, San Francisco Supervisor

Harry Britt authored local ordinance 499–85 (passed by the San Francisco Board of Supervisors on November 5, 1985, to amend Police Code Section 3801) banning AIDS discrimination; the measure became the strongest ordinance in a major city and served as the model for the United States. San Francisco's ordinance differed from other local legislation because it prohibited landlords, employers, and others from requiring testing for HIV. This excerpt provides the background information known to date behind legislation that allowed media to present a realistic face to the epidemic.

Document: Ordinance Passed by San Francisco Board of Supervisors Prohibiting Discrimination on the Basis of AIDS and Associated Conditions (November 5, 1985)

Article 38 Prohibiting Discrimination on the Basis of AIDS and Associated Conditions. Section 3801. POLICY. It is the policy of the City and County of San Francisco to eliminate discrimination based on the fact that a person has AIDS or any medical signs or symptoms related thereto. In adopting this ordinance, the Board of Supervisors does not intend to proscribe any activity the proscription of which would constitute an infringement of the free exercise of religion as guaranteed by the United States and California constitutions.

Section 3802. FINDINGS. After public hearings and consideration of testimony and documentary evidence, the Board of Supervisors finds and declares that the medical condition described as acquired immuno deficiency syndrome, and commonly known as AIDS, is a deadly disease which has the potential to affect every segment of the City's population. AIDS was first recognized in 1981. It is now seen as the top priority of the United States Public Health Service.

AIDS is the most severe manifestation of a spectrum of clinical disease caused by a virus, variously known as Human T-lymphotropic virus type III, lymphadenopathy-associated virus, or AIDS-associated retrovirus, which attacks and cripples the body's immune system by killing T-helper lymphocytes, thereby leaving the body vulnerable to opportunistic infections and malignancies. A person afflicted AIDS can suffer a variety of viral, bacterial, fungal, and protozoal infections and malignancies which eventually lead to death, usually within one year after diagnosis.

The spread of the virus has occurred only through the exchange of body fluids, that is blood, blood products, or semen, between individuals. No evidence exists to indicate that the virus can be spread by casual person-to-person contact. Medical studies of families in which one or more members have been infected with HTLV-III/LAV/ARV show no spread of the virus other than through sexual intercourse or from mother to fetus in utero. Medical studies of hospital personnel caring for AIDS patients show no spread of the virus other than through needle sticks. The public danger presented by the virus and its subsequent manifestations of AIDS-related complex and AIDS is caused by a lengthy asymptomatic period of infection during which an apparently healthy individual may unknowingly spread the disease to other persons through the exchange of blood, products, or semen. AIDS is concentrated primarily in urban areas, with the City and County of San Francisco having the largest incidence of the disease in the country. In the opinion of the scientific, medical, and public health communities, AIDS will continue to increase at a high rate within our City for the foreseeable future.

AIDS and AIDS-related complex by their nature have created a minority of our citizens who are afflicted with a seriously disabling condition whose ultimate outcome is fatal. Individuals infected with the virus represent a significant segment of our population particularly victimized due to the nature of their infection and to the present climate of misinformation, ignorance, and fear in the general population. Discrimination against victims of AIDS or AIDS-related conditions are faced with discrimination in employment, housing, business establishments, city facilities, city services, and other public accommodations. This discrimination cuts across all racial, ethnic, and economic lines. Such discrimination poses a substantial threat to the health, safety, and welfare of the community. Existing state and federal restraints on such arbitrary discrimination are inadequate to meet the particular problems of this city and county.

Source: San Francisco Police Code, Article 38. Available online at http://www.amlegal.com/nxt/gateway.dll/California/police/policecode?f=templates$fn=default.htm$3.0$vid=amlegal:sanfrancisco_ca$sync=1.

HOMESTEADING

Homesteading is an interesting conflation of ideas. It is historical and current, mental and physical, and a mix of practicality and posturing. In its current form, homesteading reflects an attitude of distancing oneself from aspects of modern society in the United States. It encourages a person to foster reliance upon oneself and the land for a number of things.

In many ways, homesteading can be considered a "back to the earth" movement. Hence, much of its focus is centered on reconnecting with nature and developing ties with the land that have been lost or forgotten. The hope is to develop a lifestyle that is based upon self-sufficiency, an ode to life before mass industrialization and manufacturing. The people who practice homesteading are attempting to remove themselves from parts of the mass consumerism.

Homesteading has evolved from being a life of necessity to one of conscious choice. Those involved see it as a more wholesome and fulfilling way to live compared with people who chose to live within the fast food, box store, and big business world. The lifestyle is, obviously, not for everyone, and those who criticize it wonder how much of a difference those who homestead make in terms of the environment, culture, and economics.

Historical Perspective

The concept of homesteading is derived from the settlement of the country and westward expansion. When the young United States made the Louisiana Purchase in 1803, taking over the lands from France, it immediately doubled in size. Though President Thomas Jefferson pushed for exploration of these acquired lands, notably with the Lewis and Clark

A settler stands outside his homestead claim in Oregon's Umpqua National Forest. The Homestead Act of 1862 honored claims on public land to anyone who would settle on it and work the land for five years. (Forest History Society)

Expedition, the territories remained sparsely populated by whites.

America was nothing if not a growing country and there was a persistent desire to move west. The Indian Removal Act, which forced Native Americans off of their lands, combined with the war against Mexico, further pushed whites into the Western areas of the country. To foster the development of these lands, President Abraham Lincoln signed the Homestead Act of 1862.

The Homestead Act had far-reaching implications. The goal of the act was to offer land to citizens who "had never taken up arms against the U.S." in the Western territories. These lands were offered at little cost, and sometimes for none at all, to willing individuals who sought to establish a home on the frontier. The basis for the Homestead Act resides with the Jeffersonian ideal of the yeoman farmer. This archetype was one of the founding principles of the country, with the notion that working farmers would comprise its backbone.

The Homestead Act allowed many people to take on lands that they otherwise might not have been able to afford. At the same time, the act motivated a strong sense of settlement in the West. Four years later, the Southern Homestead Act of 1866 was passed in an attempt to settle parts of the Southeast and stimulate the economy of the South during Reconstruction after the Civil War. In 1873, the Timber Culture Act allowed people to gain extra acreage should they plant trees on one-quarter of their lands.

While the sum total of these acts, and later ones that followed them, was to offer land cheaply to American citizens and to develop the land, it also furthered the individualistic ideology that would later be a bedrock of the American mind. Furthermore, there is the intrinsic notion that European Americans must cultivate the land, in essence, bending it to their will. Some of these aspects are intrinsic to the modern concept of homesteading.

Conservationism

The contemporary motivation toward homesteading is at least, in part, based upon the conservation movement that arose in the early 20th century. Though one could argue that Henry David Thoreau and Walt Whitman were two of the big names associated with the early conservation movement, it is John Muir who took on a visible leadership role.

As the lands of America were trampled by the two-pronged assault of a growing population and fast-developing industrialization, some people began to espouse the value of the land.

Muir saw the terrain as one that should be preserved, with two main tenets shaping his beliefs. The first was a utilitarian view, where he reasoned that people still needed to be connected to the land without the intrusion of technology or machines, that people needed to respect the land for its value of providing food and materials. The second reason behind his attempt to control the development of the land was founded in aesthetics. One aspect that makes the United States unique is how it has appreciated its own scenery.

From a Euro-colonial perspective, the United States has a short history compared to Europe. Most European artists had chosen, likely due to their patrons, to focus on various leaders, religion, the female form, and depictions of war for their content. American artists did not have the same history upon which to draw and supplanted many of these topics with the use of nature. The artists of New York's Adirondacks comprise the first major group to use landscapes, and man at home with the land.

The group of artists associated with these works is loosely defined as the Hudson River School, with notable artists like Thomas Cole, Robert Weir, the Hart Brothers, and Frederic Church, to mention a few. They saw nature and its beauty as a direct manifestation from God, and as something that should be appreciated, if not, in a way, worshipped. Artists like Winslow Homer and Ansel Adams both continued these ideals as they moved beyond that area of the country and began to showcase other regions.

Modern Homesteading

While early homesteading was essential to sustaining life, the modern version comes from the rise of the counterculture perspective. The main thrust for the movement is tied to the Hippies of the 1960s. While the Hippies are associated with a number of different messages, like free love, make peace not war, and the civil rights movement, they also advanced the idea of living off of the land. They exemplified this belief by creating communes where groups of people would attempt to live in harmony in farm-like communities.

Homesteading, in this regard, goes beyond just the food that is grown, and is a whole community. It is easy to consider the material goods, like clothing and furniture, but it also encompasses the notion of education, which is left to those in the community who feel they know what is best for the next generation.

As homesteading has moved forward, it has used the ideals from both earlier history and its more recent counterpart. The people who practice homesteading seek to make their own food, by growing the fruits, vegetables, and animals, but also to create their own energy sources to leave less of a carbon footprint. They believe in alternative medicines rather than going to hospitals, as their faith is in the fact that the natural world knows what is best. In addition, they also create their own goods and sometimes branch out into their own small-scale businesses.

In conjunction with their practices, there is also the spiritual component. While some may pray to one particular God, others find a universal God in nature. The land, in this respect, is a gift from God, and is what provides life, comfort, and enjoyment. The connection that these people feel with the land is a serious one as they have developed a lifestyle that is predicated on a sense of harmony with it. Thus, there is a reverence, and recognition, that goes beyond just the simple appreciation of landscapes.

Modern homesteaders often try to do more with less, seeking to develop a lifestyle of self-sufficiency on plots that are close to one acre in size. They see that families do not need huge plots of land to create a sustainable situation, and that with the right strictures they should manage just fine.

Homesteading is an unusual outlier in American culture. It can be tied to many aspects of the early development of the country, yet in its current form it exists as contrary to the norm. It is a hopeful ideology where its adherents seek to connect with the land; something they feel had been left behind in the ever-growing world of machination and big corporations. The idea of determining one's own food, clothes, housing, and education provides a means for escape while also setting oneself apart from the common norms of the country.

The idea of homesteading is both a homage to the country's past and an ode to current green and positive eco-friendly movements. The hope of trying to scale down and become more self-reliant is a testament to the individualistic concept of Americans.

See also

Counterculture; The Frontier; Hippies; Indian Rights; Manifest Destiny; Western Expansion/Exploration; Western Lore

P. HUSTON LADNER

Further Reading

Gehring, Abigail R. 2011. *The Homesteading Handbook: A Back to Basics Guide to Growing Your Own Food, Canning, Keeping Chickens, Generating Your Own Energy, Crafting, Herbal Medicine, and More*. New York: Skyhorse Publishing.

Gould, Rebecca Kneale. 2005. *At Home in Nature: Modern Homesteading and Spiritual Practice in America*. Berkeley, CA: University of California Press.

Hyman, Harold M. 2008. *American Singularity: The 1787 Northwest Ordinance, the 1862 Homestead and Morrill Acts, and the 1944 G.I. Bill*. Athens, GA: University of Georgia Press.

Seymour, John. 2009. *The New Complete Book of Self-Sufficiency*. London: Dorling Kindersley.

Homesteading—Primary Document

Introduction

The Homestead Act of 1862 set in motion a comprehensive plan for settling more of the Western country by making land affordable for U.S. citizens. In conjunction, this act also served to cultivate lands, turning them into productive spheres of economic growth. While behaviors developed by homesteading these lands were borne out of necessity, many people have adapted these practices to a modern lifestyle, eschewing rampant consumerism and big business. Their practices include farming, canning, carpentry, and making their own clothes in an attempt to be more self-sufficient.

Document: Homestead Act (May 20, 1862)

CHAP. LXXV. —An Act to Secure Homesteads to Actual Settlers on the Public Domain

Be it enacted by the Senate and House of Representatives of the United States of America in Congress assembled, That any person who is the head of a family, or who has arrived at the age of twenty-one years, and is a citizen of the United States, or who shall have filed his declaration of intention to become such, as required by the naturalization laws of the United States, and who has never borne arms against the

United States Government or given aid and comfort to its enemies, shall, from and after the first January, eighteen hundred and. sixty-three, be entitled to enter one quarter section or a less quantity of unappropriated public lands, upon which said person may have filed a preemption claim, or which may, at the time the application is made, be subject to preemption at one dollar and twenty-five cents, or less, per acre; or eighty acres or less of such unappropriated lands, at two dollars and fifty cents per acre, to be located in a body, in conformity to the legal subdivisions of the public lands, and after the same shall have been surveyed: Provided, That any person owning and residing on land may, under the provisions of this act, enter other land lying contiguous to his or her said land, which shall not, with the land so already owned and occupied, exceed in the aggregate one hundred and sixty acres.

SEC. 2. And be it further enacted, That the person applying for the benefit of this act shall, upon application to the register of the land office in which he or she is about to make such entry, make affidavit before the said register or receiver that he or she is the head of a family, or is twenty-one years or more of age, or shall have performed service in the army or navy of the United States, and that he has never borne arms against the Government of the United States or given aid and comfort to its enemies, and that such application is made for his or her exclusive use and benefit, and that said entry is made for the purpose of actual settlement and cultivation, and not either directly or indirectly for the use or benefit of any other person or persons whomsoever; and upon filing the said affidavit with the register or receiver, and on payment of ten dollars, he or she shall thereupon be permitted to enter the quantity of land specified: Provided, however, That no certificate shall be given or patent issued therefor until the expiration of five years from the date of such entry; and if, at the expiration of such time, or at any time within two years thereafter, the person making such entry; or, if he be dead, his widow; or in case of her death, his heirs or devisee; or in case of a widow making such entry, her heirs or devisee, in case of her death; shall prove by two credible witnesses that he, she, or they have resided upon or cultivated the same for the term of five years immediately succeeding the time of filing the affidavit aforesaid, and shall make affidavit that no part of said land has been alienated, and that he has borne rue allegiance to the Government of the United States; then, in such

case, he, she, or they, if at that time a citizen of the United States, shall be entitled to a patent, as in other cases provided for by law: And provided, further, That in case of the death of both father and mother, leaving an Infant child, or children, under twenty-one years of age, the right and fee shall ensure to the benefit of said infant child or children; and the executor, administrator, or guardian may, at any time within two years after the death of the surviving parent, and in accordance with the laws of the State in which such children for the time being have their domicil, sell said land for the benefit of said infants, but for no other purpose; and the purchaser shall acquire the absolute title by the purchase, and be entitled to a patent from the United States, on payment of the office fees and sum of money herein specified.

SEC. 3. And be it further enacted, That the register of the land office shall note all such applications on the tract books and plats of, his office, and keep a register of all such entries, and make return thereof to the General Land Office, together with the proof upon which they have been founded.

SEC. 4. And be it further enacted, That no lands acquired under the provisions of this act shall in any event become liable to the satisfaction of any debt or debts contracted prior to the issuing of the patent therefor.

SEC. 5. And be it further enacted, That if, at any time after the filing of the affidavit, as required in the second section of this act, and before the expiration of the five years aforesaid, it shall be proven, after due notice to the settler, to the satisfaction of the register of the land office, that the person having filed such affidavit shall have actually changed his or her residence, or abandoned the said land for more than six months at any time, then and in that event the land so entered shall revert to the government.

SEC. 6. And be it further enacted, That no individual shall be permitted to acquire title to more than one quarter section under the provisions of this act; and that the Commissioner of the General Land Office is hereby required to prepare and issue such rules and regulations, consistent with this act, as shall be necessary and proper to carry its provisions into effect; and that the registers and receivers of the several land offices shall be entitled to receive the same compensation for any lands entered under the provisions of this act that they are now entitled to receive when the same quantity of land is entered with money, one half to be paid by the person making the application at the time of so doing, and the other half on the issue of the certificate by the person to whom it may be issued; but this shall not be construed to enlarge the maximum of compensation now prescribed by law for any register or receiver: Provided, That nothing contained in this act shall be so construed as to impair or interfere in any manner whatever with existing preemption rights : And provided, further, That all persons who may have filed their applications for a preemption right prior to the passage of this act, shall be entitled to all privileges of this act: Provided, further, That no person who has served, or may hereafter serve, for a period of not less than fourteen days in the army or navy of the United States, either regular or volunteer, under the laws thereof, during the existence of an actual war, domestic or foreign, shall be deprived of the benefits of this act on account of not having attained the age of twenty-one years.

SEC. 7. And be it further enacted, That the fifth section of the act entitled" An act in addition to an act more effectually to provide for the punishment of certain crimes against the United States, and for other purposes," approved the third of March, in the year eighteen hundred and fifty-seven, shall extend to all oaths, affirmations, and affidavits, required or authorized by this act.

SEC. 8. And be it further enacted, That nothing in this act shall be so construed as to prevent any person who has availed him or herself of the benefits of the first section of this act, from paying the minimum price, or the price to which the same may have graduated, for the quantity of land so entered at any time before the expiration of the five years, and obtaining a patent therefor from the government, as in other cases provided by law, on making proof of settlement and cultivation as provided by existing laws granting preemption rights.

APPROVED, May 20, 1862.

Source: Homestead Act. Available at Our Documents Web site. http://www.ourdocuments.gov/doc.php?doc=31&page=transcript.

HUMAN RIGHTS

The phrase *human rights* generally refers to the idea that humans have inherent dignity simply by virtue of their humanity and that governmental and nongovernmental institutions and individuals alike are obligated to respect that inherent dignity. Contemporary human rights norms are generally codified in the various international human rights treaties and declarations crafted by nations following World War II, such as the United Nations Charter (1945), the Universal Declaration of Human Rights (1948), the International Covenant on Civil and Political Rights (1966), and the International Covenant on Economic, Social and Cultural Rights (1966). More recent international human rights conventions include the Convention Against Torture and Other Cruel, Inhuman or Degrading Treatment (1987) and the Convention on the Rights of Persons with Disabilities (2007). The U.S. government played a major role in drafting all of these documents.

However, the role of human rights in the United States began long before the 20th century, instead dating to the nation's founding. The founding fathers of the United States, many of whom had received classical educations, were heavily influenced by ideas of the Enlightenment as well as British legal documents such as the Magna Carta. These influences are reflected in their writings. For example, drawing on conceptions of British and French philosophers that assume the inherent rights of individuals by virtue of their humanity, the Declaration of Independence famously declares "that all men are created equal, that they are endowed by their Creator with certain unalienable rights, that among these are life, liberty and the pursuit of happiness." Though the founding documents explicitly limited these rights to men, successive social movements within the United States of racial minorities, women, the poor, and gay activists have challenged these limitations as violations of the underlying conception of universal human rights.

The successful movements for the abolition of slavery in the 1860s and to achieve women's suffrage in the 1920s were domestic human rights movements. Likewise, the welfare rights movement of the 1960s, which claimed a constitutional "right to live," although unsuccessful in the courts, was a human rights movement. These earlier movements did not consistently adopt the language of human rights, instead often using language to demarcate and separate their identity group—that is, "women's liberation," "black power"—rather than connect their cause to others outside of the specific group. However, in 1980, when activists founded a civil rights organization to secure equality for lesbian, gay, bisexual and transgendered (LGBT) people, they named the new organization the Human Rights Campaign Fund, directly connecting this equality movement with the more general philosophies of human rights and conveying their central argument that the rights of LGBT people are the rights of all.

As concepts of human rights have moved from philosophy and rhetoric to law, the language of human rights has become increasingly important in the United States both as a legal tool and as an organizing construct. Though the United States played a leading role in the drafting of the Universal Declaration of Human Rights and the other important human rights documents, the strictures of the Cold War deterred domestic advocacy groups from openly appealing to human rights norms. Before World War II, civil rights groups such as the National Association for the Advancement of Colored People (NAACP) were initially active in international venues, pressing for scrutiny of U.S. apartheid through appeals to the United Nations and other international human rights bodies. Similarly, U.S. women's groups such as the National Women's Party sought support for domestic women's equality in international gatherings, particularly focusing on restrictions on women's citizenship status in the United States. However, as Cold War tensions increased, the risks of associating the causes of U.S. civil rights and women's equality with international equality movements, particularly those of the Soviet Union and Eastern Europe, became too great. The threat of red-baiting and McCarthy-type hearings that could have long-term effects on individual reputations and organizational fund-raising forced civil rights and women's rights activists to focus their work in ways that were purely domestic and more incremental, without overt appeals to international human rights norms.

By the late 1970s, however, with the Cold War era well over, domestic advocates were in a position to reconnect with their human rights roots. President Jimmy Carter gave human rights a central place in his administration's foreign policy, and oversaw an increase in U.S. participation in human rights treaties. Advocacy organizations such as the New York–based Center for Constitutional Rights initiated litigation against an alleged Paraguayan torturer, *Filartiga v. Pena-Irala* (1980),

specifically intended to integrate human rights norms into domestic U.S. law by holding international human rights violators accountable in U.S. courts. In the ensuing years, international human rights groups increasingly trained their scrutiny on U.S. practices, while domestic civil rights groups also increased their human rights focus after years of neglect. The founding director of the Women's Division of Human Rights Watch, Dorothy Q. Thomas, was highly influential on both fronts. Beginning in 1990, in her writings and public speaking, she urged Human Rights Watch and other international NGOs to scrutinize the United States as they did other countries, while she also admonished groups like the NAACP that had once been international human rights leaders to re-engage with the larger human rights system. Thomas's campaign bore considerable fruit, with groups such as the Ford and Soros Foundations providing new support to U.S. organizations expanding their domestic human rights work. In 1998, Thomas was awarded a MacArthur "genius" Fellowship for her work on U.S. human rights issues.

Momentum for human rights in the United States continued to build in the first decade of the 21st century. In 1998, the Columbia University Law School in New York City founded its Human Rights Institute, addressing human rights issues both domestically and internationally. Other university-based programs followed, with a burgeoning number of law school human rights clinics taking on human rights issues as a part of student's legal training. Human rights organizations also continued to expand. In 2003, the U.S. Human Rights Network was formed, to serve as a convener and coordinator of U.S.-focused human rights organizations. The following year, the American Civil Liberties Union (ACLU) created a human rights program to promote and oversee human rights work of the ACLU affiliates across the country. Also in 2004, the National Economic and Social Rights Initiative was created to promote social and economic human rights in the United States.

Fueling these organizations was a growing domestic grassroots movement using human rights as a rallying cry. Among the most prominent was the Kensington Welfare Rights Union (KWRU), a group of low-income activists based in the Kensington neighborhood of Philadelphia. Using strategies such as marching on the United Nations and filing claims with international bodies, the KWRU effectively framed its local struggles to find stable housing in broad human rights terms. Human rights frameworks were also adopted by groups such as SisterSong, a women of color reproductive justice collective; the Coalition of Immokalee Workers, a workers' rights organization based in Florida; and United Workers, an organization led by low-wage workers in Maryland. Notably, the venerable Leadership Conference on Civil Rights, founded in 1950 as the legislative advocacy arm of the civil rights movement, changed its name in 2010 to the Leadership Conference on Civil and Human Rights.

The rise in human rights awareness in the United States has changed the nature of U.S. human rights activism. No longer looking exclusively at human rights abuses abroad, U.S. activists are now more likely to make connections between U.S. governmental and corporate policies and human rights abuses. The campaign to divest American funds from South Africa is an early example of this. More recent campaigns have involved pressure on U.S. corporations to engage in business practices that comport with human rights, such as the anti-sweatshop movement.

Greater human rights activism in the United States has also led to greater scrutiny of U.S. statements in the international arena and use of human rights legal mechanisms to promote domestic change. For example, when the U.S. government reported in 2008 to U.N. committee monitoring compliance with the International Convention on the Elimination of All Forms of Racial Discrimination, hundreds of U.S.-based organizations organized to collectively critique the U.S. report, with many of these organizations also traveling to Geneva for the U.N. committee hearing on U.S. compliance.

Greater human rights awareness in the United States has also influenced the development of domestic jurisprudence. U.S. courts have long considered international law as a matter of course, since treaties are denominated at the Supreme Law of the Land under the U.S. Constitution's Supremacy Clause. In recent years, the U.S. Supreme Court has regularly received briefing from advocates addressing domestic constitutional cases through an international human rights lens. Several justices, including Justices Stephen Breyer, Ruth Bader Ginsburg, and Sonia Sotomayor, have spoken about their interest in these materials and the U.S. Supreme Court has cited international human rights documents, such as the Universal Declaration of Human Rights and the opinions of the European Court of Human Rights, on several occasions. State courts also increasingly looked to human rights material to inform their decisions, particularly in cases involving state constitutional rights. Despite some backlash, with the states

of Oklahoma (2011) and Kansas (2012) barring judicial citation of international law, the history of the U.S. legal system and its capacity to absorb new influences suggests that the practice of considering human rights norms will continue.

See also

African American Civil Rights Movement; Capital Punishment; Diplomacy; Feminist Movement; Racism; Women's Suffrage

MARTHA F. DAVIS

Further Reading

Anderson, Carol. 2003. *Eyes Off the Prize: The United Nations and the African American Struggle for Human Rights.* Cambridge: Cambridge, UK University Press.

Ford Foundation. 2004. *Close to Home: Case Studies of Human Rights Work in the United States.* New York: Ford Foundation.

Soohoo, Cynthia, Catherine Albisa, and Martha F. Davis, eds. 2009. *Bringing Human Rights Home: A History of Human Rights in the United States.* Philadelphia, PA: University of Pennsylvania Press.

Human Rights—Primary Document

Introduction

Reproduced here is a 2011 speech delivered to the American Society of International Law by Michael Posner, assistant secretary, Bureau of Democracy, Human Rights, and Labor at the U.S. State Department. The speech is remarkable because it continues a national dialogue concerning economic and social rights in the United States that was initiated in 1941 with President Franklin Delano Roosevelt's "Four Freedoms" speech. While discussing these freedoms in the context of U.S. human rights policy abroad, Assistant Secretary Posner also trains a lens on the United States to ask what recognition and implementation of these human rights might mean for domestic policy.

Document: "The Four Freedoms Turn 70: Ensuring Economic, Political, and National Security in the 21st Century" by Michael H. Posner (March 24, 2011)

Seventy years ago, President Franklin Delano Roosevelt delivered his famous Four Freedoms speech as he was steeling the United States for war. Three years later he elaborated further on his vision of human rights and security in a State of the

Union address delivered at a moment when the democratic way of life was under assault around the world.

Roosevelt framed the war aims broadly in terms of core American values. And he warned that "enduring peace cannot be bought at the cost of other people's freedom."

Roosevelt's premise was that our liberty rested on Four Freedoms: Freedom of speech and expression, freedom to worship, freedom from fear, and freedom from want. He identified freedom of speech and freedom to worship as core civil and political rights, just as we do now. He defined "freedom from fear" as a reduction in arms, so as to diminish our collective destructive capabilities—and that's a component of the U.S. National Security Strategy to this day. And with the indelible phrase—"freedom from want"—Roosevelt linked the liberty of our people with their basic economic and social wellbeing. This concept is being echoed today on the streets of Cairo, Tunis and other Arab cities.

Roosevelt concluded with words that still guide us today: "Freedom means the supremacy of human rights everywhere."

There are many ways to think about what should or should not count as a human right. Perhaps the simplest and most compelling is that human rights reflect what a person needs in order to live a meaningful and dignified existence. It is the core belief in the supreme value of human dignity that leads us, as Americans, to embrace the idea that people should not be tortured, discriminated against, deprived of the right to choose their government, silenced, or barred from observing the religion of their choosing. As President Obama has made clear, it is this same belief in human dignity that underlies our concern for the health, education, and wellbeing of our people.

Human dignity has a political component and an economic component—and these are inexorably linked. Participation, transparency and accountability are valuable not just because they contribute to the dignity of the governed, but because they enhance the responsiveness of those who govern.

Amartya Sen, who spoke here last night, has spotlighted the connection between freedom of speech, democracy and good governance. He said elections, uncensored news reporting and unfettered public criticism prompt governments to address hunger. Freedom to criticize and make demands "promote the political incentive for governments to be responsive, caring and prompt."

In the Middle East, the public understands the connection between corruption and impunity on one hand, and lack of freedom and economic opportunity on the other. That [sic] why the story of a Tunisian vegetable vendor, who was so humiliated by local authorities that set himself ablaze, resonated around the region.

It was recognition of the importance of human dignity that guided Eleanor Roosevelt as she led the effort to persuade the United Nations to adopt the Universal Declaration of Human Rights in 1948. She used FDR's words as moral cornerstones for the international legal and institutional regimes that would later arise—regimes that address economic social and cultural rights, as well as civil and political rights.

Today I want to re-examine those moral cornerstones, the Four Freedoms, as Roosevelt defined them, and talk about three things. First, since I have just returned from Egypt, where I accompanied Secretary Clinton last week, I want to discuss how the principles embodied in the Four Freedoms are resonating in Egypt today. Second, I want to discuss how President Obama and Secretary Clinton are applying those universal principles through U.S. foreign policy in the 21st Century. And third, I want to explain how we think about the economic and social rights that derive from Roosevelt's freedom from want.

Today's national security challenges are different than those that confronted Roosevelt as he contemplated war with Nazi Germany; but they are no less consequential. In one sense our primary enemies, extremists and terrorists, are much weaker. They have no armies. But they are able to employ a kind of Jujitsu strategy by turning our highly developed communications and transportation systems against us. Given the nihilistic extremism of those attempting to wield these tools against us, it is possible for a small group to cause catastrophic damage, as we have seen from New York to Bali to Mumbai.

In this unpredictable security environment, the Obama administration is doing everything possible to protect our nation, fulfill our security commitments in Iraq and Afghanistan, and deny Al Qaeda safe haven to plot and train for future attacks. As Harold Koh, the State Department's Legal Adviser said here last year, we are committed to pursuing these security imperatives consistent with our values and while complying with all applicable domestic and international law, including the laws of war.

In his Nobel Prize lecture, President Obama promised that the United States would remain "a standard bearer in the conduct of war. That is what makes us different from those whom we fight. That is the source of our strength."

The recent turmoil in the Middle East once again demonstrates the fallacy of trying to divide America's "hard" strategic interests from our "soft" interests, including our commitment to human rights. Human security and national security are inextricably linked. As Roosevelt said, "Freedom from fear is eternally linked with freedom from want." While the United States has important strategic interests in the Middle East, the recent protests demonstrate the centrality of human rights to those interests and the links among civil, political, economic and social rights. As President Obama said last week, the United States has "made clear our support for a set of universal values, and our support for the political and economic change that the people of the region deserve."

Going forward, U.S. policy aims to help the Egyptian people achieve true stability as they build a political system that will honor the aspirations of all citizens—women and men, Muslims and Copts, bloggers and businessmen. Egyptians need the freedom from fear that the State Security police will knock on their door in the night or hack their Facebook pages. And they also need decent jobs for the nearly one-fifth of the population that is still living on less than $2 a day.

As Roosevelt put it, "People who are hungry and out of a job are the stuff of which dictatorships are made."

President Obama echoed this theme in his Nobel Prize speech in December 2009, when he said, "Just peace includes not only civil and political rights—it must encompass economic security and opportunity. For true peace is not just freedom from fear, but freedom from want."

Although the freedom from want is not explicitly contained in the U.S. Constitution, concern about the economic well-being of the American populace is deeply embedded in our nation's history and culture.

After all, in the Preamble to the Constitution, the Framers aimed to "promote the general welfare." From our earliest days, state laws and constitutions sought to promote our people's economic security. And the American Dream is predicated on the belief that allowing individuals to flourish is the best way for our nation to flourish.

Nevertheless, the United States has had reservations about the international debate on economic, social and cultural rights, for reasons I will discuss in a moment.

Certainly the Egyptian activists and government leaders we spoke with last week view political and social rights, transparency and accountability, economic and social progress as inextricably linked. Egypt's Prime Minister described his goals as promoting "freedom, democracy and social justice." Young activists told us the Tahrir Square Revolution was spurred by both the denial of basic political freedoms and the absence of jobs and economic opportunity.

When I met with Egypt's new labor minister, he stressed his efforts to restore workers' rights to free association, which he sees as a prerequisite to building a strong Egyptian economy. And when we met with Coptic Christian leaders, they spoke of a desperate need for educational reforms to combat religious bigotry and sectarian violence. Egyptians see the intersections between these issues as obvious and uncontroversial.

The United States has taken steps to provide for economic, social and cultural rights but we understand them in our own way and, at any given time, we meet them according to our domestic laws—laws that emerge from a political system based on representative democracy, free speech and free assembly.

But since the founding of the U.N., some Americans have worried that the international movement to recognize economic, social and cultural rights would obligate us to provide foreign assistance commitments that went beyond what was decided by the U.S. This has never been true. Human rights law doesn't create an obligation to any particular level of foreign assistance.

The U.S. is a leading contributor to global efforts to alleviate poverty and promote development—not because we have an obligation to but because it is in our interest. We do this through our bilateral aid programs, through our multilateral contributions, and through the American people—who annually contribute financially and through voluntary service to development and humanitarian activities around the world. President Obama has asked Congress for nearly $33 billion for our 2012 core foreign assistance budget and we annually respond to multiple humanitarian crises around the world—from Haiti to Pakistan, from Sudan to Japan. And American citizens and U.S. corporations give much more than the government, year in and year out. We also give through our service. Over the last 50 years, more than 200,000 Americans have served in 177 countries as Peace Corps volunteers.

Some have also been concerned that using the language of human rights could create new domestic legal obligations that would be enforceable through the courts and tie the hands of Congress and the states. But we have been careful to ensure that any international agreements we endorse protect the prerogatives of the federal government, as well as those of our states and localities.

Under the U.S. federal system, states take the lead on many economic, social and cultural policies. For example, all 50 states are committed through their constitutions to providing education for all children. But our federal Constitution makes no mention of rights to education, health care, or social security.

Nevertheless, as my late friend and mentor Professor Louis Henkin wrote, once economic and social rights are granted by law, they cannot be taken away without due process. And these rights also fall under the general requirement that government act rationally and afford equal protection under the law.

Our government's commitment to provide for the basic social and economic needs of our people is clear, and it reflects the will of the American people.

The people ask us to care for the sick . . . and we do. In 2009, our nation spent nearly $900 billion on Medicare and Medicaid. And as you know, last year the administration passed and signed the Affordable Care Act to expand access to health care in America.

They ask us to provide shelter for the destitute . . . and we do. In the wake of the housing crisis, last year the federal government committed almost $4 billion to target homelessness.

They ask us to educate every child, including those with physical and learning disabilities . . . and we do. This year alone, federal, state and local governments will spend close to $600 billion on education.

Some of our suspicion of the international focus on economic, social and cultural rights springs from the misuse of these demands in earlier times. For decades, the Soviet states and the Non-Aligned Movement critiqued the United States for a perceived failure to embrace economic and social rights. They used the rhetoric of economic, social and cultural rights to distract from their human rights abuses. They claimed economic rights trumped political rights, while in fact failing to provide either. We have prioritized political and civil rights because governments that are transparent and respect free speech are stable, secure and sustainable—and do the most for their people.

It is time to move forward. The Obama administration takes a holistic approach to human rights, democracy and development. Human rights do not begin after breakfast. But without breakfast, few people have the energy to make full use of their rights. As Martin Luther King once noted, an integrated lunch counter doesn't help the person who can't afford to eat there.

Therefore, we will work constructively with like-minded delegations to adopt fair and well-reasoned resolutions at the

UN that speak to the issues of economic, social and cultural rights and are consistent with our own laws and policies.

We will do this understanding that these goals must be achieved progressively, given the resources available to each government. But we will also stress that nothing justifies a government's indifference to its own people. And nothing justifies human oppression—not even spectacular economic growth.

When negotiating language on these resolutions and in our explanations of position, we will be guided by the following five considerations:

- First, economic, social and cultural rights addressed in U.N. resolutions should be expressly set forth, or reasonably derived from, the Universal Declaration and the International Covenant on Economic, Social and Cultural Rights. While the United States is not a party to the Covenant, as a signatory, we are committed to not defeating the object and purpose of the treaty.
- Second, we will only endorse language that reaffirms the "progressive realization" of these rights and prohibits discrimination.
- Third, language about enforcement must be compatible with our domestic and constitutional framework.
- Fourth, we will highlight the U.S. policy of providing food, housing, medicine and other basic requirements to people in need.
- And fifth, we will emphasize the interdependence of all rights and recognize the need for accountability and transparency in their implementation, through the democratic participation of the people.

At the same time, the U.S. will not hesitate to reject resolutions that are disingenuous, at odds with our laws, or contravene our policy interests. Just because a resolution is titled "a right to food" doesn't mean it is really about the right to food. Resolutions are not labeling exercises. Rather, they are about substance.

Finally, we will push back against the fallacy that countries may substitute human rights they like for human rights they dislike, by granting either economic or political rights. To assert that a population is not "ready" for universal human rights is to misunderstand the inherent nature of these rights and the basic obligations of governments.

All Four Freedoms are key to the Obama administration approach to human rights, national security and sustainable global prosperity.

For U.S. foreign policy today, freedom from fear means we will continue our efforts to halt the proliferation of weapons of mass destruction. It also means voting for UN Security Council resolution 1973 on Libya last week and joining other countries to enforce the resolution in order to protect Libyan civilians against a brutal regime.

Freedom to worship in foreign policy today means that Secretary Clinton makes a point of defending freedom of religion throughout the world. In Egypt she stressed that democratic transitions will only succeed when Muslims, Copts and Jews all have the opportunity to worship freely and in peace.

Freedom from want in foreign policy today means a U.S. leadership role in a global food security initiative that aims to help subsistence farmers expand their production and developing countries to develop their markets. It also means being the world's leader in global health—providing treatment for those infected by HIV, and strengthening health systems in developing countries. It also includes our recent pledge of $150 million in economic aid and democracy assistance to Egypt to help during this time of transition.

For our domestic policy today, freedom from want means this Administration will keep fighting to bring health care to more Americans, improve education to make our country more competitive, and continue to provide unemployment benefits for those who need them. Despite our budget constraints, we will continue to invest in the future of the American people.

We will also continue to urge other countries to invest in a better future for their citizens. And we stand willing to assist by pursuing an approach to development that respects human rights, involves local stakeholders, promotes transparency and accountability, and builds the institutions that underpin sustainable democracy.

This is in our moral interest, our political interest and our strategic interest. President Obama, in his National Security Strategy, put it in terms Franklin Roosevelt would have approved:

"Democracy does not merely represent our better angels," the President said, "It stands in opposition to aggression and injustice, and our support for universal rights is both fundamental to American leadership and a source of strength in the world."

Thank you.

Source: Four Freedoms Tuns 70 available at U.S. Department of State. http://www.state.gov/j/drl/rls/rm/2011/159195.htm.

I

ILLEGAL IMMIGRATION

Illegal immigration (a subset of *immigration*) has, for decades, been the subject of intense debate in local, state, and national politics in the United States. Seen as a relatively recent phenomenon, most discussions of illegal immigration center on the unauthorized migration of foreign nationals, typically perceived as Latin American, into the United States. In reality, the history of illegal immigration far predates the current controversies and the term itself has a much broader definition. Recent scholarship has demonstrated that the United States, since its founding, has attempted to control through federal and state laws the migrants entering the country and the movement of its own people within the country. Illegal immigration comes in a variety of forms. The best known is the unauthorized entrance of any foreign national into the country. Less well known, but still common, is when a foreign visitor or worker overstays his or her temporary visa and illegally remains in the United States.

During the colonial period, the British government actively worked to construct a loyal population in British North America, discouraging the emigration of Catholics and encouraging that of Protestants. In addition, the British crown passed laws governing the migration of individuals within the colonies. Most significant was the Proclamation of 1763. Issued after Pontiac's War, the Proclamation forbade the migration of Europeans west of the Appalachian Mountains in an attempt to normalize British/Native American relations and avoid further bloodshed. The Proclamation infuriated a wide range of colonists, small farmers, speculators, and politicians, many of whom ignored it, illegally settling the area. This process would be repeated throughout the 18th and 19th centuries as the United States set up Indian reservations throughout the West.

In addition to the Proclamation of 1763, the British crown nullified various attempts by the colonies to restrict the immigration of convicts and African slaves. The Declaration of Independence alludes to these restrictions on migration, as well as the Proclamation of 1763, as justifications for rebelling against the British king.

After the Revolutionary War, many of the U.S. leading politicians and public figures, including James Madison, Thomas Jefferson, and Benjamin Franklin, actively worked to encourage European immigration. Simultaneously, they urged the individual states to pass laws that restricted the immigration of convicted felons. Constitutionally, the argument could be made that the federal government could not pass any laws restricting immigration before 1808, a concession given to the slave states that prevented Congress from ending the slave trade until that date. It therefore fell to the individual states to restrict the immigration of convicts, and by 1790 several had already done so, the first restrictions on immigration in the United States.

Illegal immigrants from Mexico sit next to the tractor-trailer they rode across the border into the United States on Interstate 8, east of San Diego, on May 3, 2008. The U.S. Border Patrol agents found sixty-one men packed into the trailer during an attempt to smuggle them into the United States. (AP Photo/U.S. Border Patrol)

During the 1790s the United States found itself caught in the middle of the conflict between Great Britain and revolutionary France. Federalists supported the British, while Jeffersonian Republicans supported the French. Using anti-French sentiment stirred up by the XYZ Affair and French attacks on American merchant vessels, the Federalists passed the Alien and Sedition Acts. This set of four laws gave the federal government an unprecedented level of power to control the press, detain or deport aliens, and slow down the naturalization of new immigrants.

In 1807, Congress passed its first immigration ban by making it illegal to bring new slaves into the United States after December 31, 1807. Nonetheless, the forced migration of enslaved Africans continued illegally as slavers smuggled in thousands between 1807 and 1865. Illegally imported African slaves therefore may qualify as the first illegal immigrants into the United States. Due to the illegal nature of the trade, numbers are difficult to ascertain, so most scholars study this trade by looking at those ships that were apprehended by authorities. One example is *The Wanderer*, apprehended in 1859 off the coast of Georgia. The ship carried over 400 slaves.

Eleven years after the abolition of the slave trade, Congress passed another major set of regulations on immigration by creating a comprehensive "Passenger Act" that governed the transportation of European immigrants to the United States across the Atlantic. It mandated that incoming ships carry at least five tons of registry for every two passengers, making it more difficult for ships to be dedicated to transporting immigrants, thereby increasing the cost of passage. This, combined with a set of Supreme Court cases, solidly placed immigration under federal control. For the rest of the antebellum period, small-scale illegal immigration continued as captains and immigrants sought to evade immigration controls and avoid paying taxes upon debarkation.

Another notable example of illegal immigration came during the antebellum period when illegal immigration helped to expand U.S. territory. During the first third of the 19th century Southern slaveholders migrated, with their slaves, into Texas. While the Mexican government actively looked to recruit immigrants into its Texan frontier as a way to solidify its control over the area, it forbade the importation of slaves. In spite of its best attempts, Mexico was unable to stop the illegal immigration of slaves. In 1835, Texan slaveholders, unhappy with Mexico's attempts to end slavery and disenfranchise them, declared independence and, ten years later, joined the United States.

In 1850, the federal government passed a more stringent Fugitive Slave Act. Part of the Compromise of 1850, the act actively sought to control migration within the United States. It created a special set of federal marshals tasked with capturing escaped slaves who had migrated to the North in pursuit of freedom. In addition, it ordered state and local governments to desist from any attempts to interfere with the recovery of escaped slaves. State and local governments continued to defy the federal government by assisting escaped slaves. Throughout the next ten years, attempts to enforce the Fugitive Slave Act often met with widespread violent and nonviolent resistance. The tension between local and federal governments is mirrored today in federal attempts to apprehend and deport illegal immigrants, and city/state "sanctuary laws" that keep local law enforcement from apprehending undocumented immigrants.

Prior to 1875, the federal government's attempts to restrict immigration focused largely on the health, criminal history, and financial status of prospective immigrants. The Page Act of 1875 introduced, for the first time, a geographical and racial aspect to the government's immigration policy. It limited the immigration of unskilled laborers from Asia and banned the immigration of any Asian woman suspected of

being a prostitute. Due to the widespread belief among many immigration inspectors that most Asian women, particularly Chinese women, were prostitutes, the Page Act basically cut off any legal immigration of Chinese women. Seven years later, the Chinese Exclusion Act further restricted Asian migration. The Act's reauthorizations in 1892 and 1902 made it even more difficult for the Chinese to legally migrate to the United States. Therefore, the Chinese turned to extralegal means to enter. This included taking advantage of family reunification policies by creating fictional "paper sons" and crossing the U.S.-Canada and U.S.-Mexico border. Many prospective Chinese immigrants landed in Mexico, donned traditional Mexican attire, and entered the United States disguised as Mexicans who, at that time, had no restrictions on their migration.

The Page Act and Chinese Exclusion Act marked the beginning of the era of immigration exclusion, as Congress pushed for more restrictive immigration laws. At the time, the ideas of "scientific racism" held sway over many members of the federal government, leading nativists to devise legislation that limited or ended immigration from Asia, Southern and Eastern Europe, and Africa. In 1891, Congress created the first federal agency dedicated to immigration administration, setting up the Office of the Superintendent of Immigration as part of the Treasury Department. Twelve years later it was moved to the Department of Commerce and Labor, and then in 1913 it became a part of the Department of Labor and, in 1940, a part of the Department of Justice. The organizational shifts reflected the changing nature of immigration enforcement, as lawmakers went from viewing immigration as a matter of revenue to a matter of labor to a matter of enforcement. In 2003, the different bureaus responsible for immigration were consolidated and placed under the newly created Department of Homeland Security.

Although United States instituted a variety of new laws governing immigration late in the 19th century, federal attempts to enforce immigration policy along the U.S.-Mexico and U.S.-Canada borders during that era were few and far between. Rather, they focused their enforcement efforts on the receiving ports at Angel Island in San Francisco and Ellis Island in New York. In 1904, the federal agency in charge of immigration assigned a group of mounted watchmen to patrol the Mexican and Canadian borders. For the next two decades, these patrols focused on apprehending European and Asian immigrants who had avoided immigration agents at Ellis and Angel Islands. In spite of the best efforts of nativists, Mexican immigrants remained immune to most of the immigration restrictions passed during the era of immigration restriction, as powerful Western farmers needed Mexican agricultural labor.

In 1924, immigration restrictionists pushed the National Origins Act through Congress. The act placed stringent quotas on immigration with extensive preference given to immigrants from Northern Europe, while banning East Asian immigration. Immigrants to the United States now needed special visas, the number of which was based on the country from where they came. This created an even greater amount of potential undocumented immigrants. Therefore, Congress supplemented the National Origins Act by budgeting $1 million to create an "additional land-border patrol" and making it a misdemeanor (escalating to a felony for the second offense) to enter the United States without a visa obtained at a valid port of entry.

The onset of the Great Depression in 1929 led to a crackdown on immigration. In a dramatic shift from previous immigration policy, Herbert Hoover's administration decided to target Mexican laborers who had entered the United States without documentation. In an era of unemployment, Mexican immigrants were believed to have taken jobs from Americans. Federal, state, and local governments collaborated with one another and unemployment assistance agencies to identify undocumented Mexicans for deportation. Immigration raids rounded up Mexicans and Mexican Americans who were then forcibly repatriated to Mexico with little regard to their citizenship or legal status. News of the raids rippled through the Mexican immigrant community and thousands "voluntarily" repatriated, taking advantage of the one-way rail fares into Mexico offered by the U.S. government. Mexico's border states were soon overwhelmed with the repatriated, many of whom had grown up in the United States and were unfamiliar with their new country.

After the United States entered World War II, the government shifted its attention from deportation to recruitment. As it drafted Americans into the armed forces, the U.S. government simultaneously recruited Mexican laborers through the Bracero Program. Begun in 1942 and lasting until 1964, the program recruited over 4.5 million Mexican workers. The Bracero Program set specific standards for wages and working conditions. Some American employers circumvented the program's requirements by recruiting undocumented Mexican workers. This practice came under attack in 1954 when the Eisenhower administration initiated "Operation Wetback." The program's racist name originated from the belief that undocumented Mexican laborers avoided official border crossings by swimming across rivers. Under the auspices of "Operation Wetback," government officials deported hundreds of thousands of Mexican immigrants, many of whom had been recruited under the still ongoing Bracero Program.

Though the Bracero Program ended in 1964, the demand for inexpensive Mexican labor did not. Passed a year later, the Immigration and Naturalization Act of 1965 set, for the first time, limits on immigration from the Western Hemisphere. Between 1965 and 1986, it was illegal to immigrate to the United States without authorization, but it was not illegal to employ unauthorized immigrant labor. Therefore, the bulk of unauthorized immigrants who illegally entered the country to meet the American demand for labor were imprisoned, fined, or deported if apprehended, but their employers were not.

This changed in 1986 with the Immigration Reform and Control Act (IRCA). Throughout the 1970s and 1980s, the American public grew more concerned with the growth of illegal immigration and began to identify it with the flow of drugs from Mexico to the United States. This was due in part to a fitful economy, a concern about a "Latino invasion," and the War on Drugs. In contrast to previous immigration scares where Americans had focused on seaports, now Americans looked at their border with Mexico as the main source of unauthorized immigration. In addition, they looked at an overwhelmed immigration system that could not deal with the millions of visa applications it had received. IRCA was the legislative attempt to "solve" the issue. The law took a two-pronged approach to illegal immigration. Recognizing the "pull" of American jobs, the law set up a series of penalties for businesses that employed illegal immigrants. It also offered amnesty to undocumented immigrants who had been in the United States since 1982. The law did little to stop the flow of migrants as the employer penalties were lightly enforced and the amnesty only temporarily resolved the backlog of visa application. This law serves as the reason every new hire in the United States must fill out an I-9 form.

Six years before IRCA, the United States finally harmonized its laws related to refugees with those of the United Nations by allowing immigrants with a "well-founded fear of persecution" based on their race, religion, nationality, political opinion, or social group. This created a new set of illegal immigrants who believed that they met the "well-founded fear" standard but the government did not. Throughout the decade church and immigrant advocacy groups lobbied the federal government and initiated a variety of lawsuits to expand the government's definition of "well-founded fear," particularly in relation to Central Americans fleeing the region's civil wars in the 1980s.

The Immigration Act of 1990 expanded the number of annual visas, set up "Temporary Protected Status" for prospective refugees from El Salvador, and increased the Border Patrol's budget. Three years later, the Border Patrol initiated "Operation Hold the Line," an attempt to secure the border at El Paso. Next year, the plan was expanded to San Diego with "Operation Gatekeeper." The Border Patrol hoped that by sealing off the primary entry points and pushing illegal immigration into the more forbidding Sonoran desert, they would cut down the rate of immigration. The strategy proved costly and ineffective. Illegal immigration continued while the Border Patrol's budget exploded and more than 1,000 immigrants died in the American desert between 1993 and 1997.

The next attempt to address the issue was the Illegal Immigration Reform and Immigrant Responsibility Act of 1996. The act further strengthened penalties for illegal immigration and granted the Border Patrol even more resources. Over the next fifteen years the Border Patrol added night vision cameras, unmanned aircraft, lasers, and a fence hundreds of miles long to the U.S.-Mexico border. Hundreds of jeeps and thousands of agents patrol the border in an attempt to apprehend illegal immigrants and halt the flow of drugs and potential terrorists from entering the United States.

After the terrorist attacks of September 11, 2001, the Border Patrol's mission expanded from catching illegal immigrants to catching terrorists. Immigration and the border were now matters of national security. Therefore, the federal agencies responsible for immigration and border security shifted from the Department of Justice and Department of the Treasury to the newly created Department of Homeland Security. As these two divisions of the federal government pour more resources into securing the border, the region has become more militarized and deportations of apprehended immigrants have increased. Desperate immigrants call on unethical human smugglers in border towns across northern Mexico to help them make the dangerous trip across. In addition, illegal immigrants are less likely to return to their country of birth for fear that they could never reenter the United States.

In the early 21st century, immigration activists have contested the very phrase "illegal immigrant," arguing that only an action, rather than a person, can be "illegal." On April 2, 2013, the Associated Press (AP), one of the world's leading news organizations, announced that it would no longer allow the use of "illegal immigrant" in its stories. Instead, the AP now uses illegal to refer to the action of unauthorized entrance into a country, but describes individuals as people living in a country illegally. Similarly, it views "undocumented" as imprecise, as it is unclear what documents immigrants do not possess.

The recent linguistic complexities of discussing illegal immigration are an indication of the continued importance of the issue. In spite of increased deportations, the militarization of the U.S. border with Mexico and greater funds allocated to the Border Patrol, the Department of Homeland Security in 2009 estimated that more than 10 million unauthorized immigrants lived in the United States, the vast majority of them from North America. As long as the United States legislates who can enter its borders, illegal, undocumented, or unauthorized immigration will continue.

See also

African American Civil Rights Movement; Asian Rights Movement; Chicano Rights; Human Rights; Immigration; Nativism

JOHN ROSINBUM

Further Reading

Balderama, Francisco E., and Raymond Rodriguez. 1995. *Decade of Betrayal: Mexican Repatriation in the 1930s*. Albuquerque, NM: University of New Mexico Press.

Haines, David W., and Karen E. Rosenblum, eds. 1999. *Illegal Immigration in America: A Reference Handbook*. Westport, CT: Greenwood Press.

Hernández, Kelly Lytle. 2010. *Migra: A History of the U.S. Border Patrol*. Berkeley, CA: University of California Press.

Migration Policy Institute. *US in Focus*. http://www. migrationinformation.org/USfocus/. Accessed September 1, 2013.

Illegal Immigration—Primary Documents

Document 1: Introduction

In 1986, the U.S. government attempted to tackle the issue of undocumented immigration with the Immigration Reform and Control Act (IRCA). IRCA offered a "carrot and stick" approach to undocumented immigration, with amnesty for undocumented immigrants present in the United States since 1982 as the carrot and a two-pronged stick that dramatically increased funds for border control and promised harsh penalties for employers of illegal immigrants. The section excerpted here authorizes tens of millions of dollars in new funds for border enforcement. IRCA did little to halt undocumented immigration and many of its employer penalties were rarely enforced. It did, however, begin an era of increased funding for border control. By 2003, the United States had spent over $2.8 billion on the Border Patrol and related offices.

Document 1: Immigration Reform and Control Act (IRCA) (November 6, 1986)

SEC. 111. AUTHORIZATION OF APPROPRIATIONS FOR ENFORCEMENT AND SERVICE ACTIVITIES OF THE IMMIGRATION AND NATURALIZATION SERVICE.

(a) Two Essential Elements.—It is the sense of Congress that two essential elements of the program of immigration control established by this Act are—

(1) an increase in the border patrol and other inspection and enforcement activities of the Immigration and Naturalization Service and of other appropriate Federal agencies in order to prevent and deter the illegal entry of aliens into the United States and the violation of the terms of their entry, and

(2) an increase in examinations and other service activities of the Immigration and Naturalization Service and other appropriate Federal agencies in order to ensure prompt and efficient adjudication of petitions and applications provided for under the Immigration and Nationality Act.

(b) Increased Authorization of Appropriations for INS and EOIR.—In addition to any other amounts authorized to be appropriated, in order to carry out this Act there are authorized to be appropriated to the Department of Justice—

(1) for the Immigration and Naturalization Service, for fiscal year 1987, $422,000,000, and for fiscal year 1988, $419,000,000; and

(2) for the Executive Office of Immigration Review, for fiscal year 1987, $12,000,000, and for fiscal year 1988, $15,000,000.

Of the amounts authorized to be appropriated under paragraph (1) sufficient funds shall be available to provide for an increase in the border patrol personnel of the Immigration and Naturalization Service so that the average level of such personnel in each of fiscal years 1987 and 1988 is at least 50 percent higher than such level for fiscal year 1986.

(c) Use of Funds for Improved Services.—Of the funds appropriated to the Department of Justice for the Immigration and Naturalization Service, the Attorney General shall provide for improved immigration and naturalization services and for enhanced community outreach and in-service training of personnel of the Service. Such enhanced community outreach may include the establishment of appropriate local community taskforces to improve the working relationship between the Service and local community groups and organizations (including employers and organizations representing minorities).

(d) Supplemental Authorization of Appropriations for Wage and Hour Enforcement.—There are authorized to be appropriated, in addition to such sums as may be available for such purposes, such sums as may be necessary to the Department of Labor for enforcement activities of the Wage and Hour Division and the Office of Federal Contract Compliance Programs within the Employment Standards Administration of the Department in order to deter the employment of unauthorized aliens and remove the economic incentive for employers to exploit and use such aliens.

Source: Immigration, Reform and Control Act, available at https://www.govtrack.us/congress/bills/99/s1200.

Document 2: Introduction

Signed by Republican governor Jan Brewer in April 2010, Arizona's Support Our Law Enforcement and Safe Neighborhoods Act (originally Arizona Senate Bill 1070 and thus popularly known as Arizona SB 1070) was, at the time of its passage, the broadest and strictest state anti-illegal immigration law in the United States. Although being in the United States illegally was already a federal misdemeanor, this Arizona law also made it a state misdemeanor for any alien to be in Arizona without the proper documentation. The law also required state law enforcement officers to determine an individual's immigration status if during a "lawful stop, detention, or arrest" they had a reasonable suspicion that the person being detained was an illegal immigrant. The law was extremely controversial, raising questions of state interference in federal immigration enforcement and charges of racial profiling by state law enforcement officers. Scheduled to take effect on July 29, 2010, the most controversial parts of the measure were blocked by various legal challenges, including a lawsuit filed by the U.S. Department of Justice. In June 2012, in the case Arizona v. United States, *the U.S. Supreme Court upheld the provision calling for checks of immigration status during law enforcement stops, but struck down several other provisions because they clashed with federal law.*

Document 2: Arizona's Support Our Law Enforcement and Safe Neighborhoods Act (Arizona SB 1070) (April 23, 2010)

Cooperation and assistance in enforcement of immigration laws; indemnification

A. No official or agency of this state or a county, city, town or other political subdivision of this state may adopt a policy that limits or restricts the enforcement of federal immigration laws to less than the full extent permitted by federal law.

B. For any lawful contact made by a law enforcement official or agency of this state or a county, city, town or other political subdivision of this state where reasonable suspicion exists that the person is an alien who is unlawfully present in the United States, a reasonable attempt shall be made, when practicable, to determine the immigration status of the person. The person's immigration status shall be verified with the federal government pursuant to 8 United States code section 1373(c).

C. If an alien who is unlawfully present in the United States is convicted of a violation of state or local law, on discharge from imprisonment or assessment of any fine that is imposed, the alien shall be transferred immediately to the custody of the United States immigration and customs enforcement or the United States customs and border protection.

D. Notwithstanding any other law, a law enforcement agency may securely transport an alien who is unlawfully present in the United States and who is in the agency's custody to a federal facility in this state or to any other point of transfer into federal custody that is outside the jurisdiction of the law enforcement agency.

E. A law enforcement officer, without a warrant, may arrest a person if the officer has probable cause to believe that the person has committed any public offense that makes the person removable from the United States.

F. Except as provided in federal law, officials or agencies of this state and counties, cities, towns and other political subdivisions of this state may not be prohibited or in any way be restricted from sending, receiving or maintaining information relating to the immigration status of any individual or exchanging that information with any other federal, state or local governmental entity for the following official purposes:

1. Determining eligibility for any public benefit, service or license provided by any federal, state, local or other political subdivision of this state.
2. Verifying any claim of residence or domicile if determination of residence or domicile is required under the laws of this state or a judicial order issued pursuant to a civil or criminal proceeding in this state.
3. Confirming the identity of any person who is detained.
4. If the person is an alien, determining whether the person is in compliance with the federal registration laws prescribed by title II, chapter 7 of the federal immigration and Nationality act.

G. A person may bring an action in superior court to challenge any official or agency of this state or a county, city, town or other political subdivision of this state that adopts or implements a policy that limits or restricts the enforcement of federal immigration laws to less than the full extent permitted by federal law. If there is a judicial finding that an entity has violated this section, the court shall order any of the following:

1. That the person who brought the action recover court costs and attorney fees.

2. That the entity pay a civil penalty of not less than one thousand dollars and not more than five thousand dollars for each day that the policy has remained in effect after the filing of an action pursuant to this subsection.

H. A court shall collect the civil penalty prescribed in subsection G and remit the civil penalty to the department of public safety for deposit in the gang and immigration intelligence team enforcement mission fund established by section 41-1724.

I. A law enforcement officer is indemnified by the law enforcement officer's agency against reasonable costs and expenses, including attorney fees, incurred by the officer in connection with any action, suit or proceeding brought pursuant to this section to which the officer may be a party by reason of the officer being or having been a member of the law enforcement agency, except in relation to matters in which the officer is adjudged to have acted in bad faith.

J. This section shall be implemented in a manner consistent with federal laws regulating immigration, protecting the civil rights of all persons and respecting the privileges and immunities of United States citizens.

Source: http://www.azleg.gov/legtext/49leg/2r/bills/sb1070s.pdf.

IMMIGRATION

Immigration is one of the defining characteristics of the United States of America. The vast majority of its citizens are descendants of immigrants who arrived in the United States following the Revolutionary War and debates over immigration often reflect ongoing concerns in American society and politics. The word *immigration* in American history is traditionally understood as foreign nationals arriving in America, but America also has an important history of migration from America (emigration) and migration within America (migration). Notable examples include Mexican Repatriation (emigration) and the Oregon Trail (migration). This encyclopedia topic will largely focus on immigration to America from abroad—an immigration that continues to the present.

Historians are unsure of the exact date and method of the arrival of the first Native Americans in North America, but most agree with a reasonable degree of certainty that by 25,000 BCE, immigrants from Asia had crossed the Bering Sea and populated North America. Climate change and geological shift largely isolated the Americas from Eurasia until Columbus's voyage of "discovery" in 1492. The Spanish established the first permanent European settlement in North America in 1565 in St. Augustine, Florida. In 1598 Don Juan de Oñate led an expedition to colonize New Mexico. Nearly ten years later, British colonists settled in Jamestown, Virginia. In 1620, the Pilgrims founded the Plymouth Colony in Massachusetts. Swedish and Dutch colonists established small colonies in present-day Connecticut, Delaware, and New York during the early 17th century. French traders and priests set up trading posts and missions along the St. Lawrence River and gradually moved south into the Great Lakes region along the shores of Lakes Ontario, Huron, Michigan, and Superior. Though the Spanish established the oldest colonies, comparatively few immigrants from Europe or Africa arrived in their colonies in the Southwest. Immigrants from Western Africa and Northwestern Europe landing along the continent's Eastern seaboard formed the lion's share of North America's arrivals for the next two hundred years.

Initially, European immigrants to Eastern North America believed that they had come to a sparsely settled land. In reality, a few decades earlier, British North America had been heavily populated but the unintentional introduction of European diseases by explorers led to the collapse of many Native American groups. As more immigrants, hungry for land, arrived, they negotiated with Native American groups for their territory, often resorting to violence. In the face of violence, Native American survivors migrated west.

More than 800 Columbus area residents from eighty-eight countries participate in a U.S. citizenship ceremony as they become new citizens, April 29, 2005, in Columbus, Ohio. The state's largest naturalization ceremony put Ohio closer to achieving a goal of the George W. Bush administration of eliminating long citizen application delays. (AP Photo/Kiichiro Sato)

Pursuing new lands, European settlers followed them, continuing a cycle that lasted until the last decades of the 19th century.

Between 1619 and 1865, American, British, Dutch, French, Portuguese, and Spanish slavers brought over 380,000 African slaves to British North America as part of the Trans-Atlantic slave trade. Taken from their homes in western and central Africa by raiding parties, Africans were placed in holding cells known as barracoons along the African coast, awaiting sale to European slave ships. On the ships they endured horrific conditions, packed together in utter squalor. About one-eighth of those who boarded died by the conclusion of the (on average) two-month voyage. On January 1, 1808, the United States officially ended its citizens' participation in the Trans-Atlantic slave trade, but the domestic slave trade continued through the antebellum period. Immigration from

Africa to the United States remained quite low for the next hundred years.

European immigration slowed dramatically between 1775 and 1820 due first to the upheaval wrought by the Revolutionary War (1775–1781) and then the emigration restrictions put in place by European countries during the Napoleonic Wars (1803–1815). In 1790, Congress passed the Naturalization Act, which allowed any "free white persons" possessing "good moral character" who had resided for two years in the United States to take an oath of allegiance and become a naturalized citizen. Future discriminatory immigration legislation like the Chinese Exclusion Act of 1882 leaned heavily on this law.

After the conclusion of the Napoleonic Wars in 1815, European immigration increased significantly. The largest group of European immigrants would be Irish. Though Irish immigration is most commonly associated with the potato famine, nearly a half million Irish men and women arrived in the United States between 1820 and 1845. They worked in construction on America's first great transportation project, the Erie Canal, and as day laborers in the North's factories and domestics in the great homes of Boston and New York. In 1845 a fungus called *Phytophthora infestans* infected Ireland's potato crop, causing a massive famine. The fungus returned a year later with devastating results, destroying the majority of Ireland's food supply. When farmers ate the "seed potatoes" they had reserved for the next year, the famine only worsened in 1847. This inspired massive waves of emigration from Ireland.

Between 1845 and 1855 nearly 2 million people immigrated from Ireland, 1.5 million of whom chose the United States as their final destination. Similar to the pre-famine migration, most Irish famine immigrants settled in Northeastern cities. The Catholicism of Irish immigrants troubled many influential Protestants in American cities, and led, in part, to the rise of nativist and anti-Catholic sentiment crystallized in political organizations such as the Know-Nothing Party of the 1850s.

Irish immigration continued after the famine, but was joined by significant immigration from Central and Northern Europe. Between 1851 and 1900, more than 3.9 million Protestants, Catholics, and Jews came from the territory that, in 1871, became Germany. A more religiously diverse group than the predominantly Catholic Irish, German immigrants settled throughout the United States. Prominent German communities sprung up in Midwestern cities like Milwaukee and St. Louis, while farmers settled in the Midwest and West. Some Germans went as far west as California, in pursuit of gold. Less numerous, Scandinavian immigrants started arriving in the early 19th century, but their immigration picked up in the 1860s and continued into the 20th century, peaking in the 1880s, when over 650,000 immigrants landed in the United States. Most settled in the Great Plains and the upper Midwest in farming communities.

While millions of Irish and Northern European immigrants arrived on the U.S. Eastern seaboard, the country obtained approximately 500,000 square miles of new territory from Mexico through the Treaty of Guadalupe-Hidalgo, which concluded the Mexican-American War (1846–1848). The treaty promised property rights and U.S. citizenship to the 80,000 Mexican citizens living in the massive region, which included most of the present-day states of California, Arizona, New Mexico, Utah, Nevada, and Utah, as well as parts of Colorado and Wyoming. For many Mexicans these promises turned empty as U.S. courts ignored their land and property claims.

On January 24, 1848, while the treaty was still being negotiated, James W. Marshall, a carpenter from New Jersey, discovered gold in Northern California. A year later, President James K. Polk boasted of the discovery in his State of the Union address. Tens of thousands of immigrants, popularly known as the 49ers, rushed to California, coming from the Eastern United States, Latin America, Europe, and East Asia. California's population exploded, with the 1850 census counting more than 90,000 non-native residents, up from the approximately 13,000 non-native residents estimated to live in California in 1847. Two years later, California conducted a state census, counting more than 300,000 residents. After the rush, many of those who did not strike it rich in the gold fields stayed in California, working the farms and railroads that drew more immigrant labor during the 1860s.

Much of California's labor came from East Asia, first from China and then from Japan. Both the "pull" of previous immigrants' tales of the wealth to be had in America and the promises of unscrupulous labor agents, and the "push" of high taxes, floods and political upheaval at home prompted extensive Chinese immigration to the United States between 1860 and 1882. Once they reached California, some Chinese immigrants tried mining, but most found that anti-Chinese discrimination made filing mining claims nearly impossible. Therefore, they turned to other professions, running various small businesses and working for the railroad companies that were such a large part of California's economy from the 1860s to the end of the century. California passed a variety of anti-Chinese measures including a "foreign miners tax" that presaged the federal government's Page Act of 1875 and Chinese Exclusion Act of 1882. The Page Act of 1875 denied entry to any East Asian woman suspected of being a prostitute. Widely misunderstood, the Chinese Exclusion Act did not bar all Chinese citizens from entry; rather, it stopped unskilled Chinese immigration and denied all Chinese citizens residing in the United States the ability to apply for citizenship. Some skilled laborers were allowed in, and those living in the United States could reenter. The exemptions within the

1882 Act were written out in subsequent reauthorizations in 1892 and 1902. Chinese immigrants found a variety of ways around the Exclusion Acts, from creating "paper sons" who used American family unification policies to landing in Mexico and crossing the U.S. border with Mexico illegally.

While a small group of Japanese immigrants came to the United States prior to the 1890s, it was not until the annexation of Hawaii that Japanese immigrants began to arrive in large numbers. From 1900 to 1930, the Japanese/Japanese American population in the United States grew from 24,000 to 138,000, most residing on the West Coast. Often highly successful, Japanese immigrants owned large farms in California's Sacramento Delta, small businesses in Los Angeles, and fisheries along the West Coast in spite of facing discrimination similar to that borne by the Chinese. Unlike the Chinese, Japanese immigrants came from a country whose military remained strong and took formal discrimination as an insult. Thus, U.S. policy makers like Theodore Roosevelt did their best to prevent a "Japanese Exclusion Act." Instead, Roosevelt negotiated a "Gentleman's Agreement" in 1907 that slowed Japanese immigration while permitting both nations to save face.

Japanese and Chinese immigrants were not the only groups facing immigration restrictions at the turn of the century. As more than 17 million immigrants landed in the country between 1890 and 1920, immigration restrictionists expressed concern about the supposed "racial inferiority" of Southern and Eastern European immigrants. In addition, they claimed that these new immigrants were unwilling and unable to assimilate into American life—an accusation they also directed at Chinese and Japanese immigrants. They pointed to relatively high rates of return migration (sometimes reaching close to 50 percent), radical political ideologies (Polish anarchists were blamed for the Haymarket bombings), and immigrants' general lack of education. In 1917, restrictionists succeeded in passing a literacy test for incoming immigrants. Restrictionists' greatest triumph came in 1924 with the creation of the Border Patrol, and the passage of the Oriental Exclusion Act and the Immigration Act of 1924. These two acts banned any immigration from East Asia and instituted immigration quotas based on the percentage of foreign-born in the United States in 1890. Restrictionists chose 1890 because most Southern and Eastern European immigrants arrived after that date. This skewed the quotas toward immigrants from Northern and Western Europe. In response to labor market demands, the law put no limits on immigration from the Western Hemisphere.

During the Great Depression of the 1930s, Americans turned even more restrictionist, advocating policies that not only banned immigration but actively sent former immigrants back to their home countries. The most famous of these was Mexican Repatriation. Between 1929 and 1937 more than 450,000 Mexicans and Mexican Americans voluntarily and involuntarily returned to Mexico. Vigilante groups of European Americans in the Southwest evicted people of Mexican descent, paying no attention to their legal status. State and local governments also collaborated with the Federal Bureau of Immigration on immigration raids that forcibly deported Mexicans and Mexican-Americans.

U.S. policy toward Mexican immigrants shifted during World War II. Agricultural labor shortages brought on by soldiers leaving for the war led to the creation of the Bracero Program, which recruited Mexican citizens for temporary work permits. The program continued well after the war, finally ending in 1964. World War II brought other changes in immigration policy as "war brides" and "war husbands" married to servicemen and women were allowed into the United States under specific acts.

The destruction wrought by World War II created a massive set of displaced people in Europe and East Asia who sought refuge in the United States. Worried that the United States was about to be flooded by a host of inassimilable and penniless refugees, restrictionists succeeded in passing the 1952 Immigration and Nationality Act (McCarran-Walter Act), which abolished the 1790 law that limited citizenship to "free white persons" while hardening the immigration quotas established in 1924. The McCarran-Walter Act passed in spite of President Harry Truman's veto. Truman warned that restricting immigration was counterproductive to the U.S. goals during the Cold War, as isolation spelled disaster in the worldwide battle for countries' hearts and minds. Growing awareness of this fact, combined with the civil rights movement, led to the passage of the 1965 Immigration and Nationality Act, which ended the racist quotas that preferred European immigration and granted some special visas for refugees, primarily those fleeing communism in Eastern Europe. In addition, it provided special visas for "highly skilled" immigrants who possessed the scientific expertise and advanced degrees necessary for a modern economy.

The end of the restrictionist national origins quotas meant a substantial increase in immigrants from Africa, Asia, and Latin America. In addition, family unification policies brought in more immigrants than ever before. Though intended for Eastern Europeans, the 1965 refugee provisions let in tens of thousands of refugees fleeing from failed U.S. interventions in Iran, Vietnam, Cuba, and more. By the late 1970s, government officials began to realize what refugee advocates had said for years: the country's approach to refugees was outdated and out of step with the refugee system set up in 1951 and 1967 by the United Nations. They began a multiyear process that culminated in the Refugee Act of 1980. The act promised refugee status (and admission into the United States) to those individuals who possessed a "well-founded fear of persecution" based on their race, religion, nationality, social group or political opinion. Though the Refugee Act provided a legal framework for refugee decisions, the meaning of "well-founded fear" remained open to interpretation. Activists, refugees and government officials battled over the meaning of these three words in courtrooms, newspapers and churches.

The government categorized those who were fleeing civil wars and did not receive refugee status as "illegal immigrants." Other illegal immigrants included immigrants from around the world who entered the country illegally in search of economic opportunity and tourists who overstayed their visa. Illegal immigration grew in volume during the 1980s and 1990s, reaching a high point in the first decade of the 21st century, prior to the Great Recession. The American public focused most of its attention on illegal immigration on Latin American immigrants crossing the border with Mexico. Congress took a variety of actions to try and deal with the "problem," passing major legislation in 1986, 1990, and 1996. The 1986 Immigration Control and Reform Act is best remembered for its amnesty provisions, which offered undocumented immigrants legal status if they had lived continuously in the country since 1982. Less remembered, as it was only lightly enforced, was its inauguration of employer sanctions, which threatened to fine or imprison those who knowingly employed undocumented immigrants. This led to the I-9 statement all employees must sign before employment. The 1990 Immigration and 1996 Illegal

Immigration Reform and Immigrant Responsibility Acts attempted to further strengthen employment penalties and provide more resources to the Border Patrol along the Southern border. Neither proved to substantially hinder illegal immigration, and it was not until the economic downturn of the Great Recession that the rate of undocumented immigration decreased.

President George W. Bush (2001–2009), in tandem with many immigration advocates, hoped for further reform of the system, but met substantial legislative roadblocks and declined to go any further. President Barack Obama (2009–) attempted to enact immigration reform by offering a "path to citizenship" for undocumented immigrants, measures to strengthen border security, and to increase the amount of visas for highly skilled immigrants.

Today, the United States continues to be a nation of immigrants, with one of the largest percentages of foreign-born residents (13 percent) in nearly a century. The importance of immigration to the United States as a political, social, and cultural topic shows little sign of decreasing.

See also

Asian Rights Movement; Illegal Immigration; Nativism

JOHN ROSINBUM

Further Reading

Daniels, Roger. 2002. *Coming to America: A History of Immigration and Ethnicity in American Life*. New York: Harper Perennial.

Tichenor, Daniel J. 2002. *Dividing Lines: The Politics of Immigration Control in America*. Princeton, NJ: Princeton University Press.

Voyages Database. 2010. *Voyages: The Trans-Atlantic Slave Trade Database*. http://slavevoyages.org. Accessed April 18, 2014.

Zolberg, Aristide R. 2008. *A Nation by Design: Immigration Policy in the Fashioning of America*. Cambridge, MA: Harvard University Press.

Immigration—Primary Document

Introduction

The Immigration Act of 1924, also known as the Johnson-Reed Act, established a permanent system of immigration quotas system, reducing the temporary immigration quotas created in 1921 by more than half. The act also reduced the immigration limit from 3 to 2 percent of each foreign-born group living in the United States in 1890. By using that year, the law ignored the wave of Southern and Eastern European immigrants who came into the country between 1900 and

1920, thus preventing the quotas from realistically reflecting the actual numbers of foreign-born in the United States from those regions. Reproduced here is the enabling proclamation issued by President Calvin Coolidge, which set the initial quotas for each immigrant group.

Document: Proclamation by President Calvin Coolidge Setting Quotas Under the Immigration Act of 1924

Whereas it is provided in the act of Congress approved May 26, 1924, entitled "An act to limit the immigration of aliens into the United States, and for other purposes" that "The annual quota of any nationality shall be two per centum of the number of foreign-born individuals of such nationality resident in continental United States as determined by the United States Census of 1890, but the minimum quota of any nationality shall be 100 (Sec. 11 a). . . .

"The Secretary of State, the Secretary of Commerce, and the Secretary of Labor, jointly, shall, as soon as feasible after the enactment of this act, prepare a statement showing the number of individuals of the various nationalities resident in continental United States as determined by the United States Census of 1890, which statement shall be the population basis for the purposes of subdivision (a) of section 11 (Sec. 12 b).

"Such officials shall, jointly, report annually to the President the quota of each nationality under subdivision (a) of section 11, together with the statements, estimates, and revisions provided for in this section. The President shall proclaim and make known the quotas so reported". (Sec. 12 e).

Now, therefore I, Calvin Coolidge, President of the United States of America acting under and by virtue of the power in me vested by the aforesaid act of Congress, do hereby proclaim and make known that on and after July 1, 1924, and throughout the fiscal year 1924–1925, the quota of each nationality provided in said act shall be as follows:

COUNTRY OR AREA OF BIRTH QUOTA 1924–25

Afghanistan 100

Albania 100

Andorra 100

Arabian Peninsula 100

Armenia 124

Australia (incl. Papua, Tasmania & all islands) 121

Austria 785

Belgium 512

Bhutan 100

Bulgaria 100

Cameroon (proposed British mandate) 100

Cameroon (French mandate) 100

China 100

Czechoslovakia 3,073

Danzig, Free City of 228

Denmark 789

Egypt 100

Estonia 124

Ethiopia (Abyssinia) 100

Finland 170

France 3,954

Germany 51,227

Great Britain & Northern Ireland 34,007

Greece 100

Hungary 473

Iceland 100

India 100

Iraq (Mesopotamia) 100

Irish Free State 28,567

Italy (incl. Rhodes, Dodecanesia & Castellorizzo) 3,845

Japan 100

Latvia 142

Liberia 100

Liechtenstein 100

Lithuania 344

Luxemburg 100

Monaco 100

Morocco (French & Spanish Zones & Tangier) 100

Muscat (Oman) 100

Nauru (proposed British mandate) 100

Nepal 100

Netherlands 1,648

New Zealand (incl. appertaining islands) 100

Norway 6,453

New Guinea (& other Pacific islands under Australian mandate) 100

Palestine (with Trans-Jordan, proposed British mandate) 100

Persia 100

Poland 5,982

Portugal 503

Ruanda & Urundi (Belgium mandate) 100

Rumania 603

Russia (European & Asiatic) 2,248

Samoa, Western (proposed mandate of New Zealand) 100

San Marino 100

Siam 100

South Africa, Union of 100

South West Africa (proposed mandate of Union of South Africa) 100

Spain 131

Sweden 9,561

Switzerland 2,081

Syria & The Lebanon (French mandate) 100

Tanganiyika (proposed British mandate) 100

Togoland (proposed British mandate) 100

Togoland (French mandate) 100

Turkey 100

Yap & other Pacific islands (under Japanese Mandate 100

Yugoslavia 671

GENERAL NOTE.-The immigration quotas assigned to the various countries and quota-areas should not be regarded as having any political significance whatever, or as involving recognition of new governments, or of new boundaries, or of transfers of territory except as the United States Government has already made such recognition in a formal and official manner.... Calvin Coolidge.

> **Source:** *Statutes at Large of the United States of America, from December, 1923 to March, 1925.* Vol. XLII, Part 1. Washington, DC: Government Printing Office, 1925, pp. 153–169. Available online at http://www.upa.pdx.edu/IMS/currentprojects/TAHv3/Content/PDFs/Immigration_Act_1924.pdf.

IMPERIALISM

The founders of the United States denounced imperialism as an ancient evil. Much of the debate over the composition and adaptation of the Constitution (1787) concerned the powers of the federal government, which some delegates feared would become a quasi-monarchial regime with power concentrated at the center. Benjamin Franklin even derided the adoption of the bald eagle as a national symbol for its ancient association with imperial grandeur. Rome was ever in the minds of the republic's framers, but the Roman Republic, not imperial Rome, was the model for the new nation.

Measured against the ancient empires of Greece and Rome, the "New World" conquests of Spain, and the overseas empires of Great Britain and France, the United States was not an imperial power during its first century. The new republic expanded across the Western frontier, settling areas thinly populated by native peoples and French and Spanish colonists. Even this territorial expansion was not without controversy. Thomas Jefferson spoke of an "Empire of Liberty" in the "New World" and negotiated the Louisiana Purchase (1803), adding 828,000 square miles to the United States but condemned by opponents as unconstitutional because the national charter made no specific provision for American expansion. Journalist John L. O'Sullivan coined the term "Manifest Destiny" in an 1845 article that proclaimed "our manifest destiny [is] to overspread the continent allotted by Providence for the free development of our yearly multiplying millions." Manifest Destiny was invoked to justify the annexation of Texas (1845) and the Mexican-American War (1846–1848) actions that transformed the United States into a transcontinental power but also generated heated debate. Ralph Waldo Emerson condemned the Mexican War, but Walt Whitman praised "the great mission of peopling the New World with a noble race."

The comparisons and contrasts with America's westward expansion and the eastward march of the Russian Empire in the 18th and 19th centuries are instructive. Like the United States, Russia pushed toward the Pacific Ocean in a seemingly inevitable reach of power at the expense of weaker empires and native peoples. But with only a few exceptions, Russian settlers did not enjoy the fruits of self-rule but remained under the direct control of the central government.

The United States established a different polity for its citizens with the Northwest Ordinance (1787). Setting the precedent for how the American West would be governed, the ordinance provided for the eventual creation of new states in the frontier lands after a period of territorial tutelage under federal authority. Although the ordinance prohibited slavery within the Northwest Territory, it was generally assumed that settlers of European descent would constitute the citizenry of the new states. The spread of slavery in the new states outside the boundary of the Northwest Territory became one of

Colonel Theodore Roosevelt and his Rough Riders pose at the summit of San Juan Hill in 1898. The Rough Riders, also known as the 1st U.S. Volunteer Cavalry Regiment, were recruited largely by Roosevelt and consisted of a varied assortment of both upper- and lower-class citizen soldiers. (Library of Congress)

the issues leading to the Civil War. The U.S. policy toward the indigenous Indian nations mirrored the imperial expansion by European powers elsewhere in the world, and was likewise based on assumptions of racial or cultural superiority. American Indians were organized into reservations under federal control and were not automatically granted citizenship until 1924.

In an 1823 message to Congress, President James Monroe committed the United States to resisting any effort by European powers to reclaim the Spanish and Portuguese colonies in Latin America that had recently declared independence,

or to establish new colonies anywhere in the "New World". Although the Monroe Doctrine was an ineffective deterrent against European intrigue through much of the 19th century, it established the idea that the United States was the principal power with particular rights in the Western Hemisphere.

Although the U.S. government remained wary of expanding beyond North America, private freebooters or "filibusters" dreamed of conquest in Latin America. John L. O'Sullivan raised money for an unsuccessful invasion of Cuba in one of many failed schemes to occupy territories in the "New World." William Walker, the most notorious filibuster, landed in

Nicaragua in 1855 at the head of a small army of adventurers. He had been invited by the losing party in a recent Nicaraguan election but quickly pushed aside his hosts and installed himself as the country's president. Walker claimed the "regeneration" of Nicaragua as his mission, but laid plans to reintroduce slavery and establish a new racial hierarchy with White Anglo-Saxon Protestant settlers at the top. In 1857, Walker was driven out by the combined armies of Central America with the financial aid of Cornelius Vanderbilt, who was angered by Walker's nationalization of his Nicaraguan assets. In 1860, Walker invaded Honduras, but was captured and executed.

When Secretary of State William H. Seward negotiated the purchase from Russia of Alaska (1867), the United States acquired a territory one-fifth as large as the rest of the country. The treaty won Senate approval with great difficulty and was ridiculed as "Seward's Folly." Alaska was regarded as remote from America's interests. Only as the 19th century ended did the United States eagerly assume the role of empire in the sense of governing overseas territories with indigenous populations. Empire building was still anathema to many politicians, including President Grover Cleveland, President Benjamin Harrison, and perennial candidate William Jennings Bryan, yet an influential lobby of Americans began to press for expansion. They included Henry Cabot Lodge, Alfred T. Mahan, and Theodore Roosevelt.

The race to claim the world's remaining "backward" lands crystallized at the Berlin Conference (1884–1885), where the major European powers met to carve up Africa. The United States was represented at the conference but refused to sign the final agreement, a gesture in keeping with America's long-standing discomfort with the idea of empire. The United States was invited to Berlin because of its role in Liberia, Africa's first and at the time only republic. Liberia's roots were planted by the American Colonization Society (ACS), acting on the idea, expressed by Thomas Jefferson as early as 1777, that emancipated slaves could be removed to some place outside the United States. ACS was a philanthropic and quasi-official organization; its first expedition to the West African coast (1821) was supported by a congressional grant and a naval escort. It was a peculiarly 19th-century American enterprise, a private-public venture mixing racism, social benevolence, and evangelical Christianity.

Reminiscent of treaties with Indian nations in North America, ACS agents and U.S. Navy officers purchased the Windward Coast from local chiefs with tobacco, rum, looking glasses, and beads. Before long, the thousands of freed American slaves were settled in the colony, fought the native Africans, and reduced them to servitude. With the U.S. government denying any territorial ambitions in Africa, Liberia operated under the paternalistic rule of an ACS governor until it was granted independence in 1847. The United States occasionally cited "special ties" with Liberia and acted half-heartedly on its behalf against European encroachment. Theodore Roosevelt took greater interest in the republic than his predecessors, sending U.S. Army officers to command Liberia's defense forces and taking charge of its customs service. In a 1924 deal brokered by the State Department, Firestone Rubber Company obtained a ninety-nine year lease on a million acres of land for a rubber plantation along with other concessions, making the American corporation a dominant force in the country's political and economic life.

The rise of an explicitly imperialist ethos in the United States coincided with the final subjugation of the American Indians at Wounded Knee (1890) and the publication of Frederick Jackson Turner's seminal essay, "The Significance of the Frontier in American History" (1893). Turner was alarmed that America had reached the limits of its natural boundaries; America's distinctive system "gained new strength each time it touched a new frontier" he wrote. The imperialist lobby believed the United States would have to look elsewhere in the world if the mission of forging a distinct national spirit would continue.

Tempted by the prospect of extending the frontier into the Pacific islands, as well as exploiting natural resources and cheap labor, the imperialists welcomed the overthrow of the Hawaiian monarchy by American planter-settlers (1893) and, over the objection of President Cleveland, pushed for the islands' annexation by the United States (1898). A Darwinian spirit of competition, in which the survival of nations depended on the power and prestige of dominating distant parts of the world, fueled America's growing appetite for colonies. In 1899, the United States acquired American Samoa in a treaty with Great Britain and Germany.

In the same period, the United States seized an empire through dramatic military action in the Spanish-American War. In the Pacific, the United States gained the Philippines and Guam, and in the Caribbean, Puerto Rico and a protectorate over Cuba. The ratification of the peace treaty with Spain, which provided for the transfer of its overseas colonies to the United States, provoked sharp debate in the Senate over the desirability of imperialism, but flush with pride in victory, the imperialists carried the vote. Filipino rebels had been fighting the Spanish since 1896 and proclaimed an independent republic under Emilio Aguinaldo, but the United States refused to recognize the new nation and moved to crush resistance.

A commission appointed by President William McKinley reported that "the government of the Philippines would speedily lapse into anarchy" and fall into the hands of other powers if the United States did not assume control of the islands. "Only through American occupation, therefore, is the idea of a free, self-governing, and united Philippine commonwealth at all conceivable. And the indispensable need from the Filipino point of view of maintaining American sovereignty over the archipelago is recognized by all intelligent Filipinos and even by those insurgents who desire an American protectorate," the report continued. The "national honor" of the United States was invoked and the commission promised that a colonial regime "will prove the greatest blessing to the peoples of the Philippine Islands."

The Philippines Insurrection, or Philippines-American War, was America's first jungle counterinsurgency. The U.S Army operated with few restraints, interned civilians in concentration camps, and employed torture. The Insurrection was declared over in 1901 with the capture of Aguinaldo and his oath of allegiance to the United States, but small bands of "Irreconcilables" continued the guerrilla war for several years, and the United States also put down a rebellion by the Moros, the island chain's Muslim population (1904–1913).

Newspaper reports of brutality by U.S. troops turned the Insurrection into a topic of debate and fueled the American Anti-Imperialist League led by William Jennings Bryan and Andrew Carnegie. Mark Twain condemned U.S. policy in the islands. "I thought we should act as their protector—not try to get them under our heel," he wrote of the Filipinos. Some U.S. politicians opposed the extension of colonialism less in the interest of democratic ideals than from fear that it would open the continental United States to an influx of nonwhite immigrants.

Theodore Roosevelt had played a prominent role in the Spanish-American War as assistant secretary of the navy

and as colonel in the "Rough Riders." Upon succeeding to the presidency after McKinley's assassination (1901), his advocacy of empire gained a higher bully pulpit. Roosevelt was adamant that an American empire was not oxymoronic but in the nation's best interests and traditions. He had studied under historian John W. Burgess at Columbia, who may have imbued him with belief in the special ability of Anglo-Saxons to rule "backward peoples." Like Rudyard Kipling, Roosevelt was eager to take up "the white man's burden." Speaking at Oxford University in 1910, he praised the "white race" for spurring the "unexampled advance of civilized mankind over the world." In a Messianic American spirit that would be invoked a century later to justify the invasion of Iraq, he spoke of "our duty to the people living in barbarism," to free them "by destroying barbarism itself."

With the Roosevelt Corollary, the president expanded the scope of the Monroe Doctrine by declaring the U.S. right to intervene in the Western Hemisphere to protect American and foreign lives and property. By asserting exclusive jurisdiction over the region as "an international police power," Roosevelt precluded European moves against weak Latin American and Caribbean states and asserted the preeminence of the United States. Under this "big stick" policy, the United States sent troops to the Dominican Republic (1905) and Nicaragua (1912), and occupied Haiti from 1915 through 1934. In 1903, Roosevelt encouraged Panamanian secessionists to break away from Colombia and sent warships to support their uprising. His interest was to secure favorable conditions for the construction of the Panama Canal. The nascent Republic of Panama granted the United States perpetual title to the Canal Zone, which insured American control over a strategic shipping route comparable to Britain's role at the Suez Canal. America's quest for dominance in the region eventually led to the purchase of the Danish West Indies (1916), which became the U.S. Virgin Islands.

As with European empires, American popular culture reflected the stature associated with the possession of colonies. The label on an early 1900s cigar box depicted Uncle Sam with a bevy of black and brown natives standing before globes dotted with American flags in the Pacific and the Caribbean.

As America gained ascendance as a world power, the age of empire as it had been defined was coming to an end. The

United States embraced the historical shift more easily than the European nations. The Philippines was reorganized as a commonwealth in 1935 and granted independence in 1946; Puerto Rico became a commonwealth in 1952; and Alaska and Hawaii were admitted as states in 1959. Under Herbert Hoover and Franklin D. Roosevelt, the Roosevelt Corollary was reinvented as the Good Neighbor policy with all the Americas having a share in upholding the Monroe Doctrine and defending the Western Hemisphere. The Good Neighbor policy became the basis for the Organization of American States, founded in 1948. The United States occupied Japan and portions of Germany and Austria after World War II, not with the intention of colonizing territory but of establishing democratic states. The old rules of empire, which frankly described land and populations as spoils of war, no longer applied. Although the move was accompanied by much criticism, the United States even agreed to the Canal Zone to Panama in a 1977 treaty.

In the post–World War II international system, with the United States as a superpower confronted by Soviet and Chinese rivals, "American imperialism" took the form of a leading role in a network of alliances and client states, backed by nuclear deterrence and the economic might of the only nation to emerge from the war richer than before. "Soft power" became increasingly important, leading European intellectuals to accuse Hollywood of "colonizing the imagination" and to condemn "Coca-colonialism."

In the Western Hemisphere, old habits from the Monroe Doctrine were subsumed by the Cold War, including the overthrow of elected governments in Guatemala (1954), Chile (1973), and Grenada (1983), as well as the Bay of Pigs invasion of Cuba (1961) and the Contra campaign in Nicaragua (1980–1990). On the Pacific frontier, the United States fought major wars in Korea and Vietnam to contain communism and support friendly regimes.

After withdrawing from Vietnam, many American politicians echoed historian Paul Kennedy's cautionary phrase "imperial overreach," and were determined to pull back from overt displays of U.S. power. Confidence in the projection of force and America's world mission was regained during the Reagan years. The George W. Bush administration justified the occupation of Afghanistan and Iraq in response to 9/11 as a campaign of freedom for the inhabitants of those countries in language Theodore Roosevelt would have supported.

British historian Niall Ferguson recently argued that "the world needs an effective liberal empire and that the United States is the best candidate for the job." He added, however, that the United States is "an empire in denial," lacking the will to shoulder the burden.

See also

Antislavery; Colonization; Communism; Diplomacy; Indian Rights; Isolationism; Manifest Destiny; Peace Movement (Late 19th Century); Racism; Social Darwinism; Western Expansion/ Exploration; Western Lore

GLEN JEANSONNE AND DAVID LUHRSSEN

Further Reading

Beale, Howard K. 1956. *Theodore Roosevelt and the Rise of America to World Power*. Baltimore, MD: Johns Hopkins Press.
Harrison, Brady. 2004. *Agent of Empire: William Walker and the Imperial Self in American Literature*. Athens, GA: University of Georgia Press.
Herring, George C. 2008. *From Colony to Superpower: U.S. Foreign Relations Since 1776*. Oxford, UK: Oxford University Press.
Murphy, Cullen. 2007. *Are We Rome: The Fall of an Empire and the Fate of America*. Boston: Houghton Mifflin.

Imperialism—Primary Document

Introduction

Even before becoming president in 1901, Theodore Roosevelt advocated the creation of an American empire overseas and spoke of imperialism as a measure of a nation's masculine prowess. He considered opponents of imperialism cowardly shirkers in the struggle for mastery in a world where survival of the fittest describes the history of nations as well as the evolution of species. In the speech excerpted here, which Roosevelt delivered at the Hamilton Club in Chicago in 1899, the future president warned that the United States must not fall behind Europe, but must redouble its will to serve as a beacon to the "Old World." For Roosevelt, empire building represented the vigorous physical life he had always extolled, but writ large on the world stage.

Document: Theodore Roosevelt's Speech at the Hamilton Club in Chicago (April 10, 1899)

Thank God for the iron in the blood of our fathers, the men who upheld the wisdom of Lincoln, and bore sword or rifle in the armies of Grant! Let us, the children of the men who proved themselves equal to the mighty days, let us, the children of the men who carried the great Civil War to a triumphant conclusion, praise the God of our fathers that the ignoble counsels of peace were rejected; that the suffering and loss, the blackness of sorrow and despair, were unflinchingly faced, and the years of strife endured; for in the end the slave was freed, the Union restored, and the mighty American republic placed once more as a helmeted queen among nations.

We of this generation do not have to face a task such as that our fathers faced, but we have our tasks, and woe to us if we fail to perform them! We cannot, if we would, play the part of China, and be content to rot by inches in ignoble ease within our borders, taking no interest in what goes on beyond them, sunk in a scrambling commercialism; heedless of the higher life, the life of aspiration, of toil and risk, busying ourselves only with the wants of our bodies for the day, until suddenly we should find, beyond a shadow of question, what China has already found, that in this world the nation that has trained itself to a career of unwarlike and isolated ease is bound, in the end, to go down before other nations which have not lost the manly and adventurous qualities. If we are to be a really great people, we must strive in good faith to play a great part in the world. We cannot avoid meeting great issues. All that we can determine for ourselves is whether we shall meet them well or ill. In 1898 we could not help being brought face to face with the problem of war with Spain. All we could decide was whether we should shrink like cowards from the contest, or enter into it as beseemed a brave and high-spirited people; and, once in, whether failure or success should crown our banners.

So it is now. We cannot avoid the responsibilities that confront us in Hawaii, Cuba, Porto Rico, and the Philippines. All we can decide is whether we shall meet them in a way that will redound to the national credit, or whether we shall make of our dealings with these new problems a dark and shameful page in our history. To refuse to deal with them at all merely amounts to dealing with them badly. We have a given problem to solve. If we undertake the solution, there is, of course, always danger that we may not solve it aright; but to refuse to undertake the solution simply renders it certain that we cannot possibly solve it aright.

The timid man, the lazy man, the man who distrusts his country, the over-civilized man, who has lost the great fighting, masterful virtues, the ignorant man, and the man of dull mind, whose soul is incapable of feeling the mighty life that thrills "stern men with empires in their brains"—all these, of course, shrink from seeing the nation undertake its new duties; shrink from seeing us build a navy and an army adequate to our needs; shrink from seeing us do our share of the world's work, by bringing order out of chaos in the great, fair, tropic islands from which the valor of our soldiers and sailors has driven the Spanish flag. These are the men who fear the strenuous life, who fear the only national life which is really worth leading. They believe in that cloistered life which saps the hardy virtues in a nation, as it saps them in the individual; or else they are wedded to that base spirit of gain and greed which recognizes in commercialism the be-all and end-all of national life, instead of realizing that, though an indispensable element, it is, after all, but one of the many elements that go to make up true national greatness. No country can long endure if its foundations are not laid deep in the material prosperity which comes from thrift, from business energy and enterprise, from hard, unsparing effort in the fields of industrial activity; but neither was any nation ever yet truly great if it relied upon material prosperity alone. All honor must be paid to the architects of our material prosperity, to the great captains of industry who have built our factories and our railroads, to the strong men who toil for wealth with brain or hand; for great is the debt of the nation to these and their kind. But our debt is yet greater to the men whose highest type is to be found in a statesman like Lincoln, a soldier like Grant. They showed by their lives that they recognized the law of work, the law of strife; they toiled to win a competence for themselves and those dependent upon them; but they recognized that there were yet other and even loftier duties—duties to the nation and duties to the race.

We cannot sit huddled within our own borders and avow ourselves merely an assemblage of well-to-do hucksters who care nothing for what happens beyond. Such a policy would defeat even its own end; for as the nations grow to have ever wider and wider interests, and are brought into closer and closer contact, if we are to hold our own in the struggle for naval and commercial supremacy, we must build up our power without our own borders. We must build the isthmian canal, and we must grasp the points of vantage which will enable us to have our say in deciding the destiny of the oceans of the East and the West.

So much for the commercial side. From the standpoint of international honor the argument is even stronger. The guns that thundered off Manila and Santiago left us echoes of glory, but they also left us a legacy of duty. If we drove out a medieval tyranny only to make room for savage anarchy, we had better not have begun the task at all. It is worse than idle to say that we have no duty to perform, and can leave to their fates the islands we have conquered. Such a course would be the course of infamy. It would be followed at once by utter chaos in the wretched islands themselves. Some stronger, manlier power would have to step in and do the work, and we would have shown ourselves weaklings, unable to carry to successful completion the labors that great and high-spirited nations are eager to undertake.

The work must be done; we cannot escape our responsibility; and if we are worth our salt, we shall be glad of the chance to do the work—glad of the chance to show ourselves equal to one of the great tasks set modern civilization. But let us not deceive ourselves as to the importance of the task. Let us not be misled by vainglory into underestimating the strain it will put on our powers. Above all, let us, as we value our own self-respect, face the responsibilities with proper seriousness, courage, and high resolve. We must demand the highest order of integrity and ability in our public men who are to grapple with these new problems. We must hold to a rigid accountability those public servants who show unfaithfulness to the interests of the nation or inability to rise to the high level of the new demands upon our strength and our resources....

Our army needs complete reorganization,—not merely enlarging,—and the reorganization can only come as the result of legislation. A proper general staff should be established, and the positions of ordnance, commissary, and quartermaster officers should be filled by detail from the line. Above all, the army must be given the chance to exercise in large bodies. Never again should we see, as we saw in the Spanish war, major-generals in command of divisions who had never before commanded three companies together in the field. Yet, incredible to relate, Congress has shown a queer inability to learn some of the lessons of the war. There were large bodies of men in both branches who opposed the declaration of war, who opposed the ratification of peace, who opposed the upbuilding of the army, and who even opposed the purchase of armor at a reasonable price for the battle-ships and cruisers, thereby putting an absolute stop to the building of any new fighting-ships for the navy. If, during the years to come, any disaster should befall our arms, afloat or ashore, and thereby any shame come to the United States, remember that the blame will lie upon the men whose names appear upon the roll-calls of Congress on the wrong side of these great questions. On them will lie the burden of any loss of our soldiers and sailors, of any dishonor to the flag; and upon you and the people of this country will lie the blame if you do not repudiate, in no unmistakable way, what these men have done. The blame will not rest upon the untrained commander of untried troops, upon the civil officers of a department the organization of which has been left utterly inadequate, or upon the admiral with an insufficient number of ships; but upon the public men who have so lamentably failed in forethought as to refuse to remedy these evils long in advance, and upon the nation that stands behind those public men....

I preach to you, then, my countrymen, that our country calls not for the life of ease but for the life of strenuous endeavor. The twentieth century looms before us big with the fate of many nations. If we stand idly by, if we seek merely swollen, slothful ease and ignoble peace, if we shrink from the hard contests where men must win at hazard of their lives and at the risk of all they hold dear, then the bolder and stronger peoples will pass us by, and will win for themselves the domination of the world. Let us therefore boldly face the life of strife, resolute to do our duty well and manfully; resolute to uphold righteousness by deed and by word; resolute to be both honest and brave, to serve high ideals, yet to use practical methods. Above all, let us shrink from no strife, moral or physical, within or without the nation, provided we are certain that the strife is justified, for it is only through strife, through hard and dangerous endeavor, that we shall ultimately win the goal of true national greatness.

Source: Roosevelt, Theodore. *The Strenuous Life: Essays and Addresses.* New York: The Century Co., 1902, pp. 1–21.

INDIAN REMOVAL

Although there were instances where peaceful relations between the native inhabitants and new settlers existed—William Penn and his Religious Society of Friends (Quakers) managed to broker a successful peace treaty between the Delaware tribe and his colony in Pennsylvania—they were few and far between. The story of Indian removal, confinement to reservations, and the attempt to impose American citizenship, which finally occurred in 1924 with congressional passage of the National Immigration Origins Act, remains one of the most, if not the most, tragic examples of discrimination based on race in American history.

Prior to the establishment of the United States, many of the Native American tribes were forced to cede their lands to growing numbers of white settlers moving into interior portions of the original thirteen colonies. Some tribes, angered by colonists' appetite for more lands for farming, took up arms with the French against the British and their colonial allies during the French and Indian War (1754–1763).

Between the close of the War of 1812 and the outbreak of the Civil War, the ever-expanding frontier and abundant material resources of the young nation provided for a rapidly growing European American population. Feeling the effects of white settlement and a patriotic confidence in the future of America's progress were the land's first inhabitants. During the 1830s and 1840s, continuing a process that began prior to the creation of the new nation, many Americans endorsed the claim that the inevitable laws of progress doomed Native Americans to extinction. Justifying the removal of Indians from their land were individuals like Lewis Cass, governor of

In 1890, the U.S. Army massacred about 300 Sioux at Wounded Knee, South Dakota. Here, they bury the dead. (Library of Congress)

the Michigan Territory; South Carolina statesman and diplomat Joel R. Poinsett, who elaborated his views in *Inquiry into the Received Opinions of Philosophers and Historians on the Natural Progress of the Human Race from Barbarism to Civilization* (1834); and President Andrew Jackson, who defended the removal of the Cherokee tribe as an inevitable step in progress during his second annual message to Congress.

The process of conquest and removal had been underway prior to Jackson's decree. Shortly before the outbreak of the War of 1812, Governor William Henry Harrison of the recently organized Indiana Territory met with Shawnee chief Tecumseh in order to broker a peace agreement. Since the British and Native Americans were allied in the Ohio Valley, pressure mounted on Harrison to prevent a confrontation. Tecumseh reiterated to Harrison the Native American philosophy of land ownership. Harrison, not satisfied, managed to bypass Tecumseh and secure the cession of 3 million acres of Indian land to the United States. When Tecumseh mobilized a number of Indian tribes to save their lands, Harrison decided to attack Tecumseh's village, Prophetstown, on the mouth of the Tippecanoe River in late 1811. Tecumseh and most of his warriors were not in the village when Harrison attacked, and Prophetstown fell after two days of battle. Harrison, despite suffering more losses, burned the buildings, destroyed all the food and possessions, and immediately declared victory.

Tecumseh's dream of a united Indian confederacy died with him in battle in 1813. After the close of the War of 1812, the Native Americans of the Old Northwest Territory found themselves removed from the territories of Michigan, Ohio, and Indiana. The process of removal then continued as American statesmen, unsympathetic to Native American culture, began engineering their relocation under the guise of beneficent guardianship and paternalistic friendship.

The classic case in point was the removal of the Cherokees, who were peaceful farmers, from Georgia in the early 1830s. In 1829, the state of Georgia appropriated all Indian land within its borders, declared all Cherokee laws null and void, disallowed them from testifying in court against state citizens, and distributed their lands to white settlers in a lottery system. With the passage of the Cherokee Removal Act in May 1830, tribal chiefs appealed to the Jackson administration. But it was in vain. Even after Chief Justice John Marshall partially reversed himself in the case of *Rev. Samuel A.*

Worcester v. the State of Georgia (1832), President Jackson dismissed the ruling and condoned Georgia's appropriation of 7 million acres of land. After the Cherokee refused to move for three years, General Winfield Scott led a 7,000-man force and removed some 1,700 Cherokees in the middle of winter without prior warning. The path they were forced to travel, known as the "Trail of Tears," went to Arkansas and then to Oklahoma. Along this terrible journey nearly 100 Native Americans, including many women and children, died each day from the cold, hunger, and disease that ravaged them during their forcible removal. Some 4,000 died in all.

But the belief in inevitable "progress" and opportunity was too much for white settlers to ignore. By the 1840s "winning the West" was inextricably tied to the ideological virtue of "Manifest Destiny," the idea that the United States had a God-given right to expand its borders from the Atlantic to the Pacific Ocean. A war with Mexico gave added currency to those who believed in the righteousness of territorial expansionism.

Although the nation was preoccupied with the bloodiest conflict in its history, the Civil War (1861–1865), the Union government did manage to pass the Morrill Land Grant Act and the Homestead Act in the early 1860s, which subsequently opened the door for further development of lands west of the Mississippi River. Homesteaders' desire for good arable lands in the West, in conjunction with the development of the railroads and various business ventures, intensified white pressure upon Native Americans. This would be the main cause of recurrent Native American wars from the 1860s to 1877. It forced a mad scramble for Native American territory until most of this land was preempted for sale to advancing settlers. To the frontiersmen and the railroad magnates, the Native American had always been an obstacle in the path of westward progress; to the Native Americans, the coming of "progress" spelled the doom of the buffalo and other game on which Indian tribes depended for food, and ultimately, the destruction of their culture and way of life.

Shortly after the "War Between the States" began, the new state of Minnesota erupted into violence between the Indians and newly arrived settlers. The Eastern (Lakota) Sioux became incensed when they failed to receive their promised payments from the government; they continued to grow angrier at the injustices committed by settlers and agents from the Bureau of Indian Affairs. When they refused to yield, further violence occurred in Minnesota farms and towns. Numerous settlers were killed in the confrontation. In brutal and swift retaliation, the U.S. Army killed numerous warriors, and at Mankato thirty-eight Native Americans were hanged in public.

The new Colorado Territory was also the scene of horrific bloodshed as the Civil War raged. Arapaho and Cheyenne resented the intrusion of miners and ranchers on their sacred lands. They began raiding stage-coach stations and ranches and murdered a white family. Once again, in reprisal, Colonel J. M. Chivington surprised the Native Americans at Sand Creek in 1864, where he killed 500, including many women and children. Many of the bodies of those killed were mutilated, prompting Army General Nelson A. Miles to comment that the Sand Creek Massacre, also known as the Chivington Massacre, was "the foulest and most unjustifiable crime in the annals of America." More successfully at the Battle at Little Big Horn on June 25–26, 1876, and culminating with their last battle in December 1890 at Wounded Knee, South Dakota, Native Americans fought back against the U.S. military in a vain attempt to preserve their way of life.

It was on the Northern plains that the final bloody chapter in the long and tragic history of Native American-white warfare was written. More than any other battle, the massacre at Wounded Knee symbolized the destruction of a civilization. When a unit of the Seventh Cavalry responded to the unfounded fears of white miners and settlers to the "Ghost Dance" sweeping through the Indian tribes, the cavalry began arresting a number of Sioux men, women, and children who were traveling to the Pine Ridge Reservation in search of food and protection. The troops surrounded them and took away their weapons. As the Sioux were being disarmed, a disturbance broke out after a shot was heard. Without any warning or provocation the troops opened fire with their rifles and Gatling guns into the disarmed Sioux. Some 90 men and 200 women and children were killed. Many white Americans expressed horror and shame at the brutality.

During the thirty-odd years of the Indian wars, Native Americans desperately tried to hold onto their lands and maintain their distinctive ways of life. The smaller the area into which they were driven, the more desperately they fought back. Initially, the first encounters between the Plains Indians and settlers, for instance, were largely peaceful until

disease and the decline of game, resulting from the impact of white migration across the Plains, made the encounters violent.

Most tellingly, the rapid extermination of the buffalo in the 1870s forced many of the Native Americans already living on the reservations to move further away, while, at the same time, forcing them to become more dependent upon federal assistance for survival. Reformers sympathetic to the plight of the Native Americans pushed the idea of an agrarian-based and settled way of life, rather than the old custom of hunting, as a pathway to eliminating the violence and growing governmental assistance.

Governmental attempts to strike a balance between the growing demand for land on the part of white settlers and the Indians' determination to keep land for the various tribes led to the formal establishment of the reservation system. The idea of setting aside reserves for the tribes on land, which they were forced to surrender, was initiated during the administration of Thomas Jefferson. It was his hope that the Indians would abandon hunting and accept an agrarian way of life. After the War of 1812, many tribes already living on reservations east of the Mississippi River made the transition to farming.

The Indian Removal Act of 1830, noted earlier, forced many living on Eastern reservations to move to the Indian Territory, which consisted of the present-day states of Nebraska, Kansas, and Oklahoma. The 1851 Fort Laramie Treaty, signed by the United States and the eight major Indian nations inhabiting the Great Plains, allowed for the concentration of the Sioux in the Dakotas, the Cheyennes in the Rocky Mountain foothills, and the Comanche near Texas. No formal reservation system had been created at this point and Indians moved freely throughout these areas, continuing their long-standing practice of hunting for food.

After the Civil War, however, many of the tribes in the Great Plains and farther west ultimately were subjected to the reservation system with the Treaty of Medicine Lodge in 1867. By this time, many of the tribes were at war with the U.S. government and their subjugation was only a matter of time. The Medicine Lodge treaty permitted the U.S. government to force many of these tribes onto confined reservations in the Indian Territory or arid regions of the West unsuitable for farming.

By the 1880s there were 441 reservations in twenty-one states. The reservation system itself was marked by rampant corruption among federal Indian agents and white settlers' unquenchable demand for more land. Conditions on the reservations were deplorable, marked by abject poverty and unsanitary conditions. The agents in charge of the reservations often stole funds and supplies. Indian religious practices were banned and children were sent to boarding schools to be assimilated into European American culture.

Continuing friction led to the breaking up of reservations into individual landholdings in the 1880s and 1890s. This was achieved with passage of the Dawes Severalty Act (1887). The act allowed the president, with tribal approval, to subdivide the reservations into individual homesteads consisting of 160-acre plots—similar to the Homestead Act of 1862. It also provided that citizenship would be made available to all Native Americans should they so choose to accept; almost all refused preferring instead to adhere to their own nationality until it was imposed upon them in 1924. At that point, all Native Americans were classified as citizens of the United States, whether they wished it or not.

Subsequent legislation permitted Native Americans to lease their lands to white settlers, which many did to their own economic disadvantage. Of the 136.3 million acres of land under Native American control that the Dawes Act established, only 34.2 million remained in their possession in 1934. The Dawes Act was repealed that year and replaced with the Indian Reorganization Act. This act permitted tribes to reconstitute their old tribal government, teach their children at home, and reinstitute their old cultural way of life.

By that time, the distinctiveness of a Native American identity was confined to the reservations and the small numbers who chose to remain there. Many Indians gradually were assimilated into Euro American culture and abandoned their ancestral way of life. In 1988, the government passed the Indian Gaming Regulatory Act, thus transforming many reservations into moneymaking ventures. Slot machines and poker tables are the current method of compensation for lands, which will never be returned.

See also

Indian Rights; Manifest Destiny; Racism; Red Power Movement; Western Expansion/Exploration

CHARLES F. HOWLETT

Further Reading

Calloway, Colin G., ed. 1996. *Our Hearts Fell to the Ground: Plains Indians View of How the West Was Lost.* New York: Bedford-St. Martin's Press.

Carlson, Paul H. 1998. *The Plains Indians.* College Station, TX: Texas A&M Press.

Confederation of American Indians. 2000. *Indian Reservations: A State and Federal Handbook.* Honolulu, HI: University Press of the Pacific.

Debo, Angie. 1972. *And Still the Waters Run: The Betrayal of Five Civilized Tribes.* Princeton, NJ: Princeton University Press.

Ehle, John. 1988. *Trail of Tears: The Rise and Fall of the Cherokee Nation.* New York: Doubleday.

Foreman, Grant. 1989. *Indian Removal: The Emigration of the Five Civilized Tribes of Indians.* Norman, OU: University of Oklahoma Press.

Frantz, Klaus. 1999. *Indian Reservations of the United States.* Chicago: University of Chicago Press.

Jackson, Helen Hunt. 1994. *A Century of Dishonor.* New York: Indian Head Books. Originally published in 1883.

Leckie, William. 1963. *The Military Conquest of the Southern Plains.* Norman, OU: University of Oklahoma Press.

Slotkin, Richard. 1973. *Regeneration Through Violence: The Mythology of the American Frontier, 1600–1860.* Norman, OU: University of Oklahoma Press.

West, Elliott. 1998. *The Contested Plains: Indians, Goldseekers, and the Rush to Colorado.* Lawrence, KS: University Press of Kansas.

Indian Removal—Primary Document

Introduction

The leader of the Nez Perce tribe, Chief Joseph, refused to move from his ancestral lands in Oregon and be forced to live on an Idaho reservation. He and his tribe refused and retreated nearly a thousand miles until captured in 1877 near the Canadian border. Joseph and the remnants of his band were deported to Indian Territory (now Oklahoma), where most died of malaria and other diseases. He appealed personally to President Rutherford B. Hayes, and he and his tribe of Nez Perces were returned to the Pacific Northwest.

Document: Chief Joseph's Lament (1879)

At last I was granted permission to come to Washington and bring my friend Yellow Bull and our interpreter with me. I am glad I came. I have shaken hands with a good many friends, but there are some things I want to know which no one seems able to explain. I cannot understand how the government sends a man out to fight us, as it did General Miles, and then breaks his words. Such a government has something wrong about it....

I have heard talk and talk, but nothing is done. Good words do not last long unless they amount to something. Words do not pay for my dead people. They do not pay for my country, now overrun by white men. They do not protect my father's grave. They do not pay for my horses and cattle.

Good words do not give me back my children. Good words will not make good the promise of your war chief, General Miles. Good words will not give my people good health and stop them from dying. Good words will not get my people a home where they can live in peace and take care of themselves.

I am tired of talk that comes to nothing. It makes my heart sick when I remember all the good words and all the broken promises. There has been too much talking by men who had no right to talk. Too many misinterpretations have been made; too many misunderstandings have come up between the white men and the Indians.

If the white man wants to live in peace with the Indian, he can live in peace. There need be no trouble. Treat all men alike. Give them the same laws. Give them all an even chance to live and grow.

All men are made by the same Great Spirit Chief. They are all brothers. The earth is the mother of all people, and all people should have equal rights upon it. You might as well expect all rivers to run backward as that nay man who was born a free man should be contented penned up and denied liberty to go where he pleases. If you tie a horse to a stake, do you expect he will grow fat? If you pen an Indian up on a small spot of earth and compel him to stay there, he will not be contented nor will he grow and prosper.

I have asked some of the Great White Chiefs where they get their authority to say to the Indian that he shall stay in one place, while he sees white men going where they please. They cannot tell me.

I only ask of the government to be treated as all other men are treated. If I cannot go to my own home, let me have a home in a country where my people will not die so fast. I would like to go to Bitter Root Valley [western Montana.] There my people would be healthy; where they are now, they are dying. Three have died since I left my camp to come to Washington. When I think of our condition, my heart is heavy. I see men of my own race treated as outlaws and driven from country to country or shot down like animals.

I know that my race must change. We cannot hold our own with the white men as we are. We only ask an even chance to live as other men live. We ask to be recognized as men. We ask that the same law shall work alike on all men. If an Indian breaks the law, punish him by the law. If a white man breaks the law, punish him also.

Let me be a free man—free to travel, free to stop, free to work, free to trade where I choose, free to choose my own teachers, free to follow the religion of my fathers, free to think and talk and act for myself—and I will obey every law or submit to the penalty.

Whenever the white man treats the Indian as they treat each other, then we shall have no more wars. We shall all be alike—brothers of one father and mother, with one sky above and one country around us and one government for all. Then the Great Spirit Chief who rules above will smile upon this land and send rain to wash out the bloody spots made by brothers' hands upon the face of the earth. For this time the Indian race are waiting and praying. I hope no more groans of wounded men and women will ever go to the ear of the Great Spirit chief above, and that all people may be one people.

Source: *North American Review* 128 (April 1879): 431–432. See also Bailey, Thomas A., and David M. Kennedy, *The American Spirit, Vol. II: Since 1865*. Boston: Houghton Mifflin Co., 1998, pp. 130–132.

INDIAN RIGHTS

As the first inhabitants of the lands that now make up the United States, the American Indian groups that have survived over 500 years of European American presence possess a number of rights that are based on their tenure on the land. Although these rights are a poor substitute for what has been taken from the tribes over that history, they are important components that make up much of what defines American Indian nations today. The U.S. Constitution places the responsibility for relationships with Indian nations squarely in the hands of the federal government, but there is no single agency or code of law that defines their extent. The definitions of those rights have come into existence from a hodge-podge of acts of Congress, court decisions, and executive orders, leading to a situation where federal, state, local, and tribal officials have to deal with a sometimes contradictory bureaucracy in order to assert the rights to which American Indian people are entitled. Most of these rights—political rights, rights to natural resources, and cultural and religious rights—are defined either by the hundreds of treaties signed between the federal government and individual tribal nations or by the so-called trust relationship that defines the enduring connections between the tribal nations and the federal government.

Trust Relationship

When Europeans first arrived in North America, the relationship between themselves and the tribes was, out of necessity, one of equals. In most cases Indian peoples had the land, the

John Collier posed with Blackfeet chiefs during his tenure as commissioner of Indian Affairs, which lasted throughout Franklin Roosevelt's presidency (1933–1945). A reformer and an advocate for Native Americans, he worked to bring self-government to Native American groups. (Library of Congress)

greater numbers, and the military power. However, that situation changed as soon as Europeans had sufficient numbers and technology to defeat Indian tribes in armed conflict. The question that arose out of the early history of colonialism in North America was what the relationship would be between these autonomous Indian tribes and the new European American governments that took root. Over the course of the first 100 years of European settlement, the relationship gradually changed from a nation-to-nation connection between theoretically equal powers to one where the American Indian peoples, for the most part, were dependent upon European Americans and subservient to them within the borders of European American settlement. Early on, Puritan leaders established so-called Praying Villages, where Indian people were to live while they assimilated to European American ways of life, and the trust relationship between the tribes and the U.S. government grew out of that transition.

When the U.S. Constitution was written, its authors recognized that Indian tribes exercised sovereignty over their lands and their people in much the same way as European nations. At that time, most of the powerful Indian nations existed outside of the borders of the thirteen states, on land that was often in dispute with European colonial powers. Because the relationships with the tribes were so important to both sides in the colonial conflicts over the continent, the tribes were able to exercise a large amount of power and influence by shifting their alliances to the side that benefited them the most. This practice continued through the War of 1812, and even some tribes that were technically inside of the borders of the United States, but near the frontier with European colonial lands, such as the powerful six nations of the Haudenosaunee (Iroquois) Confederacy, were able to maintain almost complete sovereignty.

With the end of warfare with European colonial powers, however, American military power began to grow and the need for alliances with Indian tribes disappeared. The constitutional definition of the relationship had not changed—the tribes were still viewed as sovereign nations, with the federal government in charge of the relationship—but many settlers, as well as politicians back in Washington, claimed that the United States had conquered Indian land, and that now, by right of conquest, it belonged to them. As settlers moved into the fertile lands of the South, anxious to make profits growing cotton, rice, sugar, tobacco, and indigo, the conflict between Indian sovereignty and the drive for land on the part of the Americans came into sharp focus. With the election of Andrew Jackson in 1828 and the passage of the Indian Removal Act of 1830, the stage was set for a dramatic shift in the relationship between the federal government and the tribes, and the gradual diminution of their rights. Although the U.S. Supreme Court would reinforce some rights on the part of the tribes, other aspects of the relationship would be fundamentally altered, and the trust relationship established. Chief Justice John Marshall's Court ruled on three landmark cases during the 1820s and early 1830s that established the ways that the Indian nations would be viewed. In *Johnson's Lessee* v. *McIntosh*, 8 Wheat. 543 (1823), the Supreme Court stripped tribes of the right to dispose of their lands as they saw fit. The second of these cases, *Cherokee Nation v. Georgia* 5 Pet. 1 (1831), started out by doing away with the idea that Indian tribal nations were nations in the European sense, setting up a new classification known as "domestic dependent nations." This meant that, although they were still considered nations, they were subservient to the United States in all matters, and all aspects of the relationship were to be regulated by the federal government. The following year, in *Worcester* v. *Georgia*, 6 Pet. 515 (1832), the same Supreme Court placed those domestic dependent nations in a status between the federal and state governments—subject to federal law, but exempt from state law.

The "Marshall trilogy," as it came to be known, created the framework for the trust relationship. The Indian domestic dependent nations were under the protection of the federal government, and the federal government was responsible to protect their interests, including promoting their education and health, as well as negotiating equitable treaties if any Indian-owned possessions (e.g., land, water, and other natural resources) were to be transferred into non-Indian hands. This relationship created an inherent conflict of interest in many cases where the government (even the very same agencies of the government) was forced to both promote the interests of European American settlers and simultaneously protect Indian interests in the same resources. While the trust relationship was designed to protect the tribes from being taken advantage of by individuals, as well as local and state governments, the federal government often used it to diminish tribal sovereignty and rob Indian nations of their resources.

Although it can easily be argued that the trust relationship had already been broken by the consistent neglect of Indian interests and the outright subversion of the terms of treaties the United States had entered into with the tribes, official changes to the relationship made through further Supreme Court decisions further diminished Indian rights. Decisions in *United States v. Kagama*, 118 U.S. 375 (1886) and *Lone Wolf v. Hitchcock*, 187 U.S. 553 (1903) gave Congress the authority to completely change the terms of treaties the United States had signed with the tribes, effectively allowing them to deny Indian rights whenever they saw fit or make whatever use of tribal resources they wanted. This view of the disposability of Indian rights largely held sway until President Franklin D. Roosevelt's appointment of John Collier as commissioner of Indian Affairs in 1933, and the passage of Collier's Indian Reorganization Act the following year. The abandonment of federal responsibility would not be completely overturned by one zealous advocate at the head of the Bureau of Indian Affairs (BIA), as proven by the so-called Termination era that followed Collier's tenure at the BIA. Finally, in the 1960s, a renewed push for self-determination by Indian activists, echoing the themes of the African American civil rights movement of the 1950s and 1960s, got Indian rights on the national agenda. By 1975, the Indian Self-Determination and Education Assistance Act was passed, guaranteeing a new level of autonomy on the part of the tribal governments. During the 1990s President Bill Clinton went a step further, stating that the federal government would start viewing the relationship not as a trust, but rather as government-to-government relationships with the tribes. However, the federal abandonment of many of its treaty responsibilities has characterized every era of the relationship between it and the tribes. The varying emphasis on the sovereignty of American Indian tribes has, however, had an impact on the extent of Indian rights throughout American history, and this has played out in terms of the rights of the tribes to the natural resources on their lands as well as the cultural and religious rights of the people.

Natural Resource Rights

The natural resources that exist on lands held by Indian nations have always been a point of contention with American society. The resources provided, including the land itself, the water associated with the land, and the timber and mineral resources found there were of great value to non-Indians, and many treaties were written with the aim of getting those resources out of Indian hands and into the possession of non-Indian settlers and companies. Even after the treaty-making era ended in 1871, the federal government used various agreements with tribes, as well as laws like the General Allotment Act of 1887, to facilitate the transfer of natural resources to non-Indians. Often, these resources had larger meanings to Indian people, who did not view them as simple commodities, but rather as integral parts of their cultural and spiritual lives. The resource with the most direct tie to Indian lifeways was land.

Although most tribes had no concept of the individual ownership of land, tribal nations did have distinct boundaries with their neighbors, and their particular lands played a large part in their social and political structures. Additionally, especially for societies that held their ancestors in a place of honor, the loss of traditional lands meant the loss of a connection with an important and integral part of their spirituality. Many native groups went through a process in which they lost their homelands more than once. The early 19th century brought the removal of many tribes from their lands, to be moved halfway across the continent, often to Indian Territory in modern-day Oklahoma, where the federal government established much smaller reservations on which they were to live. Usually the tribes were coerced into signing treaties to legitimize the removal, but even those treaties guaranteed the land rights of the Indians to the new reservation lands. However, with the passage of the General Allotment Act and the opening of Indian Territory to non-Indian settlement, these very same tribes lost their lands again when the federal government stepped in, divided the communally held reservation into parcels for individual Indians, and then sold off the "surplus lands" to non-Indians. Further, the allotments distributed to individual Indians were now subject to property taxes and Indians, not accustomed to the non-Indian methods of farming, often accumulated debt. Between those taxes and debts, many of the individual Indians who received allotments of land ended up losing that land, which then became the property of non-Indians as well. As a result, of the lands held by Indian tribes in 1877, more than two-thirds became the property of non-Indians by the time the allotment policy ended with the passage of the Indian Reorganization Act (IRA) in 1934.

After the passage of the IRA, the Indian Claims Commission (ICC) was established to provide redress and compensation for the unjustified taking of Indian lands. The ICC worked to determine the fair market value of lands that were ceded to the United States in treaties and provide compensation to the tribes where the federal government had not paid a fair price. This could also take into account the tribes' reserved rights to the water, timber, and mineral resources found on those lands. In many cases, the ICC found that the federal government paid as low as 1/20th the fair market value of land, and recommended compensation to the tribes that were taken advantage of. However, even the payment of compensation could not make up for the loss of the role that the land played in the tribes' social, political, and spiritual lives.

Although the policy of allotment ended with the passage of the IRA, not much was done to restore any lost lands to tribes; rather, the ICC was focused on monetary compensation. However, that began to change during the self-determination era. Beginning with the bill signed by President Richard Nixon in 1970 returning Blue Lake to the people of Taos Pueblo, the federal government began seeking, in some cases, to actually increase the land base of certain Indian nations. The following year, Congress passed the Alaska Native Claims Settlement Act, which provided both compensation and 44 million acres to Alaska's native peoples. Though this effort can be described as piecemeal at best, it does represent a reversal of a trend that lasted for over 350 years.

Tied to land rights but with its own long, complex, and often-contradictory history, water rights are often just as important, because without water the land that Indians hold (mostly in the most arid parts of the nation) are useless for agriculture or many other uses. Before the early 20th century, Indian water rights were largely ignored altogether where they conflicted with the water needs of non-Indians. Though the main U.S. Supreme Court decision defining Indian water rights, *Winters v. United States* (1908), guaranteed Indians huge amounts of water, actually gaining the use of those waters was next to impossible for most Indian tribes over the majority of the 20th century. The decision in the *Winters* case, put succinctly, was that in signing treaties with the federal government that resulted in the creation of their reservations, Indians agreed to vast land cessions in return for guarantees that their reservation lands would be permanently reserved for Indian use and occupation. The Supreme Court ruled that, when the Indians did this, they reserved to themselves every right not specified in the treaty, including the right to the waters that ran in and adjacent to those lands. When the reservations were established, the Indian nations and the United States implicitly reserved, along with the land, sufficient water to fulfill the purposes of the reservations, which in most cases was farming.

However, Congress has never passed any definitive Indian water rights bills supporting or even defining their rights. According to the Winters Doctrine derived from the court case, Indian water rights are defined and governed by a body of federal law that recognizes that Indian nations have sovereignty over the water on their reservations. However, the federal government did nothing to reconcile these *Winters* rights with the prior appropriation system already in use in much of the nation, leading to inevitable conflict between Indian claims and non-Indian use of the waters. When non-Indian rights secured by prior appropriation (which recognizes the right of the first person to make beneficial use of the water as paramount), Indian tribes that had lived on their lands for centuries before the arrival of European Americans, the Indian rights were technically paramount. But, as the old saying goes, "possession being 9/10th of the law," the tribes were usually left high and literally dry. Tribes were left to go to court to gain the water to which they were legally entitled.

The situation was even worse for tribes that did not traditionally practice sedentary agriculture, as the courts generally recognized such agriculture as the paramount use for water in most of the areas in which Indians lived. With the rise of migration to the West during the 20th century and the corresponding development of urban and suburban landscapes in arid or semiarid regions, Indian water rights have constantly been under attack in the federal and state courts and in other political arenas as well. Even where the rights seem plain, the capriciousness of the courts toward Indian nations has meant that the nations have had to enter into lengthy and expensive litigation with no guarantee of success.

Since the 1980s, the federal government has promoted negotiated settlements as the best way for all parties to resolve their water claims. Rather than seeking final adjudication in the courts, the parties use the court-determined data to achieve a solution that will satisfy some of the desires of all sides rather than all of the desires of one side. Indian water needs are addressed without eliminating non-Indian water uses, although usually neither side is able to achieve all its goals. Negotiations in a land of limited water like the American West means that the Indian nations usually do not receive the full share of water determined by the Winters Doctrine; but in return they often get money for facilities or projects to put to use the water they are allocated. Such federal funding has allowed Indians to secure not only water rights but also delivered water put to beneficial use. At the same time, non-Indians gain the assurance that they will be able to continue using water without the constant threat of an assertion of *Winters* rights on the part of the Indian nations.

The presence of oil, minerals and timber on Indian lands created another area in which Native peoples were deprived of the resources they possessed. Especially in Oklahoma, where an oil boom peaked in the 1890s, shortly before the Indian lands were allotted, such discoveries had a huge impact on the ways that non-Indian people took advantage of Native Americans and satisfied their appetite for the resources that Indians possessed. The Osage people, who had a reservation in northeastern Indian Territory, were left alone until oil was discovered in 1875. However, non-Indians immediately began seeking ways to get their hands on Osage oil and gas. Many tribes like the Osage allotted their lands as directed by the federal government, but were able to hold the subsurface rights collectively, splitting the income gained by leasing the oil and mineral rights. Additionally, an influx of non-Indian lawyers into Oklahoma led to a spike in court actions to declare the owners of these headrights unfit, and many were declared wards of non-Indians who plundered their income. Intermarriage with non-Indians was another way many sought to get their hands on the wealth being pumped out of the ground.

Approximately one-third of the coalfields in the United States are on tribal lands, along with approximately 35 percent of the uranium. The trust relationship places the federal government as the trustee for the tribes, with a responsibility to see that the tribes receive as much benefit from those resources as possible. Of course, at the same time, the conflict of interest within the federal government exists when it needs those same resources, or has an interest in seeing a corporation gain the use of those resources. However, with the rise of self-determination among the tribes, and by working together in national organizations such as the Council of Energy Resource Tribes, many tribes are managing their own resources. However, the fact that the case of *Lone Wolf v. Hitchcock* (1903) gave Congress the right to impose its will upon the tribes without recourse still hangs over the all of the natural rights exercised by the tribes.

Cultural, Political, and Religious Rights

The cultural, political, and religious rights of American Indian peoples were not enumerated until the late 20th century in most cases. For the vast majority of the history of interaction between Indian peoples and non-Indians, Indians were too often denied the right to practice their religious beliefs, govern themselves, or even in many cases speak their own languages. Education in Indian boarding schools was not used as a means to preserve their cultures, but rather a way of replacing them. Just as with the policy of the allotment of tribal lands, federal policy used education as a means to encourage Indians to assimilate into non-Indian society and become indistinguishable from white Americans. And, just as with allotment, those policies began to change in 1934 with the Indian Reorganization Act.

In 1968, many of these rights were spelled out for the first time in the Indian Civil Rights Act, which guaranteed Indian people many of the same rights the Bill of Rights had guaranteed to non-Indians. The rights of Indian people as tribal nations were expanded with the passage of the Indian Self-Determination and Education Assistance Act of 1975. The passage of this act created a framework where a return to a relationship between nations could exist between the United States and Indian nations. The American Indian Religious Freedom Act of 1978 addressed their religious rights, and Indian cultural rights were reinforced by the Native American Graves Protection and Repatriation Act of 1990. Although there are still many court cases going on over the extent of American Indian rights, as of the beginning of the 21st century American Indian people were exercising greater autonomy over their lands, waters, natural resources, and personal lives than they had been allowed to do over the vast majority of American history. However, the redress of the injustices done to American Indian rights over the course of that history has been limited to the extent of the violations of law. The impact of those injustices in terms of the many deaths that occurred over the centuries; the vast amounts of income the tribes were denied; the cultural genocide engaged in by the federal, state, and local governments; and the legacy that can still be seen in the fact that American Indians are the most impoverished ethnic group in the United States have never been anywhere near adequately addressed.

See also

Indian Removal; Manifest Destiny; Red Power Movement

STEVEN L. DANVER

Further Reading

Burton, Lloyd. 1991. *American Indian Water Rights and the Limits of Law*. Lawrence, KS: University Press of Kansas.

Clow, Richmond L., and Imre Sutton. 2001. *Trusteeship in Change: Toward Tribal Autonomy in Resource Management*. Boulder, CO: University Press of Colorado.

Debo, Angie. 1966. *And Still the Waters Run: The Betrayal of the Five Civilized Tribes*. New York: Gordian Press.

Deloria, Vine, Jr. 1985. *American Indian Policy in the Twentieth Century*. Norman, OK: University of Oklahoma Press.

Deloria, Vine, Jr., and Clifford M. Lytle. 1984. *The Nations Within: The Past and Future of American Indian Sovereignty*. Austin, TX: University of Texas Press.

Deloria, Vine, Jr., and David E. Wilkins. 1999. *Tribes, Treaties, and Constitutional Tribulations*. Austin, TX: University of Texas Press.

Fixico, Donald L. 2011. *The Invasion of Indian Country in the Twentieth Century: American Capitalism and Tribal Natural Resources*. 2nd ed. Boulder: University Press of Colorado.

Hundley, Norris, Jr. 1978. "The Dark and Bloody Ground of Indian Water Rights: Confusion Elevated to Principle." *Western Historical Quarterly* 9: 454–482.

Hundley, Norris, Jr. 1982. "The 'Winters' Decision and Indian Water Rights: A Mystery Reexamined." *Western Historical Quarterly* 13: 17–42.

Jennings, Francis. 1975. *The Invasion of America: Indians, Colonialism and the Cant of Conquest*. Chapel Hill, NC: University of North Carolina Press.

McCool, Daniel. 2002. *Native Waters: Contemporary Indian Water Settlements and the Second Treaty Era*. Tucson, AZ: University of Arizona Press.

Prucha, Francis Paul. 1994. *American Indian Treaties: The History of a Political Anomaly*. Berkeley, CA: University of California Press.

Prucha, Francis Paul. 1995. *The Great Father: United States Government and the American Indians*. Lincoln, NB: University of Nebraska Press.

Indian Rights—Primary Document

Introduction

When President Franklin D. Roosevelt appointed a reformer named John Collier as commissioner of Indian Affairs in 1933, he began a fundamental change in the ways that the federal government dealt with American Indian people and nations. Policies that had dominated Indian policy, such as the forced assimilation of Indian people and the reduction of Indian-held lands, were reversed. Tribal governments were given legitimacy. Although Collier's Indian Reorganization Act was far from a panacea for Indian peoples, it did represent the beginning of an emphasis on Indian self-determination, which would come to greater fruition during the 1970s–1990s. In this document, Collier recounts the efforts of his Bureau of Indian Affairs to correct the past denials of American Indian rights.

Document: Report by John Collier, Commissioner of Indian Affairs, *Annual Report of the Secretary of the Interior* (1938)

In all our colorful American life there is no group around which there so steadfastly persists an aura compounded of glamor, suspicion, and romance as the Indian. For generations the Indian has been, and is today, the center of an amazing series of wonderings, fears, legends, hopes.

Yet those who have worked with Indians know that they are neither the cruel, warlike, irreligious savages imagined by some, nor are they the "fortunate children of nature's bounty" described by tourists who see them for an hour at some glowing ceremonial. We find the Indians, in all the basic forces and forms of life, human beings like ourselves. The majority of them are very poor people living under severely simple conditions. We know them to be deeply religious. We know them to be possessed of all the powers, intelligence, and genius within the range of human endowment. Just as we yearn to live out our own lives in our own ways, so, too, do the Indians, in their ways.

For nearly 300 years white Americans, in our zeal to carve out a nation made to order, have dealt with the Indians on the erroneous, yet tragic, assumption that the Indians were a dying race—to be liquidated. We took away their best lands; broke treaties, promises; tossed them the most nearly worthless scraps of a continent that had once been wholly theirs. But we did not liquidate their spirit. The vital spark which kept them alive was hardy. So hardy, indeed, that we now face an astounding, heartening fact.

Actually, the Indians, on the evidence of federal census rolls of the past eight years, are increasing at almost twice the rate of the population as a whole.

With this fact before us, our whole attitude toward the Indians has necessarily undergone a profound change. Dead is the centuries-old notion that the sooner we eliminated this doomed race, preferably humanely, the better. No longer can we, with even the most generous intentions, pour millions of dollars and vast reservoirs of energy, sympathy, and effort into any unproductive attempts at some single, artificial permanent solution of the Indian problem. No longer can we naively talk of or think of the "Indian problem." Our task is to help Indians meet the myriad of complex, interrelated, mutually dependent situations which develop among them according to the very best light we can get on those happenings—much as we deal with our own perplexities and opportunities.

We, therefore, define our Indian policy somewhat as follows: So productively to use the moneys appropriated by the Congress for Indians as to enable them, on good, adequate lands of their own, to earn decent livelihoods and lead self-respecting, organized lives in harmony with their own aims and ideals, as an integral part of American life. Under such a policy, the ideal end result will be the ultimate disappearance of any need for government aid or supervision. This will not happen tomorrow; perhaps not in our lifetime; but with the revitalization of Indian hope due to the actions and attitudes of this government during the last few years, that aim is a probability, and a real one....

In looking at the Indian picture as a social whole, we will consider certain broad phases—land use and industrial enterprises, health and education, roads and rehabilitation, political organization—which touch Indian life everywhere, including the 30,000 natives of Alaska for whose health, education, and social and economic advancement the Indian

Service is responsible. Lastly, this report will tell wherein the Indian Service, or the government's effort as a whole for the Indians, still falls short.

So intimately is all of Indian life tied up with the land and its utilization that to think of Indians is to think of land. The two are inseparable. Upon the land and its intelligent use depends the main future of the American Indian.

The Indian feels toward his land, not a mere ownership sense but a devotion and veneration befitting what is not only a home but a refuge. At least nine out of ten Indians remain on or near the land. When times are good, a certain number drift away to town or city to work for wages. When times become bad, home to the reservation the Indian comes, and to the comparative security which he knows is waiting for him. The Indian still has much to learn in adjusting himself to the strains of competition amid an acquisitive society; but he long ago learned how to contend with the stresses of nature. Not only does the Indian's major source of livelihood derive from the land but his social and political organizations are rooted in the soil.

A major aim, then, of the Indian Service is to help the Indians to keep and consolidate what lands they now have and to provide more and better lands upon which they may effectively carry on their lives. Just as important is the task of helping the Indian make such use of his land as will conserve the land, insure Indian self-support, and safeguard or build up the Indian's social life....

In 1887, the General Allotment Act was passed, providing that after a certain trust period, fee simple title to parcels of land should be given to individual Indians. Individual proprietorship meant loss—a paradox in view of the Indian's love for the land, yet an inevitable result, when it is understood that the Indian by tradition was not concerned with possession, did not worry about titles or recordings, but regarded the land as a fisherman might regard the sea, as a gift of nature, to be loved and feared, to be fought and revered, and to be drawn on by all as an inexhaustible source of life and strength.

The Indian let the ownership of his allotted lands slip from him. The job of taking the Indian's lands away, begun by the white man through military expeditions and treaty commissions, was completed by cash purchase—always of course, of the best lands which the Indian had left. In 1887, the Indian had remaining 130 million acres. In 1933, the Indian had left only 49 million acres, much of it waste and desert.

Since 1933, the Indian Service has made a concerted effort—an effort which is as yet but a mere beginning—to help the Indian to build back his landholdings to a point where they will provide an adequate basis for a self-sustaining economy, a self-satisfying social organization.

Source: *Annual Report of the Secretary of the Interior for the Fiscal Year Ended June 30, 1938.* Washington, DC, 1938, pp. 209–211.

INDUSTRIAL REVOLUTION

Origins and Early American Involvement

Since the origin of anatomically modern humans about 200,000 years ago in Africa and their subsequent migration to Eurasia and the Americas, they depended on their own muscles and those of the animals they domesticated to accomplish tasks. The invention of the waterwheel and its subsequent spread in the Middle Ages augmented human and animal power. In the 18th century arose a change so momentous that it has been called the Industrial Revolution. It involved the use of machines rather than mere muscle to accomplish tasks.

In the 18th century, Britain was the first to industrialize. Textiles led the way. Looking for a source of cotton, it was natural that Britain turned to the American South. The plantation system, until the rise of textile mills in the American Northeast, depended on Britain as the destination for exports. Cotton codified the early plantation system, which exported the fiber and imported slaves. In this way slaves became integral to the Industrial Revolution. The American Revolution and even more so the Civil War, by reducing cotton exports from the U.S. South, led Britain to turn to India for cotton, though this fact should not obscure the importance of American cotton to the Industrial Revolution in Britain.

The Beginnings of Industry in the American Colonies

The Industrial Revolution in the American colonies roughly coincided with the American Revolution of the last quarter

Boys worked alongside adults in the spinning room at the Olympian Cotton Mills in Columbia, South Carolina, ca. 1903. The South's connection to the Industrial Revolution had been supplying cotton for textile mills, but the region sought to expand its industrialization after the Civil War. (Library of Congress)

of the 18th century, though some scholars believe that America's Industrial Revolution predated the American Revolution by a decade or two. Rather than reinvent the wheel, the American colonies adopted the technology and methods of Britain, though it tried to stop the piracy of its technology and methods of production. The seeming abundance of wood and other sources of energy and an expanding population were two factors that led to the success of the Industrial Revolution in the American colonies. The consumerism that would fuel the Industrial Revolution in the 20th century sank roots in the colonial era, when the well-to-do imported china, cloth, and furniture from Britain. Although colonial cities existed only along the Atlantic Ocean—Boston, New York City, and Philadelphia are good examples—they grew rapidly and emerged as both producer and consumer of manufactured goods. The creation of good roads, an arduous process, eased the transportation of manufactured products from city to city. The distillation of sugar into rum and the milling of grains were quasi-industrial processes. The "Protestant work ethic" imbued in colonists the habit of diligence that would serve the Industrial Revolution well. However, capital was scarce in the colonies, forcing Americans to look toward British investors for help. Moreover Britain tried to preserve its supremacy in manufacturing and its mercantilist system by enacting several laws to cripple the development of industry in the colonies. In 1750, for example, Parliament, Britain's legislative body, outlawed the production of steel in the colonies, which must have been on a small scale. Yet colonists tended, where possible, to ignore Parliament. The American Revolution stimulated demand for shoes, hats, uniforms, guns, cannons, and powder. American manufacturers arose to meet these wartime demands. Further stimulating domestic industries, America halted the import of manufactured goods from Britain during the Revolution.

The conclusion of the American Revolution in 1783 restored a sense of normalcy, at least in this regard, between the new United States and Britain. Trade rebounded, although the Napoleonic Wars and the War of 1812 hampered this trade.

U.S. industries, having made strides in the late 18th and early 19th centuries, nonetheless lagged behind British industries. This was not a problem that troubled George Washington, Benjamin Franklin, and John Adams, who were not as forward thinking as one might imagine. They counseled a return to agriculture rather than a leap forward into industrialization. Perhaps this view is not surprising given that Washington was a plantation owner, but Franklin and Adams might have been expected to be more imaginative.

Yet in the late 18th and early 19th centuries, the United States invested heavily in textiles mills, though not all these ventures succeeded. They were important, however, in stoking domestic demand from the South's cotton. American textile mills, as did industry everywhere else, exploited child labor, a practice abhorrent by modern standards. One mill in Rhode Island employed some 100 children, whose work supervisors scrutinized.

The Debate Between Thomas Jefferson and Alexander Hamilton in the Early Republic

Thomas Jefferson, President George Washington's secretary of state and later president in his own right, had visited Britain and disliked the filth, squalor, poverty, overcrowded cities, and a despondent working class that the Industrial Revolution had spawned. He believed that industrialization threatened democracy with the rise of plutocrats. He favored the rise of the United States as a nation of free white farmers as the backbone of republican government.

Hamilton, Washington's secretary of the treasury, disagreed. He looked to the federal government as a central economic planner. He believed that the United States was destined to industrialize to the degree that Britain had. He believed that U.S. industries would one day rival and perhaps surpass those of Britain. Hamilton was a charter member of the New York Manufacturing Society. He sought to attract British engineers and investors to come to the United States to quicken the pace of industrialization. Hamilton sent a colleague to Britain to gain knowledge of British industrial methods and technology. He hoped the federal government would encourage the development of industry and as secretary of the treasury he sought to convince Washington and Congress of his views. Although he agreed with Jefferson that agriculture would remain important, Hamilton foresaw that industry would come to dominate. Hamilton believed that industry would employ surplus labor, particularly immigrants. At Hamilton's suggestion, New Jersey created the Society for Establishing Useful Manufacturers. Jefferson outlived Hamilton and toward the end of his life came to understand that the movement toward industrialization was inevitable.

Industry in 19th-Century America

With the 19th century came the growth of industry, cities, and the number of immigrants as the labor pool. Pittsburgh, Cincinnati, and St. Louis came to challenge the older cities of the East as centers of industry. By the end of the War of 1812, the United States had about 15,000 industrial workers, a modest number to be sure. These workers concentrated on the manufacture of textiles, iron, paper, and flour, and the building of roads, canals, and ultimately railroads would transport these and other manufactured goods. In the 19th century, textile mills turned to women, young and old, in hopes of employing a submissive labor force. By 1830, women comprised 80 percent of textile workers. The tradition, at least in the 19th century and still in some sectors of the U.S. economy, was to pay poor wages. Textile mills were no exception. One mill in 1846 reduced wages 25 percent. Workers quit and the mill failed. This development marked one of the few instances of economic justice. Because wages were so low, U.S. cities aggregated more than their share of destitute people, many of them immigrants. By 1850, immigrants totaled more than half the labor in U.S. textile mills.

The Civil War stoked the growth of textiles and the move toward standardization in shoe and uniform sizes. After the Civil War the production of steel leapt from 16,000 tons in 1865 to 56 million tons in 1905. Industrialist Andrew Carnegie emerged as the leader of the steel industry worldwide in the 19th century. While he amassed a colossal fortune, he treated workers poorly. They received only one holiday per year, July 4. Low wages, the surveillance of workers, and terrible conditions prompted the infamous strike at the Homestead factory in Homestead, Pennsylvania, in 1892. Carnegie was on vacation, leaving the ruthless Henry Clay Frick in charge. A shootout ensued, leaving workers and thugs dead. Newspapers condemned Carnegie, but the violence did not appear to bother him. As a penalty for the strike, he halved wages.

As the pace of work accelerated throughout U.S. industries, supervisors attempted to squeeze every drop of sweat from their exhausted workers. Unions tried to improve conditions, but had few successes in the 19th century. Indeed,

except for a brief flowering in the 20th century, unions have benefited few industrial workers. Today, the union movement appears in retreat in the United States.

The rise of science and technology in the 19th century and even more so in the 20th and 21st centuries became important sources of intellectual capital on which industries could draw. The number of patents increased during the 19th century, and Alexander Graham Bell's patent of the telephone led to a telecommunications revolution. In 1883, the United States had some 100,000 phones, rising to 12 million by 1917. America's most celebrated inventor, Thomas Edison, patented an enormous number of inventions, the most important possibly being the incandescent light bulb. Factories increasingly used electricity, on which inventor Nicola Tesla labored, to power machines.

By 1850, New York and Philadelphia had emerged as the centers of U.S. industries, though by 1880 the Midwest, Chicago in particular, had emerged to challenge the Northeast. Between 1860 and 1870 the number of factory workers quadrupled in Chicago. Cincinnati, St. Louis, and Milwaukee also emerged as industrial centers during the 19th century. Between 1860 and 1880 industrial output in the United States doubled. Between 1880 and 1900 output quadrupled.

By 1890, the products of industries tripled the value of crops and livestock in the United States. By 1894, the United States surpassed Britain as the world's biggest manufacturer. By 1914, U.S. industries produced more than the industries of Britain, France, and Germany combined. In the 19th century oilman John D. Rockefeller created Standard Oil of Ohio, which he made into a trust in 1883. Standard Oil concentrated on refining and transporting oil. The company left to others the task of drilling for oil. At first Standard Oil refined oil into kerosene, which it sold at home and abroad to light lamps. The electric light and to a lesser extent the use of natural gas as an illuminant challenged the kerosene lamp, but by then a new contraption, the automobile, had emerged to consume oil. Standard Oil now refined oil into gasoline to power the automobile. This achievement made Rockefeller the world's richest industrialist. Bill Gates today has some $40 billion; if Rockefeller of Standard Oil had the same share of American money that he had in the late 19th century, he would be worth nearly $200 billion today. Standard Oil had a near monopoly on the refinement and transport of oil, alarming purists who agreed that competition was an important component of capitalism. In 1911, the U.S. Supreme Court dissolved Standard Oil, but its component companies remained powerful and grew in size and scope. Standard Oil of California emerged as Chevron. Perhaps more important, Standard Oil of New Jersey and Standard Oil of New York merged in 1999 to form ExxonMobil, the face of Big Oil today. Cheap oil and cheap energy in general powered the Industrial Revolution.

The 20th Century

In the early 20th century Henry Ford revolutionized the automobile industry. His Model T modernized transportation, labor, and the way Americans dined, attended the cinema, dated, and lived. The automobile became indispensable to the average American and helped create a consumer culture that has been the backbone of U.S. prosperity. He stood the Carnegies of the world on their head by paying $5 per day, then a good wage. Like other industrialists, however, Ford sought to scrutinize every aspect of workers' lives. His assembly line quickened the pace of work, and at least one worker's wife complained to Ford that her husband came home from work too tired to do anything. By 1920, the center of U.S. industries had moved from the Northeast to the Midwest.

One scholar believes that the success of industry in the United States owes much to Americans' fascination with machines. Evidence suggests that the United States had more machines per capita than did the nations of Europe. The abundance of natural resources may also account of the rapidity of the Industrial Revolution in the United States. Another scholar has drawn interesting parallels between wages and machines. As wages have risen, industrialists have substituted machines for labor. The era of the robot may be the strongest manifestation of this trend.

Economies of scale tripled in the mid-20th century as U.S. industries grew larger. The defenders of monopoly argued that it was a way to regulate what would otherwise be cutthroat competition. Even late in life, Rockefeller insisted that he had brought order and stability to the oil industry. After World War II, U.S. industries came increasingly to employ minorities, as Ford Motor Company did, and women. Industry came to spawn middle management jobs that it staffed with white men who had some semblance of an education.

Industry came to the South belatedly, first through the mechanization of cotton culture. Again the machine triumphed over labor. The mechanization of the sugarcane harvest in U.S. territory Puerto Rico had a similar effect. Florida has been a different story. Machines harvest some of the sugarcane, but near Lake Okeechobee in South Florida the ground is too wet to support machines. In these instances immigrants, primarily from Jamaica, harvest the cane. The labor force is almost entirely black.

The era of cheap oil, under which U.S. industries thrived, ended in the 1970s. In 1970, U.S. oil production peaked and has since declined while demand has soared. The only way to meet U.S. demand has been through imports, much of which comes from the Middle East. In 1973, Arab nations of the Organization of Petroleum Exporting Countries (OPEC) quadrupled the price of oil, and that year and into 1974 refused to export oil to the United States in retaliation for U.S. support for Israel in the Yom Kippur War. Panicked Americans waited in long lines for gasoline and truckers parked their rigs on highways to protest high gasoline prices. In 1974, U.S. industrial production fell 10 percent. American industry, if it were to survive, would need to become more energy efficient.

Factories in Japan rose to challenge U.S. industries. Japanese automobiles contested Ford, General Motors, and Chrysler. If U.S. industries were in the doldrums, the Cold War might have been a culprit. U.S. industries, dependent on government contracts, produced armaments but seemingly lost the ability to manufacture the world's best televisions, stereos, and videocassette recorders. Industries responded by slashing wages to save themselves. Some moved to the South, which did not have a tradition of unions and high wages. The migration of Latinos to Florida, Texas, and other regions of the South served as cheap labor for industry. By 1980, the South had gained 1 million manufacturing jobs, while the Northeast and Midwest lost 2 million jobs. The Midwest became the Rust Belt. Other industries moved to Mexico, Singapore, and other regions of Asia, forever in search of the lowest wages. Ford made its popular Ranger vehicle and other models in Mexico.

The 21st Century

As industry eroded the purchasing power of American workers, government demanded austerity, firing teachers, firefighters, and police. Since the late 20th century, industrial policies have impoverished the masses and widened the gap between rich and poor. In the first years of the 21st century, the income of the richest 1 percent of Americans doubled, whereas the bottom 60 percent of wage earners saw their incomes fall. In 2000, one third of all U.S. industrial workers toiled below the poverty line. Labor is in retreat, having lost more than 3 million members in the first decade of the 21st century. In 2000, only 15 percent of industrial workers belonged to a union.

See also

Big Oil; Capitalism; Consumerism; Fordism; Immigration; Labor Movement; Mass Production; Mercantilism

CHRISTOPHER CUMO

Further Reading

Hillstrom, Kevin, and Laurie Collier Hillstrom,. eds. 2006. *Industrial Revolution in America: Automobiles.* Santa Barbara, CA: ABC-CLIO.

Kunstler, James Howard. 2000. *The Long Emergency: Surviving the Converging Catastrophes of the Twenty-First Century.* New York: Atlantic Monthly Press.

Wyatt, Lee T., III. 2009. *The Industrial Revolution.* Westport, CT: Greenwood Press, 2009.

Industrial Revolution—Primary Document

Introduction

In 1791, Secretary of the Treasury Alexander Hamilton wrote A Report on Manufactures *that he submitted to Congress. It expressed his hope for public and private capital to support America's nascent Industrial Revolution. It also was an important part of the first political, economic, and ideological controversies of the early American republic. Secretary of State Thomas Jefferson disagreed with Hamilton; Jefferson believed in a more agrarian society and a weaker central government than the one that Hamilton contemplated.*

Document: Alexander Hamilton's *Report on Manufactures* (December 5, 1791)

Of this some experience has been had in the instance of the Pennsylvania society, [for the Promotion of Manufactures and useful Arts;] but the funds of that association have been too contracted to produce more than a very small portion of the good to which the principles of it would have led. It may confidently be affirmed that there is scarcely any thing, which has been devised, better calculated to excite a general spirit of improvement than the institutions of this nature. They are truly invaluable.

In countries where there is great private wealth much may be effected by the voluntary contributions of patriotic individuals, but in a community situated like that of the United States, the public purse must supply the deficiency of private resource. In what can it be so useful as in prompting and improving the efforts of industry?

Source: press-pubs.uchicago.edu/founders/documents/a1_8_8s9.html.

INFORMATION AGE

The Information Age began in the early 1970s when information became increasingly accessible through computers and especially proliferated with the invention of the Internet. It was not an age of new information per se, but instead, a time when information became more easily accessible through digital means and was used for advanced communication, social networking, and other purposes. This new medium prompted a transformative change in the United States as people more easily gained access to information; used it for local, national, and international business transactions; and were able to more facilely and speedily communicate. The Information Age essentially launched the United States into the future as a global leader in electronic technology, advanced communication, and economics. It transformed American culture as people turned to the computer to get their news, shop, communicate with relatives, friends, and colleagues through e-mail, twitter, Facebook, and other social networking means, and for other activities.

CNN journalist Tony Silvia observed the phenomenon of the transformation of journalism in the Information Age by describing how digitization of the media has changed the way people access and perceive the news. In his book, *Global News: Perspectives on the Information Age*, he explains how "the Internet is hardly the beginning, nor will it be the end of the advanced technology that makes a journalist's job simultaneously easier and harder—easier because it makes information processing and transmission tantamount to child's play, harder because some would argue that this same technology complicates the decisions we make about what gets covered and what doesn't" (p.168). People can access the news anywhere and anytime as long as they have access to the Internet. They do not have to go to a store to purchase a magazine or newspaper because the information they need is readily and easily available on the Internet. Such is the convenience of having cable twenty-four hours a day, seven days a week, at least for those who can afford it. While the Information Age made access to information more convenient for computer users, it also has brought some unintended consequences.

Prior to the Information Age, newspaper editors had considerable control over what information was included and what was excluded. Part of this was prompted by space limitations. With the digitization of news and other information, space no longer became an issue. Furthermore, editors no longer have as much control over what information to include online because they know people have multiple methods through which they can get what they need on the Internet. As Silvia points out, this has forced media organizations to change how they deliver content to their readers. It also has resulted in many print organizations merging with larger and more profitable companies, or going out of business.

Legacy media corporations such as *The New York Times, Boston Globe,* and *Los Angeles Times* have lost hundreds of thousands of dollars due to a sharp decline in print subscriptions as a result of greater demand for online news. Other, smaller companies such as *The Baltimore Examiner, Kentucky Post, Cincinnati Post*, and *Albuquerque Tribune* went out of business. Despite the convenience of easy access to news online, the costs of the Information Age have been devastating to print media—not only newspapers and magazines, but also books.

In 2011, Borders Bookstore, one of the largest book retail stores in the United States, declared bankruptcy and went out of business. Among the many reasons for its downfall was the company's late recognition of the book industry going electronic, and companies such as Barnes and Nobles and Amazon foresaw this trend early on, and shifted their business strategies to selling books online. Electronic books were much easier to download and cheaper to purchase than print books. The popularity of the Kindle and Nook transformed the book business. But bookstores were not the only companies to embrace the popularity and profitability of electronic books.

Textbook companies also have changed how they do business with schools because students are now able to access the information they need electronically. Students no longer have to carry heavy backpacks and book bags because they can purchase and download the textbooks electronically. Additionally, the availability of electronic textbooks has reduced how much students have to spend on books each year. But these textbook companies are large enough to be able to make the shift from print to electronic without losing much money. This has not been the case for libraries.

Historically, libraries have been keepers of massive volumes of print materials. With the digitization of information, however, fewer books sit on bookshelves because many of them are available digitally online. As a result, not only are libraries facing reduced holdings, but also shrinking budgets with the tight economy. This potentially was the death knell for many libraries. While the consequences of the digitization of information have been negatively impactful to certain businesses, they have been advantageous to society in general.

An interview with Vinton Cerf, one of the inventors of ARPA (which later became the Internet), explained this phenomenon. Once someone asked him when the Sony Walkman was invented. After pulling out his Blackberry, and researching it on Google, he replied, "1981." An e-mail from another person said, "No, you're wrong, it was actually 1979." Some dueling went on before all parties agreed that it originally was invented in 1979, but proliferated in the 1980s until the compact Discman became popular and replaced it. What amazed Cerf was the possibility of having conversations with multiple people via e-mail or through other electronic means with the capability of referencing and finding what they needed within seconds. This far surpassed what Cerf and his colleagues originally had envisioned. It had not occurred to them how the digitalization of information would be so easily accessible to people who could find what they needed in seconds. Nor had they envisioned how the Information Age range would result in an integrated global network of information, business transactions, and social organizations, or as Manuel Castells puts it, a "globalization of economy, technology, and communication" (p.311). In essence, the Industrial Revolution had ended, and the post–Industrial Revolution age began.

In this post-Industrial Age, businesses functioned considerably differently as a result of computers. They needed fewer workers to perform job functions because computer-driven robots could do them more easily and efficiently. With computers, companies were able to save money by consolidating operations to make them run more efficiently and increase productivity through a more highly specialized workforce. Many of them could diversify based on which areas of their products were in the greatest demand. Prior to the 1960s and 1970s, this was not the case as high-tech industrial parks were considerably smaller in number, and had a less efficient workforce. Today, many urban and suburban communities have several high-tech industrial parks. Silicon Valley, for example, is one of the most advanced, industrialized high-tech areas in the United States. It epitomizes the Information Age as computer technicians, programmers, and specialists create logarithms enabling millions of people to instantly communicate with each other through e-mail, twitter, text messaging, and other electronic means. They also have created some of the most advanced, sophisticated software systems used by corporations globally to run more efficiently and generate greater profits. Apple Computer, for instance, has opened thousands of stores worldwide showcasing the latest in computer technology, software, and inventions. Phone companies such as AT&T, Verizon, T-Mobile, and others have cornered the cellular phone market with devices that can perform multiple tasks through applications. Each year, these companies and many others meet to showcase their latest inventions.

As journalist Silvia put it, "Digital technology has put more knowledge and information within reach of more people than any other invention known to man" (p.191). It has transformed the world by creating a system of easier and faster communication, increased efficiency, productivity, and profitability for many global companies, and created a larger global economy. However, that greater accessibility applies only to people who have access to computers. Many of the world's poor people do not have computers, and as a result, cannot access information, but that is changing as more schools in lower-income communities receive computers through government grants and donations from national and local businesses and private parties. Schools are converting traditional classrooms into virtual classrooms to take maximum advantage of technology, including digital archives filled with information that usually would be difficult or impossible to obtain without spending considerable time and money to access.

Apple Computer's motto is true: we are living in "an Apple world," meaning with the digitization of information, and advances in electronic technology, the world indeed has become more electronically and technologically driven. Some would argue that this transformation is for the better, and others for the worse. Regardless, there is considerable agreement among scholars and other experts that living in the Information Age has been beneficial to many people globally, especially as literacy rates increase, people are becoming more aware of what is happening around them thanks to the easy availability of information, communication has substantially improved, and many businesses have benefited from advanced computer software programs. In fact, each year in Las Vegas, a number of the world's electronic technology companies gather at a convention to showcase their latest inventions. For example, people no longer have to purchase a camera and wait until the film develops to get pictures. Using the camera on their cellular phones, they can point and click, and immediately upload their pictures to Facebook or Instagram, and send them as e-mail attachments to friends and relatives—and the quality of the pictures rivals those taken by cameras. Airbus, one of the world's largest aircraft manufacturers, has released a prototype of an airliner it plans to build in 2050 that includes a virtual computer station at every seat. Instead of having to bring their computers and other electronic equipment onboard, passengers will be able to access a suite of applications including their e-mail, news, other functions, and watch movies all on a virtual screen. The question surrounding the Information Age is not what new technology will emerge, but is there a limit to what the technology can do? Is there another coming age beyond the Information Age? We can only wait.

See also

Commercialization; Internet Nation; Mass Communication

DANIEL K. BUBB

Further Reading

Castells, Manuel. 2009. *The Rise of the Network Society: The Information Age: Economy, Society and Culture, Volume 1*. 2nd ed. New York: Wiley-Blackwell.

Houle, David. 2013. *Entering the Shift Age: The End of the Information Age and the New Era of Transformation*. Naperville, IL: Sourcebooks.

Silvia, Tony, ed. 2001. *Global News: Perspectives on the Information Age*. New York: Wiley-Blackwell.

Information Age—Primary Documents

Introduction

Tony Silvia was a journalist for CNN and became chair of the Department of Journalism and professor of journalism and communication studies at the University of Rhode Island. In Document 1, an excerpt from Silvia's book, Global News: Perspectives on the Information Age, *Silvia and other journalists write about how they witnessed the dramatic transformation of the news from editor-controlled content in print to the empowered consumers accessing news stories through different methods in the Information Age.*

Vinton Cerf, currently Google's chief Internet promoter, was one of the inventors of ARPA, the forerunner of the Internet. In Document 2, an interview of Cerf conducted by Donald Nielson in Mountain View, California, in November 2007, Cerf discusses how ARPA evolved, and how it eventually became the Internet, which is one of the cornerstones of the Information Age.

Document 1 Tony Silvia's *Global News: Perspectives on the Information Age* (2001)

"While working both as a writer in the CNN newsroom and as a correspondent in its features unit, I would often be in awe of a news agency with such power and reach. The very idea that my stories would be seen by millions of people in countries I would never visit, also brought with it a strong sense of responsibility."

"This book never could have been written, certainly not in the form in which it now exists, without the advent of the Internet. Most of the chapters were written, edited, rewritten, and transmitted electronically."

"Our 15-year-old son is already a columnist for an Internet Web site and communicates via e-mail with literally hundreds of readers from around the world everyday. Casey, our college-age daughter, uses the Internet to disperse knowledge about political candidates across the globe via a website operated by a group called "Project Vote Smart.""

"Whether (Ted) Turner realized it or not, his 1980 launch of CNN was perhaps the single most important action taken toward changing how we define news, from the perspectives of both content and delivery. Turner clearly had a larger ambition: to create an international news service that would expand the definition of news to include people and concerns beyond our rural and urban neighborhoods and national borders.

"Turner's concept is "news on demand," around the clock 24 hours, seven days a week. Nothing could have been more radical nor more suited to its time, for the growth of the global economy, coupled with CNN's readily available new programming, made the push to distribute CNN internationally an obvious business strategy for Turner."

"The technology of the Internet is a technology that creates expectations at the same time as it scuttles to satisfy them. Its rapidity is part of a media culture in which rapidity has replaced reflection. Rapid ease of access to information has put certain stories and categories of stories on new managers' agendas that, minus today's technology, might not have entered our collective journalistic consciousness."

Source: Silvia, Tony, ed. *Global News: Perspectives on the Information Age*. Ames, IA: Iowa State University Press, 2001, pp. xvi, xvii, 5, 6.

Document 2: Oral History Interview with Vinton Cerf by Donald Nielson in Mountain View, California (November 7, 2007)

"What intrigued me about the ARPANET was that there were computer programs interacting with each other, not just terminals interacting with remote programs but the possibility of programs interacting, and you could begin to imagine these virtual environments, not the 3-D games-based environments, but these virtual communications environments that would allow computer programs to exchange information and for some reason the idea that these programs had a life of their own and they could interact with each other that I found very intriguing."

"When this system was first designed, the whole idea was, if you follow the following rules you can build your own piece of internet and connect to it, and it should work. That's basically all the philosophy was, let anybody build anything they want to as long as it meets these requirements. What has happened is that the economics of all of this are driving towards aggregation of service providing. People for a long time, for example, when the internet was first made available to the public, most of the public got access to it by dial up modems. This had the following interesting property: You can change internet service providers by dialing a different number. So the overhead of changing was de minimis. Then broadband comes along, and suddenly it gets harder to switch providers because getting a broadband facility then means sometimes a cable pole, or fiber pole, or something, significant amounts of time and energy go into those broadband connections. And, if you want to switch, it's not a question of dialing a different number, it's a question of picking up the phone and talking to somebody about bringing another truck rollout to provide you with a different access channel. So the competition among broadband carriers is very limited in my view. In other parts of the world where there isn't very much competition either, broadband has been very successful anyway. So, if you go to South Korea, for example, something like 70 percent of the country is on broadband capability. The UK is doing very well in this regard."

"I am always stunned when I discover when I'm looking for information that it's there. I mean, sitting at the dinner table and somebody says something—I'll tell you, I was having dinner in New York. Somebody said when was the Sony Walkman invented? And so I'm sitting at the dinner table and I, you know, get my Blackberry out, and I fire up Google, and I go and look and I find 1981. And a few hours later I get an email from somebody saying, "No, you're wrong, it was actually 1979." And we have dueling, you know, back up documents to prove one or the other. But the thing is that

was a casual act. I'll give you another example of casual and stunning. I was in a hotel in Los Angeles last week, and I was on a video chat with my son, who's in Hollywood. And he says why don't we get mom on the line; she's in Washington. So we bring up a three-way video chat on the i-Chat application on the Macs. We all have the same, you know, wonderful Macs with the little television camera. So we're all three chatting away, Echo cancellation is working fine, no one's wearing headsets. And then my wife says, oh, would you like to see how the fireplace is coming? Because we're building an extra fireplace in the basement. And I said, sure. So she unplugs and she's using Wi-Fi, of course, and it's got a battery, so she just casually walks down the stairs as we're chatting away, aims the camera at the fireplace and I get to see how far the construction has gotten. And after that whole thing was over, I was thinking, I don't believe that. I mean, we used to have 17 engineers to try to figure out how to get the video set up and get the audio advance and everything else, and here are three of us, very casually, without thinking about it, had this three-way conversation, and she's wandering around with the television camera, aiming at the fireplace to tell us what's going on. And I thought, my God, have we ever come a long way from where we were in 1981 when we were trying to do video conferencing over the ARPANET and the Internet."

Source: Computer History Museum. www.computerhistory. org/collections/catalog/102658186. Also available in pdf format at http://archive.computerhistory.org/resources/access/text/ 2012/04/102658186-05-01-acc.pdf.

INTERNET NATION

In 1989, computer scientist Dr. Tim Berners-Lee submitted a proposal on his invention of a computer management system that helped people solve the problem of loss of information in complex evolving systems. Through the use of a hypertext and hyperlink system, people could more easily organize and store their computer files, communicate, and have easier access to global information through HTML. Berners-Lee's invention would ultimately become known as the World Wide Web.

Communication technology and time have played a transformative role in the economic, social, and cultural growth and development of the United States. Prior to the invention

Everything Is Easy opened in Times Square, New York City, on November 28, 2000. It was the world's largest Internet café, with 800 computers for those who wanted to stop in and log in. Internet cafés became less popular as more people obtained their own computers and then smartphones. (Pool LeFranc US/Gamma-Rapho via Getty Images)

of the telegram and telephone, people communicated by letter, which was time-consuming because the letters had to be transported by horse and, depending on the destination, took days and, in some cases, weeks to deliver. In the 19th century, the telephone sped up the communication process, enabling one person to talk to another person within minutes. Today, communication is virtually instant thanks to the Internet. With a computer and an Internet connection, one person can e-mail another, or talk face to face on computer screens within seconds. Through the Internet, people also have been able to conduct business, make bank transactions, shop, and download music within minutes and without having to leave their homes. While many types of technology have helped the United States become a globally advanced nation, arguably few technologies have had as great an impact as the Internet.

With more than two-thirds of the nation's population using the Internet for communication and a variety of other purposes, the United States has become an Internet nation.

In the early 1960s, computer scientist Joseph Licklider of the Massachusetts Institute of Technology envisioned a network where people globally could access data and communicate with each other through their computers. He invented a system called the Galactic Network, which provided this capability but was extremely limited and slow. Other MIT scholars—namely Ivan Sutherland, Bob Taylor, Lawrence Roberts, and Leonard Kleinrock—also envisioned and experimented with a similar system. Roberts was able to link a computer in Massachusetts to a computer in California, but only through a low-speed dial-up system. At the same time, the government and military were looking for ways to create a communication system that would protect the country from attack, and enable military personnel in different parts of the country to communicate with each other within seconds. In 1969, the Department of Defense contracted with scientists in California and Utah to invent a high-speed communication system. They developed ARPANET, which facilitated near-instant communication in different locations. Scientists Robert Kahn and Vinton Cerf invented the Transmission Control Protocol (TCP), a device that would accommodate and enable multiple networks communicating with each other through faster speeds. In the 1980s, private companies soon invented their own devices that would perform the same function as the TCP. Unfortunately, the dial-up connections were slower, and had weak signals that caused multiple interruptions including lost connections in the middle of a conversation or e-mail. This frustrated Internet users. Today, communications companies have faster means of connectivity for Internet users so they can connect anywhere in the country or world virtually instantly with greater reliability in connection strength. What began as an experiment by a small group of researchers has become a global commodity where hundreds of millions of people and businesses can begin communicating with each other within seconds.

The Internet has enabled many companies to increase their efficiency and productivity by allowing them to directly place orders, communicate, and process transactions within minutes. As a result, businesses also have been able to expand their operations to other parts of the world through these and other cost-saving measures thanks to the Internet. With greater speed and newer and better capabilities, more companies have been able to hook up and expand their efficiency and profitability as a result of being connected to the Internet.

While the Internet has provided many benefits for users, one of the challenges it faces is slower connectivity in rural communities. While many towns and cities in the United States have Internet broadband width access, many rural communities do not, and as a result, dial-up connection can take time and frustrate users. Additionally, some people living in urban and rural communities do not have access to the Internet because they cannot afford to own a computer. Statistics show that 75 percent of households with an income lower than $15,000 and 67 percent of households with an income between $15,000 and $35,000 have no access to the Internet because they do not have a computer or other electronic device that is connected to the Internet. Sixty percent of adults with a high school degree and 87 percent of adults with less than a high school education do not use the Internet. Also, Internet connectivity is expensive, and often bundled in packages offered by communication providers to consumers who do not need the extra amenities. Many lower and middle-class households simply do not have the budget to afford these packages, and as a result have limited or no access to the Internet. Though the country has made considerable progress using satellite technology, slow connectivity and Internet affordability continue to be problems for some Americans. Despite these problems, experts believe given how advanced the United States has become through innovations in technology that it will not be long before people and businesses in rural communities have improved access, and faster communication capability through increased broadband width or wireless Internet connectivity. Also, they believe that Internet access will become more affordable as more communications companies enter the market.

As communications technology continues to improve, so does Internet connectivity, which has become a staple of American society and culture. People can check their e-mail on their cellular phones or laptop computers as long as they have Internet access. They can conduct business on commercial passengers planes, in airport lounges, hotel atria, libraries, and in coffee shops that have Internet connectivity. Essentially, people do not have to disrupt their lives as long as they have a cellular phone or computer and Internet access. They can shop online for their favorite items and have those goods delivered to their homes. But, there are consequences that come with convenience. Many local establishments struggle to keep up with larger companies that cater to online shoppers. These merchants do not have the selection nor volume of goods to sell at competitive prices that people can buy online and have shipped to their front doors. Internet shopping has forced many "mom-and-pop" stores to either adapt to online sales or go out of business (the latter far more frequent than the former). Even medium- and larger-sized companies such as bookstores and department stores struggle to keep up with the online competition.

One other consequence of Internet use is hacking. Although there are companies that offer protection against hackers getting into Internet users accounts (that contain credit card and personal information), there are skilled hackers who can access Internet users' accounts with little effort. This is one reason why some people refuse to use the Internet, especially for banking transactions. They also fear that Internet viruses will invade their computers and destroy the hard drives containing personal information and important documents. While many computer antivirus software companies guarantee the effectiveness of their products, Internet users are not immune to "superbugs" that can completely destroy their hard drives, wipe out important information, and cost them hundreds of dollars to have new hard drives installed or in some cases have to buy a new computer. The world of cybercrime is becoming more sophisticated, and with more people using the Internet for shopping, banking, and other personal activities, they remain even more vulnerable to these sophisticated hackers.

Despite the potential dangers of connecting to the Internet, the United States will continue to be an Internet nation. Businesses, contemporary societal needs, and American culture depend on the Internet. But, can the Internet keep up with the rapidly growing and developing computer industry? With smaller, faster, and more sophisticated computers, the Internet has to be able to keep up with the applications, live streaming, and other capabilities on users' cellular phones and portable laptop computers. Despite the pressure to keep up, the Internet still has made its imprint on the country. As MIT computer and Internet pioneering scientists Barry Leiner, Vinton Cerf, David Clark, and others put it, "The Internet has revolutionized the computer and communications worlds like nothing before. The telegraph, telephone, radio, and computer have all set the stage for the Internet's unprecedented integration of capabilities. The Internet is at once a worldwide broadcasting capability, a mechanism for information dissemination, and a medium for collaboration and interaction between individuals and their computers without regard for geographic location" (p.102).

There is little doubt among these and other scholars that the Internet has been one of the most transformative technologies ever invented, but a larger and more relevant question they pose is: can people keep up with the Internet capabilities and advancements in computer technology? Recent trends show that newer generations of Americans are better able to keep up with advances in computer technology and the Internet, while older generations of Americans require more time to keep up. According to Internet researcher Roger

E. Clancy, people ages five to twenty-five showed greater use of the Internet (92 percent) compared to people ages thirty to eighty (55 percent). In fact, many college students nearly exclusively use the Internet for research and other class assignments, thereby requiring colleges to have computer labs or dorms with Internet access, and libraries enabling students to have access to the Internet and digitized books and other sources of information. Many colleges and universities offer entire degree programs online to global consumers who can afford the tuition and have access to the Internet.

No Americans will forget when Neil Armstrong, Buzz Aldrin, and other astronauts landed on the moon. They will not forget when Henry Ford introduced his Model A and Model T automobiles to the country. They will remember when the Wright brothers inaugurated the concept of flight. All of these were remarkable technological achievements. But, so was the time when computer users first were able to write and send e-mails, or access a world of information through the Internet. The Internet certainly was another hallmark of technological innovation and achievement in the United States, and will continue to make its economic, social, and cultural impact felt not only by Americans but also by other global peoples who too are able to enjoy the same benefits of being connected to the Internet.

See also

Commercialization; Consumerism; Information Age; Mass Communication; Mass Production

DANIEL K. BUBB

Further Reading

Cerf, V. G., and Kahn, R. E. 1974. "A Protocol for Packet Network Interconnection." *IEEE Trans/Comm Tech* 5 (May): 627–641.

Clancy, Roger E. 2002. *A Nation Online: How Americans Are Expanding Their Use of the Internet.* Hauppauge, NY: Nova Science Publishers.

Keefer, Alice, and Tomas Baiget. 2001. "How It All Began: A Brief History of the Internet." *Vine* 31 (September): 90–95.

Kleinrock, L. 1961. "Information Flow in Large Communication Nets." *RLE Quarterly Progress Report* (July).

Internet Nation—Primary Document

Introduction

These are excerpts from Dr. Tim Berners-Lee's "Information Management: A Proposal," which outlined a new and easier

method by which people could organize their computer files, communicate, and have easier access to global information through use of a hypertext and hyperlink system (HTML). Berners-Lee's proposal, presented in March 1989 to CERN (European Organization for Nuclear Research), would ultimately become known as the World Wide Web.

Document: "Information Management: A Proposal" by Tim Berners-Lee (March 1989)

"Many of the discussions of the future at CERN and the LHC era end with the question: how will we ever keep track of such a large project? This proposal provides an answer to such questions. Firstly, I discuss the problem of information access at CERN. Then, I introduce the idea of linked information systems, and compare them with less flexible ways of finding information. I then summarise my short experience with non-linear text systems known as "hypertext," describe what CERN needs from such a system, and what industry may provide. Finally, I suggest steps we should take to involve ourselves with hypertext now, so that individually and collectively we may understand what we are creating."

"If a CERN experiment were a static once-only development, all the information could be written in a big book. As it is, CERN is constantly changing as new ideas are produced, as new technology becomes available, and in order to get around unforeseen technical problems. When a change is necessary, it normally affects only a small part of the organisation. A local reason arises for changing a part of the experiment or detector. At this point, one has to dig around to find out what other parts and people will be affected. Keeping a book up to date becomes impractical, and the structure of the book needs to be constantly revised.

The sort of information we are discussing answers, for example, questions like:

Where is this module used?
Who wrote this code? Where does he work?
What documents exist about that concept?
Which laboratories are included in that project?

Which systems depend on this device?
What documents refer to this one?

The problems of information loss may be particularly acute at CERN, but in this case (as in certain others), CERN is a model in miniature of the rest of world in a few years time. CERN meets now some problems which the rest of the world will have to face soon. In 10 years, there may be many commercial solutions to the problems above, while today we need something to allow us to continue."

Linked Information Systems

In providing a system for manipulating this sort of information, the hope would be to allow a pool of information to develop which could grow and evolve with the organisation and the projects it describes. For this to be possible, the method of storage must not place its own restraints on the information.

This is why a "web" of notes with links (like references) between them is far more useful than a fixed hierarchical system. When describing a complex system, many people resort to diagrams with circles and arrows. Circles and arrows leave one free to describe the interrelationships between things in a way that tables, for example, do not. The system we need is like a diagram of circles and arrows, where circles and arrows can stand for anything. We can call the circles nodes, and the arrows links. Suppose each node is like a small note, summary article, or comment. I'm not over concerned here with whether it has text or graphics or both. Ideally, it represents or describes one particular person or object. In practice, it is useful for the system to be aware of the generic types of the links between items (dependences, for example), and the types of nodes (people, things, documents. . .) without imposing any limitations.

An Article in the UUCP News Scheme

The Subject field allows notes on the same topic to be linked together within a "newsgroup". The name of the newsgroup (alt.hypertext) is a hierarchical name. This particular note is expresses a problem with the strict tree structure of the scheme: this discussion is related to several areas. Note that the "References", "From" and "Subject" fields can all be used to generate links."

"A linked system takes this to the next logical step. Keywords can be nodes which stand for a concept. A keyword node is then no different from any other node. One can link documents, etc., to keywords. One can then find keywords by finding any node to which they are related. In this way, documents on similar topics are indirectly linked, through their key concepts."

"It has been difficult to assess the effect of a large system on an organisation, often because these systems never had seriously large-scale use. For this reason, we require large amounts of existing information should be accessible using any new information management system."

"The CERNDOC system provides the mechanics of storing and printing documents. A linked system would allow one to browse through concepts, documents, systems and authors, also allowing references between documents to be stored. (Once a document had been found, the existing machinery could be invoked to print it or display it)."

Incentives and CALS

"The US Department of Defence has given a big incentive to hypermedia research by, in effect, specifying hypermedia documentation for future procurement. This means that all manuals for parts for defence equipment must be provided in hypermedia form. The acronym CALS stands for ÒComputer-aided Acquisition and Logistic Support). There is also much support from the publishing industry, and from librarians whose job it is to organise information."

What Will the System Look Like?

"Let us see what components a hypertext system at CERN must have. The only way in which sufficient flexibility can be incorporated is to separate the information storage software from the information display software, with a well defined interface between them. Given the requirement for network access, it is natural to let this clean interface coincide with the physical division between the user and the remote database machine.

(A client/server split at this level also makes multi-access more easy, in that a single server process can service many clients, avoiding the problems of simultaneous access to one database by many different users.)

This division also is important in order to allow the heterogeneity which is required at CERN and would be a boon for the world in general. Therefore, an important phase in the design of the system is to define this interface. After that, the development of various forms of display program and of database server can proceed in parallel. This will have been done well if many different information sources, past, present and future, can be mapped onto the definition, and if many different human interface programs can be written over the years to take advantage of new technology and standards."

Source: "Information Management: A Proposal." CERN, March 1989. Available at http://www.w3.org/History/1989/proposal.html.

ISLAMIC FUNDAMENTALISM

Islamic Fundamentalism is a political concept based on the idea that the fundamentals of Islam, the Koran (the holy text of Islam) and the *Sunnah* (a collection of writings describing the life and actions of the Prophet Muhammad), are as sufficient to guide the Muslim world today as they were in the early years of Islam. Many Islamic Fundamentalists reject the bifurcation of religion and politics that much of the Western world inherited from the Enlightenment. Islam, they argue, is an all-encompassing system for society. It should not be relegated to the private sphere through Western-style secularism. Instead, Islamic principles should inform social relationships and Islamic law (Sharia) should provide the framework for political systems. Islamic Fundamentalism is the underlying theory behind many recent political movements in the Middle East and North Africa that have shaped American perceptions of Islam and influenced American foreign policy. Recent events with links to Islamic Fundamentalism include the Egyptian Revolution of 2011, the rise of the Muslim Brotherhood, the influence of Al Qaeda and similar terrorist groups, the Arab Spring, and the Egyptian Revolution of 2011.

The term *Fundamentalism* was coined in the United States in the 1920s to describe a Christian religious movement

An effigy of the deposed shah of Iran is burned during a demonstration outside the U.S. Embassy in Tehran in late 1979. Iran's Islamic Revolution of that year began as an uprising against Shah Mohammad Reza Pahlavi, whose autocratic rule and ties to the West were extremely unpopular in his country. (AP Photo)

that stressed adherence to the "fundamental" aspects of the Christian faith, notably the inerrancy of scripture and the virgin birth. Christian Fundamentalists rejected biblical criticism and cultural and theological liberalism. In the years since the Iranian Revolution of 1979, the concept of Islamic Fundamentalism has been used to describe a wide range of Islamic reform movements and political ideologies, including very liberal, modern reform movements that seek a cooperative relationship with the West and very strict, dogmatic movements that reject modernity, technology, and modern conceptions of human rights.

A defining feature of Islamic Fundamentalism is a sense that the modern Islamic world has become too closely aligned with the West, and as such has lost its former glory. Islamic Fundamentalists believe the earliest years of Islam represent the purest form of Islamic community. In 622 CE,

Muhammad led a small band of followers from Mecca to Medina, both cities in the Arabian Peninsula. This migration (the *Hijra*) marks the beginning of an independent Islamic religious and political community. The Muslims remained in Medina under Muhammad's leadership until his death in 632. The Prophet was succeeded by four *caliphs*, religious and political leaders who oversaw the rapid expansion of Islam throughout the Arabian Peninsula until 661. Islamic Fundamentalists attribute the many political and military successes of this early period in Islamic history to the fact that this community was united as a singular religious and political community. Rather than being relegated to the private sphere, Islam was the central belief system around which the community was organized. Because early Muslims were true to their faith, Fundamentalists argue, Islam spread quickly throughout the Middle East, North Africa, and parts of Asia.

If modern-day Muslims would return to the fundamentals of Islam, the Muslim world would once again experience the successes of Islam's early era.

In Sunni Islam, the era from the mid-8th century to the mid-13th century CE is considered the Golden Age of Islam. While most of Europe was embroiled in the Dark Ages, much of the Islamic world was united under powerful Islamic empires. During this period, Islam spread throughout North Africa and the Middle East, and the Islamic world was the center of global culture and learning. As the Western world emerged from the Dark Ages, the apex of global intellectualism shifted from cities such as Baghdad and Najaf to Paris and London. Three hundred years of Western colonialism in the Middle East and Africa resulted in much of the Muslim world being divided up into arbitrary geopolitical boundaries that benefitted the former colonizers but did not reflect the actual geopolitical situation in these territories. As a result, the Muslim world has been mired in conflict for centuries. The death knell for the glory days of political Islam was the collapse of the Ottoman Empire in 1924. The Ottoman Empire was the last transcontinental Muslim empire. With its collapse, the Muslim world was broken up into the countries we know today. No longer was the state ruled by a caliph, the religious and political leader of the *ummah* (the Muslim community). Instead, Muslim-majority countries in the Middle East and North Africa resembled secular Western nation-states. Islamic Fundamentalists believe that in order for the Muslim world to gain a degree of political stability and to compete in an increasingly globalized world, Muslims must return to the fundamentals of the faith, and Islamic principles must guide politics and society once again. Many Islamic Fundamentalists reject Western secularism and the geopolitical legacy left by European colonization. However, the rejection of these Western ideas can take countless forms throughout the Islamic world. The Medina Period (622–661 CE) and the Golden Age (8th century–13th century CE) are frequently evoked by Islamic Fundamentalists as proof that a rejection of Western secularism in favor of a new Islamic state will return the Islamic world to its former glory.

Muhammad ibn 'Abdul Wahhab (1703–1792), considered by some scholars to be the mastermind of Fundamentalism, remains one of the most influential Islamic Fundamentalist thinkers in history. Wahhab argued that the Muslims of the Medina Period in Islamic history were practicing a true and pure faith. Further, rites and rituals that developed after this early period were erroneous developments informed by centuries of fallible interpretation. In order to return to a true and pure Islam, he argued, Muslims must return to the Koran and Sunnah with a fresh new perspective. Rather than rely on interpretations of the Koran that had developed over the previous millennium, followers of Wahhab developed their own interpretations. In doing this, they were practicing *ijtihad* (the right to interpret the Koran for oneself). *Ijtihad* is a critical concept within Islamic Fundamentalism. During the medieval period, Muslim scholars argued that the gates of ijtihad had closed because Arabic, the language in which the Koran and Sunnah were written, had changed too dramatically since the time of the Prophet. Only those with a clear grasp of classical Arabic could truly grasp the spirit of those documents. Islamic Fundamentalists like Wahhab reject the idea that *ijtihad* is closed to Muslims. They argue that Muslims can and should interpret the Koran for themselves within a modern context. Wahhab's strict Fundamentalism was not widely popular during his lifetime. After being expelled from his hometown, Wahhab found an ally in a powerful political leader named Muhammad bin Saud. Together, Wahhab and Saud founded Saudi Arabia, and their descendants still rule that country. In Saudi Arabia, Fundamentalist principles have resulted in one of the most culturally conservative countries on the planet. However, many progressive reform movements in Saudi Arabia and other countries appeal to Fundamentalist principles in an effort to counteract strict conservatism. For example, Islamic feminist movements point out that Islam provides very progressive protections for women in marriage and divorce and maintains a healthy respect for women as valued members of Muslim culture. While many reform movements could be considered "Fundamentalist," reform goals differ based on interpretations of fundamental Islamic principles.

The leading Islamic Fundamentalist of the 20th century was Sayyid Qutb (1906–1966). A prominent member of the Muslim Brotherhood organization, Qutb was a staunch opponent of Egyptian president Gamal Abdel Nasser, who ruled Egypt from 1956 to 1970. Nasser's Egypt was built around the concept of pan-Arab Nationalism and Westernization. Whereas Islamic Fundamentalists like Qutb hoped for a new Egyptian state based on Islamic principles, Nasser wanted Egypt to be largely secular, modern, and Westernized. Much of Qutb's writings were concerned with the idea of Islamic justice, which he thought was inherent within Islam. The first type of justice that Fundamentalists believe Islam provides is social justice. Social justice is not provided by separating religion and politics. Rather, social justice originates from the incorporation of Islam into economic, social, governmental, and legal relationships. Secondly, Fundamentalists believe that a return to an Islamic rule of government would provide political justice. In the classical era of Islam, a ruler's political power originated from God. The Prophet Muhammad provided the precedent for this. During the Medina Period in Islamic history, Muhammad served as the religious, political, and military leader of the Muslim community. Muslims were ruled by caliphs (successors of the Prophet Muhammad) for centuries following Muhammad's death. The office of the caliph derives political authority from God. Secular political leaders, such as presidents, kings, and emperors, derive their political authority either by popular election or by force. Since Islamic Fundamentalists believe that God has provided a complete system of society in the Koran and the Sunnah, many have called for the office of the caliph to be reinstated. Even those Fundamentalists who do not want the return of the caliphate believe that Islam should be the source of political legitimacy.

Finally, Islamic Fundamentalists would agree with Qutb that Islam provides legal justice. The implementation of Islamic law (*sharia*) is both the most controversial and the most misunderstood aspect of Islamic Fundamentalism. Islamic law is derived from *sharia* (fixed revelations found in the Koran) and must be interpreted by Muslim jurists in order to have relevance within a modern political context. Most Islamic Fundamentalists would call for the implementation of Islamic law. However, because interpretations of Islamic laws differ, often substantially from one person to the next, *sharia* can have many different implications. For example, the Koran commands harsh corporal punishment for certain crimes, as in cutting off the hands of thieves (5:38) and the flogging of adulterers (24:2). As a legal code, strict interpretation of sharia is open to criticism for its harshness. Because of the inherent difficulties in implementing Islamic law, many Islamic Fundamentalists envision an Islamic state in which sharia would be one of multiple sources of legislation. Qutb's three types of justice echo sentiments made by many Islamic Fundamentalists.

Islamic Fundamentalism was a prominent ideology in North African and the Middle East throughout the 20th century, but it was not until the Iranian Revolution of 1979 that Islamic Fundamentalism was propelled to the forefront of American politics. American observers were left perplexed as a Westernized, secular, "modern" regime was toppled in favor of a heavily theocratic democracy. The assumption that secularism was a product of modernism, an assumption that undergirded much of 20th-century political theory, was shattered by the ascendency of Ayatollah Khomeini, an Islamic jurist who returned from exile to lead the new Iranian Republic. From 1979 to his death in 1989, Ayatollah Khomeini was the poster child for Islamic Fundamentalism. Khomeini's calls for a strict, conservative republic led by Islamic jurists, and especially his highly publicized fatwa, issued in 1989, calling for the assassination of British author Salman Rushdie made the revolutionary leader seem like an anachronistic religious fanatic to Western observers. To be sure, Khomeini appealed to Islamic tradition to reinforce his agenda. He believed that the Shah was too closely aligned to Western interests and that the return of Islam to the public sphere would improve the social standing of Iranians. To this extent, Ayatollah Khomeini was an Islamic Fundamentalist. Khomeini, however, considered his reforms quite progressive. The concept of a Supreme Jurist was an innovation. Though Khomeini argued that Shiite jurists were once a more powerful group within Shia Islam, his ascendancy was not a return to fundamentals but a new invention. Khomeini was a product of the very specific political and social milieu of Iran, and his thought and actions had more in common with populism than religious fanaticism. The fact that the degree to which Khomeini was Fundamentalist is under debate indicates the problematic nature of the concept of Islamic Fundamentalism. Nevertheless, the stern-faced Ayatollah Khomeini remains the indelible image of hardline Islamic Fundamentalism to many Americans, particularly those who lived through the Iranian Revolution and the Iranian Hostage Crisis.

Interest in Islamic Fundamentalism has dramatically increased in the years following the terrorist attacks of September 11, 2001. Prominent Fundamentalist thinkers such as Wahhab, Qutb, and others garnered significant attention from American academics, journalists, and politicians who wanted to learn more about the inspiration behind the terrorist attacks. While modern terrorists often cite Fundamentalist thinkers and writers, the connection between Islamic Fundamentalism and terrorism is not as clear as it may seem at first.

Islamic Fundamentalism is critical to understanding recent developments in Egypt. The Muslim Brotherhood has been a consistent oppositional voice in Egypt since the early 20th century. Echoing Qutb and other Fundamentalist thinkers, the Brotherhood has blamed Westernization, secularism, and British colonization for the political problems that have plagued Egypt since the collapse of the Ottoman Empire. After the 2011 Revolution deposed Hosni Mubarak, a Muslim Brotherhood member named Mohammed Morsi was elected president. Though the Brotherhood is not the ruling party in Egypt and the military has regained power at this writing, the organization was the driving force behind efforts to draft a new constitution and create a new Egyptian state.

Directly east of Egypt, a small disputed territory known as the Gaza Strip is currently under the control of a Muslim Brotherhood offshoot organization known as Hamas. Hamas was created in 1987 to advocate the creation of a Palestinian state in and around Israel, the West Bank, and the Gaza Strip. In the decades since its founding, Hamas has pursued a conservative, dogmatic agenda in the territories it controls. For example, Hamas has instituted strict dress and behavior codes for women and has limited music and the Internet in the Gaza Strip. Islamic Fundamentalist movements that oppose Israel are of particular importance to Americans. The United States is an ally of Israel and has agreed to protect the nation of Israel against its enemies. Therefore, the United States keeps a close watch on the politics of Palestinian Fundamentalist groups that oppose Israeli policies. While the Muslim Brotherhood and Hamas are closely associated with the politics of Egypt and Palestine, respectively, the influence of these organizations extends throughout North Africa, the Middle East, and Southeast Asia.

In the Azawad region of Northern Mali, a group of Sunni Fundamentalists began fighting the Malian government in early 2012 for the right to establish an independent Fundamentalist Islamic state in the region. The Islamist rebels had taken control of the region by April 2012 and established a short-lived Fundamentalist territory. The Fundamentalist instituted a conservative, Fundamentalist agenda in the region that included required head scarves for women, the banning of Western music and cinema, the destruction of Shiite holy sites, and the implementation of a harsh interpretation of sharia law.

Not all Fundamentalist reform movements are violent and radical. Many Islamic Fundamentalists believe that a rejection of secularism and a return of Islam into the public sphere will result in a more peaceful and respectful world for men and women, Muslims and non-Muslims. Muslim advocates for women's rights appeal to Islamic Fundamentalism to show that women were well respected members of the early Muslim community. Likewise, Fundamentalists point out that for much of Islamic history, non-Muslims were treated very well. These groups of Fundamentalists are arguing that a rejection of secularism within Muslim-majority countries will pave the way for human rights, equality, and tolerance. Islamic Fundamentalism does not necessarily entail a violent opposition to the West through a repressive system of religious authoritarianism.

Islamic Fundamentalists have conceived of Islamic tradition and history in remarkably fluid ways. With so much history from which to draw, Fundamentalists are able to find historical precedent for a wide range of ideas. Many prominent Islamist organizations from all over the world can be classified as Fundamentalist. These bodies are very different from one another because they are responding to a specific political and social situation. What makes all of these ideas and movements Fundamentalist is the desire to translate a tradition or concept from Islamic history into present-day reform movements. American interests in the Islamic world are directly affected by Islamic Fundamentalist politics, and recent developments in North African and the Middle East suggest that Islamic Fundamentalism will remain an important and influential political theory for generations to come.

See also

Diplomacy; War as Policy; War on Terror

RICHARD KENT EVANS

Further Reading

Almond, Gabriel A., R. Scott Appleby, and Emmanuel Sivan. 2003. *Strong Religion: The Rise of Fundamentalisms Around the World.* Chicago: University of Chicago Press.

Ruthven, Malise. 2007. *Fundamentalism: A Very Short Introduction.* New York: Oxford University Press.

Wood, Simon, and David Harrington Watt, eds. 2013. *Fundamentalism: Perspectives on a Contested History*. Columbia, SC: University of South Carolina Press.

Islamic Fundamentalism—Primary Document

Introduction

In the 1990s, the U.S. government grew increasingly concerned about the rise of Islamic Fundamentalism in North Africa and the Middle East. The U.S. Congress regularly invites experts to speak about issues that affect foreign policy. In 1993, the House of Representatives hosted a roundtable discussion about the nature of Islamic Fundamentalism and its potential impact on America concerns in the Middle East. In his comments from that roundtable, reproduced here, Dr. Joshua Muravchik argues that democracy is the key to long-term stability in the region and that Islamic Fundamentalism is an obstacle to realizing this goal.

Document: Dr. Joshua Muravchik of the American Enterprise Institute Speaks on Ways in Which Islamic Fundamentalism Impedes American Foreign Policy Interests (September 21, 1993)

In the last year, however, I have had a series of interesting conversations with representatives of the Mojahedin Organization, at their initiative. They came to me wanting to talk about democracy in their country. I welcomed this, not just because of my interest in democracy, but also because it may offer an answer to a terrible problem, the rise of Islamic "fundamentalism," that is fanatical, politicized and violent. In recent days, the problem of terrorism by this movement has been brought home to us with new drama and urgency.

It is also of special concern from the point of view of those who delight in the recent progress of democracy around the globe. With the collapse of the last of the great and terrible 20th century totalitarian ideological alternatives to democracy, the one remaining fierce opponent of democracy in the world is the force of this Islamic fanaticism. It is a very major

impediment to the further spread of democracy in the world, and to the consolidation of democracy in those parts of the world where it is young and fragile.

Source: U.S. House. 103rd Congress. *Panel Discussion on Islamic Fundamentalism, September 21, 1993.* Washington, DC: Government Printing Office, 1993. (139 Cong Rec E 2203).

ISOLATIONISM

Isolationism is a term that describes a foreign policy of limited involvement in the world outside the home state. It entails avoidance of political and military commitments and requires specific criteria for intervention. The most popular use of the term has been in describing U.S. foreign policy, the history of which has been widely identified as the result of tension between isolationism and intervention.

The word *isolationism* was not used until the 20th century, when it pejoratively described Midwestern progressive Republicans who eschewed U.S. membership in the League of Nations. However, the roots of U.S. isolationism as a broad foreign policy derive from the belief in American exceptionalism and moral superiority, a tradition that dates at least as far back as 1630, when John Winthrop declared the Massachusetts Bay Colony a "city upon a hill."

Washington's Farewell Address

During the American Revolution, the American colonists signed the Treaty of Amity and Commerce (1778), which established a trade relationship with France, as well as a military alliance with that nation. In 1793, as the French Revolution began its phase known as the Reign of Terror, the increased violence prompted President George Washington to distance the United States from France. Instead, he desired improved relations with Great Britain in order to make that country the chief trading partner of the United States. Washington issued the Proclamation of Neutrality (1793) in response to the continued wars between France and Great Britain.

In 1794, the United States and Great Britain signed the Jay Treaty, which gave Great Britain favorable trade conditions with the United States. Drafted by Federalist Party member

John Jay, the treaty helped defuse postwar tension over the British occupation of some North American forts, but it was also controversial; the Democratic-Republicans, led by James Madison and Thomas Jefferson, thought that a trade agreement with Britain was veiled economic colonialism and compromised U.S. sovereignty. Nevertheless, the newly independent United States looked to its former colonizer as a foreign policy guide. Britain's imperial foreign policy was famously summarized as "no permanent friends, no permanent enemies, only permanent interests."

Washington attempted to summarize American diplomatic principles in his farewell address (1796), which was interpreted as an outline of the country's isolationist policy. Washington stated: "The nation which indulges toward another an habitual hatred or an habitual fondness is in some degree a slave. It is a slave to its animosity or to its affection, either of which is sufficient to lead it astray from its duty and its interest." Washington also warned against the "insidious wiles of foreign influence" by maintaining that "history and experience prove that foreign influence is one of the most baneful foes of a republican government." In addition, the address outlined the influence of foreign trade on foreign policy, as Washington cautioned, "The great rule of conduct for us in regard to foreign nations is, in extending our commercial relations to have with them as little political connection as possible."

Finally, Washington's address iterated the idea of American exceptionalism as an influence on foreign policy: "Our detached and distant situation invites and enables us to pursue a different course." The United States was an ideal setting for isolationism, as it was geographically separate from Europe, and its agrarian economy guaranteed self-sufficiency.

Expansion Through Isolation

In an oft-quoted line, President Jefferson continued his predecessor's isolationist stance in his 1801 inaugural address when he called for "honest friendship with all nations, entangling alliances with none." However, historians have argued that the isolationism encouraged by the two presidents differed in its source. Purportedly, Washington's isolationism was more aligned with political realism, which aimed to protect the interests, and promote the survival, of the young nation, while Jefferson's isolationism was ideologically driven

by the idea of American exceptionalism. Much debate over isolationism arises from different interpretations of those ideas. However varied its origins may be, though, isolationism has never meant an inactive foreign policy. Conversely, the United States has been very active in the international arena since the Tripolitan War of 1801–1805.

During the presidency of James Monroe, many Latin American nations declared independence from the weakened Spanish Empire. Despite public pressure to recognize those new states, Secretary of State John Quincy Adams doubted the success of their revolutions; he was also afraid that recognizing those states would drag the United States into conflict with Spain, and thus into European affairs. When Greece declared its independence from the Ottoman Empire in 1821, many Americans—viewing the nation as the birthplace of democracy—called for U.S. support of the Greek War of Independence. In a speech to the House of Representatives on July 4, 1821, Adams stated the administration's view on Grecian sovereignty by delineating the costs of intervention and establishing another tenet of U.S. isolationism:

But she [the United States] goes not abroad, in search of monsters to destroy. She is the well-wisher to the freedom and independence of all. She is the champion and vindicator only of her own. She will commend the general cause by the countenance of her voice, and the benignant sympathy of her example. She well knows that by once enlisting under other banners than her own, were they even the banners of foreign independence, she would involve herself beyond the power of extrication, in all the wars of interest and intrigue, of individual avarice, envy, and ambition, which assume the colors and usurp the standard of freedom.

In spite of that relatively passive definition of American isolationism, in 1823, Monroe presented the Monroe Doctrine, which outlined U.S. plans for intervention in, and dominance over, the Western Hemisphere. The doctrine was designed to deter European countries from future colonization in the Americas. Although the doctrine espoused hemispheric intervention, it was seen as consistent with U.S. isolationist policy because of its necessity to maintain "the amicable relations existing between the United States and those [European] powers." Even as his doctrine asserted the U.S. right to intervene in the nascent Latin American governments, Monroe supported isolationism: "In the wars of the European powers in matters relating to themselves we have never taken any part, nor does it comport with our policy to do so."

Support for isolationism remained a popular theme in presidential rhetoric throughout the 19th century. Although the United States continued its active foreign policy in pursuit of trade throughout the world, the so-called creation of the U.S. Empire during the 19th century was still consistent with isolationism. The United States built its empire without becoming entangled in European affairs, as the Spanish-American War fell under the purview of the Monroe Doctrine and the consequent Philippine-American War were fought to protect U.S. economic interests. In subsequent interventions, like that which led to the construction of the Panama Canal, the United States took on the role of policing the hemisphere. In what became known as the Roosevelt Corollary to the Monroe Doctrine, President Theodore Roosevelt explained:

> It is not true that the United States feels any land hunger or entertains any projects as regards the other nations of the Western Hemisphere save such as are for their welfare. All that this country desires is to see the neighboring countries stable, orderly, and prosperous. . . . Chronic wrongdoing, or an impotence which results in a general loosening of the ties of civilized society, may in America, as elsewhere, ultimately require intervention by some civilized nation, and in the Western Hemisphere the adherence of the United States to the Monroe Doctrine may force the United States, however reluctantly, in flagrant cases of such wrongdoing or impotence, to the exercise of an international police power.

World War I

As the 20th century progressed, technological advancement made isolation less feasible. When World War I erupted in 1914, President Woodrow Wilson issued a Declaration of Neutrality (1914), and the United States avoided engagement in the conflict, despite American casualties during German U-boat attacks on passenger and merchant ships. Wilson, however, actively affirmed the Roosevelt Corollary by ordering excursions into Mexico during that country's revolution. Wilson also ordered Gen. John J. Pershing into Mexico in an unsuccessful pursuit of Pancho Villa, who had harassed Americans along the border, during 1916. Unrest on the Caribbean island of Santo Domingo, which led to the separation of Haiti and the Dominican Republic, prompted Wilson to send the U.S. Marines to restore order and occupy those countries in 1915 and 1916; the marines stayed until 1924.

Although Wilson, who campaigned under the slogan "He kept us out of war" in the 1916 presidential election, was rewarded for his ardent isolationism with a second term, he asked Congress for a declaration of war against Germany in 1917. Germany's unrestricted submarine warfare, combined with overwhelming U.S. public support, forced Wilson to initiate the first major break in the nation's isolationist policy since its inception. Some historians have argued that the U.S. policy in World War I was still isolationist, as Wilson's pretext for entering the war was German submarine attacks, not European affairs.

Still, not all Americans were convinced of the necessity of U.S. involvement in World War I. Secretary of State William Jennings Bryan, a pacifist and isolationist, already had resigned in protest over what he saw as Wilson's bellicose response to the German sinking of the passenger ship *Lusitania* in 1915. Others were skeptical of involving the United States in what they considered an ideological crusade. Sen. Robert La Follette, a Wisconsin Republican, voted against going to war because he suspected that Eastern bankers and businesses, eager to profit from the conflict, were behind the push toward war. Sen. George W. Norris, a Republican from Nebraska, likewise believed the Eastern elite would profit while ordinary Americans paid the bulk of the war expenses. Republican Senator Gerald Nye of North Dakota also criticized U.S. involvement in World War I. Nye rose to national prominence in 1934, when he called for an investigation of the munitions industry; he subsequently denounced munitions manufacturers as "merchants of death" that had undue influence in politics and led the country into war for their own gain.

In the wake of the war, Wilson took an active role in world affairs as a participant in the Paris Peace Conference and as a supporter of the League of Nations, which was a facet of his Fourteen Points speech. During the interwar period, progressive Republican senators from agrarian states, like

La Follette, were the loudest voices of isolationism. As such, they opposed the Treaty of Versailles (1919) and U.S. membership in the League of Nations. Hiram Johnson, a California Republican, supported the war but opposed the Treaty of Versailles and the League of Nations because he thought they represented "entangling alliances." Sen. William Borah, a Republican from Idaho, opposed U.S. membership in the League of Nations because he did not want the United States involved in European politics, which he considered corrupt. Those senators were disparagingly labeled "isolationists."

1921–1933: The Republican "Return to Normalcy"

While campaigning for president in 1920, Warren Harding stated that "America's present need... is normalcy." Alliances were seen as a chief cause of the war, and Harding promised to keep the country peaceful, prosperous, and politically isolated. Harding's successor, Calvin Coolidge, was determined to foster prosperity and continue the avoidance of alliances and intervention in international affairs. The Coolidge administration pushed increasingly for isolation and, as a precursor to the Good Neighbor Policy, began decreasing U.S. intervention in Latin America. Nevertheless, in keeping with the Roosevelt Corollary, Coolidge sent Henry L. Stimson to Nicaragua in 1927 to monitor elections and to help reestablish a constitutional government. Coolidge broke with isolationism in late 1928 to support the Kellogg-Briand Pact, an international attempt to outlaw war.

As the Great Depression began to ravage the international economy during 1929, isolationist sentiment increased throughout the world. Policy makers began to favor protectionism, a form of economic isolation; however, such protectionist economic policies as the 1930 Smoot-Hawley Tariff exacerbated the dire economic conditions they were designed to mollify. In that political and economic climate, the American public questioned U.S. intervention in the Western Hemisphere. As comedian Will Rogers queried in 1932, "Why are we in Nicaragua and what the hell are we doing there?"

1934–1937: The High Tide of Isolationism

In 1935, Congress passed a neutrality act in response to Italy's Ethiopian invasion. The act allowed trade with belligerents but established an embargo on arms. The act was amended in 1936 to ban loans or credit to the belligerents. In 1937, in response to the Spanish Civil War, the United States amended the act to ban arms sales to all parties, as well as U.S. travel on belligerents' ships. In order to maintain strict neutrality, President Franklin D. Roosevelt refused to recognize Japan's invasion of China as a state of war because an arms embargo, as stipulated by the neutrality act, would disproportionately hurt China and could be interpreted as taking sides. The Neutrality Act (1939) stipulated a "cash and carry" policy toward arms sales; belligerents had to pay cash for arms and use their own ships to transport them. That policy prevented the United States from helping a belligerent by extending credit and from violating blockades in shipping goods. U.S. ships and citizens were also banned from traveling through "combat zones," which were designated by presidential discretion.

As World War II erupted in Europe in 1939, former marine general Smedley D. Butler, who became known in 1932 through his criticism of U.S. foreign policy and his renunciation of his role in it, advocated a policy of isolationism. He preached, "Not a single drop of American blood should ever again be spilled on foreign soil." Butler believed that the U.S. military should be used for homeland defense only. In 1940, the America First Committee was established to keep the United States out of the war. The committee was popular with such politicians as Nye and Burton Wheeler, a Montana isolationist. Wheeler soon made a name for himself by railing against the Lend-Lease Act. Charles Lindbergh, who had visited Nazi Germany and opposed going to war against the fascist nation, also supported the committee. Historian Charles Beard opposed intervention and called for self-sufficiency in his 1940 work *A Foreign Policy for America*. After the Japanese attacked Pearl Harbor on December 7, 1941, however, many former isolationists, like senators Norris and Johnson, supported going to war. After the war, though, many isolationists renewed their skepticism toward "entangling alliances." Johnson, for example, opposed the adoption of the United Nations Charter.

The Cold War and the New Right

During the Cold War, the heightened Soviet threat and the increased economic and political power of the United States precluded a return to the isolationist policies of the previous decades. As alliances were blamed for World War I, isolationism was blamed for World War II. Traditional isolationism was all but forgotten during the Cold War period. Senator Robert Taft, an Ohio Republican who opposed U.S. membership in the North Atlantic Treaty Organization, was pejoratively called an "Old Isolationist" by prominent historian Arthur Schlesinger Jr. Though Taft despised both Germany and the Soviet Union, he considered Germany a limited threat, and he believed that the United States did not have the economic means to cover the costs of containment.

The consensus for U.S. intervention and alliances during the Cold War accompanied the emergence of Republican interventionists of the "New Right," like ardent conservative Barry Goldwater. Rife with such tenets as the domino theory, the arms race, and détente, the Cold War necessitated preventive intervention in other nations' affairs. Isolationism was, thus, considered narrow-minded and provincial.

Neo-isolationism

Since the Cold War ended in 1989, the United States has experienced a mild resurgence in the tension between isolationism and intervention. In 1989, President George Bush warned the country not to "retreat into an isolationist cocoon" and criticized politicians who were "working right now to breathe life into those old flat-Earth theories of protectionism, of isolationism." However, the criteria for intervention advocated by Bush were unclear in his policies; in 1992, Secretary of State James Baker III explained the U.S. decision not to intervene in the Yugoslavian Civil War by stating, "[W]e don't have a dog in that fight."

During the 18th century, an alliance referred mainly to commercial agreements between states. The distinction between commercial agreements and military or political alliances did not occur until the 19th century. The advancement of worldwide free trade has further blurred the distinction between military or political and commercial agreements. In 1993, Secretary of State Warren Christopher exemplified that fusion of politics and commerce by stating that the administration of President Bill Clinton had "placed economic policy at the heart of our foreign policy." Such new isolationists as antiglobalization protesters on the Left and Pat Buchanan on the Right confronted Clinton's policies of economic openness and increased free trade. Conversely,

Vice President Al Gore criticized isolationists and defended U.S. polices by stating, "These new isolationists seek nothing less than to impede President Clinton's ability to defend American interests and values." During his presidential campaign in 1999, Texas governor George W. Bush also cautioned against the stagnation and savagery that he predicted would accompany an isolationist U.S. policy in the 21st century.

The Indispensable Nation

Recent discussion of isolationism in the United States has been inextricably linked to debate about an American empire. Leftist historians like William Appleman Williams, who regarded U.S. isolationism as mythical, have posthumously become popular with both libertarians and conservative anti-imperialists. Although many agree that Williams underestimated the Soviet threat, some regard his warnings about the continuation of U.S. "imperial" motives after the Cold War as prescient. Many isolationists across the political spectrum blame the World Trade Center and Pentagon attacks of September 11, 2001, on America's interventions throughout the world. Those neo-isolationists worry that the costs of increased U.S. military and political intervention throughout the world far outweigh the benefits.

Neo-isolationists believe that a strong defense, in a nation free of "entangling alliances," will be the clearest communication of U.S. intentions and, as such, will deter attacks on the United States in the future. Subscribers to that belief note that the U.S. military is better positioned to defend other parts of the world than it is to defend the U.S. mainland, although they concede that America's two ocean borders still offer some protection. Isolationist critics of the U.S. relationship with Israel cite Washington's farewell address, which warns against such close alliances; they believe that the relationship has brought the United States unnecessary problems and limited benefits.

In 1998, Secretary of State Madeleine Albright harkened back to the Roosevelt Corollary when she identified the United States as "the indispensable nation, willing to make the world safe for. . . nations who follow the rules." Despite disagreements on theory and policy, both isolationist and interventionist stances are rooted in the essence of Albright's belief: that the United States rests at the apex of international foreign policy and is essential to the climate, whether interventionist or isolationist, of nations the world over.

See also

Anticommunism; Capitalism; Commercialization; Communism; Containment; Fascism; Human Rights; Industrial Revolution; Manifest Destiny; Military-Industrial Complex; War as Policy

PHILIP J. MACFARLANE

Further Reading

Bacevich, Andrew J. 2002. *American Empire: The Realities and Consequences of U.S. Diplomacy.* Cambridge, MA: Harvard University Press.

Boot, Max. 2003. *The Savage Wars of Peace: Small Wars and the Rise of American Power.* New York: Basic Books.

Dallek, Robert. 1998. *Franklin D. Roosevelt and American Foreign Policy, 1932–1945.* 2nd ed. New York: Oxford University Press.

Kissinger, Henry A. 1995. *Diplomacy.* New York: Simon and Schuster.

Schlesinger, Arthur M., Jr. 1952. "The New Isolationism." *Atlantic Monthly* (May).

Isolationism—Primary Document

Introduction

On December 19, 1950, President Harry S Truman's administration announced that the United States would significantly augment its military forces in Europe. To accomplish this, the president named General Dwight D. Eisenhower as the first supreme allied commander of North Atlantic Treaty Organization (NATO) forces. At the time, policy makers were concerned that the Soviets might attempt to launch an invasion of Western Europe while the West was preoccupied with the war in Korea. Truman's decision set off a brief debate on Capitol Hill over the scope of U.S. military commitments. On December 20, former Republican President Herbert Hoover provided the catalyst for the "Great Debate" during a nationally broadcast address. A paean to conservatism and isolationism, the speech cautioned that the administration's current policies were likely to bankrupt the nation. He urged that U.S. troops not be stationed in continental Europe, believing that European nations must provide for their own defense. He believed that it was a grave mistake to engage in far-flung military and political commitments and that the United States should arm itself to create a "Western Hemisphere Gibraltar of Western Civilization." Conservatives and quasi-isolationists such as Senator

Robert A. Taft, an Ohio Republican, used Hoover's address to engage Capitol Hill in a brief but noisy debate about U.S. military commitments, but most lawmakers and policy makers favored a more internationalist foreign policy, and the issue burned itself out by the spring of 1951.

Document: Former President Herbert Hoover's "Gibraltar America" Address (December 20, 1950)

Our National Policies in This Crisis

I have received hundreds of requests that I appraise the present situation and give my conclusions as to our national policies.

I speak with a deep sense of responsibility. And I speak tonight under the anxieties of every American for the nation's sons who are fighting and dying on a mission of peace and the honor of our country.

No appraisal of the world situation can be final in an unstable world. However, to find our national path we must constantly re-examine where we have arrived and at times revise our direction.

I do not propose to traverse the disastrous road by which we reached this point.

The Global Military Situation

We may first survey the global military situation. There is today only one center of aggression on the earth. That is the Communist-controlled Asian-European land mass of 800,000, people. They have probably over 300 trained and equipped combat divisions with over 30,000 tanks, 10,000 tactical planes and further large reserves they can put in action in ninety days. But they are not a great sea power. Their long-range air power is limited. This congerie of over 30 different races will some day go to pieces. But in the meantime they furnish unlimited cannon fodder.

Facing this menace on the Eastern front there are about 100,000,000 non-Communist island peoples in Japan,

Formosa, the Philippines and Korea. Aside from Korea, which I discuss later, they have probably only 12 effective combat divisions with practically no tanks, air or navy.

Facing this land mass on the South are the Indies and the Middle East of about 600,000,000 non-Communist peoples. There are about 150,000,000 further non-Communist peoples in North Africa and Latin America. Except Turkey and Formosa, these 850,000,000 non-Communist peoples have little military force which they would or could spare.

But they could contribute vital economic and moral strength. Facing this menace on the Continental European front there are about 160,000,000 further non-Communist peoples who, excluding Spain, have less than 20 combat divisions now available, few tanks and little air or naval force. And their will to defend themselves is feeble and their disunities are manifest.

Of importance in military weight at this moment there is the British Commonwealth of 150,000,000 people, with probably 30 combat divisions under arms, a superior navy, considerable air force and a few tanks.

And there are 150,000,000 people in the United States preparing 3,500,000 men into a gigantic air force and navy, with about 30 equipped combat divisions.

Thus there are 1,300,000,000 non-Communist peoples in the world of whom today only about 320,000,000 have any military potency.

Some Military Conclusions

If we weigh these military forces as they stand today we must arrive at certain basic conclusions.

a) We must face the fact that to commit the sparse ground forces of the non-Communist nations into a land war against this Communist land mass would be a war without victory, a war without a successful political terminal.

The Germans failed with a magnificent army of 240 combat divisions and with powerful air and tank forces. That

compares with only 60 divisions proposed today for the North Atlantic Pact Nations.

Even were Western Europe armed far beyond any contemplated program, we could never reach Moscow.

Therefore any attempt to make war on the Communist mass by land invasion, through the quicksands of China, India or Western Europe is sheer folly. That would be the graveyard of millions of American boys and would end in the exhaustion of this Gibraltar of Western Civilization.

b) Equally, we Americans alone with sea and air power can so control the Atlantic and Pacific Oceans that there can be no possible invasion of the Western Hemisphere by Communist armies. They can no more reach Washington in force than we can reach Moscow.

c) In this military connection we must realize the fact that the atomic bomb is a far less dominant weapon than it was once thought to be.

d) It is obvious that the United Nations have been defeated in Korea by the aggression of Communist China. There are no available forces in the world to repel them.

Even if we sacrifice more American boys to hold a bridgehead, we know we shall not succeed at the present time in the mission given to us by the 50 members of the United Nations.

Our Economic Strength

We may explore our American situation still further. The 150,000,000 American people are already economically strained by government expenditures. It must not be forgotten that we are carrying huge burdens from previous wars including obligations to veterans and $260 billions of bond and currency issues from those wars. In the fiscal year 1952, federal and local expenditures are likely to exceed $90 billions. That is more than our total savings. We must finance huge deficits by further government issues. Inflation is already moving. The dollar has in six months fallen 15 percent or 20 percent in purchasing power. But we might with stern measures avoid the economic disintegration of such a load for a very few years. If we continued long on this road the one center of resistance in the world will collapse in economic disaster.

The Diplomatic Front

We may also appraise the diplomatic front. Our great hope was in the United Nations. We have witnessed the sabotage of its primary purpose of preserving peace. It has been, down to last week, a forum for continuous smear on our honor, our ideals and our purposes.

It did stiffen up against raw aggression last July in Korea. But in its call for that military action, America had to furnish over 90 percent of the foreign forces and suffer over 90 percent of their dead and injured. That effort now comes at least to a measurable military defeat by the aggression of Communist hordes.

Whether or not the United Nations is to have a moral defeat and suffer the collapse of its whole moral stature now depends on whether it has the courage to

(a) Declare Communist China an aggressor.

(b) Refuse admission of this aggressor to its membership.

(c) Demand that each member of the United Nations cease to furnish or transport supplies of any kind to Communist China that can aid in their military operations. Such a course honestly carried out by the non-Communist nations is not economic sanctions nor does it require military actions. But it would constitute a great pressure for rectitude.

(d) For once, pass a resolution condemning the infamous lies about the United States.

Any course short of such action is appeasement.

What Should Our Policies Be?

And now I come to where we should go from here.

Two months ago I suggested a tentative alternate policy for the United States. It received a favorable reception from the large majority of our press.

Since then the crisis in the world has become even more acute. It is clear that the United Nations are defeated in Korea. It is also clear that other non-Communist nations did not or could not substantially respond to the U.N. call for arms to Korea. It is clear the U.N. cannot mobilize substantial military forces. It is clear Continental Europe has not in the three years of our aid developed that unity of purpose, and that will power necessary for its own defense. It is clear that our British friends are flirting with appeasement of Communist China. It is clear that the United Nations is in a fog of debate and indecision on whether to appease or not to appease.

In expansion of my proposals of two months ago, I now propose certain principles and action.

First. The foundation of our national policies must be to preserve for the world this Western Hemisphere Gibraltar of Western Civilization.

Second. We can, without any measure of doubt, with our own air and naval forces, hold the Atlantic and Pacific Oceans with one frontier on Britain (if she wishes to co-operate); the other, on Japan, Formosa and the Philippines. We can hold open the sea lanes for our supplies.

And I devoutly hope that a maximum of co-operation can be established between the British Commonwealth and ourselves.

Third. To do this we should arm our air and naval forces to the teeth. We have little need for large armies unless we are going to Europe or China. We should give Japan her independence and aid her in arms to defend herself. We should stiffen the defenses of our Pacific frontier in Formosa and the Philippines. We can protect this island chain by our sea and air power.

Fourth. We could, after initial outlays for more air and navy equipment, greatly reduce our expenditures, balance our budget and free ourselves from the dangers of inflation and economic degeneration.

Fifth. If we toil and sacrifice as the President has so well asked, we can continue aid to the hungry of the world. Out of our productivity, we can give aid to other nations when they have already displayed spirit and strength in defense against Communism. We have the stern duty to work and sacrifice to do it.

Sixth. We should have none of appeasement. Morally there is no appeasement of Communism. Appeasement contains more dangers than Dunkirks. We want no more Teherans and no more Yaltas. We can retrieve a battle but we cannot retrieve an appeasement. We are grateful that President Truman has denounced such a course.

Seventh. We are not blind to the need to preserve Western Civilization on the Continent of Europe or to our cultural and religious ties to it. But the prime obligation of defense of Western Continental Europe rests upon the nations of Europe. The test is whether they have the spiritual force, the will and acceptance of unity among them by their own volition. America cannot create their spiritual forces; we cannot buy them with money.

You can search all the history of mankind and there is no parallel to the effort and sacrifice we have made to elevate their spirit and to achieve their unity.

To this date it has failed. Their minds are confused with fears and disunities. They exclude Spain, although she has the will and means to fight. They higgle with Germany, although she is their frontier. They vacillate in the belief that they are in little danger and the hope to avoid again being a theatre of war. And Karl Marx has added to their confusions. They still suffer from battle shock. Their highly organized Communist parties are a menace that we must not ignore.

In both World War I and World War II (including West Germany) those nations placed more than 250 trained and equipped combat divisions in the field within sixty days with strong air and naval forces. They have more manpower and more productive capacity today than in either one of those wars. To warrant our further aid they should show they have spiritual strength and unity to avail themselves of their own resources. But it must be far more than pacts, conferences, paper promises and declarations. Today it must express itself in organized and equipped combat divisions of such huge numbers as would erect a sure dam against the red flood. And that before we land another man or another dollar on their shores. Otherwise we shall be inviting another Korea. That would be a calamity to Europe as well as to us.

Our policy in this quarter of the world should be confined to a period of watchful waiting before we take on any commitments.

National Unity

There is a proper urge in all Americans for unity in troubled times. But unless unity is based on right principles and right action it is a vain and dangerous thing.

Honest difference of views and honest debate are not disunity. They are the vital process of policy making among free men.

A right, a specific, an open foreign policy must be formulated which gives confidence in our own security before we can get behind it.

Conclusions

American eyes should now be opened to these hordes in Asia. These policies I have suggested would be no isolationism. Indeed they are the opposite. They would avoid rash involvement of our military forces in hopeless campaigns. They do not relieve us of working to our utmost. They would preserve a stronghold of Christian civilization in the world against any peradventure.

With the policies I have outlined, even without Europe, Americans have no reason for hysteria or loss of confidence in our security or our future. And in American security rests the future security of all mankind.

It would be an uneasy peace but we could carry it on with these policies indefinitely even if the Communists should attack our lines on the seas.

We can hope that in time the more than a billion of other non-Communist peoples of the world will rise to their dangers.

We can hope that sometime the evils of Communism and the crumbling of their racial controls will bring their own disintegration. It is a remote consolation, but twice before in world history Asiatic hordes have swept over a large part of the world and their racial dissensions dissolved their empires.

Our people have braved difficult and distressing situations in these three centuries we have been on this continent. We have faced our troubles without fear and we have not failed.

We shall not fail in this, even if we have to stand alone. But we need to realize the whole truth and gird ourselves for troubled times. The truth is ugly. We face it with prayer and courage. The Almighty is on our side.

Source: Hoover, Herbert. "Our National Policies in Crisis." *Vital Speeches of the Day*. 17, Issue 6 (January 1, 1951): 165.

J

JIM CROW

Origins

A set of ideas as well as laws, Jim Crow was ascendant in the South for about a century after the Civil War. The ideas predated the laws. In his *Notes on the State of Virginia* and elsewhere, Thomas Jefferson wrote that whites and blacks are separate races and that the white race was superior to the black race. These were not new ideas, but Jefferson's status as America's polymath gave them new life. At the end of the Civil War, fears arose that blacks might claim equality with whites. Equality might lead to a mingling of the races, and black men and black women might interbred with white women and men. In doing so, the black race would pollute the pure white race. It was essential, therefore, to protect racial purity. Blacks must not be allowed to mingle with whites, preserving the former's inferior status. Because Jim Crow rested on a series of laws, the best way to attack it was to dismantle its laws. The phrase *Jim Crow* derived from a 19th-century musical that featured an old black slave named Jim Crow. For this reason whites called blacks Jim Crow.

Overview

Racial attitudes, sometimes supported by the "science" of earlier eras, held that blacks were more closely related to apes than whites. In the 19th century, physician and anatomist Samuel Morton measured skulls in an attempt to demonstrate the inferiority of blacks. Louis Agassiz and Edward Cope were scientific racists. Agassiz, having trained under Georges Cuvier and occupying an endowed chair at Harvard, was particularly influential. Whites reasoned that blacks were primitive, driven by impulse rather than reason. After the American Civil War, whites in the South did not wish to live near blacks or to have any but the briefest contact with them. Jim Crow, the legal system of segregation in the South, protected whites from undesirable contact with blacks. African Americans could not go to the same schools, use the same restrooms, sit with them on trains, live near whites, enter a building through the same door as whites, and many other restrictions. These Jim Crow laws enjoyed the protection of the U.S. Constitution, according to the U.S. Supreme Court.

The states passed the overwhelming majority of these Jim Crow laws between 1877 and 1964. Until the 1920s, 90 percent of African Americans lived in the eleven states of the former Confederacy, the home of Jim Crow. The fear that black men unable to contain their sexual impulses might violate a white woman was one of the fears that preserved Jim Crow for so long.

Examples of Jim Crow abounded. A Georgia law made it illegal for white baseball players to occupy a field within two blocks of a black playground. Another Georgia law prohibited blacks from being buried in a cemetery that interred

Students watch from the windows and steps of Central High School in Little Rock, Arkansas, on October 16, 1957, as six African American students are escorted to class by the National Guard. After Governor Orval Faubus ordered state militia to prevent them from entering the school, President Dwight D. Eisenhower called upon the U.S. Army's 101st Airborne in to enforce desegregation. (Bettmann-UPI/Corbis)

whites. This law was popular throughout the South and seems to have been practiced in the North as well. In Louisiana white landlords could not rent property inhabited by whites to blacks. Along with thirty-seven other states, many of them in the North, Florida banned interracial marriage. North Carolina required separate libraries for blacks and whites. Alabama forbade white nurses from caring for black patients. In Mississippi, blacks and whites could not play pool or other games together. Mississippi, in opposition to the First Amendment, banned the publication of any text that advocated racial equality. Alabama required restaurants to construct barriers between black and white patrons. Jim Crow laws created a South in which African Americans had no value, were underpaid, and had few opportunities for advancement.

The system of Jim Crow gained strength from the fact that while the North had rejected slavery, it did not believe in racial equality. Jim Crow had political dimensions. The Democratic Party, the party of the South, denounced racial equality, whereas the most progressive Republicans, the champions of the North and cities, advocated political, social and economic equality. These Republicans were a minority of the party. The Radical Republicans favored extension of the franchise and other rights to African Americans.

Post-Reconstruction America did not help African Americans via government or its laws. President Andrew Johnson, who became president on Abraham Lincoln's death, was a racist former slave owner. Johnson insisted that only the states had the authority to define who deserved the rights of citizenship. In the immediate post–Civil War period, the

South moved quickly to segregate blacks from whites and to deprive African Americans of the rights of citizenship. Again the fear of race mixing emerged. A white and black couple who attempted to marry in Mississippi could be sentenced to prison for life. Cotton farmers throughout the South used black prison labor in conditions that were difficult to distinguish from slavery. Farmers did not pay the convicts. Rather the sheriff who furnished the convicts pocketed a bonus. The system of convict labor killed one quarter of blacks because of deplorable working conditions. Black convicts sentenced to the mines in Alabama suffered 35 percent mortality. Mine owners were satisfied because blacks drank putrid water without complaint, slept in their chains, and could not strike.

The U.S. Supreme Court accelerated the move to Jim Crow by ruling in case after case that the federal government could not interfere with the states' rights to enact laws governing race relations. One notable case involved a black man, Charles Green, who had purchased a ticket to a concert by all African American performers. He had bought the ticket from African American Fisk University. Yet, the theater refused to seat him. The police forcibly removed him. Green sued the theater. The judge, however, dismissed the case because the theater had the right to bar anyone from attendance. Not vanquished, Green appealed the ruling. The U.S. Supreme Court accepted the case in 1876, though it would take seven years to render a decision. The Court, combining the Green case with two others, ruled in 1883 in the *Civil Rights Cases* that blacks had no civil rights and that Congress could not make laws granting them putative rights (Tischauser, 18). They are commonly referred to in that way.

Louisiana, like other Southern states, segregated railroad cars. In June 1892, Homer Adolph Plessy, a shoemaker of black ancestry from New Orleans and a member of the Citizens' Committee to Test the Constitutionality of the Separate Car Law, bought a ticket and entered the white car. Because he was an octoroon and so light in complexion, he might have gone unnoticed but for the fact that he informed the conductor that he was black. The conductor had Plessy arrested, bringing on one of the U.S. Supreme Court's most infamous rulings. A lower court judge, John Ferguson, found Plessy guilty and fined him, but Plessy appealed the verdict. The state Supreme Court likewise found Plessy guilty. At this point two whites, Albion Tourgee, a novelist and former Louisiana congressman and army officer, and Samuel Phillips, former

solicitor general of the United States, encouraged Plessy to appeal his case to the U.S. Supreme Court, which accepted the case. The 1896 ruling, *Plessy v. Ferguson*, denied that Plessy had a right to integrate the railroad car. Segregation was law and he had violated it, deserving censure. Because the South believed in the inferiority of blacks it had the right to segregate the races. Discrimination was perfectly permissible.

African Americans differed on how best to respond to these laws and actions. Often viewed as an accomodationist, Booker T. Washington, head of the Tuskegee Institute in Alabama, urged blacks not to advocate too vociferously for political and social equality. Rather, they should acquire job skills, buy a business or farm, and demonstrate to whites that they were responsible citizens. This would lead to the end of Jim Crow.

To those who advocated that African Americans receive the franchise, the South required its citizens to pay a poll tax. Although only $1 or $2, the tax as well as the terrorism of the Ku Klux Klan kept blacks home on election day. Mississippi led the South in disenfranchising blacks, imposing a $2 poll tax and a literacy test. Presumably the administrator of the test graded whites more leniently than blacks. The combination of poll tax and literacy test caused both poor ill-educated blacks and whites to forgo participation in elections.

In justifying Jim Crow, whites blamed blacks for this state of affairs. By nature, blacks had criminal and violent temperaments. Not even education could mitigate these tendencies. Whites must act harshly against African Americans to prevent them from destroying the civilization that whites had built over millennia.

White author Thomas Bailey summarized the Jim Crow system in his 1914 book, *Race Orthodoxy in the South and Other Aspects of the Negro Question*. His formulation laid down the following twelve commandments:

1. The white race is superior.

2. The black race was, is, and would always be inferior.

3. Under these conditions, there can be no social equality.

4. Likewise there can be no political equality.

5. Make no laws that detract from the superiority of whites or inflate the lowly status of blacks.

6. Blacks do not deserve the same education as whites.

7. Where blacks are educated, they must be trained to serve whites.

8. Only white Southerners truly understand the mentality of blacks.

9. Blacks can aspire to be nothing more farm laborers.

10. Only the South can settle "the Negro question."

11. The most inferior white person is superior to the most advanced black person.

12. God is the source of these commandments. (Tischauser, 37)

African Americans had low intelligence, white Southerners believed. Blacks were capable of mastering only simple tasks: fixing shoes or sewing a pair of pants. Mississippi's governor in the early 20th century, James K. Vardaman, thought that blacks should have no more than three years of schooling because more education might inflate their egos and make them dangerous. In 1904, Vardaman called on the Mississippi legislature to end all funding for black schools. Throughout the South, states funded white schools as many as sixteen times more than black schools. White teachers received thrice the pay of black teachers. Teachers in black schools were not well educated, with only seven or eight years' schooling. Public colleges and universities were slow to admit black students. Only a few private academies taught African Americans the liberal arts and sciences.

Between 1910 and 1930, nearly 2 million African Americans moved north to escape Jim Crow. The North was not as accommodating as blacks had hoped. Most settled the large cities of Boston, Chicago, Cleveland, Detroit, Indianapolis, New York City, and Philadelphia. The boll weevil, which devoured cotton and deprived farm laborers of work, sent blacks north. Jim Crow marched north with them.

Jim Crow lived on despite noble military service by thousands of African Americans. President Woodrow Wilson, whose historical writings received praise from D.W. Griffith when he made the classic racist film *Birth of a Nation*, segregated every agency in the federal government. After fighting for freedom in Europe, black soldiers returned from World War I determined to abolish Jim Crow. Yet, they would need decades, not years, to accomplish this goal. Particularly troubling was the fact that the Republican presidents of the 1920s did nothing to aid African Americans, who had been their most loyal voting bloc.

The Communist Party of the United States, though it had no chance to win any election, attracted African Americans to its ranks. In 1929, the Communist Party promoted civil rights and an end to segregation. Communists gained some additional support during the Depression, but neither the downturn nor the ensuing New Deal did much to change or challenge existing segregation.

By the end of World War II, Jim Crow was front and center again. Education had reemerged as a divisive issue. A white who taught at a black school risked the revocation of his or her teaching certificate. Throughout the South blacks and whites who married risked a year in jail. In Texas and Virginia the sentence was five years. Harry Truman, who became president upon Franklin D. Roosevelt's death in 1945, used the office of president to champion civil rights and end Jim Crow, even though the majority of his party disagreed with him. He addressed the National Association for the Advancement of Colored People (NAACP), announcing these goals. In 1948, by executive order, President Truman integrated the military and demanded that the government hire and promote based on merit, not on race. In 1949, Truman backed several bills introduced into Congress to give blacks civil rights, but Southern Democrats filibustered the bills.

Yet the U.S. Supreme Court had finally turned against Jim Crow, striking down an Oklahoma law banning blacks from attending graduate school at the state's public universities. The Court ordered the University of Oklahoma to admit a black teacher to graduate studies in the College of Education. In 1950, the U.S. Supreme Court ordered the University of Texas Law School to admit its first African American law student. Other plaintiffs sought to overturn segregation in elementary and high schools. In 1951, Thurgood Marshall, a lawyer with the NAACP, filed a lawsuit on behalf of a black plaintiff in South Carolina. Marshall employed evidence that segregated schools cause irreparable harm to black children. When asked to choose a doll to play with, African American children almost universally chose a white rather than a black one because they had internalized the inferiority that Jim Crow had instilled in them. The three-judge panel ruled in favor of segregation. Marshall and the NAACP appealed the case to the U.S. Supreme Court, which, combining it with four other cases, in 1954 issued the ruling *Brown v. Board of Education*, finally overturning the legality of segregation. The ruling was unanimous, with Chief Justice Earl Warren writing the opinion. "To separate [children] from others of similar age and qualifications solely because of their race," Warren wrote, "generates a feeling of inferiority as to their status in the community that may affect their hearts and minds in ways unlikely ever to be undone" (Tischauser, 123). One must note, however, that, important as it was, the ruling applied only to public schools. It did not strike down other instances of segregation. Yet the Court, concerned about the reaction, gave schools time to implement integration. Some schools in the South remained segregated as late as 1970.

President Dwight D. Eisenhower, Truman's successor, was slow to support the U.S. Supreme Court. Legal decisions could not, he believed, change hearts and minds. Nevertheless, the courts continued their inexorable march. In 1955, a federal court outlawed segregated busing in South Carolina. That year Rosa Parks, secretary of the Montgomery, Alabama, chapter of the NAACP, refused to give up her seat to a white passenger. The bus driver had Parks arrested. Leading a boycott of the city's buses, Rev. Martin Luther King Jr. rose to prominence as a defender of civil rights. In 1956, the U.S. Supreme Court ruling in *Browder v. Gayle* overturned segregated seating on buses.

In 1957, a federal court ordered the public schools in Little Rock, Arkansas, to begin integration in 1958. When nine African American students prepared to enter Central High School in Little Rock, Arkansas governor Orval Faubus sent the National Guard to maintain order, but it did nothing to protect the students, who could not enter the school. President Eisenhower sent 1,000 troops from the 101st Airborne Division to prevent riots. The students endured a perilous year at Central High School. The next year, Arkansas closed its public schools to prevent other instances of integration.

The 1960s brought additional advances and conflicts, King's emergence as the nation's most eloquent promoter of

civil rights, and an end to Jim Crow. President Lyndon Baines Johnson, who assumed the office after John F. Kennedy's assassination and who was a Southerner, nonetheless managed to forge a governing coalition of progressive Democrats and Republicans. He shepherded the Civil Rights Act of 1964 and the Voting Rights Act of 1965 through the House and Senate. Jim Crow had finally been overturned, thus giving blacks the legal equality with whites that they had so long desired and to which they had been entitled under the U.S. Constitution.

See also

African American Civil Rights Movement; Judicial Activism; Racism; White Supremacy/Power

CHRISTOPHER CUMO

Further Reading

Cole, Stephanie, and Natalie J. Ring, eds. 2012. *The Folly of Jim Crow: Rethinking the Segregated South*. Arlington, TX: The University of Texas at Arlington.

Jordan, Winthrop. 1974. *The White Man's Burden: Historical Origins of Racism in the United States*. London: Oxford University Press.

Tischauser, Leslie V. 2012. *Jim Crow Laws*. Santa Barbara, CA: Greenwood Press.

Jim Crow—Primary Document

Introduction

An African American teacher, minister, and legislator, B.W. Arnett was born free in Brownsville, Pennsylvania, in 1838. A school teacher from 1859 to 1867, Arnett later became an African Methodist Episcopal (AME) minister and served congregations in various cities in Ohio, including Toledo and Cincinnati. He served as a bishop of the AME Church from 1888 until his death in 1906. In 1885, Arnett won election to the Ohio State Legislature, where he authored the bill that when enacted repealed Ohio's Black Laws, which had imposed strict segregation on African Americans. Arnett was an influential Republican politician in Ohio, in part due to his friendship with fellow Ohio legislator William McKinley, who was elected president of the United States in 1896. Reproduced here is an excerpt from a pamphlet containing a speech against the Black Laws that Arnett delivered before the Ohio House of Representatives on March 10, 1886.

Document: "The Black Laws" by Bishop B. W. Arnett (1886)

The denial of our civil rights in this and other States is a subject of public notoriety, denied by none but acknowledged by all to be wrong and unjust; yet, in traveling in the South we are compelled to feel its humiliating effects. It is written over the door of the waiting room, "For Colored Persons;" and in that small, and frequently dirty and dingy room, you have to go or stand on the platform and wait for the train. In Georgia they have cars marked "For Colored Passengers." There is one railroad in Alabama that has a special car for colored persons. They will not allow a white man to ride in that car; and many other roads allow the lower classes to ride in the car set apart for "Colored Persons."

One would think that at this time of our civilization, that character, and not color, would form the line of distinction in society, but such is not the case. It matters not what may be the standing or intelligence of a colored man or woman, they have to submit to the wicked laws and the more wicked prejudice of the people. It is not confined to either North or South. It is felt in this State to some extent; we feel it in the hotels, we feel it in the opera house. There are towns in this State where respectable ladies and gentlemen have been denied hotel accommodations, but such places are diminishing daily, under the growing influences of equal laws.

In the city of Cincinnati there are places where a colored man can not get accommodations for love nor money; there was a man who started an equal rights house; the colored people patronized him; his business increased; he made money. He has closed his house against his former patrons, and will not accommodate them.

Members [of the Ohio Legislature] will be astonished when I tell them that I have traveled in this free country for twenty hours without anything to eat; not because I had no money to pay for it, but because I was colored. Other passengers of a lighter hue had breakfast, dinner and supper. In traveling we are thrown in "jim crow" cars, denied the privilege of buying a berth in the sleeping coach. This monster caste stands at the doors of the theatres and skating rinks, locks the doors of the pews in our fashionable churches closes the mouths of some of the ministers in their pulpits which prevents the man of color from breaking the bread of life to his fellowmen.

This foe of my race stands at the school house door and separates the children, by reason of *color*, and denies to those who have a visible admixture of African blood in them the blessings of a graded school and equal privileges. We propose by this bill to knock this monster in the head and deprive him of his occupation, for he follows us all through life; and even some of our graveyards are under his control. The colored dead are denied burial. We call upon all friends of *Equal Rights* to assist in this struggle to secure the blessings of untrammeled liberty for ourselves and prosperity.

I am proud to stand in this presence and announce that we have lived to see the day when the leaders and platforms of all the parties of this State are in favor of the civil rights of my poor race that has suffered for so many centuries.

Source: Library of Congress. American Memory. http://memory.loc.gov/ammem/aap/aapprot.html.

JUDICIAL ACTIVISM

American courts are among the most powerful in the world. In addition to settling a wide range of criminal and civil cases, courts also interpret ambiguous laws, a process known as statutory interpretation. American courts also exercise the power of judicial review—that is, the power to strike down legislation that they believe contrary to the U.S. Constitution. Judges vary in their approach to legislation along a broad continuum, from advocates of judicial restraint to advocates of judicial activism. Those who advocate judicial restraint claim to adhere strictly to the letter of the laws whenever possible, supporting the validity of those laws as much as possible. Those who advocate judicial activism take a broader view and attempt to discern the fundamental principles underlying legislation, whether those principles have been specifically spelled out in the laws or not. Therefore, activist judges are much more likely to strike down federal legislation when such legislation is thought to violate the principles underlying the Constitution. In effect, activist judges make their own laws by selecting which laws will stand and which will not. Advocates of judicial activism often point to what they consider to be past judicial successes in advancing civil rights and liberties, thus encouraging judges to remedy injustices wherever they find them. Those who favor judicial restraint caution judges about undermining democratic processes by substituting their own judgments for those of the people's elected representatives.

The exercise of judicial review is consistent with the system of separation of powers and checks and balances that the framers of the U.S. Constitution adopted, but this power is in tension with democratic principles. Whereas the people elect members of the other two branches of government, the president appoints members of the judicial branch subject to confirmation by the U.S. Senate. Similarly, whereas members of the elected branches have fixed terms in office, members of the judiciary serve "during good behavior," or until they die,

John Marshall (1755–1835) served as chief justice from 1801 to 1835 and molded the Supreme Court as a major institution. He encouraged his colleagues to speak with one voice in a majority opinion, rather than in separate opinions that might dilute the Court's views, and spoke boldly for federal supremacy. (Library of Congress)

retire, or are impeached, convicted, and subsequently removed from office. Because of their insulation from the electorate, scholars sometimes refer to the courts, and particularly the U.S. Supreme Court, as a countermajoritarian institution.

Given this tension, it was inevitable that conflict would emerge over judicial exercises of power. Initially, Supreme Court justices all issued separate opinions on cases that came before them. When John Marshall became chief justice in 1801, he persuaded the Court to issue majority opinions to bolster its prestige. In one of the most famous of these decisions, *Marbury v. Madison* (1803), Marshall helped establish the power of judicial review of congressional legislation by declaring the Judiciary Act (1789) unconstitutional. This case set an important precedent, as Marshall asserted that the Supreme Court was constitutionally empowered to sit in judgment of the other two branches of government—a stance that ultimately made judicial activism possible.

Over the next thirty years, the Marshall Court continued to read the Constitution expansively to affirm broad federal powers. Thus, in *McCulloch v. Maryland* (1819), the Court upheld the constitutionality of the national bank as an implied power. Similarly, in *Gibbons v. Ogden* (1824), the Court held that a federal pilotage license granted under Congress's authority to regulate interstate commerce preempted a New York law that attempted to grant a steamboat monopoly on its waters. In such cases as *Dartmouth College v. Woodward* (1819), the Court took a strong stand on behalf of property rights. Similarly, in a number of cases, the Marshall Court struck down state laws that it believed to be in conflict with federal laws or treaties. In *Cohens v. Virginia* (1821), for example, the Court ruled that judgments in criminal cases could be appealed from state to federal courts, thus elevating the prestige and importance of federal courts over those of the states.

Both Presidents Thomas Jefferson and Andrew Jackson questioned what they considered the Court's attempt to monopolize constitutional interpretation. Both argued that all three branches had the responsibility of interpreting the Constitution for themselves. When Jackson vetoed a congressional bill to renew the Bank of the United States in 1832, he refused to be bound by the Supreme Court's earlier decision in *McCulloch v. Maryland* that this bank was constitutional. Later, although acknowledging that Supreme Court decisions must govern in individual cases, President Abraham Lincoln, who opposed the Court's decision in *Dred Scott v. Sandford*

(1857), cautioned the people against allowing the Court to determine all constitutional issues.

Over time, most American politicians came to recognize that the courts had a unique role to play in interpreting the U.S. Constitution, but the exact nature and extent of that role remained controversial. Justices had to decide whether to base their decisions simply on the basis of the Constitution or on the basis of more general principles for which they believed the Constitution stood. Justices also had to choose among a variety of methods of constitutional interpretation. Advocates of judicial restraint tended to base their decisions on closely interpreting the words of the document, on precedents, and on the intentions of those who formulated and ratified various constitutional provisions. Advocates of judicial activism often focused on broader constitutional principles, on what they perceived as the likely consequences of their decisions, and on what they thought the Constitution should mean within the modern context.

The Marshall Court has come down through history as an activist Court, and yet the only national law it struck down was a provision of the Judiciary Act (1789) that it voided in *Marbury v. Madison*. Moreover, although the Court headed by Chief Justice Roger B. Taney, which has been remembered as one that advocated restraint, was generally much more deferential to legislative judgments, in *Dred Scott v. Sandford* (1857), the Taney Court voided the Missouri Compromise of 1820 and declared that African Americans were not and could not be U.S. citizens. Ironically, in writing this decision, Taney claimed not to be enforcing his own views but the views of those who had originally written the Constitution. The Court's prestige suffered in the aftermath of Taney's tenure, but it took a more activist stance as the 19th century came to an end.

Although the picture is considerably more complex than many popular histories acknowledge, historians generally agree that from about 1890 to 1937, the Supreme Court was dominated by justices who favored laissez-faire economics, often finding support for decisions striking down governmental regulations in such broadly worded provisions of the Constitution as the due process clause, which was a clear case of judicial activism. For example, in *United States v. E.C. Knight Co.* (1895), the Court severely limited the reach of the Sherman Antitrust Act by distinguishing between the regulation of manufacturing (in this case, the establishment of a monopoly in sugar refining) and the subsequent commerce of such items. Likewise, the Court struck down a state law regulating the hours of bakers in *Lochner v. New York* (1905), ruling that this law impermissibly interfered with workers' freedom of contract. Similarly, in *Hammer v. Dagenhart* (1918), the Court invalidated a federal law limiting child labor on the basis that this was a matter of state rather than federal concern. In this latter case, Justice Oliver Wendell Holmes specifically accused the majority of ignoring the harms of child labor and reading its own economic views into the Constitution.

When Franklin D. Roosevelt assumed the presidency in 1933, he proposed a wide range of governmental programs that became known as the New Deal. Many of these laws repudiated laissez-faire theories of economics by calling for the exercise of broad governmental powers to deal with the Great Depression. Although it made some exceptions, the Supreme Court struck down most of the laws that it examined, relying on legal arguments that it had been developing since 1890. After being reelected in 1936, Roosevelt proposed what came to be known as the Court-packing plan. It sought to add one justice (and federal judge) up to fifteen for every justice over the age of seventy who did not retire. Although Roosevelt lost the battle for this bill, he arguably won the war.

In *West Coast Hotel Co. v. Parrish* (1937) and *National Labor Relations Board v. Jones & Laughlin Steel Corp.* (1937), both decided in 1937, the Court—in apparent reaction to Roosevelt's plan—made what is often called "the switch in time that saved nine" by giving far broader readings to congressional powers under the commerce clause (and thus exercising judicial restraint by deferring to legislation) than it had previously been willing to do. Justices were thereafter extremely deferential to governmental programs regulating the economy, although they began to look more closely at programs that impinged on the guarantees of civil rights and liberties found in the Bill of Rights and the Fourteenth Amendment.

The appointment of Chief Justice Earl Warren in 1953 brought another round of judicial activism to the Supreme Court, but it centered primarily on a more expansive definitions of civil liberties. In perhaps the most important case of the century, *Brown v. Board of Education* (1954), the Court overturned the doctrine of "separate but equal" that a previous Court had endorsed in *Plessy v. Ferguson* (1896) and that undergirded a massive system of segregation in this country. The Warren Court declared that the system of racial segregation must come to an end in schools and other public places.

Using the due process clause of the Fourteenth Amendment and a process generally known as selective incorporation, the Warren Court applied most of the provisions of the Bill of Rights, which had previously applied only to the national government, to the states as well. In such cases as *New York Times Co. v. United States* (1971)—involving attempted government suppression of the publication of the Pentagon Papers—and *New York Times Co. v. Sullivan* (1964)—dealing with the libel of public officials—the Court significantly expanded protections for First Amendment rights like freedom of speech and freedom of the press.

In a series of decisions in the 1960s, the Warren Court also gave much wider protection to the rights of criminal defendants. In *Mapp v. Ohio* (1961), for example, the Court applied the exclusionary rule to the states; in *Gideon v. Wainwright* (1963), it expanded the right to counsel; and in *Miranda v. Arizona* (1966), it insisted that police officers give their rights to suspects before interrogating them. The Court overturned an earlier decision to declare in *Baker v. Carr* (1962) that it would now consider cases of state legislative apportionment, and in *Reynolds v. Sims* (1964), it applied the principle of "one person one vote" to both houses of state legislatures. In *Griswold v. Connecticut* (1965), the Court further struck down an intrusive Connecticut birth control law by broadly interpreting the Constitution to establish a right to privacy.

Although these liberal decisions found many supporters, such judicial activism stirred considerable opposition both on and off the Court. Sometimes while indicating their own support for the liberal direction of Supreme Court decisions, such justices as Felix Frankfurter and John Marshall Harlan II advocated greater judicial restraint, arguing that the Court was going far beyond the language of the Constitution and weakening democracy by usurping the role of the people's elected representatives. In 1968, presidential candidate Richard Nixon blamed the Court's decisions for rising crime rates and promised to appoint strict constructionists to the Supreme Court if elected to the presidency.

It is not surprising that hearings over judicial appointments have sometimes become battlegrounds for advocates of judicial restraint and judicial activism. Opposition to key decisions of the Warren Court led in part to the Senate's failure to approve President Lyndon B. Johnson's efforts in 1968 to elevate liberal justice Abe Fortas to the chief justiceship.

During his tenure as president, Nixon appointed four justices to the Court, including a chief justice. Yet not only did the Court unanimously vote to deny his claim of executive privilege in the case of *United States v. Nixon* (1974) in the midst of the Watergate scandal, but it rendered some activist decisions of its own, most notably in *Roe v. Wade* (1973), where it extended the right to privacy to strike down most state laws restricting abortion. Two of Nixon's nominees to the Supreme Court sparked heated political debate, as both Clement Haynsworth and G. Harold Carswell were rejected before Harry Blackmun was finally confirmed in the vacant seat.

More than fifteen years later, President Ronald Reagan also faced opposition to his nominations when the Senate rejected his nomination of Robert Bork, the conservative critic of the judicial activism of the Warren Court, and Douglas Ginsburg, who withdrew after allegations of marijuana use. In President George Bush's administration, too, Clarence Thomas was narrowly confirmed after allegations of sexual harassment were raised against him. Although many of these disputes over appointments can be attributed to the personal conduct of the nominees, some question whether personal foibles have not been used as an excuse to prevent justices who support either activism or restraint from joining the Court.

Despite political battles over appointments, however, Nixon was in effect true to his word, as the Court under William Rehnquist, chief justice from 1986 to 2005, was generally considered one that practiced judicial restraint. One contemporary case that is often used as an example of judicial restraint is the 1989 decision in *DeShaney v. Winnebago County Department of Social Services*. After Randy DeShaney beat his son so badly that he fell into a coma and required institutionalization, his mother sued the state for damages under the due process clause of the Fourteenth Amendment, arguing that the state's social workers, who had intervened in a number of previous cases where the boy had been abused, had violated the Constitution by failing to protect him. In a 6–3 decision for the Court, Rehnquist refused to rule against the state, arguing that however tragic the boy's situation was, it was the result of his father's actions and not those of the state. In a passionate dissent, Justice Harry Blackmun (appointed by Nixon to support judicial restraint but often classified as a judicial activist) accused his brethren of giving an overly formalistic reading of the Constitution, maintaining that a formal and legalistic reading of the law could result in an injustice.

The perception of judicial activism and judicial restraint is often in the eyes of the beholder. Many of those who once welcomed far-reaching decisions by the liberal Warren Court looked askance as the Burger and Rehnquist Courts have issued more conservative decisions restricting congressional powers on federalism grounds and limiting the scope of Fourth Amendment rights against unreasonable searches and seizures. Judges who are perceived as models of restraint in one area of the law may be examples of activism in others and vice versa.

With the death of Chief Justice Rehnquist and retirement of Justice Sandra Day O'Connor, President George W. Bush appointed Chief Justice John Roberts and Justice Samuel Alito. They moved the court in a more conservative direction, prompting moderates and liberals to criticize judicial activism among conservatives. A series of decisions scaled back affirmative action, efforts to promote school integration, and attempts to limit political campaign contributions.

The Constitution and the judicial system itself impose certain interpretative limits on the extent to which judges and justices can read their own opinions into the Constitution, but the system of presidential appointment and Senate confirmation remains the ultimate control over such activism. This system of appointment and confirmation can respond both to arguments that conservative advocates of judicial restraint are likely to give inadequate attention to rights—like the right of privacy—that previous Courts have affirmed and to criticisms that more liberal advocates of judicial activism are likely to substitute their own judgment on controversial issues for those of the people. This system is likely to ensure a continuing colloquy over the roles that judges should play.

See also

Antislavery; Bill of Rights; Constitutionalism; Federalism; Freedom of Religion; Freedom of Speech; Freedom of the Press; Privacy; States' Rights (Antebellum, Memory, Contemporary)

JOHN R. VILE

Further Reading

Abraham, Henry J. 1998. *The Judicial Process.* New York: Oxford University Press.

Bork, Robert. 1997. *The Tempting of America: The Political Seduction of the Law.* New York: The Free Press.

Hickok, Eugene W., and Gary L. McDowell. 2002. *Justice vs. Law: Courts and Politics in American Society.* New York: The Free Press.

Miller, Arthur Selwyn. 1982. *Toward Increased Judicial Activism: The Political Role of the Supreme Court.* Westport, CT: Praeger.

Wolfe, Christopher. 1991. *Judicial Activism: Bulwark of Freedom or Precarious Security?* New York: Harcourt.

Judicial Activism—Primary Document

Introduction

Marbury v. Madison *was pivotal in establishing the doctrine of judicial review of laws made in Congress and thus helped to shape the government of the United States. In England, Parliament is considered to be supreme. Because it exercises such legislative sovereignty and because Great Britain has no single written constitution, a formal amendment process is not necessary. By contrast, in the United States, the Constitution is supreme over ordinary acts of legislation. If Congress wishes to alter the Constitution, it must proceed via the amending processes in Article V of the Constitution. In large part, this system emerged because of the extraordinarily important decision that Chief Justice John Marshall authored in* Marbury v. Madison *in 1803.*

Document: *Marbury v. Madison* (1803)

MR. JUSTICE MARSHALL delivered the opinion of the Court.

In the order in which the court has viewed this subject, the following questions have been considered and decided.

1. Has the applicant a right to the commission he demands?

2. If he has a right, and that right has been violated, do the laws of his country afford him a remedy?

3. If they do afford him a remedy, is it a mandamus issuing from this court?

. . . It is . . . the opinion of the court,

1. That, by signing the commission of Mr. Marbury, the President of the United States appointed him a justice of peace, for the county of Washington in the District of Columbia; and that the seal of the United States, affixed thereto by the Secretary of State, is conclusive testimony of the verity of the signature, and of the completion of the appointment; and that the appointment conferred on him a legal right to the office for the space of five years.

2. That, having this legal title to the office, he has a consequent right to the commission; a refusal to deliver which, is a plain violation of that right, for which the laws of this country afford him a remedy.

It remains to be enquired whether,

3. He is entitled to the remedy for which applies. This depends on,

    1. The nature of the writ applied for and
    2. The power of this court.

. . . This, then, is a plain case for mandamus, either to deliver the commission, or a copy of it from the record; and it only remains to be enquired, whether it can issue from this court.

The act to establish the judicial courts of the United States authorizes the Supreme Court "to issue writs of mandamus in cases warranted by the principles and usages of law, to any courts appointed, or persons holding office, under the authority of the United States."

The Secretary of State, being a person holding an office under the authority of the United States, is precisely within the letter of the description and if this court is not authorized to issue a writ of mandamus to such an officer, it must be because the law is unconstitutional, and therefore absolutely incapable of conferring the authority, and assigning the duties which its words purport to confer and assign.

The Constitution vests the whole judicial power of the United States in one supreme court, and such inferior courts as Congress shall, from time to time, ordain and establish. This power is expressly extended to all cases arising under the laws of the United States; and, consequently, in some form, may be exercised over the present case; because the right claimed is given by a law of the United States.

In the distribution of this power it is declared that "the Supreme Court shall have original jurisdiction in all cases affecting ambassadors, other public ministers and consuls, and those in which a state shall be a party. In all other cases, the Supreme Court shall have appellate jurisdiction."

It has been insisted at the bar, that, as the original grant of jurisdiction to the Supreme and inferior courts, is general, and the clause assigning original jurisdiction to the Supreme Court contains no negative or restrictive words, the power remains to the legislature to assign original jurisdiction to that court in other cases than those specified in the article which has been recited; provided those cases belong to the judicial power of the United States.

If it had been intended to leave it in the discretion of the legislature to apportion the judicial power between the Supreme and inferior courts according to the will of that body, it would certainly have been useless to have proceeded further than to have defined the judicial power, and the tribunals in which it should be vested. The subsequent part of the section is mere surplusage, is entirely without meaning. If Congress remains at liberty to give this court appellate jurisdiction, where the Constitution has declared their jurisdiction shall be original; and original jurisdiction where the Constitution has declared it shall be appellate, the distribution of jurisdiction made in the Constitution is form without substance.

Affirmative words are often, in their operation, negative of other objects than those affirmed; and in this case, a negative or exclusive sense must be given to them, or they have no operation at all.

It cannot he presumed that any clause in the Constitution is intended to be without effect; and, therefore, such a construction is inadmissible unless the words require it.

. . . To enable this court, then to issue a mandamus, it must be shown to be an exercise of appellate jurisdiction, or to be necessary to enable them to exercise appellate jurisdiction.

It has been stated at the bar that the appellate jurisdiction may be exercised in a variety of forms, and that, if it be the will of the legislature that a mandamus should be used for that purpose, that will must be obeyed. This is true, yet the jurisdiction must be appellate, not original.

It is the essential criterion of appellate jurisdiction that it revises and corrects the proceedings in a cause already instituted, and does not create that cause. Although, therefore, a mandamus may be directed to courts, yet to issue such a writ to an officer for the delivery of a paper is in effect the same as to sustain an original action for that paper, and, therefore, seems not to belong to appellate, but to original jurisdiction. Neither is it necessary, in such a case as this, to enable the court to exercise its appellate jurisdiction.

The authority, therefore, given to the Supreme Court by the act establishing the judicial courts of the United States, to issue writs of mandamus to public officers, appears not to be warranted by the Constitution; and it becomes necessary to inquire whether a jurisdiction so conferred can be exercised.

The question, whether an act repugnant to the Constitution can become the law of the land, is a question deeply interesting to the United States; but, happily, not of an intricacy proportioned to its interest. It seems only necessary to recognize certain principles, supposed to have been long and well established, to decide it.

That the people have an original right to establish, for their future government, such principles as, in their opinion, shall most conduce to their own happiness is the basis on which the whole American fabric had been erected. The exercise of this original right is a very great exertion; nor can it, nor ought it, to be frequently repeated. The principles, therefore, so established, are deemed fundamental. And as the authority from which they proceed is supreme, and can seldom act, they are designed to be permanent.

This original and supreme will organizes the government, and assigns to different departments their respective powers. It may either stop here, or establish certain limits not to be transcended by those departments.

The government of the United States is of the latter description. The powers of the legislature are defined and limited; and that those limits may not be mistaken, or forgotten, the Constitution is written. To what purpose are powers limited, and to what purpose is that limitation committed to writing, if these limits may, at any time, be passed by those intended to be restrained? The distinction between a government with limited and unlimited powers is abolished if those limits do not confine the persons on whom they are imposed, and if acts prohibited and acts allowed are of equal obligation. It is a proposition too plain to be contested, that the Constitution controls any legislative act repugnant to it; or, that the legislature may alter the Constitution by an ordinary act.

Between these alternatives there is no middle ground. The Constitution is either a superior paramount law, unchangeable by ordinary means, or it is on a level with ordinary legislative acts, and, like other acts, is alterable when the legislature shall please to alter it.

If the former part of the alternative be true, then a legislative act contrary to the Constitution is not law: if the latter part be true, then written constitutions are absurd attempts on the part of the people to limit a power in its own nature illimitable.

Certainly all those who have framed written constitutions contemplate them as forming the fundamental and paramount law of the nation, and consequently, the theory of every such government must be, that an act of the legislature, repugnant to the constitution, is void.

This theory is essentially attached to a written constitution, and is, consequently, to be considered by this court as one of the fundamental principles of our society. It is not therefore to be lost sight of in the further consideration of this subject.

If an act of the legislature, repugnant to the Constitution, is void, does it, notwithstanding its invalidity, bind the courts, and oblige them to give it effect? Or, in other words, though it be not law, does it constitute a rule as operative as if it was a law? This would be to overthrow in fact what was established in theory; and would seem at first view, an absurdity too gross to be insisted on. It shall, however, receive a more attentive consideration.

It is emphatically the province and duty of the judicial department to say what the law is. Those who apply the rule to particular cases must, of necessity, expound and interpret that rule. If two laws conflict with each other, the courts must decide on the operation of each.

So if a law be in opposition to the Constitution; if both the law and the constitution apply to a particular case, so that the court must either decide that case conformably to the law, disregarding the Constitution; or conformably to the Constitution, disregarding the law; the court must determine which of these conflicting rules governs the case. This is of the very essence of judicial duty.

If, then, the courts are to regard the Constitution, and the Constitution is superior to any ordinary act of the legislature, the Constitution, and not such ordinary act, must govern the case to which they both apply.

Those, then, who controvert the principle that the Constitution is to be considered, in court, as a paramount law, are reduced to the necessity of maintaining that courts must close their eyes on the Constitution, and see only the law.

This doctrine would subvert the very foundation of all written constitutions. It would declare that an act which, according to the principles and theory of our government, is entirely void, is yet, in practice, completely obligatory. It would declare that if the legislature shall do what is expressly forbidden, such act, notwithstanding the express prohibition, is in reality effectual. It would be giving to the legislature a practical and real omnipotence, with the same breath which professes to restrict their powers within narrow limits. It is prescribing limits and declaring that those limits may be passed at pleasure.

That it thus reduces to nothing what we have deemed the greatest improvement on political institutions—a written constitution—would of itself be sufficient, in America, where written constitutions have been viewed with so much reverence, for rejecting the construction. But the peculiar expressions of the Constitution of the United States furnish additional arguments in favor of its rejection.

The judicial power of the United States is extended to all cases arising under the Constitution.

Could it be the intention of those who gave this power to say that, in using it, the Constitution should not be looked into? That a case arising under the Constitution should be decided without examining the instrument under which it rises?

This is too extravagant to be maintained.

In some cases then, the Constitution must be looked into by the judges. And if they can open it at all, what part of it are they forbidden to read or to obey?

There are many other parts of the Constitution which serve to illustrate this subject.

It is declared that "no tax or duty shall be laid on articles exported from any state." Suppose a duty on the export of cotton, of tobacco, or of flour; and a suit instituted to recover it. Ought judgment to be rendered in such a case? Ought the judges to close their eyes on the Constitution, and see only the law?

The Constitution declares that "no bill of attainder or ex post facto law shall be passed."

If, however, such a bill should be passed and a person should be prosecuted under it; must the court condemn to death those victims who the Constitution endeavours to preserve?

"No person," says the Constitution, "shall be convicted of treason unless on the testimony of two witnesses to the same overt act, or on confession in open court."

Here the language of the Constitution is addressed especially to the courts. It prescribes, directly for them, a rule of evidence not to be departed from. If the legislature should change that rule, and declare one witness, or a confession out of court, sufficient for conviction, must the constitutional principle yield to the legislative act?

From these, and many other selections which might be made, it is apparent that the framers of the Constitution contemplated that instrument as a rule for the government of courts, as well as of the legislature.

Why otherwise does it direct the judges to take an oath to support it? This oath certainly applies in an especial manner to their conduct in their official character. How immoral to impose it on them, if they were to be used as the instruments, and the knowing instruments, for violating what they swear to support?

The oath of office, too, imposed by the legislature, is completely demonstrative of the legislative opinion on this subject. It is in these words: "I do solemnly swear that I will administer justice without respect to persons, and do equal right to the poor and to the rich; and that I will faithfully and impartially discharge all the duties incumbent on me as—, according to the best of my abilities and understanding agreeably to the Constitution and laws of the United States."

Why does a judge swear to discharge his duties agreeably to the Constitution of the United States, if that Constitution forms no rule for his government? If it is closed upon him, and cannot be inspected by him?

If such be the real state of things, this is worse than solemn mockery. To prescribe, or take this oath, becomes equally a crime.

It is also not entirely unworthy of observation that, in declaring what shall be the supreme law of the land, the Constitution itself is first mentioned; and not the laws of the United States generally, but those only which shall he made in pursuance of the Constitution, have that rank.

Thus, the particular phraseology of the Constitution of the United States confirms and strengthens the principle, supposed to be essential to all written constitutions, that a law repugnant to the Constitution is void; and that courts, as well as other departments, are bound by that instrument.

The rule must be

Discharged.

Source: Our Documents Website. http://www.ourdocuments. gov/doc.php?flash=true&doc=19&page=transcript.

_____

JUDICIAL REVIEW

Judicial review is the constitutional and legal doctrine that permits a judicial body to review the actions of the legislative and executive branches and reverse or nullify acts and decisions that are inconsistent with a constitution or other governing document. In the United States, this permits state and federal courts to declare acts of Congress, the president, and state legislatures unconstitutional and invalid when the court finds that those acts are inconsistent with the Constitution of the United States. The use of this power by the courts can play an important role in shaping the political trends across the nation.

The Constitution of the United States does not explicitly grant the judiciary the power of judicial review. In contrast with the explicit grants of power to Congress in Article I, Section 8, and the powers granted to the president in Article II, Article III of the Constitution does little more than establish the basic structure and jurisdiction of the federal judiciary, and is silent as to whether the courts can reverse an act of Congress. Article VI asserts the supremacy of the federal constitution and federal law over conflicting state laws, but does not directly authorize the courts to invalidate laws it finds to be unconstitutional.

Though the Constitution does not directly grant the courts the power to invalidate laws, its drafters were not silent on the issue. During the Constitutional Convention, the delegates debated the Virginia Plan, which vested the veto power in a Council of Revision that would include the president and federal judges. This proposal eventually failed, leaving the veto power solely with the president, because the delegates believed the courts inherently possessed the power to ignore unconstitutional laws. The drafters of Article III added the clause "arising under this Constitution" specifically to grant the courts jurisdiction to hear constitutional cases. In debates regarding granting to Congress a specific power to veto state laws, the delegates determined that it was unnecessary because the judiciary could set aside any laws that violated the federal constitution. The totality of the historical record of the convention indicates that the majority of delegates endorsed the power of judicial review.

After the delegates to the Constitutional Convention approved the Constitution and sent it to the states, delegates returned to their home states to advocate its ratification. In

A political cartoon satirizes the court-packing plan proposed by President Franklin D. Roosevelt in 1937. Roosevelt's plan represented an attempt to control Supreme Court decisions related to his New Deal legislation. Cartoon by S.J. Ray, *Kansas City Star*, August 1937. (AP Photo)

no fewer than seven of the state ratifying conventions, supporters of ratification openly declared that the Constitution authorized the power of judicial review for the courts in order to protect individual rights and limit congressional power. Three proponents of ratification, Alexander Hamilton, John Jay, and James Madison, circulated essays in support of ratification that became known as the Federalist Papers. In *The Federalist No. 78*, Hamilton argues that it is the judiciary's "duty... to declare all acts contrary to the manifest tenor of the Constitution void. Without this, all the reservations of particular rights or privileges would amount to nothing." In Hamilton's view, because the Constitution is intended to be limited, granting only specific powers to the federal government, and reserving all other powers for the states and the people themselves, the judiciary must act as "bulwarks of a limited Constitution against legislative encroachments." Hamilton argues that this power to invalidate acts of Congress does not make the judiciary superior to Congress; it simply recognizes that the courts must act as an intermediary

between the people and the legislature to ensure that the Congress neither exceeds the powers assigned to them nor takes actions directly forbidden of them.

The first exercise of judicial review in the federal courts appeared in the 1803 case of *Marbury v. Madison*. Near the end of John Adams's presidency, he appointed William Marbury as a justice of the peace for the District of Columbia. The Senate confirmed Marbury, President Adams signed the commission, and the secretary of state stamped the commission with the seal of the United States; however, the commission was not delivered to Marbury before President Adams left office and Thomas Jefferson assumed the presidency. Upon taking office, Jefferson and his secretary of state, James Madison, refused to deliver the commission of Marbury and several other "midnight" appointees, thus preventing them from exercising the duties of their office. Marbury sued Madison asking the Court to grant a judicial writ of mandamus—an order from a court—compelling Secretary Madison to deliver the commission. Under Section 13 of the Judiciary Act of 1787, the suit was to originate with the U.S. Supreme Court, meaning only the Supreme Court could hear the case.

Chief Justice John Marshall, an Adams appointee, held that that the signing of the commission by President Adams completed the appointment of Mr. Marbury and entitled him to the justice of the peace post. Marshall, who happened to have been the secretary of state who failed to deliver Marbury's commission, concluded that the Judiciary Act of 1789 granted Marbury the right to seek judicial intervention, and granted the courts the power to issue a writ to the secretary. However, because the act required the Supreme Court to hear the case under its original jurisdiction, the chief justice declared that the act itself was unconstitutional. Marshall argued that because Article III of the Constitution dictates precisely the limited types of cases where the Supreme Court has original jurisdiction and declares that in "all the other cases" it shall have appellate jurisdiction, Congress could not alter this divided jurisdiction through ordinary statute. Therefore, because the Court had no jurisdiction to hear Marbury's suit, it could not issue the writ to Secretary Madison compelling him to deliver the commission to Mr. Marbury.

In justifying his assertion of the judicial review power, Marshall expanded on many of Hamilton's arguments presented in *Federalist No. 78*. Chief Justice Marshall claimed the power to find the act unconstitutional was in the very nature of the Constitution itself. He reasoned that if the Constitution is to be the supreme law of the land, and the legislature is to have limited powers, then it follows that any act that exceeds those powers or is in conflict with the Constitution must be void. If the courts cannot find that act to be void but are instead obliged to follow that act as if it is law, then the act is effectively valid, and there is no limit to legislative power.

Though Chief Justice Marshall's decision in Marbury cemented the great power of judicial review, the Supreme Court of the United States did not invalidate another federal law until *Dred Scott v. Sandford* in 1857. The Court's decision, authored by Chief Justice Roger Taney, invalidated the Missouri Compromise, reversed the creation of free states by federal statute, and held that slaveholders could not be prevented from taking their slaves with them into new territories. This widely despised decision was one of a chain of events that ultimately precipitated the Civil War and serves as a leading example of how the use of judicial review can have wide-ranging political implications.

Since the Civil War, the courts have used the power of judicial review to invalidate federal and state laws with numerous political outcomes. During the post–Civil War Reconstruction period, the Court frustrated congressional efforts to protect freed slaves by declaring federal civil rights laws unconstitutional holding that the Fourteenth Amendment granted to Congress the power only to regulate discrimination by the state, not by private individuals. This led to an era of discriminatory Jim Crow laws across the South. However, beginning in the 1940s, the Court began to use judicial review to invalidate state laws discriminating against minorities. In *Smith v. Allwright* (1944), the Court ruled a Texas law that enforced "white-only" primary elections was unconstitutional. In *Sweatt v. Painter* (1950), the Court required the University of Texas Law School to admit an African American applicant because the segregated facilities were unequal to the white-only schools. In the landmark 1954 case of *Brown v. Board of Education*, the Court unanimously rejected state laws requiring segregated "separate but equal" public schools and required measures to desegregate schools across the nation.

The Court has also used the power of judicial review to invalidate attempts by progressives to pass labor laws designed to protect the worker. In the 1905 case of *Lochner v. New York*, the Court found that a New York state law limiting the number of hours one could work per week in a bakery was invalid because the Fourteenth Amendment's due process clause prevented any law from limiting an individual liberty of contract. This permitted a worker to contract his own labor on his own terms, regardless of any state interest in protecting the safety of bakery workers by limiting work hours. For the next thirty years, the Court would expand this right of liberty of contract with rulings that invalided state and federal laws limiting child labor, laws requiring a minimum wage, and laws that supported the right to form labor unions.

Judicial review became a key issue early in the presidency of Franklin Roosevelt. During Roosevelt's first term of office, he began to implement his New Deal programs designed to alleviate the effects of the Great Depression. The Supreme Court initially thwarted Roosevelt's efforts, repeatedly finding that New Deal programs designed to support the agriculture industry and regulate the coal industry were unconstitutional because they exceeded congressional power to tax and spend or regulate interstate commerce. The Court's repeated use of judicial review to invalidate New Deal programs prompted Roosevelt to attempt to "pack the Court" with new appointees favorable to his agenda. Many disagreed with President Roosevelt's attempt to circumvent the Court's judicial review power and viewed it as a threat to the separation of powers. The legislation failed in Congress, but the Court began upholding his legislative agenda.

Over the course of the 20th century, judicial review became a key tool to invalidate state and federal laws that violate the Bill of Rights. The First Amendment protection of free speech led the Court to invalidate federal and state laws banning flag burning, holding that it is protected symbolic speech. The Court protected the freedom of the press by invalidating prior restraint laws that prevented publication of controversial material, and limited libel laws that prevented newspapers from publishing truthful material critical of public figures. The Court invoked the establishment clause of the First Amendment to invalidate laws that required prayer in schools and held that free exercise clause forbids laws that require a student to salute the flag. Recent Court decisions have overturned state and local laws banning gun ownership holding that the Second Amendment protects an individual's right to gun ownership.

In addition to protecting individual rights enumerated in the Bill of Rights, the Court began to use judicial review to protect so-called fundamental rights. These rights are not listed specifically in the Constitution, but are viewed as fundamental to the concept of liberty. In *Griswold v. Connecticut* (1965), the Supreme Court declared that the Constitution protects a fundamental right to privacy and invalidated a state law that banned access to contraceptives for married couples. In *Skinner v. Oklahoma* (1942), the Court determined that the Constitution protected a fundamental right to procreate, and invalidated a law requiring sterilization of criminals. More recently, the Court has nullified laws that discriminated against homosexuals, overturning a Texas law, and recently the federal Defense of Marriage Act, which prevented the federal government from providing spousal benefits to same-sex couples legally married under state law.

In recent years, the Court has begun to exercise judicial review to limit congressional power under the commerce clause, reversing the trend of expanding congressional power since the New Deal. In 1995, for the first time in more than fifty years, the Court found that Congress exceeded its commerce clause power by implementing a federal law creating gun-free school zones. In a controversial 2012 decision authored by Chief Justice John Roberts, the Court found that Congress could not require individuals to purchase health insurance under its commerce clause power, but determined that the Affordable Care Act was valid because it was within the taxing power to levy a fine against those who violated the law.

See also

Judicial Activism; Separation of Powers

BRIAN HILL

Further Reading

Clinton, Robert Lowry. 1989. *"Marbury v. Madison" and Judicial Review*. Lawrence, KS: University Press of Kansas.

Federalist Paper, No. 78. (Alexander Hamilton). http://www. constitution.org/fed/federa78.htm. Accessed April 21, 2014.

Marbury v. Madison, 5 U.S. 137 (1803).

Melone, Albert P., and George Mace. 1988. *Judicial Review and American Democracy*. Ames, IO: Iowa State University Press.

Prakash, Saikrishna B., and John C. Yoo. 2003. "The Origins of Judicial Review." *University of Chicago Law Review* 70: 887–982.

Judicial Review—Primary Document

Introduction

After the Constitutional Convention of 1787 approved the new federal constitution, the delegates submitted it to the individual states for ratification and adoption. Three supporters of ratification, Alexander Hamilton, John Jay, and James Madison, wrote and published a series of essays and articles collectively labeled The Federalist. *Each document proceeded to explain the different powers and rights listed in the new constitution. This collection of essays is frequently cited as a leading source for determining the original intent and meaning of the Constitution. This essay,* Federalist No. 78, *written by Alexander Hamilton, addressed the issue of the role of the judiciary in the proposed government. Of all the eighty-five essays comprising* The Federalist, *No. 78 is the most frequently cited by U.S. Supreme Court justices.*

Document: *The Federalist* No. 78 (Alexander Hamilton) (May 28, 1788)

To the People of the State of New York:

We proceed now to an examination of the judiciary department of the proposed government.

In unfolding the defects of the existing Confederation, the utility and necessity of a federal judicature have been clearly pointed out. It is the less necessary to recapitulate the considerations there urged, as the propriety of the institution in the abstract is not disputed; the only questions which have been raised being relative to the manner of constituting it, and to its extent. To these points, therefore, our observations shall be confined.

The manner of constituting it seems to embrace these several objects: 1st. The mode of appointing the judges. 2d. The tenure by which they are to hold their places. 3d. The partition of the judiciary authority between different courts, and their relations to each other.

First. As to the mode of appointing the judges; this is the same with that of appointing the officers of the Union in general, and has been so fully discussed in the two last numbers, that nothing can be said here which would not be useless repetition.

Second. As to the tenure by which the judges are to hold their places: this chiefly concerns their duration in office; the provisions for their support; the precautions for their responsibility.

According to the plan of the convention, all judges who may be appointed by the United States are to hold their offices during good behavior; which is conformable to the most approved of the State constitutions, and among the rest, to that of this State. Its propriety having been drawn into question by the adversaries of that plan, is no light symptom of the rage for objection, which disorders their imaginations and judgments. The standard of good behavior for the continuance in office of the judicial magistracy, is certainly one of the most valuable of the modern improvements in the practice of government. In a monarchy it is an excellent barrier to the despotism of the prince; in a republic it is a no less excellent barrier to the encroachments and oppressions of the representative body. And it is the best expedient which can be devised in any government, to secure a steady, upright, and impartial administration of the laws.

Whoever attentively considers the different departments of power must perceive, that, in a government in which they are separated from each other, the judiciary, from the nature of its functions, will always be the least dangerous to the political rights of the Constitution; because it will be least in a capacity to annoy or injure them. The Executive not only dispenses the honors, but holds the sword of the community. The legislature not only commands the purse, but prescribes the rules by which the duties and rights of every citizen are to be regulated. The judiciary, on the contrary, has no influence over either the sword or the purse; no direction either of the strength or of the wealth of the society; and can take no active resolution whatever. It may truly be said to have neither FORCE nor WILL, but merely judgment; and must ultimately depend upon the aid of the executive arm even for the efficacy of its judgments.

This simple view of the matter suggests several important consequences. It proves incontestably, that the judiciary is beyond comparison the weakest of the three departments of power*; that it can never attack with success either of the other two; and that all possible care is requisite to enable it to defend itself against their attacks. It equally proves, that though individual oppression may now and then proceed from the courts of justice, the general liberty of the people can never be endangered from that quarter; I mean so long as the judiciary remains truly distinct from both the legislature and the Executive. For I agree, that "there is no liberty, if the power of judging be not separated from the legislative and executive powers."† And it proves, in the last place, that as liberty can have nothing to fear from the judiciary alone, but would have every thing to fear from its union with either of the other departments; that as all the effects of such a union must ensue from a dependence of the former on the latter, notwithstanding a nominal and apparent separation; that as, from the natural feebleness of the judiciary, it is in continual jeopardy of being overpowered, awed, or influenced by its coordinate branches; and that as nothing can contribute so much to its firmness and independence as permanency in office, this quality may therefore be justly regarded as an indispensable ingredient in its constitution, and, in a great measure, as the citadel of the public justice and the public security.

The complete independence of the courts of justice is peculiarly essential in a limited Constitution. By a limited Constitution, I understand one which contains certain specified exceptions to the legislative authority; such, for instance, as that it shall pass no bills of attainder, no *ex-post-facto* laws, and the like. Limitations of this kind can be preserved in practice no other way than through the medium of courts of justice, whose duty it must be to declare all acts contrary to the manifest tenor of the Constitution void. Without this, all the reservations of particular rights or privileges would amount to nothing.

Some perplexity respecting the rights of the courts to pronounce legislative acts void, because contrary to the Constitution, has arisen from an imagination that the doctrine would imply a superiority of the judiciary to the legislative

---

* The celebrated Montesquieu, speaking of them, says : "Of the three powers above mentioned, the judiciary is next to nothing." —"Spirit of Laws," vol. i., page 186—PUBLIUS.
†*Idem*, page 181.—PUBLIUS.

power. It is urged that the authority which can declare the acts of another void, must necessarily be superior to the one whose acts may be declared void. As this doctrine is of great importance in all the American constitutions, a brief discussion of the ground on which it rests cannot he unacceptable.

There is no position which depends on clearer principles, than that every act of a delegated authority, contrary to the tenor of the commission under which it is exercised, is void. No legislative act, therefore, contrary to the Constitution, can be valid. To deny this, would be to affirm, that the deputy is greater than his principal; that the servant is above his master; that the representatives of the people are superior to the people themselves; that men acting by virtue of powers, may do not only what their powers do not authorize, but what they forbid.

If it be said that the legislative body are themselves the constitutional judges of their own powers, and that the construction they put upon them is conclusive upon the other departments, it may be answered, that this cannot be the natural presumption, where it is not to be collected from any particular provisions in the Constitution. It is not otherwise to be supposed, that the Constitution could intend to enable the representatives of the people to substitute their *will* to that of their constituents. It is far more rational to suppose, that the courts were designed to be an intermediate body between the people and the legislature, in order, among other things, to keep the latter within the limits assigned to their authority. The interpretation of the laws is the proper and peculiar province of the courts. A constitution is, in fact, and must be regarded by the judges, as a fundamental law. It therefore belongs to them to ascertain its meaning, as well as the meaning of any particular act proceeding from the legislative body. If there should happen to be an irreconcilable variance between the two, that which has the superior obligation and validity ought, of course, to be preferred; or, in other words, the Constitution ought to be preferred to the statute, the intention of the people to the intention of their agents.

Nor does this conclusion by any means suppose a superiority of the judicial to the legislative power. It only supposes that the power of the people is superior to both; and that where the will of the legislature, declared in its statutes, stands in opposition to that of the people, declared in the Constitution,

the judges ought to be governed by the latter rather than the former. They ought to regulate their decisions by the fundamental laws, rather than by those which are not fundamental.

This exercise of judicial discretion, in determining between two contradictory laws, is exemplified in a familiar instance. It not uncommonly happens, that there are two statutes existing at one time, clashing in whole or in part with each other, and neither of them containing any repealing clause or expression. In such a case, it is the province of the courts to liquidate and fix their meaning and operation. So far as they can, by any fair construction, be reconciled to each other, reason and law conspire to dictate that this should be done; where this is impracticable, it becomes a matter of necessity to give effect to one, in exclusion of the other. The rule which has obtained in the courts for determining their relative validity is, that the last in order of time shall be preferred to the first. But this is a mere rule of construction, not derived from any positive law, but from the nature and reason of the thing. It is a rule not enjoined upon the courts by legislative provision, but adopted by themselves, as consonant to truth and propriety, for the direction of their conduct as interpreters of the law. They thought it reasonable, that between the interfering acts of an *equal* authority, that which was the last indication of its will should have the preference.

But in regard to the interfering acts of a superior and subordinate authority, of an original and derivative power, the nature and reason of the thing indicate the converse of that rule as proper to be followed. They teach us that the prior act of a superior ought to be preferred to the subsequent act of an inferior and subordinate authority; and that accordingly, whenever a particular statute contravenes the Constitution, it will be the duty of the judicial tribunals to adhere to the latter and disregard the former.

It can be of no weight to say that the courts, on the pretense of a repugnancy, may substitute their own pleasure to the constitutional intentions of the legislature. This might as well happen in the case of two contradictory statutes; or it might as well happen in every adjudication upon any single statute. The courts must declare the sense of the law; and if they should be disposed to exercise WILL instead of JUDGMENT, the consequence would equally be the substitution of their pleasure to that of the legislative body. The observation, if it prove any thing, would prove that there ought to be no judges distinct from that body.

If, then, the courts of justice are to be considered as the bulwarks of a limited Constitution against legislative encroachments, this consideration will afford a strong argument for the permanent tenure of judicial offices, since nothing will contribute so much as this to that independent spirit in the judges which must be essential to the faithful performance of so arduous a duty.

This independence of the judges is equally requisite to guard the Constitution and the rights of individuals from the effects of those ill humors, which the arts of designing men, or the influence of particular conjunctures, sometimes disseminate among the people themselves, and which, though they speedily give place to better information, and more deliberate reflection, have a tendency, in the meantime, to occasion dangerous innovations in the government, and serious oppressions of the minor party in the community. Though I trust the friends of the proposed Constitution will never concur with its enemies,* in questioning that fundamental principle of republican government, which admits the right of the people to alter or abolish the established Constitution, whenever they find it inconsistent with their happiness, yet it is not to be inferred from this principle, that the representatives of the people, whenever a momentary inclination happens to lay hold of a majority of their constituents, incompatible with the provisions in the existing Constitution, would, on that account, be justifiable in a violation of those provisions; or that the courts would be under a greater obligation to connive at infractions in this shape, than when they had proceeded wholly from the cabals of the representative body. Until the people have, by some solemn and authoritative act, annulled or changed the established form, it is binding upon themselves collectively, as well as individually; and no presumption, or even knowledge, of their sentiments, can warrant their representatives in a departure from it, prior to such an act. But it is easy to see, that it would require an uncommon portion of fortitude in the judges to do their duty as faithful guardians of the Constitution, where legislative

* *Vide* "Protest of the Minority of the Convention of Pennsylvania,: Martin's Speech, etc.—PUBLIUS.[CE1]

invasions of it had been instigated by the major voice of the community.

But it is not with a view to infractions of the Constitution only, that the independence of the judges may be an essential safeguard against the effects of occasional ill humors in the society. These sometimes extend no farther than to the injury of the private rights of particular classes of citizens, by unjust and partial laws. Here also the firmness of the judicial magistracy is of vast importance in mitigating the severity and confining the operation of such laws. It not only serves to moderate the immediate mischiefs of those which may have been passed, but it operates as a check upon the legislative body in passing them; who, perceiving that obstacles to the success of iniquitous intention are to be expected from the scruples of the courts, are in a manner compelled, by the very motives of the injustice they meditate, to qualify their attempts. This is a circumstance calculated to have more influence upon the character of our governments, than but few may be aware of. The benefits of the integrity and moderation of the judiciary have already been felt in more States than one; and though they may have displeased those whose sinister expectations they may have disappointed, they must have commanded the esteem and applause of all the virtuous and disinterested. Considerate men, of every description, ought to prize whatever will tend to beget or fortify that temper in the courts; as no man can be sure that he may not be to-morrow the victim of a spirit of injustice, by which he may be a gainer to-day. And every man must now feel, that the inevitable tendency of such a spirit is to sap the foundations of public and private confidence, and to introduce in its stead universal distrust and distress.

That inflexible and uniform adherence to the rights of the Constitution, and of individuals, which we perceive to be indispensable in the courts of justice, can certainly not be expected from judges who hold their offices by a temporary commission. Periodical appointments, however regulated, or by whomsoever made, would, in some way or other, be fatal to their necessary independence. If the power of making them was committed either to the Executive or legislature, there would be danger of an improper complaisance to the branch which possessed it; if to both, there would be an unwillingness to hazard the displeasure of either; if to the people, or to persons chosen by them for the special purpose, there would be too great a disposition to consult popularity, to justify a reliance that nothing would be consulted but the Constitution and the laws.

There is yet a further and a weightier reason for the permanency of the judicial offices, which is deducible from the nature of the qualifications they require. It has been frequently remarked, with great propriety, that a voluminous code of laws is one of the inconveniences necessarily connected with the advantages of a free government. To avoid an arbitrary discretion in the courts, it is indispensable that they should be bound down by strict rules and precedents, which serve to define and point out their duty in every particular case that comes before them; and it will readily be conceived from the variety of controversies which grow out of the folly and wickedness of mankind, that the records of those precedents must unavoidably swell to a very considerable bulk, and must demand long and laborious study to acquire a competent knowledge of them. Hence it is, that there can be but few men in the society who will have sufficient skill in the laws to qualify them for the stations of judges. And making the proper deductions for the ordinary depravity of human nature, the number must be still smaller of those who unite the requisite integrity with the requisite knowledge. These considerations apprise us, that the government can have no great option between fit character; and

that a temporary duration in office, which would naturally discourage such characters from quitting a lucrative line of practice to accept a seat on the bench, would have a tendency to throw the administration of justice into hands less able, and less well qualified, to conduct it with utility and dignity. In the present circumstances of this country, and in those in which it is likely to be for a long time to come, the disadvantages on this score would be greater than they may at first sight appear; but it must be confessed, that they are far inferior to those which present themselves under the other aspects of the subject.

Upon the whole, there can be no room to doubt that the convention acted wisely in copying from the models of those constitutions which have established *good behavior* as the tenure of their judicial offices, in point of duration; and that so far from being blamable on this account, their plan would have been inexcusably defective, if it had wanted this important feature of good government. The experience of Great Britain affords an illustrious comment on the excellence of the institution.

PUBLIUS

Source: Lodge, Henry Cabot, ed. *The Federalist: A Commentary on the Constitution of the United States.* New York: G. P. Putnam's Sons, 1902, pp. 482–491.

K

KEYNESIAN ECONOMICS

Keynesian economics, originating in the thought of English political economist John Maynard Keynes (1883–1946), is the most widely accepted economic theory in the world today. Keynesian monetary and fiscal policy has been used primarily to justify the development and maintenance of the authoritarian Welfare State.

Virtually every school of political economy today is Keynesian, based on Keynesian assumptions, or a reaction against Keynesian economics. As Nobel Laureate Milton Friedman (1912–2006) of the Monetarist (Chicago) school of political economy declared in an interview in the December 31, 1965, issue of *Time* magazine, "We are all Keynesians now."

Keynesian economics developed out of a split in classical economics between the Smithian school, based on the work of Adam Smith (1723–1790), and the Ricardian school, derived from the work of David Ricardo (1772–1823). The principal differences between the Smithian school and the Ricardian school incorporated into Keynesian theory are a rejection of Say's Law of Markets and the real bills doctrine, acceptance of the labor theory of value, and an increased economic role for the state. Austrian school economist Friedrich von Hayek (1899–1992) claimed that Keynesian economics is inherently collectivist.

Say's Law of Markets

Although not developed by Jean-Baptiste Say (1767–1832), Say best expressed what became known as "Say's Law of Markets." Say's Law is based on Smith's dictum from *The Wealth of Nations* (1776) that "consumption is the sole end and purpose of all production" (*Wealth of Nations*, III.8.).

As Say explained in *Letters to Malthus* (English translation, 1821), no one can consume a good unless that good is produced, either by means of one's own labor, land, or capital, or by the labor, land, or capital of another. Aside from charity, the only legitimate way to obtain a good for consumption is to produce it oneself, or to exchange the goods one has produced for those produced by others.

Purchases of goods produced by others are not made with "money," but with what the purchaser has produced. "Money" is only the medium through which exchanges are made. Everything else being equal and assuming there are no barriers to the acquisition and employment of labor, land, or capital, and given that production (supply) is the only source of consumption (demand), supply generates its own demand, and demand, its own supply.

If, therefore, some goods remain unsold or there is insufficient demand, the solution is not to "multiply barren consumptions," such as creating artificial demand by manipulating the currency or the money supply. Rather, the solution to economic disequilibrium is to make people who were formerly not able to produce productive through acquisition and effective employment of labor, land, and capital: "[I]f certain commodities do not sell, it is because others are not produced, and that it is the raising produce alone which opens a market for the sale of produce" (*Letters to Malthus*, I).

The Real Bills Doctrine

The "real bills doctrine" is an application of Say's Law of Markets. Money is anything that can be accepted in settlement of a debt, that is, whatever can be exchanged, "all things transferred in commerce" ("Money," *Black's Law Dictionary*). All money is therefore a contract, just as (in a sense) all contracts are money, consisting of *offer, acceptance*, and *consideration*, consideration being the thing of value being exchanged.

As explained by Henry Thornton (1760–1815), the "Father of Central Banking," in his book, *An Enquiry into the Nature and Effects of the Paper Credit of Great Britain* (1802), a "real bill" is a financial instrument (contract) conveying a property right in the present value of an existing or future marketable good that the issuer owns. If the property right conveyed is in an existing good, the instrument is a "mortgage." If in a future good, the instrument is a "bill of exchange."

A "fictitious bill" is an instrument issued by someone who does not have an ownership interest in the consideration, or in which the consideration does not have a present value. A "bill of credit" ("anticipation note") is an instrument emitted by a government backed by the present value of future tax collections in anticipation of those taxes. As the state does not own taxes that have not been collected, a bill of credit is a fictitious bill.

Mortgages and bills may either circulate directly as money in the economy, or be accepted (discounted) by commercial banks for the bank's promissory notes that circulate as money. A bank's promissory notes circulate either directly in the form of banknotes or as backing for demand deposits (checking accounts).

A central bank ensures the stability, uniformity, and adequacy of the money supply for the private sector by rediscounting mortgages and bills of member banks, and engaging in "open market operations" in private sector securities issued by nonmember banks, businesses, and individuals representing the present value of existing and future marketable goods and services. A central bank also provides emergency reserves to member banks to prevent "runs" that could precipitate a financial panic.

The Labor Theory of Value

In the Smithian school of classical economics, all production is the result of labor, land, and capital, "capital" being understood as technology. ("Circulating stock," or "financial capital," consists of money by means of which a producer engages in exchange, and is not itself productive.) In the Ricardian school, labor is the sole factor of production. Land and capital only enhance labor. In extreme forms of the labor theory of value, such as Marxism and Georgism, land produces nothing, while capital is "accumulated" or "congealed" labor.

Economic Role of the State

In the Smithian school, the economic role of the state is to remove barriers to full participation in the "economic common good." The economic common good is that vast network of institutions (e.g., money, credit, and private property) within which humanity engages in economic activity, such as production and consumption. In general, the role of the state is to ensure equal access to institutions, protect private property, police abuses, and enforce contracts: equality of opportunity. To address an emergency, the state may redistribute wealth.

In the Ricardian school, the state takes a more proactive role to effect desired results. Generally this is through manipulation of the money supply by emitting or redeeming bills of credit, and by redistributing existing wealth through taxation when manipulating the money supply proves inadequate. The role of the central bank changes from accommodating the private sector to financing government.

Keynesian monetary and fiscal policy is dictated by adherence to the principles of the Ricardian school of classical economics, adapted to the exigencies of dealing with the problem of advancing technology (capital) displacing labor in the production process when capital is not recognized as productive.

Keynesian Finance

In the Smithian school, bills of exchange as well as mortgages can be used to finance new capital. Issuing bills of exchange turns the present value of future increases in production into money. When the new capital becomes productive, a portion of the profits ("future savings") is used to redeem the bills, canceling the money. The money supply expands and contracts automatically with the needs of commerce.

The Keynesian system recognizes only past savings (mortgages) as the source of capital financing, that is, an excess of production over consumption accumulated as money (*General Theory of Employment, Interest, and Money* [1936], II.6.ii). This requires a class of wealthy persons who have the capacity to refrain from consuming all they produce: "The immense accumulations of fixed capital which, to the great benefit of mankind, were built up during the half century before the war (World War I), could never have come about in a Society where wealth was divided equitably" (*The Economic Consequences of the Peace* [1919], 2.iii.).

Confusing mortgages and bills of exchange, and thus past savings with future savings, the Keynesian system does not recognize bills of exchange as money. Further confusing private sector bills of exchange with government bills of credit, state debt is viewed as a claim on the existing wealth of society, a mortgage, instead of the present value of future tax collections, a pure credit instrument, that is, a contract based on future savings instead of past savings.

Increasing public debt in the Keynesian view only increases claims on existing wealth, not on future wealth that does not yet exist. The size of the public debt is not a primary concern, any more than is the capacity of the economy to produce the profits to be taxed in the future to retire the debt.

Because in the Keynesian system the state has a monopoly over money creation, and thus over the creation of effective demand, the only way to increase demand (and thus the demand for new capital resulting in job creation) is for the state to increase the money supply by increasing public debt. The rise in the price level that usually follows an increase in the money supply not matched by an increase in production is not considered inflation, for Keynes defined "true inflation" as a rise in the price level after full employment has been reached. A rise in the price level prior to reaching full employment is due to other causes (*General Theory*, II.10.ii, V.21.v).

Defining savings solely as reductions in consumption, a rise in the price level in the Keynesian system prior to reaching full employment "forces" savings and increases the financing available for new capital investment (and thus job

creation) by restricting consumption by the non-owning class and increasing the profits of the owning class.

Given that money represents only existing wealth and not future wealth, and that the state is the ultimate owner of the wealth of society through a monopoly on money creation and the power to tax, backing for public debt (and thus the capacity to retire the debt) always exists. It is only necessary to raise taxes to drain excess demand out of the economy if the public debt grows too great and inflation becomes a problem, and to increase the debt if there is insufficient demand in the economy and unemployment becomes a problem: the Keynesian tradeoff between inflation and unemployment.

Relying on past savings as the sole source of financing for new capital formation restricts capital ownership to the currently wealthy—the wealthier, the better—for the wealthy cannot consume all of their income and necessarily will reinvest it in new capital. Small owners are "functionless investors," for they consume the income their capital generates instead of reinvesting it to finance new capital formation. To increase the efficiency of the economy, Keynes advocated the elimination (the "euthanasia") of small ownership (*General Theory*, VI.24.ii).

Keynesian Full Employment

In the Keynesian system, labor is the sole factor of production, albeit enhanced by capital. Labor is therefore the only means of generating effective demand, even if nothing of value is produced (*General Theory*, III.10.vi).

Demand is essential in any economic system, for demand for consumer goods always drives the demand for new capital and, thus, in the Keynesian system, creates jobs. Full employment of labor, regardless of the utility of what is produced, is therefore the overriding goal of Keynesian economics.

The Keynesian Role of the State

Because employers will not voluntarily pay more than the market rate of wages, the state sets minimum wage rates and maximum rates of return, and allocates resources (*General Theory*, V.24.iii). If this is unsuccessful, the state increases or decreases effective demand by emitting or retiring bills of credit.

Because private sector commercial banks will presumably create as much money as possible up to the legal limit without regard to the needs of the economy in order to be able to make a profit by lending, regardless of the soundness of the loan, the state must strictly regulate money creation. Ideally, as in the "chartalism" of Georg Friedrich Knapp (1842–1926) from which Keynes developed his monetary theory, money creation is a state monopoly, with the state determining the amount of money to be created, and thus the desired rate of economic growth.

If the economy fails to respond to stimulus, state action must be increased to bring all aspects of economic life directly under state control. Once, however, the right formula has been developed and equilibrium has been established, state control can be relaxed, and the economy returned to its self-regulating mode of operation.

Conclusion

Despite its virtually worldwide acceptance, Keynesian economics is based on incomplete and erroneous assumptions (primarily regarding money and credit, the productiveness of capital, private property, and the role of the state) that preclude a Keynesian system from ever presenting an adequate overview of economic reality. By not taking into account the facts that private property in capital is as legitimate as private property in labor, that capital is productive in the same way that labor is productive, and that new capital can be financed with both past and future savings, most people are inhibited or prevented from acquiring private property in capital to replace the declining relative value of their labor as technology advances. This results in an increasing dependency on the state as the sole source of economic well-being, with a consequent decline in respect for the dignity of the human person, and overriding individual sovereignty and rights to achieve political goals.

See also

Constitutionalism; Right to Life; Self-Governance

M. D. GREANEY

Further Reading

Adler, Mortimer J., and Louis O. Kelso. 1958. *The Capitalist Manifesto*. New York: Random House.

Adler, Mortimer J., and Louis O. Kelso. 1961. *The New Capitalists: A Proposal to Free Economic Growth from the Slavery of Savings*. New York: Random House.

Keynes, John Maynard. 1920. *The Economic Consequences of the Peace*. New York: Harcourt, Brace.

Keynes, John Maynard. 1936. *The General Theory of Employment, Interest, and Money*. New York: Harcourt, Brace, Jovanovich.

Keynes, John Maynard. 1930. *A Treatise on Money, Volumes I and II*. New York: Harcourt, Brace, Jovanovich.

Knapp, Georg Friedrich. 1924. *The State Theory of Money*. London: Macmillan and Company.

Moulton, Harold Glenn. 1935. *The Formation of Capital*. Washington, DC: The Brookings Institution.

Moulton, Harold Glenn. 1943. *The New Philosophy of Public Debt*. Washington, DC: The Brookings Institution.

Ricardo, David. 1817. *The Principles of Political Economy and Taxation*. London: John Murray.

Say, Jean-Baptiste. 1821. *Letters to Mr. Malthus on Several Subjects of Political Economy*. London: Sherwood, Neely, and Jones.

Smith, Adam. 1776. *The Wealth of Nations*. London: W. Straham and T. Cadell.

Thornton, Henry. 1802. *An Enquiry into the Nature and Effects of the Paper Credit of Great Britain*. London: J. Hatchard.

Keynesian Economics—Primary Document

Introduction

Adam Smith built his economic theory on the premise that the sole purpose of production is consumption. From this came "Say's Law of Markets": that, everything else being equal, the only way to consume is to produce something by means of your labor or capital, or to exchange something that you have produced by means of your labor and capital, for something that someone else has produced with his or her labor or capital.

Based on his belief that only labor is productive, and that capital only enhances labor, Keynes discounted the labor-displacing effects of advancing technology, reformulated Say's Law to take into account only production by labor, and declared that Say's Law is invalid because in an advanced industrial economy supply does not generate its own demand, and demand its own supply. Examining Say's Law as explained by Say shows where Keynes suffered from flawed logic.

Document: Letter of Jean-Baptiste Say to Thomas Malthus on Political Economy and Stagnation of Commerce (1821)

. . . You say, Sir, that the distinction between productive and unproductive labor is the earner stone of *Adam Smith's* work, and that to call, as I have done, that labor productive which is not fixed in any material object, is to overthrow his work from top to bottom. No, Sir, this is not the earner stone of Adam Smith's work, since, that stone being shaken, the edifice is imperfect without being less stable. What will eternally support that excellent work is, that it proclaims in all its pages, that the *changeable value* of things is the foundation of all wealth. It is from that time that political economy is become a positive science; for the price-current of each thing is a determined quantity, the elements of which may be analised, the causes assigned, the bearings studied, and the changes foreseen. By taking away from the definition of wealth this essential character, allow me to inform you, Sir, we replunge the science into the surge, and drive it back.

Far from undermining the celebrated inquiries into the Wealth of Nations, I support them in all their essential parts; but at the stone time, I think Adam Smith has misconceived real exchangeable value, by forgetting that which is attached to productive service, which leaves no trace behind, because the whole of it is consumed. I think he has also forgotten real services, which even leave traces behind them, in material productions such as service of capital, consumed, independently of the capital itself. I think he has got into infinite obscurity, for want of having distinguished the consumption of the industrious services of an enterpriser, from the services of his capital—a distinction so real, however, that there is scarcely any commercial house that does not keep these accounts under distinct heads.

I revere Adam Smith,—he is my master. At the commencement of my career in Political Economy, whilst yet tottering, and driven on the one hand by the Doctors of the Balance of Trade, and on the other by the Doctors of Net Proceeds, I stumbled at every step, he showed me the fight road. Leaning upon his *Wealth of Nations*, which at the same time discovers to us the wealth of his genius, I learned to go alone. Now I no longer belong to any school, and shall not share the ridicule of the Reverend Jesuit Fathers who translated *Newton's* Elements, with notes. They felt that the laws of natural philosophy did not well accord with those of Loyola; they also took care to inform the public by an Advertisement, that although they had apparently shown the motion of the Earth, in order to complete the development

of celestial philosophy, they were not less under subjection to the decrees of the Pope, who did not admit this motion. I am only under the subjection of the decrees of eternal Reason, and I am not afraid to say so. *Adam Smith* has not embraced the whole of the phenomenon of the production and consumption of wealth, but he has done so much that we ought to feel grateful to him. Thanks to him, the most vague, the most obscure of sciences will soon become the most precise, and that which of all others will leave the fewest points unexplained.

Let us figure to ourselves, producers (and under this name I comprise as well the possessors of capitals and lands, as the possessors of industrious powers,) let us fancy them advancing, to meet each other with their productive services, or the profit which has resulted from them (an immaterial quality). This profit is their produce. Sometimes it is fixed on an immaterial object, which is transmitted with the immaterial produce, but which in itself is of no importance, is nothing, in political Economy: for matter, dispossessed of value, is not wealth. Sometimes it is transmitted, is sold by one, and bought by another, without being fixed in any matter. It is the advice of the Doctor or the Lawyer, the service of the Soldier or the public Officer. Every one exchanges the utility he produces against that which is produced by others, and in every one of these exchanges, which are carried to account in a book of competition, as the utility offered by *Paul* is more or less in demand than that offered by *Jacques*, it sells dearer or cheaper—that is to say, that it obtains in exchange more or less of the utility offered by the latter. It is in this sense that the influence of the demand and supply must be understood.

This, Sir, is not a doctrine advanced by way of afterthought; it is to be found in sundry parts of my *Treatise on Political Economy*; and by the help of my Epitome its coincidence with every other principle of the science, and with all the facts which serve for its basis, is fundamentally the same. It is already professed in many parts of Europe; but I earnestly desire that it may succeed in convincing you, and that it may appear to you to be worthy of being introduced into the chair, which you fill with so much eclat.

After these necessary explanations, you will not accuse me of finesse if I rest upon those laws which I have shown to be rounded on the nature of things and on the facts which issue from them.

Commodities, you say, are only exchanged for commodities: they are also exchanged for labor. If this labor be a produce that some persons sell, that others buy, and that the latter consume, it will cost me very little to call it a *Commodity*, and it will cost you very little more to assimilate other commodities to it, for they are also produce. Then comprising both under the generic name of *Produce*, you may perhaps admit that produce is bought only with produce.

Source: Letters to Malthus on Political Economy and Stagnation of Commerce by Jean Baptiste Say. Letter 1. (1821). Available at http://www.marxists.org/reference/subject/economics/say/letter1.htm.

L

LABOR MOVEMENT

The American labor movement has undergone several changes in its organizational principles, membership bases, social demands, and economic effects since its beginnings during the 19th century. The labor movement developed in response to changes in social and economic disparities in the United States and promoted legal protections, social progress, and economic benefits for the working classes. Workers with specialized skills formed craft and trade unions, while many semi-skilled or unskilled workers coalesced into broad, collective unions that included wider ranges of working-class peoples.

During the initial development of unions in the late 18th and early 19th centuries, artisans and craftsmen who spent years developing their trades and crafts formed unions to alleviate competitive practices that undercut profits and to remain viable in an expanding American marketplace. By the middle of the 19th century, artisans and craftsmen experienced the initial industrialization of the country when their advanced skills began to be replaced by machinery and production methods that simplified the abilities needed to produce specialty, hand-made products. Carpenters, shoemakers, and tailors organized within their individual trades and crafts and set prices to charge for their labor and materials, demanded a set number of working hours in a day, and shared information on markets and methods. Most industrial

workers did not actively influence the movement since most of the craft and trade unions did not allow unskilled factory workers to join their memberships. Further industrialization and manufacturing development during and after the U.S. Civil War (1861–1865) eventually diminished the influences of the trade and craft unions. Factories allowed for the reduction in waiting time and costs for consumers and, subsequently, public demand lessened for expensive specialty products. By the end of the 19th century, many artisans and craftsmen found their specialty-produced items no longer in demand and the craft and trade unions lost influence as more inclusive, broader-based workers' unions formed to represent those employed in factories.

As the nation industrialized during the Gilded Age (1870s–1890s) and Progressive Era (1890s–1920s), factories hired thousands of workers to make new products for a mostly American marketplace. One influential early workers' union, the Knights of Labor, formed as a craft union in 1869 to represent tailors, but by 1880 it expanded its base to include industrial workers in one large, powerful union that addressed social and economic disparities and workers' on-the-job safety. The leader of the Knights of Labor, Terrence Powderly, designed a platform of issues that concerned workers and, while Powderly refused to allow strikes by members of the Knights of Labor, their demands centered on the standard of an eight-hour workday across industries,

Joseph J. Ettor speaks to striking barbers during an Industrial Workers of the World (IWW) demonstration at Union Square, New York, in 1913. The IWW, a socialist union, tried to organize everyone from these barbers to miners in the Western United States. (Library of Congress)

better safety conditions, and compensation for workers injured on the job, equal pay regardless of gender for workers in the same jobs, and the end of child labor.

On May 4, 1886, the Knights of Labor gathered at Haymarket Square in Chicago to offer support to striking workers who desired the eight-hour day. During the peaceful demonstrations, as police attempted to disperse the striking workers, someone threw a dynamite bomb into the crowd, resulting in the deaths of seven policemen and four workers. The Haymarket Affair, also known as the Haymarket Riot, resulted in a highly publicized trial in which the primary evidence linked the bomb's manufacture to anarchists even though no evidence associated these individuals with the actual throwing of the bomb. By the end of the trial, eight anarchists were found guilty and seven were sentenced to capital punishment by hanging while one person was sentenced to a term of fifteen years in prison. By the time of

the executions, in November 1887, Illinois governor Richard Oglesby commuted the sentences of two of the anarchists to life terms in prison and one had committed suicide. In 1893, Illinois's new governor, John Peter Altgeld, pardoned the rest of the anarchists as the trial came under severe criticism; however, the Haymarket Affair heavily affected the labor movement by associating anarchists and political agitators with unions. Following the Haymarket Affair, membership in the Knights of Labor plummeted and their influence became less significant.

While the Knights of Labor lost its influence at the close of the 19th century, new labor movements adopted similar socioeconomic and political platforms that focused on the lives of workers, safety conditions, and lobbying for protective legislation. The Industrial Workers of the World (IWW), the Congress of Industrial Organizations (CIO), and the American Federation of Labor (AFL) rose to prominence during the Progressive Era (1890s–1920s) and represent the second surge in the American labor movement. The CIO and the AFL developed as smaller unions joined together under collective ideologies into powerful confederations, while the IWW remained focused on uniting all workers into a singular, one-world union.

The IWW formed in the summer of 1905 when industrial workers in Chicago met with socialists to draft a workers' manifesto to demand broad rights for the working classes. By 1906, the IWW established a reputation for radicalism with the adoption of strikes under the leadership of "Big" Bill Haywood (1869–1928). Haywood earned his nickname for his intimidatingly large size and musculature that developed from years spent mining coal. Haywood initially joined a miners' union where he embraced and promoted general strikes against companies and industries that refused to shorten their workdays to eight hours and abused the rights of laborers. The members of the IWW, also known as the "Wobblies," oftentimes led general strikes against businesses and manufacturers. The goals of Wobblies in a general strike included not just workers protesting and picketing a specific factory or business but also calling all workers in a specific industry to walk off the job and join the ranks of those on strike in efforts to support broad reforms for the working classes. When the United States entered World War I (1917–1918), Haywood and the Wobblies came under suspicion for promoting the end of capitalism in the United States. During World War I, the federal government passed laws to eradicate espionage and sedition, effectively limiting people's abilities to criticize the government. The Wobblies, and Haywood in particular, emphasized the need for workers to establish a socialist system for industries through the elimination of capitalism in the United States, which Haywood believed kept workers in a constant form of bondage. In 1917, the U.S. government charged Haywood, who had risen to the head of the IWW, with sedition and arrested him and one hundred other union supporters and Wobblies. Haywood and the others arrested attempted several court appeals, but were rejected by the U.S. Supreme Court. In 1921, while out of prison on bail, Haywood fled to the Soviet Union where he died seven years later in 1928. The repression of labor unions during and after World War I significantly affected the Wobblies and while the organization still exists, the membership never again matched in number or volume the aggressively political and social agitation of its early years.

The AFL and the CIO also rose to prominence during the Progressive Era but offered a much less radicalized social and political platform than the IWW. The AFL formed in 1886 when a coalition of craft unions, led by Samuel Gompers of the Cigar Makers' International Union, broke away from the Knights of Labor over a dispute on closing individual unions in efforts to centralize power and finances into the Knights of Labor. The member unions that formed the AFL elected Gompers as their president, and he continued to retain the presidency every year afterward except for 1895 until his death in 1924. Gompers and his contemporaries in the AFL based their organization on the principles of craft and trade unionism and, like the Knights of Labor, tended to dismiss general laborers and workers outside of the highly skilled crafts. As the AFL attracted more trade and craft unions, the organizing power of the Knights of Labor diminished and the AFL concentrated its organizational powers on demands for higher wages and better, safer working conditions.

The AFL came under pressure at the beginning of the 20th century when manufacturers started the open shop movement and offered employer-sponsored unions and paternalistic measures such as housing and food allowances. Such practices by employers encouraged workers that their interests were best met through their employers' largesse. Meanwhile, new production methods like the moveable assembly line allowed manufacturers to speed up the pace, which forced workers to complete tasks at increasingly faster rates, removed their abilities to leave the lines to use toilets or to get a drink of water, and oftentimes created dangerous situations that left many factory workers injured. The AFL generally supported and encouraged better and safer workplaces for its members but remained diligent in its goals, which Gompers termed "business unionism," or the ability to have the union leadership negotiate contracts through their collective bargaining with companies in a capitalist framework that provided for better wages and working conditions.

The AFL developed a more conservative platform in response to the emerging radicalism of laborers' unions organized under the CIO. The CIO formed when the Knights of Labor and the AFL rejected common laborers and unskilled or semi-skilled workers. Led by John Llewellyn Lewis of the United Mine Workers of America, the CIO broke off from the

AFL in 1935 and faced many challenges as an organization until it reunited with the AFL in 1955. John Lewis represented the radicalism felt by the common laborers, the unskilled and the semi-skilled workers who toiled in the growing number of factories in the early decades of the 20th century, and the CIO developed a social and political platform that responded to those workers' demands. The CIO supported and encouraged strikes by its member unions against manufacturers and businesses, and launched several successful strikes in the steel industries and meatpacking industries, where the CIO maintained its strongest base of member union support.

During the presidential race of 1932, the CIO organized its member unions to provide political support for Democratic candidate Franklin Delano Roosevelt. After Roosevelt took office in March 1933, the economic and social impacts of the Great Depression levied a heavy toll on industrial workers. Roosevelt's administration designed a series of federal programs promoted to the public as a "New Deal" designed to help alleviate the hardships felt by many workers who lost their jobs in the national economic collapse. Roosevelt's New Deal policies not only included the creation of temporary federal jobs programs, but also introduced federal protective legislation for industrial workers.

New Deal protective legislation included the 1933 National Industrial Recovery Act (NIRA), which was designed to allow the federal government to control prices in industries to stimulate the economy after a major deflation. NIRA provided protection for workers and the labor movement by defending unions engaged in negotiations with companies and forced companies to recognize and bargain with unions. When the Supreme Court declared the National Industrial Recovery Act unconstitutional in the summer of 1935, Roosevelt implemented a similar program with the National Labor Relations Act that same year, also known as the Wagner Act for Senator Robert F. Wagner (D-NY). The National Labor Relations Act formed the basis of federal labor laws by allowing private-sector workers and employees to form and join unions, demand that companies ing engage in collective bargaining with unions, and allowing unionized workers the right to strike if contracts with companies could not be negotiated. The National Labor Relations Act also established a federal committee, the National Labor Relations Board, to oversee compliance with the regulations put on companies.

Following the passage of the National Labor Relations Act, memberships in the partner unions of the AFL and CIO expanded in large numbers, yet women and minority workers often remained unwelcome in the union movement. During the Progressive Era, women workers created their own unions and merged with women's clubs to form the Women's Trade Union League in 1903. The Women's Trade Union League (WTUL) fought for political and social reforms for all workers, but especially for women and children who worked long hours in often horrendous conditions. While officially one of the member unions of the AFL, in its early years, the WTUL and issues related to women's employment, child labor, and their workplace safety were ignored by the AFL. In 1911, the disaster of the Triangle Shirtwaist Factory in New York City brought national attention to the plight of women and children workers when the factory caught fire and 146 people, of those 123 women and older children, died from the blaze, smoke inhalation, or by jumping from the upper windows of the ten-story building. The subsequent investigation revealed that the owners of the factory had locked the doors to the exits and stairwells and the workers could not escape the fire. The disaster led to the rise in support of women's unions and the creation of legislation that improved safety conditions in factories and attracted public attention to sweatshop labor. The WTUL also partnered with women's groups and organizations to lobby for the end of child labor and in 1938 helped pass the Fair Labor Standards Act. The Fair Labor Standards Act did not end child labor in the United States, but it did set strict guidelines for the use of children's labor that allowed for family businesses and family farms to use child labor as well as allowed for teenaged children to be employed on a strictly enforced part-time basis.

In the late 1940s and 1950s, the labor movement fell under increasing attacks as the fear of communism spread in the United States following the end of World War II (1941–1945). Many of the unions supported collectivism, and some had started with the support of radicals who were socialists and communists. Senator Joseph McCarthy (R-Wisconsin) led the calls for purging the unions of radical members, especially socialists and communists, by inflating Americans' fear of communism during the beginning of the Cold War era in the late 1940s and early 1950s. McCarthy demanded that the unions dismiss their radical members and pressured groups such as the AFL and CIO to disband any union from their organizations that refused to dismiss their radical members. The AFL and CIO reunited into one collective union organization in 1955 to offset some of the damage done by McCarthy's accusations but, deeply affected by the purging of its radical elements, by the 1970s retained less influence with the working classes.

While the AFL-CIO struggled in the postwar years, certain powerful individual unions rose to dominate the labor movement. During the 1970s, the International Brotherhood of Teamsters, representing semi-truck drivers and shipping and receiving workers, gained notoriety for its tactics in negotiations and for embezzling money, while the United Automobile Workers experienced the defeat of being unable to organize workers in foreign car industries in the American South while competing with new automation that decreased the need for workers. While the AFL-CIO struggled to maintain the integrity of its member unions, the United Farm Workers of America experienced many hard-won successes in organizing mostly migrant workers into the union movement. In the 1960s, the National Farm Workers Association led by Cesar Chavez partnered with the Agricultural Workers Organizing Committee led by Larry Itliong to promote migrant workers' rights and organized the United Farm Workers into a strike on grape farmers who paid their workers low wages, denied them unemployment benefits, and oftentimes harassed workers both off and on the job.

The United Farm Workers joined the AFL-CIO in 1972 and exposed the emerging needs of new sectors of the American labor movement. Agricultural workers were not the only newer group to join the union movement in the latter part of the 20th century. During the 1970s and 1980s, professional unions organized to represent the demands of workers in clerical and office support positions, teachers and professors, police and fire department members and in the public sector. In 1981, the Professional Air Traffic Controllers Organization, which had formed in 1968, engaged in a strike against the U.S. Civil Service clauses that restricted its abilities to negotiate for better pay and working conditions. President Ronald Reagan used the power of the Taft-Hartley Act passed in 1947 that forbade strikes by government employees in the interest of national safety and ordered that striking air traffic controllers return to work or lose their jobs. When many of the controllers refused to return to work, Reagan ordered military

personnel to replace some of them and transferred other public air traffic controllers in attempts to alleviate the congestion in air traffic caused by the strike. By October 1981, Reagan's tactics worked to break the strike and the Federal Labor Relations Authority decertified the Professional Air Traffic Controllers Organization so it could no longer represent its members.

At the close of the 20th century, the increase in service-oriented jobs gave rise to the emergence of service workers' unions such as the Service Employees International Union, which represents more than 2 million workers in the public and private sectors. While the influences of such newer unions represent a shift in the American labor movement, the rapid increase in their union membership suggests that the goals that inspired the earlier labor movements in the United States remain key issues to working Americans. The need for reliable and steady employment, safe working conditions, regulations on companies, and improved wages and benefits still remain important aspects of working people's lives and the American labor movement continues to adjust to these needs in a changing labor force.

See also

Communism; Fordism; Industrial Revolution; Progressivism; Unionization

ANITA ANTHONY-VANORSDAL

Further Reading

Breitzer, Susan Roth. 2009. "Loved Labor's Losses: The Congress of Industrial Organizations and the Effects of McCarthyism." *History Compass* 7, no. 5: 1400–1415.

Buhle, Paul. 2005. "The Legacy of the IWW." *Monthly Review* 57, no. 2: 13. Available at http://isreview.org/issue/86/legacy-iww

Dubofsky, Melvin, and Joseph McCartin. 2000. *We Shall Be All: A History of the Industrial Workers of the World*. Bloomington, IN: University of Indiana Press.

Fones-Wolf, Elizabeth, and Ken Fones-Wolf. 1994. "Rank-and-File Rebellions and AFL Interference in the Affairs of National Unions: The Gompers Era." *Labor History* 35, no. 2: 237–259.

Kirkby, Diane. 1987. "The Wage-Earning Woman and the State: The National Women's Trade Union League and Protective Labor Legislation, 1903–1923." *Labor History* 28, no. 1: 54–74.

Martens, Allison M. 2009. 2009. "Working Women or Women Workers? The Women's Trade Union League and the Transformation of the American Constitutional Order." *Studies in American Political Development* 23, no. 2: 143–170.

Oestreicher, Richard. 1981. "Socialism and the Knights of Labor in Detroit, 1877–1886." *Labor History* 22, no. 1: 5–30.

Labor Movement—Primary Document

Introduction

Many labor unions faced severe persecution from industries when workers began to join the union movement. The following excerpt written by Industrial Workers of the World (IWW) leader William L. "Big Bill" Haywood in 1919 attempted to draw public attention to the plight of workers who joined the IWW. Published in pamphlet form and distributed to workers and their communities, these informative calls to action helped organizations such as the IWW retain their memberships and represented a working-class American collective consciousness.

Document: "With Drops of Blood the History of the Industrial Workers of the World Has Been Written" by "Big Bill" Haywood (1919)

Ever since the I.W.W. was organized in June, 1905, there has been an inquisitorial campaign against its life and growth, inaugurated by the Chambers of Commerce, Profiteers, large and small, and authorities of State and Nation in temporary power. The Industrial Workers of the World is a Labor organization composed of sober, honest, industrious men and women. Its chief purposes are to abolish the system of wage slavery and to improve the conditions of those who toil. This organization has been foully dealt with; drops of blood, bitter tears of anguish, frightful heart pains have marked its every step in its onward march of progress . . . We charge that I.W.W. MEMBERS have been murdered . . . many who have given up their lives on the altar of Greed, sacrificed in the ages-long struggle for Industrial Freedom. We charge that many thousands of members of this organization have been imprisoned, on most occasions arrested without warrant and held without charge . . . We charge that members of the I.W.W. have been cruelly and inhumanly beaten. Hundreds of members can show scars upon their lacerated bodies that were inflicted upon them when they were compelled to run the gauntlet . . . We charge that I.W.W. members have been denied the right of citizenship, and in each instance the judge frankly told the applicants that they were refused on account of membership in the Industrial Workers of the World . . . We charge that members of this organization have been exiled from the shores of this land for no other reason than because of their membership in the I.W.W . . . others have been slipped through without a chance of communicating with friends or conferring with counsel . . . We charge that the homes of members which are supposed to be sacred have been invaded. Their private and personal property has been rummaged and seized. In some cases these invasions have taken place in the night time without warrant . . . We charge that members of the I.W.W. have been denied the privilege of defense. This being an organization of working men who had little or no funds of their own, it was necessary to appeal to the membership and the working class generally for funds to provide a proper defense. The postal authorities, acting under orders from the Postmaster-General at Washington, D.C., have deliberately prevented the transportation of our appeals, our subscription lists, our newspapers. These have been piled up in the post offices and we have never received a return of the stamps affixed for mailing . . . We charge that members of the I.W.W. have suffered cruel and unusual punishment. At Fresno, California, where the jail was crowded with members, the Fire Department was called and a stream of water was turned upon the helpless men. Their only protection was mattresses and blankets—one man had his eye torn out by the water . . . We charge that members of this organization have been unjustly accused and framed . . . Our literature, our letters and telegrams, pamphlets and songs have been misinterpreted and used against us. We ask the reader how long these terrible persecutions are going to be permitted to continue? This communication is addressed to the working class of the world. This is a voice from the men and women employed in the industries. It is a demand for a square deal. The out rages that have been imposed upon us will yet be suffered by you, if you do not help us in our need. Our fight is your fight. We want you to stand shoulder to shoulder with us. Funds are necessary . . . .

Source: Haywood, William Llewellyn "Big Bill." "With Drops of Blood: The History of the Industrial Workers of the World Has Been Written." Chicago, 1919. Available online at Library of Congress, American Memory. http://memory.loc.gov/cgi-bin/query/r?ammem/rbpe:@field%28DOCID+@lit%28rbpe01805500%29%29.

LIBERALISM

The word *liberal* is one of the most controversial words in our political lexicon. It is subject to raging debates about the role and size of government, political attack ads, esoteric discussions about public policy and, of course, the Democratic Party. Yet liberalism is also misunderstood and diffuse, meaning certain things to one group and something else to another. Liberalism, however, has played a major role in the economic and political development of the United States. From its more classical meaning to its 20th-century understanding, liberalism continues to reflect the American Dream of both separation from the "Old World" and the belief in government to use its power to pursue social and economic justice and human progress.

Classical liberalism was greatly concerned with private property and markets. Central to classical liberalism was

Governor Franklin D. Roosevelt of New York delivers his acceptance speech at the Democratic National Convention in Chicago, July 2, 1932. He pledged a "New Deal" for the American people and set the tone for liberal politics in America into the 1960s, and beyond. (AP Photo)

the ability of people to enter into contracts in the workplace. If government controlled these mechanisms then individual freedom was denied. Intellectuals and philosophers have debated how best to free the individual from the power of the state. The French Revolution—arguably the most important development in the West over the past 300 years—was in part fought over new ideas for freedom from the ancient order of absolutism and divine rule for monarchs. In addition, the American Revolution and the foundation of the United States brought new notions about freedom and the individual. The United States vigorously maintained the idea that private property is central to the notion of freedom. While the Civil War changed Americans conception of freedom, the coming Gilded Age forced the country to grapple with what freedom really meant. The debates would make Americans reconsider the role of government, the economy, and freedom in the new context of massive economic inequality.

During the Gilded Age, many Americans, in response to transformative economic and social change and progress, began asking questions about the staggering levels of economic inequality, political elitism, and power inequities that defined the era. Labor unions, Populist organizations, silver advocates, academics, journalists, farmers, African Americans, and others took umbrage at the stark differences between the precious few who controlled capital, wealth, and opportunity, and the millions and millions of people who toiled for little wages, often in great physical danger with nothing in the way of hope for economic and social mobility. These people—farmers, African Americans, academics, miners, laborers, and women—loosely made up what would become known as the Progressives.

The Progressives were not monolithic, nor were they confined to one region of the United States. These people were white and black, poor and affluent, unlettered and highly educated, workers and those wanted to work, men and women. Further, their interests differed according to what they deemed most important. In fact, the only group that found itself almost completely ignored was African Americans, who were subject to Jim Crow laws, lynchings, and conditions as close to slavery as they could possibly be without the chains. As the 19th century ended and the 20th century began, the Progressive Era attracted supporters on a national level.

The assassination of President William McKinley in 1901 ushered in a new era of progressive presidents. Theodore Roosevelt (TR) challenged Big Money and brought greater scrutiny to the private sector. Moreover, TR embraced environmentalism and instituted new government programs to benefit average Americans. William Howard Taft followed Roosevelt into the White House and continued many of TR's policies. After a contentious election in 1912, academician and politician Woodrow Wilson took over the reins of government. In the process he talked of a New Freedom, one that would supposedly play down the role of government, but actually oversaw the creation of the Federal Reserve, the Federal Trade Commission, and the federal income tax system. Equally important, President Wilson entered the United States into World War I. A war that destroyed many people's faith in reason and human progress, it also brought about Wilsonian Internationalism, which after World War II would become a mainstay of American foreign policy. But the harsh repression perpetuated on millions of American by the Wilson administration helped to end the progressive movement. Before the war ended, however, women, who fiercely advocated for voting rights and supported the war effort, won the franchise in 1920. Nevertheless, liberalism was on the wane.

The 1920s were supposed to mark a "return to normalcy." Free enterprise and consumerism replaced war, hardship, advocacy, and liberalism as Americans primary focus in the so-called "Roaring '20s" changed. Furthermore, xenophobia, racism, and antilabor sentiment took the place of Progressive impulses. Three presidents—Warren G. Harding, Calvin Coolidge, and Herbert Hoover—presided over a booming, if not unequal, economy and provided a steely backbone to conservatism. The unregulated economy and overheated stock market, however, led to the crash of the stock market in 1929. And the next three and a half years nearly destroyed the confidence of tens of millions of Americans in the capacity of conservatism to protect the average American and control the harshness of unregulated capitalism. In the process, a New York patrician and member of the American version of an aristocracy rose to the head of the Democratic Party and, after an easy election victory over Hoover, the presidency. Franklin D. Roosevelt (FDR) promised bold and frequent experimentation in resolving the economic crisis that had brought America to its knees. Furthermore, FDR promised Americans a New Deal, one that would redefine government, its role, and liberalism itself.

FDR entered the White House in March 1933 as more than quarter of all working-age Americans were unemployed. In winning the Oval Office, FDR created a new, dynamic Democratic Party that became truly national in scope and representation. Building on the political work of the Democratic Party's 1928 presidential nominee, Al Smith, FDR brought African Americans, Jews, immigrants, academics, labor unions, lawyers, Southerners, old progressives, and others into the Democratic fold as an electoral and governing coalition. These groups would form the nucleus of the Democratic Party for nearly fifty years.

As FDR moved into the White House, he was followed by an army of lawyers, political operatives, social workers, academics, and others hungry to redefine the role of government. The economic and political catastrophe created an opportunity for government to become activist in nature. And Roosevelt moved aggressively to seize the moment and put liberalism in to action.

FDR immediately moved to shore up the nation's banking system. Also, his administration persuaded Congress to sign fifteen pieces of legislation into law. The famed one hundred days would become the measure by which all future presidents would be measured. The New Deal, which roughly lasted from 1933 to 1938, focused on two different but interconnected goals: economic recovery and economic security. Consequently, liberalism acquired its modern meaning: activist government interjects itself into the private sector, and eventually, into social justice issues to improve the quality of life of the masses; moreover, liberal governance and policy curb the harsh excesses of capitalism through regulation and provide for the security of the least fortunate, the aged, and others that life had not smiled upon. World War II and the Cold War strengthened liberalism and helped to bring about a massive transformation of American racial and social practices.

World War II and the Allies' fight against Nazism, militarism, and totalitarianism strengthened liberalism by striking out against hatred, human rights abuses, and assisting in the defeat of the old order: an order defined by political and economic elites and ending or helping to end the colonial rule of European nations throughout the Third World, especially in Africa. Some of these accomplishments would take decades to come to fruition. Others were apparent as the ruins of major cities in Europe and Japan were still smoldering.

FDR tried to use the war effort to help the liberal cause. Roosevelt even delivered his famous speech calling for a Second Bill of Rights in 1944. After the war, as the Cold War began in earnest, the United States and its citizens debated which political direction the nation should go. Labor disputes and political unrest seized the nation in 1945 and 1946. Republicans seized control of Congress in the 1946 midterm elections. Even FDR's death, and the rise of Vice President Harry Truman, whose Fair Deal program would largely be stymied by Congress, did little in the way of providing momentum for liberal legislation. By 1948, Richard Nixon and others in Washington were charging various individuals as communists and subversives. Liberalism was suspect. Its ideological proximity to communism and socialism, in the context of the Cold War, made it increasingly dangerous to be identified as a liberal. In response, self-identified liberals found new ways to define themselves.

Prominent liberals such as Eleanor Roosevelt, Harry Truman, Arthur Schlesinger Jr., Averell Harriman, and others began to redefine liberalism as dedicated to capitalism, unwavering in support of government involvement in society, and fiercely anticommunist. Liberalism was called the Vital Center after Schlesinger published a book by the same name in 1949. Over the next two decades, the liberal consensus governed American political thought so thoroughly that Republicans could not be electorally viable nationally unless candidates accepted liberal articles of faith about government.

Mainstream liberals of the 1940s and 1950s, however, played down the importance of civil rights and women's rights because of desires not to embarrass the United States internationally in its cold war against the Soviet Union. Liberals harassed civil rights leaders by questioning their loyalty, accusing some of communist sympathies and warning African Americans and others that they were pressing to hard and fast; incrementalism should be pursued, not rapid social change.

Secularism has also been a mainstay of liberalism. This is especially true as it relates to much of postwar liberalism. Belief in science and reason eclipsed traditional religious faith. Even before Richard Nixon and Ronald Reagan, conservatives had long attracted faith-based groups. In the early postwar years, religious figures such as Billy Graham captivated millions with crusades, television programs, and literature. The Cold War's emphasis on differences between the United States and the Soviet Union underscored religious and secular differences. For instance, communism's disdain for organized religion made the Soviet Union a Godless state, damaging to the interests of the faithful. Capitalism was supposedly wrapped in both scripture and God. Many Americans thought of private property and free enterprise as ordained by the Almighty. Many liberals were openly contemptuous of religiosity. As the United States relaxed social mores in the 1950s and 1960s, those cleavages between the Left and the Right became more pronounced. *Playboy*, women's rights, civil rights, beatniks, free love, birth control, and other things contributed to the profound divisions within the American body politic. Furthermore, during this time, liberalism underwent another shift, a shift that incorporated many aspects of the old economic liberalism of the New Deal while embracing the social liberalism of the 1950s and 1960s.

The 1960s were a watershed era for the United States. The assassinations of President John F. Kennedy, Malcolm X, Dr. Martin Luther King Jr., and Senator Robert F. Kennedy still haunt America today. Further, the embrace of pacifism, antiwar rhetoric, challenging of social conventions, and support for minority and underrepresented groups signaled a new era for liberalism. In the process, it produced divisions that continue well into the 21st century. During and after the passage of the legislation that comprised John F. Kennedy's "New Frontier" and Lyndon B. Johnson's "Great Society," liberalism grew to mean support for the environment, civil rights, women's rights, defendant rights, LGBT rights, welfare recipients, Native American rights, anti-militarism, and a host of other things, including personal freedom, that changed the way in which Americans viewed themselves and their government. Along with consumerism and technology these new elements joined with older notions of liberalism to make up the Democratic Party in the 1980s, 1990s, and 2000s.

Today, liberalism remains a hotly debated topic in the United States. While conservatives have somewhat succeeded in making liberalism a profane and corrupt ideology, most Americans have come to enjoy liberal public policy. Americans will display anger when politicians discuss reforming Social Security, Medicare/Medicaid, public education, labor protections, and other assorted liberal policies enacted during the past eighty years. People enjoy having something of a social safety net to protect them from the harshness of capitalism. Moreover, most Americans love the relaxed social mores that allow them to "hook up," divorce, engage in sex out-of-wedlock, and eschew religion in favor of earthly and secular pursuits. Liberalism has come to mean a strong belief in the power of the state to confer benefits to the masses. Even conservatives have become enamored with the power of the state to interfere in the private sector and the lives of individuals. At the end of the day liberalism's meaning continues to evolve and develop as the times change. Finally, despite arguments to the contrary, liberalism remains alive and well.

See also

African American Civil Rights Movement; Anticommunism; Chicano Rights; Conservatism; Gay Rights; Great Society; Indian Rights; Libertarianism; Progressivism; Women's Rights Movement (19th Century)

DARYL A. CARTER

Further Reading

Brinkley, Alan. 2000. *Liberalism and Its Discontents.* Cambridge, MA: Harvard University Press.

Cohen, Lizabeth. 2007. *Making a New Deal: Industrial Workers in Chicago, 1919–1939.* 2nd ed. New York: Cambridge University Press.

Flanagan, Maureen A. 2006. *America Reformed: Progressives and Progressivisms, 1890s–1920s.* New York: Oxford University Press.

MacKenzie, Calvin G., and Robert Weisbrot. 2008. *The Liberal Hour: Washington and the Politics of Change in the 1960s.* New York: Penguin Group.

Schlesinger, Arthur M., Jr. 2007. *The Vital Center: The Politics of Freedom.* New York: Transaction Publishers.

Liberalism—Primary Document

Introduction

Franklin Roosevelt's 1932 acceptance speech at the Democratic National Convention in Chicago was a major moment in American political history. Roosevelt makes his argument not only for his candidacy but for political change. The speech was a harbinger of things to come, a vehicle whereby Roosevelt told the American people of a New Deal he was offering to the nation, a New Deal that would redefine government and American society.

Document: Franklin D. Roosevelt's Acceptance Speech to the Democratic National Convention (July 2, 1932)

. . . Never in history have the interests of all the people been so united in a single economic problem. Picture to yourself, for instance, the great groups of property owned by millions of our citizens, represented by credits issued in the form of bonds and mortgages—Government bonds of all kinds, Federal, State, county, municipal; bonds of industrial companies, of utility companies; mortgages on real estate in farms and cities, and finally the vast investments of the Nation in the railroads. What is the measure of the security of each of those groups? We know well that in our complicated, interrelated credit structure if any one of these credit groups collapses they may all collapse. Danger to one is danger to all.

How, I ask, has the present Administration in Washington treated the interrelationship of these credit groups? The answer is clear: It has not recognized that interrelationship existed at all. Why, the Nation asks, has Washington failed to understand that all of these groups, each and every one, the top of the pyramid and the bottom of the pyramid, must be considered together, that each and every one of them is dependent on every other; each and every one of them affecting the whole financial fabric?

Statesmanship and vision, my friends, require relief to all at the same time.

Just one word or two on taxes, the taxes that all of us pay toward the cost of Government of all kinds.

I know something of taxes. For three long years I have been going up and down this country preaching that Government—Federal and State and local—costs too much. I shall not stop that preaching. As an immediate program of action we must abolish useless offices. We must eliminate unnecessary functions of Government—functions, in fact, that are not definitely essential to the continuance of Government. We must merge, we must consolidate subdivisions of Government, and, like the private citizen, give up luxuries which we can no longer afford.

By our example at Washington itself, we shall have the opportunity of pointing the way of economy to local government, for let us remember well that out of every tax dollar in the average State in this Nation, 40 cents enter the treasury in Washington, D.C., 10 or 12 cents only go to the State capitals, and 48 cents are consumed by the costs of local government in counties and cities and towns.

I propose to you, my friends, and through you, that Government of all kinds, big and little, be made solvent and that the example be set by the President of the United States and his Cabinet.

And talking about setting a definite example, I congratulate this convention for having had the courage fearlessly to write into its declaration of principles what an overwhelming majority here assembled really thinks about the 18th Amendment. This convention wants repeal. Your candidate wants repeal. And I am confident that the United States of America wants repeal.

Two years ago the platform on which I ran for Governor the second time contained substantially the same provision. The overwhelming sentiment of the people of my State, as shown by the vote of that year, extends, I know, to the people of many of the other States. I say to you now that from this date on the 18th Amendment is doomed. When that happens, we as Democrats must and will, rightly and morally, enable the States to protect themselves against the importation of intoxicating liquor where such importation may violate their State laws. We must rightly and morally prevent the return of the saloon.

To go back to this dry subject of finance, because it all ties in together—the 18th Amendment has something to do with finance, too—in a comprehensive planning for the reconstruction of the great credit groups, including Government credit, I list an important place for that prize statement of principle in the platform here adopted calling for the letting in of the light of day on issues of securities, foreign and domestic, which are offered for sale to the investing public.

My friends, you and I as common-sense citizens know that it would help to protect the savings of the country from the dis-

honesty of crooks and from the lack of honor of some men in high financial places. Publicity is the enemy of crookedness.

And now one word about unemployment, and incidentally about agriculture. I have favored the use of certain types of public works as a further emergency means of stimulating employment and the issuance of bonds to pay for such public works, but I have pointed out that no economic end is served if we merely build without building for a necessary purpose. Such works, of course, should insofar as possible be self-sustaining if they are to be financed by the issuing of bonds. So as to spread the points of all kinds as widely as possible, we must take definite steps to shorten the working day and the working week.

Let us use common sense and business sense. Just as one example, we know that a very hopeful and immediate means of relief, both for the unemployed and for agriculture, will come from a wide plan of the converting of many millions of acres of marginal and unused land into timberland through reforestation. There are tens of millions of acres east of the Mississippi River alone in abandoned farms, in cut-over land, now growing up in worthless brush. Why, every European Nation has a definite land policy, and has had one for generations. We have none. Having none, we face a future of soil erosion and timber famine. It is clear that economic foresight and immediate employment march hand in hand in the call for the reforestation of these vast areas.

In so doing, employment can be given to a million men. That is the kind of public work that is self-sustaining, and therefore capable of being financed by the issuance of bonds which are made secure by the fact that the growth of tremendous crops will provide adequate security for the investment.

Yes, I have a very definite program for providing employment by that means. I have done it, and I am doing it today in the State of New York. I know that the Democratic Party can do it successfully in the Nation. That will put men to work, and that is an example of the action that we are going to have....

Source: Franklin D. Roosevelt: "Address Accepting the Presidential Nomination at the Democratic National Convention in Chicago," July 2, 1932. Online by Gerhard Peters and John T. Woolley, *The American Presidency Project.* http://www.presidency.ucsb.edu/ws/?pid=75174.

LIBERTARIANISM

Literally, *libertarianism* means a strong belief in liberty. It is a cult of personal freedom, a faith in the natural rights to life, liberty and property, respecting the similar rights of others, and a set of political philosophies to live the life of one's own choice without undesired state intervention. The libertarians strive for a free world of abundance, peace, prosperity, and pleasure for everyone. The concept of laissez faire (French for "let us do") aptly reveals the notion of libertarians. Adhering to the criteria of mutual respect and good will, libertarians regard liberty as the opposite of over-government, the basis of civilization, and the essential quality of human life. They believe that private property and personal freedom are far more substantial than political freedoms like the right to vote and the right to hold an office. The philosophy of libertarianism is the combination of liberty, responsibility, and tolerance. Every individual is free to do as he or she chooses with his or her life and property, as long as the person and property of other individuals is not harmed or violated. In the libertarian view, the law should forbid only those actions that involve the initiation of force against those who have not themselves used force—actions, like fraud, kidnapping, rape, robbery, and murder. The core idea of libertarianism is "as much liberty as possible" and "as little government as necessary."

The stand of libertarianism is neither "Left" nor "Right," nor even the combination of the two. They side with neither liberals nor conservatives. The reason is that the liberals favor personal liberty but believe in governmental intervention in the economy; and the conservatives favor economic freedom but strive to curtail individual liberty.

The moderate libertarians, however, tend to liberalism, in as much as the latter favors civil liberties. They also incline toward conservatives, because the latter support private property ownership and economic liberty. In the United States, the Libertarian Political Party tends to be liberal on social issues, and inclines toward conservatives on economic issues. Ronald Reagan said in 1975, "I believe the very heart and soul of conservatism is libertarianism." There are libertarian factions within both the Democratic and Republican parties; but neither party can fully align with libertarian thought. The Libertarian Party adheres, in general, to the principles of "maximizing individual liberty" and "avoiding excessive government interference" with the operation of the free market, individual ownership, and personal property.

The libertarian movement can be divided into two groups—absolutist and moderate. The absolutist libertarians are extremists for they believe in entire elimination of government interference in private property and personal liberty. They oppose the rules set up by religious values and traditional marriage. The moderates believe in limited government. They want state only to enforce law and order. The term *libertarian* in its metaphysical connotations refers to the thinkers who believe in the free will as against the determinists or—necessitarians. William Belsham for the first time used the term libertarian in metaphysics in 1789, to contradict the determinist school that opposed the concept of free will.

Libertarianism, in its essence, is a device that enables individuals to fulfill their visions by assuming responsibility for the consequence of their acts and co-operating for the common good without compulsion, because "we move in and out of the herd," that is to say, people think alone but have to act with others. In fact, because libertarianism is a set of related political philosophies, there is no consensus on its definition. However, it seems safe to hold that libertarianism is a combined system of thought that favors the transformation of society by reform or revolution and that strives to hand over the power from the authority of the coercive state to the voluntary associations of citizens, co-operative societies, and free markets. The U.S. Libertarian political party, created in 1971, emphasizes "funding government" by voluntary associations and limiting the governmental power only to protect individuals from "coercion and violence." Attaching liability to liberty, libertarians suggest that individuals are subject to certain principled rules for adjucating disputes—one who has been proved demonstrating a lack of respect for the rights of others should be subject to sanctions as constraint on the transgressor's freedom. The libertarian movement praises the Constitution of the United States as setting the limit to the proper scope of the national government. The Libertarian Party accuses both the Democratic and Republican parties of overstepping constitutional limits. The Party also opposed the Patriot Act, and the Iraq War, as well as government regulation of drugs and prostitution, and bans on same sex-marriage. Libertarians also oppose government funding for abortion, taking the fetus to be a person. They even oppose restrictions on pornography. They are in favor of the privatization of education, and strongly support school choice. They stress the elimination of the public school system, universal health care, taxes, and the welfare state.

Both sides of the Atlantic have influenced American libertarian thought, as have a variety of authors and literary genres. English political philosopher Herbert Spencer is widely considered the first systematic libertarian writer. Some of the eminent libertarianism oriented-writers have been William Graham Summer, William Godwin, J. S. Mill, Frederic Bastiat, William Leggett, Henry David Thoreau, Carl Menger, Isabel Paterson, Emile Armand, Mikhail Bakunin, Kropotkin, Robert Nozick, novelist Ayn Rand, and Josiah Warren.

Libertarianism, as a political philosophy, is divided on three principal questions, which render it various forms and nomenclatures:

1. The ethical theory: whether actions are determined to be morally deontological (or consequential (meaning that they have favorable results). Consequential libertarians argue that a free market and strong private property rights bring about beneficial consequences. According to deontologists, natural rights exist, so the initiation of force and fraud should never take place.

2. The legitimacy of private property: whether private property is legitimate or can be curtailed. This issue gives birth to propertarian and non-propertarian forms of libertarianism. The propertarian libertarianism supports the free market and recognizes private property as the sole source of legitimate authority. Non-propertarian libertarianism stresses abolishing authoritarian institutions that subordinate the majority to an owning class elite.

3. The legitimacy of the state: whether or not the state is desirable. This question gives rise to such ideologies as anarchism, monarchism, mutualism, collectivism, and state socialism.

Early in the 21st century, libertarianism enjoyed a renaissance in the United States. The Tea Party Movement of 2009 was supposed to be a major outlet for libertarian ideas. The movement advocates rigorous adherence to the U.S. Constitution, lower taxes, property rights, and individual liberty. The libertarians oppose health care and other welfare state programs. Current research and surveys found considerable support for at least some of the elements of libertarianism. One of the pollsters in 2006 concluded that Americans may be classified as "fiscally conservative and socially liberal or libertarian." "Liberty" for libertarians includes freedom to do everything, provided that it does not injure the freedom of others. They believe that the personal freedom of thought, expression, occupation of choice, association, enjoyment of life to the full, and ownership of property are not only sine qua non for self-development but also for making the world a far better place for all people.

See also
Conservatism; Liberalism

RAJENDRA BAHADUR SINGH

Further Reading
Hospers, John. 1971. *Libertarianism: A Political Philosophy for Tomorrow.* Santa Barbara, CA: Reason Press.
Huebert, Jacob H. 2010. *Libertarianism Today.* Westport, CT: Praeger.
Miron, Jeffrey A. 2010. *Libertarianism from A to Z.* New York: Basic Books.
Nozick, Robert. 1974. *Anarchy, State, and Utopia.* New York: Basic Books.
Otsuka, Michael. 2005. *Libertarianism Without Inequality.* New York: Oxford University Press.
Rand, Ayn. 1957. *Atlas Shrugged.* New York: Random House.

Libertarianism—Primary Document

Introduction

The Libertarian Party, founded in 1971, tends to be more socially liberal than Democrats and more economically conservative than Republicans. The 1972 Libertarian Party Platform outlines the early party's views and principles. Throughout the platform, individual liberty is stressed along with a laissez-faire economic and foreign policy ideology. Libertarians believed a government's sole responsibility is to protect the rights of its citizens, and that the government should have minimal intervention in its citizens' lives, including ending all government subsidizing and standards for schools, repealing any population control legislation (regarding abortion or birth control), and removing any and all censorship.

Document: Libertarian Party Platform (June 17, 1972)

The Party of Principle

Adopted in Convention, Denver, Colorado, June 17–18, 1972

Statement of Principles

Adopted unanimously by the delegates to the first national convention of the Libertarian Party, on June 17, 1972.

We, the members of the Libertarian Party, challenge the cult of the omnipotent state, and defend the rights of the individual.

We hold that each individual has the right to exercise sole dominion over his own life, and has the right to live his life in whatever manner he chooses, so long as he does not forcibly interfere with the equal right of others to live their lives in whatever manner they choose.

Governments throughout history have regularly operated on the opposite principle, that the State has the right to dispose of the lives of individuals and the fruits of their labor. Even within the United States, all political parties other than our own grant to government the right to regulate the life of the individual and seize the fruits of his labor without his consent.

We, on the contrary, deny the right of any government to do these things, and hold that the sole function of government is the protection of the rights of each individual: namely (1) the right to life—and accordingly we support laws prohibiting the initiation of physical force against others; (2) the right to liberty of speech and action—and accordingly we oppose all attempts by government to abridge the freedom of speech and press, as well as government censorship in any form; and (3) the right to property—and accordingly we oppose all government interference with private property, such as confiscation, nationalization, and eminent domain, and support laws which prohibit robbery, trespass, fraud and misrepresentation.

Since government has only one legitimate function, the protection of individual rights, we oppose all interference by government in the areas of voluntary and contractual relations among individuals. Men should not be forced to sacrifice their lives and property for the benefit of others. They should be left free by government to deal with one another as free traders on a free market; and the resultant economic system, the only one compatible with the protection of man's rights, is laissez-faire capitalism.

Individual Rights and Civil Order

The protection of individual rights is the only proper purpose of government. No conflict exists between civil order and individual rights. Both concepts are based on the same fundamental principle: that no individual, group, or government may initiate force against any other individual, group, or government. Government is instituted to protect individual rights. Government is constitutionally limited so as to prevent the infringement of individual rights by the government itself.

Crime

We hold that no action which does not infringe the rights of others can properly be termed a crime. We favor the repeal of all laws creating "crimes without victims" now incorporated in Federal, state and local laws—such as laws on voluntary sexual relations, drug use, gambling, and attempted suicide. We support impartial and consistent enforcement of laws designed to protect individual rights—regardless of the motivation for which these laws may be violated.

Due Process for Criminally Accused

Until such time as a person is proved guilty of a crime, that person should be accorded all possible respect for his individual rights. We are thus opposed to reduction of present safeguards for the rights of the criminally accused. Specifically, we are opposed to preventive detention, so-called "no-knock laws" and all other similar measures which threaten existing rights. We further pledge to do all possible to give life to the Sixth

Amendment's guarantee of a speedy trial, and shall work for appropriate legislation to this end. We support full restitution for all loss suffered by persons arrested, indicted, imprisoned, tried, or otherwise injured in the course of criminal proceedings against them which do not result in their conviction. We look ultimately to the voluntary funding of this restitution.

Freedom of Speech and the Press

We pledge to oppose all forms of censorship, whatever the medium involved. Recent events have demonstrated that the already precarious First Amendment rights of the broadcasting industry are becoming still more precarious. Regulation of broadcasting can no longer be tolerated. We shall support legislation to repeal the Federal Communications Act, and to provide for private ownership of broadcasting rights, thus giving broadcasting First Amendment parity with other communications media. We support repeal of pornography laws.

Protection of Privacy

Electronic and other covert government surveillance of citizens should be restricted to activity which can be shown beforehand, under high, clearly defined standards of probable cause, to be criminal and to present immediate and grave danger to other citizens. The National Census and other government compilations of data on citizens should be conducted on a strictly voluntary basis.

The Right to Keep and Bear Arms

In recognition of the fact that the individual is his own last source of self-defense, the authors of the Constitution guaranteed, in the Second Amendment, the right of the people to keep and bear arms. This reasoning remains valid today. We pledge to uphold that guarantee. We oppose compulsory arms registration.

Volunteer Army

We oppose the draft (Selective Service), believing that the use of force to require individuals to serve in the armed forces or anywhere else is a violation of their rights, and that a well-paid volunteer army is a more effective means of national defense than the involuntary servitude exemplified

by the draft. We recommend a complete review and possible reform of the Uniform Code of Military Justice, to guarantee effective and equal protection of rights under the law to all members of the U.S. armed forces, and to promote thereby the morale, dignity, and sense of justice within the military which are indispensable to its efficient and effective operation. We further pledge to work for a declaration of unconditional amnesty for all who have been convicted of, or who now stand accused of, draft evasion and for all military deserters who were draftees.

Property Rights

We hold that property rights are individual rights and, as such, are entitled to the same respect and protection as all other individual rights. We further hold that the owner of property has the full right to control, use, dispose of, or in any manner enjoy his property without interference, until and unless the exercise of his control infringes the valid rights of others. We shall thus oppose restrictions upon the use of property which do not have as their sole end the protection of valid rights.

Unions and Collective Bargaining

We support the right of free men to voluntarily associate in, or to establish, labor unions. We support the concept that an employer may recognize a union as the collective bargaining agent of some or all of his employees. We oppose governmental interference in bargaining, such as compulsory arbitration or the obligation to bargain. We demand that the National Labor Relations Act be repealed. We recognize voluntary contracts between employers and labor unions as being legally and morally binding on the parties to such contracts.

Trade and the Economy

Because each person has the right to offer his goods and services to others on the free market, and because government interference can only harm such free activity, we oppose all intervention by government into the area of economics. The only proper role of government in the economic realm is to protect property rights, adjudicate disputes and protect contracts, and provide a legal framework in which voluntary trade is protected. All efforts by government to redistribute wealth, or to control or manage trade, are improper in a free society.

Money

We favor the establishment of a sound money system. We thus support the private ownership of gold, and demand repeal of all legal tender laws.

The Economy

Government intervention in the economy imperils both the material prosperity and personal freedom of every American. We therefore support the following specific immediate reforms:

(a) reduction of both taxes and government spending;

(b) an end to deficit budgets;

(c) a halt to inflationary monetary policies, and elimination, with all deliberate speed, of the Federal Reserve System;

(d) the removal of all governmental impediments to free trade—including the repeal of the National Labor Relations Act, the Interstate Commerce Act, all antitrust laws, and the abolition of the Department of Agriculture, as the most pressing and critical impediments;

(e) and the repeal of all controls on wages, prices, rents, profits, production, and interest rates.

Subsidies

In order to achieve a free economy in which government victimizes no one for the benefit of anyone else, we oppose all government subsidies to business, labor, education, agriculture, science, the arts, or any other special interests. Those who have entered into these activities with promises of government subsidy will be forewarned by being given a cutoff date beyond which all government aid to their enterprise will be terminated. Relief or exemption from involuntary taxation shall not be considered a subsidy.

Tariffs and Quotas

Like subsidies, tariffs and quotas serve only to give special treatment to favored interests and to diminish the welfare of other citizens. We therefore support abolition of all tariffs and quotas as well as the Tariff Commission and the Customs Court.

Interim Reforms

In order to effect our long-range goals, we recommend, among others, the following interim measures: the adoption of the Liberty Amendment, and provision for greater use of the referendum for reducing or repealing taxes.

Long-Range Goals

Since we believe that every man is entitled to keep the fruits of his labor, we are opposed to all government activity which consists of the forcible collection money or goods from citizens in violation of their individual rights. Specifically, we support the eventual repeal of all taxation. We support a system of voluntary fees for services rendered as a method for financing government in a free society.

Domestic Ills

Government intervention in current problems, such as crime, pollution, defraud of consumers, health problems, overpopulation, decaying cities, and poverty, is properly limited to protection of individual rights. In those areas where individual rights or voluntary relations are not involved, we support an immediate reduction of government's present role, and ultimately, a total withdrawal of government intervention, together with the establishment of a legal framework in which private, voluntary solutions to these problems can be developed and implemented.

Pollution

We support the development of an objective system defining individual property rights to air and water. We hold that ambiguities in the area of these rights (e.g. concepts such as "public property") are a primary cause of our deteriorating environment. Whereas we maintain that no one has the right to violate the legitimate property rights of others by pollution, we shall strenuously oppose all attempts to transform the defense of such rights into any restriction of the efforts of individuals to advance technology, to expand production, or to use their property peacefully.

Consumer Protection

We shall support strong and effective laws against fraud and misrepresentation. We shall oppose, however, that present and prospective so-called "consumer-protection" legislation which infringes upon voluntary trade.

Overpopulation

We support an end to all subsidies for childbearing built into our present laws, including all welfare plans and the provision of tax-supported services for children. We further support the repeal of all laws restricting voluntary birth control or voluntary termination of pregnancies during their first hundred days. We shall oppose all coercive measures to control population growth.

Education

We support the repeal of all compulsory education laws, and an end to government operation, regulation, and subsidy of schools. We call for an immediate end of compulsory busing.

Poverty and Unemployment

We support repeal of all laws which impede the ability of any person to find employment—including, but not limited to, minimum wage laws, so-called "protective" labor legislation for women and children, governmental restrictions on the establishment of private day-care centers, the National Labor Relations Act, and licensing requirements. We oppose all government welfare and relief projects and "aid to the poor" programs, inasmuch as they are not within the proper role of government, and do contribute to unemployment. All aid to the poor should come from private sources.

Foreign Policy

The principles which guide a legitimate government in its relationships with other governments are the same as those which guide relationships among individuals and relationships between individuals and governments. It must protect itself and its citizens against the initiation of force from other nations. While we recognize the existence of totalitarian governments, we do not recognize them as *legitimate* governments. We will grant them no moral sanction. We will not deal with them as if they were proper governments. To do so is to ignore the rights of their victims

and rob those victims of the knowledge that we know they have been wronged.

▪ ECONOMIC

Foreign Aid

We support an end to the Federal foreign aid program.

Ownership in Unclaimed Property

We pledge to oppose recognition of claims by fiat, by nations or international bodies, of presently unclaimed property, such as the ocean floor and planetary bodies. We urge the development of objective standards for recognizing claims of ownership in such property.

Currency Exchange Rates

We pledge to oppose all governmental attempts to peg or regulate currency exchange rates. International trade can truly be free only when currency exchange rates reflect the free market value of respective currencies.

▪ MILITARY

Military Alliances

The United States should abandon its attempts to act as policeman for the world, and should enter into alliances only with countries whose continued free existence is vital to the protection of the freedom of all American citizens. Under such an alliance, the United States may offer the protection of its nuclear umbrella, but our allies would provide their own conventional defense capabilities. We should in particular disengage from any present alliances which include despotic governments.

Military Capability

We shall support the maintenance of a sufficient military establishment to defend the United States against aggression. We should have a sufficient nuclear capacity to convince any potential aggressor that it cannot hope to survive a first strike against the United States. But, as our foreign commitments are reduced, and as our allies assume their share of the burden of providing a conventional war capability, we should be able to reduce the size of our conventional defense, and thus reduce the overall cost and size of our total defense establishment.

▪ DIPLOMATIC

Diplomatic Recognition

The United States should establish a scheme of recognition consistent with the principles of a free society, the primary principle being that, while individuals everywhere in the world have unalienable rights, governments which enslave individuals have no legitimacy whatsoever.

Secession

We shall support recognition of the right to secede. Political units or areas which do secede should be recognized by the United States as independent political entities where: (1) secession is supported by a majority within the political unit, (2) the majority does not attempt suppression of the dissenting minority, and (3) the government of the new entity is at least as compatible with human freedom as that from which it seceded.

The United Nations

We support withdrawal of the United States from the United Nations. We further support a Constitutional Amendment designed to prohibit the United States from entering into any treaty under which it relinquishes any portion of its sovereignty.

Source: Minor/Third Party Platforms: "Libertarian Party Platform of 1972," June 17, 1972. Online by Gerhard Peters and John T. Woolley, *The American Presidency Project*. http://www.presidency.ucsb.edu/ws/?pid=29615.

LITERACY

The condition of being literate (able to read, write, and be skillful in the use of words) is key to American democracy; in any society literacy brings strength as only a knowledgeable populace can test and innovate ideas. The notion of self-education fostered by literacy is core to the American cultural identity that came out of the Great Awakening. Within the broader idea of enduring democracy where government by the people is exercised either directly or through elected representatives, a well-read and knowledgeable populace is mandatory. Literacy as an idea is seminal to the First Amendment of the U.S. Constitution that protects civil liberties, including the free expression of religion, the right to peacefully assemble, free speech, and the right to petition the government. If any group is intentionally excluded from literacy education, that group is effectively disenfranchised. Today, social media have revolutionized how American society perceives literacy and literacy education, so that basic skills such as cursive writing that has historically been a hallmark of literacy have been dropped from elementary school curriculum in some states.

Illiteracy within a given society reflects an "educational underclass" with symptoms seen in the disposed: the homeless, the unemployed, and families on welfare. This educational underclass comes with individuals who are developmentally or intellectually challenged, those who attend inferior inner-city or rural schools, those who enter the school system later than piers or those in families who relocate frequently, and immigrants with limited education and literacy in their native languages.

While today illiteracy has not had a color bar, in the past it has, primarily during slavery and by law. Literacy is tied to self-identity. The ability to read provides a sense of self-worth, opening up the world of new ideas. The institutional push to matriculate or marginalize minority groups within English-only systems has led regulation limiting literacy education to control or suppress the upward mobility of certain groups feared to be subversive to the status quo.

Economic interests and social control have driven literacy in America. Industries with low-skilled workers do not require an educated workforce, but highly skilled jobs require highly literate workers. In 2006, the National Commission on Adult Literacy (http://www.nationalcommissiononadultliteracy.org/about.html) was established to address this issue, but the underlying ideas of literacy education date back to cultural origins of the United States.

Before the American Revolution, England established the King's English as the standard for literacy in the British colonies. Theology mandated literacy and historically the most significant literacy movements have been church-driven. Already demographically multicultural, various denominations cultivated knowledgeable readers to grow congregations. *The New England Primer* for Protestants became the most widely used schoolbook in America during the 17th

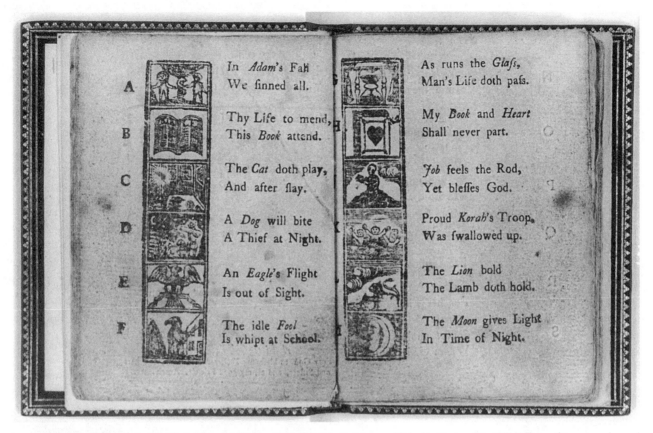

A page illustrated with lessons in the alphabet from A to M from *McGuffey's Eclectic Primer*, published in Cincinnati in 1849. Millions of Americans learned their ABCs from this book. (Library of Congress)

and 18th centuries. Women were literate enough to teach young children but not enough to challenge male heads of households. Women could assemble to read and discuss religious texts privately, but in public could not discuss male-dominated fields like politics, economics, and science that shaped community action.

During the early republic, American lexicographer Noah Webster (1758–1843) led the movement to standardize spelling and punctuation of the English language in the United States. He published *The American Spelling Book* (1783) as a means of promoting American nationalism and achieving cultural independence from England. With westward expansion, public education was limited, so literacy education occurred at home, in one-room (common) schools, and in church-based programs.

Literacy as an idea is linked to industry, which was considered an American virtue. Literacy education in the United States emerged with secular Sunday schools (also

called First Day Societies), seasonal schools that met once a week to provide basic instruction in reading for children and adults. Tracts written in a lively and entertaining style became the predominant genre for literacy education. They usually were written in easy language for children, and then children brought them home and taught other members of their family how to read. Irish-born publisher of chapbooks (small pamphlets containing popular literature of the day) and Bibles, Mathew Carey (1760–1839) immigrated to become a founding member of the First Day Society, America's first secular Sunday school established in Philadelphia in 1790 to promote literacy education. The first Sunday-School Union in America was established in Philadelphia in 1791 and the Hartford Evangelical Tract Society was established in 1815.

The American Sunday-School Union (ASSU) was established in Philadelphia in 1817 as a coalition of local Protestant Sunday-school groups, and was established in 1824. The

Union's goals included establishing Sunday schools as well as providing communities with libraries and materials for religious instruction. This nonsectarian organization pioneered the development of a distribution network for American literature on diverse topics considered relevant to being well read in health, history, travel, biography, and science. The Union provided the educational materials and training to children and adults on the frontier as they established networks of Sunday schools. Writers from many denominations—in a single generation—produced quality literature so widely read that it caused a complete revolution in the reading habits and tastes of American youth.

By 1830, the ASSU deliberately set out to create indigenous children's literature, following the model of More's Cheap Repository Tracts. During the 1840s, many stories were written to instill in children the values and morals needed to become good citizens. The Union commissioned American writers to create stories with American subjects and settings. The Union published its books in attractive smaller formats that appealed to children, and American artists and engravers illustrated many of the books. They were modestly priced to be affordable. These books remained influential until the 1860s when public libraries began to provide easy access to attractive children's literature. The American Tract Society (ATS) was established in 1825 to consolidate the publishing ventures of diverse Bible societies, gospel tract ministries, and denominations, including the New York Tract Society (founded in 1812) and the New England Tract Society (founded in 1814). They were more ephemeral because of the publisher's system for distribution: ATS established a network of colporteurs (traveling salesmen of Christian literature) that sold and distributed literature, led services, and provided counseling in communities.

Not all regions and populations put the same emphasis on literacy, but they understood its importance. The Nat Turner Rebellion in Virginia in 1831 led to retaliatory measures that created a large illiterate population in the American South: it was estimated that at the start of the Civil War, less than 5 percent of individuals of African descent in America were literate.

McGuffey Eclectic Readers were the most popular and widely distributed school books in America between 1836 and 1960; during the Civil War they were sent to schools in the South when other textbooks from the North were banned.

Far more popular than *The New England Primer* and Noah Webster's blue-backed *Speller*, William Holmes McGuffey (1800–1873) formatted the series with short passages of prose or verse illustrated with wood engravings and accompanies with questions to test the pupil's comprehension of words and morals imbedded in passages. The upper-graded McGuffey readers contained extracts from works by famous authors that were sometimes the only means that high school or academy students could learn about literature. Because boys were more likely to attend schools, most of the content was geared toward male readers.

A second large movement to promote American literacy rates occurred after the Civil War when former slaves were taught to read. Economic interests and social control in the Southern plantation system required submission of slaves. Literacy would open the world of ideas and subsequently a sense of self-worth that led to upward mobility. During the Reconstruction era from 1865 to 1877, after the Emancipation, organizations including the African Methodist Episcopal Church, the American Missionary Association, and the Society of Friends dispatched teachers and books, including the King James Bible to the South. Agents from the Freedman's Bureau and U.S. Army personnel protected, and sometimes even organized, supported, and taught in black schools during this adult literacy crusade.

Although blacks had established political structures without great literacy levels, having literacy (knowledge of English literature, civics, history, mathematics and surveying, and geography) rates increased empowered black communities to expand these structures.

A third large movement was government-supported and occurred in conjunction with the civil rights movement but has largely been underfunded. In 1984, the Center for Applied Technology (CAST; http://www.cast.org/) was established to expand opportunities to develop reading skills and enthusiasm for literacy education for at-risk groups. The Supreme Court decision in *Brown v. Board of Education* (1954) desegregated public schools, finding that separate-but-equal schools fostered educational inequity, and leading the way for school integration. The National Literacy Act (1991) established the National Institute for Literacy to enhance and coordinate adult literacy programs for adults in the United States to expand work opportunities and ultimately quality of life.

The continuing mandate of literacy education is training the American work force to remain competitive in a fluid global economy. The Carnegie Review (http://carnegie.org/programs/past-commissions-councils-and-task-forces/carnegie-council-for-advancing-adolescent-literacy) has found that American fifteen-year-olds are struggling to demonstrate international standards for literacy and the concern remains that this has serious implications for their futures in higher education and in the workforce. In the past, students had school libraries where they could access quality reading materials and assistance, but many public schools no longer have school libraries with literacy education, so book distribution is still necessary. The U.S. Department of Education continues the never-ending work to motivate children to read and establish adult literacy programs to increase American productivity, but the results are as consistent as the agency's funding.

See also

American Missionary Movement; Industrial Revolution; Second Great Awakening; War on Poverty

MEREDITH ELIASSEN

Further Reading

Gordon, Edward E., and Elaine H. Gordon. 2003. *Literacy in America: Historic Journey and Contemporary Solutions.* Westport, CT: Praeger.

Hunter, Carman St. John. 1979. *Adult Literacy in the United States: A Report to the Ford Foundation.* New York: McGraw-Hill.

Knight, Edgar W. 1953. *A Documentary History of Education in the South before 1860.* Chapel Hill, NC: University of North Carolina Press.

Monaghan, E.J. 2005. *Learning to Read and Write in Colonial America.* Boston: University of Massachusetts Press.

Webber, Thomas. 1978. *Deep Like the Rivers: Education in the Slave Quarter Community, 1831–1865.* New York: W.W. Norton.

Literacy—Primary Document

Introduction

On August 21, 1831, Nathanial "Nat" Turner (1800–1831) led a slave rebellion in Southampton County, Virginia, that killed fifty-six white men, women, and children. The white militia quickly quelled the violence. Over fifty-five blacks involved with the rebellion were killed and 200 who were not involved were killed in retaliation. Turner, who was literate, highly intelligent, and able to sway and organize others, evaded arrest for two months, but was finally captured, convicted, and executed. The rebellion ignited deep fear and polarized political moderates and slaveholders and led to anti-literacy legislation that oppressed slaves and free blacks alike in the South. The law, excerpted here, prohibited education and the right to assemble for slaves and free blacks, curtailed basic civil rights for free blacks, and only white ministers could preside over black congregations.

Document: Retaliatory Legislation Enacted in Virginia After the Nat Turner Rebellion to Prohibit the Teaching of Slaves, Free Negroes, or Mulattoes to Read or Write (1831)

4. Be it further enacted, That all meetings of free negroes or mulattoes, at any school-house, church, meeting-house or other place for teaching them reading or writing, either in the day or night, under whatsoever pretext, shall be deemed and considered as an unlawful assembly; and any justice of the county or corporation, wherein such assemblage shall be, either from his own knowledge, or on the information of others, of such unlawful assemblage or meeting, shall issue his warrant, directed to any sworn officer or officers, authorizing him or them, to enter the house or houses where such unlawful assemblage or meeting may be, for the purpose of apprehending or dispersing such free negroes or mulattoes, and to inflict corporal punishment on the offender or offenders, at the discretion of any justice of the peace, not exceeding twenty lashes.

5. Be it further enacted, That if any white person or persons assemble with free negroes or mulattoes, at any school-house, church, meeting-house, or other place for the purpose of instructing such free negroes or mulattoes to read or write, such person or persons shall, on conviction thereof, be fined in a sum not exceeding fifty dollars, and moreover may be imprisoned at the discretion of a jury, not exceeding two months.

6. Be it further enacted, That if any white person for pay or compensation, shall assemble with any slaves for the purpose of teaching, and shall teach any slave to read or write, such person, or any white person or persons contracting with such teacher so to act, who shall offend as aforesaid,

shall, for each offence, be fined at the discretion of a jury, in a sum of not less than ten, nor exceeding one hundred dollars, to he recovered on an information or indictment.

7. The judges of the superior courts of law, and the attorneys prosecuting for the commonwealth, in the county and corporation courts, are hereby required to give this act in charge to their several grand juries.

8. This act shall be in force from the first day of June next.

Source: *Supplement to the Revised Code of the Laws of Virginia, Being a Collection of All the Acts of the General Assembly of a Public and Permanent Nature Passed Since the Year 1819, with a General Index.* Richmond: Printed by Samuel Shepherd & Co., 1833, chapter 186.

LOST CAUSE

After four years of fighting in the Civil War, white Southerners remained unrepentant despite their defeat at the hands of the North. Yet with their landscape completely ruined, almost 25 percent of their military-age male population killed and thousands more permanently wounded, and their slave-based social and economic system destroyed, white Southerners, especially former Confederate leaders, needed to justify these losses in the war's aftermath. In the process, these former Confederates created a new memorial school of the conflict, known as the Lost Cause, to address these concerns. Borrowing the term from the title of book on the Civil War by the wartime editor of *the Richmond Examiner*, Edward A. Pollard, white Southerners constructed this view that attempted to overlook slavery, emancipation, and their interconnection with the Civil War to justify Southern secession and the Confederacy's role in the conflict. Initially, only white Southerners accepted this narrative, but it eventually grew to become the prominent memorial school used in both the North and South. Even today, Americans deal with the Lost Cause in Civil War memory.

The term *Lost Cause* first appeared with the publication of Pollard's book *The Lost Cause: A New Southern History of the War of the Confederates* in 1867. Pollard provided the first example of the sectionalist memory that would emerge in the 19th century. Following Pollard's justifications of

Southern secession and its role in the Civil War, many prominent Confederates, especially former Confederates General Jubal A. Early and President Jefferson Davis, promoted and spread the ideas of the Lost Cause in the postwar years. Early and other Confederate veterans contributed a number of articles to the *Southern Historical Society Papers* explaining their views on the war during and after Reconstruction. Davis published his history of the war titled *The Rise and Fall of the Confederate Government* in 1881. Primarily, these leaders as well as numerous other Confederate veterans created a new image of the conflict and what caused the war through their speeches, writings, ceremonies, and memoirs.

Their approach included ignoring the role slavery played in the cause of the Civil War. The white Southerners claimed that slavery was not the critical sectional issue that led to Southern secession. Instead, the conflict started because of cultural differences and disparities in nationalistic thought between the two sections. Southerners believed that "states' rights" overrode the power of the federal government, but Abraham Lincoln and the Republican Party would overwhelm the power of the states. To protect their states' rights, then, the Southern states needed to secede.

In addition, the Lost Cause claimed the South would have given up slavery eventually without the war. Despite evidence to the contrary, Southerners claimed the institution of slavery was no longer economically viable for the South and the institution would have disappeared. Thus, it was the agitating actions of radical abolitionists in the North, primarily in New England, that led to secession. They wanted to change the South's society to reflect the Northern states, which pushed Southerners past their limits and led to secession and war. Although abolitionist arguments accentuated the inhumanity and brutality of slavery, white Southerners claimed the slaves were treated well and African Americans actually benefited from the institution. According to the Lost Cause, Southern secession came about because of Northerners' actions prior to 1860, which justified the South's reaction to Lincoln's election that year.

Most importantly for many white Southerners, the Lost Cause asserted that the Confederacy was never truly defeated. Instead, by 1865, Union manpower and industry simply overwhelmed the South. Southern leaders were considered far superior to their Union counterparts, as Robert E. Lee and Thomas J. "Stonewall" Jackson showed during the

D.W. Griffith's 1915 film *Birth of a Nation*, which was about the American Civil War/Reconstruction and white domination by the Ku Klux Klan (KKK), sparked major controversy throughout the country and contributed to the reemergence of the KKK. (Library of Congress)

war. Union General Ulysses S. Grant was branded a "butcher" of his troops who showed no concern for the enlisted men and Union General William T. Sherman exemplified the uncivilized lengths to which Northerners would go for victory. Thus, the more chivalrous Southern soldiers were overwhelmed by a horde of barbaric Yankees rather than defeated by those armies. By ignoring the failure of Confederate command and Union success in the Western Theater, Lost Cause advocates could prove the South's martial superiority in the Virginia Theater. In the fighting between Gettysburg and Richmond, they claimed, the Confederate Army of Northern Virginia won every battle except the Battle of Gettysburg. Even the defeat at Gettysburg would not have happened, according to the military standards of the Lost Cause, if Stonewall Jackson, the best general on either side, had been alive in July 1863. Only the Union's war of attrition caused the collapse of the Confederacy. Thus, Southern honor and manhood remained intact despite the Union victory.

But Union commanders and armies were not the only ones who received attacks from Lost Cause memorialists. General James Longstreet, commander of the Army of Northern Virginia's First Corps during the war, fell into disrepute in the South in the 1870s and 1880s. Although the troops who served under Longstreet supported their former commander after the war, General Early, in placing blame for Confederate failure, blamed Longstreet for a number of Confederate defeats, including the loss at Gettysburg and the failure to capture Knoxville, Tennessee, in 1863. In an attempt to defend his reputation, Longstreet pushed the blame onto other commanders, including his former superior and Lost Cause martyr Robert E. Lee. He also became a "Scalawag," a pejorative term for post–Civil War Southerners who became and cooperated with Republicans; Longstreet backed Ulysses Grant for president in 1868 and received a patronage appointment. With these actions, additional veteran Confederate commanders attacked Longstreet in writing, which helped destroy his reputation with common Southerners in the postwar years.

An additional aspect, albeit not as central, is an emphasis on the state of Virginia in Lost Cause mythology. Numerous parts of the Lost Cause place Virginia in a prominent position in Confederate memory, and many important Lost Cause figures have connections to Virginia. For example, Lee and Jackson as well as Confederate cavalry commander J.E.B. Stuart, another Lost Cause hero killed during the Battle of Yellow

Tavern in May 1864, were Virginians. And both Early and William Mahone, former Confederate generals and leaders in the creation of the Lost Cause mythology, hailed from Virginia. Also, much of the Lost Cause argument concentrates on the fighting in Virginia to promote the martial superiority of white Southerners over the Northern Unionists. Virginia had a strong connection in both Lost Cause memory and in the creation of the Lost Cause.

At first, only white Southerners accepted this memorial school. Throughout Reconstruction, African Americans and white Northerners, especially Union veterans, emphasized the emancipationist and Unionist legacies of the conflict. They stressed the fact that the Union victory had preserved the United States and ended the horrific institution of slavery that blighted the nation's overall quality. Union veterans, both white and black, followed this reasoning for the remainder of their lives. Even as late as the 1920s, these former soldiers argued against the rising power of the Lost Cause in American memory and the interpretation of the war. Although they used common valor in combat to reconcile with some of their Southern neighbors, the veterans on both sides reflected sectionalism in their personal memories of the conflict.

Having become disillusioned with Reconstruction by the mid-1870s and to placate the bitter white Southerners who survived the war and Reconstruction, however, many non-veteran white Northerners and Southerners had created a new reconciliation movement based on the Lost Cause. By 1877, the Lost Cause gained ground as the common narrative of the war for white Americans, especially once Reconstruction ended. Primarily, reconciliation ignored the differences between the Union and Confederacy that caused the war, especially slavery. Instead, they focused on the common valor and bravery of white soldiers from both sides and disregarded the role of African Americans in the conflict. Reconciliation began to become a reality on the basis of white supremacy and Lost Cause mythology throughout the United States.

In addition, ancestral organizations, such as the Sons of Confederate Veterans, United Daughters of the Confederacy, and the Sons of Union Veterans, played a greater role in reconciliation and the Lost Cause once the veterans' generation started to die out in the late 1910s and veterans' organizations, such as the United Confederate Veterans and Grand Army of the Republic, began to lose political power. These ancestral organizations also emphasized the courage of the common soldiers over the sectional issues that caused secession for memorializing the conflict. Primarily, they focused on public displays of memorialization from parades and battlefield preservation to the construction of monuments. These attempts at memorialization, however, did not include African Americans in the process, whether holding a parade for Memorial Day or constructing monuments to the common soldiers. With the concentration on the martial events between 1861 and 1865, these organizations also avoided discussing the history of secession and overlooked the reasons for the conflict in the process. By ignoring the uncomfortable history of slavery and secession, these groups supported a memory that all white Americans could accept as the common experience of the Civil War.

In addition to ignoring the role of slavery in secession and the Civil War, Lost Cause mythology and white Americans overlooked the role African Americans played in combat. White Americans rarely mentioned the presence of the United States Colored Troops in the Union forces and played down any actions they participated in during the conflict. The emphasis on white troops also helped reunify Americans by promoting the perceived superiority of whites in society. The Supreme Court decision in *Plessy v. Ferguson* (1896) and the ability of white soldiers to "defend and protect" black Cubans in the Spanish-American War in 1898 solidified this belief and supported the ideas created by the Lost Cause.

Popular culture, especially film in the early 20th century, and popular historical writing also solidified the presence of the Lost Cause in Civil War memory. With the growth of movies in the 1910s, the Civil War was a popular topic for filmmakers. *The Birth of a Nation* (1915) was the first major film to portray the Civil War and Reconstruction. D. W. Griffith's four-hour epic, based on Thomas Dixon's popular novel *The Clansman* (1905), brought the Lost Cause to an even larger number of Americans. *Birth of a Nation*, the highest grossing film in history until 1939, glorified both the Confederate cause during the war and the Ku Klux Klan, a terrorist organization in the Reconstruction era. Following *Birth of a Nation*, the popular novel and film *Gone with the Wind* (1936 and 1939 respectively) lionized the Old South. Depicting happy, contented slaves and the chivalrous plantation system in the Deep South, *Gone with the Wind* overcame *Birth of a Nation*'s grosses and continues to be one of the most popular Civil

War films of all time. The exposure of the Lost Cause through these films and popular histories congealed the presence of the Lost Cause in American memory.

Academic historians also followed Lost Cause teachings. Few professors examined the institution of slavery in their works. Once they did start to study the topic, similar to the Lost Cause leaders of the 19th century, they ignored the slaves' experiences and emphasized the economics of the institution. In military history, academic historians followed the tradition of finding honor in the men who fought on both sides. The commanders, however, did not receive a similar treatment. Many studies continued to spread the image of General Grant as a butchering alcoholic. Similarly, General Sherman received unfavorable examinations of his command in Georgia and the Carolinas where, they claimed, he created "total war" tactics. And General Longstreet's reputation continued to fall. Generals Lee and Jackson, however, were deified in both academic and popular histories as the last of the chivalrous commanders who existed in the United States before the Civil War. The work of Douglas Southall Freeman, who wrote a multivolume biography of Robert E. Lee and multiple books on his subordinates, followed this perspective and was extremely popular throughout the 1930s and 1940s. The Lost Cause had infiltrated all aspects of Civil War interpretation and memory by the early 20th century.

New interpretive trends starting in the late 1940s and 1950s changed the field of Civil War history. Historians began questioning the previously held assumptions about slavery and examined the darker sides of American history. By focusing on the experiences of African Americans and probing the uncomfortable aspects of history, historians brought new perspectives to the war's memory. Although many popular histories continued the Lost Cause trend, academic historians introduced interpretations that would change how Americans perceived the conflict. But the Lost Cause had become such a powerful memorial school that it even infiltrated popular historian Shelby Foote's three-volume history of the conflict and the interpretation of the conflict by the National Park Service.

The rise of the civil rights movement in the 1950s exposed even more questions about what Americans knew about the Civil War era and the Old South. The approaching Civil War Centennial in the 1960s, working in conjunction with the civil rights movement, forced public and academic Civil War historians to deal with the contradictions that the civil rights movement exposed. The popularity of the Civil War grew, but historians published numerous studies on antebellum slavery and the Civil War that questioned long-held assumptions. Primarily, historians included the role of African Americans and emancipation in the Union war effort. In addition, popular histories on the war, especially the ones written by Bruce Catton, provided more balanced perspectives that increased the reputations and popularity of Union commanders, while still honoring their counterparts with the Confederacy.

Although Americans had started to question the Lost Cause, it has survived throughout changes in the Civil War narrative. More historians questioned the established narrative in the late 1960s and early 1970s. The disillusionment Americans felt in the aftermath of the Vietnam War also contributed to the reversal of Lost Cause mythology. Many Americans doubted the glorification of combat that the Lost Cause provided with the widespread exposure of the Vietnam experience. With African Americans gaining a larger voice in the historical profession as well as historical perspectives, their role, and the role of emancipation, returned to prominence in the story of the Civil War.

Despite these changes, however, Americans continue to face Lost Cause mythology in popular culture, especially films such as *Gettysburg* (1993) and *Gods and Generals* (2003), and in the rise of neo-Confederate organizations, which spread Lost Cause teachings and have recently promoted the idea of black Confederate soldiers despite evidence against their participation. Additionally, the work of ancestral groups and private organizations erected numerous monuments dedicated to the Lost Cause that Americans can still find today. For example, Manassas National Battlefield owns an enormous statue to Lost Cause hero Stonewall Jackson. The city of Richmond has an entire avenue with monuments to Lee, Jackson, Davis, and J.E.B. Stuart. And, in Georgia, Americans can find Stone Mountain, an enormous relief statue of Davis, Lee, and Jackson. Although the Lost Cause has lost some of its centrality in American memory, it continues to survive generational changes and still influences Civil War memory today.

See also

Abolition; African American Civil Rights Movement; Antislavery; Chattel Slavery; Federalism; Industrial Revolution; Modernizization; Nullification; Patriotism; Racism; Reconstruction; Secession; Sectionalism; Self-Governance; Southern Rights Movement; States' Rights (Antebellum, Memory, Contemporary); White Supremacy/Power

MICHAEL BURNS

Further Reading

Blight, David W. 2002. *Race and Reunion: The Civil War in American Memory*. Cambridge, MA: Belknap Press of Harvard University Press.

Gallagher, Gary W. 2008. *Causes Won, Lost, and Forgotten: How Hollywood and Popular Art Shape What We Know About the Civil War*. Chapel Hill, NC: University of North Carolina Press.

Gallagher, Gary W., and Alan T. Nolan, eds. 2000. *The Myth of the Lost Cause and Civil War History*. Bloomington: Indiana University Press.

Osterweis, Rollin G. 1973. *The Myth of the Lost Cause, 1865–1900*. Hamden, CT: Archon Books.

Lost Cause—Primary Document

Introduction

Edward Pollard provided some of the earliest apologetic rhetoric for Southern secession and its role in the Civil War. The following paragraphs from chapter four of his book The Lost Cause *explain the reason for Southern secession in the aftermath of Abraham Lincoln's election in 1860. In the process, Pollard plays down slavery as part of the cause and ignores the secession committees' obvious pronouncements about slavery being the central reason for secession. Instead, Pollard points to the physical threat of the Republican Party against the people of the South.*

Document: Edward A. Pollard's *The Lost Cause: A New Southern History of the War of the Confederates* (1866)

In the face of this sectional triumph there was plainly no protection for the South in the future. There was none in power; for the superiour [*sic*] political strength of the North was now beyond dispute. There was none in public opinion; for that, all the political history of America showed, was the slave of the majority. There was none in the courts; for the Dred Scott decision had been denounced in the Chicago platform as a dangerous heresy, and the doctrine upon which Mr. Lincoln had been elected had been actually declared illegal by the supreme judicial authority of the country.

In Congress the Northern States had 183 votes; the South, if unanimous, 120. If then the North was prepared to act in a mass its power was irresistible; and the election of Mr. Lincoln plainly showed that it was prepared so to act and to carry out a sectional design . . . . the South prepared to go out of a Union which no longer afforded any guaranty [*sic*] for her rights or any permanent sense of security, and which had brought her under the domination of a section, the designs of which, carried into legislation, would destroy her institutions, and even involve the lives of her people.

Such was the true and overwhelming significance of Mr. Lincoln's election to the people of the South. They saw in it the era of a sectional domination, which they proposed to encounter, not by *revolution*, properly so called, not by an attempt to recover by arms their constitutional rights in the Union, but simply to escape by withdrawal from the confederation, and the resumption of their original character of independent States.

But again it was urged by the apologists of Mr. Lincoln's election that such escape of the South from its results was unfair, in view of the fact that during most of the preceding period of the Union, the South had held in its hands the administration at Washington, and had but little reason now to complain that it had passed to those of the rival section.

This view was not without plausibility, and yet as fallacious as that which appealed to the perceptive rule of majorities in America. The South had held power at Washington for a long time; but that power threatened nothing in the North, sought noting from it, desired to disturb nothing in it. It had no aggressive intent; it stood constantly on the defensive. It had no sectional history; it was associated with a general prosperity of the country. 'Do not forget,' said Senator Hammond of South Carolina, when Mr. Seward boasted in the United States Senate that the North was about to take control at Washington,—'it can never be forgotten—it is written on the brightest page of human history—that we, the slaveholders of the South, took our country in her infancy, and, after ruling her for sixty of seventy years of her existence, we shall surrender her to you without a stain upon her honour [*sic*], boundless in prosperity, incalculable in her strength, the wonder and the admiration of the world. Time will show what you will make of her; but no time can ever diminish in our glory or your responsibility.'

When the South held power, it was only to the North a certain absence from office, a certain exclusion from patronage. But when the North was to obtain it, acting not as a party, but a people united on a geographical idea, it was something more than a negative evil or disappointment to the South; it was the enthronement at Washington of a sectional despotism that threatened the institutions, the property, and the lives of the people of the Southern States. Power in the hands of the South affected the patronage of a political party in the North. Power in the hands of the North affected the safety and happiness of every individual in the South. It was simply determined by the South to withdraw from a game where the stakes were so unequal, and where her loss would have been ruin

Source: Pollard, Edward A. *The Lost Cause: A New Southern History of the War of the Confederates*. New York: E. B. Treat and Co., 1866, pp. 80–81.

M

MANIFEST DESTINY

Throughout the 19th century, Americans pushed the frontiers of settlement further westward from the Atlantic seaboard to the Pacific Ocean. Believing that God foreordained westward expansion, Americans convinced themselves that the nation's ultimate calling was to instill American ideals of independence, equality, and freedom across the continent. In this ethnocentric quest, Americans extended their physical territory and promoted social, economic, and political changes. The migrations of Americans to the West supplanted native peoples, created opportunities to exploit natural resources and build settlements, altered economic and political arrangements for the country, ignited wars, and drew a diverse population of Americans with varied cultural backgrounds west of the Mississippi River.

Convinced by their own proclamations, many Americans believed that westward expansion remained a right given by God and that it was their ultimate calling, or destiny, to promote and proclaim American ideas of morality and equality. In 1839, as growing numbers of Americans migrated across the Great Plains and into the far West, John O'Sullivan wrote of the moral inspirations that guided many Americans westward. O'Sullivan served as the editor and cofounder of *The United States Magazine and Democratic Review* and penned an 1845 article on the country's future greatness. O'Sullivan wrote, "We must onward to the fulfillment of our mission—to the entire development of the principle of our organization—freedom of conscience, freedom of person, freedom of trade and business pursuits, universality of freedom and equality. This is our high destiny, and in nature's eternal, inevitable decree of cause and effect we must accomplish it.... Who, then, can doubt that our country is destined to be the great nation of futurity?"

This "destiny" for greatness could be accomplished only if Americans migrated westward and focused on transplanting democracy and capitalism across the continent. Many settlers believed that God set aside the land for them and sought to dispossess Native Americans of their lands and cultures as these divergent cultures seemed incapable of assimilating to the settlers' American ideals.

During the first fifty years of the 19th century, treaties with Native Americans and the Mexican and French governments increased the geographic size of the United States and provided opportunities for personal advancement and achievements for Americans. Due in part to increased hostilities with Native Americans, most significantly the Iroquois, many Americans remained on their farmlands east of the Appalachian Mountains during the 18th century. The French and Indian War (also part of the European Seven Years' War, 1756–1763) allied French settlers in Canada and the Northern colonies with Native American groups who desired the end of American expansion west of the Appalachians. The

John Gast's 1873 painting *American Progress* depicts an allegorical female figure of America leading settlers, telegraph lines, and railroads into the untamed West. The concept of Manifest Destiny represented in the painting related to the belief that the United States had a moral and divine mandate to colonize the lands west of the Mississippi River and bring "civilization" and technology along. (Library of Congress)

French and British wanted to obtain dominance in their colonies around the world, and in the American colonies, the fight for dominance by these empires resulted in the creation of enormous war debts and new treaties between Native American tribal groups and the British government that promised to keep American settlers east of the Appalachian Mountains to avoid more costly wars. By the ratification of the U.S. Constitution in 1788, however, farmers and land speculators already violated the newly obsolete British treaties and had left the constraints of exhausted soils on Eastern farms to search for new lands and natural resources west of the Appalachians. The outright violation of former and then-current treaties with Native Americans continued during President Andrew Jackson's administration (1829–1837). Ultimately,

President Jackson decided that the removal of Native Americans to far western lands would provide land for Americans while ensuring their safety as well. Jackson's decision to use the U.S. Army to remove the Cherokee, Seminole, Creek, Choctaw, and several other tribal groups in Florida created a desperate situation where thousands of native peoples died on a forced march to Oklahoma in the 1830s, oftentimes referred to as the Trail of Tears, and forecast Native American removals to reservations on undesirable lands.

While the removal of Native Americans from their lands created less-hostile conditions for American settlements, large tracts of land west of the Mississippi River mostly belonged to France and Mexico. In 1803, President Thomas Jefferson secured an enormous amount of land in the middle portion of what is now the United States in the Louisiana Purchase. But the high tide of Manifest Destiny came in the mid-19th century with the acquisition of the modern American Southwest. The presidential election of 1844 turned on the issue of adding to American territory: Democrat James Polk narrowly defeated Whig Henry Clay after advocating obtaining new lands. The addition of the Republic of Texas and lands in the Southwest in the 1840s drew more Americans west following the Mexican-American War (1846–1848) and established a pattern of territorial expansion through wars. The Treaty of Guadalupe Hidalgo ended the Mexican-American War and added approximately half a million square miles of highly valuable land to the United States with the acquisition of Texas and the former Mexican territories in the Southwest and created new borders between the United States and Mexico. By the final purchase of a small northern segment of land from Mexico in 1853, the United States had more than doubled its land mass since the end of the Revolutionary War.

The accumulation of such massive physical territory by the federal government created political issues. By the Civil War, the United States freely gave land away to nearly any American who qualified for a newly established federal land grant. Land grants such as the Homestead Act, passed by Congress in May 1862 and signed into law by President Abraham Lincoln, intended to open large amounts of territory to Americans for further settlements and farming. The initial Homestead Act provided those who migrated to federal lands in the West with 160 acres to build a home and family farm and required that free or low-cost federally owned land be made available to those who were at least twenty-one years of age or the head of their household and never had taken up arms against the United States (the Homestead Acts were signed into law during the Civil War and concerns over Southern slaveholders' potential migrations kept Congress from extending the act to secessionists). If those simple conditions were met, individuals, including women and former slaves, applied for federal land grants, promised to improve the lands, and filed for deeds of title. While the Homestead Acts required residency on the land, the availability of free land attracted land speculators who accumulated large tracts of Midwestern and Great Plains lands and sold those lands later to farmers for significant profits.

Following the U.S. Civil War (1861–1865), thousands of former slaves from the South migrated to the Western frontiers and joined with immigrants in settling towns and cities and establishing homesteads. African American settlers brought their families and belongings with them in their Western migrations, and many viewed the West as their biblical Canaan. This belief in a "promised land" in the West helped earn African American settlers the nickname "Exodusters" in reference to similarities with the biblical story in the Book of Exodus about the freeing of the Israelites from slavery in Egypt and their search for a homeland. Immigrants searched for similar opportunities as well. Thousands of immigrants from disparate regions of the world made the Great Plains and the West their new homes. Eastern and mostly Western Europeans settled across vast areas of the farming regions in the Great Plains, and immigrants from Asian countries and empires arrived on the Californian coast with dreams of returning to their homelands with money earned building the railroads and infrastructure that would bring thousands of more settlers to the West.

The discovery of gold in California in 1849 and in the Black Hills of the Dakota Territory in 1874 gave further impetus to the U.S. government to secure land in the West for settlement as more Americans left their farms and towns for a chance at the reportedly large amounts of gold available for those willing and able to do the work. For those unwilling or uninterested in gold mining, business ventures such as dry goods stores, brothels, and saloons that catered to the gold miners presented opportunities for enterprising businessmen to gain fortunes. Cities such as San Francisco quickly rose to phenomenal wealth and size during the California gold rush and provided miners with needed supplies, information from the Eastern states, and entertainment. Gold rushes such as in the Black Hills of the Dakotas and in the American River area of California brought thousands of mostly young men to the West and supplanted Native Americans, providing impetus for the Plains Indians to engage in warfare against American settlers who oftentimes violated federal land treaties by trespassing on lands reserved for Native Americans.

The discovery of gold in the Black Hills of the Dakota Territory, in particular, created hostilities between Americans and Native Americans on the frontier and drew many more settlers and adventure-seekers. Relatively few Americans ventured into the Black Hills prior to the U.S. Civil War as the Cheyenne and Lakota considered the Black Hills a sacred and holy place and protected the area by attacking American settlers and escaping into the Black Hills for refuge. Following the U.S. Civil War, more American settlers migrated to the Dakotas and demanded a military presence in the Black Hills as a safeguard against attacks by the Lakota and Cheyenne. The American Army, led by Lieutenant Colonel George A. Custer, entered the Black Hills in 1874 to establish the validity of a gold discovery. The veracity of journalists and Custer's claims that gold flowed from the hills remains in doubt but, once the "discovery" was made known to American settlers in the area, attempts to enter the Black Hills for mining began in earnest even though the army tried to keep settlers and miners out of the Hills in efforts to honor treaties made with Indians in the 1860s. Even though the army kept settlers and miners from the Black Hills for a brief period of time, by the spring of 1875 the numbers of whites in the area increased significantly and the army was unable to keep them away any longer. In 1874, American settlers in the Black Hills numbered approximately 800 people, but the confirmation of gold in the Hills and the continued presence of the army attracted an estimated 10,000 miners and fortune-seekers by the end of 1875. The U.S. government, in an attempt to pacify and placate the Native Americans, invited several leaders to Washington, D.C., in the spring of 1875 to resolve the issues involved with the Black Hills. The Native American leaders refused to relinquish the Black Hills and negated any offers or compromises attempted by the federal government. This led President Ulysses S. Grant to order the Natives onto reservations. When the tribes refused, the army pursued, eventually leading to the Battle of Little Big Horn and, subsequently, Indian submission or flight to Canada.

The Great Plains Indian Wars of the last quarter of the 19th century resulted from encroachments by American settlers/miners like that of the Black Hills. Thousands of Native peoples who survived the wars were removed by federal authorities to designated reservations by the end of the 19th century.

In 1893, responding to the finding of the 1890 decennial census that the frontier had closed with the spread of American settlement, historian Frederick Jackson Turner gave a lecture on the frontier and the lingering effects of Manifest Destiny at the annual meeting of the American Historical Association, held in conjunction with the Chicago World's Fair. Turner believed that ever-changing frontier experiences consistently drove Americans to define their independence, freedoms, and what essentially made them Americans. Turner believed that the end of western migrations across the continent ultimately halted American social, economic, and political progress, and separated the United States into four sections, or regions of North, South, East, and West with distinct characteristics that defined and were defined by their inhabitants' identities and interests. The creation of this sectionalism or regionalism, according to Turner, inspired competing interests and furthered sectional strife among Americans. By 1899, however, the surrender of former Spanish colonies in the Spanish-American War allowed Americans to once again apply the principles of Manifest Destiny to the acquisition of Cuba, Puerto Rico, and the Philippines.

At the beginning of the 20th century, the principles of Manifest Destiny that Americans claimed for a hundred years seemed less imperative than they had been during the 19th century. Having accomplished the spread of American settlement and the advancement of American ideals from the Atlantic Ocean in the East to the Pacific Ocean in the West, the United States began to appear as an empire in the acquisition of the former Spanish colonies. The belief in a manifest destiny ordained by God for the spread of American ideals of independence, freedom, rights, and obligations was tested severely by the Philippine-American War (1899–1902) as Filipinos demanded these same ideals for their own country free from American controls. Americans could no longer claim what John O'Sullivan wrote sixty years earlier, that America was "chosen; and her high example shall smite unto death the tyranny of kings, hierarchs, and oligarchs, and carry the glad tidings of peace and good will. . . Who, then, can doubt that our country is destined to be the great nation of futurity?"

See also

Diplomacy; Exodusters; Homesteading; Imperialism; Indian Removal; Western Expansion/Lore

ANITA ANTHONY-VANORSDAL

Further Reading

Correia, David. 2009. "Making Destiny Manifest: United States Territorial Expansion and the Dispossession of Two Mexican Property Claims in New Mexico, 1824–1899." *Journal of Historical Geography* 35: 87–103.
Hansen, Zeynep K., and Gary D. Libecap. 2004. "The Allocation of Property Rights to Land: U.S. Land Policy and Farm Failure in

the Northern Great Plains." *Explorations in Economic History* 41: 103–129.

Horsman, Reginald. 1986. *Race and Manifest Destiny: The Origins of American Racial Anglo-Saxonism.* Cambridge, MA: Harvard University Press.

Lasch, Christopher. 1958. "The Anti-Imperialists, the Philippines, and the Inequality of Man." *Journal of Southern History* 24: 319–331.

Longstreet, Stephen. 1970. *War Cries on Horseback: The Story of the Indian Wars of the Great Plains.* Garden City, NY: Doubleday Press.

Painter, Nell Irvin. 1976. *Exodusters: Black Migration to Kansas After Reconstruction.* New York: Alfred A. Knopf.

Turner, Frederick Jackson. 1925. "The Significance of the Section in American History." *The Wisconsin Magazine of History* 8: 255–280.

Welch, Richard E., Jr. 1979. *Response to Imperialism: The United States and the Philippine-American War, 1899–1902.* Chapel Hill, NC: University of North Carolina Press.

Manifest Destiny—Primary Document

Introduction

Convinced by their own proclamations, many Americans believed that westward expansion remained a right given by God and that it was their ultimate calling, or destiny, to promote and proclaim American ideas of morality and equality. In 1839, as growing numbers of Americans migrated across the Great Plains and into the far West, John O'Sullivan wrote of the moral inspirations that guided many Americans westward. O'Sullivan served as the editor and cofounder of The United States Magazine and Democratic Review *and penned an article on the country's future greatness, which, though it did not use the term manifest destiny, captured the spirit of the concept.*

Document: "The Great Nation of Futurity" by John L. O'Sullivan (November 1839)

The American people having derived their origin from many other nations, and the Declaration of National Independence being entirely based on the great principle of human equality, these facts demonstrate at once our disconnected position as regards any other nation; that we have, in reality, but little connection with the past history of any of them, and still less with all antiquity, its glories, or its crimes. On the contrary, our national birth was the beginning of a new history, the formation and progress of an untried political system, which separates us from the past and connects us with the future only; and so far as regards the entire development of the natural rights of man, in moral, political, and national life, we may confidently assume that our country is destined to be *the great nation* of futurity.

It is so destined, because the principle upon which a nation is organized fixes its destiny, and that of equality is perfect, is universal. It presides in all the operations of the physical world, and it is also the conscious law of the soul—the self-evident dictate of morality, which accurately defines the duty of man to man, and consequently man's rights as man. Besides, the truthful annals of any nation furnish abundant evidence, that its happiness, its greatness, its duration, were always proportionate to the democratic equality in its system of government.

How many nations have had their decline and fall, because the equal rights of the minority were trampled on by the despotism of the majority; or the interests of the many sacrificed to the aristocracy of the few; or the rights and interests of all given up to the monarchy of one? These three kinds of government have figured so frequently and so largely in the ages that have passed away, that their history, through all time to come, can only furnish a resemblance. Like causes produce like effects, and the true philosopher of history will easily discern the principle of equality, or of privilege, working out its inevitable result. The first is regenerative, because it is natural and right; the latter is destructive to society, because it is unnatural and wrong.

What friend of human liberty, civilization, and refinement, can cast his view over the past history of the monarchies and aristocracies of antiquity, and not deplore that they ever existed? What philanthropist can contemplate the oppressions, the cruelties, and injustice inflicted by them on the masses of mankind, and not turn with moral horror from the retrospect?

America is destined for better deeds. It is our unparalleled glory that we have no reminiscences of battle fields, but in defence of humanity, of the oppressed of all nations, of the rights of conscience, the rights of personal enfranchisement. Our annals describe no scenes of horrid carnage, where men were led on by hundreds of thousands to slay one another, dupes and victims to emperors, kings, nobles, demons in the human form called heroes. We have had patriots to defend our homes, our liberties, but no aspirants to crowns or thrones; nor have the American people ever suffered themselves to be led on by wicked ambition to depopulate the land, to spread desolation far and wide, that a human being might be placed on a seat of supremacy.

We have no interest in the scenes of antiquity, only as lessons of avoidance of nearly all their examples. The expansive future is our arena, and for our history. We are entering on its untrodden space, with the truths of God in our minds, beneficent objects in our hearts, and with a clear conscience unsullied by the past. We are the nation of human progress, and who will, what can, set limits to our onward march? Providence is with us, and no earthly power can. We point to the everlasting truth on the first page of our national declaration, and we proclaim to the millions of other lands, that "the gates of hell—" the powers of aristocracy and monarchy—"shall not prevail against it."

The far-reaching, the boundless future will be the era of American greatness. In its magnificent domain of space and time, the nation of many nations is destined to manifest to mankind the excellence of divine principles; to establish on earth the noblest temple ever dedicated to the worship of the Most High—the Sacred and the True. Its floor shall be a hemisphere—its roof the firmament of the star-studded heavens, and its congregation an Union of many Republics, comprising hundreds of happy millions, calling, owning no man master, but governed by God's natural and moral law of equality, the law of brotherhood—of "peace and good will amongst men."

But although the mighty constituent truth upon which our social and political system is founded will assuredly work out the glorious destiny herein shadowed forth, yet there are many untoward circumstances to retard our progress, to procrastinate the entire fruition of the greatest good to the human race. There is a tendency to imitativeness, prevailing amongst our professional and literary men, subversive of originality of thought, and wholly unfavorable to progress. Being in early life devoted to the study of the laws, institutions, and antiquities of other nations, they are far behind the mind and movement of the age in which they live: so much so, that the spirit of improvement, as well as of enfranchisement, exists chiefly in the great masses—the agricultural and mechanical population.

This propensity to imitate foreign nations is absurd and injurious. It is absurd, for we have never yet drawn on our mental resources that we have not found them ample and of unsurpassed excellence; witness our constitutions of government, where we had no foreign ones to imitate. It is injurious, for never have we followed foreign examples in legislation; witness our laws, our charters of monopoly, that we did not inflict evil on ourselves, subverting common right, in violation of common sense and common justice. The halls of legislation and the courts of law in a Republic are necessarily the public schools of the adult population. If, in these institutions, foreign precedents are legislated, and foreign decisions adjudged over again, is it to be wondered at that an imitative propensity predominates amongst professional and business men. Taught to look abroad for the highest standards of law, judicial wisdom, and literary excellence, the native sense is subjugated to a most obsequious idolatry of the tastes, sentiments, and prejudices of Europe. Hence our legislation, jurisprudence, literature, are more reflective of foreign aristocracy than of American democracy.

European governments have plunged themselves in debt, designating burthens on the people "national blessings." Our State Legislatures, humbly imitating their pernicious example, have pawned, bonded the property, labor, and credit of their constituents to the subjects of monarchy. It is by our own labor, and with our own materials, that our internal improvements are constructed, but our British-law-trained legislators have enacted that we shall be in debt for them, paying interest, but never to become owners. With various climates, soils, natural resources, and products, beyond any other country, and producing more real capital annually than any other sixteen millions of people on earth, we are, nevertheless, borrowers, paying tribute to the money powers of Europe.

Our business men have also conned the lesson of example, and devoted themselves body and mind to the promotion of foreign interests. If States can steep themselves in debt, with any propriety in times of peace, why may not merchants import merchandise on credit? If the one can bond the labor and property of generations yet unborn, why may not the other contract debts against the yearly crops and daily labor of their contemporary fellow citizens?

And our literature!—Oh, when will it breathe the spirit of our republican institutions? When will it be imbued with the God-like aspiration of intellectual freedom—the elevating principle of equality? When will it assert *its* national independence, and speak the soul—the heart of the American people? Why cannot our literati comprehend the matchless sublimity of our position amongst the nations of the world—our high destiny—and cease bending the knee to foreign idolatry, false tastes, false doctrines, false principles? When will they be inspired by the magnificent scenery of our own world, imbibe the fresh enthusiasm of a new heaven and a new earth, and soar upon the expanded wings of truth and liberty? Is not nature as original—her truths as captivating—her aspects as various, as lovely, as grand—her Promethean fire as glowing in this, our Western hemisphere, as in that of the East? And above all, is not our private life as morally beautiful and good—is not our public life as politically right, as indicative of the brightest prospects of humanity, and therefore as inspiring of the highest conceptions? Why, then, do our authors aim at no higher degree of merit, than a successful imitation of English writers of celebrity?

But with all the retrograde tendencies of our laws, our judicature, our colleges, our literature, still they are compelled to follow the mighty impulse of the age; they are carried onward by the increasing tide of progress; and though they cast many a longing look behind, they cannot stay the glorious movement of the masses, nor induce them to venerate the rubbish, the prejudices, the superstitions of other times

and other lands, the theocracy of priests, the divine right of kings, the aristocracy of blood, the metaphysics of colleges, the irrational stuff of law libraries. Already the brightest hopes of philanthropy, the most enlarged speculations of true philosophy, are inspired by the indications perceptible amongst the mechanical and agricultural population. There, with predominating influence, beats the vigorous national heart of America, propelling the onward march of the multitude, propagating and extending, through the present and the future, the powerful purpose of soul, which, in the seventeenth century, sought a refuge among savages, and reared in the wilderness the sacred altars of intellectual freedom. This was the seed that produced individual equality, and political liberty, as its natural fruit; and this is our true nationality. American patriotism is not of soil; we are not aborigines, nor of ancestry, for we are of all nations; but it is essentially personal enfranchisement, for "where liberty dwells," said Franklin, the sage of the Revolution, "there is my country."

Such is our distinguishing characteristic, our popular instinct, and never yet has any public functionary stood forth for the rights of conscience against any, or all, sects desirous of predominating over such right, that he was not sustained by the people. And when a venerated patriot of the Revolution appealed to his fellow-citizens against the overshadowing power of a monarch institution, they came in their strength, and the moneyed despot was brought low. Corporate powers and privileges shrink to nothing when brought in conflict against the rights of individuals. Hence it is that our professional, literary, or commercial aristocracy, have no faith in the virtue, intelligence or capability of the people. The latter have never responded to their exotic sentiments nor promoted their views of a strong government irresponsible to the popular majority, to the will of the masses.

Yes, we are the nation of progress, of individual freedom, of universal enfranchisement. Equality of rights is the cynosure of our union of States, the grand exemplar of the correlative equality of individuals; and while truth sheds its effulgence, we cannot retrograde, without dissolving the one and subverting the other. We must onward to the fulfillment of our mission—to the entire development of the principle of our organization—freedom of conscience, freedom of person, freedom of trade and business pursuits, universality of freedom and equality. This is our high destiny, and in nature's eternal, inevitable decree of cause and effect we must accomplish it. All this will be our future history, to establish on earth the moral dignity and salvation of man—the immutable truth and beneficence of God. For this blessed mission to the nations of the world, which are shut out from the life-giving light of truth, has America been chosen; and her high example shall smite unto death the tyranny of kings, hierarchs, and oligarchs, and carry the glad tidings of peace and good will where myriads now endure an existence scarcely more enviable than that of beasts of the field. Who, then, can doubt that our country is destined to be the great nation of futurity?

Source: O'Sullivan, John L. "The Nation of Great Futurity." *The United States Magazine and Democratic Review* VI, no. XXIII (November 1839): 426–430.

MARRIAGE

Most cultures have a formal mechanism for publicly recognizing certain deep emotional bonds between individuals who are not blood-related. In America, as in most Judeo-Christian societies, the term *marriage* is used to denote such relationships. While marriage in America has its roots in religious practice, both the state and federal governments have exerted tight control over it. Laws dictate who can marry and who can officiate over a marriage, and marriages are not recognized by the government until the parties to the marriage obtain a government license. Laws require that parties to a marriage make a public undertaking that the marriage is consensual. Once individuals are married, a new legal regime controls their affairs, governing property ownership, inheritance, and responsibilities for marital children. Precisely because of the very public entanglement of marriage and law, the scope and meaning of marriage has been contested repeatedly throughout American history.

By most accounts, before the arrival of Europeans, Native Americans held marriage ceremonies that formally recognized emotional bonds and alliances. Some of these marriages were couplings between two individuals, both same-sex and opposite sex. Others were group marriages between an older man and younger women, or an older and younger couple.

The arrival of European immigrants brought a different conception that directly connected marriage with property and control. The eminent British jurist William H. Blackstone wrote in 1765, "By marriage, the husband and wife are one person in law: that is, the very being or legal existence of the woman is suspended during the marriage. . . and consolidated into that of the husband" (Blackstone, 430). Under this British family law regime, adopted wholesale by the early colonies, married women in America had no independent legal existence; they were, essentially, denied the rights and responsibilities of citizenship in the new nation.

African American slaves in America were entirely excluded from legal marriage, at least until the early 1700s. Quite simply, enslaved blacks were not allowed to legally marry. However, as slave owners sought ways to stabilize and perpetuate their profits, they hit upon slave marriage as a solution. They reasoned that marriage would lead to reliable reproduction cycles that would better allow them to renew and exploit the labor provided by their slaves. Some marital slave families resided on a single plantation, while others visited spouses at neighboring plantations once or twice a week. Still, these unions were fragile, and slave owners might suddenly separate families if they believed it would lead to economic gain.

By the mid-19th century, there were stirrings of liberation among both women and African Americans that would have profound impacts on marriage laws in America. In 1848, at Seneca Falls, New York, a gathering of women and men drafted the Declaration of Sentiments, charging that man has "made woman, if married, in the eye of the law, civilly dead" (Stanton, 1848). A rallying cry for the first wave of American feminists, the Declaration built on and contributed to the rapid spread of Married Women's Property Acts in states throughout the 19th century, which allowed married women some measure of control over the property of the marriage.

African American marriages also changed profoundly after the Reconstruction period (1865–1877), when the marriages of black Americans were finally recognized by law. Now legitimated, these marriages were also expected to conform to legal strictures regarding marriage—for example, prohibitions on adultery—a situation that was sometimes used against black Americans as a tool of social control by the dominant white culture.

In particular, anti-miscegenation laws that broadly barred mixing of the races through marriage made clear that blacks and whites, as well as Asians, were not yet truly equal with respect to marriage. As late as 1967, when the U.S. Supreme Court issued its landmark decision in *Loving v. Virginia* holding that state restrictions on marriage between blacks and whites violated the equal protection clause of the U.S. Constitution, sixteen states still retained and enforced such laws.

In the late 20th century, gay rights groups modeled their own advocacy efforts to attain marriage equality on the earlier examples provided by American blacks and women. Like those groups, individuals interested in same-sex marriage confronted a legal firewall that excluded them from thousands of federal and state benefits routinely accorded to married couples, from visitation rights to inheritance rights to immigration sponsorship to joint tax returns. Grassroots advocacy on the state level led a number of states, such as New York (2011), to legislatively expand their marriage laws to recognize same-sex marriages. At the same time, in some states, such as Iowa (2009) and Massachusetts (2004), state high courts ruled that state constitutions required marriage equality. The majority of states (e.g., Louisiana [1999] and Alaska [1998]) and the federal government (1996) reacted against marriage equality efforts by adopting new laws defining marriage as exclusively between a man and a woman. Many believe that, just as in *Loving v. Virginia*, the U.S. Supreme Court will ultimately decide whether marriage equality is protected under the federal equal protection clause or whether states have the prerogative to ban same-sex marriages.

While some gay rights groups have decried the gay rights movement's focus on marriage equality to the detriment of other civil rights issues, the fact that many activists see it as a critical equality issue underscores the significant place that marriage holds in American culture. Yet, ironically, while marriage remains a life goal for more than 80 percent of high school students, a Pew Research Center report showed that as of December 2011, just 51 percent of all American adults were actually married. Concerned about increases in non-marital births, some states—with federal support—have initiated modest marriage promotion programs targeting low-income recipients of public benefits on the theory that increased marriage rates will result in decreased poverty. At the same time, American popular culture has retained a fascination with marriages that are still outside of legal bounds, such as the Fundamentalist Mormon polygamous marriage popularized in the Home Box Office television show *Big Love* (2006–2011). In short, the symbolic and cultural significance of marriage in America remains robust, despite the drop in marriage rates.

See also

Feminist Movement; Miscegenation; Mormonism; Reconstruction; Women's Rights Movement (19th century)

MARTHA F. DAVIS

Further Reading

Blackstone, William. 1765–1769. *Commentaries on the Laws of England*. 4 vols. Oxford, UK: Clarendon Press.

Chakkalakal, Tess. 2012. *Novel Bondage: Slavery, Marriage and Freedom in Nineteenth Century America*. Urbana, IL: University of Illinois Press.

Cott, Nancy. 2000. *Public Vows: A History of Marriage and the Nation*. Cambridge, MA: Harvard University Press.

Fry, Richard. 2012. "No Reversal in Decline of Marriage, Pew Research Social & Demographic Trends." http://www.pewsocialtrends.org/2012/11/20/no-reversal-in-decline-of-marriage/. Accessed February 10, 2013.

Stanton, Elizabeth Cady. "The Declaration of Sentiments." http://www.nps.gov/wori/historyculture/declaration-of-sentiments.htm. Accessed February 10, 2013.

Marriage—Primary Document

Introduction

Following emancipation, the federal Freedmen's Bureau was authorized to issue marriage certificates to former slaves who could now legally marry even as states were slow to adjust their laws to these new realities. As the attached document indicates, former slaves Joseph and Mary Province had cohabited for twenty-one years and had a nineteen-year-old son. The formal recognition of families like theirs was an important confirmation of their freedom and citizenship status. The Provinces obtained a certificate of marriage from the Freedmen's Bureau in 1866, one year before Tennessee's state laws were adjusted to recognize such marriages.

Document: Marriage Certificate for Joseph and Mary Province (February 26, 1866)

Bureau Refugees, Freedmen and Abandoned Lands.

By the authority of Circular No. 5, dated Assistant Commissioner's Office Ky. And Tenn., Nashville, Feb. 26, 1866, I certify that I have this day united *Joseph Province* and *Mary Province used to belong to W. Hallem*, colored, in the bonds of matrimony, they having been living together as man and wife for about *Twenty one* years past, and have had, as the result thereof, the following children, viz:

> *Stephen Province Aged about 19 years. Stephen went off with Genl. Wilders command of U.S. Troops in 1863. And was heard from at Louisville Ky soon after Hood's raid to Nashville, probably went by the name of Sanders or Calhoun.*

In witness whereof, I have hereunto set my hand in duplicate at office in Lebanon, Wilson County, Tennessee, April 23, 1866.

S.B.F.C. Barr, Sup't

Wilson County.

> **Source:** National Archives. Available at http://research.archives .gov/description/595017.

Edward R. Murrow reports the evening news on CBS Radio in 1954. Murrow began his career reporting on the radio and influenced American views of World War II with his brilliant reporting from London. His television reporting in the early 1950s set a standard of excellence rarely equalled since. (Library of Congress)

MASS COMMUNICATION

Mass communication refers to how groups and individuals reach large portions of the population and shape the views and actions of those they are reaching. Throughout American history, mass communication has taken a variety of forms, changing with population growth, continental expansion, and, perhaps most importantly, technology. It also has evolved with the fields that comprise it, including advertising and journalism from their beginnings, and, eventually, broadcasting.

The most critical events in American mass communication may well have taken place long before European settlement of the United States. Between 3,000 and 5,000 years ago, Egyptians developed hieroglyphics and papyrus, thus devising both a way to impart information and a means of distributing it more widely than in just one place. The Chinese began printing about 1,000 years ago, and the efforts of Johannes Gutenburg and others in the 15th century led to

the growth of printing presses, which sped and eased the dissemination of information, from Bibles to textbooks.

Although Benjamin Harris's *Publick Occurrences, Both Foreign and Domestic* became the first colonial newspaper when he began publishing it in Boston in 1690, the honor of being the founding fathers of American mass communication may belong to the Franklins. In 1721, James Franklin started printing *The New England Courant* and his younger brother Benjamin served as his apprentice before going on to Philadelphia, where he printed newspapers, published *Poor Richard's Almanack*, and helped found the public library—all important to promoting mass communication by making information available and disseminating it widely. While Benjamin Franklin represented colonial interests in England during the 1760s and early 1770s, the colonists increasingly turned to existing means of mass communications by writing letters, posting flyers, contributing to colonial newspapers, and gathering in coffeehouses. Pamphlets, and thus the combination of knowing how to talk to the masses and the ability to print material for them to read, played a large role, and none larger than *Common Sense*, written by Thomas Paine and appearing early in 1776, followed by his *Crisis* series. Hundreds of thousands of colonists read and took inspiration from him. John Adams commented that Paine had said nothing that he had not already said, but Paine put it in a way that the common people could more easily understand and appreciate, making him a pioneer of American mass communications.

As the 19th century unfolded, technology produced the means of truly communicating to the masses. The invention of the telegraph, perfected by Samuel F. B. Morse in 1844, sped the transmission of information. Advances in transportation—steamboats, improved roads, and railroads—eased the distribution of newspapers, magazines, and books. In the 1830s and 1840s, a group of New York City publishers and editors devised what became known as the "penny press" because they sold their dailies for 1 cent. They sought to reach not the elite, but the increasingly powerful masses, which grew the "common man's" participation in the political process. At the same time, industrialization and the rise of a market society were bringing more people from farms to cities and into contact with one another, and inspiring entrepreneurs to find ways to attract business through mass advertising. James Gordon Bennett's *New York Herald* specialized in news coverage, as did Horace Greeley's *New York Tribune*, but Greeley also opened his columns to a wide array of thinkers and reformers ranging from dietary advisor Sylvester Graham (he proposed that his followers take better care of themselves by eating a certain cracker) to a European correspondent, Karl Marx. Perhaps as significant as Greeley's New York City circulation, he also produced a weekly edition distributed throughout the country, and his political views—first Whig and then Republican, always antislavery—had an impact well beyond the East, encouraging more ideological unity among Northerners against the "peculiar institution" and during wartime. Advertisers also saw opportunity in being able to reach a diverse urban market, but also take a more specialized approach in weekly newspapers and magazines.

The Civil War fostered new technologies, and continuing urban expansion, population growth, and innovations after the Civil War also continued to revolutionize mass communication. With the transatlantic cable and telephone making communication ever more instantaneous, in the late 19th century, publishers like Joseph Pulitzer and William Randolph Hearst pioneered what became known as "Yellow Journalism" due to their fight over who would publish a color comic strip; more important, "Yellow Journalism" represented what would later be associated with tabloids and sensationalism. Magazines like *Harper's* and *Frank Leslie's Illustrated Newspaper* benefited from inventions like George Eastman's development of photographic film and Congress granting them discount postal rates. Magazines also helped lead Americans toward a different political point of view: early in the 20th century, magazines published muckraking journalists and their reports, most notably Lincoln Steffens's investigations of urban corruption that led to his book *Shame of the Cities*, and Ida Tarbell's probe into Standard Oil that affected and reflected new attitudes toward antitrust laws. Just as the rise of mass communication helped unite Northerners before and during the Civil War, the public's access to muckrakers and their information helped foster the Progressive movement. The invention of motion pictures also provided a crucial means of mass communication, and even had a political impact: D. W. Griffith's filming of *Birth of a Nation* cemented for many Americans a view of American history that took decades for historians to undo; during the Great Depression, films about gangsters who had been poor and ended up robbing from the rich gave organized crime a far better reputation than it deserved.

The inventions by Guglielmo Marconi and Nikolai Tesla, who perfected wireless transmission in the late 19th and early 20th centuries, bore fruit with the beginnings of radio in the United States in the 1920s. This was another important step in mass communications. Americans could instantly hear others in distant cities. Federal licensing of 50,000-watt "clear channel" stations meant that some radio stations could be heard across the country: WSM-AM-650 could be heard in thirty-eight states, for example, and powerhouses like WLW-AM-710 in Cincinnati and WGN-AM-720 in Chicago broadcast well beyond their communities. David Sarnoff and Radio Corporation of America formed the National Broadcasting Company with two networks (the latter eventually became the American Broadcasting Company), while young entrepreneur William S. Paley bought the fledgling Columbia Broadcasting System and expanded it—and the rise of these networks meant that the same forms of entertainment reached homes across the country, while public opinion surveys and rating services helped determine what proved most popular with consumers. The expansion of major advertising agencies such as New York–based BBD&O (Batten, Barton, Durstein, and Osborne) joined with radio and its rating measurements to make New York City the nation's media capital and thus a trendsetter and tastemaker in mass communication.

Radio and film demonstrated the power of mass communications. During the 1930s, Franklin Roosevelt delivered a series of "Fireside Chats," becoming the first president to use radio regularly and effectively, but demagogues like Father Charles Coughlin, whose radio show devolved from supporting FDR to making anti-Semitic pronouncements, served as an example of the less admirable uses of genuinely mass communication. As World War II spread in Europe and to the United States, the broadcasts of Edward R. Murrow on CBS made Americans more aware of the threats they faced from foreign dictators than they could have been without being able to listen to his broadcasts. In the same period, movies (much like radio, but with the important difference of being visual) became important not just as entertainment, but also for introducing Americans to different cultures to which they had not been previously exposed—and, during the war, encouraging support for the war effort. Other new forms of journalism also promoted the idea of mass communication: in 1923, Yale classmates Briton Hadden and Henry Luce founded *Time*, a weekly newsmagazine, and Luce later followed with *Life*, which pioneered in photojournalism, and *Fortune*, which covered business—all widely distributed, and all highly influential on the general public and on political and business leaders.

Ultimately, a newer technology reduced the impact of radio, film, and magazines: television. First developed in the 1920s, it showed signs of advancement in the late 1930s and early 1940s with the first sports telecasts and the first television commercial aired in 1941 on NBC's experimental station. World War II slowed its march, but with the war's end, television became the newest mass medium. Many criticized its use for entertainment purposes—radio comedian

Fred Allen said television was called a medium because so little on it was well done, and Federal Communications Commissioner Newton Minow described its programming in the early 1960s as a "vast wasteland." But live coverage of daily news and special events as well as documentaries provided Americans with instantaneous communications and new means of learning about the world around them, and affected public opinion; television showed Senator Joseph McCarthy's hearings about alleged communist infiltration in the U.S. Army and helped end his reign, and news video of the violence directed at civil rights advocates helped that movement gain support and achieve legislative changes. Also, "entertainment" shows over the years have addressed or even shaped social issues, from Mary Richards of *The Mary Tyler Moore Show* encouraging young women to pursue careers without seeking permanent relationships to *M*A*S*H* demonstrating the horrors and stupidity of war—and such shows have affected fashion trends and public opinion in a variety of ways.

In the late 20th and early 21st centuries, mass communication took on still other new forms affected by further technological advances. Joining the major television networks were numerous smaller networks and cable systems that included a variety of different programs and programming forms. Similarly, the rise of the Internet meant that the masses could communicate and be communicated with on a different level than they had before. Such sites as Facebook and Google could collect information that would help determine what advertisements would appear on the computer screen—a sign of how mass communication has an impact on our daily lives, and how it can be both for the masses and catering to the individual.

See also

African American Civil Rights Movement; Anticommunism, Anti-Semitism; Antislavery; Consumerism; Information Age; Internet Nation; Muckraking; Pop Culture; Progressivism; Yellow Journalism

MICHAEL S. GREEN

Further Reading

Brinkley, Alan. 2010. *The Publisher: Henry Luce and His American Century*. New York: Vintage Books.
Emery, Michael, Edwin Emery, and Nancy Roberts. 1997. *The Press and America: An Interpretive History of the Mass Media*. 9th ed. Upper Saddle River, NJ: Pearson.

Howe, Daniel Walker. 2007. *What Hath God Wrought: The Transformation of America, 1815–1848*. New York: Oxford University Press.

Mass Communication—Primary Document

Introduction

In 1958, the award-winning broadcast journalist Edward R. Murrow spoke to the Radio-Television News Directors Association convention in Chicago. He had been fighting his employers at CBS for several years over what he could say and show on the air. His speech, excerpted here, reflects his concerns over the uses and abuses of a popular medium of mass communication, and its impact.

Document: Edward R. Murrow's Speech to the Radio-Television News Directors Association (October 15, 1958)

This just might do nobody any good. At the end of this discourse a few people may accuse this reporter of fouling his own comfortable nest, and your organization may be accused of having given hospitality to heretical and even dangerous thoughts. But the elaborate structure of networks, advertising agencies and sponsors will not be shaken or altered. It is my desire, if not my duty, to try to talk to you journeymen with some candor about what is happening to radio and television.

I have no technical advice or counsel to offer those of you who labor in this vineyard that produces words and pictures. You will forgive me for not telling you that instruments with which you work are miraculous, that your responsibility is unprecedented or that your aspirations are frequently frustrated. It is not necessary to remind you that the fact that your voice is amplified to the degree where it reaches from one end of the country to the other does not confer upon you greater wisdom or understanding than you possessed when your voice reached only from one end of the bar to the other. All of these things you know.

You should also know at the outset that, in the manner of witnesses before Congressional committees, I appear here voluntarily—by invitation—that I am an employee of the Columbia Broadcasting System, that I am neither an officer nor a director of that corporation and that these remarks are of a "do-it-yourself" nature. If what I have to say is irresponsible, then I alone am responsible for the saying of it. Seeking neither approbation from my employers, nor new sponsors, nor acclaim from the critics of radio and television, I cannot well be disappointed. Believing that potentially the commercial system of broadcasting as practiced in this country is the best and freest yet devised, I have decided to express my concern about what I believe to be happening to radio and television. These instruments have been good to me beyond my due. There exists in my mind no reasonable grounds for personal complaint. I have no feud, either with my employers, any sponsors, or with the professional critics of radio and television. But I am seized with an abiding fear regarding what these two instruments are doing to our society, our culture and our heritage.

Our history will be what we make it. And if there are any historians about 50 or 100 years from now, and there should be preserved the kinescopes for one week of all three networks, they will there find recorded in black and white, or color, evidence of decadence, escapism and insulation from the realities of the world in which we live. I invite your attention to the television schedules of all networks between the hours of 8 and 11 p.m., Eastern Time. Here you will find only fleeting and spasmodic reference to the fact that this nation is in mortal danger. There are, it is true, occasional informative programs presented in that intellectual ghetto on Sunday afternoons. But during the daily peak viewing periods, television in the main insulates us from the realities of the world in which we live. If this state of affairs continues, we may alter an advertising slogan to read: LOOK NOW, PAY LATER.

For surely we shall pay for using this most powerful instrument of communication to insulate the citizenry from the hard and demanding realities which must be faced if we are to survive. I mean the word survive literally. If there were to be a competition in indifference, or perhaps in insulation from reality, then Nero and his fiddle, Chamberlain and his umbrella, could not find a place on an early afternoon sustaining show. If Hollywood were to run out of Indians, the program schedules would be mangled beyond all recognition. Then some courageous soul with a small budget might be able to do a documentary telling what, in fact, we have done—and are still doing—to the Indians in this country. But that would be unpleasant. And we must at all costs shield the sensitive citizens from anything that is unpleasant.

I am entirely persuaded that the American public is more reasonable, restrained and more mature than most of our industry's program planners believe. Their fear of controversy is not warranted by the evidence. I have reason to know, as do many of you, that when the evidence on a controversial subject is fairly and calmly presented, the public recognizes it for what it is—an effort to illuminate rather than to agitate....

Recently, network spokesmen have been disposed to complain that the professional critics of television have been "rather beastly." There have been hints that somehow competition for the advertising dollar has caused the critics of print to gang up on television and radio. This reporter has no desire to defend the critics. They have space in which to do that on their own behalf. But it remains a fact that the newspapers and magazines are the only instruments of mass communication which remain free from sustained and regular critical comment. If the network spokesmen are so anguished about what appears in print, let them come forth and engage in a little sustained and regular comment regarding newspapers and magazines. It is an ancient and sad fact that most people in network television, and radio, have an exaggerated regard for what appears in print. And there have been cases where executives have refused to make even private comment on a program for which they were responsible until they heard the reviews in print. This is hardly an exhibition of confidence.

The oldest excuse of the networks for their timidity is their youth. Their spokesmen say, "We are young; we have not developed the traditions nor acquired the experience of the older media." If they but knew it, they are building those traditions, creating those precedents every day. Each time they yield to a voice from Washington or any political pressure, each time they eliminate something that might offend some section of the community, they are creating their own body of precedent and tradition. They are, in fact, not content to be "half safe."

Nowhere is this better illustrated than by the fact that the chairman of the Federal Communications Commission publicly prods broadcasters to engage in their legal right to editorialize. Of course, to undertake an editorial policy, overt and clearly labeled, and obviously unsponsored, requires a station or a network to be responsible. Most stations today probably do not have the manpower to assume this responsibility, but the manpower could be recruited. Editorials would not be profitable; if they had a cutting edge, they might even offend. It is much easier, much less troublesome, to use the money-making machine of television and radio merely as a conduit through which to channel anything that is not libelous, obscene or defamatory. In that way one has the illusion of power without responsibility....

One of the basic troubles with radio and television news is that both instruments have grown up as an incompatible combination of show business, advertising and news. Each of the three is a rather bizarre and demanding profession. And when you get all three under one roof, the dust never settles. The top management of the networks, with a few notable exceptions, has been trained in advertising, research, sales or show business. But by the nature of the corporate structure, they also make the final and crucial decisions having to do with news and public affairs. Frequently they have neither the time nor the competence to do this. It is not easy for the same small group of men to decide whether to buy a new station for millions of dollars, build a new building, alter the rate card, buy a new Western, sell a soap opera, decide what defensive line to take in connection with the latest Congressional inquiry, how much money to spend on promoting a new program, what additions or deletions should be made in the existing covey or clutch of vice-presidents, and at the same time—frequently on the same long day—to give mature, thoughtful consideration to the manifold problems that confront those who are charged with the responsibility for news and public affairs.

Sometimes there is a clash between the public interest and the corporate interest. A telephone call or a letter from the proper quarter in Washington is treated rather more seriously than a communication from an irate but not politically potent viewer. It is tempting enough to give away a little air time for frequently irresponsible and unwarranted utterances in an effort to temper the wind of criticism ....

So it seems that we cannot rely on philanthropic support or foundation subsidies; we cannot follow the "sustaining route"—the networks cannot pay all the freight—and the F.C.C. cannot or will not discipline those who abuse the facilities that belong to the public. What, then, is the answer? Do we merely stay in our comfortable nests, concluding that the obligation of these instruments has been discharged when we work at the job of informing the public for a minimum of time? Or do we believe that the preservation of the Republic is a seven-day-a-week job, demanding more awareness, better skills and more perseverance than we have yet contemplated?

I am frightened by the imbalance, the constant striving to reach the largest possible audience for everything; by the absence of a sustained study of the state of the nation. Heywood Broun once said, "No body politic is healthy until it begins to itch." I would like television to produce some itching pills rather than this endless outpouring of tranquilizers. It can be done. Maybe it won't be, but it could. Let us not shoot the wrong piano player. Do not be deluded into believing that the titular heads of the networks control what appears on their networks. They all have better taste. All are responsible to stockholders, and in my experience all are honorable men. But they must schedule what they can sell in the public market.

And this brings us to the nub of the question. In one sense it rather revolves around the phrase heard frequently along Madison Avenue: The Corporate Image. I am not precisely sure what this phrase means, but I would imagine that it reflects a desire on the part of the corporations who pay the advertising bills to have the public image, or believe that they are not merely bodies with no souls, panting in pursuit of elusive dollars. They would like us to believe that they can distinguish between the public good and the private or corporate gain. So the question is this: Are the big corporations who pay the freight for radio and television programs wise to use that time exclusively for the sale of goods and services? Is it in their own interest and that of the stockholders so to do? The sponsor of an hour's television program is not buying

merely the six minutes devoted to commercial message. He is determining, within broad limits, the sum total of the impact of the entire hour. If he always, invariably, reaches for the largest possible audience, then this process of insulation, of escape from reality, will continue to be massively financed, and its apologist will continue to make winsome speeches about giving the public what it wants, or "letting the public decide ...."

Let us have a little competition. Not only in selling soap, cigarettes and automobiles, but in informing a troubled, apprehensive but receptive public. Why should not each of the 20 or 30 big corporations which dominate radio and television decide that they will give up one or two of their regularly scheduled programs each year, turn the time over to the networks and say in effect: "This is a tiny tithe, just a little bit of our profits. On this particular night we aren't going to try to sell cigarettes or automobiles; this is merely a gesture to indicate our belief in the importance of ideas." The networks should, and I think would, pay for the cost of producing the program. The advertiser, the sponsor, would get name credit but would have nothing to do with the content of the program. Would this blemish the corporate image? Would the stockholders object? I think not. For if the premise upon which our pluralistic society rests, which as I understand it is that if the people are given sufficient undiluted information, they will then somehow, even after long, sober second thoughts, reach the right decision—if that premise is wrong, then not only the corporate image but the corporations are done for ....

This instrument can teach, it can illuminate; yes, and it can even inspire. But it can do so only to the extent that humans are determined to use it to those ends. Otherwise it is merely wires and lights in a box. There is a great and perhaps decisive battle to be fought against ignorance, intolerance and indifference. This weapon of television could be useful.

Source: American Masters. Available at http://www.pbs.org/wnet/americanmasters/education/lesson39_organizer1.html.

MASS PRODUCTION

Meatpacking

Many Americans intuit automaker Henry Ford as the founder of mass production. Indeed, he coined the phrase, by which he meant the replication of a product in huge quantities, in the 1920s. But in important ways the meatpacking industry, anticipating Ford, was a mass producer of beef, pork, and chicken, and so serves as a useful place to start a discussion of mass production.

In early America, meatpacking was a small-scale and not entirely coherent process, but it matured after the Civil War. Mechanization, an essential feature of mass production, transformed meatpacking into a year-round, rapid technological process. The industry emerged as the first U.S. economic activity to use an assembly line of sorts, better called a disassembly line because as a carcass moved from station to station, each worker dismembered part of it for packaging and transit. It is not true, therefore, that Ford invented the assembly line.

In 1850, U.S. meatpackers produced $12 million of beef and pork. By 1919, the amount had risen to $4.2 billion. In its heyday, the meatpacking industry employed more people than any other activity, the automobile industry surpassing it in the 20th century. The spread of railroads throughout the United States also hastened the shipping of large amounts of meat, and the use of the refrigerated car after the Civil War made possible the production and transit of mass quantities of beef and pork. Chicago, and to a lesser extent Saint Louis and Cincinnati, arose in the second half of the 19th century as centers of the mass production of beef and pork. As would be true of Ford Motor Company, employees in the meatpacking industry were largely unskilled and taught to perform a very narrow range of tasks. Many immigrants, particularly from Eastern Europe, toiled for little pay. The disassembly line moved quickly, setting an exhausting pace and precipitating numerous injuries. Because of mechanization, by 1880, five workers could dismember 80 carcasses per hour and by 1890 120 carcasses per hour. With these gains in productivity, a meatpacker could process a single carcass for only 42 cents in labor costs.

Yet the industry was not without critics. Perhaps the most influential was the American journalist Upton Sinclair, whose novel, *The Jungle* (1906), detailed the filth, squalor, and miserable working conditions in the meatpacking industry. Sinclair hoped his exposé would provoke a backlash against meatpackers' terrible treatment of workers. Instead, Americans, convinced that their meat was unsafe to eat, demanded that government regulate the wholesomeness of their beef and pork, and President Theodore Roosevelt and Congress created new agencies to do just that.

Henry Ford and the Apogee of Mass Production

Ford visited meatpackers, absorbing their methods of mass production, including the assembly line. Despite the contributions of the meatpackers, many historians name Ford the exemplar of mass production.

Not particularly well educated, Henry Ford held a series of temporary jobs as a youth. As early as 1891, Ford was drawn to the nascent automobile and began tinkering with it. For a time he raced cars, an avocation at which he excelled. With

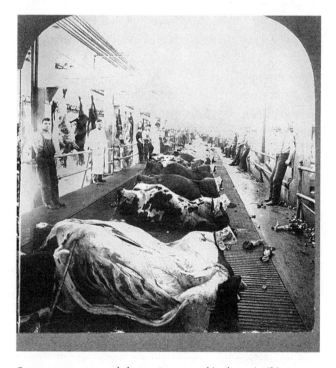

Carcasses on a conveyor belt at an Armour packing house in Chicago, ca. 1909, were converted into cuts of meat distributed throughout the region. Only a few years before, the publication of Upton Sinclair's novel *The Jungle* helped inspire federal laws requiring the inspection of food like this. (Library of Congress)

the creation of Ford Motor Company in Detroit, Ford vowed to price the automobile within the means of the average American. This goal required the adoption of the methods of mass production because the profit from a single car would be small, but aggregated over millions of sales, Ford stood to profit handsomely.

In 1908, he priced the new Model T at $850, a competitive price, but he believed he could do better. In 1913, he introduced the assembly line to quicken production. As was true regarding the meatpackers, labor on the assembly line was unskilled and performed a narrow range of tasks. Yet Ford broke with tradition by paying $5 per day and hiring African Americans. One should note, however, that the pay was not automatic. Ford established a sociology department to scrutinize the daily lives of workers. Only those who lived up to his ideals of clean living earned $5 per day. By 1916, the Model T cost only $360. Demand soared and Ford became America's first mass producer of the automobile. To mass-produce the automobile ever more cheaply, Ford simplified the design and construction of the Model T. A standardizer, Ford, once he had found success with the Model T, produced no other type of car for several years. He painted every car black because black paint dried fastest. He used interchangeable parts as innovators had done before him.

Sales grew accordingly. In 1911, the Ford Motor Company sold nearly 40,000 Model Ts, in 1913, 182,311, in 1917, 740,770, and in 1921, more than 1 million. By then, more than half of all cars purchased in the United States were Model Ts. By 1927, the last year of production, Ford had sold more than 15 million Model Ts during its long and celebrated tenure.

Yet Ford, and mass production, had their critics. Perhaps the most influential or at least popular was actor Charlie Chaplin, whose 1936 film *Modern Times* emphasized the dehumanizing repetitiveness of the assembly line. Mass production turned workers into automatons.

Because the automobile, thanks to Ford, was ubiquitous, it affected the daily lives of Americans. The automobile allowed people to live farther from work and quickened the move from city to suburb, particularly after World War II. In the early days of the automobile, physicians used it to make house calls. Families took Sunday drives after church and to vacation destinations. Young men and women used the automobile, as they had used the bicycle, to flee from parental supervision. They parked at a secluded spot and engaged in intimate moments. Banks, restaurants, and even funeral homes all provided their customers with drive-in service. Mass production had helped create mass consumption.

The Factory Farm

Modern agribusiness, known in some circles as factory farming, may be the most enduring legacy of mass production. The factory farm combines the techniques of mass production on a grand scale and of science and technology. The humble tomato may serve as an example. Machines shake tomato vines, causing them to shed their fruit when still green. Farmers follow this procedure to produce a hard, tough tomato that will withstand rough handling and last longer at the grocery store. This trade comes at the expense of flavor and nutrition. Once gathered, green tomatoes are sprayed with ethylene gas, which reddens them to give tomatoes the appearance, if not the reality, of ripeness. Attendant businesses—restaurants, grocers, pizza joints—all depend on the tomato, a connection to be explored later.

Like Ford and the Model T, agribusiness simplifies farming by mass-producing a small number of commodities: corn and soybeans in the Corn Belt and wheat on the Great Plains. One author has called U.S. agribusiness "assembly-line farming," as if to strengthen the connection with the auto industry (Miller, 16). The use of fertilizers, herbicides, insecticides, and fungicides on a large scale minimizes the cost of labor, a tenet of mass production. The reliance of petrochemicals makes agribusiness reliant on fossil fuels. Another way of minimizing crops is the planting of genetically modified (GM) crops. U.S. agrochemical company Monsanto has engineered varieties of soybeans and corn that do not die when exposed to the herbicide Roundup, which Monsanto also owns. The farmer need only spray his or her field with Roundup to kill all weeds without harm to his or her corn and soybeans. No hand weeding is necessary.

So productive are America's large farms that they exported 161,000 tons of meat in 1960 and 4.5 million tons in 2006. In the United States, large farms mass-produce 74 percent of chickens, 68 percent of eggs, 50 percent of pork, and 43 percent of beef. North Carolina alone mass-produces more than 10 million pigs per year. As a result of these numbers, stockmen must rid their farms of 20 million tons of manure per year. The mass producers of poultry house up to 70,000 chickens in a single building, almost all of them infected with *Escherichia coli* bacteria. The American diet, if it is moving from beef and pork to chicken, will only encourage the production of ever-larger numbers of chickens. In 2008, U.S. factory farms mass-produced 11 billion livestock, 300 million of them being chickens and 70 million of them being pigs.

Advocates of agribusiness believe that the mass production of food is the most efficient way to feed a planet of some 7 billion people. As population rises still higher, agribusiness must produce ever more food. Yet critics, appealing to the Jeffersonian vision of the United States as a nation of small farms, are uncomfortable with the mass production of food, sure that it ruins the environment and abuses livestock. Others note that the preoccupation with corn and soybeans provides cheap calories and protein but little else in the way of nutrients. Concentration should be on growing vegetables. The mass production of food has led many Americans to become obese, making them more at risk for diabetes, heart disease, and cancer. Others charge that the mass production of food is wasteful and unhealthy. Too many Americans eat too many fatty meats.

The McDonaldization of America

One scholar refers to McDonald's as a "fast food factory" (Ritzer, 40). He calls "McDonaldization" a phenomenon by which the methods of mass production have come to dominate the United States (Ritzer, 1). The tomato found a buyer among fast-food restaurants, among them McDonalds. As early as 1937, brothers Mac and Dick McDonald, in the midst of the Great Depression, opened their first fast-food restaurant, focusing on assembly line methods of production and standardized, limited menus. They broke cooking into a step-by-step process. Each worker performed one step in the process. In 1955, amid the rise of mass consumption, entrepreneur Ray Kroc bought his first McDonald's franchise.

By 2010, McDonald's recorded $24.1 billion in revenues and $4.9 billion in profits, making McDonald's the face of mass-produced fast food. By that year, McDonald's served 64 million customers per day and had 14,000 franchises in the United States. Even the most remote location in the United States is no more than 107 miles from a McDonald's. Saturating television with commercials, McDonald's stokes consumerism, an essential feature of mass production, and other fast-food companies have done the same. The Big Mac, like the Model T, is a uniform commodity mass-produced by the same standardized methods.

Labor, like workers in meatpacking and Ford, is unskilled and often young and part time. McDonald's labor is rock bottom cheap, in part because part-time workers receive no medical benefits. Like Ford, McDonald's has resisted the encroachment of unions.

It would be difficult to find an American who has never visited a McDonald's, so vast is the company's reach. A poll of young students revealed that 96 percent were familiar with the character Ronald McDonald. Only Santa Claus had greater name recognition. So ubiquitous is McDonald's that the Pentagon, New York's Times Square, and the Grand Canyon all have franchises. The company makes no secret of its desire to control every aspect of the mass production of fast food. In theory at least, this mentality should cause the extinction of Burger King, Kentucky Fried Chicken, and others—even Starbucks, whose coffee must compete against McDonald's brew. Indeed, coffee is a good example of worldwide McDonaldization. Grown in the tropics, coffee is a staple on some large farms, which pay workers very little, allowing McDonald's to acquire coffee beans (coffee is not a true bean) cheaply. Keeping costs low, one may recall, is a tenet of mass production. Like meatpacking and Ford, McDonald's pursues efficiency as a method to lower costs still farther.

Standardization, a tenet of mass production, means that McDonald's food will be the same no matter where it is purchased. McDonald's gives every customer the same experience. If an Egg McMuffin is not a delicacy, neither is it tasteless. The consumer walks away satiated. Even the worker, performing the same tasks ad infinitum, is a standardized, interchangeable part. One critic notes that a standardized, limited menu and uncomfortable seats cause diners to eat quickly and leave, opening space for still more customers. As meatpackers and Ford saw so clearly in the late 19th and early 20th centuries, and even in a 21st century society that many call postindustrial, mass production entails mass consumption, and both continue.

See also

Agrarianism; Capitalism; Consumerism; Fordism; Industrial Revolution

CHRISTOPHER CUMO

Further Reading

Batchelor, Ray. 1994. *Henry Ford: Mass Production, Modernism and Design.* Manchester and New York: Manchester University Press.

Miller, Debra A., ed. 2010. *Factory Farming.* Detroit, MI: Greenhaven Press.

Ritzer, George. 2013. *The McDonaldization of Society.* Los Angeles: SAGE.

Skaggs, Jimmy M. 1986. *Prime Cut: Livestock Raising and Meatpacking in the United States, 1607–1983.* College Station, TX: Texas A & M University Press.

Mass Production—Primary Document

Introduction

In 1916, John F. Dodge and Horace E. Dodge sued the Ford Motor Company and Henry Ford, claiming that he should have provided more shareholder dividends to them instead of cutting the price of his Model T. The Dodge brothers won their lawsuit, prompting Ford to cash out his stockholders within the next few years so that he could more easily control his production, prices, and workers. The transcript of Ford's responses to questions from Elliott G. Stevenson, the attorney for the Dodges, discusses his business plan and the role of mass production in it.

Document: Testimony of Henry Ford in Lawsuit Brought by John F. and Horace E. Dodge (1916)

Stevenson: To what extent have you considered the necessity for increased facilities for production of cars?

Ford: We expect to increase it double.

Stevenson: To double; that is, you produced 500,000 cars, with the old plant, as we speak of it, as up to July 31st, 1916?

Ford: Yes, sir.

Stevenson: And you are duplicating that plant, or more than duplicating it?

Ford: About duplicating it.

Stevenson: Your policy is to increase the production to a million cars per annum?

Ford: Yes, sir.

Stevenson: Yes. You are not satisfied with producing five hundred thousand cars per annum?

Ford: The demand was not satisfied.

Stevenson: The demand was not satisfied?

Ford: No.

Stevenson: Do you mean that the Ford Motor Company during the year 1915 and '16, when it produced and sold 500,000 cars, could not meet the demand?

Ford: Could not quite meet the demand; and, besides, we left the price—

Stevenson: What is that?

Ford: We left the price as it was the preceding car [*sic*].

Stevenson: That is, you left the price in 1915 and '16 the same as the year 1913 and '14?

Ford: Left the price the same in 1916.

Stevenson: What?

Ford: We left the price the same in 1916 as we did in 1915.

Stevenson: Your fiscal year ends July 31st, 1916?

Ford: Yes, sir.

Stevenson: So that year would include from July 31st, 1915, to July 31st, 1916?

Ford: Yes, sir.

Stevenson: And you left the price of the car—

Ford: Yes, sir.

Stevenson: The same for 1915–16 as for 1914–15?

Ford: Yes; for the purpose of accumulating money to make these extensions.

Stevenson: You found that even with the old price, and the increased production to 500,000 cars a year, you were unable to keep up with the demand for the car?

Ford: Just about.

Stevenson: Just about?

Ford: Yes.

Stevenson: So far as your experience of 1915 and '16 was concerned, you had good reason to believe that you could duplicate that production and sell it at the same price during the next year, didn't you?

Ford: Yes, but that isn't our policy.

Stevenson: Well, that is, you are satisfied you could do that?

Ford: No, we couldn't do it.

Stevenson: What is that?

Ford: No, we couldn't do it; not keep the same price.

Stevenson: Not, and produce the same number of cars?

Ford: Not and keep the same price.

Stevenson: Why not?

Ford: Because the price was too high.

Stevenson: Well, you could not meet the demand the year before, you say?

Ford: That has been always our policy, to reduce the price.

Stevenson: You said, in answer to my question, that you produced 500,000 cars, and that they did not meet the demand; was that true, or wasn't it?

Ford: When?

Stevenson: For the year 1915 and '16?

Ford: I don't know as to '15 and 16; I don't know anything about it.

Stevenson: The year ending the 31st of July, 1916; that is the end of your fiscal year, is it?

Ford: Yes, sir.

Stevenson: I mean the year preceding that?

Ford: The year preceding that?

Stevenson: Yes, the year that this financial statement that we have referred to, covered and represented.

Ford: 1916 was the financial statement.

Stevenson: Do you call that the 1916 business?

Ford: Yes.

Stevenson: We will call it the 1916 business; then, for the year of 1916, you produced 500,000 cars, and you sold them?

Ford: Yes, sir.

Stevenson: And you said that didn't meet the demand, those 500,000 cars?

Ford: Not quite.

Stevenson: Not quite; so that you had no reason to believe, from the experience of 1916, that you could not sell 500,000 more cars in 1917?

Ford: No.

Stevenson: At the same price, had you?

Ford: Yes, sir, we did.

Stevenson: What reason did you have?

Ford: The price was too high.

Stevenson: Why was the price too high, if you were able to sell them?

Ford: Because we looked ahead to know what we could sell the next year.

Stevenson: How could you know what you could sell the next year?

Ford: Just from the way we run our business.

Stevenson: Tell us that secret, how you judge, when you were able to do it in 1916, you were not able to meet the demand, that you could not do it the next year?

Ford: The only thing that makes anything not sell is because the price is too high.

Stevenson: You say you do not think it is right to make so much profits? What is this business being continued for, and why is it being enlarged?

Ford: To do as much as possible for everybody concerned.

Stevenson: What do you mean by "doing as much good as possible"?

Ford: To make money and use it, give employment, and send out the car where the people can use it.

Stevenson: Is that all? Haven't you said that you had money enough yourself, and you were going to run the Ford Motor Company thereafter to employ just as many people as you could, to give them the benefits of the high wages that you paid, and to give the public the benefit of a low priced car?

Ford: I suppose I have, and incidentally make money.

Stevenson: Incidentally make money?

Ford: Yes, sir.

Stevenson: But your controlling feature, so far as your policy, since you have got all the money you want, is to employ a great army of men at high wages, to reduce the selling price of your car, so that a lot of people can buy it at a cheap price, and give everybody a car that wants one?

Ford: If you give all that, the money will fall into your hands; you can't get out of it.

Source: State of Michigan. Circuit Court of Wayne County. Transcript of the Testimony of Henry Ford. *John F. and Horace E. Dodge v. Ford Motor Co., Henry Ford, et. al.* No. 56660 (1916).

MERCANTILISM

This economic theory was particularly influential in early modern Europe, and had significant effects on the development of the thirteen colonies that became the United States and other New World colonies that later became part of the United States. Mercantilism provided one of the intellectual theories behind the establishment and governance of European colonies in the Americas, the West Indies, and the Far East from the late 15th through the early 19th centuries. Mercantile theory stipulated that each nation should seek to find a favorable balance of trade with the rest of the world by increasing domestic production, encouraging exports, and reducing imports. The amount of wealth available in the world, as measured in specie and bullion, was a fixed quantity. Therefore, a favorable balance of trade strengthened country, while a negative balance of trade weakened the state. Colonies reinforced this system by providing a low-cost source of raw materials and a closed market for the exports of the home country. In theory, mercantilism created a closed economic system for each empire, but this theory suffered from inconsistent enforcement of trade laws and the opposing economic interests of the home country and the colonies.

Trade in scare commodities flourished between the near east and Italy through the 13th and 14th centuries. Control of that trade was a source of wealth. The Spanish discovery of gold and silver in the new world, combined with the trading experience of the Italian city-states, helped create a fundamental reassessment of the medieval economy. For the first time, the economic interests of a kingdom now encompassed a multicontinental empire. In order to ensure that the proceeds of colonization only benefited Spain, bullion exports became a crown monopoly. A percentage was paid directly to the treasury, while the rest was heavily regulated in order to prevent other European empires such as France or England from benefiting from trade within the Spanish Empire. The close links between trade and national authority structures was a feature of the mercantile system; in many ways trade existed for the economic benefit of the crown. Early expressions of the mercantile theory appear as early as 1581. In *A Discourse of the Common Weal of This Realm of ENGLAND*, "W.S." hypothesized that the prosperity of England was dependent upon maintaining a favorable balance of trade. Later works, such as Thomas Mun's 1664 work *England's Treasure by Forraign Trade*, expanded on theory promoted by "W.S."

The link between a closed system of trade and the good of the nation found its ultimate expression in the creation of royal trading companies in England, the Netherlands, and France during the 16th century. In England, the East India Company was established in 1600 to monopolize English trade with India and China, thereby creating an English trade in the Far East rather than rely on foreign merchants. The Dutch East India Company was established in 1602 to control all trade between the East Indies and the Netherlands. The French crown established a similar company with similar goals in 1664. Other monopoly companies controlled other sectors of English foreign trade. The Royal African Company was established in 1660 to monopolize trade in West African gold and slaves. The North American fur trade was monopolized with the creation of the Hudson's Bay Company in 1670. The European trading companies shared several characteristics. Each company was closely tied to their respective governments, maintained a monopoly of all legal trade within their designated spheres of activity, and exercised governmental authority over their trading posts. For example, the East India Company was authorized by Charles II in 1670 to mint money, raise armies, and maintain criminal and civil rule over all holdings in India.

The expansion of immigration and settlement in the "New World" presented a different series of challenges under the mercantile theory. Expansive settlement patterns provided particular challenges to Great Britain. The new colonies could not be governed as company holdings; this required a slightly different form of regulating trade without establishing company government as well. In the case of England, the Navigation Acts were the legal manifestation of the modified mercantilist framework. The Navigation Acts were first passed in order to curtail Dutch trade with English sugar colonies in the Caribbean and restrict the carrying trade between the Dutch and the North American colonies. The provisions of the acts directed that colonial commerce could be carried only in English ships, all foreign merchants were excluded from the colonies, and certain enumerated goods could be traded only to England and English colonies. The Navigation Acts were retained and expanded during the restoration. The 1660 edition decreed that certain enumerated products such as cotton, sugar, and tobacco could be exported only to England or to other

English colonies. Further modifications in 1663 decreed that all European goods that were imported to the colonies or colonial goods exported to Europe must first pass through England and then be re-exported. The navigation laws were expanded in 1673 to provide for a system of duties and customs officials in the colonies to ensure that laws pertaining to enumerated goods were followed. This economic policy sought to direct colonial trade through England or to other English possessions, thereby ensuring the profits of that commerce.

The mercantile system was an effective tool that encouraged trade between Britain (England until the 1707 Act of Union, Great Britain after), the mainland British colonies, and British colonies in the Caribbean. Basic necessity as well as profit and strategic interests drove this trade. Many of the material underpinnings of industrial and colonial development were supplied through a system of Trans-Atlantic trade in staple goods. Trade in North American foodstuffs provided the base materials that allowed for the existence of the West Indian plantation economy, the growth of the North Atlantic fisheries, and also provided an important source of money for colonial traders enabling them to consume English manufactured goods. Colonies contributed to the overall wealth of the empire by providing an internal source of previously imported goods such as naval stores, sugar, and tobacco while providing a market for finished British goods. British colonies lacked a large-scale manufacturing base while England's manufacturing capacity was growing. In turn, imports of colonial foodstuffs helped foster the evolution of the English economy from an agricultural base to an industrial economy. The exchange of unfinished commodities for luxury and manufactured goods created a trade deficit for the colonies; this gap was closed through the profits created by a series of exceptions to the navigation laws that permitted colonials to trade with other empires.

It was the legalized leakages within mercantilism that created a practical economic system that allowed the theory of mercantilism to work into the 18th century. There were certain exceptions to the navigation statutes. The most important exception was the trade in salt and wine to the colonies from Southern Europe in exchange for salt fish, rice, and grain from the colonies to Southern Europe. These exceptions in the Navigation Acts provided an essential leakage within the theatrically closed mercantile economic system.

The British American colonies created a large trade surplus with Southern Europe by exchanging staple food crops for salt and wine. The profit from this trade eased the colonial balance of payments deficit with Britain, thereby enriching both the metropolis and the colonies at the expense of Spain and Portugal. Much of this trade surplus was in the form of cash or bills of exchange that enabled colonial consumers to continue to purchase manufactures from Britain. In addition, salt imports allowed for the expansion of the highly profitable salt cod industry, which generated more exports to Southern Europe as well as a source of food for enslaved Caribbean plantation workers.

By the mid-18th century, problems with illegal trade increased. This was particularly true in the sugar trade. In 1733, the Molasses Act was created in order to ensure that colonial consumers purchased more expensive sugar products from the British West Indies rather than cheaper goods from the French, Dutch, or Spanish sugar colonies by increasing taxation on imported sugar products. The tax could not be collected due to smuggling, tax evasion, and the intimidation of customs officials in the colonies. As the 18th-century economy grew more complex, economic interactions in the Atlantic world increasingly occurred without regard for political boundaries that divided the region, or for the laws that intended to enforce the mercantile system. The enforcement problem exposed by the Molasses Act was a symptom of a larger systemic problem within the mercantile system. Mercantilism was a successful system only if there was a reasonable balance between the imports and exports in both the mother country and each of the colonies. In addition, the system could not function if the colonial economies diversified away from the production of staples products. An example of this conflict was the Iron Act of 1750. Under the Iron Act, it was illegal for the colonies to produce any finished iron products or steel despite the demand of the local markets because local production would compete with imported British manufactures. Much like the Sugar Act, the Iron Act proved to be unenforceable due to the demand for those products and the inability of the British government to enforce the law. While diversification was not possible for Newfoundland, the Caribbean colonies or, to a lesser extent, the plantation economies of the American South, diversification was becoming a reality for the middle colonies and New England by the mid-18th century.

The events of the 1750s exposed the vast distance between the mercantile system as a theory and as it was practiced. The diversification away from the classical triangle trade to a system of multiple triangle trades oftentimes removed Britain from the trade networks entirely. The accepted leakages that contributed to the benefit of both mother country and the colonies had expanded to a vast system of quasi-legal and illegal trade networks that did not always benefit Britain. The Seven Years' War left Great Britain with a large national debt. This economic factor, combined with the knowledge that many of the laws designed to enrich Britain through mercantile trade were being openly flouted if not ignored, enraged many imperial officials. A series of efforts to enforce the trade acts as both an economic revenue measure and a matter of authority poisoned British-colonial relations during the 1760s and 1770s.

American independence in 1776 reconfigured the political geography of the Atlantic world. Great Britain retained a mercantilist system in theory, but the practical challenges of enforcing trade regulations excluding American products from the empire proved to be difficult to enforce as the Navigation Acts during the colonial era. Mercantilism also faced serious philosophical challenges. Mercantile theory depended on the belief that the amount of wealth in the world was fixed, and the wealth of the empire could be measured only by the amount of gold and silver in the treasury. This belief was challenged in Adam Smith's influential 1776 work *The Wealth of Nations*. According to Smith, wealth consisted not of gold or silver, but what gold and silver could buy in the marketplace. Hoarding specie, therefore, was illogical. David Ricardo expanded on the importance of trade to national wealth in his 1817 work *On the Principals of Political Economy and Taxation*; according to Ricardo, trade itself was a source of wealth. Despite the theoretical challenges posed by the classical economists, the mercantile system persisted. The Corn Laws, which prohibited grain importation into Great Britain, were passed in 1815 in order to limit competition for domestic farm production. The law was repealed in 1846; the laws reflect the last effort to enforce a strict mercantile system. The growth of free trade ideals in the mid-19th century also impacted the remaining royal trading companies. The Indian Mutiny of 1857 resulted in the holdings of the East India Company being nationalized in 1858, while the land holdings of the Hudson's Bay Company were transferred to the Dominion of Canada in 1870.

See also

Capitalism; Colonization; Free Trade; Imperialism

PATRICK CALLAWAY

Further Reading

Gomes, Leonard. 1987. *Foreign Trade and the National Economy: Mercantilist and Classical Perspectives*. New York: St. Martin's Press.

McCusker, John J., and Russell R. Menard. 1985. *The Economy of British North America, 1607–1789*. Chapel Hill, NC: University of North Carolina Press.

Wallerstein, Immanuel. 2011. *The Modern World System, Book II*. 2nd ed. Berkeley, CA: University of California Press.

Mercantilism—Primary Document

Introduction

The Sugar Act of 1764, also known as the American Revenue Act or the American Duties Act, was intended to reinforce colonial trade restrictions under the Navigation Acts. Interest in this legislation was sparked by the need to increase revenue in the wake of the Seven Years' War, by the political pressure brought to bear on Parliament by the West India lobby, and by the realization of imperial officials that colonial smuggling was common. This effort to reestablish imperial authority over colonial trade was met with resistance in the colonies; the Sugar Act was ultimately unenforceable due to popular resistance. This excerpt from the act provides the rationale for the legislation as a revenue measure, as well as argues for taxes on colonial imports as a mercantilist measure.

Document: Sugar Act (April 5, 1764)

An act for granting certain duties in the British colonies and plantations in America, for continuing, amending, and making perpetual, an act passed in the sixth year of the reign of his late majesty King George the Second, (inituled, An act for the better securing and encouraging the trade of his Majesty's sugar colonies in America;) for applying the produce of such duties, and of the duties to arise by virtue of the said act, towards defraying the expences of defending, protecting, and securing the said colonies and plantations; for explaining an act made in the twenty fifth year of the reign of King Charles the Second, (intituled, An act for the encouragement of the Greenland and Eastland trades, and for the better securing the plantation trade;) and for altering and disallowing several drawbacks on exports from this kingdom, and more effectually preventing the clandestine conveyance of goods to and from the said colonies and plantation, and improving and securing the trade between the same and Great Britain.

Whereas it is expedient that new provisions and regulations should be established for improving the revenue of this kingdom, and for extending and securing the navigation and commerce between Great Britain and your Majesty's dominions in America, which, by the peace, have been so happily enlarged: and whereas it is just and necessary, that a revenue be raised, in your Majesty's said dominions in America, for defraying the expences of defending, protecting, and securing the same; we, your Majesty's most dutiful and loyal subjects, the commons of Great Britain, in parliament assembled, being desirous to make some provision, in this present session of parliament, towards raising the said revenue in America, have resolved to give and grant unto your Majesty the several rates and duties herein after-mentioned; and do most humbly beseech your Majesty that it may be enacted; and be it enacted by the King's most excellent majesty, by and with the advice and consent of the lords spiritual and temporal, and commons, in this present parliament assembled, and by the authority of the same, That from and after the twenty ninth day of September, one thousand seven hundred and sixty four, there shall be raised, levied, collected, and paid, unto his Majesty, his heirs and successors, for and upon all white or clayed sugars of the produce or manufacture of any colony or plantation in America, not under the dominion of his Majesty, his heirs and successors; for and upon indigo, and coffee of foreign produce or manufacture; for and upon wines (except French wine;) for and upon all wrought silks, bengals, and stuffs, mixed with silk or herbs of the manufacture of Persia, China, or East India, and all callico painted, dyed, printed, or stained there; and for and upon all foreign linen cloth called Cambrick and French Lawns, which shall be imported or brought into any colony or plantation in America, which now is, or hereafter may be, under the dominion of his Majesty, his heirs and successors, the several rates and duties following....

Source: Avalon Project. 2013. "Great Britain: Parliament—The Sugar Act: 1764." Available at http://avalon.law.yale.edu/18th_century/sugar_act_1764.asp.

MILITARY-INDUSTRIAL COMPLEX

On January 17, 1961, President Dwight D. Eisenhower delivered his farewell address to the nation. In it, Eisenhower warned Americans against the growth of a "military-industrial complex" in the Cold War era. Fearing that the connection between the U.S. military, defense industry, and politicians—including the federal executive and legislative branches, lobbyists, and state governments, among others—could overwhelm Americans if it went unchecked, Eisenhower made the population aware of a growing concern he had as president. Although Eisenhower's term is the most commonly used, this interconnection could be termed the political-military-industrial complex. In addition, the military-industrial complex could include the work of academics and components of health care. Any version of this idea contains one main component: the fear that a coalition of interests, including defense companies, military officers, civilian bureaucrats, scientists, and others, dictate the direction of foreign and domestic policy in the United States.

The idea of a military-industrial complex has a longer history than many Americans believe. Before the late 19th century, many nations collaborated with private companies to create new weapons and technology during wartime, but not during peacetime. One historian tracks a version of the military-industrial complex back to the 19th-century U.S. Navy. The modern concept of a military-industrial complex, however, did not exist until the mid-20th century. Prior to World War I, the U.S. military relied on government-run arsenals, such as the U.S. Armory and Arsenal at Harper's Ferry in modern-day West Virginia. Initially, the U.S. military was supplied through government-run industrial projects.

With America's entrance into World War I, however, the unprepared nation had to mobilize its industry quickly to build up the military. But the federal government lacked the ability to launch a massive mobilization effort and turned to private businesses for assistance. During the conflict, the United States used the skills of big business leaders to help organize the resources and industry needed to fight the war. This led to the U.S. military directly dealing with corporations and creating contracts with them during the mobilization effort. From April 1916 to June 1919, for example, the U.S. Army pushed $14.5 billion into private enterprises. In addition, businessmen on temporary loan from their own corporations headed the War Industries Board, an organization

President Dwight D. Eisenhower shown giving his farewell television address to the nation from the White House in Washington, January 18, 1961. His warning about a military-industrial complex followed his long military career and eight years as civilian commander-in-chief. (AP Photo/Bill Allen)

that controlled the production and distribution of military supplies. For the first time in American history, the U.S. military worked directly with corporations, including on the creation of defense contracts. The rapid need for a military buildup caused the United States to take the first steps toward the military-industrial complex.

With the outbreak of World War II in 1939, President Franklin Delano Roosevelt's administration prepared for the mass mobilization of industry for military needs in case the United States entered the conflict at any point. For this purpose, instead of creating a "super agency" similar to the War Industries Board, Roosevelt constructed a number of "gentlemen's agreements" with private corporations for wartime production. Under these, businesses agreed to devote up to 50 percent of their manufacturing capacity to wartime needs.

In addition, the government would control prices and production for these businesses in a time of war so they would neither hike up the prices nor run low on supplies. Thus, the administration controlled private corporations once the United States entered the conflict. Primarily, corporations like Ford, Boeing, and Lockheed produced wartime materiel, such as planes, tanks, and jeeps, and private weapons companies like Colt's Manufacturing Company and Winchester Repeating Arms Company manufactured and distributed firearms for the American forces.

In addition to the new relationship between corporations and the federal government, the rapid development and improvements in military equipment and weapons caused the administration to increase funding for scientific research and development. While Ford, Boeing, and Winchester manufactured materials and weapons like B-24 Liberators, B-17 Flying Fortresses, and M1 Garands respectively, the National Defense Research Committee, eventually the Office of Scientific Research and Development, obtained funds and resources for new scientific research for the military. These new funds led to the establishment and development of national research laboratories, such as the Los Alamos National Laboratory in New Mexico, and projects dealing with new weapons, such as the reactor research taking place at the University of Chicago—a major part of the Manhattan Project and the construction of the first nuclear bombs. These new connections between industrial production, scientific research, and federal funding established the system that President Eisenhower would term the military-industrial complex.

Prior to and during World War II, Eisenhower experienced the federalized mobilization of industry and research for the military firsthand. While he approved the move during the conflict, he hoped this system would disband after the war, believing that this mobilization was unconstitutional. But the influence of air power during World War II, the development of atomic weapons, and the emergence of the Cold War dramatically and fundamentally changed Americans' assumptions about the U.S. military's place in the world. This change caused the United States to keep pace with its wartime production in peacetime.

After an initial drop in production in the year immediately following World War II, defense manufacturing once again increased as the Department of Defense (DOD), in response to the belief that the United States had been caught unprepared for World War II, vowed to keep an established military machine in preparation for the ensuing clashes between the United States and Soviet Union. For the first time in U.S. history, the government sustained a large, permanent defense establishment as a response to the rising tensions of the Cold War. For example, during the Korean War, considered one of the first "hot" conflicts in the Cold War, the United States committed 70 percent of all government spending to the military.

This process of defense expansion heated up with the so-called missile gap between the United States and Soviet Union. The majority of Americans believed the Soviet Union was producing more missiles and military materiel than the United States, making the United States vulnerable to future Soviet assaults, especially after the Soviets launched the *Sputnik* satellite in 1957. As a result of this increasingly widespread belief in the differences in military capabilities, Democrats in Congress throughout the 1950s called for additional defense spending and production.

During his time as president, Eisenhower looked to create an American military policy that balanced the duties, budget, and role of the three main branches, the Army, Navy, and Air Force. Eisenhower developed his "New Look" military in the hopes of cutting much of the defense budget to streamline the military. He believed that an increase in nuclear armaments would allow the United States to step away from possessing a traditional, large-scale military and make it more cost-effective. Eisenhower succeeded in building up America's nuclear armaments. In 1952, the United States possessed about 1,000 nuclear warheads. By Eisenhower's farewell speech in 1961, America's stockpile grew to approximately 23,000 nuclear warheads. In addition, air power overwhelmed the traditional strength of ground forces. Believing that future conflicts would include primarily nuclear weapons, Eisenhower desired a stronger air force to deliver these weapons. But the national response to the *Sputnik* launch and continued pressure from Congressional Democrats and the Pentagon, which wanted to maintain a standing traditional army, turned Eisenhower away from his "New Look" military and a return to increased military spending, although he had reduced military spending from 70 percent during the Korean War to 50 percent of the federal budget. From his experience as president, Eisenhower developed his concept of the military-industrial complex and brought it to Americans' attentions in his farewell speech in 1961.

Although Eisenhower warned Americans against the military-industrial complex that had developed out of World War II, the perceived Soviet threat during the Cold War justified the enormous defense spending that had developed since 1945. Despite this justification, Eisenhower's warning seemed to be coming true. Once John F. Kennedy entered the White House, the United States took on an increasingly prominent role in the conflict in Vietnam and this intervention caused an increase in military spending. For example, the DOD bought up 72 percent of aeronautics production, 34 percent of all electronics components, and 26 percent of transportation equipment between 1960 and 1973—the years of greatest U.S. involvement in Vietnam.

Even without these incredible figures, the public perception of the military-industrial complex increased during the Vietnam War. For example, in 1966, Dow Chemical, a plastic manufacturing company based in Midland, Michigan, received a defense contract for the manufacturing of 75,000 tons of Napalm-B, a new type of incendiary jelly that had already been used against the North Vietnamese. The American public's knowledge of what Napalm did in Vietnam caused a massive backlash against this new contract, leading to Dow being considered the poster child for corporate cooperation with the military during an unjust war. Thus, industry became synonymous with militarism during Vietnam. Although Dow was one of the minor defense contractors, its contract highlighted the concept of the military-industrial complex during the Vietnam War.

Strangely, Eisenhower's term did not receive widespread usage until late in the conflict with North Vietnam. Most Americans had not considered Eisenhower's phrase important when he delivered his farewell speech in 1961. But increased disillusionment with the war in Vietnam caused many Americans to revisit the military-industrial complex that Eisenhower warned against. Political scientist Martin Medhurst notes that the term "military-industrial complex" had not appeared in print until 1969, once the United States became entrenched in the quagmire of Vietnam. During the conflict, however, Americans became increasingly aware of the presence of the military-industrial complex. Politically, it became a target of the New Left. This group used it as a scapegoat for America's entrance into the Vietnam War, explaining that the United States sent troops to Vietnam in order to satisfy the hunger of warmongering Americans and the defense industry within the military-industrial complex. In addition, a congressional report on defense spending in 1969 found numerous problems between the Pentagon and its contractors, including cost overruns, inefficiency, and lack of accountability, but Congress still provided the funds for this inefficient system.

Despite these reports, prices continued to grow for basic equipment and the federal government paid out on delinquent contracts throughout the 1970s and 1980s leading to the belief that the military used these contracts to prop up failing defense companies. For example, Lockheed Aircraft, the country's largest defense contractor in the mid-1960s, received a $1.9 billion contract from the air force for the construction of a fleet of C-5A military transport planes, despite the Pentagon suggesting buying the Boeing 747. Yet, after declaring multimillion dollar losses in 1969 and 1970 and requesting a $600 million federal loan, the company received a loan up to $250 million from the federal government. Eventually, by 1989, when the last C-5A was constructed, Lockheed manufactured only a fraction of the fleet at triple the estimated cost.

The fall of the Soviet Union in 1991 and the consequent end of the Cold War instigated a small reduction in defense spending between 1990 and 2001. In turn the idea of the military-industrial complex disappeared from America's public consciousness. The terrorist attacks of September 11, 2001, and the subsequent wars in Afghanistan and Iraq, however, renewed the perception of the military-industrial complex in the United States. Primarily, the new interest in the military-industrial complex extends from the U.S. war with Iraq. Some Americans believe that the defense industry needs to innovate and display their new products to keep contracts. The connections between defense contractor Halliburton and George W. Bush's vice president, Dick Cheney, led many to believe that the billions going to Halliburton for the wars in Iraq and Afghanistan were simply to prop up the military-industrial complex. In addition, for many Americans, the privatization of American security, as seen through the Blackwater security firm, and the length of the conflicts in Afghanistan and Iraq have rehabilitated the fear of the military-industrial complex in the 21st century.

See also

Anticommunism; Antiwar Movement (Vietnam Era); Big Oil; Communism; Conservatism; Containment; Counterculture; Diplomacy; Foreign Interventionism; Hippies; Imperialism; New Left Movement; Nuclear Power Movement; Nuclear Proliferation; Violent Protest; Weapons of Mass Destruction (WMDs)

Michael Burns

Further Reading

Hackemer, Kurt. 2001. *The U.S. Navy and the Origins of the Military-Industrial Complex, 1847–1883.* Annapolis, MD: Naval Institute Press.

Hartung, William D. 2010. *Prophets of War: Lockheed Martin and the Making of the Military-Industrial Complex.* New York: Nation Books.

Ledbetter, James. 2011. *Unwarranted Influence: Dwight D. Eisenhower and the Military Industrial Complex.* New Haven, CT: Yale University Press.

Mieczkowski, Yanek. *Eisenhower's Sputnik Moment: The Race for Space and World Prestige*. Ithaca, NY: Cornell University Press, 2013.

Pursell, Carroll W., Jr., compiler. 1972. *The Military-Industrial Complex*. New York: Harper and Row.

Military Industrial Complex—Primary Document

Introduction

In this speech, delivered three days before leaving office as a farewell to the nation, President Dwight D. Eisenhower addressed his concerns over the creation of a large and complex defense industry. He sought to warn Americans against the growth of this complex relationship between the government and private defense industry. He recognized the need for military spending and growth during the Cold War, but wanted to suggest that Americans beware of unchecked spending and growth. It is in this speech that Eisenhower popularized the term military-industrial complex.

Document: President Dwight D. Eisenhower's Farewell Address to the Nation (January 17, 1961)

My fellow Americans:

Three days from now, after half a century in the service of our country, I shall lay down the responsibilities of office as, in traditional and solemn ceremony, the authority of the Presidency is vested in my successor.

This evening I come to you with a message of leave-taking and farewell, and to share a few final thoughts with you, my countrymen.

Like every other citizen, I wish the new President, and all who will labor with him, Godspeed. I pray that the coming years will be blessed with peace and prosperity for all.

Our people expect their President and the Congress to find essential agreement on issues of great moment, the wise resolution of which will better shape the future of the Nation.

My own relations with the Congress, which began on a remote and tenuous basis when, long ago, a member of the Senate appointed me to West Point, have since ranged to the intimate during the war and immediate post-war period, and, finally, to the mutually interdependent during these past eight years.

In this final relationship, the Congress and the Administration have, on most vital issues, cooperated well, to serve the national good rather than mere partisanship, and so have assured that the business of the Nation should go forward. So, my official relationship with the Congress ends in a feeling, on my part, of gratitude that we have been able to do so much together.

We now stand ten years past the midpoint of a century that has witnessed four major wars among great nations. Three of these involved our own country. Despite these holocausts America is today the strongest, the most influential and most productive nation in the world. Understandably proud of this pre-eminence, we yet realize that America's leadership and prestige depend, not merely upon our unmatched material progress, riches and military strength, but on how we use our power in the interests of world peace and human betterment.

Throughout America's adventure in free government, our basic purposes have been to keep the peace; to foster progress in human achievement, and to enhance liberty, dignity and integrity among people and among nations. To strive for less would be unworthy of a free and religious people. Any failure traceable to arrogance, or our lack of comprehension or readiness to sacrifice would inflict upon us grievous hurt both at home and abroad.

Progress toward these noble goals is persistently threatened by the conflict now engulfing the world. It commands our whole attention, absorbs our very beings. We face a hostile ideology—global in scope, atheistic in character, ruthless in purpose, and insidious in method. Unhappily the danger it poses promises to be of indefinite duration. To meet it successfully, there is called for, not so much the emotional and transitory sacrifices of crisis, but rather those which enable us to carry forward steadily, surely, and without complaint the burdens of a prolonged and complex struggle—with liberty the stake. Only thus shall we remain, despite every provocation, on our charted course toward permanent peace and human betterment.

Crises there will continue to be. In meeting them, whether foreign or domestic, great or small, there is a recurring temptation to feel that some spectacular and costly action could become the miraculous solution to all current difficulties. A huge increase in newer elements of our defense; development of unrealistic programs to cure every ill in agriculture; a dramatic expansion in basic and applied research—these and many other possibilities, each possibly promising in itself, may be suggested as the only way to the road we wish to travel.

But each proposal must be weighed in the light of a broader consideration: the need to maintain balance in and among national programs—balance between the private and the public economy, balance between cost and hoped for advantage—balance between the clearly necessary and the comfortably desirable; balance between our essential requirements as a nation and the duties imposed by the nation upon the individual; balance between actions of the moment and the national welfare of the future. Good judgment seeks balance and progress; lack of it eventually finds imbalance and frustration.

The record of many decades stands as proof that our people and their government have, in the main, understood these truths and have responded to them well, in the face of stress and threat. But threats, new in kind or degree, constantly arise. I mention two only.

A vital element in keeping the peace is our military establishment. Our arms must be mighty, ready for instant action, so that no potential aggressor may be tempted to risk his own destruction.

Our military organization today bears little relation to that known by any of my predecessors in peacetime, or indeed by the fighting men of World War II or Korea.

Until the latest of our world conflicts, the United States had no armaments industry. American makers of plowshares could, with time and as required, make swords as well. But now we can no longer risk emergency improvisation of national defense; we have been compelled to create a permanent armaments industry of vast proportions. Added to this, three and a half million men and women are directly engaged in the defense establishment. We annually spend on military security more than the net income of all United States corporations.

This conjunction of an immense military establishment and a large arms industry is new in the American experience. The total influence—economic, political, even spiritual—is felt in every city, every State house, every office of the Federal government. We recognize the imperative need for this development. Yet we must not fail to comprehend its grave implications. Our toil, resources and livelihood are all involved; so is the very structure of our society.

In the councils of government, we must guard against the acquisition of unwarranted influence, whether sought or unsought, by the military-industrial complex. The potential for the disastrous rise of misplaced power exists and will persist.

We must never let the weight of this combination endanger our liberties or democratic processes. We should take nothing for granted. Only an alert and knowledgeable citizenry can compel the proper meshing of the huge industrial and military machinery of defense with our peaceful methods and goals, so that security and liberty may prosper together.

Akin to, and largely responsible for the sweeping changes in our industrial-military posture, has been the technological revolution during recent decades.

In this revolution, research has become central; it also becomes more formalized, complex, and costly. A steadily increasing share is conducted for, by, or at the direction of, the Federal government.

Today, the solitary inventor, tinkering in his shop, has been overshadowed by task forces of scientists in laboratories and testing fields. In the same fashion, the free university, historically the fountainhead of free ideas and scientific discovery, has experienced a revolution in the conduct of research.

Partly because of the huge costs involved, a government contract becomes virtually a substitute for intellectual curiosity. For every old blackboard there are now hundreds of new electronic computers.

The prospect of domination of the nation's scholars by Federal employment, project allocations, and the power of money is ever present—and is gravely to be regarded.

Yet, in holding scientific research and discovery in respect, as we should, we must also be alert to the equal and opposite danger that public policy could itself become the captive of a scientific-technological elite.

It is the task of statesmanship to mold, to balance, and to integrate these and other forces, new and old, within the principles of our democratic system—ever aiming toward the supreme goals of our free society.

Another factor in maintaining balance involves the element of time. As we peer into society's future, we—you and I, and our government—must avoid the impulse to live only for today, plundering, for our own ease and convenience, the precious resources of tomorrow. We cannot mortgage the material assets of our grandchildren without risking the loss also of their political and spiritual heritage. We want democracy to survive for all generations to come, not to become the insolvent phantom of tomorrow.

Down the long lane of the history yet to be written America knows that this world of ours, ever growing smaller, must avoid becoming a community of dreadful fear and hate, and be, instead, a proud confederation of mutual trust and respect.

Such a confederation must be one of equals. The weakest must come to the conference table with the same confidence as do we, protected as we are by our moral, economic, and military strength. That table, though scarred by many past frustrations, cannot be abandoned for the certain agony of the battlefield.

Disarmament, with mutual honor and confidence, is a continuing imperative. Together we must learn how to compose differences, not with arms, but with intellect and decent purpose. Because this need is so sharp and apparent I confess that I lay down my official responsibilities in this field with a definite sense of disappointment. As one who has witnessed the horror and the lingering sadness of war—as one who knows that another war could utterly destroy this civilization which has been so slowly and painfully built over thousands of years—I wish I could say tonight that a lasting peace is in sight.

Happily, I can say that war has been avoided. Steady progress toward our ultimate goal has been made. But, so much remains to be done. As a private citizen, I shall never cease to do what little I can to help the world advance along that road.

So—in this my last good night to you as your President—I thank you for the many opportunities you have given me for public service in war and peace. I trust that in that service you find some things worthy; as for the rest of it, I know you will find ways to improve performance in the future.

You and I—my fellow citizens—need to be strong in our faith that all nations, under God, will reach the goal of peace with justice. May we be ever unswerving in devotion to principle, confident but humble with power, diligent in pursuit of the Nation's great goals.

To all the peoples of the world, I once more give expression to America's prayerful and continuing aspiration:

We pray that peoples of all faiths, all races, all nations, may have their great human needs satisfied; that those now denied opportunity shall come to enjoy it to the full; that all who yearn for freedom may experience its spiritual blessings; that those who have freedom will understand, also, its heavy responsibilities; that all who are insensitive to the needs of others will learn charity; that the scourges of poverty, disease and ignorance will be made to disappear from the earth, and that, in the goodness of time, all peoples will come to live together in a peace guaranteed by the binding force of mutual respect and love.

Source: Dwight D. Eisenhower: "Farewell Radio and Television Address to the American People," January 17, 1961. Online by Gerhard Peters and John T. Woolley, *The American Presidency Project*. http://www.presidency.ucsb.edu/ws/?pid=12086.

MISCEGENATION

Since its earliest days as a collection of English colonies, the United States has been concerned with miscegenation, or romantic or sexual relations between the races, largely because it is the most intimate and profound of all interracial relationships. Virtually all of the nation's minorities, from Native Americans to African Americans to Asian Americans, have faced discrimination in this area. Only in recent decades has the United States accepted miscegenation legally, but racism related to it continues to exist in American society.

As more Africans arrived in the Southern colonies in the mid-17th century, settlers increasingly worried about the possibility of interracial marriage. In 1664, Maryland passed a law barring the marriage of whites with slaves and indentured servants who were African or of mixed race. In 1691, Virginia prohibited free blacks and whites from marrying, and Maryland followed the next year. Other colonies, including Pennsylvania and Massachusetts, did the same. By the time of independence, more than half of the colonies barred interracial marriage, but Pennsylvania repealed its ban in 1780 as part of a series of laws that reduced restrictions on free blacks. Under pressure from abolitionists, Massachusetts finally repealed its law in 1843.

Although Southern slave states technically banned them, sexual relations between slaves and masters were a common occurrence in the South. The best known example of such a relationship is that of Thomas Jefferson and his slave, Sally Hemings, and historians now largely agree that Jefferson fathered several children with Hemings. Additionally, a significant number of masters had sexual relations with their female slaves and produced children. In an era in which society viewed white women as pure and lacking in sexual impulses, masters often used slave women to satisfy their urges and demonstrate their dominance, producing offspring.

Ironically, the word *miscegenation* emerged not in the South, but in the North. The Democratic Party coined it during its campaign against Abraham Lincoln's reelection to a second term as president. Democrats often used the derogatory term *black Republicans* to characterize their opponents, thereby reminding their potential supporters that the other side had some sympathy toward African Americans. In 1863, they published a pamphlet, *Miscegenation: The Theory of the Blending of the Races, Applied to the American White Man and Negro*. It was anonymous, but the authors were two journalists from *The New York World*, a leading Democratic Party organ. They claimed to be expressing the views of the Republican Party—that its goal was to turn the United States into a mixed-race society of mulattos. As a political tactic, it failed: Lincoln won reelection handily. But the word had been created and would spread, as would opposition to the idea.

Dozens of states had laws preventing interracial marriage at some point in their histories, demonstrating that this racism was not confined to the South. In the West, for instance, the Motion Picture Production Code or Hays Code of 1930 barred the depiction of miscegenation in films. But Asians were the primary target for anti-miscegenation laws in the late 19th- and early 20th-century West, as whites feared losing their dominance to the Chinese and Japanese immigrants flooding into the region. Among the legal challenges to these laws was *Kirby v. Kirby* (1921), which unsuccessfully argued that Arizona's anti-miscegenation ban technically made it illegal for a mixed-race individual to marry anyone. However, it was not until *Perez v. Sharp* (1948) that a court overturned any such law, in this case California's. The plaintiff's lawyers successfully compared anti-miscegenation laws to the views of Adolf Hitler, while experts argued that race was an inconsequential category of human definition because culture, not race, was responsible for human difference.

Despite this victory, many states maintained bans on interracial marriage, and there were occasional efforts to enshrine a ban on miscegenation in the Constitution through the amending process. Finally, the Supreme Court overturned Virginia's anti-miscegenation law in the landmark case of *Loving v. Virginia* (1967). In 1958, Mildred and Richard Loving wed in Washington, D.C., where Virginia's anti-miscegenation law did not apply, but when they went back to Virginia, they were arrested. Told to leave the state as a way to avoid prison, they appealed the ruling. By ruling that Virginia's ban violated the Fourteenth Amendment, the Supreme Court effectively made all such laws unconstitutional in a unanimous opinion written by Chief Justice Earl Warren.

The decision in *Loving v. Virginia* eliminated legal obstacles to intermarriage, and public opinion increasingly supported mixed marriages. The number of interracial marriages consistently rose in the late 20th and early 21st centuries. In addition to the civil rights movements, especially in the 1960s, popular culture played a role in gaining acceptance: the 1970s television show *The Jeffersons* featured a white husband and black wife whose daughter married the son of the title characters.

Social and cultural obstacles remained. The Fundamentalist Bob Jones University only lifted its ban on interracial dating in 2000. In a well-publicized incident in 2009, for instance, a justice of the peace in Louisiana refused to marry to an interracial couple because racial mixing violated his personal views; the couple in question sued the judge, who was forced to resign his position. In the same year, a new president of the United States took office, the son of Barack Obama, a black Kenyan economist studying at the University of Hawaii, and the former Ann Dunham, a white woman born in Wichita, Kansas. President Obama's political rise demonstrated that the idea of miscegenation or mixed marriage had indeed gained wider acceptance, even as some of his supporters accused his critics of basing their opposition to him on the color of his skin.

See also

Abolition; African American Civil Rights Movement; Sex in American Society

BRYAN KVET

Further Reading

Pascoe, Peggy. 2008. *What Comes Naturally: Miscegenation Law and the Making of Race in America.* New York: Oxford University Press.

Smith, John David, ed. 1993. *Racial Determinism and the Fear of Miscegenation, post-1900.* New York: Garland Publishing.

Smith, John David, ed. 1993. *Racial Determinism and the Fear of Miscegenation, pre-1900.* New York: Garland Publishing.

Williamson, Joel. 1995. *New People: Miscegenation and Mulattoes in the United States.* Baton Rouge: Louisiana State University Press.

Miscegenation—Primary Documents

Introduction

Reproduced here are two anti-Republican cartoons produced by G. W. Bromley and Company in 1864. The cartoons are meant to show that Republican support for racial equality will lead to an undesirable mixing of races if President Abraham Lincoln is reelected in the 1864 presidential campaign. The first cartoon, entitled "Miscegenation or the millennium of abolitionism," is the second in the Bromley series of anti-Lincoln

satires. In it, Lincoln and other Republican and abolitionist leaders consort with various black women. The second cartoon, entitled "The Miscegenation Ball"—the fourth in the Bromley series—depicts a miscegenation ball held at Lincoln campaign headquarters in New York, where black women again mingle with Republican leaders.

Document 1: Cartoon: "Miscegenation or the Millennium of Abolitionism" (1864) (Illustration, page 665)

Document 2: Cartoon: "The Miscegenation Ball" (1864) (Illustration, page 666)

MISSIONARY MOVEMENT

See AMERICAN MISSIONARY MOVEMENT

MODERN MEDICINE

As a practice to heal the human body, medicine has existed and evolved since the dawn of man. However, it was not until the adoption of the scientific method for diagnosis and treatment in the late 18th century that modern medicine was born. Early on, the development of more effective medical practices progressed slowly. But by the 19th century, the pace of discoveries and innovations began to accelerate resulting in the boon that occurred during the 20th century. By that time, the institution of modern medicine had become a daunting empire that formed an integral part of the social, political, and economic fabric of American life. Perhaps due to the perceived monopoly by the traditional medical establishment, some critics have argued for the legitimizing of alternative medicine, and others have decried the mounting costs of modern medicine. In an attempt to address the rising price of medical care, in 2010 the U.S. government passed a health care reform act.

"Miscegenation or the Millennium of Abolitionism" (1864). (Library of Congress. http://www.loc.gov/pictures/item/2008661680/.)

Primitive and ancient medicine was often tied to religion and philosophies that helped people make sense of the world. An accurate understanding of how the body worked took many years to develop. In this regard, the Greek physician Galen (131–200 BCE) was a trailblazer. He wrote hundreds of books on anatomy (eighty still exist today) that expanded human knowledge of the working of the body. Unfortunately, some of his conclusions were in error, and the misinformation was adopted in Europe for more than a thousand years. Notably, the advent of the printing press dramatically increased the dissemination of evolving medical knowledge. However, it was not until the discovery of microorganisms with the use of a microscope by Antonie Philips van Leeuwenhoek (1632–1723) that physicians began to scientifically identify and prevent certain illnesses.

As it was in so many other ways, the Civil War proved to be a turning point in the history of modern medicine. The U.S. government expanded the army's medical department while the U.S. Sanitary Commission formed to help serve soldiers and their families. Because so many soldiers in the North and the South died not of wounds but of diseases and infections, sometimes resulting from their wounds, Americans became more conscious of the need for improving surgical techniques and treatment and research facilities. The war also sped up the professionalization of nursing.

In the late 19th century, the adoption of the scientific method ushered in the era of modern medicine. Louis Pasteur (1822–1895), a French chemist and microbiologist, was an innovator who established the germ theory of disease. In

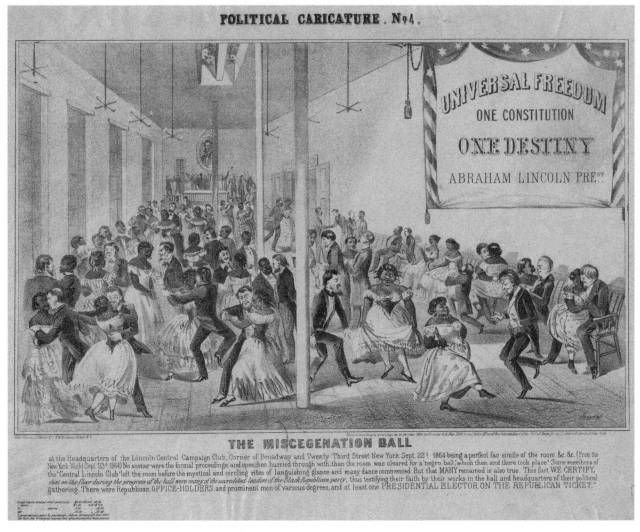

"The Miscegenation Ball" (1864). (Library of Congress. http://www.loc.gov/pictures/item/2008661682/.)

1879, Pasteur developed a vaccine for chicken cholera, which was the first vaccine developed in a laboratory. He developed an anthrax vaccine in 1881 and a rabies vaccine the next year. In later years, by building on Pasteur's successes with microbiology, other scientists also developed various vaccines. In 1897, a team of scientists working for the German company Bayer AG developed aspirin, and the pain medication quickly became a huge seller around the world. These and other discoveries charted the slow but determined progress of modern medicine in the 19th century.

Researchers continued the momentum in the 20th century by building on past discoveries but at a much more accelerated pace. For example, in 1901 Karl Landsteiner (1868–1943) received the Nobel Prize for discovering and identifying different human blood types. In 1906, Frederick Hopkins (1861–1947), also a Nobel Prize recipient, discovered vitamins. In 1921, another Nobel Prize winner, Sir Frederick Banting (1891–1955) discovered insulin. Oral anesthesia, a tremendous advancement in surgical procedures, had been used by Crawford Long (1815–1878), an American pharmacist and surgeon, as early as 1842. In 1921, Fidel Pages (1886–1923), a military surgeon, developed a technique for epidural anesthesia. Vaccines for diphtheria, whooping cough, tuberculosis, and tetanus were all developed in the 1920s. However, one of the greatest modern medicine milestones of the 20th was the development of penicillin in 1928 by Sir Alexander Fleming (1881–1955). Fleming, a Nobel Prize winner, provided the world with the

President Barack Obama, center, stands with, from left, Dr. Mona Mangat of St. Petersburg, FL; Dr. Hershey Garner of Fayetteville, AK; Dr. Richard Evans of Dover-Foxcroft, ME; and Dr. Amanda McKinney of Beatrice, NE, in the Rose Garden of the White House in Washington, October 5, 2009, during an event with doctors from around the country to discuss health care reform. (AP Photo/Susan Walsh)

first antibiotic to fight infections. The contribution of penicillin to modern medicine was vast. Surely, millions of lives were saved because of it.

During the second half of the century, numerous other innovations occurred: the world's first dialysis machine was developed (1943); the first effective cancer chemotherapy drug was developed (1946); the pain medication Tylenol was developed (1948); the first polio vaccine was developed (1952); the heart-lung machine to aid in open heart surgery was invented (1953); the first human kidney transplant was performed (1954); the first implantable pacemaker was developed (1958); in vitro fertilization was introduced (1959); the cardiopulmonary resuscitation device was invented (1960); the first oral contraceptive was approved by the FDA (1960); the first human liver (1963), lung (1963), pancreas (1966), and heart (1967) transplants were performed; the CAT scan was invented (1971); laser eye surgery was performed for the first time (1973); and liposuction was performed successfully (1974). Perhaps one of the most impressive accomplishments of modern medicine in the 20th century was the eradication of smallpox in the late 1970s, making it the first disease in human history ever to be completely wiped out by human intervention.

As the printing press had done centuries before, the invention of the World Wide Web in 1989 was a windfall for modern medicine. The Internet eased the spread of medical information at a rate that had never been possible before. More astoundingly, the Web enabled doctors to administer treatment from great distances. For example, in 2001, Jacques Marescaux performed gallbladder surgery on a patient in France from New York with the use of a remotely controlled robot. In 2007, doctors successfully implanted the very first "bionic" eye on a blind patient. But the proliferation of Web sites about medicine and diseases led to another problem: people trying to treat or diagnose themselves according to what they read online.

As with the use of certain medical technologies, research in medical genetics, often made possible or easier through these technological advances, has sometimes created ethical controversies. For example, as scientists have engaged in animal cloning and continued efforts to map the entire human genome, some critics charged that doctors have stepped out of their human roles by attempting to "play god." Evidence of their humanity could be found in the countless medical errors that occurred every year and in the greed-induced overmedication of patients by some doctors simply for profit. The bottom line was that doctors were fraught with human foibles, and, although genetic manipulation offered hope for combating certain illnesses, it also opened a Pandora's Box.

Other criticism stemmed from anti-medical establishment groups. For example, some proponents of alternative medicine have pointed out that mainstream medical practices taught in conventional medical schools have only existed for a couple of centuries, while natural remedies have served humanity for thousands of years. Furthermore, naturalists argued that sometimes alternative medicine could be used advantageously in conjunction with traditional medicine. At other times when traditional medicine offered no hope, alternative medicine served a crucial role. These groups, therefore, were appalled at the fact that modern medicine enjoyed an acceptance and legitimacy that alternative medicine did not. In essence, the pedestal on which modern medicine had been placed gave it a tremendous advantage over alternative medicine that was deemed unfair, because it created a monopoly. Furthermore, some critics contended that the medical establishment had purposely attempted to discredit alternative medicine. For example, in 1976, a group of chiropractors filed a lawsuit against the American Medical Association (AMA) for violation of the Sherman Anti-Trust Act. Two years later, the U.S. Supreme Court ruled that the AMA was, in fact, guilty of attempting to suppress chiropractic care. In 1993, David Eisenberg published a Harvard survey that showed that one-third of Americans used some form of alternative therapy. The medical establishment took note, and in 1998 *The Journal of the American Medical Association* (JAMA) published a special issue dedicated to the topic of alternative medicine. In 2000, President Bill Clinton created the White House Commission on Complementary and Alternative Medicine Policy.

Although these were positive steps for proponents of alternative medicine, the roots of the traditional medical establishment remained unscathed, because they have enveloped social, political, and economic facets of American life for more than two hundred years. Another aspect of modern medicine that caused widespread concern was escalating costs. Doctors demanded high salaries due to their much-needed and specialized training. Malpractice lawsuits further drove prices up. Research required funding. Pharmaceutical companies charged high prices for medications. Exasperating matters, health insurance rates skyrocketed. Critics charged that the benefits of modern medicine were mostly enjoyed by the rich, because the poor could not afford it. Certainly, serious and expensive diseases to treat such as tuberculosis were more deadly for the poor than the wealthy. In an attempt to address these inequalities, government programs like Medicare and Medicaid were put in place. However, many middle-class families remained at a disadvantage, because they earned too much income to qualify for government aid yet earned too little to afford high insurance costs. In 1994, Clinton proposed a health care reform plan that was defeated in Congress. In 2010, President Barack Obama's Affordable Care Act passed Congress in an effort to address the high cost of health care. While the provisions of "Obamacare," as it came to be called, gradually took effect, it continued to remain a source and subject of political controversy as Republicans in particular objected to it.

The passage of Obamacare promised change in some ways and codified it in others. For example, it led to more information-sharing, which advances in computer technology had long since made possible and encouraged. Medicine also changed as, increasingly, other aspects of American life such as gender roles evolved: men traditionally had been doctors while women had been nurses, but that began changing more markedly in the 1960s and has continued to do so. Continuing studies of such matters as diet kept producing changes: more medications to reduce cholesterol and other contributors to cardiovascular disease promised to produce longer lives while moving away from the use of preservatives in foods meant that some of what had been thought true proved otherwise; thus, many who gave up butter for margarine went back to the more natural product. Such changes demonstrated that medicine is, like the other sciences, not set in stone, and a reflection of other social forces.

See also

Disease Eradication; Internet Nation

ROLANDO AVILA

Further Reading

Bynum, W. F. 2006. *The Western Medical Tradition: 1800 to 2000.* New York: Cambridge University Press.

Duffy, John. 1993. *From Humors to Medical Science: A History of American Medicine.* Urbana, IL: University of Illinois Press.

King, Lester S. 1991. *Transformations in American Medicine: From Benjamin Rush to William Osler.* Baltimore, MD: Johns Hopkins University Press.

Reiser, Stanley Joel. 1981. *Medicine in the Reign of Technology.* Cambridge, UK: Cambridge University Press.

Starr, Paul. 1982. *The Social Transformation of American Medicine.* New York: Basic Books.

Modern Medicine—Primary Document

Introduction

Physician V.M. Synge delivered his inaugural address to the Dublin University Biological Association on November 7, 1925. Synge's address, "A Criticism of Modern Medicine," was later published in The Irish Journal of Medical Science *(January 1926, Volume 1, Issue 1, pp. 20–28). Synge's criticism resonated strongly enough among medical professionals that the editors of* The Journal of the American Medical Association *(JAMA) responded to Synge's ideas later that same year. In the editorial (presented here), the editors of JAMA agreed with Synge that the only way to improve modern medical practices was by examining them critically. For example, while it was true that modern medicine had improved human life in some ways, it had not terminated disease or human suffering. Also, medical practitioners were too reliant on new tests rather than human observation of "signs and symptoms." Due to their obsession, awe, and reverence for new and unproven scientific developments, practitioners had developed a blind faith in science, which was nothing more than a superstitious reliance on tools. In other words, doctors were allowing the scientific approach to medicine to destroy the human art of medicine. According to both Synge and the editors of the JAMA, it was only when both art and science were combined and weighed out equally that true medical advancements would come about.*

Document: "A Criticism of Modern Medicine," a *Journal of the American Medical Association* Editorial (April 10, 1926)

A conscientious reviewer of the history of medicine would probably admit that within the last century, and largely within half that period, medical science and art have advanced with a speed incomparably greater than at any pervious time. Philosophical speculation has given way to experimentation as medicine has kept pace with the advancement of medical knowledge along with the evolution of culture; and medicine can proudly boast of many conquests that deserve to be called marvelous.

Synge has urged that it is often more useful to criticize than to applaud, because without dissatisfaction, without criticism, progress is impossible. To be content is to cease to advance. Synge has therefore frankly presented a series of cogent criticism and comments, some of which seem worth repeating at a time when the needs, the shortcomings, the failures and the misdirections of medical training are being investigated vigorously in several quarters. There can be no offense in any effort to promote an advance, particularly since, despite medical progress, the incidence of all diseases is not decreasing; in fact, the incidence of some diseases is markedly increasing. Like many writers in this country, Synge stresses the belief that the tendency of modern diagnosis is to neglect the evidence furnished by signs and symptoms, and to place undue reliance on special tests. Thus, we are told bluntly that the roentgen ray, by simplifying diagnosis, has made clinicians lazy. "The science of errors is, unfortunately, a neglected branch of study." This statement embodies an appreciation of the readiness of present-day student and practitioner alike to accept so-called evidence at face value and without adequate discussion. Thus, some serologic reactions are frankly misleading. We are, in Synge's judgment, too ready to apply unfinished biochemical research to clinical purposes. A discovery is heralded, and straightaway it is applied to purposes of diagnosis or treatment regardless of possible limitations or fallacies. . . .

It sounds like a platitude, yet one welcomed by the "practical doctor," to hear that observation, experience and sound judgment are more important in clinical medicine than are measurements with delicate instruments. . . . We find somewhat greater sympathy with Synge's animadversions at the spread of certain fashions and foibles. Vaccines become a panacea, and every conceivable disease is treated with them. Drugs must now be given hypodermically or intravenously instead of by mouth, because a few drugs have been found to more efficacious when so given. . . .

Synge alleges, with much justification, that the belief in the magical and the irrational has increased because the critical faculty has been dulled by so many new wonders. . . . Is it not better to share the more optimistic outlook of Synge in his admonition:

Hard and conscientious work, accurate observation, sound reasoning, a mind free from obsessions and superstitions, a firm belief in the possibilities of medicine as an art and as a science; these are the things which have raised medicine to its present greatness; these are the things which will carry it onward always.

Source: Editorial. "A Criticism of Modern Medicine." *The Journal of the American Medical Association* 233 (April 10, 1926): 1132.

MODERNIZATION

In comparison to other advanced democracies, the United States has undergone its own unique set of experiences that have put it on the path to modernization. Various outcomes to these experiences have led to exponential growth in technological advancements and lifestyle improvements. The birth of this process can primarily be found in the American Revolution and corresponding events surrounding that period of time. Furthermore, the origins of the Industrial Revolution (a period of time beginning primarily in the early 1800s when the use of fossil fuels led to massive growth in technology and standard of living due to more efficient use of machines in labor) also played an important role. More enhanced technology in both transportation and communication resulting from this so-called revolution have led to increasing connectivity domestically and internationally for Americans. This entry will discuss some of the most prominent phases of modernization in U.S history and how the United States has closely followed the *theory of modernization* (a notion that when democracy and capitalism are carried out, development will occur more rapidly in almost all regards).

First, the question of what constitutes "modern" or "a state of modernity" in Western society must be defined. In general, when a country is considered modern, it means that it values rationalism, secularism, materialism, technological advancement, and in some cases, the bureaucratic model of governance. Furthermore, modern societies place a high emphasis on individual freedom and to a degree, collective equality.

America's first step toward modernization comes to light with the ratification of its Constitution in 1788 after the American Revolution. Not only was the U.S. Constitution a break

New York City's Woolworth building, pictured in 1930, was once the world's tallest building. Built in 1913 and designed by Cass Gilbert, the architect who later designed the U.S. Supreme Court building in Washington, D.C., the Woolworth building is still among New York's major skyscrapers. (AP Photo)

from the political norms of monarchical Europe, but it was a major jump in the direction of rationalism and the secularization of the state from religious influence and conversely the state's establishment of religion. As pointed out in the First Amendment, "Congress shall make no law respecting an establishment of religion, or prohibiting the free exercise thereof" (The Bill of Rights). Essentially, this amendment placed a wall of separation between government and religion both in a state religion, as was prevalent in Europe, and restricting anyone from the free practice of their religious beliefs. Since that time, the United States has become an increasingly secular country, especially in light of the evolution of judicial interpretation regarding the freedom of religion.

As mentioned, the catalyst for modernization was the Industrial Revolution. In the United States, the growth of industry through technological advancements was apparent in major inventions such as the cotton gin, which made the harvest of cotton—the Southern states' biggest cash crop—increasingly efficient. Additionally, the use of the steamboat on U.S. waterways enhanced the capabilities of farmers and factories to transport their products hundreds of miles to the eastern seaboard for sale. Although these innovations played a significant role in America's modernization, other driving forces also catalyzed the growth of the United States. This modernizing growth can be categorized into three phases that will be briefly discussed next.

Economic Modernization

The United States' first phase of modernization took place with the transition from slavery and the transatlantic triangle (a system of trade between North America, Europe, and Africa that entailed raw materials, manufactured goods, and slaves), and a mercantilist system to the beginnings of a strong capitalist democratic republic. To clarify, this phase can essentially be characterized as an economic modernization from a mere mercantilist system (when the economy is paramount to the survival of the state and functions to serve its needs to a functioning capitalist economy that encourages open markets and international trade). After the U.S Civil War (1861–1865), laissez-faire capitalism (a form of capitalism that enjoys little to no governmental interference in the markets, including the allowance of monopolies at the expense of consumers and the environment) was encouraged, leading to the vast growth of corporations and big business. Due to political forces described in the next section, economic modernization in the United States took on a new form that headed in the direction of more social democratic policies. Generally, these policies attempted to curtail the ill effects of big business and put government's hand in the markets.

Political Modernization

In connection to economic modernization, political modernization also began after the Civil War as an opposing force to laissez-faire capitalism and powerful private sector entities. This is seen in the expansion of the federal civil service or, as it is more commonly called, the American bureaucracy. Also known as the rise of the administrative state, this political modernization was pushed by President Woodrow Wilson from his days as a college professor. Inspired by German

philosopher Max Weber and his theory on democracy and economy, Wilson sought to end political corruption through the growth of an expert bureaucracy. The Pendleton Act of 1883, passed after a disappointed patronage seeker assassinated President James Garfield, began this process by ending appointment to administrative positions as a political favor, forcing a merit system approach. Out of all this, numerous administrative agencies supported by progressives such as Wilson came into existence to combat unregulated monopolies and unfair business practices and corruption in the government itself. In addition to corruption, progressives sought to use the government to solve a wave of new challenges threatening the United States. From the founding, societal problems were generally taken care of on a local level of governance. But with the threat of world war on the horizon during the early 1900s and later with large-scale economic depression, the U.S. political field transformed to a more centralized state where much more was expected of government to fix the serious problems plaguing the country.

Technological Modernization

The last phase of modernization to be discussed largely took place after World War II. The threat of nuclear weapons during the Cold War (a time when opposing forces, democracy and communism, were under threat of nuclear fallout and war in the 1950s to 1990s) heightened the idea that the United States could not risk falling behind the Soviet Union technologically. With the Cold War threat, technological advances grew exponentially as scientists from both the Soviet Union and the United States furiously worked on their respective space programs and military weaponry. It was during this time that space travel became a reality and the United States placed a man on the moon for the first time. Also, nuclear weapons technology became more apparent within both competing military powers.

Another aspect of technological modernization worth mentioning is that of the American media and the growing connectivity of people through Internet capabilities. Currently, the methods of sharing information are limitless in non-authoritarian states such as the United States. During the height of the Vietnam War in the 1960s and 1970s, Americans, for the first time, experienced televised reports of war. To some, graphic images of war that were shown by media outlets were a factor that led to the wide disapproval of American involvement in Vietnam. Also, it is important to note that most information before that time originated from newspapers and radio, much less reactive forms of media. Since then, rudimentary sources became increasingly obsolete methods of obtaining information to be replaced with televised news reporting and later on, the advent of Internet communication and social media. Examining how much the United States has changed since its founding, modernization has left America almost unrecognizable in comparison with its appearance over two hundred years ago.

See also

Bill of Rights; Capitalism; Civil Service Reform; Democracy; Freedom of Religion; Industrial Revolution; Mercantilism; Progressivism; Separation of Church and State; Spoils System

ADAM M. BREWER

Further Reading

Herring, George C. 2011. *From Colony to Superpower: U.S. Foreign Relations Since 1776.* New York: Oxford University Press.

O'Neil, Patrick. 2010. *Essentials of Comparative Politics.* New York: W.W. Norton & Company.

Modernization—Primary Document

Introduction

Felix von Luckner was a German naval officer who gained a great reputation during World War I for his daring naval exploits and his avoidance of casualties. In 1926, von Luckner, who was known as the "Seadevil," began a successful speaking tour in the United States, where he even received a new car from Henry Ford. In this excerpt from his travelogue, Seadevil Conquers America, *von Luckner describes the skyscrapers that made New York City the very example of modernization in the 1920s.*

Document: *Seadevil Conquers America* by Felix von Luckner (1928)

When I first visited New York, years ago, the skyscrapers were few in number and were considered quite exceptional; today they determine the character of the city's physical appearance. Whether they are beautiful or not, I don't know. But they are stupendous and it makes a deep impression to look down from the thirtieth or fortieth story, to see little pointed buildings and then realize that these are churches. Above all, the skyscrapers are necessities in a city like New York in which so much business is concentrated and which lies on a small rocky island. Unable to expand in space, it must grow into the air.

To get a single overall view, we visited the Woolworth Building. This immense structure of steel and stone, the highest in New York, was executed in pure Gothic style and dedicated as a cathedral of commerce. It is 792 feet high, and has fifty-six stories, with three more in the tower. It has become a sort of trademark for New York. In the evening, lit up, it seems fairylike. The view from the tower is overwhelming. All around are the suburbs; in the distance, the Statue of Liberty and the great bridges across the East River to Brooklyn. Far below is the tiny City Hall, and before it at midday is the bustle of the anthouse. Toward Wall Street, downtown, is a little cemetery in which the tombstones seem like tiny pebbles.

It must not be supposed that the skyscrapers are limited to commercial uses. That may have been true to begin with, but they are now being put up for residential purposes as well, especially in the vicinity of Central Park. And why not? As far as comfort is concerned, it matters not whether one lives on the second story of an old house or on the twentieth or thirtieth of a new one; the elevators ceaselessly run up and down. And such quarters have the advantages of height, which Americans like; they shut out the street noises, are accessible to sunlight and to good fresh air. Rents are, however, not cheap in New York. A six-room apartment in a desirable neighborhood and good house will not be found for less than $3,000 a year.

Source: Luckner, Felix von. *Seadevil Conquers America* [Seeteufel erobert Amerika.] Leipzig: Koehler and Amelang, 1928. Available online at http://americainclass.org/sources/becomingmodern/modernity/text5/colcommentarysky.pdf.

MONETARY POLICY

Monetary policy is the broad set of actions taken to influence the availability of money or credit in the economy, and is usually the responsibility of a nation's central bank, such as the Federal Reserve System in the United States. Monetary policy affects the supply of money or interest rates using different policies. These include altering the discount rate at which the central bank lends to other banks, raising or lowering the reserve ratio banks are required to hold against liabilities thereby changing the supply of money available for lending, or open market operations of buying or sells securities to add or subtract from the money supply or alter interest rates. While often discussed in technical economic jargon, both the purpose and conduct of monetary policy have been hotly debated by American politicians and policy makers. The purposes of monetary policy emphasized, at different times, promoting employment, maintaining stable prices and low inflation, and supporting the convertibility of money into some commodity, usually gold, at a fixed rate, among others. Similarly, decision makers altered between adhering to automatic rules for setting policy and allowing greater discretion in pursuit of these goals. The means and ends of policy, and its contribution to overall prosperity, therefore, have evolved over time with changes in prevailing economic theory as well as political ideology.

The U.S. Constitution only briefly mentioned monetary policy, with Section 1, Article 8, investing Congress with the power to "coin money" and "regulate the value thereof." Since the founding of the country a variety of institutions have, officially or unofficially, made and implemented monetary policy. These include the First (1791–1811) and Second (1816–1836) Bank of the United States, the Department of the Treasury, and, since its creation in 1913, the Federal Reserve System. While the First and Second Bank encountered political opposition for being too active in the economy, Congress created the Federal Reserve as a decentralized institution to oversee a passive monetary policy based upon the gold standard and the real bills doctrine. Over time, however, the Federal Reserve became more centralized and increasingly influential as the goals of monetary policy changed and its implementation dictated a more active approach.

Even before its formal adoption with the Gold Standard Act (1900), the seemingly automatic and mechanical precepts of the gold standard guided American monetary policy. Countries adhering to the rules of the gold standard agreed to convert currency, such as dollars or pounds sterling, into gold at a fixed rate. Additionally, the so-called price-specie mechanism described by the Scottish philosopher David Hume appeared to allow the gold standard to operate with only a passive monetary policy. According to Hume, when

a country on the gold standard imported more than it exported, it funded the excess by paying out gold, the reduction in the supply of gold prompted a corresponding decline in amount of currency in circulation since there was less gold to back it, which lowered prices and increased interest rates as money became dear. Falling prices, however, made the country's exports more competitive while high interest rates attracted investors, automatically reversing the process and resulting, over the long term, in relative equilibrium. In practice the gold standard was not nearly so automatic, subject to periodic suspensions of convertibility, particularly during periods of economic crisis or war, and strenuously opposed by supporters of monetary expansion, like free silver advocate and long-time Democratic presidential nominee William Jennings Bryan. In the main, however, the gold standard seemed to provide clear guidance for monetary policy that only required policy makers maintain convertibility and passively allow gold to freely move in and out of the country.

Adherence to the "real bills" doctrine offered a similarly passive approach to monetary policy. Real bills dictated that the central bank rediscount, or lend to banks, against short-term commercial paper collateralized by commercial or agricultural (i.e., real) products. According to the theory, monetary policy passively aided the expansion or contraction of currency based upon the needs of the market. Adherents to the real bills theory believed that this prevented an inflationary overexpansion of the supply of money. Real bills, therefore, assessed the quality of credit, privileging uses deemed productive and discouraging credit judged as speculative. Combined with the ideology of the gold standard, policy makers conducted monetary policy by passively applying a set of rules rather than actively intervening in the market at the discretion of central bankers to influence specific targets such as inflation or employment.

In the middle of the 20th century, shifts in economic theory and political leadership at first threatened and then revived the fortunes of monetary policy as a tool for economic management. Monetary policy lost much of its importance with the onset of the Great Depression and the collapse of the gold standard in the 1930s. Critics charged that adherence to the gold standard and real bills doctrines exacerbated the crisis by requiring monetary contraction and then preventing expansion as the economy declined. The failure of banks and other lending institutions further aggravated the crisis. While it was believed that monetary policy could constrain inflation, its ability to prompt expansion was doubted, a condition many at the time likened to "pushing on string." Instead, fiscal policy became more important, particularly deficit spending to stimulate demand, a measure supported by the adherents of the British economist John Maynard Keynes. These attitudes prevailed during the years of the Great Depression and World War II, and monetary policy only slowly regained its perceived relevance during the 1950s. The revival was helped, in part, by the coming to office of Dwight Eisenhower, more conservative than the preceding Franklin Roosevelt and Harry Truman administrations. Eisenhower's fiscal conservatism made him more skeptical of Keynesian solutions and, therefore, willing to look to monetary policy as an alternative.

Monetary policy played an active role in supporting domestic goals of low unemployment and international aims of restoring the convertibility of the dollar into gold at a fixed rate under the renewed gold standard adopted at Bretton Woods (1944). After the European resumption of gold convertibility in 1958, however, monetary policy makers continued to prioritize American domestic issues ahead of maintaining the gold value of the dollar. The Federal Reserve used monetary policy, including open market operation, to influence interest rates and support Treasury deficit financing of domestic social welfare spending and Cold War defense and national security commitments. These included President Lyndon Johnson's Great Society programs as well as the Vietnam War. The active use of monetary policy to promote employment at home represented an important shift from the pre–Great Depression experience of a passive effort to provide currency elasticity. Furthermore, critics charged that presidential administrations exercised undue political influence over the Federal Reserve, compromising its independence. These accusations were heightened by the progressive centralization of power within the central bank. An expansive monetary policy, therefore, played a role in promoting inflation and helped precipitate the so-called Great Inflation of the mid-1960s through the mid-1980s. During the period prices rose rapidly as the supply of money expanded. Average annual consumer price inflation topped 13 percent by 1980. Inflation also contributed to end of the gold standard as the supply of dollars exceeded the nation's ability to convert

them into gold at a fixed rate. Consequently, the United States abandoned gold convertibility in 1971 and adopted a floating exchange rate by 1973.

Monetarism, popularized by the economist Milton Friedman, offered an alternative to the discretionary monetary policy blamed for the Great Inflation. Monetarism favored controlling inflation rather than actively promoting employment. It drew on the work of economists dating back to the beginning of the 20th century, such as Irving Fisher. Monetarists argued that policy should be guided by rules rather than discretion to prevent political influence. Furthermore, they focused on the growth of the quantity of money, rather than other economic indicators such as interest rates. According to Friedman, the Federal Reserve failed to prevent a decline in the quantity of money during the 1930s and thereby transformed a recession into the Great Depression, while a similar failure to check the rapid growth in the quantity of money caused the Great Inflation. Paul Volcker (1979–1987), the Federal Reserve Board chair during the Jimmy Carter and Ronald Reagan administrations, generally followed monetarist policy in combating the Great Inflation. Volcker limited the growth of the money supply even as this caused large swings in interest rates and contributed to a brief recession. The pain of high interest rates and recession helped discredit the monetarist emphasis on controlling the money supply, although inflation fell dramatically.

At the end of the 20th century, monetary policy continued to evolve in response to the economic and political context. Policy makers abandoned the monetarist targeting of monetary aggregates but retained a rules-based structure cognizant of the need to maintain low inflation. These policies again shifted in response to the 2008 financial crisis, as the Federal Reserve used discretionary emergency action to prevent banking collapses and followed a policy of monetary ease, in part to help combat high rates of unemployment.

See also
Bimetallism; Capitalism; Keynesian Economics; Libertarianism; National Bank/Federal Reserve System

Timothy W. Wintour

Further Reading
Axilrod, Stephen H. 2011. *Inside the Fed: Monetary Policy and Its Management, Martin Through Greenspan to Bernanke.* Cambridge, MA: MIT Press.

Friedman, Milton, and Anna Schwartz Jacobson. 1971. *A Monetary History of the United States, 1867–1960.* Princeton, NJ: Princeton University Press.

Hetzel, Robert L. 2008. *The Monetary Policy of the Federal Reserve: A History.* New York: Cambridge University Press.

Timberlake, Richard H., Jr. 1993. *Monetary Policy in the United States: An Intellectual and Institutional History.* Chicago: University of Chicago Press.

Monetary Policy—Primary Document

Introduction

Irving Fisher (1867–1947), a professor of political economy at Yale University, played a leading role in the development of a quantity theory of money. Fisher's macroeconomic beliefs, established in his book The Purchasing Power of Money, *and elsewhere, helped lay the foundation of later monetarist critiques by Milton Friedman and others. Fisher's work predated the adoption of the Federal Reserve Act in 1913, but varieties of monetarism began to have their greatest impact on monetary policy during the late 20th century. In the preface from* The Purchasing Power of Money, *reproduced here, Fisher not only set out the case for a scientific approach to money but also connected the topic to larger social and political interests.*

Document: Preface of Irving Fisher's *The Purchasing Power of Money: Its Determination and Relation to Credit Interest and Crises* (1912)

Preface to the First Edition

THE purpose of this book is to set forth the principles determining the purchasing power of money and to apply those principles to the study of historical changes in that purchasing power, including in particular the recent change in "the cost of living," which has aroused world-wide discussion.

If the principles here advocated are correct, the purchasing power of money—or its reciprocal, the level of prices—depends exclusively on five definite factors: (1) the volume of money in circulation; (2) its velocity of circulation; (3) the volume of bank deposits subject to check; (4) its velocity;

and (5) the volume of trade. Each of these five magnitudes is extremely definite, and their relation to the purchasing power of money is definitely expressed by an "equation of exchange." In my opinion, the branch of economics which treats of these five regulators of purchasing power ought to be recognized and ultimately will be recognized as an exact science, capable of precise formulation, demonstration, and statistical verification.

The main contentions of this book are at bottom simply a restatement and amplification of the old" quantity theory" of money. With certain corrections in the usual statements of that theory, it may still be called fundamentally sound. What has long been needed is a candid re-examination and revision of that venerable theory rather than its repudiation.

Yet in the voluminous literature on money, there seems to be very little that approaches accurate formulation and rigorous demonstration,—whether theoretical or statistical.

In making this attempt at reconstruction, I have the satisfaction of finding myself for once a conservative rather than a radical in economic theory. It has seemed to me a scandal that academic economists have, through outside clamor, been led into disagreements over the fundamental propositions concerning money. This is due to the confusion in which the subject has been thrown by reason of the political controversies with which it has become entangled.

As some one has said, it would seem that even the theorems of Euclid would be challenged and doubted if they should be appealed to by one political party as against another. At any rate, since the "quantity theory" has become the subject of political dispute, it has lost prestige and has even come to be regarded by many as an exploded fallacy. The attempts by promoters of unsound money to make an improper use of the quantity theory—as in the first Bryan campaign—led many sound money men to the utter repudiation of the quantity theory. The consequence has been that, especially in America, the quantity theory needs to be reintroduced into general knowledge.

Besides aiming to set forth the principles affecting the purchasing power of money, this book aims to illustrate and verify those principles by historical facts and statistics. In particular, the recent rise in prices is examined in detail and traced to its several causes.

The study of the principles and facts concerning the purchasing power of money is of far more than academic interest. Such questions affect the welfare of every in habitant of the civilized world. At each turn of the tide of prices, millions of persons are benefited and other millions are injured.

For a hundred years the world has been suffering from periodic changes in the level of prices, producing alternate crises and depressions of trade. Only by knowledge, both of the principles and of the facts involved, can such fluctuations in future be prevented or mitigated, and only by such knowledge can the losses which they entail be avoided or reduced. It is not too much to say that the evils of a variable monetary standard are among the most serious economic evils with which civilization has to deal; and the practical problem of finding a solution of the difficulty is of international extent and importance. I have proposed, very tentatively, a remedy for the evils of monetary instability. But the time is not yet ripe for the acceptance of any working plan. What is at present most needed is a clear and general public understanding of principles and facts.

Toward such an end this book aims to contribute:—

1. A reconstruction of the quantity theory.

2. A discussion of the best form of index number.

3. Some mechanical methods of representing visually the determination of the level of prices.

4. A practical method of estimating the velocity of circulation of money.

5. The ascertainment statistically of the bank deposits in the United States which are *subject to check*, as distinct from "individual deposits," as usually published.

6. An improved statistical evaluation of the volume of trade, as well as of the remaining elements in the equation of exchange.

7. A thorough statistical verification of the (reconstructed) quantity theory of money.

As it is quite impossible to do justice to some of these subjects without the use of mathematics, these have been freely introduced, but have been relegated, so far as possible, to Appendices. This plan, which is in accordance with that previously adopted in *The Nature of Capital and Income* and *The Rate of Interest*, leaves the text almost wholly nonmathematical....

Source: Fisher, Irving. *The Purchasing Power of Money: Its Determination and Relation to Credit Interest and Crises.* New York: The MacMillan Company, 1912, pp. 7–9. Available online at http://books.google.com/books?id=YjcuAAAAYAA-J&printsec=frontcover&dq=irving+fisher+purchasing+power&hl=en&sa=X&ei=JKD-UcCeLu2yygG69oDQDw&ved=0C-DoQ6AEwAA#v=onepage&q=irving%20fisher%20purchasing%20power&f=false.

MONROE DOCTRINE

The growing spirit of national pride following the stalemate between the United States and Great Britain in the War of 1812, Napoleon's defeat on the European continent in 1815, and the ongoing independence movements in Latin America had a profound impact on the young United States. American foreign policy makers understood the importance of freedom movements in Spanish America as potential markets for the exchange of goods and commodities. Certainly, the development of an independent foreign policy based on U.S. national interests, as embodied in the Monroe Doctrine, was the major diplomatic achievement of the new nation's first generation of political leaders.

The Congress of Vienna (1815) and the Holy Alliance (1818), which was inspired by Russian tsar Alexander I, were attempts by the restored European monarchs to maintain control over their colonial possessions. Russia still held on to the vast and unexplored territory of Alaska and sought to maintain its rights over the Pacific waters. Great Britain remained in charge of Canada and numerous islands in the Caribbean. Spain, despite the independence spirit sweeping Mexico and nations to the south, remained firmly in control of Cuba and Puerto Rico. France and the Netherlands ruled in French and Dutch Guiana as well as some islands in the Caribbean. The acquisition of the Louisiana Territory in 1803 and the preservation of the young

This painting by Allyn Cox depicts President James Monroe (left) meeting with his cabinet to discuss the Monroe Doctrine in 1823. Secretary of State John Quincy Adams stands at the globe. (Office of the Curator, Architect of the Capitol)

nation after the war with Great Britain in 1812 reinforced the notion that "Manifest Destiny"—the fulfillment of the natural boundaries from the Atlantic to the Pacific—was now within reach. The revolutions in Mexico and other Latin America countries between 1808 and 1822 to rid the yoke of imperialist domination by Spain and Portugal gave added weight to a developing American foreign policy.

The final expulsion of Spanish armies from Latin America in the spring of 1822 would be followed by a sharp rise in U.S. trade with the new countries. President James Monroe extended formal diplomatic recognition to La Plata, Chile, Peru, Colombia, and Mexico. Riding the crest of nationalistic fervor, Secretary of State John Quincy Adams,

Monroe's successor in that office and later as president, urged American diplomats to concentrate their efforts on acquiring favorable trading rights with the newly independent nations to the South. Adams was clear in his instructions that he did not want these new nations to exchange their former Spanish hegemony for English commercial absolutism.

The new British foreign secretary, George Canning, was also resolutely determined to prevent any restoration of Spanish rule in the Americas while seeking to maintain favorable commercial rights for English shipping, which was the basis for Adams's warning to his diplomats. In August 1823, Canning entered into discussions with the American minister to England, Richard Rush. The topic of their discussion focused on the success of the French military in Spain. Rush was confident that the British would never permit France to interfere with Latin American independence or to acquire territory by means of cession or conquest. Canning inquired whether the American government would join England in adopting such a policy. Rush later responded by letter that if the foreign secretary agreed to recognize the independence of the new Latin American republics, he would initiate such a joint statement without direct authorization from Washington. When Canning vaguely mentioned future recognition, Rush then referred matters back to Adams and Monroe.

Adams did not trust the British or their intentions and persuaded Monroe to make an announcement without British participation. In his annual message to Congress on December 2, 1823, President Monroe announced an American foreign policy that years later would be named after him. Three specific actions were undertaken. First, Secretary of State Adams sent a strong note of protest to Russia, asserting American rights to sail in the Pacific waters. Second, the United States, without qualification, recognized the complete and full independence of the revolutionary governments of Latin America. Third, the principle of independence in foreign affairs was reaffirmed while asserting U.S. rights to protect the Western Hemisphere for economic and security reasons.

In the course of his famous message, President Monroe, reaffirming his own economic nationalistic sentiments, issued four clear declarations: (1) colonization by European powers in the Western Hemisphere was no longer an option; (2) any attempt by any European country to establish colonies in the New World or efforts to gain political control of any American country would be considered an unfriendly act; (3) the United States would not interfere in the affairs of European nations or in the affairs of their colonies currently established in the Western Hemisphere; and (4) Europe must not in any way disturb the political status of any free country in the Americas.

The Monroe Doctrine was primarily concerned with two important principles. The first, noncolonization, was aimed at preventing any European power in the future from forming new colonies in the Western Hemisphere. The doctrine strengthened the U.S. hegemony in the Americas and served as a measure of continental security. This principle was primarily directed at Tsar Alexander, who, in 1821, announced

that Russian dominion extended southward from Alaska along the Pacific to the fifty-first parallel. The second principle, nonintervention, was a two-sided coin: the United States would be precluded from taking part in European wars, reinforcing the distinct differences in political systems; and, conversely, it implicitly deemed "unfriendly" any efforts by European powers to oppress or control the futures of the independent countries of the New World. This aspect committed the United States to a leading role in world politics and would be demonstrated by the Roosevelt Corollary to the Monroe Doctrine in the early 20th century.

Overseas, the immediate effect of Monroe's pronouncement was hardly earth shattering. The statesmen in Europe dismissed it as "blustering," "monstrous," and "arrogant." Yet no formal protests were delivered from the heads of government in Europe. Latin American capitals received the message with cordial respect. However, when Washington failed to negotiate military alliances with Colombia and Brazil, disillusionment quickly surfaced as to the intentions of the United States. Nevertheless, the most remarkable aspect to the entire diplomatic journey was that the upstart United States managed to issue such a bold statement without the military power to back it up. European powers were too concerned about maintaining the balance of power in their own backyard. Consequently, they paid very little attention to Monroe's message.

At home, the public's response was positive and enthusiastic. The anti-European, anti-British thrust of the message reached a receptive audience. The United States proclaimed a policy of "America for Americans." Latin Americans felt emboldened by the message, despite the lack of a military alliance with the United States, and resisted all forms of European intervention. Great Britain kept its part of the bargain and did not interfere. Canning remained firm in his commitment to prevent future revolutions and colonial expansion in Latin America. Nevertheless, he made sure to notify the government leaders in Latin America that England—through the Polignac Memorandum and the British Navy—and not the brash, upstart United States was responsible for warning off the Holy Alliance from recapturing the Latin colonies for Spain.

Actually, Great Britain was most responsible for giving the Monroe Doctrine its lasting strength. Because the British Navy controlled the Atlantic seas, it was with Great Britain's consent that United States ships were able to sail freely between Europe and the "New World." What helped foster the doctrine's viability was the reality that British merchants were primarily interested in preserving the independence of the emerging nations in Central and South America for commercial purposes. The first sign of interference from any European power signaled British willingness to side with the United States.

The Monroe Doctrine was grounded on the ideas of security and a growing awareness of the nation's developing economic potential. It represented a direct warning to the European powers that the United States was concerned about the affairs of all nations in the Western Hemisphere. It also revealed the growing strength of nationalism within the young country.

The Monroe Doctrine became a major cornerstone of U.S. foreign policy. It was not, however, referred to by that name until the 1850s. Prior to the nation's bloodiest conflict, the Civil War (1861–1865), European powers gradually took notice that the policy existed. Monroe's message, despite its anti-imperialist rhetoric, would be employed by future generations to further America's diplomatic interests in the name of "hemispheric solidarity" and "republic principles," including Theodore Roosevelt's "Big Stick" policy, the construction of the Panama Canal, and William Howard Taft's more amicable policy of "Dollar Diplomacy." In the aftermath of World War I the doctrine's role as protector of U.S. interests resurfaced when the military was deployed to the Caribbean nations of Haiti and Nicaragua to suppress revolutionary movements. Eventually, the negativity surrounding the doctrine's application was replaced by President Franklin D. Roosevelt's Good Neighbor Policy in the 1930s. However, during the Cuban Missile Crisis of 1962 and again in Nicaragua in the 1980s, while not invoking the Monroe Doctrine by name, the United States clearly was determined to protect its national security interests or seek the overthrow of governments hostile to a nation's democratic principles.

Although President Monroe's 1823 message to Congress was not widely recognized until years later, it symbolized the growing importance of the young nation on the global stage. The doctrine established a permanent precedent for U.S. actions in dealing with other American states. Its application took on added importance by the turn of the new century when the United States assumed a leading position in world politics and economic dominance. In terms of foreign policy, it extended the country's domestic principle of "Manifest Destiny," for better or worse.

See also
Diplomacy; Imperialism

CHARLES F. HOWLETT

Further Reading
Ammon, Harry. 1990. *James Monroe: The Quest for National Identity*. Charlottesville, VA: University of Virginia Press.

Bemis, Samuel Flagg. 1949. *John Quincy Adams and the Foundations of American Foreign Policy*. New York: Alfred A. Knopf.

Bemis, Samuel Flagg. 1943. *The Latin American Policy of the United States: An Historical Interpretation*. New York: Harcourt, Brace.

Cunningham, Noble F., Jr. 1996. *The Presidency of James Monroe*. Lawrence, VA: University Press of Kansas.

Dangerfield, George. 1965. *The Awakening of American Nationalism, 1815–1828*. New York: Harper & Row.

May, Ernest. 1975. *The Making of the Monroe Doctrine*. Cambridge, MA: Harvard University Press.

Perkins, Dexter. 1955. *A History of the Monroe Doctrine*. Boston: Little, Brown.

Sexton, Jay. 2011. *The Monroe Doctrine: Empire and Nation in the Nineteenth Century*. New York: Hill and Wang.

Monroe Doctrine—Primary Document

Introduction

In his annual message to Congress on December 2, 1823, President James Monroe denounced European subjugation on the American continents. That denunciation became famous as the Monroe Doctrine.

Document: President James Monroe's 1823 Message to Congress Spelling Out the Monroe Doctrine (December 2, 1823)

Fellow citizens of the Senate and House of Representatives:

Many important subjects will claim your attention during the present session, of which I shall endeavor to give, in aid of your deliberations, a just idea in this communication. I undertake this duty with diffidence, from the vast extent of the interests on which I have to treat and of their great importance to every portion of our Union. I enter on it with zeal from a thorough conviction that there never was a period since the establishment of our revolution when, regarding the condition of the civilized world and its bearing on us, there was greater necessity for devotion in the public servants to their respective duties, or for virtue, patriotism, and union in our constituents.

Meeting in you a new Congress, I deem it proper to present this view of public affairs in greater detail than might otherwise be necessary. I do it, however, with peculiar satisfaction, from a knowledge that in this respect I shall comply more fully with the sound principles of our government. The people being with us exclusively the sovereign, it is indispensable that full information be laid before them on all important subjects, to enable them to exercise that high power with complete effect. If kept in the dark, they must be incompetent to it. We are all liable to error, and those who are engaged in the management of public affairs are more subject to excitement and to be led astray by their particular interests and passions than the great body of our constituents, who, living at home in the pursuit of their ordinary avocations, are calm but deeply interested spectators of events and of the conduct of those who are parties to them. To the people every department of the government and every individual in each are responsible, and the more full their information the better they can judge of the wisdom of the policy pursued and of the conduct of each in regard to it. From their dispassionate judgment much aid may always be obtained, while their approbation will form the greatest incentive and most gratifying reward for virtuous actions and the dread of their censure the best security against the abuse of their confidence. Their interests in all vital questions are the same, and the bond, by sentiment as well as by interest, will be proportionably strengthened as they are better informed of the real state of public affairs, especially in difficult conjunctures. It is by such knowledge that local prejudices and jealousies are surmounted, and that a national policy, extending its fostering care and protection to all the great interests of our Union, is formed and steadily adhered to....

At the proposal of the Russian imperial government, made through the minister of the emperor residing here, a full power and instructions have been transmitted to the minister of the United States at St. Petersburg to arrange by amicable negotiation the respective rights and interests of the two nations on the northwest coast of this continent. A similar proposal had been made by his imperial Majesty to the government of Great Britain, which has likewise been acceded to. The government of the United States has been desirous by this friendly proceeding of manifesting the great value which they have invariably attached to the friendship of the emperor and their solicitude to cultivate the best understanding with his government. In the discussions to which this interest has given rise and in the arrangements by which they may terminate the occasion has been judged proper for asserting, as a principle in which the rights and interests of the United States are involved, that the American continents, by the free and independent condition which they have assumed and maintain, are henceforth not to be considered as subjects for future colonization by any European powers....

It was stated at the commencement of the last session that a great effort was then making in Spain and Portugal to improve the condition of the people of those countries, and that it appeared to be conducted with extraordinary moderation. It need scarcely be remarked that the result has been so far very different from what was then anticipated. Of events in that quarter of the globe, with which we have so much intercourse and from which we derive our origin, we have always been anxious and interested spectators. The citizens of the United States cherish sentiments the most friendly in favor of the liberty and happiness of their fellow men on that side of the Atlantic. In the wars of the European powers in matters relating to themselves, we have never taken any part, nor does it comport with our policy so to do. It is only when our rights are invaded or seriously menaced that we resent injuries or make preparation for our defense. With the movements in this hemisphere we are of necessity more immediately connected, and by causes which must be obvious to all enlightened and impartial observers. The political system of the allied powers is essentially different in this respect from that of America. This difference proceeds from that which exists in their respective governments; and to the defense of our own, which has been achieved by the loss of so much blood and treasure, and matured by the wisdom of their most enlightened citizens, and under which we have enjoyed unexampled felicity, this whole nation is devoted. We owe it, therefore, to candor and to the amicable relations existing between the United States and those powers to declare that we should consider any attempt on their part to extend their system to any portion of this hemisphere as dangerous to our peace and safety. With the existing colonies or dependencies of any European power, we have not interfered and shall not interfere. But with the governments who have declared their independence and maintained it, and whose independence we have, on great consideration and on just principles, acknowledged, we could not view any interposition for the purpose of oppressing them, or controlling in any other manner their destiny, by any European power in any other light than as the manifestation of an unfriendly disposition toward the United States. In the war between those new governments and Spain, we declared our neutrality at the time of their recognition, and to this we have adhered, and shall continue to adhere, provided no change shall occur which, in the judgment of the competent authorities of this government, shall make a corresponding change on the part of the United States indispensable to their security.

The late events in Spain and Portugal show that Europe is still unsettled. Of this important fact no stronger proof can be adduced than that the allied powers should have thought it proper, on any principle satisfactory to themselves, to have interposed by force in the internal concerns of Spain. To what extent such interposition may be carried, on the same principle, is a question in which all independent powers whose governments differ from theirs are interested, even those most remote, and surely none more so than the United States. Our policy in regard to Europe, which was adopted at an early stage of the wars which have so long agitated that quarter of the globe, nevertheless remains the same, which is, not to interfere in the internal concerns of any of its powers; to consider the government de facto as the legitimate government for us; to cultivate friendly relations with it, and to preserve those relations by a frank, firm, and manly policy, meeting in all instances the just claims of every power, submitting to injuries from none. But in regard to those continents, circumstances are eminently and conspicuously different. It is impossible that the allied powers should extend their political system to any portion of either continent without endangering our peace and happiness; nor can anyone believe that our southern brethren, if left to themselves, would adopt it of their own accord. It is equally impossible, therefore, that we should behold such interposition in any form with indifference. If we look to the comparative strength and resources of Spain and those new governments, and their distance from each other, it must be obvious that she can never subdue them. It is still the true policy of the United States to leave the parties to themselves in the hope that other powers will pursue the same course.

Source: Richardson, James D., ed. *A Compilation of the Messages and Papers of the Presidents.* Vol. 2. New York: Bureau of National Literature, Inc., 1897, pp. 207–219.

MORAL MAJORITY

The Moral Majority, the conservative evangelical Christian political action group founded by Baptist preacher Jerry Falwell in 1979, had its roots in the changes in the American zeitgeist that transpired during the late 1960s and early 1970s. The sexual revolution that accompanied the rise of the counterculture during the 1960s challenged the dominance of evangelical views on morality in the United States. The feminist movement of the 1970s that took many women out of the home and into the workplace challenged the evangelical views of a God-ordained, patriarchal society. The tipping point began in 1973, when the U.S. Supreme Court delivered its decision in *Roe v. Wade*, guaranteeing abortion rights to American women. As many evangelicals viewed America as a special nation, smiled upon by God because of its morality and biblical values, such changes threatened the very core of their identity, both as Christians and as Americans.

Before the late 1970s, however, many Christian leaders eschewed partisan politics. In many quarters, it was considered ungodly to engage in partisan talk from the pulpit. The church was viewed as being above politics among white evangelicals; historically, African American churches had been more active. The election of 1976 was both a bellwether event and the last straw for conservative Christians. The election of Jimmy Carter—a self-proclaimed born again Christian—encouraged conservatives that America was

Moral Majority Leader Rev. Jerry Falwell, right, during his antipornography demonstration, September 1, 1985. Two years before, *Hustler* magazine had published a parody about Falwell's sex life; Falwell sued for libel and ultimately lost his case before the U.S. Supreme Court, which held that reasonable people would not have believed the satire. (Shelly Katz/The LIFE Images Collection/Getty Images)

ready for an actively political voice from the church. But the liberal nature of Carter's politics (or more liberal than Christian leaders might have expected) disillusioned many evangelicals, especially in the South. The perceived downfall of the United States religiously, socially, and politically, combined with increases in urban crime and racial polarization and an economy in recession, caused many American evangelicals to abandon the Democratic Party that had for so long been the dominant force in the South, in favor of the Republican Party.

Jerry Falwell was no newcomer when he founded the Moral Majority in 1979. In 1956, he had started the Thomas Road Baptist Church in Lynchburg, Virginia, and within a year was televising his services on a program called the *Old-Time Gospel Hour*. However, for most of the first two decades of his ministry, Falwell opposed political involvement on the part of the clergy, especially during the civil rights

protests of the 1950s and 1960s—a movement he personally opposed. By 1971, the *Old-Time Gospel Hour* was broadcast nationwide, and as the decade wore on his views about involvement began to change, especially after *Roe v. Wade*. In 1976, Falwell embarked on nationwide "I Love America" rallies that blended patriotic and religious themes, with the clean-cut students of Liberty University, a school he had personally founded, providing the musical and visual backdrop. As gay and lesbian Americans began to protest for equal rights in much the same way that African Americans had done two decades earlier, Falwell was outspoken in his opposition, claiming that those forces that he saw as bringing down America were no more than a vocal minority. He stated in his 1987 autobiography *Strength for the Journey*, "I was convinced that there was a 'moral majority' out there among these more than 200 million Americans sufficient in number to turn back the flood tide of moral permissiveness, family breakdown and general capitulation to evil and to foreign policies such as Marxism-Leninism."

Falwell, along with cofounder Paul Weyrich (a conservative Catholic), began the Moral Majority at a fortuitous time. With a vision of creating a movement that would include not only Fundamentalist Christians like himself, but also conservative Catholics, Jews, and even atheists, he was ready to bring his views of how to turn America around to a national audience. With the nation disillusioned after a decade of economic difficulty, conservative Christians saw the election of 1980 as their time to get America to turn back to what they saw as the godly principles on which it had been founded. Religious conservatism merged with political conservatism when Republican candidate Ronald Reagan told a largely conservative meeting of the Religious Roundtable in Dallas in August 1980 that "you can't endorse me, but I want you to know that I endorse you." Falwell and the Moral Majority, along with other conservative Christian groups, quickly lined up behind Reagan and helped ensure a landslide victory in the presidential election that November. Unlike Carter, Reagan supported every facet of the Moral Majority's stated agenda: supporting the traditional definition of family, conservative views on gender roles, and censorship of pornography; while opposing the Supreme Court's ban on organized prayer in public schools, equal rights for women and especially abortion rights.

Falwell claimed much of the credit for the Republican victories for the Moral Majority, both in the presidential race and in congressional races, in 1980. There can be little doubt that the group was influential, establishing local chapters in all fifty states, holding voter registration and education drives to increase the numbers of conservative Christians going to the ballot box, and pioneering the idea of a national organization targeting specific members of Congress for defeat. Falwell consolidated his position as the preeminent voice for the political Religious Right by naming to the Moral Majority's board of directors a large number of influential Fundamentalist ministers, such as Tim LaHaye, Charles Stanley, and James Kennedy. In its heyday during the early 1980s, the Moral Majority claimed over 4 million members, though others dispute these claims as wildly inflated. Regardless, the organization was influential, as Reagan's political preferences largely mirrored the Religious Right. Though actual members of the Moral Majority were not appointed to office, Reagan did appoint a conservative Christian who opposed abortion rights, C. Everett Koop, as surgeon general.

Though the organization was powerful and influential during the early 1980s—largely based on Falwell's personality and television presence—its local chapters were less effective. In only two states were county chapters established, and the fact that the organization was organized like the Baptist denomination—with complete independence at the local level—brought with it a lack of unity in terms of political strategy. After the election of Reagan in 1980 and the organization's victories in terms of membership and influence during the first half of the decade, the large-scale fund-raising that was the lifeblood of the national organization began to drop off. This occurred for a number of reasons. Reagan's landslide reelection in 1984 made the urgency that characterized the 1980 campaign seem less necessary. Scandals that brought down fellow evangelical leaders such as Jimmy Swaggart and Jim and Tammy Faye Bakker had tarnished the reputation of the Religious Right in the eyes of many Americans. Falwell, who had brought American Fundamentalism with him as he rose in popularity, also helped diminish its influence as many Americans began to see him as judgmental and extreme. His penchant for making controversial statements, which had done so much to bring public attention to his cause in the early years, turned on him as well. By 1987, Falwell resigned as the president of the Moral Majority, and in 1989, claiming that the organization had accomplished its mission, Falwell disbanded the group. He attempted to revive the Moral Majority in 2004, but it failed to gain any traction and he died three years later.

The Moral Majority left a mixed legacy. In terms of its stated goals, it accomplished little: abortion was still legal, pornography had not been diminished, the gay rights movement was stronger than ever, and women were still bucking the Fundamentalist opinion that they should primarily be mothers and homemakers. However, its influence continued long after the organization folded. Other groups quickly took up the Moral Majority's mantle at the leadership of the conservative Christian political movement. The Christian Coalition, founded the same year that the Moral Majority disbanded, by fellow televangelist Pat Robertson and conservative activist Ralph Reed continued to support the same causes and use many of the tactics pioneered by Falwell and the Moral Majority. Falwell himself handed off the mantle of the movement to radio psychologist James Dobson and his organization, Focus on the Family. Though the political switch of the South from primarily supporting the Democratic to backing the Republican Party cannot be attributed to Falwell, the large number of his followers who lived in that region certainly contributed to the changes. Largely thanks to Falwell's efforts, the Religious Right would remain a potent political force in American politics for at least another two decades after his organization's decline.

See also

Christian Fundamentalism; Conservatism; Gay Rights; Pro-Choice Movement; Pop Culture; Right to Life

STEVEN L. DANVER

Further Reading

Falwell, Jerry. 1987. *Strength for the Journey.* New York: Simon and Schuster.

Lichtman, Allan J. 2008. *White Protestant Nation: The Rise of the American Conservative Movement.* New York: Grove Press.

Martin, William. 1996. *With God on Our Side: The Rise of the Religious Right in America.* New York: Broadway Books.

Moen, Matthew C. 1992. *The Transformation of the Christian Right.* Tuscaloosa, AL: University of Alabama Press.

Snowball, David. 1992. *Continuity and Change in the Rhetoric of the Moral Majority.* New York: Praeger.

Williams, Daniel K. 2010. *God's Own Party: The Making of the Christian Right.* New York: Oxford University Press.

Moral Majority—Primary Documents

Document 1: Introduction

Jerry Falwell founded the Moral Majority in 1979 as a religious answer to the increasing secularism he saw in American society, which had its roots in the counterculture of the 1960s. Southern evangelicals, long an exclusive constituency of the Democratic Party, followed Falwell to the Republican Party beginning with the election of Ronald Reagan in 1980. In this excerpt from Falwell's seminal call to religious and political conservatism, Listen America, *he encapsulates the reasons for his movement.*

Document 1: *Listen America* by Jerry Falwell (1980)

We must reverse the trend America finds herself in today. Young people between the ages of twenty-five and forty have been born and reared in a different world than Americans of years past. The television set has been their primary baby-sitter. From the television set they have learned situation ethics and immorality—they have learned a loss of respect for human life. They have learned to disrespect the family as God has established it. They have been educated in a public-school system that is permeated with secular humanism. They have been taught that the Bible is just another book of literature. They have been taught that there are no absolutes in our world today. They have been introduced to the drug culture. They have been reared by the family and the public school in a society that is greatly void of discipline and character-building. These same young people have been reared under the influence of a government that has taught them socialism and welfarism. They have been taught to believe that the world owes them a living whether they work or not.

I believe that America was built on integrity, on faith in God, and on hard work. I do not believe that anyone has ever been successful in life without being willing to add that last ingredient—diligence or hard work. We now have second- and third-generation welfare recipients. Welfare is not always wrong. There are those who do need welfare, but we have reared a generation that understands neither the dignity nor the importance of work.

Every American who looks at the facts must share a deep concern and burden for our country. We are not unduly concerned when we say that there are some very dark clouds on America's horizon. I am not a pessimist, but it is indeed a time for truth. If Americans will face the truth, our nation can be turned around and can be saved from the evils and the destruction that have fallen upon every other nation that has turned its back on God.

There is no excuse for what is happening in our country. We must, from the highest office in the land right down to the shoe shine boy in the airport, have a return to biblical basics. If the Congress of our United States will take its stand on that which is right and wrong, and if our President, our judiciary system, and our state and local leaders will take their stand on holy living, we can turn this country around.

I personally feel that the home and the family are still held in reverence by the vast majority of the American public.

I believe there is still a vast number of Americans who love their country, are patriotic, and are willing to sacrifice for her. I remember the time when it was positive to be patriotic, and as far as I am concerned, it still is. I remember as a boy, when the flag was raised, everyone stood proudly and put his hand upon his heart and pledged allegiance with gratitude. I remember when the band struck up "The Stars and Stripes Forever," we stood and goose pimples would run all over me. I remember when I was in elementary school during World War II, when every report from the other shores meant something to us. We were not out demonstrating against our boys who were dying in Europe and Asia. We were praying for them and thanking God for them and buying war bonds to help pay for the materials and artillery they needed to fight and win and come back.

I believe that Americans want to see this country come back to basics, back to values, back to biblical morality, back to sensibility, and back to patriotism. Americans are looking for leadership and guidance. It is fair to ask the question, "If 84 per cent of the American people still believe in morality, why is America having such internal problems?" We must look for the answer to the highest places in every level of government. We have a lack of leadership in America. But Americans have been lax in voting in and out of office the right and the wrong people.

My responsibility as a preacher of the Gospel is one of influence, not of control, and that is the responsibility of each individual citizen. Through the ballot box Americans must provide for strong moral leadership at every level. If our country will get back on the track in sensibility and moral sanity, the crises that I have herein mentioned will work out in the course of time and with God's blessings.

It is now time to take a stand on certain moral issues, and we can only stand if we have leaders. We must stand against the Equal Rights Amendment, the feminist revolution, and the homosexual revolution. We must have a revival in this country....

As a preacher of the Gospel, I not only believe in prayer and preaching, I also believe in good citizenship. If a labor union in America has the right to organize and improve its working conditions, then I believe that the churches and the pastors, the priests, and the rabbis of America have a responsibility, not just the right, to see to it that the moral climate and conscience of Americans is such that this nation can be healed inwardly. If it is healed inwardly, then it will heal itself outwardly....

Americans have been silent much too long. We have stood by and watched as American power and influence have been systematically weakened in every sphere of the world. We are not a perfect nation, but we are still a free nation because we have the blessing of God upon us. We must continue to follow in a path that will ensure that blessing....

Let us never forget that as our Constitution declares, we are endowed by our Creator with certain inalienable rights. It is only as we abide by those laws established by our Creator that He will continue to bless us with these rights. We are endowed our rights to freedom and liberty and the pursuit of happiness by the God who created man to be free and equal.

The hope of reversing the trends of decay in our republic now lies with the Christian public in America. We cannot expect help from the liberals. They certainly are not going to call our nation back to righteousness and neither are the pornographers, the smut peddlers, and those who are corrupting our youth. Moral Americans must be willing to put their reputations, their fortunes, and their very lives on the line for this great nation of ours. Would that we had the courage of our forefathers who knew the great responsibility that freedom carries with it....

Our Founding Fathers separated church and state in function, but never intended to establish a government void of God. As is evidenced by our Constitution, good people in America must exert an influence and provide a conscience and climate of morality in which it is difficult to go wrong, not difficult for people to go right in America.

I am positive in my belief regarding the Constitution that God led in the development of that document, and as a result, we here in America have enjoyed 204 years of unparalleled freedom. The most positive people in the world are people who believe the Bible to be the Word of God. The Bible contains a positive message. It is a message written by 40 men over a period of approximately 1,500 years under divine inspiration.

It is God's message of love, redemption, and deliverance for a fallen race. What could be more positive than the message of redemption in the Bible? But God will force Himself upon no man. Each individual American must make His choice....

Americans must no longer linger in ignorance and apathy. We cannot be silent about the sins that are destroying this nation. The choice is ours. We must turn America around or prepare for inevitable destruction. I am listening to the sounds that threaten to take away our liberties in America. And I have listened to God's admonitions and His direction—the only hopes of saving America. Are you listening too?

Source: Falwell, Jerry. *Listen America*. New York: Doubleday, 1980, pp. 17–23. Copyright © 1980 by Jerry Falwell. Rights held by Doubleday, a division of Bantam Doubleday Dell Publishing Group, Inc.

Document 2: Introduction

From the founding of the Moral Majority in 1979 through the early 1980s, the group exercised a profound influence on the rhetoric of religion in public spaces in the United States. The group (and larger conservative religious movements) had a beneficial and symbiotic relationship with candidate and President Ronald Reagan. Reagan spoke the words that the movement wanted to hear, and in return they gave him their unwavering support. This 1984 speech by Reagan is a case in point.

Document 2: Remarks at an Ecumenical Prayer Breakfast in Dallas, Texas, by President Ronald Reagan (August 23, 1984)

These past few weeks it seems that we've all been hearing a lot of talk about religion and its role in politics, religion and its place in the political life of the Nation. And I think it's appropriate today, at a prayer breakfast for 17,000 citizens in the State of Texas during a great political convention, that this issue be addressed.

I don't speak as a theologian or a scholar, only as one who's lived a little more than his threescore ten—which has been a source of annoyance to some—[laughter]—and as one who has been active in the political life of the Nation for roughly four decades and now who's served the past three and a half years in our highest office. I speak, I think I can say, as one who has seen much, who has loved his country, and who's seen it change in many ways.

I believe that faith and religion play a critical role in the political life of our nation—and always has—and that the church—and by that I mean all churches, all denominations—has had a strong influence on the state. And this has worked to our benefit as a nation.

Those who created our country—the Founding Fathers and Mothers—understood that there is a divine order, which transcends the human order. They saw the state, in fact, as a form of moral order and felt that the bedrock of moral order is religion.

The Mayflower Compact began with the words, "In the name of God, amen." The Declaration of Independence appeals to "Nature's God" and the "Creator" and "the Supreme Judge of the world." Congress was given a chaplain, and the oaths of office are oaths before God.

James Madison in the Federalist Papers admitted that in the creation of our Republic he perceived the hand of the Almighty. John Jay, the first Chief Justice of the Supreme Court, warned that we must never forget the God from whom our blessings flowed.

George Washington referred to religion's profound and unsurpassed place in the heart of our nation quite directly in his Farewell Address in 1796. Seven years earlier, France had erected a government that was intended to be purely secular. This new government would be grounded on reason rather than the law of God. By 1796 the French Revolution had known the Reign of Terror.

And Washington voiced reservations about the idea that there could be a wise policy without a firm moral and religious foundation. He said, "Of all the dispositions and habits which lead to political prosperity, Religion and morality are indispensable supports. In vain would that man (call himself a patriot) who (would) labour to subvert these...finest props of the duties of men and citizens. The mere Politician. . . (and) the pious man ought to respect and to cherish (religion and morality)." And he added, ". . . let us with caution indulge the supposition, that morality can be maintained without religion."

I believe that George Washington knew the City of Man cannot survive without the City of God, that the Visible City will perish without the Invisible City.

Religion played not only a strong role in our national life; it played a positive role. The abolitionist movement was at heart a moral and religious movement; so was the modern civil rights struggle. And throughout this time, the state was tolerant of religious belief, expression, and practice. Society, too, was tolerant.

But in the 1960's this began to change. We began to make great steps toward secularizing our nation and removing religion from its honored place.

In 1962 the Supreme Court in the New York prayer case banned the compulsory saying of prayers. In 1963 the Court banned the reading of the Bible in our public schools. From that point on, the courts pushed the meaning of the ruling ever outward, so that now our children are not allowed voluntary prayer. We even had to pass a law—we passed a special law in the Congress just a few weeks ago to allow student prayer groups the same access to schoolrooms after classes that a young Marxist society, for example, would already enjoy with no opposition.

The 1962 decision opened the way to a flood of similar suits. Once religion had been made vulnerable, a series of assaults were made in one court after another, on one issue after another. Cases were started to argue against tax-exempt status for churches. Suits were brought to abolish the words "under God" from the Pledge of Allegiance and to remove "In God We Trust" from public documents and from our currency.

Today there are those who are fighting to make sure voluntary prayer is not returned to the classrooms. And the frustrating thing for the great majority of Americans who support and understand the special importance of religion in the national life—the frustrating thing is that those who are attacking religion claim they are doing it in the name of tolerance, freedom, and openmindedness. Question: Isn't the real truth that they are intolerant of religion? [Applause] They refuse to tolerate its importance in our lives.

If all the children of our country studied together all of the many religions in our country, wouldn't they learn greater tolerance of each other's beliefs? If children prayed together, would they not understand what they have in common, and would this not, indeed, bring them closer, and is this not to be desired? So, I submit to you that those who claim to be fighting for tolerance on this issue may not be tolerant at all.

When John Kennedy was running for President in 1960, he said that his church would not dictate his Presidency any more than he would speak for his church. Just so, and proper. But John Kennedy was speaking in an America in which the role of religion—and by that I mean the role of all churches—was secure. Abortion was not a political issue. Prayer was not a political issue. The right of church schools to operate was not a political issue. And it was broadly acknowledged that religious leaders had a right and a duty to speak out on the issues of the day. They held a place of respect, and a politician who spoke to or of them with a lack of respect would not long survive in the political arena.

It was acknowledged then that religion held a special place, occupied a special territory in the hearts of the citizenry. The climate has changed greatly since then. And since it has, it logically follows that religion needs defenders against those who care only for the interests of the state.

There are, these days, many questions on which religious leaders are obliged to offer their moral and theological guidance, and such guidance is a good and necessary thing. To know how a church and its members feel on a public issue expands the parameters of debate. It does not narrow the debate; it expands it.

The truth is, politics and morality are inseparable. And as morality's foundation is religion, religion and politics are necessarily related. We need religion as a guide. We need it because we are imperfect, and our government needs the church, because only those humble enough to admit they're sinners can bring to democracy the tolerance it requires in order to survive.

A state is nothing more than a reflection of its citizens; the more decent the citizens, the more decent the state. If you practice a religion, whether you're Catholic, Protestant, Jewish, or guided by some other faith, then your private life will be influenced by a sense of moral obligation, and so, too, will your public life. One affects the other. The churches of America do not exist by the grace of the state; the churches of America are not mere citizens of the state. The churches of America exist apart; they have their own vantage point, their own authority. Religion is its own realm; it makes its own claims.

We establish no religion in this country, nor will we ever. We command no worship. We mandate no belief. But we poison our society when we remove its theological underpinnings. We court corruption when we leave it bereft of belief. All are free to believe or not believe; all are free to practice a faith or not. But those who believe must be free to speak of and act on their belief, to apply moral teaching to public questions.

I submit to you that the tolerant society is open to and encouraging of all religions. And this does not weaken us; it strengthens us, it makes us strong. You know, if we look back through history to all those great civilizations, those great nations that rose up to even world dominance and then deteriorated, declined, and fell, we find they all had one thing in common. One of the significant forerunners of their fall was their turning away from their God or gods.

Without God, there is no virtue, because there's no prompting of the conscience. Without God, we're mired in the material, that flat world that tells us only what the senses perceive. Without God, there is a coarsening of the society. And without God, democracy will not and cannot long endure. If we ever forget that we're one nation under God, then we will be a nation gone under.

If I could just make a personal statement of my own—in these three-and-a-half years I have understood and known better than ever before the words of Lincoln, when he said that he would be the greatest fool on this footstool called Earth if he ever thought that for one moment he could perform the duties of that office without help from One who is stronger than all.

I thank you, thank you for inviting us here today. Thank you for your kindness and your patience. May God keep you, and may we, all of us, keep God.

Source: *The Public Papers of Ronald Reagan*, The Ronald Reagan Presidential Library, National Archives and Records Administration. Available at http://www.reagan.utexas.edu/archives/speeches/1984/82384a.htm.

MORMONISM

The Church of Jesus Christ of Latter-day Saints began in New York's "burned-over district" during the early decades of the 19th century. Nicknamed "Mormonism," and its followers, "Mormons," by nonmembers, both labels reference the Book of Mormon and are considered acceptable. Authorized shortened versions of the religion and its adherents include "the Church," or "the Church of Jesus Christ," and "Latter-day Saints," (LDS) or "Saints."

The beginning of Mormonism may be traced to two waves of religious fervor in the United States that helped to develop the climate necessary for its birth. Both the Great Awakening and the Second Great Awakening helped to reorient Christian thinking and establish evangelistic patterns that encouraged personal contact with God and an increased lay participation in church matters. Due to the timing of Mormonism's appearance and to its experiments at communal pooling of resources (as part of the law of consecration), the beginning of the church is also frequently connected to the utopian movement.

Mormonism is theologically similar to yet distinct from other Christian denominations. One founding principle is the idea that the church is a reorganization of Christ's original church. Latter-day Saints believe that the primitive organization Christ established during his mortal ministry on earth and its authorized priesthood power were removed from the earth due to widespread apostasy following the deaths of the Twelve Apostles. This true church was reorganized and restored beginning in 1820 under the direction of Joseph

Smith Jr. For this reason Mormonism does not embrace a number of traditional Christian doctrines or creeds that were generated after the close of the New Testament. Latter-day Saints also maintain that miracles and direct revelation continue to occur and are necessary in order to guide the church and its members. For this reason the religion is directed by a living prophet-president who holds the proper priesthood authority to govern.

The church divides its history into the following six periods:

1. New York Period (1820–1830)

The foundation of Mormonism is traced to Joseph Smith's First Vision at age fourteen. This occurred near his home in upstate New York in the spring of 1820. At that time, young Joseph had a vision in which God and Jesus Christ appeared to him. Later, an angel named Moroni visited in 1823 to inform him of an ancient religious record located in the Hill Cumorah near Palmyra, New York. Smith translated this record and published it in 1830 as the Book of Mormon. That same year in Fayette, New York, the Church of Jesus Christ was also officially organized on April 6. At that time, six original members and a small group of believers sustained Smith as the religion's first prophet, seer, and revelator of this dispensation or time period. Early proselytizing efforts resulted in the formation of several congregations located in New York and Pennsylvania. Even prior to its official organization, believers experienced a great deal of hostility.

2. Ohio-Missouri Period (1831–1838)

As turmoil surrounding the new religion increased, Smith directed the church to move further west into Ohio and Missouri. Establishing their headquarters in Kirtland, Ohio, members constructed a modern temple and dedicated it on March 27, 1836. While internal strife, external mob violence, and massive bank failures resulted in a migration of members to Illinois, vigorous missionary efforts also attracted large numbers of immigrant members from overseas. These conversions served as the main source of growth for the church in the future.

3. Nauvoo Period (1839–1846)

Forced from their homes in Ohio and Missouri, church members established the city of Nauvoo, Illinois, along the banks of a bend in the Mississippi River in 1839. Growing in size to match that of the city of Chicago, Nauvoo became the new headquarters of the church and the site of a second temple. The Female Relief Society of Nauvoo was established in 1842. Originally founded to sew work shirts for temple laborers, this auxiliary continues today simply as the Relief Society. It is the oldest and largest women's organization in the world. Smith introduced the principle of plural marriage during the 1840s, though the practice did not become widespread until the 1850s. Increasing hostility eventually resulted in the assassination of Joseph Smith and his brother Hyrum on June 27, 1844, at Carthage, Illinois. The event helped to spur a new migration toward the Salt Lake Valley in what was, at that time, the northern edge of Mexico.

4. Pioneering the West (1846–1898)

Under the direction of Brigham Young, an exodus of Latter-day Saints from Illinois began during the winter of 1846. U.S. military leaders approached the migrants at Council Bluffs, Iowa, to recruit volunteers for the Mexican-American War. As a result, the Mormon Battalion was mustered into service on July 16, 1846. They undertook a 2,030-mile march to San Diego, one of the longest in military history. At approximately the same time this group was mustered out of service, the first body of pioneers entered the Salt Lake Valley on July 24, 1847. The church next instituted a widespread expansion effort throughout the Great Basin region. It also renewed overseas missionary efforts. In 1857, conflicts with the government resulted in the U.S. Army arriving in Utah to subdue what was believed to be an uprising against federal authority dubbed "the Mormon War." Associated with this unrest was a tragedy known as the Mountain Meadows Massacre. During this event, local Mormons, spurred by hysteria and fear, attacked a passing migrant train, killing 120 individuals. Toward the end of the Pioneer Period, in 1890, the church discontinued its practice of plural marriage.

5. Expansion of the Church (1899–1950)

The practice of Saints migrating to the central headquarters of the church ended during the 1920s due to growing membership numbers outside of Utah. Church leadership also embraced new technologies on a large scale. The church's semi-annual General Conference was broadcast for the first time over the radio in 1924 and televised in 1949. A modern welfare program was instituted in 1936 during the Great Depression to encourage members to be self-supporting and to care for the destitute.

6. The Worldwide Church (1951–present)

Tremendous international growth marked the last half of the 20th century as church membership reached 1 million in 1997. Other notable events included the removal of racial barriers to the priesthood in 1978 and the correlation of all church programs and objectives under the direction of centralized church leadership.

Splinter and Fundamentalist organizations have periodically emerged from the main church, usually appearing after a major event such as the martyrdom of Joseph Smith Jr. or the end of the practice of polygamy. The most notable of these independent groups is the Reorganized Church of Jesus Christ of Latter-day Saints, now the Community of Christ. Founded by Joseph Smith's son, Joseph Smith, III, the headquarters of this religion is located in Independence, Missouri.

Scriptural Canon

The scriptural canon of the Church of Jesus Christ is commonly referred to as the standard works. It is comprised of four volumes, including the Holy Bible, the Book of Mormon, the Doctrine and Covenants (D&C), and the Pearl of Great Price. Mormons revere the bedrock of Christianity, the Bible, while believing that it contains some translation errors. The King James Version is accepted as the religion's official English translation.

The Book of Mormon is considered a companion to the Holy Bible. It is an account of several groups of ancient people who migrated to the Western Hemisphere from the Holy Land. Mormon, the prophet-historian for whom the record is named, abridged portions of the history and religious teachings of these inhabitants onto metal plates before the account's burial. Moroni, as an angel, later appeared to Joseph Smith with instructions related to the location, purpose, and care of the plates. Since that time, the book has been translated into approximately ninety-three languages and by 2011, 150 million copies had been printed.

The third and fourth volumes in the standard works are the Doctrine and Covenants (D&C) and the Pearl of Great Price. The D&C is a collection of inspired declarations provided through Smith and later prophet-presidents. The Pearl of Great Price is comprised of selections taken from Smith's various revelations, translations of ancient texts, and writings that relate to important aspects of church doctrine.

Structure

Two counselors, as part of the First Presidency, and a Quorum of Twelve Apostles support the prophet-president in leading the church worldwide. Locally, congregations are divided into regional geographic units referred to as stakes and wards and are presided over by male priesthood holders who have been called to do so, with women overseeing those organizations designed to address the needs of females and children.

Meeting on a regular basis, active members serve in positions that carry out church functions and objectives in caring for each other. Missionary work is considered an important aspect of this church service, with all active members participating as member-missionaries. Full-time missionary work is carried on voluntarily. All worthy young males are encouraged to serve two-year missions and young women are permitted to serve for eighteen months. Older or retired couples are also encouraged to serve full-time missions of varying lengths both locally and abroad. More than 50,000 full-time missionaries currently serve in approximately 152 nations. This number is rising rapidly. In October 2012, the missionary age requirements for young adults were lowered from nineteen years of age to eighteen for males, and from twenty-one to nineteen for females.

Doctrines and Beliefs

Several beliefs and doctrines of the church are unique to Mormonism, including its view of the Trinity or Godhead as three separate individuals. While God and Jesus have physical bodies, only the Holy Ghost exists as a spirit. Personal revelation is also a central doctrine as members rely on personal guidance from God regarding personal or private matters.

Practicing Mormons subscribe to a moral code that promotes sexually chaste lifestyles and a health code (the Word of Wisdom) that discourages the use of coffee, tea, alcohol, and illegal drugs. It also promotes other beneficial health habits. Members support the church and its functions through donations or a 10 percent tithing. The church uses these monies to finance the construction and operation of building projects as well as the funding of various programs.

Latter-day Saints believe that more than existing with God as angels for eternity, faithful people will have the opportunity to progress toward godhood themselves as part of an eternal family. For this reason, the family is considered the foundational unit of the church. Marriage is also viewed as ordained of God with children being an important and welcome aspect of this. This belief also dictates specific gender roles within the family with fathers serving as primary provider and mothers as nurturers. Together both parents share the responsibility for child-rearing.

Temples are considered houses of the Lord and holy places of learning and worship. Due to the solemn and sacred nature of these edifices, only those members who have fully prepared themselves may enter. The Church's 130 temples perform ordinances that unite families eternally with God. Consequently, Mormons uphold celestial or eternal marriage as a worthy goal for all.

Conclusion

In 2013, church membership comprised approximately 1.7 percent of the U.S. population, with a worldwide membership of more than 14 million. Since its inception, Mormonism has periodically attracted a great deal of attention from outside sources. Over the past decade, it has received much media attention. For example, in 2012, Mitt Romney became the first Mormon nominated by a major political party to run for president of the United States. Other events also created such intense interest that some media members dubbed the year 2012 "the Mormon moment."

See also

Great Awakening; Second Great Awakening; Utopian Movements

DANETTE TURNER

Further Reading

Allen, James B., and Glen M. Leonard. 1976. *The Story of the Latter-day Saints.* Salt Lake City, UT: Deseret Book.

Bushman, Richard L. 2008. *Mormonism: A Very Short Introduction.* New York: Oxford University Press.

Church of Jesus Christ of Latter-day Saints. www.lds.org. Accessed April 22, 2014.

Joseph Smith Papers. http://josephsmithpapers.org/. Accessed April 22, 2014.

Mormonism—Primary Document

Introduction

Written by Joseph Smith and published in 1842, the Articles of Faith *outline thirteen basic beliefs of the Church of Jesus Christ of Latter-day Saints. The* Articles *are currently included as part of the* Pearl of Great Price, *one of the four Standard Works of the LDS Church comprising materials produced by Joseph Smith and published in early church periodicals.*

Document: *Articles of Faith* (1842)

1. We believe in God, the Eternal Father, and in his Son, Jesus Christ, and in the Holy Ghost.

2. We believe that men will be punished for their own sins, and not for Adam's transgression.

3. We believe that through the Atonement of Christ, all mankind may be saved, by obedience to the laws and ordinances of the Gospel.

4. We believe that the first principles and ordinances of the Gospel are: first, Faith in the Lord Jesus Christ; second, Repentance; third, Baptism by immersion for the remission of sins; fourth, Laying on of hands for the gift of the Holy Ghost.

5. We believe that a man must be called of God, by prophecy, and by the laying on of hands by those who are in authority, to preach the Gospel and administer in the ordinances thereof.

6. We believe in the same organization that existed in the Primitive Church, namely, apostles, prophets, pastors, teachers, evangelists, and so forth.

7. We believe in the gift of tongues, prophecy, revelation, visions, healing, interpretation of tongues, and so forth.

8. We believe the Bible to be the word of God as far as it is translated correctly; we also believe the Book of Mormon to be the word of God.

9. We believe all that God has revealed, all that He does now reveal, and we believe that He will yet reveal many great and important things pertaining to the Kingdom of God.

10. We believe in the literal gathering of Israel and in the restoration of the Ten Tribes; that Zion (the New Jerusalem) will be built upon the American continent; that Christ will reign personally upon the earth; and, that the earth will be renewed and receive its paradisiacal glory.

11. We clam the privilege of worshiping Almighty God according to the dictates of our own conscience, and allow all men the same privilege, let them worship how, where, or what they may.

12. We believe in being subject to kings, presidents, rulers, and magistrates, in obeying, honoring, and sustaining the law.

13. We believe in being honest, true, chaste, benevolent, virtuous, and in doing good to all men; indeed, we may say that we follow the admonition of Paul—We believe all things, we hope all things, we have endured many things, and hope to be able to endure all things. If there is anything virtuous, lovely, or of good report or praiseworthy, we seek after these things.

Source: *Articles of Faith*. From the Church of Jesus Christ of Latter-day Saints. Used by permission.

MUCKRAKING

Part of the Progressive Era's crusade for reforms in business and government around the turn to the 20th century, muckrakers were investigative journalists who wanted to shed light on corruption. Through their articles and books exposing the "wrongdoing" of big business or political agents, muckrakers influenced primarily America's middle class to push for the reforms that came in the first two decades of the century.

Background

Many historians believe the muckrakers were influenced by the "Yellow Journalism" that was made popular in the late 19th century by such publishers as William Randolph Hearst and Joseph Pulitzer. These early investigative journalists would expose wrongdoing and corruption in order to stir up public anger and thus sell more papers. Accuracy was often exchanged for sensationalism; it was about circulation, not righting a social wrong. On the eve of the new century, journalists and editors started demanding more facts; thus, the rise of the muckraker.

Often considered to be the first example of muckraking, Julius Chambers committed himself to the Bloomingdale Asylum in 1872 in order to expose its horrors to *New York Tribune*'s audience. Other historians claim the first muckraker was Henry Demarest Lloyd. Lloyd blasted Standard Oil in an 1881 issue of *The Atlantic Monthly* and his critical examination of monopolies was expanded into *Wealth Against Commonwealth* in 1894.

The height of the phenomenon, however, came in 1902 when *McClure's* ran articles such as Ida Tarbell's exposé on John D. Rockefeller's Standard Oil, Lincoln Steffens's on the corruption of big city political machines, and Ray Stannard Baker's work on the problems within coal mines and the unions. Besides these famous series, editor S.S. McClure himself wrote an editorial denouncing such corrupt entities as politicians, employers, and judges. The issue containing the editorial (January 1903) sold out quickly as many Americans agreed with the overall argument that something had become wrong with the "American character."

Some of the other leading examples of muckrakers and their major topics include: David Graham Phillips of *Cosmopolitan* highlighted corruption in the U.S. Senate, Samuel Hopkins Adams uncovered the fraudulent claims made by the pharmaceutical industry, Charles Edward Russell covered such topics as prison reform and corruption in the beef industry, and Jacob Riis' important work, *How the Other Half Lives*, allowed those of the middle and upper classes to realize the horrors of extreme poverty in the slums of America's large cities. Riis' book included heart-wrenching photos—many depicting children—and added tremendously to its impact.

The term *muckraker* can be traced back to *Pilgrim's Progress*, John Bunyan's 17th-century classic Christian work, in which "the Man with the Muck-rake" took a stand against "filth." However, it took the mighty force of President Theodore Roosevelt's reference to Bunyan's "Man with the Muck-rake" in a 1906 speech to actually christen the journalists with their famous moniker. Ironically, Roosevelt was speaking of them in primarily negative terms, essentially saying that by focusing so much on the "filth," the journalists were ignoring all the positives (or the "celestial crown" referred to in *Pilgrim's Progress*). "Muckrakers are often indispensable to the well being of society, but only if they know when to stop raking the muck."

Roosevelt was concerned that many of the reformers were advocating socialism, such as Upton Sinclair did in *The Jungle*, although Roosevelt's progressive agenda benefited from the public outcry that the muckrakers helped to create. Despite President Roosevelt's criticisms or fears, soon the title of "muckraker" became a badge of honor for the writers and mainstream America rejected socialism as the answer. For example (and much to Sinclair's dismay), *The Jungle*'s argument for socialism was largely ignored for the much juicier details of Chicago's meatpacking industry.

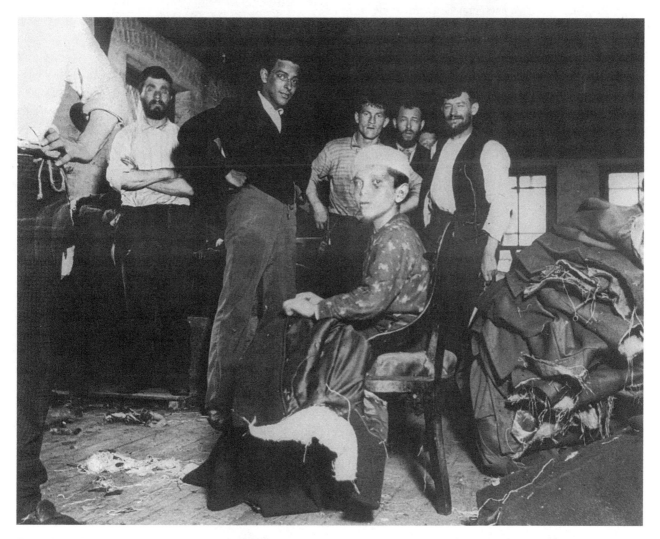

This Jacob Riis photograph shows a twelve-year-old boy working in a sweatshop while men watched in 1889. Riis's photographs and the book based on them—*How the Other Half Lives*—were part of this social reform movement. (Library of Congress)

Major Muckraking Works

An early reforming pioneer was Jacob Riis who, besides using investigative writing to bring about positive change, used powerful photographs as well. One of the first pioneers in flash photography, Riis's pictures of impoverished New Yorkers shocked readers of the middle and upper classes.

Jacob Riis was born in Denmark, immigrated to New York when he was twenty-one, and spent several years in real poverty until he was able to find some financial security in carpentry and sales. Receiving some training in newspaper editing, he became involved in several papers and eventually became a police reporter. That enabled him to become familiar with the crime-ridden, poverty-stricken slums. He began writing about the conditions he witnessed, but felt his words were inadequate. He started photographing some scenes, yet so many of the locations were dark and dismally lit that many of the actual photos showed very little. Once the German innovation of flash powder came, Riis and several friends realized its potential in lighting subjects to be photographed. He would put magnesium powder in a frying pan, remove the camera's lens cap, light the powder, and then replace the cap. He could now document the worst of the slums and what happened at night.

Riis supplemented his police reporting with showing his pictures and speaking, primarily at churches, until *Scribner's Magazine* published an article in 1889 and he was soon offered a book deal. *How the Other Half Lives: Studies Among the Tenements of New York* sold well, and even though some critics charged him with exaggerating, there is no doubt that he made enormous strides in making people aware of the plight of the slums. During his time as a police commissioner, Theodore Roosevelt asked Riis to accompany him sometimes when he would walk the city and check if the patrolmen were in place. Roosevelt publicly praised Riis's work many times, which is ironic, considering his later attitudes toward those who "raked the muck."

Often, the most significant series of articles would later be published as a complete book. For example, two years after the first of Ida Tarbell's nineteen articles had been in *McClure's*, they were published by McClure, Phillips, and Company as *The History of the Standard Oil Company*. Tarbell analyzed hundreds of thousands of pages of documents relating to all aspects of Standard Oil, from all over the country.

She then did meticulous interviews with current and former employees, executives, competitors, lawyers, and government officials. Special focus was given to John D. Rockefeller's rise within the oil industry and his strong-arm tactics against any company or individual that got the way of his ambitions. She also did an in-depth profile of the tycoon, even though Rockefeller had been retired for several years and she was never able to interview Rockefeller himself. It was the first profile of its kind in American journalism.

Tarbell's work proved highly influential. Besides the side effect of advancing women's rights, Tarbell's work greatly inspired other journalists to explore other areas of corruption. *The History of the Standard Oil Company* also contributed greatly to the breakup of Standard Oil by the U.S. Supreme Court for violating the Sherman Antitrust Act.

Just like Tarbell's book, Steffens's *The Shame of the Cities* was a collection of the articles that had run in *McClure's* and published in 1904 by McClure, Phillips, and Company. New York reporter Steffens focused on the political "machines" in large American cities (St. Louis, Chicago, Minneapolis, Pittsburgh, Philadelphia, and New York). More than a simple exposé on municipal corruption, his intention was to criticize the public's complicity in the corruption and make average people face their responsibility for allowing the "shame" to continue.

According to Steffens, "Business men are the sources of evil." Whether bankers, business owners or managers, brokers, or other such men, they are only out for their own profit. The politicians, judges, and police then continue the chain of corruption by accepting bribes to participate or look the other way. Steffens was truly shocked by how often this sort of politician would be reelected because so much of the public was naïve, duped, or benefiting from the graft. Election fraud was also rampant. Fictitious names filled the assessor's roles or other officials passed along names of deceased people and arranged for people to vote as such.

The Shame of the Cities received immediate acclaim and reviews. Steffens became a highly sought-after speaker, was offered a job as editor of a London magazine, and was even used to sell cigars. More importantly, his work was as significant as Tarbell's in launching muckraking and the successes of the Progressive Era.

In 1905, Upton Sinclair broke into muckraking with a new type of medium—fiction. Sinclair was employed by a socialist newspaper, *Appeal to Reason*, and had spent six months researching Chicago's meatpacking industry, including roughly two months undercover in the factories themselves. The newspaper published his political fiction exposé in serial form, but it gained little recognition until Doubleday published it as the novel *The Jungle* in 1906. (Five previous publishers had turned it down due to its shocking content). The fictitious story of Jurgis Rudkus, a Lithuanian immigrant, and his family's struggles to survive quickly fascinated Americans. The reader follows Jurgis through his struggles to find and/or keep employment, children dying of freezing temperatures or drowning in mud, a woman having to trade sexual favors to keep her job, unsavory con-men, and above all else, the horrible conditions at the meatpacking plants: diseased meat being sold to the public, workers being disfigured or permanently crippled, rats and falling into the mixers, workers themselves falling into the tubs of rendered lard, and so on. Eventually, Jurgis is introduced to socialism and finally finds purpose and a supportive community.

Sinclair had intended the work not only to highlight the horrors of the meatpacking industry, but also as a larger insight into the hardships of immigrant families and especially the exploitive nature of capitalism (and thus the solution of socialism). According to the introduction of the novel, he intended to "set forth the breaking of human hearts by a system which exploits the labor of men and women for profit." In reality, it failed in this expectation for most of his readers (middle- or upper-class) were not going to be swayed that far to the Left. However, Americans were so shocked at the conditions of the plants and the safety of their food, that President Roosevelt ordered a federal government investigation and found Sinclair's writing to be quite accurate. The Meat Inspection Act and Pure Food and Drug Act were the eventual results.

A somewhat bitter Upton Sinclair went on to write more muckraking books such as *The Brass Check*, a criticism of the Yellow Journalism techniques popularized by William Randolph Hearst. He ran for various political positions—both as a Socialist and then as a Democrat—but never won any of the elections. Even though Sinclair was disappointed by the impact of *The Jungle* and what Americans focused on, it is considered one of the most significant and influential muckraking works.

Impact

The impact of muckraking is tied up with that of the larger Progressive Era, but no one can doubt that it was profound, for without the journalists, Progressivism would never have achieved such support among the people. Muckrakers gave Progressive reformers a national voice. The problems and weaknesses that can arise from strict laissez-faire capitalism and democracy were exposed; however, they relied on the democratic process to fix the "wrongs." If Americans were made aware of the corruption and government is brought closer to the people, then the corrections will come whenever ballots are cast. Some have called the faith that democracy would restore balance naïve, yet the results are clear.

The creation of the first child labor laws, restructuring of the U.S. Navy, legislation strengthening the Sherman Anti-Trust Act, the Meat Inspection Act, the Pure Food and Drug Act, and the Seventeenth Amendment's direct election of senators all resulted from scandals and wrongdoings exposed by muckrakers. The overall decline of corruption within cities—among the machines, police, judges, and politicians—were also influenced by the movement and went a long way in restoring the "character" of which Americans took pride The Progressive Era ended with World War I, yet the muckrakers had established a standard of journalism and paved the way for future investigative reporters. Others followed in the print media, including I. F. Stone, who spent decades ferreting out corruption and secrets in Washington, D.C., and Seymour Hersh, who uncovered the My Lai massacre during the Vietnam War; the term also was applied to Bob Woodward and Carl Bernstein of *The Washington Post* for their coverage of Watergate, and other reporters who have uncovered business and government wrongdoing. Later, broadcast and Internet media entered the fray, ranging from the investigative reports on such network broadcasts as the CBS News magazine *Sixty Minutes* to Glenn Greenwald's work based on the National Security Agency leaks by contract employee Edward Snowden. Not all muckrakers have been popular, or even correct, but they have continued the digging that the early 20th-century reporters made famous.

See also

Big Oil; Internet Nation; Progressivism; Yellow Journalism

Samantha Warber

Further Reading

Brady, Kathleen. 1984. *Ida Tarbell: Portrait of a Muckraker*. New York: Putnam.

Filler, Louis. 1976. *Progressivism and Muckraking*. New York: R.R. Bowker Co.

Fitzpatrick, Ellen F., ed. 1999. *Muckraking: Three Landmark Articles*. Boston: Bedford/St. Martin's Press.

Geiger, Louis. 1966. "Muckrakers: Then and Now." *Journalism Quarterly* (June): 469–476.

Serrin, Judith, and William Serrin. 2002. *Muckraking!: The Journalism That Changed America*. New York: the New Press.

Shapiro, Herbert. 1968. *The Muckracker and American Society*. Boston: D.C. Heath.

Muckracking—Primary Documents

Document 1: Introduction

President Theodore Roosevelt in his famous "Muck-rake speech" lashed out against those disparaging him. Although the label stuck to journalists, Roosevelt was speaking out against all of his detractors.

Document 1: "The Man with the Muck-rake" by President Theodore Roosevelt (April 14, 1906)

Over a century ago Washington laid the corner stone of the Capitol in what was then little more than a tract of wooded wilderness here beside the Potomac. We now find it necessary to provide by great additional buildings for the business of the government.

This growth in the need for the housing of the government is but a proof and example of the way in which the nation has grown and the sphere of action of the national government has grown. We now administer the affairs of a nation in which the extraordinary growth of population has been outstripped by the growth of wealth in complex interests. The material problems that face us today are not such as they were in Washington's time, but the underlying facts of human nature are the same now as they were then. Under altered external form we war with the same tendencies toward evil that were evident in Washington's time, and are helped by the same tendencies for good. It is about some of these that I wish to say a word today.

In Bunyan's "Pilgrim's Progress" you may recall the description of the Man with the Muck Rake, the man who could look no way but downward, with the muck rake in his hand; who was offered a celestial crown for his muck rake, but who would neither look up nor regard the crown he was offered, but continued to rake to himself the filth of the floor.

In "Pilgrim's Progress" the Man with the Muck Rake is set forth as the example of him whose vision is fixed on carnal instead of spiritual things. Yet he also typifies the man who in this life consistently refuses to see aught that is lofty, and fixes his eyes with solemn intentness only on that which is vile and debasing.

Now, it is very necessary that we should not flinch from seeing what is vile and debasing. There is filth on the floor, and it must be scraped up with the muck rake; and there are times and places where this service is the most needed of all the services that can be performed. But the man who never does anything else, who never thinks or speaks or writes, save of his feats with the muck rake, speedily becomes, not a help but one of the most potent forces for evil.

There are in the body politic, economic and social, many and grave evils, and there is urgent necessity for the sternest war upon them. There should be relentless exposure of and attack upon every evil man, whether politician or business man, every evil practice, whether in politics, business, or social life. I hail as a benefactor every writer or speaker, every man who, on the platform or in a book, magazine, or newspaper, with merciless severity makes such attack, provided always that he in his turn remembers that the attack is of use only if it is absolutely truthful.

The liar is no whit better than the thief, and if his mendacity takes the form of slander he may be worse than most thieves. It puts a premium upon knavery untruthfully to attack an honest man, or even with hysterical exaggeration to assail a bad man with untruth.

An epidemic of indiscriminate assault upon character does no good, but very great harm. The soul of every scoundrel is gladdened whenever an honest man is assailed, or even when a scoundrel is untruthfully assailed.

Now, it is easy to twist out of shape what I have just said, easy to affect to misunderstand it, and if it is slurred over in repetition not difficult really to misunderstand it. Some persons are sincerely incapable of understanding that to denounce mud slinging does not mean the endorsement of whitewashing; and both the interested individuals who need whitewashing and those others who practice mud slinging like to encourage such confusion of ideas.

One of the chief counts against those who make indiscriminate assault upon men in business or men in public life is that they invite a reaction which is sure to tell powerfully in favor of the unscrupulous scoundrel who really ought to be attacked, who ought to be exposed, who ought, if possible, to be put in the penitentiary. If Aristides is praised overmuch as just, people get tired of hearing it; and over-censure of the unjust finally and from similar reasons results in their favor.

Any excess is almost sure to invite a reaction; and, unfortunately, the reactions instead of taking the form of punishment of those guilty of the excess, is apt to take the form either of punishment of the unoffending or of giving immunity, and even strength, to offenders. The effort to make financial or political profit out of the destruction of character can only result in public calamity. Gross and reckless assaults on character, whether on the stump or in newspaper, magazine, or book, create a morbid and vicious public sentiment, and at the same time act as a profound deterrent to able men of normal sensitiveness and tend to prevent them from entering the public service at any price.

As an instance in point, I may mention that one serious difficulty encountered in getting the right type of men to dig the Panama canal is the certainty that they will be exposed, both without, and, I am sorry to say, sometimes within, Congress, to utterly reckless assaults on their character and capacity.

At the risk of repetition let me say again that my plea is not for immunity to, but for the most unsparing exposure of, the politician who betrays his trust, of the big business man who makes or spends his fortune in illegitimate or corrupt ways. There should be a resolute effort to hunt every such man out of the position he has disgraced. Expose the crime, and hunt down the criminal; but remember that even in the case of

crime, if it is attacked in sensational, lurid, and untruthful fashion, the attack may do more damage to the public mind than the crime itself.

It is because I feel that there should be no rest in the endless war against the forces of evil that I ask the war be conducted with sanity as well as with resolution. The men with the muck rakes are often indispensable to the well being of society; but only if they know when to stop raking the muck, and to look upward to the celestial crown above them, to the crown of worthy endeavor. There are beautiful things above and round about them; and if they gradually grow to feel that the whole world is nothing but muck, their power of usefulness is gone.

If the whole picture is painted black there remains no hue whereby to single out the rascals for distinction from their fellows. Such painting finally induces a kind of moral color blindness; and people affected by it come to the conclusion that no man is really black, and no man really white, but they are all gray.

In other words, they neither believe in the truth of the attack, nor in the honesty of the man who is attacked; they grow as suspicious of the accusation as of the offense; it becomes well nigh hopeless to stir them either to wrath against wrongdoing or to enthusiasm for what is right; and such a mental attitude in the public gives hope to every knave, and is the despair of honest men. To assail the great and admitted evils of our political and industrial life with such crude and sweeping generalizations as to include decent men in the general condemnation means the searing of the public con science. There results a general attitude either of cynical belief in and indifference to public corruption or else of a distrustful inability to discriminate between the good and the bad. Either attitude is fraught with untold damage to the country as a whole.

The fool who has not sense to discriminate between what is good and what is bad is well nigh as dangerous as the man who does discriminate and yet chooses the bad. There is nothing more distressing to every good patriot, to every good American, than the hard, scoffing spirit which treats the allegation of dishonesty in a public man as a cause for laughter. Such laughter is worse than the crackling of thorns under a pot, for it denotes not merely the vacant mind, but the heart in which high emotions have been choked before they could grow to fruition. There is any amount of good in the world, and there never was a time when loftier and more disinterested work for the betterment of mankind was being done than now. The forces that tend for evil are great and terrible, but the forces of truth and love and courage and honesty and generosity and sympathy are also stronger than ever before. It is a foolish and timid, no less than a wicked thing, to blink the fact that the forces of evil are strong, but it is even worse to fail to take into account the strength of the forces that tell for good.

Hysterical sensationalism is the poorest weapon wherewith to fight for lasting righteousness. The men who with stern sobriety and truth assail the many evils of our time, whether in the public press, or in magazines, or in books, are the leaders and allies of all engaged in the work for social and political betterment. But if they give good reason for distrust of what they say, if they chill the ardor of those who demand truth as a primary virtue, they thereby betray the good cause and play into the hands of the very men against whom they are nominally at war. . . .

At this moment we are passing through a period of great unrest-social, political, and industrial unrest. It is of the utmost importance for our future that this should prove to be not the unrest of mere rebelliousness against life, of mere dissatisfaction with the inevitable inequality of conditions, but the unrest of a resolute and eager ambition to secure the betterment of the individual and the nation.

So far as this movement of agitation throughout the country takes the form of a fierce discontent with evil, of a determination to punish the authors of evil, whether in industry or politics, the feeling is to be heartily welcomed as a sign of healthy life.

If, on the other hand, it turns into a mere crusade of appetite against appetite, of a contest between the brutal greed of the "have nots" and the brutal greed of the "haves," then it has no significance for good, but only for evil. If it seeks to establish a line of cleavage, not along the line which divides good men from bad, but along that other line, running at right angles thereto, which divides those who are well off from those who are less well off, then it will be fraught with immeasurable harm to the body politic.

We can no more and no less afford to condone evil in the man of capital than evil in the man of no capital. The wealthy man who exults because there is a failure of justice in the effort to bring some trust magnate to account for his misdeeds is as bad as, and no worse than, the so-called labor leader who clamorously strives to excite a foul class feeling on behalf of some other labor leader who is implicated in murder. One attitude is as bad as the other, and no worse; in each case the accused is entitled to exact justice; and in neither case is there need of action by others which can be construed into an expression of sympathy for crime.

It is a prime necessity that if the present unrest is to result in permanent good the emotion shall be translated into action, and that the action shall be marked by honesty, sanity, and self-restraint. There is mighty little good in a mere spasm of reform. The reform that counts is that which comes through steady, continuous growth; violent emotionalism leads to exhaustion.

It is important to this people to grapple with the problems connected with the amassing of enormous fortunes, and the use of those fortunes, both corporate and individual, in business. We should discriminate in the sharpest way between fortunes well won and fortunes ill won; between those gained as an incident to performing great services to the community as a whole and those gained in evil fashion by keeping just within the limits of mere law honesty. Of course, no amount of charity in spending such fortunes in any way compensates for misconduct in making them.

As a matter of personal conviction, and without pretending to discuss the details or formulate the system, I feel that we shall ultimately have to consider the adoption of some such scheme as that of a progressive tax on all fortunes, beyond a certain amount, either given in life or devised or bequeathed upon death to any individual—a tax so framed as to put it out of the power of the owner of one of these enormous fortunes to hand on more than a certain amount to any one individual; the tax of course, to be imposed by the national and not the state government. Such taxation should, of course, be aimed merely at the inheritance or transmission in their entirety of those fortunes swollen beyond all healthy limits. Again, the national government must in some form exercise supervision over corporations engaged in interstate business—and all large corporations engaged in interstate business—whether by license or otherwise, so as to permit us to deal with the far reaching evils of overcapitalization.

This year we are making a beginning in the direction of serious effort to settle some of these economic problems by the railway rate legislation. Such legislation, if so framed, as I am sure it will be, as to secure definite and tangible results, will amount to something of itself; and it will amount to a great deal more in so far as it is taken as a first step in the direction of a policy of superintendence and control over corporate wealth engaged in interstate commerce; this superintendence and control not to be exercised in a spirit of malevolence toward the men who have created the wealth, but with the firm purpose both to do justice to them and to see that they in their turn do justice to the public at large.

The first requisite in the public servants who are to deal in this shape with corporations, whether as legislators or as executives, is honesty. This honesty can be no respecter of persons. There can be no such thing as unilateral honesty. The danger is not really from corrupt corporations; it springs from the corruption itself, whether exercised for or against corporations.

The eighth commandment reads, "Thou shalt not steal." It does not read, "Thou shalt not steal from the rich man." It does not read, "Thou shalt not steal from the poor man." It reads simply and plainly, "Thou shalt not steal."

No good whatever will come from that warped and mock morality which denounces the misdeeds of men of wealth and forgets the misdeeds practiced at their expense; which denounces bribery, but blinds itself to blackmail; which foams with rage if a corporation secures favors by improper methods, and merely leers with hideous mirth if the corporation is itself wronged.

The only public servant who can be trusted honestly to protect the rights of the public against the misdeeds of a corporation is that public man who will just as surely protect the corporation itself from wrongful aggression.

If a public man is willing to yield to popular clamor and do wrong to the men of wealth or to rich corporations, it may be set down as certain that if the opportunity comes he will secretly and furtively do wrong to the public in the interest of a corporation.

But in addition to honesty, we need sanity. No honesty will make a public man useful if that man is timid or foolish, if he is a hot-headed zealot or an impracticable visionary. As we strive for reform we find that it is not at all merely the case of a long uphill pull. On the contrary, there is almost as much of breeching work as of collar work. To depend only on traces means that there will soon be a runaway and an upset.

The men of wealth who today are trying to prevent the regulation and control of their business in the interest of the public by the proper government authorities will not succeed, in my judgment, in checking the progress of the movement. But if they did succeed they would find that they had sown the wind and would surely reap the whirlwind, for they would ultimately provoke the violent excesses which accompany a reform coming by convulsion instead of by steady and natural growth.

On the other hand, the wild preachers of unrest and discontent, the wild agitators against the entire existing order, the men who act crookedly, whether because of sinister design or from mere puzzle headedness, the men who preach destruction without proposing any substitute for what they intend to destroy, or who propose a substitute which would be far worse than the existing evils—all these men are the most dangerous opponents of real reform. If they get their way they will lead the people into a deeper pit than any into which they could fall under the present system. If they fail to get their way they will still do incalculable harm by provoking the kind of reaction which in its revolt against the senseless evil of their teaching would enthrone more securely than ever the evils which their misguided followers believe they are attacking.

More important than aught else is the development of the broadest sympathy of man for man. The welfare of the wage worker, the welfare of the tiller of the soil, upon these depend the welfare of the entire country; their good is not to be sought in pulling down others; but their good must be the prime object of all our statesmanship.

Materially we must strive to secure a broader economic opportunity for all men, so that each shall have a better chance to show the stuff of which he is made. Spiritually and ethically we must strive to bring about clean living and right thinking. We appreciate that the things of the body are important; but we appreciate also that the things of the soul are immeasurably more important.

The foundation stone of national life is, and ever must be, the high individual character of the average citizen.

Source: American Rhetoric Web site. "Top 100 Speeches." Available at http://www.americanrhetoric.com/speeches/teddy rooseveltmuckrake.htm.

Document 2: Introduction

One achievement of the muckrakers was passage of the Pure Food and Drug Act of 1906, which had been strongly pushed by President Theodore Roosevelt. The act stemmed in large part from muckraker efforts to heighten public awareness regarding the dangers of improperly or carelessly prepared foods and the dangers of addiction and death arising from the unregulated sale of patent medicines. The act created the Food and Drug Administration (FDA), which was tasked with testing all foods and drugs meant for human consumption. It also required prescriptions from licensed doctors for the purchase and use of some drugs, and it required warning labels on addictive drugs.

Document 2: Pure Food and Drug Act (June 30, 1906)

An Act for preventing the manufacture, sale, or transportation of adulterated or misbranded or poisonous or deleterious foods, drugs, medicines, and liquors, and for regulating traffic therein, and for other purposes.

Be it enacted by the Senate and House of Representatives of the United States of America in Congress assembled, That it shall be unlawful for any person to manufacture within any Territory or the District of Columbia any article of food or drug which is adulterated or misbranded, within the meaning of this Act; and any person who shall violate any of the provisions of this section shall be guilty of a misdemeanor, and for each offense shall, upon conviction thereof, be fined not to exceed five hundred dollars, or shall be sentenced to one year's imprisonment, for each subsequent offense and conviction thereof shall be fined not less than one thousand dollars or sentenced to one year's imprisonment, or both such fine and imprisonment, in the discretion of the court.

SEC. 2 That the introduction into any State or Territory or the District of Columbia from any other State or Territory or the District of Columbia, from any other State or Territory or the District of Columbia, or to any foreign country, or shipment to any foreign country of any article of food or drugs which is adulterated or misbranded, within the meaning of this Act, is hereby prohibited; and any person who shall ship or deliver for shipment from any State or Territory or the District of Columbia to any other State or Territory or the District of Columbia, or to a foreign country, or who shall receive in any State or Territory or the District of Columbia, or foreign country, and having so received, shall deliver, in original unbroken packages, for pay or otherwise, or offer to deliver to any other person, any such article so adulterated or misbranded within the meaning of this Act, or any person who shall sell or offer for sale in the District of Columbia or the Territories of the United States any such adulterated or misbranded foods or drugs, or export or offer to export the same to any foreign country, shall be guilty of a misdemeanor, and for such offense be fined not exceeding two hundred dollars for the first offense, and upon conviction for each subsequent offense not exceeding three hundred dollars or be imprisoned not exceeding one year, or both, in the discretion of the court: Provided, That no article shall be deemed misbranded or adulterated within the provisions of this Act when intended for export to any foreign country and prepared or packed according to the specifications or directions of the foreign purchaser when no substance is used in the preparation or packing thereof in conflict with the laws of the foreign country to which said article is intended to be shipped; but if said article shall be in fact sold or offered for sale for domestic use or consumption, then this proviso shall not exempt said article from the operation of any of the other provisions of this Act.

SEC. 3 That the Secretary of the Treasury, the Secretary of Agriculture, and the Secretary of Commerce and Labor shall make uniform rules and regulations for carrying out the provisions of this Act, including the collection and examination of specimens of foods and drugs manufactured or offered for sale in the District of Columbia, or in any Territory of the United States, or which shall be offered for sale in unbroken packages in any State other than that in which they shall have been respectively manufactured or produced, or which shall be received from any foreign country, or intended for shipment to any foreign country, which may be submitted for examination by the chief health, food, or drug officer of any State, Territory, or the District of Columbia, or at any domestic or foreign port through which such product is offered for interstate commerce, or for export or import between the United States and any foreign port or country.

SEC. 4 That the examinations of specimens of foods and drugs shall be made in the Bureau of chemistry of the Department of Agriculture, or under the direction and supervision of such Bureau, for the purpose of determining from such examinations whether such articles are adulterated or misbranded within the meaning of this Act; and if it shall appear from any such examination that any of such specimens is adulterated or misbranded within the meaning of this act, the Secretary of Agriculture shall cause notice thereof to be given to the party from whom such sample was obtained. Any party so notified shall be given an opportunity to be heard, under such rules and regulations as may be prescribed as aforesaid, and if it appears that any of the provisions of this act have been violated by such party, then the Secretary of Agriculture shall at once certify the facts to the proper United States district attorney, with a copy of the results of the analysis or the examination of such article duly authenticated by the analyst or officer making such examination, under the oath of such officer. After judgment of the court, notice shall be given by publication in such

manner as may be prescribed by the rules and regulations aforesaid.

SEC. 5 That it shall be the duty of each district attorney to whom the Secretary of Agriculture shall report any violation of this Act, or to whom any health or food or drug officer or agent of any State, Territory, or the District of Columbia shall present satisfactory evidence of any such violation, to cause appropriate proceedings to be commenced and prosecuted in the proper courts of the United States, without delay, for the enforcement of the penalties as in such case herein provided.

SEC.6 That the term "drug," as used in this Act, shall include all medicines and preparations recognized in the United States Pharmacopoeia or National Formulary for internal or external use, and any substance or mixture of substances intended to be used for the cure, mitigation, or prevention of disease of either man or other animals. The term "food," as used herein, shall include all articles used for food, drink, confectionery, or condiment by man or other animals, whether simple, mixed, or compound.

SEC. 7 That for the purposes of this Act an article shall be deemed to be adulterated: In case of drugs: First. If, when a drug is sold under or by a name recognized in the United States Pharmacopoeia or National formulary, it differs from the standard of strength, quality, or purity, as determined by the test laid down in the United States Pharmacopoeia or National Formulary official at the time of investigation: Provided, That no drug defined in the United States Pharmacopoeia or National Formulary shall be deemed to be adulterated under this provision if the standard of strength, quality, or purity be plainly stated upon the bottle, box, or other container thereof although the standard may differ from that determined by the test laid down in the United States Pharmacopoeia or National Formulary. Second. If its strength or purity fall below the professed standard or quality under which it is sold. In the case of confectionery: If it contains terra alba, barites, talc, chrome yellow, or other mineral substance or poisonous color or flavor, or other ingredient deleterious or detrimental to health, or any vinous, malt or spirituous liquor or compound or narcotic drug. In the case of food:

First. If any substance has been mixed and packed with it so as to reduce or lower or injuriously affect its quality or strength.

Second. If any substance has been substituted wholly or in part for the article.

Third. If any valuable constituent of the article has been wholly or in part abstracted.

Fourth. If it be mixed, colored powdered, coated, or stained in a manner whereby damage or inferiority is concealed.

Fifth. If it contain any added poisonous or other added deleterious ingredient which may render such article injurious to health: Provided, That when in the preparation of food products for shipment they are preserved by any external application applied in such manner that the preservative is necessarily removed mechanically, or by maceration in water, or otherwise, and directions for the removal of said preservative shall be printed on the covering or the package, the provisions of this act shall be construed as applying only when said products are ready for consumption.

Sixth. If it consists in whole or in part of a filthy, decomposed, or putrid animal or vegetable substance, or any portion of an animal unfit for food, whether manufactured or not, or if it is the product of a diseased animal, or one that has died otherwise than by slaughter.

SEC. 8 That the term "misbranded," as used herein, shall apply to all drugs, or articles of food, or articles which enter into the composition of food, the package or label of which shall bear any statement, design, or device regarding such article, or the ingredients or substances contained therein which shall be false or misleading in any particular, and to any food or drug product which is falsely branded as the State, territory, or country in which it is manufactured or produced . . . .

SEC. 9 That no dealer shall be prosecuted under the provisions of this Act when he can establish a guaranty signed by the wholesaler, jobber, manufacturer, or other party residing in the united States, from whom he purchases such articles to the effect that the same is not adulterated or misbranded within the meaning of this Act, designating it. Said guaranty, to afford protection, shall contain the name and address of the party or parties making the sale of such articles to such dealer, and such case said party or parties shall be amenable to the prosecutions, fines, and other penalties which would attach, in due course, to the dealer under the provisions of this Act . . . .

SEC. 13 That this Act shall be in force and effect from and after the first day of January, nineteen hundred and seven. Approved, June 30, 1906

Source: *United States Statutes at Large* (59th Cong., Sess. I, Chapter 3915), pp. 768–772.

N

NATIONAL BANK/FEDERAL RESERVE SYSTEM

The Federal Reserve System, sometimes referred to as the Fed, functions as the central bank of the United States. Central banks are generally held responsible for monetary policy, using different methods to expand or contract the supply of money in accordance with the needs of the economy. Monetary policies are often adopted in the pursuit of one or more goals, including providing sufficient money to meet the demands of business, preventing inflation or deflation and ensuring stable prices, promoting employment, or maintaining the value of the nation's currency relative to that of another country or to a commodity such as gold or silver.

Additionally, modern central banks such as the Fed are often responsible for regulating member banks and other financial institutions. While central banks are often tasked with public functions such as monetary policy or regulation, they work closely with private financial interests. Over the course of the nation's history, Americans have debated the structure, responsibilities, and even the need for a central bank, adopting and abandoning a number of solutions prior to settling on the Federal Reserve System.

The first attempt to provide the new American republic with a national bank came at the recommendation of the first secretary of the treasury, Alexander Hamilton. In response to Hamilton's proposal, Congress approved a twenty-year charter for the (First) Bank of the United States (1791–1811), headquartered in Philadelphia, Pennsylvania. The government provided 20 percent of the bank's initial $10 million capital, with the remainder coming from private stockholders. The bank served the needs of private business, making loans and issuing notes that circulated throughout the economy. At the same time, the First Bank acted as the American government's fiscal agent by collecting taxes, handling official funds, making payments, and facilitating borrowing, further enhancing its influence and ability to lend. The size and scope of the bank allowed it to function as a central bank, expanding or contracting loans to alter the supply of money. It also acted as an informal regulator of state banks, redeeming notes issued by the smaller institutions for specie (usually gold or silver) and curtailing their ability to lend. The bank encountered opposition almost immediately. State bankers resented the First Bank's ability to curtail their lending and envied its role as fiscal agent to the national government. The First Bank's lending policies favored short-term credit to Northern manufacturers rather than long-term credit to Southern and Western agricultural interests and thereby aroused further opposition from farmers and their political supporters, such as Thomas Jefferson and his party. As a result, the First Bank's charter was allowed to expire in 1811.

At the front center four of the first Federal Reserve Board of Governors members (front, left to right), Paul M. Warburg, John S. Williams, Charles S. Hamlin, Frederic A. Delano, pose with a group of bankers and governors in Washington, D.C., 1914. (Library of Congress)

With the expiration of the First Bank of the United States in 1811 and the subsequent outbreak of the War of 1812, the American government turned to smaller, state chartered banks to assist in financing the conflict. Advocates of a new national bank argued that reliance on these state banks resulted in the proliferation of small, economically unstable institutions. Critics pointed to suspension of specie payments by state banks and charged that their operations resulted in an inflationary proliferation of credit. Members of Congress, supported by business interests who favored stable money, such as John Jacob Astor, responded by chartering a new national bank, the Second Bank of the United States (1816–1836). Supporters hoped that the bank would reestablish a stable currency, resume species payments, and help spur the economy out of its postwar decline.

The structure and operations of the Second Bank were similar to those of the First Bank in many ways, only on a larger scale. Indeed, the Second Bank began its life occupying the same building in Philadelphia as its predecessor before moving several years later. The Second Bank commenced operations on a twenty-year charter with an initial capitalization of $35 million, compared to the $10 million of the First Bank. While it was a private institution, the government again provided 20 percent of the initial capitalization and in return received the power to appoint five of the twenty-five members of the board of directors. Similar to the First Bank, the Second Bank acted as the government's fiscal agent, making and receiving payments. Additionally, the bank made direct loans and its large specie reserves allowed its bank notes to circulate as a stable paper currency. Over its life the

Second Bank opened twenty-five branch offices across the country, giving it a wide geographic influence that enhanced its ability to provide credit and finance westward economic and territorial expansion.

The Second Bank's very scope and size, however, also contained the seeds of its own eventual demise. The bank's large holdings of state banknotes enabled it to exert pressure on monetary conditions, as well as constrict the lending of these smaller institutions, effectively allowing it to act as an informal central bank. When the Second Bank desired to constrain lending, it redeemed some of its state banknote holdings for specie, forcing the state bank to reduce its lending proportionally. The Second Bank, therefore, became a political target for state bankers who resented its privileged position as the government's fiscal agent as well as its influence over their own institutions and profits. It also became a bogey man for farmers and small entrepreneurs whose ability to borrow and pay existing debts suffered when the Second Bank acted to limit the availability of credit. While state bankers and farmers opposed what they believed were the bank's overly restrictive practices, others criticized it for perceived profligacy in circulating its own paper bank notes. These advocates of so-called hard money argued that only specie should be used as a medium of exchange.

President Andrew Jackson (1829–1837) was the Second Bank's greatest opponent. Jackson's mix of views conflicted with the operations of the bank on almost every point. In addition to being a hard money advocate, Jackson was a populist-style champion of private citizens who believed the Second Bank served the narrow interests of private privileged elites at the expense of the public. Jackson's assertions about the bank as a servant of wealthy privilege gained credence when, following the president's withdrawal of government funds, Second Bank head Nicholas Biddle used the institution's powers to engineer a financial crisis. The aristocratic Biddle hoped to pressure the administration to redeposit the funds, but only reinforced the critical view of the bank. While Jackson was unable to "kill" the Second Bank, as he desired, he did succeed in preventing a renewal of its charter, which expired in 1836.

Between the closure of the Second Bank in 1836 and the passage of the Federal Reserve Act in December 1913, the United States possessed no central banking institution. In its absence, states adopted so-called free banking laws,

inaugurating the Free Bank era (1837–1863); these laws eased the requirements for establishing state chartered banks, leading to their proliferation. Instead of a stable, uniform currency, as the Second Bank hoped to provide, a wide variety of state banknotes, legitimate and counterfeit, circulated, often redeemable for only a fraction of their face value. Furthermore, some banks issued far more notes than they could ever hope to redeem, making them vulnerable to collapse and threatening the safety of deposits.

This situation continued until the outbreak of the Civil War in 1861 and a renewed effort by Congress and the Treasury to impose a uniform and stable currency. The most significant step came with the passage of the National Banking Acts of 1863 and 1864, marking the beginning of the National Banking era (1863–1913). Under the terms of the law, banks possessing a national charter could issue national banknotes. The federal government encouraged their adoption in a number of ways. First, the notes were convertible into specie at the issuing bank. Reserves of U.S. Treasury securities, which could be sold and used to redeem the notes should the issuing bank fail to pay out specie, further guaranteed their value. Second, national banknotes were accepted for the payment of most federal taxes, encouraging their use. Third, the federal government imposed a 10 percent tax on state banknotes, discouraging their further circulation. Ultimately, the acts succeeded in creating a stable and uniform national currency.

Despite these reforms, periodic crises continued to plague the American banking system. The United States experienced financial crises of differing magnitudes in 1873, 1884, 1890, 1893 and 1907. The last of these crises, in 1907, abated only when a consortium of private bankers led by J.P. Morgan cooperated to provide liquidity to banks that were solvent but found themselves squeezed by the temporary panic. As a private citizen, Morgan had, in effect, acted as a lender of last resort during the crisis, a function associated with central banks, prompting advocates of reform call for a more official alternative. In addition to acting as a lender of last resort to stem financial crises, advocates of a central bank saw at least two other benefits. First, a central bank could use its influence to provide a more elastic currency. An elastic currency would ease seasonal fluctuations in interest rates, which tended to rise or fall according to the needs of agriculture. A more elastic currency would, therefore, provide a more stable financial environment. Second, bankers desired a central bank at which they could rediscount commercial paper used to finance business transactions. Rediscounting added additional flexibility to the American money market; it further served the needs of an industrializing American economy, and it allowed U.S. banks to compete with their British counterparts who already enjoyed rediscounting services of the Bank of England.

The passage of the Federal Reserve Act in 1913 attempted to resolve the perceived insufficiencies of the Free Bank and National Bank eras, as well as address issues that had generated opposition to the earlier First and Second Banks. The Fed was intended to be a bank for banks, serving other financial institutions, rather than making loans to commercial enterprises as had previous national banks. The Fed's founders also adopted a decentralized organizational structure to defuse bankers' fears of an institution beholden to political interests, as well as forestall public concern of a central bank serving only the interests of wealthy elites. The Fed was composed of twelve regional reserve banks located in cities across the country: Boston, New York, Philadelphia, Cleveland, Richmond, Atlanta, Chicago, St. Louis, Minneapolis, Kansas City, Dallas and San Francisco. Additionally, the legislation created a board of governors headquartered in Washington, D.C. The Reserve Banks were administered by a board of directors comprising local banking, commercial, industrial, and agricultural interests, as well as appointees of the board of governors. The Washington-based board included five presidential appointees, later expanded to seven, confirmed by the Senate. Board members now serve fourteen-year terms, with the chair serving for four years. Initially the comptroller of the currency and the secretary of the treasury sat as ex-officio members of the board until their removal with the passage of the Banking Act of 1935. Additionally, at the outset, the regional Reserve Banks enjoyed a great deal of autonomy in setting and enacting policy, further reducing fears of a powerful central bank, similar to the First or Second Banks. The Fed's purpose was also narrowly defined and focused on discounting commercial paper "drawn for agricultural, industrial, or commercial purposes" thereby providing elasticity to the currency lacking in the late nineteenth century.

The Federal Reserve uses three broad policy tools to alter the supply of money and credit, and thereby influence economic conditions. First, the Fed controls the discount rate, the rate at which it lends money to other banks. Raising or lowering the discount rate increases or decreases the cost of borrowing. Second, the Fed sets reserve requirements, the amount of funds banks hold against liabilities such as deposits. The lower the reserve ratio, the more banks have available to lend. Third, open market operations allow the Fed to buy securities from or sell them to banks. Buying securities increases the amount of money banks have available to lend, while selling securities decreases loanable funds.

Over time, the Federal Reserve's organization structure and institutional goals evolved to meet changing economic and political conditions, as well as overcome perceived shortcomings in the original legislation. These changes turned the Fed from a decentralized and narrowly focused organization into a modern central bank with broad objectives and substantial powers. When originally adopted, the Federal Reserve Act included a twenty-year time limit, similar to the twenty-year charters for the First and Second Banks. With the passage of the McFadden Act (1927), Congress made the Fed a permanent body, avoiding a repetition of earlier political squabbles over re-chartering. Additionally, during the early years of operation, the regional Reserve Banks enjoyed significant autonomy in setting policy. While they often cooperated, disputes over specific discount rates and open market operations, as well as ideological beliefs about the role of the central bank, inhibited the Fed's response to the onset of the Great Depression. Consequently, Congress enhanced and centralized the powers of the Federal Reserve, particularly with the passage of the Banking Act of 1935. The 1935 law created the Federal Open Market Committee (FOMC) to oversee open market operations. Made up of the seven members of the board and five Reserve Bank heads, the chairman of the board also serves as chair of the FOMC with the head of the Federal Reserve Bank of New York serving as vice chair.

The mission of the Federal Reserve also changed to accommodate new goals. At its conception, the Fed's mission was to provide an elastic currency, expanding and contracting the supply of money to accommodate seasonal fluctuations. Additionally, the Fed helped preserve the nation's commitment to the gold standard, the promise to convert dollars to gold at a fixed price, which served as the basis for the international economy. With periodic interruptions caused by the world wars, the United States remained on the gold standard until 1971–1973, when President Richard Nixon abandoned the link to gold in favor of floating exchange rates. During the 1930s and 1940s, assisting domestic economic recovery and financing the American effort in World War II became the Fed's primary concern. In response to the stagflation (high inflation and low economic growth) of the 1970s, the Humphrey-Hawkins Act (1977) formalized the so-called dual mandate, requiring the Federal Reserve to seek both price stability and low unemployment. Humphrey-Hawkins also increased the imperative of Fed transparency, requiring the chairman of the board to appear semi-annually before Congress and testify on the state of monetary policy.

Since the 1990s, the Federal Reserve has assumed a greater role in ensuring the stability of the American, and global, financial system. At the same time the central bank has come under increasing scrutiny by its critics. Calls to audit or even abolish the central bank, while unlikely in the near term, demonstrate persistent misgivings about the concentrated economic and political power of such institutions on the part of Americans.

See also

Bimetallism; Capitalism; Keynesian Economics; Monetary Policy; Progressivism

TIMOTHY W. WINTOUR

Further Reading

Livingston, James. 1986. *Origins of the Federal Reserve System: Money, Class, and Corporate Capitalism, 1890–1913*. Ithaca, NY: Cornell University Press.

Timberlake, Richard H., Jr. 1978. *The Origins of Central Banking in the United States*. Cambridge, MA: Harvard University Press.

Wood, John H. 2009. *A History of Central Banking in Great Britain and the United States*. New York: Cambridge University Press.

National Bank/Federal Reserve System—Primary Document

Introduction

In 1790, Secretary of the Treasury Alexander Hamilton submitted reports to Congress that might be described as his vision for the new American republic's economy. He talked in one report about the public debt. In this report, he explained the value of a national bank. What he had to say proved controversial. Secretary of State Thomas Jefferson, and others who preferred a more strict construction of the U.S. Constitution,

questioned whether it was legal, much less wise, to create such a bank. Hamilton ultimately triumphed, with the Bank of the United States winning approval in 1791.

Document: Alexander Hamilton's *Second Report on the Further Provision Necessary for Establishing Public Credit* (December 13, 1790)

[To the Speaker of the House of Representatives]

In obedience to the order of the House of Representatives of the ninth day of August last,154 requiring the Secretary of the Treasury to prepare and report on this day such further provision as may, in his opinion, be necessary for establishing the public Credit

The said Secretary further respectfully reports

That from a conviction (as suggested in his report No. 1155 herewith presented) That a National Bank is an Institution of primary importance to the prosperous administration of the Finances, and would be of the greatest utility in the operations connected with the support of the Public Credit, his attention has been drawn to devising the plan of such an institution, upon a scale, which will entitle it to the confidence, and be likely to render it equal to the exigencies of the Public.

Previously to entering upon the detail of this plan, he entreats the indulgence of the House, towards some preliminary reflections naturally arising out of the subject, which he hopes will be deemed, neither useless, nor out of place. Public opinion being the ultimate arbiter of every measure of Government, it can scarcely appear improper, in deference to that, to accompany the origination of any new proposition with explanations, which the superior information of those, to whom it is immediately addressed, would render superfluous.

It is a fact well understood, that public Banks have found admission and patronage among the principal and most enlightened commercial nations. They have successively obtained in Italy, Germany, Holland, England and France, as well as in the United States. And it is a circumstance, which cannot but have considerable weight, in a candid estimate of their tendency, that after an experience of centuries, there exists not a question about their utility in the countries in which they have been so long established. Theorists and men of business unite in the acknowledgment of it.

Trade and industry, wherever they have been tried, have been indebted to them for important aid. And Government has been repeatedly under the greatest obligations to them, in dangerous and distressing emergencies. That of the United States, as well in some of the most critical conjunctures of the late war, as since the peace, has received assistance from those established among us, with which it could not have dispensed.

With this two fold evidence before us, it might be expected, that there would be a perfect union of opinions in their favour. Yet doubts have been entertained; jealousies and prejudices have circulated: and though the experiment is every day dissipating them, within the spheres in which effects are best known; yet there are still persons by whom they have not been entirely renounced. To give a full and accurate view of the subject would be to make a Treatise of a report; but there are certain aspects in which it may be cursorily exhibited, which may perhaps conduce to a just impression of its merits. These will involve a comparison of the advantages, with the disadvantages, real or supposed, of such institutions.

The following are among the principal advantages of a Bank.

First. The augmentation of the active or productive capital of a country. Gold and Silver, when they are employed merely as the instruments of exchange and alienation, have been not improperly denominated dead Stock; but when deposited in Banks, to become the basis of a paper circulation, which takes their character and place, as the signs or representatives of value, they then acquire life, or, in other words, an active and productive quality. This idea, which appears rather subtile [*sic*] and abstract, in a general form, may be made obvious and palpable, by entering into a few particulars. It is evident, for instance, that the money, which a merchant keeps in his chest, waiting for a favourable opportunity to employ it,

produces nothing 'till that opportunity arrives. But if instead of locking it up in this manner, he either deposits it in a Bank, or invests it in the Stock of a Bank, it yields a profit, during the interval; in which he partakes, or not, according to the choice he may have made of being a depositor or a proprietor; and when any advantageous speculation offers, in order to be able to embrace it, he has only to withdraw his money, if a depositor, or if a proprietor to obtain a loan from the Bank, or to dispose of his Stock; an alternative seldom or never attended with difficulty, when the affairs of the institution are in a prosperous train. His money thus deposited or invested, is a fund, upon which himself and others can borrow to a much larger amount. It is a well established fact, that Banks in good credit can circulate a far greater sum than the actual quantum of their capital in Gold & Silver. The extent of the possible excess seems indeterminate; though it has been conjecturally stated at the proportions of two and three to one. This faculty is produced in various ways. First. A great proportion of the notes, which are issued and pass current as Cash, are indefinitely suspended in circulation, from the confidence which each holder has, that he can at any moment turn them into gold and silver. Secondly, Every loan, which a Bank makes is, in its first shape, a credit given to the borrower on its books, the amount of which it stands ready to pay, either in its own notes, or in gold or silver, at his option. But, in a great number of cases, no actual payment is made in either. The Borrower frequently, by a check or order, transfers his credit to some other person, to whom he has a payment to make; who, in his turn, is as often content with a similar credit, because he is satisfied, that he can, whenever he pleases, either convert it into cash, or pass it to some other hand, as an equivalent for it. And in this manner the credit keeps circulating, performing in every stage the office of money, till it is extinguished by a discount with some person, who has a payment to make to the Bank, to an equal or greater amount. Thus large sums are lent and paid, frequently through a variety of hands, without the intervention of a single piece of coin. Thirdly, There is always a large quantity of gold and silver in the repositories of the Bank, besides its own Stock, which is placed there, with a view partly to its safe keeping and partly to the accommodation of an institution, which is itself a source of general accommodation. These deposits are of immense consequence in the operations of a Bank. Though liable to be redrawn at any moment, experience proves, that the money so much oftener changes proprietors than place, and that what is drawn out is generally so speedily replaced, as to authorise the counting upon the sums deposited, as an *effective fund;* which, concurring with the Stock of the Bank, enables it to extend its loans, and to answer all the demands for coin, whether in consequence of those loans, or arising from the occasional return of its notes.

These different circumstances explain the manner, in which the ability of a bank to circulate a greater sum, than its actual capital in coin, is acquired. This however must be gradual; and must be preceded by a firm establishment of confidence; a confidence which may be bestowed on the most rational grounds; since the excess in question will always be bottomed on good security of one kind or another. This, every well conducted Bank carefully requires, before it will consent to advance either its money or its credit; and where there is an auxiliary capital (as will be the case in the plan hereafter submitted) which, together with the capital in coin, define the boundary, that shall not be exceeded by the engagements of the Bank, the security may, consistently with all the maxims of a reasonable circumspection be regarded as complete.

The same circumstances illustrate the truth of the position, that it is one of the properties of Banks to increase the active capital of a country. This, in other words is the sum of them. The money of one individual, while he is waiting for an opportunity to employ it, by being either deposited in the Bank for safe keeping, or invested in its Stock, is in a condition to administer to the wants of others, without being put out of his own reach, when occasion presents. This yields an extra profit, arising from what is paid for the use of his money by others, when he could not himself make use of it; and keeps the money itself in a state of incessant activity. In the almost infinite vicissitudes and competitions of mercantile enterprise, there never can be danger of an intermission of demand, or that the money will remain for a moment idle in the vaults of the Bank. This additional employment given to money, and the faculty of a bank to lend and circulate a greater sum than the amount of its stock in coin are to all the purposes of trade and industry an absolute increase of capital. Purchases and undertakings, in general, can be carried on by any given sum of bank paper or credit, as effectually as by an equal sum of gold and silver. And thus by contributing

to enlarge the mass of industrious and commercial enterprise, banks become nurseries of national wealth: a consequence, as satisfactorily verified by experience, as it is clearly deducible in theory.

Secondly. Greater facility to the Government in obtaining pecuniary aids, especially in sudden emergencies. This is another and an undisputed advantage of public banks: one, which as already remarked, has been realised in signal instances, among ourselves. The reason is obvious: The capitals of a great number of individuals are, by this operation, collected to a point, and placed under one direction. The mass, formed by this union, is in a certain sense magnified by the credit attached to it: And while this mass is always ready, and can at once be put in motion, in aid of the Government, the interest of the bank to afford that aid, independent of regard to the public safety and welfare, is a sure pledge for its disposition to go as far in its compliances, as can in prudence be desired. There is in the nature of things, as will be more particularly noticed in another place, an intimate connection of interest between the government and the Bank of a Nation.

Thirdly. The facilitating of the payment of taxes. This advantage is produced in two ways. Those who are in a situation to have access to the Bank can have the assistance of loans to answer with punctuality the public calls upon them. This accommodation has been sensibly felt in the payment of the duties heretofore laid, by those who reside where establishments of this nature exist. This however, though an extensive, is not an universal benefit. The other way, in which the effect here contemplated is produced, and in which the benefit is general, is the increasing of the quantity of circulating medium and the quickening of circulation. The manner in which the first happens has already been traced. The last may require some illustration. When payments are to be made between different places, having an intercourse of business with each other, if there happen to be no private bills, at market, and there are no Bank notes, which have a currency in both, the consequence is, that coin must be remitted. This is attended with trouble, delay, expence and risk. If on the contrary, there are bank notes current in both places, the transmission of these by the post, or any other speedy, or convenient conveyance answers the purpose; and these again, in the alternations of demand, are frequently returned, very soon after, to the place from whence they were first sent: Whence the transportation and retransportation of the metals are obviated; and a more convenient and more expeditious medium of payment is substituted. Nor is this all. The metals, instead of being suspended from their usual functions, during this process of vibration from place to place, continue in activity, and administer still to the ordinary circulation; which of course is prevented from suffering either diminution or stagnation. These circumstances are additional causes of what, in a practical sense, or to the purposes of business, may be called greater plenty of money. And it is evident, that whatever enhances the quantity of circulating money adds to the ease, with which every industrious member of the community may acquire that portion of it, of which he stands in need; and enables him the better to pay his taxes, as well as to supply his other wants. Even where the circulation of the bank paper is not general, it must still have the same effect, though in a less degree. For whatever furnishes additional supplies to the channels of circulation, in one quarter, naturally contributes to keep the streams fuller elsewhere. This last view of the subject serves both to illustrate the position, that Banks tend to facilitate the payment of taxes; and to exemplify their utility to business of every kind, in which money is an agent. . . .

Abandoning, therefore, ideas, which however agreeable or desirable, are neither practicable nor safe, the following plan for the constitution of a National Bank is respectfully submitted to the consideration of the House.

I. The capital Stock of the Bank shall not exceed ten Millions of Dollars, divided into Twenty five thousand shares, each share being four hundred Dollars; to raise which sum, subscriptions shall be opened on the first monday of april next, and shall continue open, until the whole shall be subscribed. Bodies politic as well as individuals may subscribe.

II. The amount of each share shall be payable, one fourth in gold and silver coin, and three fourths in that part of the public debt, which according to the loan proposed by the Act making provision for the debt of the United States,159 shall bear an accruing interest at the time of payment of six per centum per annum.

III. The respective sums subscribed shall be payable in four equal parts, as well specie as debt, in succession, and at the distance of six calendar months from each other; the first payment to be made at the time of subscription. If there shall be a failure in any subsequent payment, the party failing shall lose the benefit of any dividend which may have accrued, prior to the time for making such payment, and during the delay of the same.

IV. The Subscribers to the Bank and their successors shall be incorporated, and shall so continue until the final redemption of that part of its stock, which shall consist of the public debt.

V. The capacity of the corporation to hold real and personal estate shall be limited to fifteen millions of Dollars, including the amount of its capital, or original stock. The lands and tenements, which it shall be permitted to hold, shall be only such as shall be requisite for the immediate accommodation of the institution; and such as shall have been bona fide mortgaged to it by way of security, or conveyed to it in satisfaction of debts previously contracted, in the usual course of its dealings, or purchased at sales upon judgments which shall have been obtained for such debts.

VI. The totality of the debts of the company, whether by bond, bill, note, or other contract, (credits for deposits excepted) shall never exceed the amount of its capital stock. In case of excess, the Directors, under whose administration it shall happen, shall be liable for it in their private or separate capacities. Those who may have dissented may excuse themselves from this responsibility by immediately giving notice of the fact and their dissent to the President of the United States, and to the Stockholders, at a general meeting to be called by the President of the Bank at their request.

VII. The Company may sell or demise its lands and tenements, or may sell the whole, or any part of the public Debt, whereof its Stock shall consist; but shall *trade* in nothing, except bills of exchange, gold and silver bullion, or in the sale of goods pledged for money lent: nor shall take more than at the rate of six per centum, per annum, upon its loans or discounts.

VIII. No loan shall be made by the bank, for the use or on account of the Government of the United States, or of either of them to an amount exceeding fifty thousand Dollars, or of any foreign prince or State; unless previously authorised by a law of the United States.

IX. The Stock of the Bank shall be transferable according to such rules as shall be instituted by the Company in that behalf.

X. The affairs of the Bank shall be under the management of Twenty five Directors, one of whom shall be the President. And there shall be on the first monday of January, in each year, a choice of Directors, by plurality of suffrages of the Stockholders, to serve for a year. The Directors at their first meeting, after each election, shall choose one of their number as President.

XI. The number of votes, to which each Stockholder shall be entitled, shall be according to the number of shares he shall hold in the proportions following, that is to say, for one share and not more than two shares one vote; for every two shares, above two and not exceeding ten, one vote; for every four shares above ten and not exceeding thirty, one vote; for every six shares above thirty and not exceeding sixty, one vote; for every eight shares above sixty and not exceeding one hundred, one vote; and for every ten shares above one hundred, one vote; but no person, copartnership, or body politic, shall be entitled to a greater number than thirty votes. And after the first election, no share or shares shall confer a right of suffrage, which shall not have been holden three calendar months previous to the day of election. Stockholders actually resident within the United States and none other may vote in elections by proxy.

XII. Not more than three fourths of the Directors in office, exclusive of the President, shall be eligible for the next succeeding year. But the Director who shall be President at the time of an election may always be reelected.

XIII. None but a Stockholder being a citizen of the United States, shall be eligible as a Director.

XIV. Any number of Stockholders not less than sixty, who together shall be proprietors of two hundred shares, or upwards, shall have power at any time to call a general meeting of the Stockholders, for purposes relative to the Institution; giving at least six weeks notice in two public gazettes of the place where the Bank is kept, and specifying in such notice the object of the meeting.

XV. In case of the death, resignation, absence from the United States, or removal of a Director by the Stockholders, his place may be filled by a new choice for the remainder of the year.

XVI. No Director shall be entitled to any emolument, unless the same shall have been allowed by the Stockholders at a General meeting. The Stockholders shall make such compensation to the President, for his extraordinary attendance at the Bank, as shall appear to them reasonable.

XVII. Not less than seven Directors shall constitute a Board for the transaction of business.

XVIII. Every Cashier, or Treasurer, before he enters on the duties of his office shall be required to give bond, with two or more sureties, to the satisfaction of the Directors, in a sum not less than twenty thousand Dollars, with condition for his good behaviour.

XIX. Half yearly dividends shall be made of so much of the profits of the Bank as shall appear to the Directors advisable: And once in every three years the Directors shall lay before the Stockholders, at a General Meeting, for their information, an exact and particular statement of the debts, which shall have remained unpaid, after the expiration of the original credit, for a period of treble the term of that credit; and of the surplus of profit, if any, after deducting losses and dividends.

XX. The bills and notes of the Bank originally made payable, or which shall have become payable on demand, in gold and silver coin, shall be receivable in all payments to the United States.

XXI. The Officer at the head of the Treasury Department of the United States, shall be furnished from time to time, as often as he may require, not exceeding once a week, with statements of the amount of the capital Stock of the Bank and of the debts due to the same; of the monies deposited therein; of the notes in circulation, and of the Cash in hand; and shall have a right to inspect such general account in the books of the bank as shall relate to the said statements; provided, that this shall not be construed to imply a right of inspecting this account of any private individual or individuals with the Bank.

XXII. No similar institution shall be established by any future act of the United States, during the continuance of the one hereby proposed to be established.

XXIII. It shall be lawful for the Directors of the Bank to establish offices, wheresoever they shall think fit, within the United States, for the purposes of discount and deposit only, and upon the same terms, and in the same manner, as shall be practiced at the Bank; and to commit the management of the said offices, and the making of the said discounts, either to Agents specially appointed by them, or to such persons as may be chosen by the Stockholders residing at the place where any such office shall be, under such agreements and subject to such regulations as they shall deem proper; not being contrary to law or to the Constitution of the Bank.

XXIV. And lastly. The President of the United States shall be authorised to cause a subscription to be made to the Stock of the said Company, on behalf of the United States, to an amount not exceeding two Millions of Dollars, to be paid out of the monies which shall be borrowed by virtue of either of the Acts, the one entitled "an Act making provision for the debt of the United States," and the other entitled "An Act making provision for the reduction of the Public Debt"; borrowing of the bank an equal sum, to be applied to the purposes for which the said monies shall have been procured, reimbursable in ten years by equal annual instalments; or at any time sooner, or in any greater proportions, that the Government may think fit. . . .

Source: National Archives. Founders Online. Available at http://founders.archives.gov/?q=national%20bank&s=1511311111&r=104.

NATIVISM

Nativism, similar to xenophobia, implies a favoring of native inhabitants and a prejudice toward outsiders, particularly foreigners. At various times throughout the American past, nativism in the form of anti-Catholicism, anti-Semitism, and anti-immigrant sentiment has dominated public opinion and political circles. Americans frequently lapse into nativism during times of economic decline, warfare, and heavy immigration, when they feel economically, socially, and politically threatened by new as well as long-standing "foreigners."

Nativism has often surfaced during times of stress in American culture. During the late 18th century, for instance, nativism became widespread for the first time in the history of the United States due to the instability of the new national government. A young and fragile nation with a weak military and a relatively open political system, the United States in the 1790s became a growing attraction for immigrants from Europe. Yet many Americans feared the rising tide of French immigrants fleeing the violent French Revolution. Despite the assistance rendered by the French to the United States during the American Revolution, Americans feared the newcomers, who might bring radical ideas to upset the American political scene.

This climate of xenophobia continued into the early 19th century due in part to the growth in slavery and American Indian warfare then taking place. Holding African Americans in bondage and taking Indian lands by military force placed white Americans in a mind-set of racial exclusiveness and homogeneity, an ethos that also supported nativism.

Anti-Catholicism represented a strong focus of nativism during the mid-1900s. Following the massive immigration of 2 million Irish Catholics to the United States during the 1840s and 1850s, American Protestants became fearful of contamination by the alleged cultural inferiority of Irish people. Those new American Catholics were labeled as subversive and linked to foreign influence and anti-American behavior. Many Protestant Americans reasoned that the pope would soon become a powerful political figure within the United States. In response, large numbers of American Protestants attempted to limit the teaching of Catholicism in public schools. In 1834, Americans burned an Ursuline convent school at Charlestown, Massachusetts. In 1844, a mob attacked Irish neighborhoods and churches. A decade later, when the papal nuncio visited the United States in 1853, a large German and American Protestant mob numbering 1,200 people fought with police outside the Cincinnati cathedral where the dignitary was staying.

Organizations formed the backbone of anti-Catholic nativism in the mid-19th century. Anchoring the nativist movement, the United American Mechanics was a working-class, white, Protestant organization that targeted groups that it felt threatened the rights of American workingmen. By 1855, more than 50,000 men belonged to the ritual-bound organization. The large membership was due in part to the recent arrival of Irish workers. The emergence of the Know-Nothing Party also illustrates the high level of organization achieved during this period of nativism. Founded in New York City in 1849 as the Order of the Star-Spangled Banner, the organization grew into the most powerful nativist association prior to the formation of the Ku Klux Klan in the late 1860s.

Taking its name from its ritual of secrecy, the Know-Nothing Party grew into a powerful political force that shaped the outcome of presidential elections in the 1850s. The national debate over slavery disrupted American politics and provided space for third parties to form. The Know-Nothings capitalized on that development. During elections in the mid-1850s, the party won several seats in Congress as well as many state governorships. In 1856, the party ran ex-president Millard Fillmore for the executive office and received more than 900,000 votes. Espousing goals of electing native-born leaders and mandating caps on immigration quotas, the political movement also supported calls for limitations on the amount of property owned by the Catholic Church in the

Members of the Ku Klux Klan (KKK) burn a cross in Swainsboro, Georgia, in February 1948. The KKK is a series of white supremacist organizations claiming lineal descent from the original KKK, which began in the U.S. South after the American Civil War of the 1860s. The KKK uses many forms of terror, most notably lynching, against groups such as African Americans and Catholics. (Library of Congress)

United States. The movement waned, however, when slavery split the nation in two during the Civil War.

Anti-Catholic nativism resurfaced in the late 19th century due to the growing power of the Catholic Church in the United States. During the 1884 presidential election, nativism became a political force once again. Several anti-Catholic organizations flourished and declined in the 1880s. In 1887, the American Protective Association was founded. Highly secretive, like the Know-Nothings, it quietly supported anti-Catholic candidates. It counted more than 100,000 members (including African Americans, women, and immigrants) who pledged to reduce the influence of Catholicism

in American politics. The organization's sway declined as public fear of Catholics waned and its leaders found other outlets for nativist sentiment.

In the Western United States, Chinese immigrants endured a nativist movement that reached fruition in California during the 1870s and 1880s. The discovery of gold in 1849 induced hundreds of thousands of Chinese people, predominantly men, to migrate to California. The economic competition they represented in the gold fields motivated white American miners to pass a miner's tax to push Chinese (and other foreign miners) out of the Sierra Nevada Mountains, where most of the gold was located. The Chinese became business owners and railroad workers in the late 1860s and 1870s and established "Chinatowns" in Western cities to survive economically.

After a severe recession and a series of bitter industrial strikes hit the United States in the 1870s, anti-Chinese sentiment grew in California. The movement received widespread support from the Irish working class and was led by Denis Kearney, an Irish worker and political activist in San Francisco. The anti-Chinese movement also drew strong support from unions and newspapers across the nation. The Knights of Labor, a popular labor union, pushed Congress in the late 1870s to restrict Chinese competition with white workers. Congress eventually passed a bill known as the Chinese Exclusion Act (1882), restricting the immigration of Chinese into the United States to only a few individuals each year.

Although the Chinese could no longer immigrate to America, those already here continued to endure abuse. In 1885, a coalition of disaffected workers attempted to instigate a boycott against Chinese-manufactured cigars in San Francisco. A speaker endorsed by the Knights of Labor stated of the event, "This is the old irrepressible conflict between slave and white labor. God grant there may be survival of the fittest." Violence became a byproduct of anti-Chinese nativism. In the late 1880s, a Chinatown at the Union Pacific Railroad coal mine in Rock Springs, Wyoming, was burned to the ground and the bystanders shot by an angry mob of unemployed miners. The day after the fire, twenty-eight Chinese were found dead. Anti-Chinese nativism continued into the 1890s. The American Federation of Labor, the largest labor union in the United States during that time, agitated Congress to extend the Chinese Exclusion Act when it came up for renewal in 1892.

In addition to anti-Catholic and anti-Chinese sentiment, anti-Semitism also served as a focal point for nativist thought in the 19th century. Rooted in Christian stereotypes of Jews as greedy and insular people dominated by a mysterious religion hostile to Christianity, anti-Semitism exercised a deeper and more lasting influence on American culture than anti-Catholicism. Immigration served as a catalyst for anti-Semitism in much the same way as it did for anti-Catholic sentiment; anti-Semitism increased markedly when millions of Jews from eastern Europe immigrated to the United States in the late 19th and early 20th centuries.

Encouraged by the proliferation of propaganda by political groups hostile to Jewish influence in Europe, discrimination against Jews became commonplace in American life. Anti-Semitism also increased due to the upward social movement of successful German Jews who first arrived in the 1850s. Despite anti-Semitic nativism, Jewish Americans achieved economic and political success by the late 19th century that unfortunately brought a backlash from white, Anglo-Saxon Protestants.

Representing several wings of nativist thought, the Ku Klux Klan (KKK) has kept nativism alive in America since the early post–Civil War period. Founded by ex-Confederate general Nathan Forrest in 1866, the KKK began as an organization to keep African Americans and federal sympathizers from rising to economic, social, and political equality with white Southerners during Reconstruction, when the North attempted to reform the South. The Klan started at Pulaski, Tennessee, and adopted the rituals of the Sons of Malta, a nonpolitical group operating at that time. The organization reached its heyday between 1866 and 1870 and between 1915 and 1950. Its origins clearly reveal a connection to nativist groups like the Know-Nothings, which flourished during the antebellum period but did not survive the Civil War.

The Klan's targets following World War I were predictable: African Americans, Jews, and Catholics. Though the Klan focused mostly on blacks until 1915, the second KKK increased its anti-Catholic and anti-Semitic emphasis. The Klan targeted Jewish business owners and white Catholics who sympathized with African Americans in their quest to achieve equality following the end of slavery. Renamed the Knights of the Ku Klux Klan, the revived group bore the indelible stamp of its founder and visionary, a Georgian named William Simmons. Like other leaders of nativist organizations, Simmons excelled at joining and operating volunteer organizations. He hired an Atlanta public relations organization called the Southern Publicity Association to disseminate Klan rhetoric, a tactic that helped the Klan rise to the height of its power by the mid-20th century.

The end of World War I promised a flood of war refugees, particularly from the new Soviet Union. American Protestants believed they would bring anarchy and bloodshed to the U.S. political and social scene. In the 1920s, however, the Klan began to lose members following the passage of the Immigration Act (1924), which severely cut back immigration from Southern and Eastern Europe. By the end of the 1920s, following an era of prosperity for the white middle class, the Klan had only 82,000 members. The 1928 election, however, was shaped by Klan anti-Catholic rhetoric. Democratic presidential candidate Alfred E. Smith lost to Republican Herbert Hoover due in part to Smith's Catholic background, a fact he could not shake during the election race.

The Klan became a well-run business enterprise after World War II, when 2 million Americans joined its ranks. In small rural towns across the South, many white Americans became angry toward African Americans and the federal government for supporting the civil rights movement. The Klan offered them an answer to the decline of white control over economic and political power. Joining the KKK became a badge of social status and manhood. Separate auxiliaries for women had also been created, so Klan activity was often a family affair. According to the Federal Bureau of Investigation, the Klan in the 1950s and 1960s was responsible for the deaths of numerous civil rights leaders, including National Association for the Advancement of Colored People organizer Medgar Evers. Sheriffs, policemen, and even judges in Southern cities were often members of the Klan, so prosecution of its murders rarely resulted.

The post–World War II era Cold War brought a new type of nativism to the United States. The rise of communism in the Soviet Union and witch hunts for communists in the United States in the 1950s created a new bogeyman to replace the Jew, Catholic, and immigrant. Indeed, prominent prosecutors of the Red Scare, like Joseph McCarthy, were Catholics. Nevertheless, presidential candidate John F. Kennedy was forced to deal with his Catholic past, a sign that fear of Catholics remained firmly rooted in the American national character. Still, Kennedy became the first Catholic president, an unthinkable development for Americans between 1850 and 1960.

Like other forms of prejudice, nativism as a cultural movement became more internal and personal in the late 20th century. It no longer produced many organizations that claimed a wide national following, though anti-immigrant groups and the KKK continued to flourish.

During the last twenty years, two foci of nativism have remained: anti-Semitism and anti-immigrant sentiment. Hatred and mistrust of Jews still retains a stronghold on the American national character due in part to a Jewish American

subculture that promotes education and economic success. Many Jews have been propelled into roles of political and economic power—for example, Senator Joseph Lieberman, the Democratic vice presidential candidate in the 2000 election.

Heavy immigration from Mexico and China since 1980 and the perceived problem of border control in Southwestern states fueled a resurgence of nativism in Florida, California, New York, Texas, and Arizona in the 1990s. Like the white-male, working-class fear of Chinese immigrant workers in the 1870s in California, a disgruntled white working class once again supported anti-immigrant sentiment in California. In 1994, Pete Wilson won his second term as governor of California by "playing the race card" and condemning the high level of Mexican immigration to California (and by implication, other states like Texas). Nativism will undoubtedly continue to be a part of American politics and culture in the years to come.

See also
Americanization; Anti-Semitism; Catholicism; Christian Fundamentalism; Illegal Immigration; Immigration Racism; White Supremacy

JASON NEWMAN

Further Reading
Anbinder, Tyler G. 1994. *Nativism and Slavery: The Northern Know Nothings and the Politics of the 1850s.* New York: Oxford University Press.

Billington, Ray Allen 1964. *The Protestant Crusade, 1800–1860: A Study of the Origins of American Nativism.* New York: Quadrangle Books.

Higham, John. 2002. *Strangers in the Land: Patterns of American Nativism, 1860–1925.* Reprint ed. New Brunswick, NJ: Rutgers University Press.

Jackson, Kenneth T. 1992. *The Ku Klux Klan in the City, 1915–1930.* Reprint ed. Chicago: Ivan R. Dee.

Reimers, David M. 1999. *Unwelcome Strangers: American Identity and the Turn Against Immigration.* New York: Columbia University Press.

Nativism—Primary Document

Introduction

In 1855, the American (or Know-Nothing) Party was formed from dissident factions of the Whig Party and members of the national Know-Nothing organization. On February 22, 1856, at its first national convention in Philadelphia, the party adopted this platform but did not take a clear position on slavery. The American Party nominated Millard Fillmore of New York for president and Andrew Donelson of Tennessee for vice president as its candidates for the election of 1856, but they lost to James Buchanan of the Democratic Party, capturing 22 percent of the popular vote and eight electoral votes, winning just one of the thirty-one states. By the election, however, the party had already begun to splinter over the slavery issue.

Document: American Party Platform (1856)

I. An humble acknowledgment to the Supreme Being who rules one universe, for His protecting care vouchsafed to our fathers in their revolutionary struggle, and hitherto manifested to us, their descendants, in the preservation of the liberties, the independence and the union of these states.

II. The perpetuation of the Federal Union, as the palladium of our civil and religious liberties, and the only sure bulwark of American independence.

III. *Americans must rule America;* and to this end, *native*-born citizens should be selected for all state, federal, or municipal offices of government employment, in preference to naturalized citizens—*nevertheless,*

IV. Persons born of American parents residing temporarily abroad, shall be entitled to all the rights of native-born citizens; but

V. No person should be selected for political station (whether of native or foreign birth), who recognizes any alliance or obligation of any description to any foreign prince, potentate or power, who refuses to recognize the federal and state constitutions (each within its own sphere), as paramount to all other laws, as rules of particular [political] action.

VI. The unequalled recognition and maintenance of the reserved rights of the several states, and the cultivation of harmony and fraternal goodwill between the citizens of the several states, and to this end, non-interference by Congress with questions appertaining solely to the individual states, and non-intervention by each state with the affairs of any other state.

VII. The recognition of the right of the native-born and naturalized citizens of the United States, permanently residing in any territory thereof, to frame their constitutions and laws, and to regulate their domestic and social

affairs in their own mode, subject only to the provisions of the federal Constitution, with the right of admission into the Union whenever they have the requisite population for one representative in Congress. *Provided, always,* That none but those who are citizens of the United States, under the Constitution and laws thereof, and who have a fixed residence in any such territory, are to participate in the formation of the constitution, or in the enactment of laws for said territory or state.

VIII. An enforcement of the principles that no state or territory can admit other than nativeborn citizens to the right of suffrage, or of holding political office unless such persons shall have been naturalized according to the laws of the United States.

IX. A change in the laws of naturalization, making a continued residence of twenty-one years, of all not heretofore provided for, an indispensable requisite for citizenship hereafter, and excluding all paupers or persons convicted of crime from landing upon our shores; but no interference with the vested rights of foreigners.

X. Opposition to any union between Church and State; no interference with religious faith or worship, and no test oaths for office, except those indicated in the 5th section of this platform.

XI. Free and thorough investigation into any and all alleged abuses of public functionaries, and a strict economy in public expenditures.

XII. The maintenance and enforcement of all laws until said laws shall be repealed, or shall be declared null and void by competent judicial authority.

XIII. Opposition to the reckless and unwise policy of the present administration in the general management of our national affairs, and more especially as shown in removing "Americans" (by designation) and conservatives in principle, from office, and placing foreigners and ultraists in their places, as shown in a truckling subserviency to the stronger, and an insolent and cowardly bravado toward the weaker powers; as shown in reopening sectional agitation, by the repeal of the Missouri Compromise; as shown in granting to unnaturalized foreigners the right of suffrage in Kansas and Nebraska, as shown in its vacillating course on the Kansas and Nebraska question; as shown in the removal of Judge Bronson from the collectorship of New York upon false and untenable grounds; as shown in the corruptions which pervade some of the departments of the government; as shown in disgracing meritorious naval officers through prejudice or caprice; as shown in the blundering mismanagement of our foreign relations.

XIV. Therefore, to remedy existing evils, and prevent the disastrous consequences otherwise resulting therefrom, we would build up the "American Party" upon the principles hereinbefore stated eschewing all sectional questions, and uniting upon those purely national, and admitting into said party all American citizens (referred to in the 3rd, 4th, and 5th sections) who openly avow the principles and opinions heretofore expressed, and who will subscribe their names to this platform. *Provided nevertheless*, that a majority of those members present at any meeting of a local council where an applicant applies for membership in the American party, may, for any reason by them deemed sufficient, deny admission to such applicant.

XV. A free and open discussion of all political principles embraced in our platform.

Source: Greeley, Horace, and John F. Cleveland. *A Political Text-book for 1860*. New York: Tribune Association, 1860.

NEW LEFT MOVEMENT

Although the New Left did not have a distinct beginning and traits that determine inclusion are disputed, historians oftentimes use a broad criterion to identify individuals and groups that were involved in the political movement. The New Left was comprised of several different movements, each with multiple organizations supporting their cause, which had varying immediate goals but a shared purpose for their actions. This unique structure has prompted the New Left to be considered a "movement of movements." The New Left was especially active between roughly 1955 and 1975, which is known as the "long Sixties" for its political activist spirit that began and extended beyond the decade of the 1960s. The New Left was in lineage with, yet distinct from, the Old Left Marxism that the Soviet Union embraced. Throughout the long Sixties, New Left individuals and organizations sought broad-scale social and political reforms with civil disobedience and agitation strategies that included protest, educational workshops, radical literature, and eventually militancy.

Marxism was a major influence of the New Left, but it was manifested very differently than it was in the Soviet Union.

Soviet Marxism required hardline Communist Party membership, while the New Left did not claim loyalty to one formal organization. Moreover, the New Left changed the focus of who would initiate social and political transformation. Old Left Marxism focused on labor where change was believed to begin with the working-class people, but the New Left believed that intellectuals, who were mostly middle class, were the wheels of reform.

Consequently, humanist philosophers like Albert Camus and Jean-Paul Sartre, Frankfurt school critical theorists Herbert Marcuse and Theodor Adorno, Marxists like Che Guevara and Rosa Luxemburg, and sociologist C. Wright Mills were influential in the foundation of New Left thought. The written works and political activism of these 20th-century intellectuals reconfigured Marxist ideology and became a heavy influence within New Left politics in both the United States and Great Britain. Western humanist ideals guided the New Left political movements and social programs during the long Sixties, which were exhibited in the strategies and goals of the various movements within the broader movement.

The label "New Left" is commonly applied to individuals and organizations that used a particular form of political strategy known as agitation politics. Rather than enacting change within the existing political system, agitation politics direct their efforts from outside the system. Many perceived the existing political and social institutions, often grouped together into what was called the "Establishment," as unjust and ineffective. Instead, New Left strategies involved mass demonstrations and protests, sit-ins and teach-in workshops, boycotts, and eventually militancy. Political and social reform was thought to begin with large groups of people, which required an emphasis on education and participatory democracy. New Left movements utilized these strategies at different times and in different ways, but they have become a defining feature of the "movement of movements."

Although there was no definitive beginning to the New Left movement, many assert that the early civil rights movement's demonstrations and programs displayed strategies that would be utilized later in the New Left. Shortly after World War II, African American individuals and organizations began to practice civil disobedience through protests, sit-ins, boycotts, Freedom Rides, and other forms of demonstration in order to combat widespread segregation and racism. Individuals such as Rosa Parks, Martin Luther King Jr.,

Malcolm X, Bayard Rustin, and many others organized mass demonstrations beginning around 1955. Civil rights organizations like the Southern Christian Leadership Conference, Student Non-violent Coordinating Committee, and the National Association for the Advancement of Colored People took similar actions to secure civil rights for African Americans in the United States. Major events in the civil rights movement that occurred between 1955 and 1965, which include the Montgomery Bus Boycott in 1956, Little Rock Central High School desegregation in 1957, Freedom Rides in 1961, March on Washington in 1963, and Mississippi Freedom Summer of 1964, set a standard for social movements that would soon follow.

Baby boomers began to enter higher education in the early 1960s and, after witnessing the successful efforts of the civil rights movement in their formative years, acknowledged the potential for social reform that the mass of university students collectively held. In 1962, University of Michigan student Tom Hayden drafted a manifesto that sharply criticized American society and politics, but offered policy recommendations and a utopian vision of the future. The manifesto, entitled the *Port Huron Statement*, became the key piece of literature for the nationwide student activist organization, Students for a Democratic Society (SDS). SDS advocated nonviolent civil disobedience and participatory democracy through workshops, demonstrations, and literature for both students on campus and individuals in major cities. Many SDS members created their own university publications and other underground newspapers, which included *The SDS Viewpoint, SDS Bulletin, New Left Notes*, and *The Movement*. SDS continued until the late 1960s when several key members defected and formed the militant Weathermen organization.

Numerous universities witnessed waves of activism throughout the long Sixties where students criticized the ongoing war in Vietnam, *in loco parentis* administrative regulations, depersonalized treatment, and restrictions on various freedoms. The most notable display of student activism took place at the University of California at Berkeley during the 1964–1965 academic year. Politically active students became increasingly frustrated in response to a ban on political activities on campus. On October 1, 1964, thousands of student protestors surrounded a police vehicle and prevented it from transporting graduate student Jack Weinberg, who refused to show his identification, for thirty-two hours. The incident sparked a series of sit-ins at the Sproul Hall student

center where students, such as Mario Savio, Bettina Aptheker, Michael Rossman, and Jackie Goldberg, gave speeches on the issue of free speech at the university. Animosity between the students and administration continued for months, and arguably years, in what became known as the Berkeley Free Speech movement. Radical student organizations and publications fueled campus unrest nationwide throughout the late 1960s and early 1970s, which represented the higher education movement within the broader New Left movement.

Although white middle-class academics were a major force of the New Left, various race-oriented organizations were equally active. Minority groups in primarily urban areas sought autonomy from institutional systems that they perceived as unjust. Organizations like the Black Panthers, Chicano Brown Berets, Young Lords, Young Patriots, and the American Indian Movement formed socialist communities that provided protection, education, and employment for their ethnic groups. Each minority organization advocated its own movement—like the Black Panthers and the broader Black Power movement—but some organizations formed coalitions to fight a common cause, which was seen in the original Chicago Rainbow Coalition struggle against urban renewal. These organizations openly carried weapons and trained for self-defense, which caused the FBI to frequently monitor and infiltrate them in fear of violent overthrows of the U.S. government. Due to constant legal, leadership, and financial difficulties, many race-oriented organizations phased out during the early 1970s along with a significant portion of other New Left movements.

One movement within the New Left, however, began to flourish in the early 1970s: women's liberation. The women's liberation movement was significantly different from the suffragettes and early feminists who fought for legal and political rights. Instead, individuals within the broad and loosely organized women's liberation movement challenged gender discrimination and social constraints, especially those on the body. Although there was not one unified organization that represented the women's liberation, organizations like the National Organization for Women, Women's Equity Action League, and Federally Employed Women were formed in the late 1960s to represent the movement. Many of these groups, as well as grassroots women's liberation groups, were divided on controversial issues like abortion rights and birth control, but many agreed on the elimination of wage inequality, sexual discrimination in education and employment, and a wide range of discriminatory social practices. The women's liberation movement rapidly grew in the early and mid-1970s while younger individuals utilized an existing New Left network through literature and the older generation sought to establish a separate movement.

The New Left experienced a wave of militancy toward the end of the long Sixties, which either represented or initiated an end to the movement of movements on the whole. Violent riots, such as the 1968 Democratic National Convention and race riots in Los Angeles and Detroit, prompted heavy police and National Guard presence. Many responded to their presence with further violence, as they perceived the forces as aggressive and authoritarian. In the early 1970s, the militant offshoot of SDS called the Weathermen carried out bombings on banks and government buildings, including the Pentagon, and declared war on the U.S. government. The Weathermen, as well as the entire New Left, lost traction in the public sphere after the United States signed a peace treaty with Vietnam at the Paris Peace Accords in 1973. Many of the organizations of the New Left broke into smaller, less radical organizations that supported specific causes. Radical New Leftists went "underground" or started rural communes, while moderate individuals embraced the Democratic Party. Interestingly, some New Leftists, including former *Ramparts* editor David Horowitz and Wisconsin school historian Ronald Radosh, shifted far Right on the political spectrum and became staunch conservatives. Although the strategy of agitation politics remained, the end of the Vietnam War and activist spirit of the long Sixties caused widespread disillusionment and an end of the "movement of movements" known as the New Left political movement.

See also

African American Civil Rights Movement; Black Power Movement; Chicano Rights; Civil Disobedience; Counterculture; Higher Education Movement; Indian Rights; Student Rights Movement

IAN POST

Further Reading

Gosse, Van. 2002. "A Movement of Movements: The Definition and Periodization of the New Left." In Jean-Christophe Agnew and Roy Rosenzweig, eds. *A Companion to Post-1945 America.* Malden, MA: Blackwell, pp. 277–302.

McMillian, John, and Paul Buhle. 2008. *New Left Revisited.* Philadelphia, PA: Temple University Press.

Mills, C. Wright. 1960. "Letter to the New Left." *New Left Review* 5 (September–October): 18–23.

Sixties Project. "Rules of the Black Panther Party." Viet Nam Generation Inc. and the Institute of Advanced Technology in the Humanities. http://www2.iath.virginia.edu/sixties/HTML_docs/Resources/Primary/Manifestos/Panther_rules.html. Accessed June 9, 2014.

Students for a Democratic Society. 1962. "The Port Huron Statement of the Students for a Democratic Society." http://coursesa.matrix.msu.edu/~hst306/documents/huron.html. Accessed June 9, 2014.

New Left Movement—Primary Document

Introduction

C. Wright Mills published his "Letter to the New Left" in the September-October 1960 issue of The New Left Review. *Mills was an American sociologist who taught at Columbia University from 1946 until his death in 1962. His written works on American imperialism, the middle and working class, and political power were influential in New Left thought. In this letter, addressed to those who identified with the New Left in the United States and Great Britain, Mills distinguished the New Left from the Old Left and aimed to inspire individuals to break from apathy. The letter, although written early in the New Left movement, deconstructs the key characteristics of New Left politics, as well as the problems that were perceived in the existing political and social systems.*

Document: "Letter to the New Left" by C. Wright Mills (1960)

… We who have been consistently radical in the moral terms of our work throughout the postwar period are often amused nowadays that various writers—sensing another shift in fashion—begin to call upon intellectuals to work once more in ways that are politically explicit. But we shouldn't be merely amused—we ought to try to make their shift more than a fashion change.

The end-of-ideology is on the way out because it stands for the refusal to work out an explicit political philosophy. And alert men everywhere today do feel the need of such a philosophy. What we should do is to continue directly to confront this need. In doing so, it may be useful to keep in mind that to have a working political philosophy means to have a philosophy that enables you to work. And for that, at least four kinds of work are needed, each of them at once intellectual and political.

In these terms, think—for a moment longer—of the end-of-ideology:

(1) It is a kindergarten fact that any political reflection that is of possible public significance is *ideological*: in its terms, policies, institutions, men of power are criticised or approved. In this respect, the end-of-ideology stands, negatively, for the attempt to withdraw oneself and one's work from political relevance; positively, it is an ideology of political complacency which seems the only way now open for many writers to acquiesce in or to justify the *status quo*.

(2) So far as orienting *theories* of society and of history are concerned, the end-of-ideology stands for, and presumably stands upon, a fetishism of empiricism: more academically, upon a pretentious methodology used to state trivialities about unimportant social areas; more essayistically, upon a naive journalistic empiricism—which I have already characterised above—and upon a cultural gossip in which "answers" to the vital and pivotal issues are merely assumed. Thus political bias masquerades as epistomological excellence, and there are no orienting theories.

(3) So far as the *historic agency of change* is concerned, the end-of-ideology stands upon the identification of such agencies with going institutions; perhaps upon their piecemeal reform, but never upon the search for agencies that might be used or that might themselves make for a structural change of society. The problem of agency is never posed as a problem to solve, as our problem. Instead there is talk of the need to be pragmatic, flexible, open. Surely all this, has already been adequately dealt with: such a view makes sense politically only if the blind drift of human affairs is in general beneficent.

(4) So far as political and human *ideals* are concerned, the end-of-ideology stands for a denial of their relevance—except as abstract ikons. Merely to hold such ideals seriously is in this view "utopian".

But enough. Where do *we* stand on each of these four aspects of political philosophy? Various of us are of course at work on each of them, and all of us are generally aware of our needs in regard to each. As for the articulation of ideals: there I think your magazines have done their best work so far. That is *your* meaning—is it not?—of the emphasis upon cultural affairs. As for ideological analysis, and the rhetoric with which to carry it out: I don't think any of us are nearly good enough, but that will come with further advance on the two fronts where we are weakest: theories of society, history, human nature; and the major problem—ideas about the historical agencies of structural change.

We have frequently been told by an assorted variety of dead-end people that the meanings of Left and of Right are now liquidated, by history and by reason. I think we should answer them in some such way as this:

The Right, among other things, means—what you are doing, celebrating society as it is, a going concern. Left means, or ought to mean, just the opposite. It means: structural criticism and reportage and theories of society, which at some point or another are focussed politically as demands and programmes. These criticisms, demands, theories, programmes are guided morally by the humanist and secular ideals of Western civilisation—above all, reason and freedom and justice. To be "Left" means to connect up cultural with political criticism, and both with demands and programmes. And it means all this inside *every* country of the world.

Only one more point of definition: absence of public issues there may well be, but this is not due to any absence of problems or of contradictions, antagonistic and otherwise. Impersonal and structural changes have not eliminated problems or issues. Their absence from many discussions—that *is* an ideological condition, regulated in the first place by whether or not intellectuals detect and state problems as potential *issues* for probable publics, and as *troubles* for a variety of individuals. One indispensable means of such work on these central tasks is what can only be described as ideological analysis. To be actively Left, among other things, is to carry on just such analysis.

To take seriously the problem of the need for a political orientation is not of course to seek for A Fanatical and Apocalyptic Vision, for An Infallible and Monolithic Lever of Change, for Dogmatic Ideology, for A Startling New Rhetoric, for Treacherous Abstractions—and all the other bogeymen of the dead-enders. These are of course "the extremes", the straw men, the red herrings, used by our political enemies as the polar opposite of where they think they stand.

They tell us, for example, that ordinary men can't always be political "heroes". Who said they could? But keep looking around you; and why not search out the conditions of such heroism as men do and might display? They tell us we are too "impatient", that our "pretentious" theories are not well enough grounded. That is true, but neither are they trivial; why don't they get to work, refuting or grounding them? They tell us we "don't really understand" Russia—and China— today. That is true; we don't; neither do they; we are studying it. They tell us we are "ominous" in our formulations. That is true: we do have enough imagination to be frightened—and we don't have to hide it: we are not afraid we'll panic. They tell us we "are grinding axes". Of course we are: we do have, among other points of view, morally grounded ones; and we are aware of them. They tell us, in their wisdom, we don't understand that The Struggle is Without End. True: we want to change its form, its focus, its object.

We are frequently accused of being "utopian"—in our criticisms and in our proposals; and along with this, of basing our hopes for a New Left *politics* "merely on reason", or more concretely, upon the intelligentsia in its broadest sense.

There is truth in these charges. But must we not ask: what now is really meant by utopian? And: Is not our utopianism a major source of our strength? "Utopian" nowadays I think refers to any criticism or proposal that transcends the up-close milieux of a scatter of individuals: the milieux which men and women can understand directly and which they can reasonably hope directly to change. In this exact sense, our theoretical work is indeed utopian—in my own case, at least, deliberately so. What needs to be understood, and what needs to be changed, is not merely first this and then that detail of some institution or policy. If there is to be a politics of a New Left, what needs to be analysed is the *structure* of institutions, the *foundation* of policies. In this sense, both in its criticisms and in its proposals, our work is necessarily structural—and so, *for us*, just now—utopian.

Which brings us face to face with the most important issue of political reflection—and of political action—in our time:

the problem of the historical agency of change, of the social and institutional means of structural change. There are several points about this problem I would like to put to you.

First, the historic agencies of change for liberals of the capitalist societies have been an array of voluntary associations, coming to a political climax in a parliamentary or congressional system. For socialists of almost all varieties, the historic agency has been the working class—and later the peasantry; also parties and unions variously composed of members of the working class or (to blur, for now, a great problem) of political parties acting in its name—"representing its interests".

I cannot avoid the view that in both cases, the historic agency (in the advanced capitalist countries) has either collapsed or become most ambiguous: so far as structural change is concerned, *these* don't seem to be at once available and effective as *our* agency any more. I know this is a debatable point among us, and among many others as well; I am by no means certain about it. But surely the fact of it—if it be that—ought not to be taken as an excuse for moaning and withdrawal (as it is by some of those who have become involved with the end-of-ideology); it ought not to be bypassed (as it is by many Soviet scholars and publicists, who in their reflections upon the course of advanced capitalist societies simply refuse to admit the political condition and attitudes of the working class).

Is anything more certain than that in 1970—indeed this time next year—our situation will be quite different, and— the chances are high—decisively so? But of course, that isn't saying much. The seeming collapse of our historic agencies of change ought to be taken as a problem, an issue, a trouble—in fact, as *the* political problem which *we* must turn into issue and trouble.

Second, is it not obvious that when we talk about the collapse of agencies of change, we cannot seriously mean that such agencies do not exist. On the contrary, the means of history-making—of decision and of the enforcement of decision—have never in world history been so enlarged and so available to such small circles of men on both sides of The Curtains as they now are. My own conception of the shape of power—the theory of the power elite—I feel no need to argue here. This theory has been fortunate in its critics, from the most diverse points of political view, and I have learned from several of these critics. But I have not seen, as of this date, any analysis of the idea that causes me to modify any of its essential features.

The point that is immediately relevant does seem obvious: what is utopian for us is not at all utopian for the presidium of the Central Committee in Moscow, or the higher circles of the Presidency in Washington, or—recent events make evident—for the men of SAC and CIA. The historic agencies of change that have collapsed are those which were at least thought to be open to *the left* inside the advanced Western nations: those who have wished for structural changes of these societies. Many things follow from this obvious fact; of many of them, I am sure, we are not yet adequately aware.

Third, what I do not quite understand about some New-Left writers is why they cling so mightily to "the working class" of the advanced capitalist societies as *the* historic agency, or even as the most important agency, in the face of the really impressive historical evidence that now stands against this expectation.

Such a labour metaphysic, I think, is a legacy from Victorian Marxism that is now quite unrealistic.

It is an historically specific idea that has been turned into an a-historical and unspecific hope....

Source: Mills, C. Wright. "Letter to the New Left." *New Left Review* no. 5 (September–October 1960): 18–23.

NONVIOLENT RESISTANCE

The history of social change in the United States over the past fifty years has provided many important speeches and events from various groups of people. Of these, one of the most vital times was the civil rights movement, in the 1950s and 1960s. This particular era centered on the American South, where the African American population was concentrated in significant numbers and where racial inequality in education, economic opportunity, and the political and legal processes was most blatant. Many leaders from within the African American community and beyond rose up in order to help promote change in their communities. These important people included Martin Luther King Jr., Rosa Parks, Malcolm X, Andrew Goodman, and others.

Hundreds of followers were inspired by the movement, and assisted these leaders in various ways. These people risked—and sometimes lost—their lives in the name of freedom and equality. This transition in American society became the leading use of nonviolent resistance, which included nonviolent protest. The action of using this design seemed new to some, but the ideas behind the movement were much older. Nonviolent resistance is the practice of achieving goals through protest, political cooperation, civil disobedience, and other messages that do not use violence. Nonviolent resistance is often correlated with civil resistance. Both of these processes show people who operate together with nonviolence and peaceful gatherings in order to make a statement or share their viewpoint.

Beginning in the late 19th century, state and local governments passed segregation laws, known as Jim Crow laws, and mandated restrictions on voting qualifications that left the black population economically and politically powerless. The movement therefore primarily addressed three areas of discrimination in America: education, social segregation, and voting rights. In reference to the later segregation issues in the South, many of the key leaders throughout history have gotten their ideas from Mohandas Gandhi.

From Gandhi's writings came several new ideas and inspirations about nonviolent resistance. He stated that there were two main ways of countering injustice in society. One way was to "smash the head of the man who perpetrates injustice and get your own head smashed in the process." He explained, "Pride makes a victorious nation bad tempered." The second way or method in the difficult task of combating injustice was explained as a situation where one does not have to break another's head, also commonly known as "*satyagraha.*"

Gandhi believed that his taking the vow of *brahmacharya* had allowed him the focus to come up with the concept of *satyagraha* in late 1906. Needing a new term for resistance, Gandhi chose the term *satyagraha*, which literally means "truth force." In the very simplest sense, *satyagraha* is passive

Whites pour sugar, ketchup, and mustard on the heads of sit-in demonstrators at a restaurant lunch counter in Jackson, Mississippi, on June 12, 1963. The protestors were standing up against Jim Crow segregated eating areas. This sit-in demonstration is an example of peaceful protest, during which the demonstrators simply refuse to leave despite harassment. (AP Photo)

resistance. However, Gandhi believed the English phrase of "passive resistance" did not represent the true spirit of resistance since passive resistance was often associated with the weak and was a tactic that could potentially be conducted in anger. In practice, *satyagraha* was a focused and forceful nonviolent resistance to a particular injustice.

A practitioner of *satyagraha* also would never take advantage of an opponent's problems. A *satyagrahi* (a person using *satyagraha*) would resist the injustice by refusing to follow an unjust law. In doing so, he would not be angry, would put

up freely with physical assaults to his person and the confiscation of his property, and would not use foul language to smear his opponent. The goal was not for there to be a winner and loser of the battle, but rather, that all would eventually see and understand the "truth" and agree to rescind the unjust law.

The true test came in 1930, when Gandhi used this technique by walking to the sea with seventy-eight disciples to break the salt tax laws. "Day by day the tension mounted," reports one writer, "as all India followed the elderly Mahatma plodding through the countryside on his crusade." Then the dramatic moment came; as hundreds of congressmen and government officials watched, Gandhi made salt from the sea, breaking the law and setting the rest of India into a "semi-comic frenzy of producing uneatable salt." It was a supremely successful "attention-getting device." Immediately, congressional organizations set about to use the other attention-getting devices, such as demonstrations, mass meetings, and picketing. These concepts would later influence Martin Luther King Jr.

Nonviolent resistance had been familiar to Dr. King from early in his adult life. As King moved on to the seminary, he began to pass countless hours studying social philosophers, including Plato, Aristotle, Rousseau, Hobbes, Bentham, Mill, and Locke. King later stated that he was first introduced to the concept of nonviolence as a freshman at Morehouse College, when he read Henry David Thoreau's *Essay on Civil Disobedience*. Having grown up in Atlanta and witnessed segregation and racism every day, King was "fascinated by the idea of refusing to cooperate with an evil system."

According to Thoreau, government has done little to change the course of history. "Government never of itself furthered enterprise. . . . It does not keep the country free. It does not settle the west. It does not educate. The character within the American people has done all that has been accomplished; and it would have done somewhat more if the government had not sometimes got in its way," Thoreau wrote. He argued that government rarely proves itself useful and that it derives its power from the majority because they are the strongest group, not because they hold the most legitimate viewpoint. Thoreau believed that all change came from the inherent goodness in human nature. He believed that government was a barrier to positive change. Would America have initiated positive social and racial change without government interference? He contends that people's first obligation is to do what they believe is right and not to follow the law dictated by the majority. This idea is mentioned in many civil rights documents and articles, as well as movies like *The Great Debaters* (2007).

Dr. King believed that the Christian doctrine of love, operating through Gandhi's method of nonviolence, was one of the most potent weapons available to oppressed people in their struggle for freedom. He explained through his own writings that he did not experience the power of nonviolent direct action firsthand until the start of the Montgomery Bus Boycott in 1955. It was during the boycott that Dr. King personally enacted Gandhi in principle with the guidance of those around him.

Several years later, in 1959, King traveled to India with his wife, Coretta Scott King, and Lawrence D. Reddick on a visit, which was cosponsored by the American Friends Service Committee. During the five-week trip, King met with the Gandhi family, as well as with Indian activists and officials, including Prime Minister Jawaharlal Nehru. In his 1959 Palm Sunday sermon, King preached on the significance of Gandhi's salt march and his fast as part of his effort to end discrimination against India's untouchables. King ultimately believed that the Gandhian approach of nonviolent resistance would "bring about a solution to the race problem in America."

King later came to understand how nonviolence could become a way of life and how it could be applied to all situations. As King's career and involvement in a nonviolent struggle went on, his words began to echo Gandhi's own sentiments. For example, in King's discussion of civil disobedience, he says that "an individual who breaks a law that conscience tells him is unjust, and who willingly accepts the penalty of imprisonment in order to arouse the conscience of the community over its injustice, is in reality expressing the highest respect for law."

Similarly, King later said, "In no sense do I advocate evading or defying the law, as would the rabid segregationist. That would lead to anarchy. One who breaks an unjust law must do so openly, lovingly, and with a willingness to accept the penalty." These statements echo the words of the Mahatma himself, who always taught respect for the law, provided it is consistent with the truth.

Eventually, he called the principle of nonviolent resistance the "guiding light of our movement." King's notion of nonviolence had six key principles:

- Number one is that one can resist evil without resorting to violence.
- Number two is that non violence seeks to win the friendship and understanding of the opponent.
- Number three states that evil itself not the people committing the evil acts should be opposed.

- Number four states that those committed to non-violence must be willing to suffer without retaliation and suffering itself can be redemptive.

- Number five states that nonviolent resistance of voids external physical violence an internal islands of spirit as well.

- Number six states that the nonviolent resister must have a deep faith in the future stemming from the conviction that "the universe is on the side of justice."

King discusses his pilgrimage to nonviolence in his first book titled *Stride for Freedom* (1958). His later books and articles also capture what he described in his first book as his "courageous confrontation of evil by the power of love" and his transition toward nonviolent resistance.

Following the end of World War II, three of the most influential groups in the civil rights movement were the Congress of Racial Equality (CORE), the Southern Christian Leadership Conference (SCLC), and the Student Nonviolent Coordinating Committee (SNCC). CORE was founded in Chicago in 1942. Another organization was the SCLC, which Dr. King organized in 1957. The third organization, SNCC, began in North Carolina in 1960. All of these groups were pivotal in bringing about social change in America. Further than just the spontaneous and planned student protests, many organizations were formed in order to fight for civil rights using Gandhi's model of nonviolent action.

The group CORE promoted better race relations and vowed to end racial discrimination in the United States. One of its first protests was in Chicago in 1943 at a coffee shop. One of its most successful projects was sending more than 1,000 Freedom Riders on buses throughout the South in 1961. Its goal was to test segregation laws and ultimately end segregation on interstate bus routes. This group also sponsored the 1963 Civil Rights March on Washington.

The SCLC was organized as a base of operations in the South to build a national platform in order to speak about segregation and civil rights. It focused its principles on nonviolent civil disobedience, and quickly became a major force in the movement. Most of its organization worked in the South and conducted leadership training programs to help citizens become better educated on its project. An example of its efforts comes from January 1965, when King and the SCLC joined with SNCC, the Dallas County Voters League (Alabama), and other local African American activists in a voting rights campaign in Selma where, in spite of repeated registration attempts by local blacks, only 2 percent were on the voting rolls. The SCLC had chosen to focus its efforts in Selma, anticipating that the notorious brutality of local law enforcement under Sheriff Jim Clark would attract national attention and pressure President Lyndon B. Johnson and Congress to enact new national voting rights legislation. This group also played a major role in the civil rights March on Washington when King gave his famous *I Have a Dream* speech.

SNCC was originally inspired in Greensboro, North Carolina; in order to promote sit-ins, the members conducted numerous gatherings throughout the South. This group was devoted to nonviolent resistance under the leadership of Stokely Carmichael who would eventually coin the phrase Black Power. This type of strategy requires tremendous courage and self-control, as well as a willingness to endure pain and sometimes even death. The strength of nonviolence lies in its ability to dramatically reduce the moral legitimacy of those who persist in using violent strategies against nonviolent opposition. This loss of legitimacy can, in turn, contribute to coalition-building efforts leading to widespread condemnation of parties using violent strategies and often the imposition of sanctions by the international community. In essence, nonviolent resistance is a strategy for countering the power of violent force with the power of the integrative system. Many nonviolent techniques can also be effective when used against illegitimate abuses of legal, political, or other types of force.

In the end, the efforts and readings from the many famous leaders, paid off. On August 6, in the presence of King and other civil rights leaders, President Johnson signed the Voting Rights Act of 1965. Recalling "the outrage of Selma," Johnson called the right to vote "the most powerful instrument ever devised by man for breaking down injustice and destroying the terrible walls which imprison men because they are different from other men." In his annual address to the SCLC a few days later, King noted that "Montgomery led to the Civil Rights Acts of 1957 and 1960; Birmingham inspired the Civil Rights Act of 1964, and Selma produced the voting rights legislation of 1965" (King, 11). The teachings of nonviolent resistance and the influences of Thoreau and Gandhi had worked once again.

Nor was the civil rights movement alone. It influenced others to pursue similar policies, and it followed in the footsteps of earlier movements—sometimes consciously, sometimes not. Even before the early days of the roaring twenties, women gathered to seek their right to vote through many types of demonstrations. Demonstrations for women's suffrage in the United States led to the passage and ratification of the constitutional amendment guaranteeing women the right to vote in 1920. Nonviolent resistance was present in European history during World War II. It was the 1940s where nonviolent resistance to the Nazis grew evident. The tradition of nonviolence had deep roots, and remains an important part of rights movements worldwide.

See also

African American Civil Rights Movement; Black Power Movement; Civil Disobedience; Romanticism

ERICA ROBINSON

Further Reading

Library of Congress. History of African Americans Online Exhibit. http://www.history.navy.mil/index.html. Accessed June 9, 2014.

Branch, Taylor. 1988. *Parting the Waters: America in the King Years, 1954–1963.* New York: Simon and Schuster.

King, Martin Luther, Jr. 2001. "Address at Conclusion of the Selma to Montgomery March." In Clayborne Carson and Kirk Shepard, eds. *A Call to Conscience: The Landmark Speeches of Dr. Martin Luther King, Jr.* New York: Grand Central Publishing.

Sargent, Frederic O. 2004. *The Civil Rights Revolution: Events and Leaders, 1955–1968.* Jefferson, NC: McFarland & Co.

Nonviolent Resistance—Primary Document

Introduction

In 1962, pacifists who opposed war and particularly the use and spread of nuclear weapons staged a "Walk for Peace" from New Hampshire to Washington, D.C. They used the same tactics of nonviolent resistance being employed at the time by Dr. Martin Luther King Jr. and other leaders of the national civil rights movement. When the protestors reached Washington, they began peacefully demonstrating at the White House and picketing at the Pentagon. Arrested by police for creating a "public hazard," many of the demonstrators went limp and had to be carried away. Thus, they assumed the classic pose of civil disobedience for the television camera crews and newspaper reporters who covered the demonstrations. All those arrested received suspended sentences and were released on probation, except for Huw Williams, who demanded a jury trial. The following article from Esquire magazine described the nonviolent philosophy and actions of the peace marchers.

Document: "Doom and Passion Along Rt. 45" by Thomas B. Morgan (November 1962)

THIRTEEN pacifists, who seemed to think that a peace march might help belay the arms race, one hot afternoon not long ago found themselves trudging along a highway outside of Woodbury, New Jersey. They were elapsing yet another leg of a seven-hundred-mile "Walk for Peace" which had begun seven weeks earlier in Hanover, New Hampshire, and would end two weeks hence in Washington, D.C. At the moment, the Walk was led by Joel Kent and Marshall Bush, a sixty-year old blind man. Kent was a tired-looking, gaunt scarecrow, aged forty, wearing a ragged white shirt and black trousers. He earned his living raising trees in Jamaica, Vermont. He was one of six peace-walkers who had come all the way from Hanover, through Massachusetts, across New York's midsection, down the Hudson River Valley, and into the flatlands of New Jersey. Bush, whom Kent held lightly at the elbow, was a latecomer, sturdy, white-haired, and neatly dressed in a sport shirt and slacks. Back home in Lancaster, Pennsylvania, he owned a vending machine business. He had joined the walk south of Camden, planning to leave it sixty miles later—about three days afoot—in Wilmington, Delaware. And now, even though he had begun to ache from sunburn, he persisted in carrying the Walk's leading sign, a circle of wood on an aluminum pole, WALK FOR PEACE / HANOVER, N.H. TO WASHINGTON, D.C. He also carried his red-tipped white cane, using it to feel for curbings and potholes.

Behind the tree farmer and the blind man, ten others walked, single file. They had come about fifteen miles since morning. They had six miles between them and the day's terminus, Paulsboro, New Jersey.

Time was passing and the walkers became more certain that they had become part of an Organism, a multilegged creature of the road that lived in space without an awareness of time passing. Ever since Hanover, walkers had shared the feeling that the Walk was itself an entity, a thing with a separate existence. But this feeling was always strongest late in the afternoon when still there were longer, more tiring miles to go. They would feel it then most keenly, almost as a loss of personality.

The only thing that mattered to the Organism was mileage—feet, yards, blocks, spaces on the motor oil map of the Atlantic seaboard. The Walk has one dimension: distance. In the time sense, there was no past. What had been happening since leaving Hanover the day before Easter had been occurring *somewhere*—in Springfield, Troy, Poughkeepsie, or Camden—but not some*time* in the past.

When had the rock been thrown at the Walk through the window of a meeting hall? Answer: Hudson, New York.

Similarly, the future was timeless. What might happen next would not happen *then*, but in a place farther south, down the road a piece, yonder. Tomorrow would not be a Saturday in June. It would be the day the Walk reached Chester, Pennsylvania. It would be Chester, Pa. Day.

And the present had become timeless, too.

The Walk had no tenses here in the thinly populated sand flats of New Jersey, Route 41 now forking into Route 45, surrounded by scrubby trees and billboards and the blur of compact cars and the murmuring of innumerable youknowwhats. Mostly, as the sun moved lower, the Organism walked heads down, each personality suspended in this later afternoon timelessness, staring at the tops of his shoes, his sneakers, boots, her sandals, his brogans, loafers, oxfords, chukkas, all scuffed and dust covered and breaking down, picking them up and laying them flat, one dog in front of the other, gingerly on the side away from the blisters, stiffly because of the shin splint or the knot in the hamstring—and hardly ever wondering what time it might be. In logic, in truth, time made no difference once the day's mileage had been set, twenty one miles today—that is, 36,960 paces—seventeen miles yesterday, fifteen tomorrow, and so on and on—*this* was what one had to get over. This was the suffering over seven hundred miles in nine weeks that made the point for them.

From a passing car, a boy shouted, "Hey, look out for the Bombbbb!"

In the ranks, Jon Robison, nineteen, carried a sign. He had been with the Walk since Kingston, New York, but could not go all the way to Washington because his parents wanted him home in time for summer school. He wore a T-shirt and khakis, with a recorder stuck in his belt. When it was someone else's turn to carry the sign, he would play tunes on the recorder as he walked. His shoes had fallen apart and were now held together with black tape.

DEFEND FREEDOM, Jon's sign read, WITH NONVIOLENT RESISTANCE.

Another sign, NO BOMB TESTS / EAST OR WEST, was held by Larry Coopersmith, eighteen-year-old son of a contractor in the New York garment industry. "My father forbade me to come on this Walk," he says. "So, I packed up and here I am. I called up home later and he said, 'Son—you bastard!' He thinks I'm a Communist. He's very conservative. My father is about as close as there is to a pure capitalist. He's a contractor in a business where everyone cuts everyone else's throat. He is honest, so he gets his throat cut quite often." Coopersmith wore a striped polo shirt, shorts, anklets, and paper thin oxfords. His feet hurt. "All I brought with me was four dollars," he says. "Someone back up the road gave me three dollars toward a new pair of shoes, but I never got any more money from anyone so I spent the three dollars on cigarettes."

Bringing up the rear, Penny Young, eighteen, carried a man-sized sign. She was from upstate Illinois, a pretty, plump, apple-checked young lady with boyish bobbed hair. She wore a fresh blouse, plaid skirt, high, white teen-ager socks and sneakers. She was a veteran of "peace actions" against the Electric Boat Company, manufacturers of Polaris submarines, and against the Atomic Energy Commission. The latter occurred in New York, involved sitting in at A.E.C. headquarters, and won Penny a five-day sentence in the women's jail in Greenwich Village. "It was an educational experience," she says, "especially learning how much worse they make those girls by putting them in jail. The girls thought that anyone like me with short hair couldn't be straight, so they descended on me. I said, 'Look, girls, I'm straight.' After that, I got along all right. My father called and said he'd be in jail with me if it weren't for his job. See, I could go to jail with dignity and take whatever they could dish out.…

Source: Morgan, Thomas B. "Doom and Passion along Rt. 45." *Esquire*, November, 1962. Available online at http://www.trussel.com/passion.htm.

NUCLEAR POWER MOVEMENT
Origins and the First Use of Nuclear Power

The atom dates to the ideas of ancient Greek philosopher Democritus. Roman writer Lucretius carried Democritus's ideas forward, though only in 1905 did German physicist Albert Einstein establish, in his famous equation $E = mc^2$, that humankind could unleash tremendous energy from the atom. Because E equals energy, m equals mass, and c equals the velocity of light, a huge number, even a small amount of mass yields enormous energy.

In the 1930s German chemists Otto Hahn and Lise Meitner split an atom, deriving energy that proved Einstein right. With the Nazis intent on conquest and mass extermination, the United States feared that Germany would seek to build an atomic bomb. Indeed, Nobel laureate Werner Heisenberg led this effort but, unknown to the United States, made no progress. When the United States entered World War II in December 1941, President Franklin Delano Roosevelt created the Manhattan Project. Although Einstein had come to the United States, he was a pacifist and would not contribute to the Manhattan Project. Nobel laureate Enrico Fermi, who had also settled in the United States, instead became the central figure in the Manhattan Project. Its success led to the ruination of Hiroshima and Nagasaki, Japan. Ever since, humankind has lived with the possibility, Nobel laureate William Faulkner reminded Americans in the 1950s, of nuclear annihilation.

The Atom for Peace

But by the 1950s there were advocates of the peaceful use of nuclear energy. If one could split uranium or plutonium atoms in a large tank of water, the resultant energy would boil the water, giving off steam. The steam would turn a turbine as it rushed through the turbine, generating electricity. The most hopeful Americans believed that clean nuclear power could replace the generation of electricity by coal, oil, or natural gas. Indeed, as early as 1945, one Irish physicist predicted the generation of electricity from nuclear energy. American science writers, eager to promote any novelty, followed this physicist in seeking to predict what the future of nuclear power might be.

Although the nuclear power plant would come to be the most important use of nuclear energy, in the early decades after World War II ideas abounded about a myriad uses of nuclear energy. In 1958, Ford Motor Company attempted to design a nuclear powered car. Books and magazines joined the bandwagon that nuclear energy might power the future. Schools taught students about the peaceful uses of nuclear power. U.S. Army General Leslie Groves, who had overseen the Manhattan Project, now wrote about nuclear powered trains, airplanes, and automobiles. Disney even premiered a film, *Our Friend the Atom*. In this way, a movement arose in the United States committed to nuclear power. These Americans were primarily college educated and were quick to applaud the efforts to build a future based on nuclear power and believed that the peaceful use of nuclear power was almost unlimited.

The U.S. Atomic Energy Commission boasted that the extraction of electricity from nuclear power would be "too cheap to meter" (Melosi, 154). Even with this enthusiasm, the progress toward nuclear power was not as rapid as it might have been given that the federal government assigned priority to the development of ever more destructive nuclear weapons. Yet not everyone in the military embraced the bomb. Admiral Hyman G. Rickover put his energies into converting the U.S. Navy to nuclear power. Nuclear energy came to power submarines, aircraft carriers, and other naval vessels. As a result of Rickover's efforts, in 1954 the Navy launched the submarine USS *Nautilus*, the world's first nuclear-powered watercraft. The navy's nuclear reactor became the model for the civilian nuclear power plant.

In 1954, the year of USS *Nautilus*'s launching, engineers in Shippingport, Pennsylvania, began construction of the world's first civilian nuclear power plant. Yet President Dwight D. Eisenhower, fearing the coming of a recession that year, cut the Atomic Energy Commission's plan to build four more nuclear power plants and a nuclear airplane. At the

Newsmen and spectators stand in front of the main gate of the Three Mile Island Nuclear Generating Station in Middletown, Pennsylvania, April 2, 1979. (AP Photo/Jack Kanthal)

same time, the president was enthusiastic about the prospect of nuclear power to generate almost unlimited electricity. Eisenhower did not want the United States to monopolize the peaceful uses of nuclear power but instead to share its knowledge with other nations, as British Prime Minister Winston Churchill had hoped during World War II. In 1954, Congress enacted the Atomic Energy Act, which urged the private sector to take a larger role in the development of nuclear power plants. General Electric and Westinghouse responded to this challenge, but many other firms, under the illusion that the United States had almost unlimited supplies of coal, oil, and natural gas, expressed little interest.

In September 1955, the Atomic Energy Commission announced its intention of building seven additional nuclear power plants. Construction of these and other nuclear power plants began in the 1960s. In 1966, U.S. utilities placed orders for twenty-one new nuclear power plants and in 1967 for thirty-one more. By 1969, the United States had nearly 100 nuclear power plants. Environmentalists were wary of nuclear power, though one might argue that fossil fuels were the real problem. The oil crisis of 1973 and 1974 forced Americans to the dismal realization that their access to oil came at a huge cost. The proponents of nuclear power saw their opportunity to promote nuclear power as an alternative to the generation of electricity by burning oil. Others sought compromise with Saudi Arabia and the other Arab oil exporters so that the United States could renew imports of Middle Eastern oil. The quadrupling of the price of oil in 1973 alone undercut the idea of appeasement and strengthened those who promoted nuclear power. However, environmental concerns intensified in the late 1970s and into the 1980s, and Americans opposed the attempt of utilities to pass on the cost of the construction of nuclear power plants by raising the price of electricity.

Setbacks for Nuclear Power

The worst blow to nuclear power in U.S. history came in 1979 when one nuclear power plant at Three Mile Island, Pennsylvania, suffered a partial meltdown, releasing toxic radiation into the atmosphere. Radiation poisoning can be fatal, and so the outcry from Americans was loud and sustained. Fossil fuels had never caused such trouble. Perhaps nuclear power was not the solution to America's energy woes. These sentiments peaked in 1986, when Americans learned of the worst nuclear power plant disaster in history, occurring at the Chernobyl nuclear reactor in Ukraine, which was then part of the Soviet Union. Survivors came forward with gruesome accounts of their friends' deaths. One, a veteran of the war between Afghanistan and the Soviet Union, wished he had been killed then to be spared the horrors he witnessed at Chernobyl. The accident killed 238 people outright, and perhaps 50,000 Ukrainians were exposed to low levels of radiation. The Soviet Union had to resettle 130,000 residents because radiation had contaminated their homes, farms, and water.

In the United States, the proponents of nuclear power tried to dismiss Chernobyl as an anomaly unlikely ever to be repeated. One American physicist put the odds of another Chernobyl at 1 per 10,000 years, but environmentalists petitioned for an end to the use of nuclear power. U.S. physicist Alvin M. Weinberg, hoping cooler heads would prevail, urged the United States and other nations to build 6,000 new plants in the next sixty years. The Massachusetts Institute of Technology's Center for Energy Policy Research applauded Weinberg's vision and emphasized that nuclear power was a clean source of electricity at a time when Americans were beginning to realize that the burning of fossil fuels might cause a greenhouse effect. Indeed, global temperatures were and are rising.

The 21st Century

By the 21st century the United States had decommissioned old nuclear power plants faster than it built new ones, causing the proportion of electricity generated by nuclear power to decline. Yet some states have had success. South Carolina, New Jersey, Vermont, and New Hampshire generate more than half their electricity from nuclear power. Nationwide, nuclear power generates about 22 percent of electricity, second only to coal and comfortably ahead of hydroelectric power, oil, and natural gas.

Though the fallout from the Fukushima nuclear power plant disaster in 2011 remains to be seen, the most bullish have termed the 21st century a renaissance of nuclear power. Although the United States does not derive as great a proportion of electricity from nuclear power as do France and Scandinavia, its commitment to nuclear power appears, at the moment at least, to be adamantine. Today the United States has 104 nuclear power plants, which generate about 20 percent (there appears to be variance in the figures) of U.S. electricity. Thirty-one states have at least one nuclear power plant. Whatever their differences, presidents George W. Bush and Barack Obama share a commitment to the growth of nuclear energy. The rising acrimony over the culpability of fossil fuels in altering earth's climate may bring more environmentalists to the cause of nuclear power.

See also

Environmental Movement; Military-Industrial Complex; Nuclear Proliferation

CHRISTOPHER CUMO

Further Reading

Levy, Solomon. 2007. *50 Years in Nuclear Power: A Retrospective*. La Grange Park, IL: American Nuclear Society.

Melosi, Martin V. 2013. *Atomic Age America*. Boston: Pearson.

Nuclear Power Movement—Primary Document

Introduction

This excerpt from the staff report on the accident at Three Mile Island emphasizes the role of journalism in focusing a public debate about the safety of nuclear power. In tracing the reaction of agencies and the media, the report demonstrates the value of intelligent and careful reporting and distribution of information, and how little was actually known about nuclear power and its potential effects.

Document: Staff Report to the President's Commission on the Accident at Three Mile Island (October 1979)

I. Summary of Reports from Public's Right to Information Task Force

For every group even remotely connected to the nuclear power industry, the accident at Three Mile Island (TMI)

was a time of truth. The training of plant personnel, the durability of equipment, the planning of civil defense officials, the responsiveness of public health officers—all were tested under harrowing conditions in the glare of national publicity. Members of the news media and public information officials were also tested far more severely than ever before in the history of the nuclear debate. Journalists were not unfamiliar with most of the issues in this debate. Battles between pro- and anti-nuclear forces, sit-ins at plant sites, acrimonious public hearings, and statements of "visible" experts have alerted the public and the media to such issues as radioactive waste disposal and the health hazards from low-level radiation. One study, prepared by the Battelle Human Affairs Research Center, estimates that there has been a 400 percent increase in print media coverage of nuclear power issues between 1972 and 1976....

Overview of Findings

The quality of information available to the public in potentially life-threatening situation is of critical importance. This information has a significant bearing on the capacity of people to respond to the accident, on their emotional health, and on their willingness to accept guidance from responsible public officials. Those managing the accident, as well as journalists, must meet a rigorous standard in providing timely, accurate, and understandable information to the public.

During the accident at Three Mile Island, neither public information officials nor journalists served the public's right to know in a manner that must be achieved in the event of future accidents. Each side failed for different reasons, and to a different degree. The most common explanations—that the utility lied, that the NRC covered up to protect the nuclear industry, or that the media engaged in an orgy of sensationalism—do not hit the mark. Indeed, reporters often showed great skill in piecing together the story, and some NRC officials disclosed information that was truly alarming and damaging to the industry's image because they thought the public had a right to know it. Even the utility's shortcomings in the public information area (and there were many) are attributable in part to self-deception, as well as to a lack of candor. Given the enormous investment at stake for Met Ed, the company's unwillingness to recognize the severity of

damage to the reactor is not surprising. But such hesitancy presents serious problems for serving the public's right to know during the early stages of an accident.

The public information problems of Met Ed and the NRC were rooted in a lack of planning. Neither expected that an accident of this magnitude—one that went on for days, requiring evacuation planning—would ever happen. In a sense they were victims of their own reassurances about the safety of nuclear power. As a result, neither had a "disaster" public information plan. Neither had personnel trained in disaster public relations. Coordination between the utility and the NRC was so weak that responsibility for informing the public in the first crucial hours of the accident was undefined. The NRC did not know when, or whether, to send its own public information people to the site; when or where to set up an NRC press center. Met Ed's public information department was an operation with low status and no policy input. It had never dealt with a national press corps. It was experienced at producing educational materials promoting nuclear power, but inexperienced at fielding specific questions about nuclear power from critics or journalists. The utility did not have an appropriate spokesperson during the accident. The job fell to John Herbein, the vice president for generations, and he proved unsuited to the task.

Perhaps the most serious failure in the planning stage was that neither the utility nor the NRC made provision for getting information from people who had it (in the control room and at the site) to people who needed it. This group included other utility executives, the governor of Pennsylvania, the NRC's Incident Response Center (IRC) in Bethesda, public information officials, journalists, and members of the public. These people all needed information to make technical decisions in managing the accident, or to make decisions on evacuation and public health.

Met Ed officials at the company's headquarters in Reading, Pa., or officials with the parent company, General Public Utilities (GPU) in New Jersey often did not know what employees at the plant knew. NRC officials in Bethesda did not know what their colleagues from the Region I office knew, nor did they know what Met Ed was planning. These fundamental communication problems persisted for the first days of the accident. The internal communication problem proved particularly damaging to Met Ed because the inadequate flow of information was often mistaken for intentional coverup. On the morning of the first day of the accident, for example, while Met Ed President Walter Creitz was telling some reporters that there had been small off-site radiation releases, Met Ed public information officials in the same building were telling reporters there had been none. Creitz and Blaine Fabian, Met Ed's public information head, had neglected to pass on this information to their own staff. This is one reason the utility lost credibility early in the accident. In addition, little effort was made by the NRC (until day six) to supply the media with technical briefers who could answer questions. Met Ed was almost as deficient in this regard. Both organizations left reporters pretty much to their own devices.

Given this confusion among sources, and given that reporters are almost entirely dependent on such sources for their information, it is not surprising that news media coverage of the accident in the first few days was also confused. For a number of issues during the accident—such as the danger posed by the hydrogen bubble or the size of a radiation release which led to evacuation concerns on Friday—it is obvious that the only type of "accurate" reporting possible under the circumstances was the presentation of contradictory and competing statements from a variety of officials.

The news media were also somewhat unprepared, and this added to the prevailing confusion. While it is a goal of many journalistic organizations to develop specialists who are expert in particular areas (such as business reporting, science and medical reporting, or national political reporting), few reporters who covered TMI had more than a rudimentary knowledge of nuclear power. Some, by their own admission, did not know how a pressurized, light water reactor worked, or what a meltdown was. Few knew what questions to ask about radiation releases so that their reports could help the public evaluate health risks.

A number of reporters in the first group to arrive were assigned to the story because they were available, and because they could cover almost anything on short notice—not because they had nuclear power as a regular "beat." Good journalists can absorb vast amounts of unfamiliar material while on the job; that happened during TMI, but the effort

required to make sense of the story was enormous. It was not like covering a political campaign or an airplane hijacking, where at least the vocabulary of the sources and the vocabulary of the reporters are the same.

The nuclear industry has developed its own language, and this was a handicap for the many journalists who did not speak it. A seemingly simple question of whether the core of the reactor had been uncovered and damaged elicited responses couched in terms of "ruptured fuel pins," "pinholes in the cladding," "melted cladding," "cladding oxidation," "failed fuel," "fuel damage," "fuel oxidation," "structural fuel damage," or "core melt." The distinctions are real, but for reporters not speaking the language, it was like suffering from color blindness at a watercolor exhibition. William Dornsife, a nuclear engineer with the Pennsylvania Bureau of Radiation Protection (BRP), describes the language problem:

It was an experience. . . considering the technical questions I was being asked and the lack of understanding of my answers. It's difficult for an engineer to respond to a technical question with anything except a technical response. And I knew by the questions I was getting back that the press people just didn't understand what was going on, and I knew there was going to be a real problem about getting information out to the public.

Neither Met Ed nor the NRC provided enough technical briefers in the first 5 days of the accident to help journalists interpret what they were being told.

Reporters also arrived with different objectives. Some were science writers with an interest in the reactor. Some were medical writers with an interest in public health and safety. Others were sent to write "color" stories and focus on reactions of citizens and evacuees. It would have been difficult under ideal circumstances for a public information program to serve the many needs of the reporters who covered the accident. Given the information program in place when the reporters arrived, it proved to be an impossibility.

In the important first few days of the accident, when evacuation decisions had to be made, the public's right to know was not served because the conditions under which all parties operated were such that the public's right to know could not be served. Imagine, for a moment, the problems confronting a reporter who arrived at the TMI site Wednesday afternoon. Met Ed had no central information facility. No one was distributing schematics of the plant or answering basic technical questions about the reactor. No one was describing what a general emergency was or why it was important. There was no central source, or good source, of up-to-date radiation information (not Wednesday, and not any day during the first week, when this was, arguably, the most crucial type of information for the public). There were no telephone facilities for reporters. The utility was answering phone queries from its Reading headquarters nearly 60 miles from the site, but the information being dispensed was late and, as it turned out, much too optimistic about conditions in the plant. There was no official spokesman for the utility until John Herbein took the part at an impromptu press conference early Wednesday afternoon. But no transcript was made of his remarks to aid reporters or Met Ed public information people who missed the press conference....

Source: www.threemileisland.org/downloads/192.pdf.

NUCLEAR PROLIFERATION

Nuclear proliferation primarily refers to the spread of nuclear weapons and the limiting of access to radioactive material. The proliferation of nuclear weapons has been a critical issue for the U.S. government since the world entered the nuclear era following World War II.

The terrible effects of nuclear weapons, as demonstrated by the two bombs dropped on Japan in 1945, means that the world community has a vested interest in limiting or preventing proliferation. As the world's first nuclear power, and the only one thus far to have used nuclear weapons in war, the United States of America has taken an active role in the effort to limit or stop many countries and terrorist groups from obtaining them.

A three-stage, liquid-fueled ICBM (scrag) in a November 7, 1968, military parade in Red Square in honor of the fifty-first anniversary of the great October Revolution, Moscow, USSR. (Sovfoto/UIG via Getty Images)

Since 1945, the capabilities of nuclear weapons have greatly increased. The bomb dropped on Hiroshima was equivalent to 13,000 tons of TNT. Within ten years, the development of hydrogen bombs increased the destructive power of a nuclear weapon to the equivalent of 1 million tons. A war between nuclear powers would assure mutual destruction, so that the mere threat of using one has proven to be a deterrent and has given nations incentive to pursue diplomacy instead of military action. This somewhat positive effect of nuclear proliferation emerged after World War II, when the world's two largest powers, the Soviet Union and the United States, built large nuclear arsenals. From 1945 to 1991, despite being ideological foes, the two countries never engaged in a large-scale war against each other, and both sides had an interest in avoiding a nuclear war. Thus, nuclear powers have been more cautious in going to war with each other, and in this sense, nuclear proliferation has had a positive effect.

Such positive effects, however, are tempered by the increased risk when nuclear powers have disagreements or go to war. Accidental detonations or a power's failure to secure its nuclear arsenals is of great concern to the United States. For example, political unrest in Pakistan has led to American fears that terrorist groups might one day gain access to nuclear materials. This problem has become worse in the 21st century, largely because of actions during the Cold War, during which the Soviet Union and the United States engaged in nuclear proliferation by aiding their allies in obtaining these weapons.

After World War II, the United States attempted to maintain its monopoly on nuclear weapons. The goal, as detailed in the Baruch Plan, was to allow other nations access to nuclear technology for peaceful purposes while having the United Nations regulate any production and use of nuclear materials such as plutonium and uranium. Soviet protests, as well as the American refusal to destroy its arsenal, prevented the plan from being enacted. What followed was a nearly fifty-year period in which an arms race between the United States and the Soviet Union led to the greatest proliferation of nuclear weapons in history.

Ideological differences, in addition to the massive costs of World War II (the Soviets lost approximately 20 million people compared to around 415,000 American soldiers killed), drove the Soviet desire to obtain a nuclear weapon. This was achieved, partly due to Soviet espionage, in 1949, when the nation tested its first atomic bomb. From 1949 onward, the actions of both superpowers largely determined the degree of nuclear proliferation throughout the world.

When the Korean War began in 1950, the United States and its allies in the United Nations found themselves facing two Soviet-backed powers: North Korea and the People's Republic of China. Although war with the Soviet Union itself was avoided, the American consideration of using nuclear weapons against the Chinese drove the communist country's desire to build a nuclear weapon of its own. Shortly after the war, Great Britain, with the help of the United States, detonated its first nuclear bomb in 1952. France followed in 1960 and then came the People's Republic of China in 1964 (with Soviet aid). From this period onward, the aforementioned nuclear powers competed to increase their arsenals in the hope of deterring their enemies. For no two countries was this as true as for the United States and the Soviet Union. At the height of the Cold War, the two powers controlled 70,000 nuclear weapons (primarily in the form of long range missiles known as ICBMs) with a destructive power equivalent to 6,000 pounds of TNT for each person in the world. Tension and fear of nuclear war peaked during the Cuban Missile Crisis of 1962 and during a renewed arms race between the United States and the Soviet Union in the early 1980s.

With so much destructive capability and so much at stake, nuclear powers began a greater effort to prevent nuclear proliferation. The five nuclear powers (the United States, the Soviet Union, Great Britain, France, and the People's Republic of China) feared that a worldwide nuclear arms race would have dangerous and catastrophic consequences. From these fears arose numerous treaties. The Nuclear Nonproliferation Treaty, created by the United Nations in 1968, is one of the largest. Countries that signed the treaty agreed not to pursue the development of nuclear weapons. Those that already possessed them could keep existing weapons as long as they made an attempt to downsize their arsenals.

From an American perspective, the Nuclear Nonproliferation Treaty had many benefits. The United States could maintain an arsenal sufficient to check Soviet threats and deter the creation of new, potentially hostile nuclear powers. The treaty marked a significant step in stemming nuclear proliferation but was not without criticism. American and Soviet militaries still possessed massive nuclear arsenals. Also, without the support of these two powers the United Nations would be unlikely to have the influence to stop nuclear proliferation. Many nations, such as South Africa, Israel, India, and Pakistan, refused to sign the treaty and continued to pursue and create nuclear weapons (South Africa signed in 1994 after destroying its weapons).

During the Cold War, the stance of the United States toward nuclear proliferation fluctuated. After aiding Great Britain in obtaining its own bomb, it did little to aid the further spread of technology and weapons to its allies. Instead, America concentrated on increasing its own arsenal while improving its technological capabilities. Early in the 21st century, the United States possesses the most capable and advanced nuclear arsenal in the world. This has been the result of a massive Cold War buildup. While certain U.S. presidents sought to downsize the number of weapons possessed by the country (such as Richard Nixon in the 1970s), others sought to increase it. Ronald Reagan was one such president. He maintained that a massive military buildup would weaken the Soviet Union and place enormous pressure on its economy as it tried to keep up. During Reagan's presidency in the 1980s American's fears of a nuclear war increased. Tension eased after 1985, when Mikhail Gorbachev, a self-styled reformer, assumed leadership of the Soviet Union. Six years later, the superpower ceased to exist, and the United States of America emerged victorious from the Cold War. A new age of nuclear proliferation began.

It is far easier and cheaper to build a nuclear weapon in the 21st century than it was before. In order to stop nuclear proliferation the United States has adapted a variety of methods, most often relying on a combination of diplomacy and the threat of military action. There are numerous instances since the Cold War in which the United States has employed these tactics.

The collapse of the world's other largest nuclear power raised significant concern in the United States. Chief among these was the ability of Russia and other former Soviet nations to secure their arsenals. Fifteen countries gained their independence after the Soviet collapse in 1991. Some, like Lithuania, did not inherit any nuclear weapons. Others, like Ukraine, Kazakhstan, and Belarus, inherited large arsenals. Under pressure and through negotiations most of these nations gradually signed the Nuclear Nonproliferation Treaty and surrendered their weapons.

As the Russian economy reeled in the early 1990s, the United States provided financial and technical aid to help secure the old Soviet arsenal. There also existed reports that nuclear material had been smuggled out of Eastern Europe and sold. Most troubling was the claim of a Russian general that a number of briefcase-sized tactical nuclear bombs had gone missing. In this chaotic time, American aid and security was critical to safeguarding former Soviet nuclear weapons.

Security efforts were accompanied by the Strategic Arms Reduction Treaty (START), the negotiations for which began in 1991. The treaty's goal was ambitious, requiring a reduction of nuclear warheads possessed by Russia and the United States to 2,500 by the year 2007. Both nations were slow to meet this goal. A continuation of the original Strategic Arms Reduction Treaty, titled New START, was announced by President Barack Obama and Russian president Dmitry Medvedev in 2010. New START seeks for both sides to limit their nuclear weapons to approximately 1,500 by 2021.

The United Nations achieved an important milestone in 1995, when 170 nations agreed to reduce the spread of nuclear weapons and ultimately eliminate the world's stockpile. In the 21st century, however, nuclear proliferation continues to be a concern. The Nuclear Nonproliferation Treaty has sought to end nations from obtaining weapons, but has not entirely succeeded. Thus, the United States has taken a significant role in policing this problem.

Hostile nations in the pursuit of nuclear weapons have often been labeled "rogue" by the U.S. government. Rogue nations often pursue nuclear weapons for purposes other than defense. Another concern is that nations such as North Korea, Iraq, or Iran might provide terrorist groups with nuclear material for an attack on the United States. This was the justification the Bush administration used for the invasion of Iraq in 2003 following the September 11 terrorist attacks in 2001. In the case of North Korea and Iran, the United States has used a combination of diplomacy and the threat of military force. Strict economic sanctions, along with a large presence of American troops along the 38th parallel in Korea and the Middle East near Iran, have tempered and delayed both nations' pursuit of nuclear weapons. For North Korea, which announced it had successfully tested a nuclear weapon in 2006, sanctions and diplomacy to decommission their nuclear program have produced mixed results.

It is likely that nuclear proliferation will continue throughout the 21st century and beyond. The high stakes involved mean that the global community has a vested interest in stopping it. As the world's strongest power, the United States remains instrumental to these efforts.

See also

Military Industrial Complex; Weapons of Mass Destruction (WMDs)

JUSTIN G. RISKUS

Further Reading

Bender, David L., and Bruno Leone. 1992. *Nuclear Proliferation: Opposing Viewpoints*. Farmington Hills, MI: Greenhaven Press.

Cheney, Glenn Alan. 1999. *Nuclear Proliferation: The Problems and Possibilities*. London: Franklin Watts.

Curtis, Charles B. 2006. "Curbing the Demand for Mass Destruction." *Annals of the American Academy of Political and Social Science* 607: 27–32.

Margulies, Philip. 2008. *Nuclear Nonproliferation*. New York: Facts on File.

Nuclear Proliferation—Primary Document

Introduction

In 1939, Albert Einstein wrote a letter to Franklin D. Roosevelt, warning the U.S. president of German efforts to build a nuclear bomb. The letter was the beginnings of real concern within the United States over nuclear proliferation and of the consequences of U.S. failure to keep up with developments in nuclear weaponry.

Document: Letter of Albert Einstein to President Franklin D. Roosevelt (August 2, 1939)

Albert Einstein
Old Grove Rd.
Nassau Point
Peconic, Long Island
August 2nd, 1939

F.D. Roosevelt
President of the United States,
White House
Washington, D.C.

Sir:

Some recent work by E. Fermi and L. Szilard, which has been communicated to me in manuscript, leads me to expect that the element uranium may be turned into a new and important source of energy in the immediate future. Certain aspects of the situation which has arisen seem to call for watchfulness and, if necessary, quick action on the part of the Administration. I believe therefore that it is my duty to bring to your attention the following facts and recommendations:

In the course of the last four months it has been made probable—through the work of Joliot in France as well as Fermi and Szilard in America—that it may become possible to set up a nuclear chain reaction in a large mass of uranium, by which vast amounts of power and large quantities of new radium-like elements would be generated. Now it appears almost certain that this could be achieved in the immediate future.

This new phenomenon would also lead to the construction of bombs, and it is conceivable—though much less certain—that extremely powerful bombs of a new type may thus be constructed. A single bomb of this type, carried by boat and exploded in a port, might very well destroy the whole port together with some of the surrounding territory. However, such bombs might very well prove to be too heavy for transportation by air.

The United States has only very poor ores of uranium in moderate quantities. There is some good ore in Canada and the former Czechoslovakia, while the most important source of uranium is Belgian Congo.

In view of this situation you may think it desirable to have some permanent contact maintained between the Administration and the group of physicists working on chain reactions in America. One possible way of achieving this might be for you to entrust with this task a person who has your confidence and who could perhaps serve in an unofficial capacity. His task might comprise the following:

1. to approach Government Departments, keep them informed of the further development, and put forward recommendations for Government action, giving particular attention to the problem of securing a supply of uranium ore for the United States;

2. to speed up the experimental work, which is at present being carried on within the limits of the budgets of University laboratories, by providing funds, if such funds be required, through his contacts with private persons who are willing to make contributions for this cause, and perhaps also by obtaining the co-operation of industrial laboratories which have the necessary equipment.

I understand that Germany has actually stopped the sale of uranium from the Czechoslovakian mines which she has taken over. That she should have taken such early action might perhaps be understood on the ground that the son of the German Under-Secretary of State, von Weizsäcker, is attached to the Kaiser-Wilhelm-Institut in Berlin where some of the American work on uranium is now being repeated.

Yours very truly,

ALBERT EINSTEIN

Source: National Archives. Available at http://research.archives .gov/description/593374.

NULLIFICATION

Nullification is a political doctrine developed in the United States during the late 1790s in an effort to rebalance the authority of the federal government and the authority of state governments under the Constitution. There were various interpretations of the nullification doctrine. Under one variation, the states could directly ignore and decline to enforce the operation of any federal laws that were unconstitutional in the judgment of the state governments. Another major variation stipulated that the states could recommend (but not require) that Congress reexamine legislation that the state governments found objectionable. These assertions of authority, however, were not accepted by most in the federal government. Opponents of state nullification argued that state review of federal laws violated Article VI of the Constitution (the Supremacy Clause) as well as Article III, which empowers the judicial branch to judge the constitutionality of the law.

During the Quasi-war with France in 1798, critics of the John Adams administration expressed concern over the expansion of federal authority under the Alien and Sedition Acts, which empowered the federal government to regulate political speech and popular criticism of governmental actions. These critics saw the expansion of federal authority as a threat to the rights of free speech and free press, and believed that the powers of the state governments could form an effective bulwark against perceived violations of the Constitution. The most articulate versions of the nullification doctrine appeared in the Virginia and Kentucky Resolutions of 1798. The resolutions were written by Vice President Thomas Jefferson (Kentucky Resolutions) and James Madison (Virginia Resolutions), although the documents' authorship remained a secret at the time. According to Jefferson's writing, the Constitution was a compact that granted limited and defined powers to the federal government. All other powers were reserved to the states or to the individual as outlined in the Tenth Amendment. The several states created the federal structure; therefore only the states were competent to judge the lawfulness of the actions of the federal government. It was absurd to expect the federal judiciary to check the powers of the federal government, so legally and logically it was up to the states to operate as an unbiased protector of the rights of the states and the people under the constitution. For Jefferson, any federal laws that did not stem from a directly delineated power of the federal government or were in violation of the Constitution were void because the power to create such laws did not exist.

Madison's Virginia Resolutions argued a similar but not identical theory as Jefferson's Kentucky Resolutions. The Virginia Resolutions cited many of the same concerns; however, Madison expressed discomfort over the potential complications of a literal application of the nullification doctrine to the American political system. In Madison's milder interpretation, the actions of the federal government were outside of the bounds set forth by the Constitution. The states had the right to collectively protest the actions of the federal government and appeal for a redress of grievances, but Madison's appeal fell short of declaring that the states possessed the right to impose changes on federal laws.

There is dispute over whether the Resolutions were meant as a political maneuver or as a serious policy recommendation. None of the other states adopted either resolution, and there was no immediate impact. The intent of the resolutions and the expected outcomes were never clarified. The election of Jefferson to the presidency in 1800 ended the immediate causes of protest. The nullification theory, however, remained in two distinct forms: one that allowed for the states to compel the repeal of federal law either through veto power or through disobedience and another that provided the states the right to request the federal government to review federal policies but without the power to compel any changes.

The judiciary was the weakest branch of the federal government in the early republic. The role of the courts expanded with the 1803 *Marbury v. Madison* Supreme Court decision that reaffirmed judicial oversight of the law as a function of the judicial branch. According to Chief Justice John Marshall, the Supreme Court was the appropriate body to regulate conflict between the various elements of the federal system as well as to judge the operation of two conflicting laws. Although *Marbury v. Madison* did not directly address the issue of federal and state powers, this affirmation of the role of the courts reinforced Articles III and VI of the Constitution and tacitly rejected the theory that the states possessed an oversight power over the federal government.

Conflicts between local and national authority persisted after *Marbury v. Madison*. Disputes over taxation and trade policies were particularly bitter. In 1807, President Jefferson signed the Embargo Act into law; this prohibited all external trade. Many citizens simply ignored the law, and customs enforcement efforts were ineffective. Many state legislatures, particularly in New England, issued a series of appeals to Congress and the president advocating a repeal of the law as an attack on the liberties of the people. This form followed the pattern set by the Virginia Resolutions, and although practical enforcement remained a problem, the crisis ended before the states drifted toward the more radical Jeffersonian interpretation of nullification. The War of 1812 created another constitutional crisis. In 1814, the Hartford Convention Report advocated for the states (primarily in New England) to reassert some ill-defined measure of authority over the federal government to curtail the expansion of federal authority and to prevent the federal government from enacting trade regulations, admitting new states, or declaring war without the support of a supermajority in Congress. These changes would have rebalanced the relationship between state and national

authority under the Constitution, but the war ended before any of the recommended changes could be enacted.

The near-disaster of the War of 1812 exposed the need for a more powerful national government, a more robust system of taxation to fund the expanding government, and for a system of tariffs to protect the growth of domestic industry. The Tariff of 1828 was passed by the John Quincy Adams administration and was widely supported in the North; the law provided little benefit for the primarily agrarian South. The newly elected President Andrew Jackson later signed the Tariff of 1832, which retained the tariff at a lower rate. Vice President (and later Senator) John C. Calhoun of South Carolina led the opposition to the tariffs. Calhoun and the South Carolina Assembly argued that the tariff was illegal and unconstitutional; therefore, the state could nullify the law. This constitutional crisis exploded in late 1832. President Jackson threatened to invade South Carolina with federal troops in order to ensure the tariff laws were enforced, while South Carolina began to arm for defense. Other states, particularly in the South, supported protests against the tariffs, but none was willing to support South Carolina's efforts with force. A compromise that retained a lower tariff rate was reached; although the immediate crisis passed, the Nullification Crisis exposed a dangerous conflict between national and state interpretations of the constitutional union.

The most significant manifestation of the nullification doctrine was the Civil War. Prior protests such as the Virginia and Kentucky Resolutions questioned the division of authority under the political union of the Constitution. By 1860, conflicts between North and South over economic policy, the political organization of the West, and slavery changed the debate from nullification and the exercise of authority under the Constitution to a reexamination of the constitutional compact as a political idea. The outbreak of war in April 1861 resulted in a most extreme form of nullification that saw not only the rejection of federal authority over particular pieces of legislation such as trade policy or taxation, but also the wholesale rejection of the federal authority over the states of the South. The Southern declaration of independence, essentially, nullified the Constitution.

Although the victory of the central government in the Civil War ended the political application of the nullification doctrine, nullification through non-enforcement of the law remained a feature of American politics, particularly in regards to minority rights. Nullification as a political doctrine was not explicitly declared illegal until the Supreme Court's *Cooper v. Aaron* decision of 1958. The Court ruled that the states were legally obligated to enforce federal laws that conflicted with state law. The justices cited the supremacy clause of the Constitution, which subordinated state law to federal law, and the 1803 *Marbury v. Madison* case that established the principle of federal judicial review. According to the court, these two statues prohibited the states from nullifying federal laws under any circumstances.

See also

Anti-Federalism; Constitutionalism; Federalism; Reconstruction

PATRICK CALLAWAY

Further Reading

Freehling, William W. 1966. *Prelude to the Civil War: The Nullification Controversy in South Carolina, 1816–1836.* New York: Harper and Row.

Sharp, James Roger. 1993. *American Politics in the Early Republic: The New Nation in Crisis.* New Haven, CT: Yale University Press.

Watkins, William J., Jr. 2004. *Reclaiming the American Revolution: The Kentucky and Virginia Resolutions and Their Legacy.* New York: Palgrave Macmillan.

Nullification—Primary Documents

Introduction

The Kentucky and Virginia Resolutions of 1798 were political statements of the Kentucky and Virginia legislatures declaring the recently enacted federal Alien and Sedition Acts to be unconstitutional. Although their authorship was kept secret, Thomas Jefferson wrote the Kentucky Resolution and James Madison drafted the Virginia Resolution. The Kentucky Resolution proclaimed the power of states to nullify any federals laws that they believed contravened the U.S. Constitution. The resolutions presented Jefferson's compact theory of the Constitution, as well as his belief that the states provided an important check against any potential abuse of power by the federal government. Besides being a fundamental exposition of the nullification doctrine, the resolutions are important expressions of the states' rights and strict constructionist views of federal-state relations and constitutional interpretation.

Document 1: Kentucky Resolution (November 19, 1798)

1. *Resolved*, That the several states composing the United States of America are not united on the principle of unlimited submission to their general government; but that, by compact, under the style and title of a Constitution for the United States, and of amendments thereto, they constituted a general government for special purposes, delegated to that government certain definite powers, reserving, each state to itself, the residuary mass of right to their own self-government; and that whensoever the general government assumes undelegated powers, its acts are unauthoritative, void, and of no force; that to this compact each state acceded as a state, and is an integral party; that this government, created by this compact, was not made the exclusive or final judge of the extent of the powers delegated to itself, since that would have made its discretion, and not the Constitution, the measure of its powers; but that, as in all other cases of compact among powers having no common judge, *each party has an equal right to judge for itself, as well of infractions as of the mode and measure of redress.*

2. *Resolved*, That the Constitution of the United States having delegated to Congress a power to punish treason, counterfeiting the securities and current coin of the United States, piracies and felonies committed on the high seas, and offences against the laws of nations, and no other crimes, whatsoever; and it being true, as a general principle, and one of the amendments to the Constitution having also declared, that "the powers not delegated to the United States by the Constitution, nor prohibited by it to the states, are reserved to the states respectively, or to the people,"—therefore, also, the same act of Congress, passed on the 14th day of July, 1798, and entitled "An Act in Addition to the Act entitled 'An Act for the Punishment of certain Crimes against the United States;'" as also the act passed by them on the 27th day of June, 1798, entitled "An Act to punish Frauds committed on the Bank of the United States," (and all other their acts which assume to create, define, or punish crimes other than those so enumerated in the Constitution,) are altogether void, and of no force; and that the power to create, define, and punish, such other crimes is reserved, and of right appertains, solely

and exclusively, to the respective states, each within its own territory.

3. *Resolved*, That it is true, as a general principle, and is also expressly declared by one of the amendments to the Constitution, that "the powers not delegated to the United States by the Constitution, nor prohibited by it to the states, are reserved to the states respectively, or to the people;" and that, no power over the freedom of religion, freedom of speech, or freedom of the press, being delegated to the United States by the Constitution, nor prohibited by it to the States, all lawful powers respecting the same did of right remain, and were reserved to the states, or the people; that thus was manifested their determination to retain to themselves the right of judging how far the licentiousness of speech, and of the press, may be abridged without lessening their useful freedom, and how far those abuses which cannot be separated from their use, should be tolerated rather than the use be destroyed; and thus also they guarded against all abridgment, by the United States, of the freedom of religious principles and exercises, and retained to themselves the right of protecting the same, as this, stated by a law passed on the general demand of its citizens, had already protected them from all human restraint or interference; and that, in addition to this general principle and express declaration, another and more special provision has been made by one of the amendments to the Constitution, which expressly declares, that "Congress shall make no law respecting an establishment of religion, or prohibiting the free exercise thereof, or abridging the freedom of speech, or of the press," thereby guarding, in the same sentence, and under the same words, the freedom of religion, of speech, and of the press, insomuch that whatever violated either throws down the sanctuary which covers the others,—and that libels, falsehood, and defamation, equally with heresy and false religion, are withheld from the cognizance of federal tribunals. That therefore the act of Congress of the United States, passed on the 14th of July, 1798, entitled "An Act in Addition to the Act entitled 'An Act for the Punishment of certain Crimes against the United States,'" which does abridge the freedom of the press, is not law, but is altogether void, and of no force.

4. *Resolved*, That alien friends are under the jurisdiction and protection of the laws of the state wherein they are; that no power over them has been delegated to the United States, nor prohibited to the individual states, distinct from their power over citizens; and it being true, as a general principle, and one of the amendments to the Constitution having also declared, that "the powers not delegated to the United States by the Constitution, nor prohibited by it to the states, are reserved to the states, respectively, or to the people," the act of the Congress of the United States, passed on the 22d day of July, 1798, entitled "An Act concerning Aliens," which assumes powers over alien friends not delegated by the Constitution, is not law, but is altogether void and of no force.

5. *Resolved*. That, in addition to the general principle, as well as the express declaration, that powers not delegated are reserved, another and more special provision inserted in the Constitution from abundant caution, has declared, "that the migration or importation of such persons as any of the states now existing shall think proper to admit, shall not be prohibited by the Congress prior to the year 1808." That this commonwealth does admit the migration of alien friends described as the subject of the said act concerning aliens; that a provision against prohibiting their migration is a provision against all acts equivalent thereto, or it would be nugatory; that to remove them, when migrated, is equivalent to a prohibition of their migration, and is, therefore, contrary to the said provision of the Constitution, and *void*.

6. *Resolved*, That the imprisonment of a person under the protection of the laws of this commonwealth, on his failure to obey the simple order of the President to depart out of the United States, as is undertaken by the said act entitled, "An Act concerning Aliens," is contrary to the Constitution, one amendment in which has provided, that "no person shall be deprived of liberty without due process of law;" and that another having provided, "that, in all criminal prosecutions, the accused shall enjoy the right of a public trial by an impartial jury, to be informed as to the nature and cause of the accusation, to be confronted with the witnesses against him, to have compulsory process for obtaining witnesses in his favor, and to have assistance of counsel for his defence," the same act undertaking to authorize the President to remove a person out of the United States who is under the protection of the law, on his own suspicion, without jury, without public trial, without confrontation of the witnesses against him, without having witnesses in his favor, without defence, without counsel—contrary to these provisions also of the

Constitution—is therefore not law, but utterly void, and of no force.

That transferring the power of judging any person who is under the protection of the laws, from the courts to the President of the United States, as is undertaken by the same act concerning aliens, is against the article of the Constitution which provides, that "the judicial power of the United States shall be vested in the courts, the judges of which shall hold their offices during good behavior," and that the said act is void for that reason also; and it is further to be noted that this transfer of judiciary power is to that magistrate of the general government who already possesses all the executive, and a qualified negative on all legislative powers.

7. *Resolved*, That the construction applied by the general government (as is evident by sundry of their proceedings) to those parts of the Constitution of the United States which delegate to Congress power to lay and collect taxes, duties, imposts, excises; to pay the debts, and provide for the common defence and general welfare, of the United States, and to make all laws which shall be necessary and proper for carrying into execution the powers vested by the Constitution in the government of the United States, or any department thereof, goes to the destruction of all limits prescribed to their powers by the Constitution; that words meant by the instrument to be subsidiary only to the execution of the limited powers, ought not to be so construed as themselves to give unlimited powers, nor a part to be taken as to destroy the whole residue of the instrument; that the proceedings of the general government, under color of those articles, will be a fit and necessary subject for revisal and correction at a time of greater tranquillity, while those specified in the preceding resolutions call for immediate redress.

8. *Resolved*, That the preceding resolutions be transmitted to the senators and representatives in Congress from this commonwealth, who are enjoined to present the same to their respective houses, and to use their best endeavors to procure, at the next session of Congress, a repeal of the aforesaid unconstitutional and obnoxious acts.

9. *Resolved*, lastly, That the governor of this commonwealth be, and is, authorized and requested to communicate the preceding resolutions to the legislatures of the several states,

to assure them that this commonwealth considers union for special national purposes, and particularly for those specified in their late federal compact, to be friendly to the peace, happiness, and prosperity, of all the states; that, faithful to that compact, according to the plain intent and meaning in which it was understood and acceded to by the several parties, it is sincerely anxious for its preservation; that it does also believe, that, to take from the states all the powers of self-government and transfer them to a general and consolidated government, without regard to the special government, and reservations solemnly agreed to in that compact, is not for the peace, happiness, or prosperity of these states; and that, therefore, this commonwealth is determined, as it doubts not its co-states are, to submit to undelegated and consequently unlimited powers in no man, or body of men, on earth; that, if the acts before specified should stand, these conclusions would flow from them—that the general government may place any act they think proper on the list of crimes, and punish it themselves, whether enumerated or not enumerated by the Constitution as cognizable by them; that they may transfer its cognizance to the President, or any other person, who may himself be the accuser, counsel, judge, and jury, whose suspicions may be the evidence, his order the sentence, his officer the executioner, and his breast the sole record of the transaction; that a very numerous and valuable description of the inhabitants of these states, being, by this precedent, reduced, as outlaws, to absolute dominion of one man, and the barriers of the Constitution thus swept from us all, no rampart now remains against the passions and the power of a majority of Congress, to protect from a like exportation, or other grievous punishment, the minority of the same body, the legislatures, judges, governors, and counsellors of the states, nor their other peaceable inhabitants, who may venture to reclaim the constitutional rights and liberties of the states and people, or who for other causes, good or bad, may be obnoxious to the view, or marked by the suspicions, of the President, or be thought dangerous to his or their elections, or other interests, public or personal; that the friendless alien has been selected as the safest subject of a first experiment; but the citizen will soon follow, or rather has already followed; for already has a Sedition Act marked him as a prey: That these and successive acts of the same character, unless arrested on the threshold, may tend to drive these states into revolution and blood, and will furnish new calumnies against republican governments, and new pretexts for those who wish it to be believed that man cannot be governed but by a rod of iron; that it would be a dangerous delusion were a confidence in the men of our choice to silence our fears for the safety of our rights; that confidence is every where the parent of despotism; free government is founded in jealousy, and not in confidence; it is jealousy, and not confidence, which prescribes limited constitutions to bind down those whom we are obliged to trust with power; that our Constitution has accordingly fixed the limits to which, and no farther, our confidence may go; and let the honest advocate of confidence read the Alien and Sedition Acts, and say if the Constitution has not been wise in fixing limits to the government it created, and whether we should be wise in destroying those limits; let him say what the government is, if it be not a tyranny, which the men of our choice have conferred on the President, and the President of our choice has assented to and accepted, over the friendly strangers, to whom the mild spirit of our country and its laws had pledged hospitality and protection; that the men of our choice have more respected the bare suspicions of the President than the solid rights of innocence, the claims of justification, the sacred force of truth, and the forms and substance of law and justice.

In questions of power, then, let no more be said of confidence in man, but bind him down from mischief by the chains of the Constitution. That this commonwealth does therefore call on its co-states for an expression of their sentiments on the acts concerning aliens, and for the punishment of certain crimes herein before specified, plainly declaring whether these acts are or are not authorized by the federal compact. And it doubts not that their sense will be so announced as to prove their attachment to limited government, whether general or particular, and that the rights and liberties of their co-states will be exposed to no dangers by remaining embarked on a common bottom with their own; but they will concur with this commonwealth in considering the said acts as so palpably against the Constitution as to amount to an undisguised declaration that the compact is not meant to be the measure of the powers of the general government, but that it will proceed in the exercise over these states of all powers whatsoever. That they will view this as seizing the rights of the states, and consolidating them in the hands of the general government, with a power assumed to bind the states, not merely in cases made federal, but in all cases whatsoever,

by laws made, not with their consent, but by others against their consent; that this would be to surrender the form of government we have chosen, and live under one deriving its powers from its own will, and not from our authority; and that the co-states, recurring to their natural rights not made federal, will concur in declaring these void and of no force, and will each unite with this commonwealth in requesting their repeal at the next session of Congress. . . .

Approved November 19, 1798.

Source: Constitution Society. 2013. "The Kentucky Resolution." Available at http://www.constitution.org/cons/kent1798.htm.

Document 2: Virginia Resolution (December 24, 1798)

RESOLVED, That the General Assembly of Virginia, doth unequivocally express a firm resolution to maintain and defend the Constitution of the United States, and the Constitution of this State, against every aggression either foreign or domestic, and that they will support the government of the United States in all measures warranted by the former.

That this assembly most solemnly declares a warm attachment to the Union of the States, to maintain which it pledges all its powers; and that for this end, it is their duty to watch over and oppose every infraction of those principles which constitute the only basis of that Union, because a faithful observance of them, can alone secure it's existence and the public happiness.

That this Assembly doth explicitly and peremptorily declare, that it views the powers of the federal government, as resulting from the compact, to which the states are parties; as limited by the plain sense and intention of the instrument constituting the compact; as no further valid that they are authorized by the grants enumerated in that compact; and that in case of a deliberate, palpable, and dangerous exercise of other powers, not granted by the said compact, the states who are parties thereto, have the right, and are in duty bound, to interpose for arresting the progress of the evil, and for maintaining within their respective limits, the authorities, rights and liberties appertaining to them.

That the General Assembly doth also express its deep regret, that a spirit has in sundry instances, been manifested by the federal government, to enlarge its powers by forced constructions of the constitutional charter which defines them; and that implications have appeared of a design to expound certain general phrases (which having been copied from the very limited grant of power, in the former articles of confederation were the less liable to be misconstrued) so as to destroy the meaning and effect, of the particular enumeration which necessarily explains and limits the general phrases; and so as to consolidate the states by degrees, into one sovereignty, the obvious tendency and inevitable consequence of which would be, to transform the present republican system of the United States, into an absolute, or at best a mixed monarchy.

That the General Assembly doth particularly protest against the palpable and alarming infractions of the Constitution, in the two late cases of the "Alien and Sedition Acts" passed at the last session of Congress; the first of which exercises a power no where delegated to the federal government, and which by uniting legislative and judicial powers to those of executive, subverts the general principles of free government; as well as the particular organization, and positive provisions of the federal constitution; and the other of which acts, exercises in like manner, a power not delegated by the constitution, but on the contrary, expressly and positively forbidden by one of the amendments thereto; a power, which more than any other, ought to produce universal alarm, because it is levelled against that right of freely examining public characters and measures, and of free communication among the people thereon, which has ever been justly deemed, the only effectual guardian of every other right.

That this state having by its Convention, which ratified the federal Constitution, expressly declared, that among other essential rights, the Liberty of Conscience and of the Press cannot be cancelled, abridged, restrained, or modified by any authority of the United States," and from its extreme anxiety to guard these rights from every possible attack of sophistry or ambition, having with other states, recommended an amendment for that purpose, which amendment was, in due time, annexed to the Constitution; it would mark a reproachable inconsistency, and criminal degeneracy, if an indifference were now shewn, to the most palpable violation of one of the Rights, thus declared and secured; and to the establishment of a precedent which may be fatal to the other.

That the good people of this commonwealth, having ever felt, and continuing to feel, the most sincere affection for their brethren of the other states; the truest anxiety for establishing and perpetuating the union of all; and the most scrupulous fidelity to that constitution, which is the pledge of mutual friendship, and the instrument of mutual happiness; the General Assembly doth solemnly appeal to the like dispositions of the other states, in confidence that they will concur with this commonwealth in declaring, as it does hereby declare, that the acts aforesaid, are unconstitutional; and that the necessary and proper measures will be taken by each, for co-operating with this state, in maintaining the Authorities, Rights, and Liberties, referred to the States respectively, or to the people.

That the Governor be desired, to transmit a copy of the foregoing Resolutions to the executive authority of each of the other states, with a request that the same may be communicated to the Legislature thereof; and that a copy be furnished to each of the Senators and Representatives representing this state in the Congress of the United States.

Agreed to by the Senate, December 24, 1798.

Source: Constitution Society. 2013. "Virginia Resolution." Available at http://www.constitution.org/cons/virg1798.htm.

O

OCCUPY MOVEMENT

The Occupy Movement is a 21st-century protest against social and economic inequality, focusing on the lack of actual democracy and on the disastrous consequences of the current financial system on people's everyday life. The most famous political slogan of the movement, "we are the 99%," pointing out the unfair distribution of wealth in United States, summarizes the key arguments of the protest. Characterized by assemblies and a horizontal decision-making process, the Occupy Movement aimed to build a different and better world.

Although the first and most famous "occupy" action was held in New York City under the name of Occupy Wall Street, several similar experiences occurred contemporaneously in other U.S. cities. The expression "occupy movement" began in other countries around the world, particularly in English-speaking ones. Typically, except for the case of Occupy Wall Street, the various local "occupy" actions took the name of the city where the protest was based. The sizes of protests and encampments varied, from a few dozen up to thousands. The largest camp, after the one in Zuccotti Park in New York City, was in Oakland, with assemblies with up to 3000 people and a general strike (which resulted in the shutdown of the commercial and industrial port of Oakland) on November 2, 2011, which gathered about 25,000 marchers.

Origins

The Occupy Movement can be considered as part of a larger protest movement: some analysts connect it both to the Arab Spring and to the 15M Spanish movement (often called the Indignados Movement) and to analogous European movements; other analysts and scholars focus more on the connection with the European movements, which actually share a lot of features with the Occupy Movement.

Indeed, on May 15, 2011, in Barcelona, Madrid, and other Spanish cities, people rose up and gathered in assemblies in central downtown squares, under the slogan *toma la plaza* (i.e., "take the square"), contesting the representation of Spanish democratic system, under the slogan *no nos representan* (i.e., "they don't represent us"). In a few days the protest spread to other cities around Spain and around Europe, including Belgium and France.

The protest movement continued through June and July and a march reached the Spanish capital on July 23, 2011. Afterward, another march was organized in order to reach Brussels in October to take part in the Global Protest Day on October 15. On September 17, on international Anti-Banks Day, the first group of Occupy Wall Street gathered in downtown Manhattan and about 200 people slept over at Zuccotti Park. On the same day various assemblies gathered both in Europe (London, Brussels, Paris, and Spain) and in United

Protesters of corporate greed gather at the New York Stock Exchange in New York City on September 30, 2008, the day after the record-breaking 777-point drop in the Dow Jones Index. (Shutterstock.com)

following months), the idea spread quite autonomously and largely. Indeed, after circulating among *Adbusters* activists, it joined other activist milieu in United States. In an article published in September, a few days after the NYC occupation, a senior editor of *Adbusters* defined the evolution of the protest as a "snowball."

In fact, the decision of an international day of demonstration against banks was connected with the idea of occupying Wall Street on the same day and it was itself a preparatory step toward the international day of mobilization, planned for October 15, 2011 (five months after the beginning in Spain). The connection between European and American movements was quite strong from the beginning and it was mostly based on social media. The hacker group Anonymous contributed to the establishment of these connections and the mask of V for Vendetta, symbol of the Anonymous group, became present in Occupy demonstrations around the world.

Goals

Although not always clear outside, and particularly in the representation provided by the media, the goals of the Occupy Movement are defined and recognizable. Indeed, the key topics targeted by the protest were the power of financial system, the lack in democracy, and the strong connection between the financial and the political power. The slogan itself, in fact, combines the two aspects since the 1 percent includes both of these components, while the 99 percent are "normal people" (and implicitly victims of the functioning of the system). However, the claim for specific demands was not homogeneous, although some exceptions existed, as in the demand for the introduction of a Robin Hood tax (conceptually close to the Tobin Tax). Indeed, the Occupy Movement's main feature, especially at very beginning, was its aspect of "reaction" against the current conditions of life while creating international connections among people involved.

Common features, common claims, and common methodologies provided the Occupy Movement with an international dimension, while it maintained a strong connection with the local level. The main targets of the movement were banks and the financial system and its power of influence on political choices. Despite the lack of actual claims and demands, in most of the cases the aim of the occupiers was to build a different model of society. Indeed, according to some

States (e.g., San Francisco). By mid-October, the number of occupy assemblies had increased notably and on October 15, one hundred U.S. cities had an occupied square.

A call for a gathering in Manhattan on September 17 had begun circulating in June. The European movement spread to the founder of the Canadian-based *Adbusters* magazine, who called for a peaceful occupation of Wall Street. By June 9, a Web site was registered under the address www.occupywallstreet.org, and was connected to the Web site platform created just after the 15M (www.takethesquare.net). Despite the role of *Adbusters* (which also attracted some criticism inside the movement in the analysts, such as Judith Butler, the absence of demands was consistent with the ideology of the movement since raising actual demands would have implied a legitimization of the power structures they were intended to fight. The reinvention of society proposed by the Occupy Movement included a different economical model not based on banks' power: a different political model, based on participatory democracy and social justice. In this framework the internationalization of the movement was consistent with this new model of society.

Structure and Functioning

Assemblies of the Occupy Movement shared almost the same structure and functioning system. Indeed, the basic common features were the tent camps, the assemblies, and the decision making process. Differences existed among different occupations based on the size and level of participation. The two biggest camps in United States were at Zuccotti Park in Manhattan and in Oakland, California. Most of the camps had a cooking and an eating space. In some cases, other dedicated spaces existed, such as praying space and children's space.

Most of the assemblies were divided into working groups and subgroups. In almost every Occupy there was a group in charge of communication and contact with media and another group for legal issues. Besides the system of the assemblies, the Occupy Movement largely used social network and social media to exchange and share information, to organize gatherings and to represent itself outside. In addition to the usual tools such as mailing lists, Twitter and Facebook, software for simultaneously working on one document and for voice communication (often in open-source version, consistently with the political view of the movement) were broadly used.

Methods

The methodology shared and widely accepted among the different Occupy groups around the United States was to make every decision in assembly, trying to reach the highest *consensus*. In order to do so, a set of communication tools was established, in particular specific gestures, both in United States and in Europe, to allow a horizontal, fair, and balanced participation to the decision-making process. These hand signals, for the most part influenced by the deaf communication system, but also from other previous experiences (such as the spokes-councils of the antiglobalization movement at

the end of the 1990s), aimed to increase participation and to allow everyone to express his or her opinion during the assembly. Such a set of signals was recognizable in every assembly in United States as well as in other countries and included the following signs:

- raise hand to express the willingness to talk
- point out the person speaking moving the fingers to give a direct response to the topic discussed
- a "C" made with fingers to ask for clarification
- a "T" made with the two hands to ask for translation (in multilingual assemblies)
- a sort of triangle made with fingers to make a point of order or to say something urgent
- raise and shake hands to show agreement
- shake hands down to show disagreement
- rotate hands to say that the intervention is too long or off-topic
- cross arms to block a decision

To ease the decision-making process, the specific role of facilitators was established. Usually working groups on facilitation existed. Each facilitation group used different techniques but a couple of common and shared practices existed around the United States: namely the so-called "stack" and the "mic-check." A stack was an open queue of speakers that everyone could join in order to express an opinion about a debated topic (usually proposed by working groups); the goal of the mic-check, quite common in small assemblies, was at the same time to amplify speakers' voices, to keep interventions short and to keep assembly's attention high: indeed the mechanism of the mic-check was a repetition of what someone was saying by people gathered in assembly.

Characteristics

One of the most remarkable characteristics of the Occupy Movement is the presence of camps. It became the special feature, which contributed to distinguish it from other protest movements. Although not necessary in order to gather in assembly and despite people belonging to the movement were much greater than the ones actually occupying the space, every single city where an Occupy group gathered had a camp with tents. Sometimes very small, as the one in Chicago, or sometimes extremely large, as the one in Oakland, camps were not sized according to the size or the importance of the city. Differently from 15M camps, almost always located in squares, Occupy camps had different kinds of locations such as parks and streets. The choice of the location was usually related to symbolic buildings or had practical reasons such as accessibility or safety.

A relevant characteristic of the Occupy Movement is the commitment to nonviolence that is one of the reasons the movement was connected to the figure of Gene Sharp, philosopher and professor of political science, considered a theorist of nonviolence and nonviolent struggle. Indeed, all over the United States as well as at the international level, the participants in the Occupy Movement underlined their nonviolent political practice, for which political analysts and thinkers, such as Manuel Castells and Naomi Klein, hailed them. Despite some sporadic cases of violence, the only known violent episodes concerned some clashes with the police (the most relevant in New York City and Oakland) where, indeed, most of the responsibility, as alleged by the protesters, fell on the police.

Protesters gathering in the Occupy Movement had various political backgrounds and relevant differences among cities around the United States extended beyond motivations and previous social and/or political engagement. The protesters included students, migrant workers, and socially marginalized groups. In some cases, namely in Oakland, the presence of war veterans was remarkable. Despite the absence of any defined political color, a slight form of anarchism has been identified as part of the political context of the Occupy Movement, although protesters neither officially recognized nor presented it a component of the movement.

Reactions

Because of its peculiarities, the movement produced multiple reactions. On the one hand, local authorities dealt with the occupation as any other demonstration: cases of clashes with the police occurred in different cities. In New York, people were arrested from the very beginning of the protest, with at least 80 people arrested on September 24, more than 700 on October 1 while demonstrating on the Brooklyn Bridge, and about 100 on October 15. On the same day, a Global Day of Protest, similar events occurred in other U.S. cities, including both demonstrations and arrests.

In many cases the violent actions of police and the use of pepper spray against the protesters have been reported, and widely criticized. Oakland authorities' reaction was particularly hostile: the police cleared and closed the camp in front of Oakland City Hall on October 25 with violent consequences, including an Iraq War veteran belonging to the Occupy Movement suffering a skull fracture. A similar episode occurred in the same city a week later, on November 2, when police shot a journalist who was filming ongoing clashes between police and protesters. In several cases around the United States, journalists had been arrested while covering the Occupy Movement. Episodes of police violence also occurred in some university Occupations such as OccupyCal. Nevertheless, generally speaking, local authorities accepted the presence of occupy camps and allowed them to stay for at least several months. In some cases, members of city councils even expressed their approval and/or support for the movement.

The movement provoked interested reaction among thinkers, scholars, and analysts such as Butler, Castells, Klein, and Noam Chomsky. Several studies in 2012 concerned the topic in the United States, in Europe, and worldwide. The stories ranged from political analysis to collections of episodes (sometimes authored by the activists themselves). Since the beginning of 2012, three months after the first occupation in New York City, some American universities began providing courses related to the Occupy Movement.

Role of Social Media

Compared with other protest movements, Occupy made an extremely interesting use of traditional as well as less traditional social media and Web tools. Facebook, Twitter, Skype, and many open-source communication and data elaboration software enabled protesters to establish connections with other branches of the movement and to represent Occupy to the public. Independent journalists and media experts contributed to media coverage and communication and the use of social media also included the distribution of video of demonstrations as well as live streams of events. Another substantial contribution of the social media communication was that it compelled traditional media to give attention to the movement, keeping the interest high. From many points of view, such a use of social media, the actions were extremely consistent with the proposed horizontal approach of the movement, facilitating the participation of each member. After the closure of all the camps around United States and worldwide, most of the ongoing activities of the Occupy Movement take advantage of media and Web technologies tools.

Occupations in United States

Protesters gathered in about thirty cities around United States. Most of the states had camps and assemblies just in one main city: Georgia (Atlanta), Illinois (Chicago), Massachusetts (Boston), Missouri (St. Louis), Nevada (Las Vegas), Ohio (Cincinnati), Rhode Island (Providence), Tennessee (Nashville), Utah (Salt Lake City), Virginia (Charlottesville), and Washington (Seattle). In some other cases, two or three cities were involved: Oregon (Ashland, Eugene, and Salem), Pennsylvania (Philadelphia and Pittsburgh), Arizona (Phoenix and Tucson), and Texas (Austin, Houston, and Dallas), as well as New York (where, besides Occupy Wall Street, occupations took place in Buffalo and Rochester). Among all the states, California was the one with highest presence of the Occupy Movement, which gathered in at least seven cities: San Francisco, San Jose, San Diego, Berkeley, Sacramento, Los Angeles, and Oakland. An Occupation also took place in Washington, D.C.

The role of California is even more underlined by the fact that among the Occupations that took place inside universities, four involved California campuses (UC Berkeley, UC Davis, UC Irvine, and San Francisco State University). An Occupy Harvard also took place. Although more focused on student issues (e.g., cuts, fees, funding, and access to education), their protests were strongly linked to the Occupy Movement both on a theoretical plane and on a more practical one. They coordinated with the local Occupy groups (the occupation of UC Berkeley, called OccupyCal, with the Occupy Berkeley camp and for Occupy Harvard with the Occupy Boston camp). In most of the cases, a coordination existed among Occupations in the same state with substantial interactions and reciprocal support.

Future

Although all the camps had been cleared by the first months of 2012, the Occupy Movement keeps connections between its members in United States and internationally; the use of social media contributes to the maintenance of this network. Indeed, the movement itself can be considered a relevant milestone in the current political and economic situation; it had an influence on the U.S. political dialogue as well as on normal people lives and imagery. Whatever their opinion, the majority of U.S. citizens are aware of the existence of the Occupy Movement.

See also
Civil Disobedience; Nonviolent Resistance

ELISABETTA CANGELOSI

Further Reading
Chomsky, Noam. 2012. *Occupy*. New York: Zuccotti Park Press.
Flank, L. 2011. *Voices from the 99 Percent: An Oral History of the Occupy Wall Street Movement*. St Petersburg, FL: Red and Black Publishing.
"Occupy Movement." 2012. *CQ Researcher* 22, no. 2 (January 13): 25–52.
Schrager, A., and D. Lang. 2012. *Dreaming in Public: The Building of the Occupy Movement*. Oxford, UK: New Internationalist Publications Ltd.
Time Magazine Editors. 2011. *What Is Occupy*. New York: TIME Books.
Van Gelder, S. 2011. *This Changes Everything: Occupy Wall Street and the 99% Movement*. San Francisco, CA: *Yes* Magazine, Berret-Koheler Publishers.
"Writers for the 99%." 2012. *Occupying Wall Street. The Inside Story of an Action That Changed America*. New York and London: OR Books.

Occupy Movement—Primary Document

Introduction

In reaction to the Occupy Movement that had been brewing in Manhattan since September 2011, President Barack Obama held a press conference on October 6 about the state of the economy, which was at the heart of the Occupy Movement. In his opening remarks, Obama emphasized his views on the importance of creating jobs to strengthen the economy. During the question-and-answer portion of the press conference, Obama was faced with questions about the Occupy Movement, and expressed his understanding of the people's frustration at the American financial system and that imperative to a healthy financial system are banks and other financial organizations that operate for the public's best interest instead of with hidden fees and confusing practices.

Document: News Conference by President Barack Obama (October 6, 2011)

. . . Q Thank you, Mr. President. As you travel the country, you also take credit for tightening regulations on Wall Street through the Dodd-Frank law, and about your efforts to combat income inequality. There's this movement—Occupy Wall Street—which has spread from Wall Street to other cities. They clearly don't think that you or Republicans have done enough, that you're in fact part of the problem.

Are you following this movement, and what would you say to its—people that are attracted to it?

THE PRESIDENT: Obviously I've heard of it. I've seen it on television. I think it expresses the frustrations that the American people feel—that we had the biggest financial crisis since the Great Depression, huge collateral damage all throughout the country, all across Main Street, and yet you're still seeing some of the same folks who acted irresponsibly trying to fight efforts to crack down on abusive practices that got us into this problem in the first place.

So, yes, I think people are frustrated, and the protestors are giving voice to a more broad-based frustration about how our financial system works. Now, keep in mind I have said before and I will continue to repeat, we have to have a strong, effective financial sector in order for us to grow. And I used up a lot of political capital, and I've got the dings and bruises to prove it, in order to make sure that we prevented a financial meltdown, and that banks stayed afloat. And that was the right thing to do, because had we seen a financial collapse then the damage to the American economy would have been even worse.

But what I've also said is that for us to have a healthy financial system, that requires that banks and other financial institutions compete on the basis of the best service and the best products and the best price, and it can't be competing on the basis of hidden fees, deceptive practices, or derivative cocktails that nobody understands and that expose the entire economy to enormous risks. That's what Dodd-Frank was designed to do. It was designed to make sure that we didn't have the necessity of taxpayer bailouts; that we said, you know what? We're going to be able to control these situations so that if these guys get into trouble, we can isolate them, quarantine them, and let them fail. It says that we're going to have a consumer watchdog on the job, all the time, who's going to make sure that they are dealing with customers in a fair way, and we're eliminating hidden fees on credit cards, and mortgage brokers are going to have to—actually have to be straight with people about what they're purchasing.

And what we've seen over the last year is not only did the financial sector—with the Republican Party in Congress—fight us every inch of the way, but now you've got these same folks suggesting that we should roll back all those reforms and go back to the way it was before the crisis. Today, my understanding is we're going to have a hearing on Richard Cordray, who is my nominee to head up the Consumer Financial Protection Bureau. He would be America's chief consumer watchdog when it comes to financial products. This is a guy who is well regarded in his home state of Ohio, has been the treasurer of Ohio, the attorney general of Ohio. Republicans and Democrats in Ohio all say that he is a serious person who looks out for consumers. He has a good reputation. And Republicans have threatened not to confirm him not because of anything he's done, but because they want to roll back the whole notion of having a consumer watchdog.

You've got Republican presidential candidates whose main economic policy proposals is, we'll get rid of the financial reforms that are designed to prevent the abuses that got us into this mess in the first place. That does not make sense to the American people. They are frustrated by it. And they will continue to be frustrated by it until they get a sense that everybody is playing by the same set of rules, and that you're rewarded for responsibility and doing the right thing as opposed to gaining the system.

So I'm going to be fighting every inch of the way here in Washington to make sure that we have a consumer watchdog that is preventing abusive practices by the financial sector.

I will be hugely supportive of banks and financial institutions that are doing the right thing by their customers. We need them to be lending. We need them to be lending more to small businesses. We need them to help do what traditionally banks and financial services are supposed to be doing, which is providing business and families resources to make productive investments that will actually build the economy. But until the American people see that happening, yes, they are going to continue to express frustrations about what they see as two sets of rules.

Q: Do you think Occupy Wall Street has the potential to be a tea party movement in 2012?

THE PRESIDENT: What I think is that the American people understand that not everybody has been following the rules; that Wall Street is an example of that; that folks who are working hard every single day, getting up, going to the job, loyal to their companies, that that used to be the essence of the American Dream. That's how you got ahead—the old-fashioned way. And these days, a lot of folks who are doing the right thing aren't rewarded, and a lot of folks who aren't doing the right thing are rewarded.

And that's going to express itself politically in 2012 and beyond until people feel like once again we're getting back to some old-fashioned American values in which, if you're a banker, then you are making your money by making prudent loans to businesses and individuals to build plants and equipment and hire workers that are creating goods and products that are building the economy and benefitting everybody.

Jake Tapper.

Q: Thank you, Mr. President. Just to follow up on Jackie's question—one of the reasons why so many of the people of the Occupy Wall Street protests are so angry is because, as you say, so many people on Wall Street did not follow the rules, but your administration hasn't really been very aggressive in prosecuting. In fact, I don't think any Wall Street executives have gone to jail despite the rampant corruption and malfeasance that did take place. So I was wondering if you'd comment on that.

And then just as a separate question—as you're watching the Solyndra and Fast and Furious controversies play out, I'm wondering if it gives you any pause about any of the decision-making going on in your administration—some of the emails that Democrats puts out indicating that people at the Office of Management and Budget were concerned about the Department of Energy; some of the emails going on with the Attorney General saying he didn't know about the details of Fast and Furious. Are you worried at all about how this is—how your administration is running?

THE PRESIDENT: Well, first on the issue of prosecutions on Wall Street, one of the biggest problems about the collapse of Lehmans and the subsequent financial crisis and the whole subprime lending fiasco is that a lot of that stuff wasn't necessarily illegal, it was just immoral or inappropriate or reckless. That's exactly why we needed to pass Dodd-Frank, to prohibit some of these practices.

The financial sector is very creative and they are always looking for ways to make money. That's their job. And if there are loopholes and rules that can be bent and arbitrage to be had, they will take advantage of it. So without commenting on particular prosecutions—obviously that's not my job; that's the Attorney General's job—I think part of people's frustrations, part of my frustration, was a lot of practices that should not have been allowed weren't necessarily against the law, but they had a huge destructive impact. And that's why it was important for us to put in place financial rules that protect the American people from reckless decision-making and irresponsible behavior.

Now, with respect to Solyndra and Fast and Furious, I think I've been very clear that I have complete confidence in Attorney General Holder in how he handles his office. He has been very aggressive in going after gun running and cash transactions that are going to

these transnational drug cartels in Mexico. There has been a lot of cooperation between the United States and Mexico on this front. He's indicated that he was not aware of what was happening in Fast and Furious; certainly I was not. And I think both he and I would have been very unhappy if somebody had suggested that guns were allowed to pass through that could have been prevented by the United States of America.

He has assigned an Inspector General to look into how exactly this happened, and I have complete confidence in him and I've got complete confidence in the process to figure out who, in fact, was responsible for that decision and how it got made.

Solyndra—this is a loan guarantee program that predates me that historically has had support from Democrats and Republicans as well. And the idea is pretty straightforward: If we are going to be able to compete in the 21st century, then we've got to dominate cutting-edge technologies, we've got to dominate cutting-edge manufacturing. Clean energy is part of that package of technologies of the future that have to be based here in the United States if we're going to be able to succeed.

Now, the loan guarantee program is designed to meet a particular need in the marketplace, which is—a lot of these small startups, they can get angel investors, they can get several million dollars to get a company going, but it's very hard for them to then scale up, particularly if these are new cutting-edge technologies. It's hard for them to find private investors. And part of what's happening is China and Europe, other countries, are putting enormous subsidies into these companies and giving them incentives to move offshore. Even if the technology was developed in the United States, they end up going to China because the Chinese government will say, we're going to help you get started. We'll help you scale up. We'll give you low-interest loans or no-interest loans. We will give siting. We will do whatever it takes for you to get started here.

And that's part of the reason why a lot of technologies that developed here, we've now lost the lead in—solar energy, wind energy. And so what the loan guarantee program was designed to do was to close that gap and say, let's see if we can help some of those folks locate here and create jobs here in the United States.

Now, we knew from the start that the loan guarantee program was going to entail some risk, by definition. If it was a risk-free proposition, then we wouldn't have to worry about it. But the overall portfolio has been successful. It has allowed us to help companies, for example, start advanced battery manufacturing here in the United States. It's helped create jobs. There were going to be some companies that did not work out; Solyndra was one of them. But the process by which the decision was made was on the merits. It was straightforward. And of course there were going to be debates internally when you're dealing with something as complicated as this.

But I have confidence that the decisions were made based on what would be good for the American economy and the American people and putting people back to work.

And by the way, let me make one last point about this. I heard there was a Republican member of Congress who's engaging in oversight on this, and despite the fact that all of them in the past have been supportive of this loan guarantee program, he concluded, you know what? We can't compete against China when it comes to solar energy. Well, you know what? I don't buy that. I'm not going to surrender to other countries' technological leads that could end up determining whether or not we're building a strong middle class in this country. And so we're going to have to keep on pushing hard to make sure that manufacturing is located here, new businesses are located here, and new technologies are developed here. And there are going to be times where it doesn't work out, but I'm not going to cave to the competition when they are heavily subsidizing all these industries.

Q: Just a follow-up on Wall Street. Are you satisfied with how aggressive your administration has been when it comes to prosecuting? Because I know a lot of it was legal, but a lot of was not. There was fraud that took place.

THE PRESIDENT: Right. Well, let me say this: The President can't go around saying, prosecute somebody. But as a general principle, if somebody is engaged in fraudulent actions, they need to be prosecuted. If they violated laws on the books, they need to be prosecuted. And that's the Attorney General's job, and I know that Attorney General Holder, U.S. attorneys all across the country, they take that job very seriously. Okay?...

Source: The White House, Office of the Press Secretary. October 6, 2011. *News Conference by the President.* Available at http://www.whitehouse.gov/the-press-office/2011/10/06/news-conference-president.